Human Resource Director's Portfolio of Personnel Forms, Records, and Reports

AXEL R. GRANHOLM

PRENTICE HALL
Englewood Cliffs, New Jersey 07632

Prentice-Hall International (UK) Limited, *London*
Prentice-Hall of Australia Pty. Limited, *Sydney*
Prentice-Hall Canada, Inc., *Toronto*
Prentice-Hall Hispanoamericana, S.A., *Mexico*
Prentice-Hall of India Private Limited, *New Delhi*
Prentice-Hall of Japan, Inc., *Tokyo*
Simon & Schuster Asia Pte. Ltd., *Singapore*
Editora Prentice-Hall do Brasil, Ltda., *Rio de Janeiro*

©1988 by

PRENTICE-HALL, Inc.

Englewood Cliffs, NJ

10 9 8 7 6 5 4 3 2 1

Library of Congress Cataloging-in-Publication Data

Granholm, Axel R. (Axel Richard)
  Human resource director's portfolio of personnel forms, records,
and reports / Axel R. Granholm.

    p.   cm.
  Includes index.
  ISBN 0-13-445842-7
  1. Personnel procedure manuals.   2. Personnel records—Handbooks,
manuals, etc.   3. Personnel management—Handbooks, manuals, etc.
I. Title.
HF5549.5.C62G73   1988
658.3—dc19   88-12612
                                                    CIP

ISBN 0-13-445842-7

PRENTICE HALL
BUSINESS & PROFESSIONAL DIVISION
A division of Simon & Schuster
Englewood Cliffs, New Jersey 07632

PRINTED IN THE UNITED STATES OF AMERICA

For his lifelong determination to succeed despite many obstacles, and his courage in fighting a losing battle with cancer, this book is dedicated to my father.

Major Axel V. Granholm, USAF
July 10, 1910–August 5, 1949

About the Author

Axel Richard Granholm has 27 years of diversified human resources management experience with major companies at the corporate-level including ACF Industries, Bell Telephone Laboratories, Exxon Research and Engineering Company, and McGraw-Hill. His experience also includes international management responsibilities with National Bulk Carriers/Universe Tankships, Ltd./Princess Hotels International, a $3 billion holding company with 28,000 employees engaged worldwide in banking, real estate, luxury hotels, mining, oil exploration and refining, ocean shipping, and agricultural companies.

Mr. Granholm's positions have ranged from the trainee to the corporate HRM officer level and include all human resources specializations. He is known for his innovativeness and technical skills in formulating maximally effective HRM systems, policies, and procedures.

An alumnus of Rutgers College and the Graduate School of Rutgers, The State University of New Jersey, he earned a bachelors degree in social science and English, and a masters degree in psychology.

Mr. Granholm currently is a senior-level program analyst at the headquarters of the Federal Aviation Administration in Washington, D.C. Prior to being promoted to this position on the staff of the Associate Administrator for Development and Logistics, he served as the Human Resource Planning Officer for the FAA Technical Center at Atlantic City International Airport, New Jersey.

What This Book Will Do for You

Human Resource Director's Portfolio of Personnel Forms, Records, and Reports is a comprehensive, how-to-do-it manual of current forms, records, and reports with step-by-step procedures and sample policies for use by human resource directors. This portfolio has been carefully constructed to meet human resource management requirements of all types and sizes of business organizations including solutions to common problems.

It covers all levels of employees, including hourly, salaried, managerial, executive, and professional. And, it's fully up-to-date on current law and human resource practice. For example, you'll find forms covering new types of benefits, programs, and services.

Today's universal challenge for HR Directors is to more efficiently and effectively provide cost effective administrative services. Increased profitability goals demand HRM cost savings while improving the quality of service. This manual provides the detailed guidelines needed to design, implement, administer, and evaluate the success of maximally effective HRM programs. It offers practical techniques for use by the HR Director in promoting a productive bottom line-oriented partnership with management.

Here are some of the ways you and your firm can stand to benefit from the portfolio:

- *Promote* successful recruiting efforts through developing specific selection criteria for each position requirement
- *Accommodate* handicapped employees through job analysis
- *Standardize* position descriptions to eliminate costly duplication of effort
- *Plan* management succession to ensure operational continuity
- *Announce* job opportunities to your employees
- *Match employees* to job openings by using a skill inventory system and save recruitment costs
- *Prepare and place* your own economical and effective help wanted ads
- *Promote* the merits of your company as an employer
- *Control* the overall recruitment, selection, and placement process to minimize the expenditure of valuable line manager time
- *Create* cost effective working relationships with employment agencies
- *Improve* reference checking to decrease turnover
- *Identify* bogus college degrees to avoid hiring dishonest and unqualified individuals
- *Introduce* a candidate host program to improve your job offer acceptance/rejection ratio
- *Enhance* your employee orientation and follow-up process to ensure successful job placements

- *Design and implement* individual development plans which meet employees' company-related career needs, promote advancement, and encourage retention of a skilled workforce
- *Provide* a professional exchange program to broaden the experience and overall value of employees to the company
- *Develop* your own training programs and save consultant costs
- *Set-up* an effective MBO program which promotes profitability
- *Create* objective performance standards which weed out unsatisfactory performers
- *Ensure* employee understanding of work rules to provide the basis for disciplinary action
- *Reward* employees for long-term company service with financial and social recognition
- *Determine* relative value of jobs/positions through a point factor evaluation approach
- *Build* wage and salary ranges
- *Ensure* competitiveness of compensation programs through wage and salary surveys
- *Install* an annual salary review system to plan merit increases and control the merit increase budget
- *Reward* employees for special achievements
- *Provide* competitive benefits to retain productive employees
- *Control* hospital costs through employee audits
- *Calculate* social security retirement benefits
- *Promote* successful retirements through employee planning
- *Provide* employees with statements on the dollar value of their benefits
- *Use* one form to process ALL personnel status changes
- *Introduce* a combination personnel folder and record
- *Determine* employee overtime exemption status by using a checklist
- *Identify* and control absence abuses through improved records systems
- *Reward* perfect attendance with an attendance award program
- *Promote* more efficient and cost-effective employee relocations
- *Reduce* workmens compensation costs through improved safety program inspections
- *Assist* employees in resolving personal problems to increase productivity
- *Provide* competitive allowances and benefits in motivating expatriate employees
- *Use* separation questionnaire and exit interview to identify problems which create turnover
- *Offer* outplacement assistance to reduce unemployment insurance costs
- *Use* workforce planning techniques to meet company operating plan requirements
- *Consider* HRM information system techniques for computerized personnel records, data, and report generation.

The Human Resource Director's Portfolio of Forms, Records, and Reports has been carefully organized to make it as easy to use as possible. Related forms and procedures have been grouped into 14 major chapters. You'll find procedures for preparing each form. Following many sets of procedures and their form is a specimen form to make sure that all details are complete. In addition to the table of contents, a list of the forms, records, and reports is provided in the front of the book. A detailed index is also included so that you can almost instantly locate the particular form you need.

You can use its suggested approaches to improve current procedures and quickly introduce new procedural processes. You can extract the recommended forms in their entirety, or adapt them to meet your specific needs. The portfolio will prove to be an invaluable reference tool for all your administrative needs.

Axel R. Granholm

Acknowledgments

Very special thanks to my wife for encouraging and helping me to write this book. Veronica always was supportive and understanding as countless frustrations were encountered along the way. She never hesitated to help with the typing, preparing artwork, and the many other tasks that were required. She showed me how to find time in our very busy schedule, during a year of many transitions and changes in our life, to meet the requirements of this major undertaking. My thirteen-year-old daughter also was very patient with her busy dad, the writer, who was not able to give her enough of his time. Elise, thanks for all of your understanding. Thanks also to the many contributors who helped by providing materials for the book. Each is acknowledged in respective sections of the book.

Contents

CHAPTER 3. SELECTION 127

List of Figures

Figure

Figure

Figure

Figure

Figure

Figure

CHAPTER 1

Human Resources Planning for Meeting Company Operating Plan Objectives

As a human resources (HR) director, your ability to design and provide effective workforce planning tools is the foundation for building a partnership with management. This chapter provides the basis for your success in defining the workforce implications of your company's operating plan. It will guide you in forecasting the numbers and types of employees needed for each organizational unit based on the work requirements generated by the operating plan. It also offers analysis techniques for defining and describing job/position requirements, including associated knowledge and skills, to provide the basis for properly identifying qualified candidates both within and outside the company. Techniques for preparing job and position descriptions, including cost-effective Standard Position Descriptions, are explained with samples. The need for a formal replacement planning procedure to ensure management continuity is met by a Succession Planning Chart process.

1.1 HR REQUIREMENTS ASSESSMENT WORKSHEET: AN APPROACH IN WORKFORCE PLANNING

Your company's operating plan begins with a sales forecast for the next fiscal or calendar year. For example, a small manufacturer of mobile telephones obtains contracts it believes will guarantee a 40 percent increase in sales. It also projects an additional 10 percent growth through other sales. This 50 percent increase in demand for its product requires a critical assessment of associated workforce implications. The firm must not unsystematically hire additional electronics assemblers and other types of employees to meet what, at first glance, appears to require increasing the workforce by 50 percent.

The HR director and management must first work as equal partners in assessing techniques to increase the productivity of the existing workforce. Some representative areas for consideration are:

1. Can work groups be organized more effectively to increase productivity?
2. Can work methods be improved through techniques such as job enrichment, quality circles, and incentive rewards?
3. What automated and other advanced technology can be introduced to expedite the manufacturing process? How can employee participation in these decisions promote acceptance?
4. What intervention strategies can be introduced to reduce costly controllable turnover and the associated loss of highly productive employees with extensive company experience?
5. Which employees, elsewhere in the company, might qualify for trainee positions as electronics assemblers?
6. To what extent is the use of overtime economically sound compared with adding more employees to the workforce?
7. Can some part-time and/or temporary employees be hired to help meet needs?

Based on these types of assessments and resultant actions, let us assume that the process yields an estimated 20 percent increase in overall productivity. Requirements now involve planning to achieve the remaining 30 percent. This planning requires sound judgments regarding the relative increase in workforce requirements for each of the company's functions as shown below.

Function	Increase of Workforce (%)
Manufacturing	30
Sales	20
Engineering	10
Administration	10

The partnership has decided to place primary growth emphasis on the manufacturing function to achieve the projected 30 percent increase in work requirements. The sales function also is targeted for relatively substantial growth—a 20 percent increase in workforce—to promote increased marketing efforts that will assure the continued growth of the company. Recognizing that substantial increases in production will require additional administrative support, a 10 percent allocation is planned for the administrative function. The engineering function also receives a 10 percent allocation to ensure the increase in product design and development activities that is required to remain competitive in the rapidly changing high technology communications industry.

Because manufacturing is the function designated for primary growth, we'll use this function and the electronics assembler position in the example of how the HR Requirements Assessment Worksheet (Figure 1.1) is used to define the workforce implications of the company's operating plan.

Procedures for Using the HR Requirements Assessment Worksheet

Here is the format for completing an HR Requirements Assessment Worksheet:

Job/Position Titles—List all job/position titles for the organization, function, or project. Group job/position families.

A. *# of Ees.*—Enter respective number of employees on payroll as of the date of the analysis (date shown on From line in heading).

B. *Losses*—Project employee losses for the assessment period (From and To in heading). Include planned and estimated attrition as follows:

RET.—Planned retirements
TERM.—Planned terminations of marginal performers
TRAN.—Planned transfers/promotions out of the organization
PROM.—Planned promotions (loss to new job/position within organization)
RIF.—Planned reduction-in-force/layoffs
SEP.—Estimated voluntary separations (resignation to accept another position, etc.)
OTHER—Miscellaneous (specify with footnotes)
TOTAL—Total of all columns in section B. Losses

C. *Gains*—Project employee additions.

TRAN.—Planned transfers into organization
PROM.—Planned promotions (gain from job/position within organization)
OTHER—Miscellaneous (specify with footnotes)
TOTAL—Total of all columns in section C. Gains

D. *Ees.*—Calculate number of employees adjusted for losses and gains ($D = A - B + C$).

E. *Repl.*—Calculate number of replacement employees required or not required due to the respective number of losses and gains ($E = A - D$).

F. *Adj. Factor*—Adjustment factor used to increase/decrease workforce to meet operating plan requirements (expressed as decimal equivalent of appropriate percentage). Enter appropriate decimal.

G. *Ees.*—Calculate number of employees to be added (reduced in RIF) to meet operating plan requirements ($G = A \times F$).

H. *Hire*—Estimated number of hires needed to meet replacement and operating plan additional employee requirements ($H = E + G$).

Example of the HR Requirements Assessment Worksheet

The HR Requirements Assessment Worksheet shown in Figure 1.1A provides a systematic approach for use by the HR director in workforce planning. The example shows how it is used to project the number of hires needed in each assembler job category to meet operating plan growth requirements.

The lead assembler category shown has four employees at the start of the assessment period (A. # of Ees.). Through the review of personnel records and discussions with management to assess potential losses (B. Losses), it is determined that one of these individuals is eligible for retirement (Ret.), another is scheduled for promotion to a supervisory position (Prom.), and past experience regarding turnover predicts that one of these individuals probably will leave the company for employment with a competitor (Sep.). In summary, three of these four employees are potential losses.

In assessing gains (C. Gains) it is determined that three senior assemblers will qualify for and be promoted to lead assembler positions during the assessment period (Prom.).

The next step involves calculating the net effect of losses and gains for Column D. Ees. By using the formula of $A - B + C = D$, we determine that $4 - 3 + 3 = 4$. By subtracting this result from Column A, $4 - 4 = 0$, it is determined that no replacement employees are required. Accordingly, a 0 is entered in Column E. Repl. $(A - D)$.

The proposed adjustment factor shown in Column F. Adj. Factor is .30. This decimal equivalent of the specified 30 percent increase percentage is used in Column G. Ees. $(A \times F)$. This step estimates the number of additional employees that must be added to the current workforce to meet growth requirements. The current number of lead assembler jobs shown in Column A. # of Ees. is four. Multiplying 4 by .30 yields 1.2, which rounds off to 1.

The result shown in Column G. Ees. plus the number of replacement employees shown in Column E. Repl. yields the total estimated number of lead assemblers that are needed to meet replacement requirements and growth objectives. The computation for column H. Hire $(E + G)$ is $0 + 1 = 1$ lead assembler hiring requirement.

HR REQUIREMENTS ASSESSMENT WORKSHEET

Organization/Function/Project _____

Page _____ of _____ Pages

From _____ To _____

Job/Position Titles	A. # of Ees.	B. Losses								C. Gains				D. Ees. (A – B + C)	E. Repl. (A – D)	F. Adj. Factor	G. Ees. (A × F)	H. Hire (E + G)
		Ret.	Term.	Tran.	Prom.	Rif	Sep.	Other	Total	Tran.	Prom.	Other	Total					

Figure 1.1 HR requirements assessment worksheet

HR REQUIREMENTS ASSESSMENT WORKSHEET

Organization/Function/Project   Manufacturing

From   1/1/XX   To   12/31/XX

Job/Position Titles	A. # of Ees.	B. Losses								C. Gains				D. Ees. (A − B + C)	E. Repl. (A − D)	F. Adj. Factor	G. Ees. (A × F)	H. Hire (E + G)
		Ret.	Term.	Tran.	Prom.	Rif	Sep.	Other	Total	Tran.	Prom.	Other	Total					
Assembler, lead	4	1	0	0	1	0	1	0	3	0	3	0	3	4	0	.30	1	1
Assembler, senior	10	0	0	0	3	0	1	0	4	0	5	0	5	11	(1)	.30	3	2
Assembler	25	0	1	0	5	0	3	0	9	0	5	0	5	21	4	.30	8	12
Assembler, trainee	10	0	2	0	5	0	2	0	9	2	0	0	2	3	7	.30	3	10

Figure 1.1A   HR requirements assessment worksheet

6

1.2 RECRUITMENT REQUIREMENTS PLAN

The Recruitment Requirements Plan shown in Figure 1.2 is used as a worksheet for adjusting the estimated hires data obtained from Column H of the HR Requirements Assessment Worksheet. Job/position title and associated Column H data are transferred to the corresponding columns of the Recruitment Requirements Plan worksheet—that is, "job/position titles" and "estimated hires."

Estimated hiring requirements data now are used as a basis for working with management in making critical judgments regarding absolutely essential needs. The HR director and management assess how to best achieve the optimum balance of skill/experience levels needed to meet operating plan requirements. This must be accomplished to ensure that promotion-from-within policy objectives and affirmative action goals are maximized.

The example provided in Figure 1.2A shows realignment adjustments of projected hiring requirements. It was decided that the recruitment of a lead assembler and two senior assemblers is essential if production objectives are to be met. This is reflected by no realignment adjustments and planned hires, which remain the same as estimated hires. It also was decided that eight of twelve assembler positions were to be reallocated to increase planned hires for trainee assemblers from ten to eighteen. The result is the cost savings associated with hiring at absolutely essential skill levels, and the enhancement of the company's promotion-from-within policy. Projected experienced-level hires are reduced from fifteen to seven, and projected entry-level hires are increased from ten to eighteen.

The affirmative action targets section is not completed in the example because commitments are based on a company's particular statistical requirements. Given the general types of affirmative action problems experienced by companies, you would probably find emphasis being placed on targets involving the higher level positions and the trainee positions.

Recruitment Requirements Plan

Organization/Function/Project_____

Job/Position Titles	Estimated Hires	Realignment Adjustments + or (−)	Planned Hires	Affirmative Action Targets				
				Females	Other Minority	Vets	Handicap	Total

Figure 1.2   Recruitment requirements plan

Recruitment Requirements Plan

Organization/Function/Project   Manufacturing

Job/Position Titles	Estimated Hires	Realignment Adjustments + or (−)	Planned Hires	Affirmative Action Targets				
				Females	Other Minority	Vets	Handicap	Total
Assembler, lead	1	0	1					
Assembler, senior	2	0	2					
Assembler	12	(8)	4					
Assembler, trainee	10	8	18					
TOTALS	25	0	25					

Figure 1.2A   Recruitment requirements plan

1.3 POSITION ANALYSIS FORM: A STEP-BY-STEP ANALYSIS OF A SECRETARIAL POSITION

The Position Analysis Form shown in Figure 1.3 provides the basis for identifying four or five of a job/position's major duties and responsibilities, then assessing these work functions to identify the associated skills and abilities an incumbent must have to perform successfully.

Some of the most essential benefits yielded by this process include:

1. *Definition of Recruitment Requirements.* The specific functional requirements of a job/position must be spelled out in order to recruit effectively. Requisite candidate skills must be defined and assigned priorities in terms of those that are essential for hiring versus those that can be obtained through on-the-job or other specialized training.
2. *Relative Value.* Defining the requirements of a job/position provides the basis for comparison to other jobs/positions to determine relative worth. This is the first step in developing a viable compensation program for employees.*
3. *Training Needs Assessment.* A job/position analysis of an existing position which identifies new or expanded duties and responsibilities leads to the establishment of specialized training requirements for the incumbent.
4. *Establishing Performance Objectives.* Careful identification of duties and responsibilities and associated goals leads to the establishment of measurable performance standards.

The Position Analysis form is designed for completion by an incumbent who is instructed to prepare the "duties and responsibilities" section. He or she is requested to "describe the four or five major functions of your position." A sample of a form that was completed for a nonrelated job/position may be provided as an example in those cases where specific guidance is required. The employee's statements should be written in the present tense and first-person ("I") form, for example, read, write, coordinate, and so on. This personalized approach facilitates the individual's responses as compared with the impersonal active verbs used in job/position descriptions (for example, the incumbent reads, writes, coordinates, and so on). An example of a secretary's functional descriptions is provided in Figure 1.3A.

After the incumbent provides this information, his or her immediate supervisor reviews the entries to suggest additions or corrections as required. Mutual agreement regarding content is essential if the varied benefits of the form are to be realized.

Next, the supervisor assesses each function to identify and specify the requisite skills and abilities in the requirement section. For each of the four or five major functions, up to five related skills and abilities should be listed (A, B, C, and so on). An example of the supervisor's assessments is shown in Figure 1.3B.

If the Position Analysis form is being completed for a new position without an incumbent, the supervisor completes both sections of the form. Since this process also will provide much of the basis for preparing the official job/position description, the supervisor completes the duties and responsibilities section by beginning each sentence with an action verb, for example, the incumbent reads, evaluates, writes, takes, and so on. This permits verbatim transcription of this information for inclusion in the job/position description format.

---

* *Note:* For an alternative approach that ties into a point factor position evaluation process, see the Position Analysis Questionnaire in Section 8.2.

Position Analysis

Job/Position Title _____

Organization/Function/Project _____

Duties and Responsibilities (Describe the 4 or 5 major functions of your position)	Requirements (Specify related skills, abilities, etc.)
1.	A. B. C. D. E.
2.	A. B. C. D. E.
3.	A. B. C. D. E.
4.	A. B. C. D. E.
5.	A. B. C. D. E.

Prepared by: _____ Date: _____   Reviewed by: _____ Date: _____

Figure 1.3 Position analysis

Position Analysis

Job/Position Title __Secretary__

Organization/Function/Project __Accounting Department__

Duties and Responsibilities (Describe the 4 or 5 major functions of your position)	Requirements (Specify related skills, abilities, etc.)
1. Read and evaluate a wide variety of written materials to maintain files, process forms, review outgoing documents for completeness and accuracy, and to collect and compile information.	A. B. C. D. E.
2. Write responses to requests for routine information.	A. B. C. D. E.
3. Deal with others in person and over the telephone to clarify or exchange information, schedule meetings, and provide guidance and assistance.	A. B. C. D. E.
4. Take dictation and type correspondence, reports, and other materials in final format.	A. B. C. D. E.
5. Coordinate a variety of office activities for manager such as making appointments, arranging meetings and travel, and processing routine administrative actions.	A. B. C. D. E.

Prepared by: _____ Date: _____

Reviewed by: _____ Date: _____

Figure 1.3A Position analysis

Position Analysis

Job/Position Title ___Secretary___

Organization/Function/Project ___Accounting Department___

Duties and Responsibilities (Describe the 4 or 5 major functions of your position)	Requirements (Specify related skills, abilities, etc.)
1. Read and evaluate a wide variety of written materials to maintain files, process forms, review outgoing documents for completeness and accuracy, and to collect and compile information.	A. Ability to read and interpret written material. B. Ability to review material for accuracy. C. Ability to organize material. D. Ability to collect and compile information. E.
2. Write responses to requests for routine information.	A. Ability to write routine correspondence. B. C. D. E.
3. Deal with others in person and over the telephone to clarify or exchange information, schedule meetings, and provide guidance and assistance.	A. Skills in interpersonal relationships. B. Ability to communicate orally. C. Knowledge of the organization's operations. D. E.
4. Take dictation and type correspondence, reports, and other materials in final format.	A. Skill in typing. B. Skill in taking dictation. C. Knowledge of spelling, grammar, punctuation. D. E.
5. Coordinate a variety of office activities for manager such as making appointments, arranging meetings and travel, and processing routine administrative actions.	A. Ability to prioritize work. B. Ability to make arrangements for conferences, meetings. C. Knowledge of company policies and procedures. D. E.

Prepared by: _____ Date: _____   Reviewed by: _____ Date: _____

Figure 1.3B Position analysis

1.4 ANALYSIS OF POSITION REQUIREMENTS WORKSHEET

This worksheet (Figure 1.4) is used by the supervisor to reach definitive conclusions regarding the relative importance of requirements yielded through the completion of the Position Analysis form.

Figure 1.4A provides an example of the completed Analysis of Position Requirements Worksheet as follows: The first column "#", is completed by transcribing the numbers corresponding to each skill and ability identified through the position analysis process, for example, 1A., 1B., and so on.

The second column, "position requirements," is completed by summarizing each statement from the Position Analysis form to facilitate comparisons. For example, "1B. Ability to review material for accuracy" becomes "1B. Review for accuracy."

The third column, "ranking," requires the supervisor to make critical assessments concerning the relative degree of importance of each factor. The example shows the ranking for each of the 14 Position Requirements.

The fourth column, "essential," is then used to designate those requirements a candidate must have to be qualified for the position.

The fifth column, "preferred," is completed for those requirements which, although not essential, would be brought to the position by an ideal candidate.

The "On Job Training" column is used to designate those preferred requirements that could be obtained through guided work experience in the position.

The "specialized training" column also is used to designate those preferred requirements that could be obtained through formal skill training while on the job. The incumbent can take a course in stenography, business writing, and so on.

The supervisor now is prepared to provide meaningful recruitment requirement guidelines to the HR director. He or she also has the basis for creating a meaningful structure of performance evaluation criteria for the new incumbent.

Analysis of Position Requirements Worksheet

Page _____ of _____ Pages

Organization/Function/Project _____

Job/Position Title _____

#	Position Requirements	Ranking	Essential	Preferred	On Job Training	Specialized Training

Figure 1.4   Analysis of position requirements worksheet

Analysis of Position Requirements Worksheet

Page _____ of _____ Pages

Organization/Function/Project ___Accounting_____

Job/Position Title ___Secretary_____

#	Position Requirements	Ranking	Essential	Preferred	On Job Training	Specialized Training
1A.	Read and interpret written material	8	x			
1B.	Review for accuracy	5	x			
1C.	Organize material	2	x			
1D.	Collect and compile information	9		x	x	
2A.	Write routine correspondence	10		x		x
3A.	Apply interpersonal effectiveness	6	x			
3B.	Communicate orally	7	x			
3C.	Apply organizational knowledge	13		x	x	
4A.	Typing	3	x			
4B.	Taking dictation	11		x		x
4C.	Apply spelling, grammar, and punctuation rules	4	x			
5A.	Prioritize work	1	x			
5B.	Make arrangements	12		x	x	
5C.	Apply company policies and procedures	14		x	x	

Specialized Training: 2A.—Business Writing Course, 4B.—Stenography Course.

Date _____ Prepared By _____

Figure 1.4A   Analysis of position requirements worksheet

1.5 POSITION ANALYSIS: IDENTIFYING ACCOMMODATIONS FOR HANDICAPPED EMPLOYEES

An Accommodations Checklist for Handicapped Employees (Figure 1.5) provides an example of how the job analysis process, which identifies the specific tasks and associated complications presented to the handicapped employee, can be used to systematically identify necessary accommodations. The checklist focuses on the unique types of accommodations that would be required to effectively employ a visually impaired or blind, deaf, or paralyzed individual as a computer programmer.

Through effective job analysis procedures, the HR director can readily develop similar data for a wide variety of positions which, when reasonable accommodations are introduced, are well suited for handicapped employees. The job analysis process provides an understanding of job requirements and the work environment. Associated requirements are compared with the handicapped individual's physical or mental limitations to identify and understand the incompatibilities. The development of a listing of potential remedies is then needed to determine the most reasonable methods for resolving the problems that have been identified.

The analysis of functional job requirements (the tasks to be performed) involves the following considerations:

1. What methods, tools, equipment, and so on are required to perform the work?
2. What physical movements or mental processes are needed to perform the tasks?
3. How much physical effort is required and/or how complex are the mental processes?
4. How much time is required to perform each task? How frequently are the tasks performed?

The United States Office of Personnel Management's pamphlet, "Handbook of Job Analysis for Reasonable Accommodation,"* provides an excellent step-by-step example of this process. It also includes an appendix with definitions for all the types of functional limitation categories, which are listed below.

1. Difficulty in interpreting information
2. Limitation of sight
3. Limitation of hearing
4. Limitation of speech
5. Susceptibility to fainting, dizziness, seizures
6. Uncoordination
7. Limitation of stamina
8. Difficulty in moving head
9. Limitation of sensation
10. Difficulty in lifting and reaching with arms
11. Difficulty in handling and fingering
12. Inability to use upper extremities
13. Difficulty in sitting
14. Difficulty in using lower extremities
15. Poor balance

* "Handbook of Job Analysis for Reasonable Accommodation," Personnel Management Series 720-B, U.S. Office of Personnel Management (Washington, DC: U.S. Government Printing Office, 1982) pp. 15–17.

Accommodations Checklist for Handicapped Employees

Through the job analysis process, which identifies the specific tasks and associated complications presented to the handicapped employee, you can systematically identify necessary accommodations for a computer programmer:

VISUALLY IMPAIRED/BLIND

— Provide magnification device to achieve required level of correction. Provide reader or Braille materials.
— Provide special telephone with enlarged numbers/Braille keys on telephone.
— Modify CRT to achieve required magnification. Add voice output feature to CRT.
— Color Code reference materials/Braille labels.

DEAF

— Provide all communication in writing.
— Train individual(s) to communicate with employee in sign language.
— Provide teletype capability between employee and supervisor.
— Facilitate face-to-face communication (lip reading) through seating arrangements.
— Assign another individual to receive and make calls.
— Provide written instructions to alert employee in emergency situations.

PARALYZED

— Arrange CRT hardcopy output if unable to use pencil, but able to operate keyboard.
— Have another employee transcribe information per verbal instructions.
— Arrange work area to facilitate wheelchair movements.
— Place reference materials on desk or within reach.
— Provide assistance in obtaining special references not available in work area, or not within reach.
— Assign disabled parking area near entrance. Provide entrance ramp and automatic door opening device.
— Ensure access to and required accommodations to use all workplace areas (elevator, restroom, cafeteria, and so on).

Figure 1.5 Accommodations checklist for handicapped employees

1.6 POSITION DESIGN WORKBOOK: DEFINING THE OVERALL PURPOSE, DUTIES, AND RESPONSIBILITIES OF A NEW POSITION

A Position Design Workbook (Figure 1.6) is used to provide step-by-step assistance to the supervisor or manager in defining the duties and responsibilities of each new administrative, professional, or managerial position. This process entails completing a Position Design Worksheet to provide details concerning the following position requirements.

A. Knowledge

"Describe the knowledge required by defining the amount and type of education and experience needed for successful performance."

B. Mental Application

"Describe the typical decisions the incumbent will be called upon to make, and indicate the extent to which he or she must seek guidance in making these decisions. To what degree does the position require creating, developing, and executing plans and procedures independently? Explain the extent to which the work is governed by established practices, rules, regulations, and so on as compared with work that requires the application of creativity and originality."

C. Programs and Projects

"Describe the incumbent's responsibility for the planning, development, organization, implementation, and direction of specific assignments, programs, and operations. Indicate the extent to which these responsibilities are governed by policy and practice, their scope, their complexities in terms of the difficulty and problems involved, and the level of authority vested in the position."

D. Supervision

"If a nonsupervisory position, describe the type and amount of direction received and the incumbent's functional responsibilities, if any, for the training of lower-level employees. If supervisory, list the titles of positions that report directly to the incumbent. Indicate the title of the incumbent's immediate supervisor or manager."

E. Accountability

"Describe the kind, amount, and scope of the incumbent's responsibility for the maintenance and conservation of assets (buildings, equipment, inventory, and so on), for producing income, and for exercising control over the allocation and utilization of resources."

F. Policies and Methods

"Describe the incumbent's responsibility for the formulation, interpretation, and execution of policies, procedures, and methods. Specify the incumbent's organizational level and the extent of the incumbent's influence on company operations. Provide details concerning records and reports for which he or she is responsible."

G. Relationships

"Describe the contacts the incumbent regularly has both within and outside the company. What is the level of these contacts? What impact do they have on company operations?"

Describing each of these position requirements is accomplished by referring to associated Factor Level Definitions, which are provided on pages 5 through 9 of the Workbook. For example, preparation of the wording for the "A. Knowledge" portion of the worksheet is accomplished by referring to page 5 of the Factor Level Definitions. This page describes seven factor levels for "A. Knowledge." The appropriate factor level is selected, and essential wording (college degree or equivalent, a specified number of years of experience, and so on) is retained in writing an appropriate description of the position's educational and experience requirements.

As explained in the instructions section of the sample Position Design Workbook, this approach allows management to participate in the position evaluation process. They actually use the same Factor Level Definitions in preparing a Position Design Worksheet that the HRM division uses to classify positions into appropriate salary grades.

This position evaluation process is described in Section 8.3, Position Evaluation Worksheet.

```
┌─────────────────────────────────────────────────────────┐
│         ┌───────────────────────────────────┐           │
│         │      POSITION DESIGN WORKBOOK      │           │
│         └───────────────────────────────────┘           │
```

INSTRUCTIONS: This workbook has been prepared by the Human Resources Management Division for providing the step-by-step assistance needed by managers and supervisors in defining the duties and responsibilities of a new administrative, professional, or managerial position. The completed Position Design Worksheet offers the information needed by the HRM division to prepare an official position description, and to determine the salary grade for the position.

The workbook contains a Position Design Worksheet, five pages of Factor Level Definitions that are used in its completion, and a sample of a completed Position Design Worksheet for a new position as mechanical engineer.

Completion of the Position Design Worksheet begins with defining the major purpose/objective/function of the proposed position in the "I. General Function" section. For example, the mechanical engineer position shown in the sample of a completed worksheet is described as: "Performs design engineering assignments involving the preparation of layouts and detailed drawings for elements of office building mechanical systems (heating, ventilating, air conditioning, plumbing, and steam distribution)."

Next, the specific duties and responsibilities of the proposed position, and associated educational and experience requirements, are defined by completing the seven items included in the "II. Position Requirements" section. The first item is "A. Knowledge," the second is "B. Mental Application" and so on. Each is completed by referring to respective Factor Level Definitions as follows:

A.   Knowledge . . . . Page 5

B.   Mental Application . . . . Pages 5 and 6

C.   Programs and Projects . . . . Pages 6 and 7

D.   Supervision . . . . Page 7

E.   Accountability . . . . Page 8

F.   Policies and Methods . . . . Pages 8 and 9

G.   Relationships . . . . Page 9

Completion of the first item, "A. Knowledge," is accomplished by reviewing the Factor Level definitions provided on page 5, A. Knowledge. If the position under consideration requires a college graduate with a minimal amount of related experience (less than 3 years) or a nondegreed individual with equivalent work experience, then Factor Level 3 is appropriate. You then reflect associated wording in completing this portion of the worksheet. "Requires the equivalent of a college degree in skills acquired either academically or through specialized business experience" becomes "requires a college degree in mechanical engineering or its equivalent in terms of professional knowledge obtained through specialized work experience.

–Page 1–

Figure 1.6 Position design workbook

continued

Working knowledge of related engineering disciplines, particularly structural and electrical, is essential.

A thoroughly prepared Position Design Worksheet ensures that the HRM division has the information needed for properly classifying a position. You, as a member of management, participate in the position evaluation process by reflecting appropriate factor levels in describing position requirements. The higher the factor level, the higher the number of points scored. The higher the number of overall points scored, the higher the salary grade for a position. The HRM division's role is to review each of your 7 Position Requirements descriptions, determine the appropriate factor level for each, and then convert these factor levels into position evaluation plan points. The total points scored for the 7 Position Requirements are converted into a tentative salary grade for the position. The HRM division assures comparability with other positions at the proposed salary grade level, then assigns an approved salary grade and title for the position.

Should you have any questions or need assistance with the preparation of this Position Design Worksheet, please contact: (insert name, title, room number, and telephone extension of designated individual).

–Page 2–

Figure 1.6 *(cont.)*

```
┌─────────────────────────────────────────────────────────────────┐
│                                                                   │
│        ┌──────────────────────────────────────────────┐          │
│        │         POSITION DESIGN WORKSHEET—            │          │
│        │  PROFESSIONAL/ADMINISTRATIVE/MANAGERIAL       │          │
│        └──────────────────────────────────────────────┘          │
│                                                                   │
│   Proposed position title _____          │
│                                                                   │
│   Company location _____           │
│                                                                   │
│   Organization/function/project _____          │
│                                                                   │
│   Division _____           │
│                                                                   │
│   Reports to (position title) _____         │
│                                                                   │
│   I.   General Function—State the major purpose/objective/        │
│        function of the proposed position.                         │
│                                                                   │
│                                                                   │
│                                                                   │
│                                                                   │
│   II.  Position Requirements—Provide details regarding the        │
│        duties and responsibilities of the position and the        │
│        associated educational and experience requirements,        │
│        by completing each of the following items.                 │
│                                                                   │
│        A.   Knowledge—Describe the knowledge required by          │
│             defining the amount and type of education and         │
│             experience needed for successful performance.         │
│                                                                   │
│                                                                   │
│                                                                   │
│                                                                   │
│        B.   Mental Application—Describe the typical decisions     │
│             the incumbent will be called upon to make, and        │
│             indicate the extent to which he or she must seek      │
│             guidance in making these decisions. To what degree    │
│             does the position require creating, developing, and   │
│             executing plans and procedures independently?         │
│             Explain the extent to which the work is governed by   │
│             established practices, rules, regulations, and so on,  │
│             as compared with work that requires the application   │
│             of creativity and originality.                        │
│                                                                   │
│                                                                   │
│                                                                   │
│                          –Page 3–                                 │
│                                                                   │
└─────────────────────────────────────────────────────────────────┘
```

Figure 1.6 *(cont.)*

C. Programs and Projects—Describe the incumbent's responsibility for the planning, development, organization, implementation, and direction of specific assignments, programs, and operations. Indicate the extent to which these responsibilities are governed by policy and practice, their scope, their complexities in terms of difficulty and problems involved, and the level of authority vested in the position.

D. Supervision—If a nonsupervisory position, describe the type and amount of direction received and the incumbent's functional responsibilities, if any, for the training of lower-level employees. If supervisory, list the titles of positions that report directly to the incumbent. Indicate the title of the incumbent's immediate supervisor or manager.

E. Accountability—Describe the kind, amount, and scope of the incumbent's responsibility for the maintenance and conservation of assets (buildings, equipment, inventory, and so on), for producing income, and for exercising control over the allocation and utilization of resources.

F. Policies and Methods—Describe the incumbent's responsibility for the formulation, interpretation, and execution of policies, procedures, and methods. Specify the incumbent's organizational level and the extent of the incumbent's influence on company operations. Provide details concerning records and reports for which he or she is responsible.

G. Relationships—Describe the contacts the incumbent regularly has both within and outside the company. What is the level of these contacts? What impact do they have on company operations?

Prepared by _____ Date _____

Position title _____

Reviewed by _____ Date _____

Position title _____

Figure 1.6 (cont.)

```
┌─────────────────────────────────┐
│      FACTOR LEVEL DEFINITIONS   │
└─────────────────────────────────┘
```

A. Knowledge

Factor Level	Definitions
1	Ordinarily requires the education acquired by graduation from high school, related experience of up to 1 or 2 years, and only those skills acquired through such education and limited experience.
2	Requires two years of college or the equivalent, related experience of 2 or 3 years, and skill and proficiency in a semi-professional occupation or specialized business function.
3	Requires the equivalent of a college degree in skills acquired either academically or through specialized business experience.
4	Requires the equivalent of a college degree with business or academic training in applicable subjects; 3 or 4 years related experience; and skills in a professional or advanced business function having a direct bearing on the products or services of the company.
5	Requires the equivalent of a college degree; 4 or 5 years of related business experience; and managerial or administrative skills at department head level or equivalent in administrative, professional, or scientific functions.
6	Requires broad and intensive knowledge acquired by full academic training; 5 to 7 years of applicable experience; and skills in planning, organizing, controlling, and administering in a management position.
7	Requires intensive knowledge of a broad field of business enterprise acquired by sufficient academic training; 7 to 10 years applicable experience; skills in planning, organizing, integrating viewpoints of people; motivating department heads; and experience in administering an important business function at the officer level.

B. Mental Application

Factor Level	Definitions
1	Work is well organized and supervised. Offers some opportunity for ingenuity in applying accepted methods, with concentrated attention to the examination of details to make logical decisions from limited alternatives.
2	Work requires individual to devise own methods under close supervision; make choices from knowledge of accepted methods; examine details of specialized subjects; make decisions within scope of own assignments; and to compose reports and correspondence.

–Page 5–

Figure 1.6 *(cont.)*

3   Work requires ingenuity in planning and implementing projects under general supervision; examines advanced subjects, and uses independent judgment to make decisions under established policies. Prepares reports requiring technical concepts.

4   Work requires individual to devise own methods; assist in the development of methods used by others; exercise ingenuity; analyze situations and apply judgment required to make decisions of an administrative nature; and prepare and edit reports and other materials involving technical concepts.

5   Work requires originality, initiative, and ingenuity to devise departmental methods; solve problems not covered by procedures; and make administrative or supervisory decisions.

6   Work requires high degree of originality, initiative, and ingenuity needed for operating a department or major function under general direction and to analyze situations of a highly complex nature and make major policy decisions subject only to officer approval.

7   Work requires highest degree of originality, initiative, and ingenuity as required to manage an important major function involving a number of departmental activities. Analyzes interdepartmental or functional situations to make decisions in situations requiring policy formulation, and approves actions of subordinates within broad limits of authority.

C.   Programs and Projects

Factor Level	Definitions
1	Projects are on an assigned basis involving well defined tasks, approved methods, and standard procedures.
2	Projects have a relation to product or services but are not complex in nature. The possibility for errors is slight. Requires interpretation and application of known facts by using approved methods or following precedents.
3	Projects are complex in nature. Requires originality and the application of related knowledge within accepted standard practice.
4	Projects are diversified or specialized in nature. Requires selections from a broad range of procedures, and the analysis of facts to determine appropriate actions. Creative ability to improve or develop a product or service for an established program is essential.
5	Projects are diversified and highly technical with direct effect on products or services. Requires extensive subject matter knowledge and ability to adapt and modify procedures to meet new situations and conditions.

Figure 1.6 *(cont.)*

6   Work involves planning, direction, and supervision of numerous projects that are part of an overall program. Applies extensive subject matter and policy and procedural knowledge in devising new methods. Accomplishes objectives independently.

7   Work requires the development and administration of programs at the departmental level based on an appraisal of facts, trends, and anticipated results that relate to overall company objectives.

8   Work requires the development, implementation, and administration of programs of an important division-level function of the company. Incumbent usually is an officer of the company.

D. Supervision

Factor Level	Definitions
1	Works under direct supervision. Receives detailed instructions and guidance. Does not supervise others, but may assist with the instruction and training of new employees.
2	Works under general instructions. May supervise and train a small unit of semi-skilled or clerical employees as a group leader.
3	Works under general instructions of a department manager. Responsible for a small group of employees assigned to a project.
4	Works under general supervision of a major department manager. While usually responsible for a section, could be the manager of a small staff function or department.
5	Works under the general direction of a division manager with responsibility for the supervision of a major department under defined limits of authority.
6	Works under direction of an officer or top functional executive. Directs a major corporate staff function or division-level organization, or serves as a key assistant to a corporate officer.
7	Works under direction of an officer or a top functional executive. Directs a major activity that may involve operations at more than one location.
8	Works under the direction of a chief executive officer. Responsible for the direction of a major function through managers who are directly responsible for their activities. Incumbent is an officer and/or top functional executive of the company.

–Page 7–

Figure 1.6 *(cont.)*

E. Accountability

Factor Level	Description
1	Responsible for the proper use and care of assigned equipment and materials. Influences costs only through the degree of personal efficiency.
2	Responsible for the proper use and care of highly valuable equipment and supplies. Nature of work may indirectly affect company costs and profitability.
3	Work involves direct responsibility for the control, preservation, and efficient utilization of equipment and/or facilities. Effectiveness results in controlling expenses.
4	As a supervisor, incumbent is responsible for the control, protection, and efficient use of equipment and/or facilities. Efforts have an important influence on the production of income and the control of costs.
5	Responsible and accountable as a department-level manager for the control, protection, and efficient use of the equipment and facilities of a department. Efforts directly affect the production of income and the control of costs.
6	Responsible and directly accountable to a corporate officer for the control and efficient utilization of equipment and facilities of a major function or division. Responsible for the production of income and the control of costs by the organizational unit(s) managed.
7	Responsible as a key executive for the effective control and efficient use of equipment companywide, or for a group of major company organizations. Directly responsibile for the production of income and the control of costs.
8	Responsible as an officer for the acquisition, maintenance, and efficient use of all equipment and facilities. Full responsibility for the production of income and the control of expenditures in meeting operating plan profitability objectives.

F. Policies and Methods

Factor Level	Definitions
1	Performs work according to well defined policies, procedures, and methods, which apply to a particular activity.
2	Responsible for interpreting policies and applying associated procedures and methods to a particular activity.

–Page 8–

Figure 1.6 (cont.)

3	Responsible for interpreting and applying methods and procedures. Ensures that policies are maintained and that interpretations by others are in accordance with established standards.
4	Responsible for formulating policies and/or recommending modifications of policies and procedures to meet changing conditions and generally improve operations.
5	As a manager, is responsible for initiating and developing major policies. Interprets company policy as required by complex requirements.
6	As an officer, responsible for promoting and contributing to the formulation of organizationwide policies. Ensures that policies and procedures are properly interpreted and applied throughout the functions for which the position is held accountable.

G. Relationships

Factor Level	Definition
1	Few and irregular external relationships. Internal relationships largely are with individuals in own immediate organization.
2	Limited external contacts with customers, vendors, staff, and other company representatives. Department-wide and occasional interdepartmental contacts.
3	Extensive external contacts involve significant importance. For example, meetings with management level personnel of other companies regarding customer relations issues. Requires extensive interdepartmental contacts, and occasional contacts with company management.
4	Extensive external contacts on a management level regarding company projects. Internal relationships on all levels are primarily at the division level in scope and purpose.
5	Direct and regular external contacts with the top management of other companies, with important representatives of the community, government agencies, and so on. Internal contacts are companywide and primarily at the officer level.

–Page 9–

Figure 1.6 *(cont.)*

```
┌─────────────────────────────────────────────────────────────┐
│           ┌──────────────────────────────────┐               │
│           │   POSITION DESIGN WORKSHEET—      │               │
│           │ PROFESSIONAL/ADMINISTRATIVE/      │               │
│           │         MANAGERIAL                │               │
│           └──────────────────────────────────┘               │
```

Proposed position title _____ Mechanical Engineer _____

Company location _____ Philadelphia, PA _____

Organization/function/project _____ Design Engineering Department _____

Division _____ Engineering Services Division _____

Reports to (position title) _____ Manager, Design Engineering _____

I. General Function—State the major purpose/objective/function of the proposed position.

Performs design engineering assignments involving the preparation of layouts and detail drawings for elements of office building mechanical systems (heating, ventilating, air conditioning, plumbing, and steam distribution).

II. Position Requirements—Provide details regarding the duties and responsibilities of the position, and the associated educational and experience requirements, by completing each of the following items.

A. Knowledge—Describe the knowledge required by defining the amount and type of education and experience needed for successful performance.

Requires a college degree in mechanical engineering or its equivalent in terms of professional knowledge obtained through specialized work experience. Working knowledge of related engineering disciplines, particularly structural and electrical, is essential.

B. Mental Application—Describe the typical decisions the incumbent will be called upon to make, and indicate the extent to which he or she must seek guidance in making these decisions. To what degree does the position require independently creating, developing, and executing plans and procedures? Explain the extent to which the work is governed by established practices, rules, regulations, and so on, as compared with work requiring the application of creativity and originality.

Receives assignments with specific instructions concerning objectives and procedures to be used, and detailed guidance needed to solve problems; however, repetitive work is performed independently. Some ingenuity is required in selecting appropriate guidelines and deciding between alternative problem-solving approaches.

C. Programs and Projects—Describe the incumbent's responsibility for the planning, development, organization, implementation, and direction of specific assignments, programs, and operations. Indicate the extent to which these responsibilities are governed by policy and practice, their scope, their complexities in terms of difficulty and problems involved, and the level of authority vested in the position.

Figure 1.6 *(cont.)*

Performs assignments, as assigned by supervision, that require applying standard engineering principles, methods, and practices for solving well defined problems through specified standard procedures. Prepares layout and detail drawings for routine projects or portions of larger and more complex projects. Performs calculations. Reviews contractor drawings to ensure adherence to specifications.

D. Supervision—If nonsupervisory, describe the type and amount of direction received and the incumbent's functional responsibilities, if any, for the training of lower-level employees. If supervisory, list the titles of positions that report directly to the incumbent. Indicate the title of the incumbent's immediate supervisor or manager.

Works under the direct supervision of the supervisor or higher-level engineers. Receives detailed instructions and guidance.

E. Accountability—Describe the kind, amount, and scope of the incumbent's responsibility for the maintenance and conservation of assets (buildings, equipment, inventory, and so on), for producing income, and for exercising control over the allocation and utilization of resources.

Requires effective application of professional skills in providing adequate designs while relieving higher-level engineers from performing routine work.

F. Policies and Methods—Describe the incumbent's responsibility for the formulation, interpretation, and execution of policies, procedures, and methods. Specify the incumbent's organizational level and the extent of the incumbent's influence on company operations. Provide details concerning records and reports for which he or she is responsible.

Performs duties in accordance with well defined established methods and procedures.

G. Relationships—Describe the contacts the incumbent has regularly both within and outside the company. What is the level of these contacts? What impact do they have on company operations?

Requires personal contacts with other engineers and technicians within the immediate office, and limited external contacts with company construction engineering personnel, and design engineering contractor personnel. Obtains advice, assistance, or information regarding the condition of existing facilities. Reports on status or results of work.

Prepared by	John T. White	Date	9/17/88
Position title	Manager, Design Engineering Department		
Reviewed by	Paul C. Brown	Date	9/23/88
Position title	Director, Engineering Services Division		

Figure 1.6 *(cont.)*

1.7 JOB/POSITION DESCRIPTION FORMATS

This section provides four examples of position descriptions that represent the principle approaches currently in use. All the examples provide a general statement on the overall purpose of the position followed by a section for describing in detail specific duties and responsibilities. Functions are described through the use of active verbs (see Section 1.8, Listing of Active Verbs for Describing Employee Work Functions).

Figure 1.7A is a short, but very complete, description of a typical secretary's job responsibilities. Because this type of a position is very much the same wherever it is found throughout the organization, it lends itself to standardization. (Standardization is further explained in Section 1.9, Standardized Position Descriptions.)

Figure 1.7B is an excellent example of a complete and precisely defined listing of the specific duties and responsibilities of a position. You can readily understand precisely what is required; however, the example does not provide for contingencies. The inclusion of a final statement such as "performs other related duties as assigned" would provide the flexibility needed to avoid problems. Otherwise, if the incumbent's supervisor decides to add another function to the position (which has been written in what appears to be an all-inclusive description of functions), questions surface regarding workload, value of the position, and so on.

It also should be noted that the last section of the job description defines "secretarial and administrative duties." This is an excellent example of a hybrid position that has grown to be more than secretarial. As a facilities coordinator with the responsibility for performing a wide variety of functions on behalf of the manager, the incumbent performs the duties of assistant manager/administrative assistant/secretary.

Figure 1.7C offers an example of a position description that describes the functions performed by a store manager in a chain of convenience stores. It is a "standardized position description" that adequately defines the role of all store managers throughout the company and specifies their requisite qualifications.

Figure 1.7D is an example of an overseas position with an expatriate incumbent. This position specification for the director of personnel and industrial relations is typical of the varied approaches used internationally. For example, this Brazilian version includes volume of work statistics, the goals to be achieved by the actions performed, and emphasis on how the legal requirements of the company to the government are being met by the incumbent.

The Position Design Workbook, as explained in Section 1.6, also serves as the basis for preparing a special position description format. This Position Specification format readily facilitates the position evaluation process. A sample of this type of special position description is provided in Section 7.3 of Chapter 7, Wage and Salary Administration.

Position Description

Position Title: Secretary

Division: Manufacturing

Department: Production Engineering

Section: N/A   Location: Detroit

Reports to: Manager, Production Engineering

GENERAL FUNCTION: The incumbent participates in the management of the office by performing routine administrative functions on behalf of the supervisor. Based on a sound working knowledge of the organization and its functions, the incumbent resolves problems associated with the administrative operations of the office.

DUTIES AND RESPONSIBILITIES: Receives calls and greets visitors. Directs callers and visitors to appropriate staff members. Resolves routine matters based on knowledge of the programs or operations. Responds orally or in writing to routine requests for information and maintains supervisor's calendar; schedules appointments based on knowledge of commitments and interests.

Receives and reviews mail. Determines which items require supervisory review, and routes others to appropriate staff members. Maintains suspense records on action items and follows up to ensure timely completions.

Types all kinds of letters, memoranda, and documents. Sets up general statistical summaries and other complex typing requirements.

Keeps current on administrative practice revisions on such matters as the preparation and processing of correspondence, reports, and forms. Prepares correspondence from rough drafts, notes, or oral instructions. Ensures proper spelling, grammar, format, and arrangement of material. Takes and transcribes dictation.

Provides guidance and assistance concerning regulations and procedures to the organization's employees.

Figure 1.7A Position description

Job Description

Company Unit: <u>Administrative Services</u>

Position: <u>Facilities Coordinator</u>

Reports to: <u>Facilities Administration Manager</u>

A. Function

The primary function of the Facilities Coordinator position is to assume the following job responsibilities:
1. Organization and maintenance of employee cafeteria records.
2. Backup for Cafeteria Supervisor.
3. Process sale and transfer of office furniture and equipment.
4. Maintenance of records relating to construction/renovations.
5. Exterior landscape administration.
6. Interior landscape administration.
7. Office furniture distribution and repair.
8. Secretarial and administrative duties for Manager.

B. Specific Responsibilities
1. Organization and maintenance of employee cafeteria records:
   a. Audit, verify, and record daily receipts.
   b. Prepare monthly sales tax, operating reports, and associated cost analyses for management.
   c. Audit vendor invoices to assure accuracy of charges and prepare payment vouchers.
   d. Maintain personnel records and operational files.
2. Backup for Cafeteria Supervisor:
   a. Act in a supervisory capacity in the absence of the Cafeteria Supervisor to ensure smooth operations.
   b. Assume responsibility for ordering food and supplies as necessary.
3. Process sale and transfer of office furniture and equipment (fixed assets):
   a. Prepare paperwork for the sale of depreciated fixed assets (determine book value, validity of sale, etc.)
   b. Maintain file with all related information.
4. Maintenance of records relating to construction/renovations:
   a. Audit invoices from vendors for payment and prepare vouchers and paperwork.
   b. Maintain files for correspondence, contracts, permits, etc.
   c. Act as liaison between on-side construction office and internal departments.
5. Exterior landscape administration:
   a. Advise landscaper of any matter requiring special attention.
   b. Oversee work performed by landscaper to ensure that established schedule is adhered to and that all contracted work is completed.
   c. Arrange annually for start-up of lawn sprinkler system.
   d. Audit invoices for payment.

Figure 1.7B   Job description

continued

6. Interior landscape administration:
   a. Arrange for acquisition of all new office plants and monitor purchase orders.
   b. Oversee work by vendor; advise when replacements are needed, or if any special attention is required.
   c. Act as liaison between vendor and company departments.
   d. Maintain inventory.
7. Office furniture distribution and repair:
   a. Upon receipt from vendor, arrange for delivery and handle paperwork.
   b. Assign fixed asset numbers when required and maintain listing regarding description, location, etc.
   c. Report service requests or repairs to Maintenance Department or vendor for completion; oversee repairs by vendor.
   d. Prepare paperwork for transfers, returns, exchanges.
8. Secretarial and administrative duties:
   a. Prepare correspondence to outside vendors; maintain all departmental records, and establish policies relating to position, when necessary.
   b. Maintain contact with outside vendors to guarantee that work is done on timely basis.
   c. Responsible for all secretarial and administrative duties for manager including word processing, typing, filing, and telex transmissions.

(Date)

Figure 1.7B *(cont.)*

Position Description

Position: Store Manager

I. Overall Requirements

Responsible for profitably managing all phases of store operations. Must effectively and efficiently plan, organize, lead, coordinate, and control material and human resources in maximizing sales while minimizing operating expenses. Requires sufficient experience with the company or comparable retailing operation(s) to meet performance standards. Former department managers from major retail chains and managers of convenience or small department stores typically are qualified for this position. Specific P&L responsibility and experience in all phases of store operations are essential.

Candidates for Associate Manager/Trainee positions must have similar retail experience at comparably lower levels.

II. Duties and Responsibilities

1.   Merchandising—Ensures maximum possible sales through effectively organizing and implementing inventory control, ordering, display, promotional, and customer service functions.
2.   Customer Relations—Promotes company image as a service-oriented neighborhood convenience store. Participates in civic groups and community activities as the company's representative.
3.   Security—Controls stock, physical assets, and cash in accordance with company policies and procedures.
4.   Housekeeping—Maintains the highest possible standard of store cleanliness and orderliness as required to promote customer development and ensure that safety standards are achieved.
5.   Administration—Submits accurate and timely reports on all phases of store operations. Analyzes trends and historical data to improve P&L position. Maintains required store records in compliance with company policy and procedures.
6.   Human Resources Management—Recruits, selects, trains, develops, leads, and retains well qualified employees. Promotes positive morale and builds team spirit as required to achieve store goals.

Figure 1.7C Position description

Position Specification

Position Title: __Director of Personnel and Industrial Relations__

Division: __Personnel and Industrial Relations__

Department: __N/A__

Location: __Monte da Prata, Brasil__

Reports to: __Assistant Executive Director, Administration__

GENERAL JOB DESCRIPTION: Plans, organizes, directs, coordinates, and controls the overall personnel and industrial relations functions of MINAS, LTDA. and affiliated companies. Promotes more efficient and effective utilization of personnel to achieve associated cost savings. Provides systematic basis for more cost-conscious recruitment, selection, placement, and development of employees.

MAJOR DUTIES AND RESPONSIBILITIES:

I. Functional

Recruitment and Selection—Directs the planning and implementation of recruitment programs, domestically and internationally, as required to fill approximately 4,500 personnel requisitions annually. Promotes utilization of professional selection techniques in ensuring satisfactory placements, thereby reducing costly employee turnover.

Personnel Administration—Directs the systematic processing of approximately 1,200 personnel status changes each month (admission of new employees; employee status changes such as transfers, promotions, and salary adjustments; employee benefit administration; and demissions of resigned and terminated employees). Ensures compliance with prompt admission-demission requirements in order to minimize compensation paid to transient personnel.

Labor Relations—Directs labor relations activities involving the company attorney and outside counsel as required to represent company interests and minimize costs involved in labor court settlements. Represents company in syndicate-federation matters relating to organized labor groups.

Safety—Ensures that legally required and other necessary safety at work programs are developed and implemented in promoting the health and welfare of employees. Promotes safety consciousness of employees through campaigns, instructions, and frequent inspections thereby reducing accidents and costly lost-time.

Education—Provides overall direction, in accordance with legal and company policy requirements, as necessary to ensure that standards of education are continuously maintained throughout the company-sponsored schooling facilities provided for children and young adults.

Security—Directs the overall asset and public protection programs as required to protect the extensive capital investments of the company, and to ensure that degree of law and order needed for the protection and general welfare of residents in company communities.

Figure 1.7D Position specification

continued

Training—Promotes cost-reduction through the effective in-house orientation of new employees to ensure satisfactory placements and the retention of personnel. Provides skill-level advancement through a wide variety of training programs with emphasis on critically-needed skills not readily available through recruitment. Arranges special training programs through coordination with heavy equipment suppliers as essential to promote the proper operation, maintenance, and maximum serviceability of costly and critically-needed machines.

Public and Community Relations—Directs the centralized planning and effective implementation of promotional orientation programs for visitors. Coordinates all social and recreational activities. Serves as principal company representative with responsibility for social club facilities and operations. Provides social assistance services (family assistance, etc.). Provides employee communications and publications as required for promoting community development.

II. Other

Coordinates with related U.S.-based companies concerning the development and implementation of policies and procedures for expatriate employees. Assists expatriate and third-country nationals in visa processing activities.

Figure 1.7D *(cont.)*

1.8 LISTING OF ACTIVE VERBS FOR DESCRIBING EMPLOYEE WORK FUNCTIONS

The basic rule for writing job/position descriptions is to use active verbs to begin sentences. They provide the focus for the reader to see and readily understand the actions being described. This listing will be helpful in jogging your memory to fully describe duties and responsibilities.

Acts	Develops	Inventories	Reconciles
Advises	Devises	Investigates	Records
Allocates	Diagnoses		Regulates
Analyses	Directs	Joins	Reports
Appoints	Discusses		Requests
Appraises	Documents	Leads	Researches
Arranges	Drafts	Lists	Resolves
Assigns	Duplicates		Responds
Assists		Maintains	Reviews
Authorizes	Enforces	Makes	Revises
	Estimates	Manages	
Builds	Evaluates	Matches	Schedules
	Examines	Measures	Selects
Calculates	Executes	Mediates	Separates
Calibrates	Experiments	Meets	Serves
Chooses	Explains	Monitors	Settles
Classifies			Solves
Collects	Files	Negotiates	Sorts
Compares	Forecasts	Notes	Studies
Composes	Formulates		Suggests
Computes		Observes	Summarizes
Conducts	Grades	Offers	Supervises
Confers	Guides	Organizes	Supplies
Consults			
Contrasts	Helps	Places	Tabulates
Controls	Holds	Plans	Tests
Coordinates		Posts	Times
Counsels	Identifies	Prepares	Tracks
Counts	Implements	Prescribes	Trains
	Indexes	Promotes	Transcribes
Decides	Initiates	Provides	Translates
Defines	Inspects	Purchases	
Delegates	Instructs		Verifies
Demonstrates	Interacts	Ranks	
Designs	Interprets	Rates	Weighs
Determines	Interviews	Recommends	

1.9 STANDARDIZED POSITION DESCRIPTIONS

It is counterproductive to write separate descriptions for jobs/positions which are indistinguishable except for their locations within the company. These types of descriptions should be standardized.

Representative samples of standardized position descriptions for secretarial and clerical positions, grouped whenever possible within the framework of job families, are provided as follows.

Executive Secretary (Figure 1.9A)

This job/position family, involving an entry-level III position as an internal advancement prospect for employees classified as a secretary, includes three levels intended to incorporate administrative assistant-type functions for key executives. Requisite educational and experience factors are stipulated for each level. For example, an Executive Secretary III position requires three to five years of experience as a secretary. The top position is designated as an Executive Secretary I to preclude the future addition of unnecessary levels.

Secretary (Figure 1.9B)

The description provides for the flexibility of assisting one or more managers. The statement of preference for company experience as a stenographer provides the path for advancement from stenographer (entry-level) to secretary (after 2 years) and to executive secretary (after 3 more years).

Stenographer (Figure 1.9C)

This entry-level position provides company experience in applying basic secretarial skills.

Clerk-Typist (Figure 1.9D)

A job family beginning with a trainee-level position offers rapid progression to the senior level in approximately three years.

File Clerk (Figure 1.9E)

A structure comparable to the clerk-typist family is provided. Both job families offer entry-level opportunities for commercial high school students as summer employment program participants. This provides three months of work experience for students between their junior and senior years. It is credited as company experience if they return for regular employment after graduation. (A summer employment program gives a company an excellent opportunity to identify outstanding performers for regular employment offers. It also supplements the workforce to accommodate needs that result from employee vacations.)

The standardized position description technique is recommended for *all* wage positions; they are uniformly similar for each job category. Written to be all inclusive statements of duties, each job is differentiated only by the level of the incumbent's experience and skill.

Standard Position Description

Position Title: <u>Executive Secretary</u>   FLSA: Exempt

Provides general administrative assistance to one or more executives at the General Manager level or above. *Requires expert secretarial skills, 1–2 years of special business education, and a minimum of 3 years experience as a secretary. Company experience is preferred as work requires knowledge of company organization, policies, and personnel.* Duties and responsibilities include dictation, typing, and general administrative functions. Work typically involves exposure to highly confidential information.

Level	Definition
III (3–5)	Provides assistance to an executive at the General Manager level. Records and transcribes dictation involving varied vocabulary and technical terms; may transcribe recorded dictation. Types variety of materials from copy. Composes letters for executive from general instructions. Maintains records and files. Opens and organizes mail to include routing inquiries to appropriate members of organization. Receives telephone calls and callers. Arranges meetings. Makes appointments and maintains executive's calendar. Relays messages from executive to subordinates. Reviews reports prepared by others to ensure procedural and typographical accuracy prior to submitting them for approval. Compiles special reports, summaries, and digests. May supervise work of lower-level secretarial and/or clerical personnel.
II (5–8)	Provides assistance to an executive at the vice-president level.
I (8+)	Provides assistance to an executive at the senior vice-president level.

Effective Date: (   ) = Years of experience required

Approved: _____
                        Human Resources Director

Figure 1.9A Standard position description (executive secretary)

Standard Position Description

Position Title: <u>Secretary</u>   FLSA: Non-Exempt

Provides general secretarial assistance to one or more managers. *Requires graduation from a commercial high school, competent stenographic and typing skills, and 2 years of related experience. Company experience as stenographer is preferred.* Work does not involve exposure to highly confidential information. Assignments are performed routinely under established guidelines.

Records and transcribes dictation involving varied vocabulary and technical terms; may transcribe recorded dictation. Types variety of materials from copy. Opens, organizes, and routes mail. Receives telephone calls and callers; makes appointments and maintains calendar for Manager. May compile data or reports. Maintains records and files. May perform variety of related assignments as directed.

Effective Date:

Approved: _____
                       Human Resources Director

Figure 1.9B Standard position description (secretary)

Standard Position Description

Position Title: Stenographer   FLSA: Non-Exempt

Assigned to two or more professional or administrative employees with high volume dictation requirements. *Requires graduation from a commercial high school, competent stenographic and typic skills, and one year of related experience.*

Primary function is to record and transcribe dictation involving varied vocabulary and technical terms. May do straight-copy typing of variety of materials; compose routine letters from general instructions; and perform a variety of clerical duties such as maintaining follow-up files, compiling information or assembling materials for reports, recording data, filing, and other similar work requiring some judgment.

Effective Date:

Approved: _____
                          Human Resources Director

Figure 1.9C Standard position description (stenographer)

Standard Position Description

Position Title: <u>Clerk-Typist</u>   FLSA: Non-Exempt

Level	Definition
III (0–1)	Trainee position for *commercial high school student or recent graduate* (summer employment between Junior and Senior years, or the first 12 months of regular employment).
II (1–3)	Performs general typing assignments requiring competent skills and the application of basic judgment, and clerical functions involving moderately difficult office practices. Types copies from longhand or typed drafts which frequently include technical terms. May type forms, form letters, and formats for duplication processes. Sets up and types basic tables, or types more complicated tables which have been already set up and spaced properly. Prepares, maintains, compares, checks, and files statements, tabulations, and reports. May be required to answer telephones, sort and distribute mail, operate business machines, or any other related duties as assigned. *A commercial high school graduate with 1–3 years of related experience is required.*
I (3 +)	A senior-level position involving general and highly complicated typing. Requires expert skills and the application of complex judgments in accomplishing difficult office practices. Types tables, reports, and briefs from rough and involved drafts; extensive knowledge of a foreign language and/or technical terms may be essential. Responsible for correct spelling, syllabication, and punctuation of material. May combine material from several sources into one typed document. Plans, lays out, and types complicated statistical tables requiring uniformity and balance in spacing. Prepares, maintains, compares, checks, and files statements, tabulations, and reports. May be required to answer telephones, sort or distribute mail, operate business machines, or any other related duties as assigned. May supervise the work of lower level clerk-typists.

Effective Date: (   ) = Years of Experience Required

Approved: _____
                    Human Resources Director

Figure 1.9D   Standard position description (clerk-typist)

44

Standard Position Description

Position Title: <u>File Clerk</u>   FLSA: Non-Exempt

Level	Definition
III (0–1)	*Trainee position for commercial high school student or recent graduate (summer employment between Junior and Senior years, or the first 12 months of regular employment).*
II (1–3)	Performs routine filing of materials which have been already classified, or which are easily classified (alphabetical, chronological, or numerical filing system). Locates and forwards materials as requested. Performs clerical tasks as required to maintain and service files. May use typewriter in connection with file work.
I (3 +)	A senior-level position involving the performance of complex filing operations. Classifies, indexes, and files materials such as records, reports, correspondence, and technical documents. Prepares index and cross reference aids. Keeps records of materials removed from files. Locates and selects materials as required to meet general information requests. May use typewriter in connection with file work. May supervise the work of lower-level File Clerks.

Effective Date: ( ) = Years of Experience Required

Approved: _____
                       Human Resources Director

Figure 1.9E   Standard position description (file clerk)

1.10 EMPLOYEE SKILL IDENTIFICATION SYSTEM

This system is designed to accommodate both small and large companies. It can be used manually through a file retrieval technique, or it can be used for providing a computer data bank of specific human resource capabilities that can be retrieved through automated techniques.

The Employee Skill Identification System form (Figure 1.10) can be printed on card stock to facilitate manual retrieval techniques. Information needed for identifying employee skills is provided in boxes at the top of the form; this readily permits manual searches for data contained in eleven boxes. For example, the boxes contain coded information as explained in the INSTRUCTIONS section of the form.

If an electronics engineer with a Masters Degree, recent product design experience for at least seven years, and at least two years of supervisory experience is needed at the company's plant in Cleveland, the search begins by screening cards filed together for all electronics engineers throughout the company. Those employees identified in Box 5 as having a Masters Degree are scanned through Boxes 1–4 to find the code for product design engineering and the requisite number of recent years of experience. Boxes 10 and 11 are then reviewed to determine whether apparent candidates are interested in relocating to the Cleveland area. The personnel files of those who appear to meet requisite criteria then are reviewed to select the best qualified candidates for consideration.

An essential ingredient for the success of this system is to have all employees update their Employee Skill Identification System form/card annually.

A manual system should be based on filing cards by educational skill code. As in the example, all electronics engineers are filed together. When a new project is being proposed, and the HR director is called upon to provide data on electronics engineers with specific types and amounts of experience, this may be accomplished readily through reviewing this portion of the file.

Automated systems offer many advantages if your needs justify the associated expenses. The data base must be created and/or revised as new employees are added, revised when employees leave the company, and updated periodically for all employees to ensure continued accuracy of data.

Employee Skill Identification System

INSTRUCTIONS: Please print legibly in ink.

Items ⓵–⓸ *Experience Category Codes*—Select codes from the attached listing to designate your primary skill in item I, secondary skill in item 2, etc. *Example:* If your primary skill is Tax Accounting, enter AC11 in item I.

Ⓐ *Amount of Experience*—Enter the total amount of related experience for each code you select.

Ⓑ *Most Recent Year*—Enter the most recent year that you performed this type of work, e.g., 83.

Item ⓹ *Educational Qualifications:*

Ⓒ *Educational Skill Code*—Select and enter the code which best describes the primary emphasis of your educational background: e.g., Electronics Engineering is E 3 0 7 .

Ⓓ *Educational Level Code*—Select and enter the appropriate code, e.g., Doctorate is Ⓓ.

Item ⓺ *Total Years of Supervisory Experience*—Enter your best estimate by adding all periods throughout your career when you performed supervisory responsibilities.

Item ⓻ *Total Years of Work Experience*—If you are a college graduate, you would normally calculate from the time after your degree was awarded when you began career employment.

Item ⓼ *Fluency in Foreign Languages*—Enter appropriate codes for languages you speak, read, and write fluently.

Item ⓽ *Current Company Work Location*—Enter appropriate code.

Item ⓾ *Willing to Relocate?* Assume a promotional opportunity. Enter Ⓨ for "Yes" or Ⓝ for "No."

Item ⑪ *Relocation Preferences*—Enter Company Work Location Codes to designate your 1st, 2nd, and 3rd preference from top to bottom.

COMMENTS: (Provide any clarifications needed regarding your choices):

Name _____ Date _____ Social Security No. ☐☐☐☐☐☐

Figure 1.10 Employee skill identification system

1.11 EMPLOYEE SKILL INVENTORY CATEGORY—CODES INDEX

Items 1 through 4: Experience Category Codes

BUSINESS

Accounting
AC01-Accounts Payable
AC02-Accounts Receivable
AC03-Auditing
AC04-Collections
AC05-Cost Analysis
AC06-Credit
AC07-Fixed Assets
AC08-General
AC09-General Ledger
AC10-Payroll
AC11-Tax

FACILITIES MANAGEMENT

FA01-Construction
FA02-Distribution
FA03-Document Control
FA04-Facilities Planning
FA05-Library
FA06-Mail Service
FA07-Maintenance
FA08-Office Automation
FA09-Office Methods and Systems
FA10-Office Services
FA11-Printing
FA12-Property Management
FA13-Real Estate Acquisition
FA14-Records Management
FA15-Repairs
FA16-Security
FA17-Shipping and Receiving/Distribution
FA18-Supplies
FA19-Telephone Service/Communications
FA20-Traffic Management

FINANCE/ECONOMICS

FN01-Budgeting
FN02-Financial Planning/Forecasting
FN03-Funds Investment

FN04-Funds Transfer
FN05-Insurance
FN06-Reporting

HUMAN RESOURCES MANAGEMENT/PERSONNEL

HR01-Benefits
HR02-Compensation
HR03-EEO/AA
HR04-Employee Assistance
HR05-Employee Development
HR06-Employee Relations
HR07-Employment/Staffing
HR08-Industrial Hygiene
HR09-Industrial Medicine/Preventative Medicine
HR10-Information Systems/Records
HR11-Labor Relations
HR12-Organizational Development
HR13-Planning and Evaluation
HR14-Psychological Testing/Research
HR15-Safety

LEGAL

LE01-Arbitration
LE02-Contracts
LE03-General Business Advisory
LE04-Government Relations
LE05-International Relations
LE06-Leases
LE07-Litigation

MANUFACTURING/PRODUCTION

MP01-Cost Estimation
MP02-Inventory Control
MP03-Methods Analysis
MP04-Production Control
MP05-Project Management
MP06-Quality Assurance
MP07-Reliability Assessment
MP08-Resource Requirements Planning
MP09-Schedule Control

MARKETING

MA01-Advertising
MA02-Community Relations
MA03-Government Relations
MA04-Planning

MA05-Public Relations

MA06-Research

MA07-Sales

MA08-Sales Promotion

MISCELLANEOUS (GENERAL ADMINISTRATIVE)

GA01-Data Analysis

GA02-Data Collection

GA03-Editing

GA04-Graphics

GA05-Indexing

GA06-Proposal Development

GA07-Report Preparation

GA08-Scheduling

GA09-Word Processing

GA10-Writing—General

GA11-Writing—Technical

PURCHASING

PG01-Contract Administration

PG02-Contract Negotiation

PG03-Expediting

PG04-Leasing

PG05-Procurement

COMPUTER SCIENCE

CS01-Computer Operations—Hardware

CS02-Computer Operations—Software

CS03-Computer Security

CS04-Data Base Development

CS05-Data Entry

CS06-File Maintenance

CS07-Performance Analysis-Failure Correction

CS08-Performance Assessment

CS09-Planning and Scheduling

CS10-Processing Control

CS11-Programming

CS12-Software Design

CS13-Software Development

CS14-Software Documentation

CS15-Software Maintenance

CS16-Systems Analysis

CS17-Systems Design

CS18-Systems Development

CS19-Systems Testing

ENGINEERING

    EN01-Applied Research
    EN02-Consulting
    EN03-Design
    EN04-Development
    EN05-Feasibility Studies
    EN06-Implementation (Installation/Construction)
    EN07-Planning
    EN08-Project Management
    EN09-Test and Evaluation

MATHEMATICS AND SCIENCE

    MS01-Differential Equations
    MS02-Mathematical Modeling
    MS03-Monte Carlo
    MS04-Numerical Analysis
    MS05-Operations Research
    MS06-Statistical Analysis

TRADES/CRAFTS/TECHNICIANS/OPERATIVES/SERVICE WORKERS/LABORERS

    TR01-Assembler
    TR02-Aircraft Mechanic
    TR03-Asphalt Worker
    TR04-Automobile Mechanic
    TR05-Baker
    TR06-Boiler Plant Operator
    TR07-Boilermaker
    TR08-Carpenter
    TR09-Cement Finisher
    TR10-Cook
    TR11-Crane Operator
    TR12-Electrician
    TR13-Electrician (High Voltage)
    TR14-Electronics Technician
    TR15-Electroplater
    TR16-Elevator Mechanic
    TR17-Equipment Operator—Heavy
    TR18-Equipment Cleaner
    TR19-Food Service Worker
    TR20-Fork Lift Operator
    TR21-Gardener
    TR22-Heating/Boiler Plant Mechanic
    TR23-Heavy Equipment Mechanic
    TR24-Heavy Equipment Operator
    TR25-Inspector
    TR26-Instrument Maker

TR27-Janitor
TR28-Laboratory Worker
TR29-Laborer
TR30-Machinist
TR31-Machine Tool Operator
TR32-Maintenance Mechanic
TR33-Mason
TR34-Materials Expediter
TR35-Model Maker
TR36-Motor Vehicle Operator
TR37-Office Machine Repairer
TR38-Packer
TR39-Painter
TR40-Pipefitter
TR41-Plasterer
TR42-Plumber
TR43-Production Worker
TR44-Rigger
TR45-Roofer
TR46-Sandblaster
TR47-Sheet Metal Mechanic
TR48-Sign Painter
TR49-Store Worker
TR50-Telephone Mechanic
TR51-Toolmaker
TR52-Tools and Parts Attendant
TR53-Warehouse Worker
TR54-Welder
TR55-Woodcrafter

Item 5 C: Educational Skill Codes

BUSINESS

B100-Accounting
B101-Administration (General)
B102-Banking
B103-Commerce
B104-Economics
B105-Finance
B106-Human Resources/Personnel
B107-Industrial Health and Safety
B108-Industrial Relations
B109-Logistics
B110-Market Research
B111-Marketing/Advertising
B112-Production/Manufacturing
B113-Retailing
B114-Sales
B115-Other (Specify in comments section)

COMPUTER SCIENCE

C200-Computer Science
C201-Information Processing
C202-Programming
C203-Systems Analysis
C204-Other (Specify in comments section)

ENGINEERING

E300-Aerospace
E301-Agricultural
E302-Architectural
E303-Bio-engineering
E304-Chemical
E305-Civil
E306-Electrical
E307-Electronics
E308-General
E309-Industrial
E310-Marine
E311-Mechanical
E312-Medical
E313-Metallurgical
E314-Mining
E315-Nuclear
E316-Petroleum
E317-Other (Specify in comments section)

MATHEMATICS AND SCIENCE

S400-Applied Mathematics
S401-Astronomy
S402-Bacteriology
S403-Chemistry
S404-Forestry
S405-General
S406-Geology
S407-Metallurgy
S408-Minerology
S409-Oceanography
S410-Operations Research
S411-Physics
S412-Statistics
S413-Other (Specify in comments section)

MISCELLANEOUS

M500-Graphic Arts
M501-Journalism
M502-Law
M503-Liberal Arts

M504-Library Science
M505-Medical Technology
M506-Medicine
M507-Nursing—Industrial
M508-Photography
M509-Printing
M510-Secretarial Administration
M511-Technical Illustration
M512-Technical Writing
M513-Word Processing
M514-Other (Specify in comments section)

Item 5 D: Educational Level Codes

N = Non-High School Graduate
H = High School Graduate
C = Commercial High School Graduate
V = Vocational High School Graduate
S = Secretarial School Graduate
A = Associate Degree
B = Bachelors Degree
M = Masters Degree
D = Doctorate
P = Post-Doctorate

Item 8: Fluency in Foreign Language Codes

01-Arabic
02-Chinese
03-Dutch
04-French
05-German
06-Greek
07-Hebrew
08-Hindi
09-Italian
10-Japanese
11-Pakistan
12-Persian
13-Portuguese
14-Russian
15-Spanish
16-Thai
17-Turkish
18-Vietnamese

1.12 SUCCESSION PLANNING CHART: MANAGEMENT POSITIONS

Based on the premise that all existing management positions are essential for the success of your company because sound organizational planning has eliminated unnecessary positions, a formal replacement planning procedure is needed to ensure management continuity. In addition to maintaining current assessments of each incumbent's performance problems, developmental requirements, and potential for promotion, the system must identify successors by:

1. *Identifying the few top performers* who are or will be ready for promotion in the near term (within 2 years), and designating one or more target positions for their candidacy. Designated positions are the basis for providing highly promotable individuals with special assignments and executive training which encourage their further development and retention with the company while waiting for the next higher position.
2. *Identifying highly satisfactory* performers who potentially can qualify for promotion to a higher-level position within 2–5 years. In designating such individuals as successors, the company must design and implement appropriate individual development plans to ensure readiness for advancement within the stipulated time frames.
3. *Identifying satisfactory performers* whose growth normally is based on the potential of their current positions. These performers have achieved the highest level their personal capabilities will permit. They are not promotable, and block the position they hold until retirement. Although they may hold the position for a substantial number of years until retirement eligibility, successors must be designated to cover all contingencies.
4. *Identifying marginal performers* who may not be qualified for their positions. Successors must be lined up to ensure immediate readiness to assume these positions. Targeted successors may include nonsupervisory employees who have demonstrated advancement potential. In the absence of suitable successors, recruitment planning must be initiated to guarantee continuity in the event that a decision is made to terminate the services of the managers in question.

Sound planning requires vertical integration with adequate designees to assure full succession coverage of all management positions. If a top performer has very high promotability for a number of positions, it is recommended that he or she only be designated as the primary successor for one position. This does not preclude having this same individual designated as a secondary candidate for other positions. Should a position for which this individual was designated as a secondary candidate become available, the choice between this top performer and the primary candidate would be decided based on the following considerations.

1. If the top performer is made to wait until the primary position becomes available, what is the associated risk factor of losing him or her to another company?
2. How much longer must the top performer wait for the other position? Does he or she understand, through special assignments and other ties to the primary position, that succession in the near term is a possibility?
3. Would it be advisable to place the top performer in the position "temporarily," and have the primary successor wait until this individual moves to his or her

targeted position? What is the risk factor of losing the primary successor who would be passed over?

Any movement within this vertically integrated structure causes chain reactions which must be optimally planned and smoothly executed if the effectiveness of a company's management team is to be maintained.

To facilitate the planning process, the use of a Succession Planning Chart system is recommended (Figure 1.12). The chart provides the basis for depicting each management position as follows.

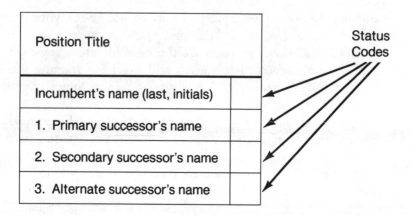

The chart is partially completed by the key manager of the organization by following these steps.

1. Enter the position titles in ink. An assistant manager/director position with line management responsibility should be shown in the upper left-hand box.
2. Draw connecting lines between boxes to properly represent reporting relationships. (The placement of an assistant manager-type position in the upper left-hand box facilitates this process.)
3. Enter in pencil the names of incumbents.
4. Check the status code listing to determine the appropriate designation for all incumbents (exclude yourself); enter this code in the status code box provided next to each incumbent's name.
5. To the extent possible in considering qualified successors within the organization in question, designate the names and status codes of primary/secondary/alternate successors in the appropriate boxes.
6. If you have identified individuals in other organizations that potentially may be successors, include their names only. When all charts are integrated into a proposed Master Succession Plan by the HR director, top management will make decisions regarding the overall succession strategy. You will receive a copy of the completed Succession Planning Chart for your organization to enable you to continuously review and update its contents as changes occur. Top management will review the overall integration of succession planning at the end of each quarter.

Status Codes

P1	=	Promotable within 1 year
P2	=	Promotable in 2 years
P3	=	Promotable in 3 years
P4	=	Promotable in 4 years
P5	=	Promotable in 5 years
PX	=	Promotable in more than 5 years
NP	=	Not Promotable (Satisfactorily performing incumbent with no promotion potential)
NR	=	Not suitable for retention (marginally performing incumbent)
R1	=	Retirement within 1 year
R2	=	Retirement in 2 years
R3	=	Retirement in 3 years
R4	=	Retirement in 4 years
R5	=	Retirement in 5 years
RX	=	Retirement in more than 5 years

Succession Planning Chart

Organization/Function/Project _____

Date Prepared _____
Date Reviewed _____
Date Reviewed _____
Date Reviewed _____
Date Reviewed _____

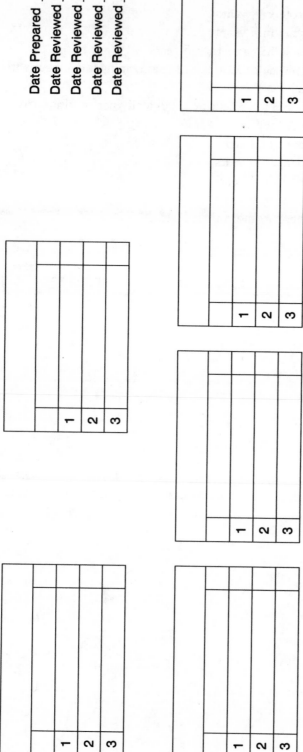
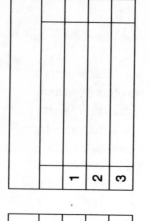
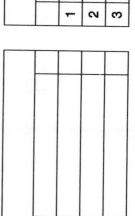
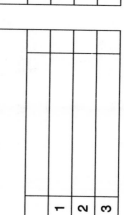
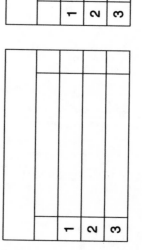

Figure 1.12 Succession planning chart

CHAPTER 2

Recruitment

This bottom line-oriented function is highly visible and measurable. Line management has little tolerance for new employees that are not on board within the specified time frames. A results-oriented framework with management participation in all steps of the process is essential for cooperation and understanding. The challenge for the HR director is to provide those unique methods and procedures that promote success.

Defining management's specific human resource requirements and obtaining approval to initiate appropriate recruitment actions is yielded through job analysis processes and using these three specialized personnel requisition forms:

1. Personnel Requisition
2. Campus Recruitment Personnel Requisition
3. Temporary Agency Employee Requisition

To complete the Personnel Requisition (see Figure 2.1), management is asked to participate by recommending recruitment plans and advertising programs to meet their requirements. They also participate in the design of appropriate advertisements through assisting in the preparation of the Help Wanted Advertisement Worksheet (see Figure 2.7).

When recruitment action is requested by a manager through the completion of a Personnel Requisition, a completed Employee Skill Identification System (ESIS) Search Request form (see Figure 2.6) must be attached. The completed Personnel Requisition also contains information necessary for preparing job posting announcements under the provisions of the Internal Placement Program. Outside recruitment action will be initiated *only* if suitable candidates are not identified internally.

Effective Internal Placement Program position-posting techniques issue listings of professional-level employee transfer and promotion opportunities at all company locations by the headquarter's HRM organization (see Figure 2.10), and listings of all job/position opportunities available at each location for local employees (see Figure 2.11).

Building close working relationships with employment agencies will enable you to supplement your recruitment capabilities; effective agency cooperation can be encouraged by using an Associated Agency Policy agreement (see Figure 2.15).

A properly constructed Applicant Resource File system (see Figure 2.20) can yield highly successful results.

Selling the company as a potential employer through Company Description Sheets (see Figure 2.17) and well organized invitations for interview letters (see Figure 2.22) leads to greater recruitment effectiveness.

Records such as the Help Wanted Advertisement Log (see Figure 2.9), Temporary Employee Agency Log (see Figure 2.26), and Employment Agency Fee Log (see Figure 2.27) provide cost control data.

2.1 PERSONNEL REQUISITION: DEFINING AND AUTHORIZING INTERNAL AND EXTERNAL RECRUITMENT ACTION

The Personnel Requisition (Figure 2.1) is designed to be $8\frac{1}{2} \times 14$ inches. This longer-than-normal page stands out on a desk filled with paperwork. To further ensure that this high priority form does not get lost in the shuffle, it should be printed on colored paper stock.

The procedure for completing the Personnel Requisition follows.

Employment Category, Shift, and Work Schedule. Specify appropriate categories as indicated.

Type of Recruitment. Specify reason for the recruitment action. An unbudgeted addition to a staff requires an explanation of why there is a need for the position. This explanation provides the basis for management assessment and approval/disapproval action.

Position Requirements. The requisitioner is required to attach the official job/position description and provide summary information. This summary requires a brief synopsis of major duties and responsibilities; details regarding essential education, experience, and special skills; and the specification of any special requirements such as fluency in a foreign language or willingness to travel. The contents of the description are used to prepare job posting, advertising, and employment agency announcement materials. The benefit of having a requisitioning manager provide this information is to have him or her focus on the essential requirements needed by an incumbent. Enhanced understanding of what is essential for the position will expedite the selection process. It avoids unnecessary confusion which results when specific needs are not defined until candidates are being considered.

Recommended Recruitment Plan. The understanding that no external recruitment action will be initiated until it is determined that no suitable candidate is available within the company is further reinforced in this section. The manager is required to attach a completed ESIS Search Request form (see Figure 2.6) to initiate the required internal job/position-to-employee matching process. This section also encourages the manager's participation in the external recruitment planning process by having him or her recommend advertising media and employment agencies. If the manager has an outside candidate in mind for the position, a so-called "targeted candidate," the individual's résumé is attached.

Personnel Requisition

No. _____ Date _____

Position Title _____ Grade _____

Organization _____ Location _____

Reports to (Name & Title) _____

Employment Category:

☐ Permanent full-time

☐ Temporary full-time
(Less than one year)

☐ Permanent part-time

☐ Call-in
(Indefinite full part-time)

Shift: ☐1st ☐2nd ☐3rd

Work Schedule:

	Mon	Tues	Wed	Thu	Fri	Sat	Sun
From							
To							

Type of Requirement:

☐ Addition to staff—budgeted

☐ Addition to staff—not budgeted

Explanation _____

_____

_____

☐ Replacement for employee:

Name _____

Title _____

Separation date _____

Position Requirements: Attach job/position description and provide the following information for job posting, advertising, and employment agency announcements.

Brief Description of Major Duties and Responsibilities

Details of Education, Experience, and Special Skills Required

Special Requirements (e.g., ability to speak foreign language, willingness to travel or relocate, etc.)

Recommended Recruitment Plan: Attach complete ESIS (Employee Skill Identification System) Search Request form, and provide the following information for outside recruitment planning in the event that neither the ESIS nor the Internal Placement Program posting system yields suitable candidates.

Recommended Advertisements (specify media and data).

Other [specify recommended employment agencies, targeted candidates (attach résumés), etc.]

Approvals:

Hire: Name_____ Date Employed_____ Ee # _____

Figure 2.1 Personnel requisition

2.2 CAMPUS RECRUITMENT PERSONNEL REQUISITION

The Campus Recruitment Personnel Requisition form (Figure 2.2), which includes three sections, is distributed to all hiring organizations each summer with a cover memorandum requesting completion. The memorandum emphasizes the need for the accurate assessments of:

I. Permanent Position Requirements

Each requirement is defined in terms of the position title, type of degree, major/specialization, and the initial work assignment. This breakdown of requirements provides the basis for a consolidated listing, prepared by the HRM organization, of companywide college recruitment requirements.

II. Summer Employment Program Requirements

Each student and faculty participant requirement is specified in terms of position title, major/specialization, and proposed project assignment. Position titles are designated as follows: a student between his or her junior and senior years is a college associate (specialization is designated, for example, electronics engineering); a graduate student is a graduate associate (specialization), and a faculty member is a faculty associate (specialization).

The "proposed project assignment" section is used to specify meaningful summer work experiences. Projects that simply provide "busy work" defeat the purpose of promoting sound college relations. High priority, viable work assignments that promote company objectives while enhancing individual career objectives are essential. Student interests must be matched with related project activities. Similarly, graduate student and faculty member research objectives must be accommodated by appropriate work experiences which also benefit the company. Meaningful summer work provides the encouragement needed to attract these high caliber undergraduates and graduate students to the company as permanent employees; it also encourages participating faculty members to promote the company as an employer with professionally rewarding opportunities.

III. Recommended Colleges/Universities

For each recruitment requirement specified in sections I and II, the organization's coordinator is required to recommend sources. For example, if Rutgers University is recommended for BSEE and BSME permanent candidates and BSME undergraduate participants for the summer employment program, the position codes for both requirements are entered next to the school name. For example, in accordance with the instructions shown at the bottom of the form, the position code(s) column entry might be "P1, P2, S1." *Note:* Each organization should have its own numerical designation. When preparing the companywide listing of College Recruitment Requirements, the HRM organization modifies position codes to include organizational designations. If this organization was designated as 200, P1 becomes P201, S1 becomes S201, and so on.

The organization's coordinator also is asked to designate faculty contacts who relate to current recruitment objectives at that campus. If a professor in the college's electronics engineering department participated in the company's summer employment program, he or she would be an excellent source of information for considering which undergraduate and graduate students should be considered for next year's program. He or she also can keep the company posted of the progress of students under consideration for permanent employment—both former summer employment program participants and others who have been identified as excellent career employment prospects.

The requirement for specifying the organization's campus representative ideally involves selecting an alumnus, preferably one who was graduated in recent years, who can easily establish rapport with and relate to candidates. As an alumnus, this individual also can readily establish effective contacts with former professors to identify their most promising students.

Campus Recruitment Personnel Requisition

Organization _____ Location _____ School Year of Sept. _____ to June _____

Coordinator _____

I. Permanent Position Requirements:

Code	#	Position Title	Type of Degree	Major/Specialization	Initial Work Assignment

II. Summer Employment Program Requirements:

Position Code	# of Students	# of Faculty	Position Title	Major/Specialization	Proposed Project Assignment

III. Recommended Colleges/Universities:

Position Code(s)	School Name	Location	Faculty Contacts Name	Dept.	Organization's Campus Rep.	Proposed Visit Date(s)

Approvals _____ _____

Position Codes: P + Number = Permanent Position Requirement
S + Number = Summer Position Requirement

Example: P2 designates a Permanent Position Requirement which is specified versus appropriate college(s) in Section III.

Figure 2.2 Campus recruitment personnel requisition

2.3 TEMPORARY AGENCY EMPLOYEE REQUISITION

The authorization of temporary agency employee requirements should be based on a company policy that ensures the following conditions have been met.

1. The work required cannot be performed by the organization's regular staff even if a reasonable amount of overtime is authorized.
2. The work required is of such a nature that it cannot be referred to the office services department (clerical services and the like).
3. The work required cannot be postponed until an employee returns from vacation, or some other relatively short period of absence. Absences of one week or less are not considered sufficient to justify the hiring of temporary employees.

The Temporary Agency Employee Requisition (Figure 2.3) includes provisions for specifying the following types of information.

- Position Required. The position title, organization, location, and reports to (name and title).
- Requirement Schedule. The dates must be listed (shown as from and through on the form). In addition to defining the duration of the requirement, this schedule provides the basis for ensuring adherence to the company's policy of not replacing employees who are absent for one week or less. The "hours of work" section is particularly helpful in specifying irregular hours and only certain days when the temporary employee will be required.
- Reason for Requirement. The "replacement of absent employee" section provides the background information needed to assess the duration of the absence. The "addition to meet workload needs" section requires an explanation of the needs and also should include the reasons why the existing staff and normal overtime cannot meet peak workload requirements (for example end-of-year consolidation activities).
- Summary of Required Skills. Highly specific and realistic requirements based on the work in question are delineated in this section. For example: "Must be able to set up and type complicated ledger sheets and statistical charts and graphs quickly and accurately. Typing 55 wpm and prior related experience is essential." Sufficient information must be provided to form the basis for the order which will be placed by the HRM organization with the temporary agency.

Temporary Agency Employee Requisition

Position Required

Title _____

Organization _____ Location _____

Reports to (Name & Title) _____

Requirement Schedule

Dates: From _____   Through _____

	Mon	Tues	Wed	Thu	Fri	Sat	Sun
Hours of From							
Work: To							

Reason for Requirement

☐ Replacement of Absent Employee

   Name of Employee _____

   Reason for Absence _____

   Dates of Absence: From _____   Through _____

☐ Addition to Meet Workload Needs

   Explanation: _____

   _____

   _____

   _____

   _____

   _____

   _____

Summary of Required Skills

   _____

   _____

   _____

   _____

   _____

   _____

   _____

Approvals: _____ _____ _____ _____
               Signature   Date   Signature   Date

Figure 2.3   Temporary agency employee requisition

2.4 EXECUTIVE SPECIFICATIONS QUESTIONNAIRE: DEFINING THE DETAILS OF AN EXECUTIVE SEARCH REQUIREMENT

Management's decision, based on thorough succession planning and assessments that no qualified candidate is available internally, may require turning to an executive search firm with specifications regarding the ideal candidate. The HR director can be critically important to the success of this initial contact by assisting management in preparing realistic definitions of absolutely essential qualifications versus optimum candidate qualifications. Factors that would disqualify an individual also should be defined. Similarly, a sound appraisal of proposed compensation should be formulated based on an assessment of market factors and equitable internal relationships. The Executive Specifications Questionnaire (Figure 2.4) provides the framework for yielding these essential requirement definitions.

The following steps are necessary for completing the questionnaire.

1. Specify why the position is needed, and what is essential for success in performing the basic functions of the position. If an incumbent is being replaced, the specific factors which led to a termination decision are defined.
2. Describe the ideal candidate in terms of education, experience, abilities, attitude, manner of relating to others, managerial/working style, prior performance indicators, appearance, and personality.
3. Define absolutely essential criteria for an acceptable candidate versus the criteria used for describing the ideal candidate.
4. Specify "knockout" factors that would eliminate a candidate.
5. Consider possible sources of qualified candidates.
6. Estimate starting salary and other compensation requirements.

Executive Specifications Questionnaire

Position Title _____

Reports to _____

Location _____

1. Why is the position subject to recruitment action at this time? If it is a new position, explain its basic role and define what is essential for success. If the incumbent is being replaced, what specific factors resulted in the decision to terminate his or her services? What expectations, goals, etc. were not met?

2. Describe the ideal candidate in terms of the following criteria:

   A. Educational background

   B. Experience

   C. Abilities/skills

   D. Attitude

   E. Manner of relating to others

   F. Managerial style/working style

   G. Prior performance indicators

   H. Appearance

   I. Presentation

3. Now that you have defined the ideal candidate, further qualify your answers to Question 2 to give a bottom-line definition of your minimum expectations for a qualified candidate:

   A. Educational background

   B. Experience

   C. Abilities/skills

   D. Attitude

   E. Manner of Relating to others

   F. Managerial style/working style

Figure 2.4 Executive specifications questionnaire

continued

G. Prior performance indicators

H. Appearance

I. Presentation

4. What factors would eliminate a candidate? Picture your ideal candidate and consider those things that such an individual would not do under any circumstances. What personality quirks, unusual mannerisms, unacceptable speech patterns, behaviors, etc., would make him or her not "fit in"?

5. Consider where suitable candidates might be found. Do you know anyone whom you think might be well suited for the position? What companies would have such an individual? At what locations? Who could you contact for recommendations?

6. Review the compensation of comparable positions, both within and outside the company, to establish your best estimates of starting salary and incentive compensation requirements:

A. Starting Salary $_____

B. Hiring Bonus $_____

C. Incentive Bonus $_____

D. Other (Specify) $_____

_____

Completed by _____ Date _____

Figure 2.4 *(cont.)*

2.5 EXECUTIVE SEARCH CONTRACTS

Third-party objectivity and effectiveness in targeting high level executives for key positions is provided by executive search firms such as Boyden Associates, Halbrecht Associates, and Haskell & Stern. These firms are members of the Association of Executive Search Consultants, Inc., which promotes professionalism and ethical practices.

When faced with a high priority executive recruitment requirement which must be met without delay, an executive search firm is prepared to initiate efforts to identify and present several well qualified candidates within a 30–60 day period. The search begins with research techniques that selectively identify candidates who meet the overall prior employment and career potential specifications profile. In-depth interviews then are conducted with chosen executives to identify those who best fit the position's professional and personal requirements. This process leads to the selection of several individuals who are recommended for interviews. An assessment report and background information is provided to the company on each of these final candidates.

The executive search firm's fee is $33\frac{1}{3}$ percent of the annual starting salary and bonus compensation, plus out-of-pocket expenses such as those incurred for travel by the firm's associates and candidates. Fee payment is made in three installments: (1) an initial nonrefundable installment as a retainer, (2) a second payment after 30 days, and (3) a third installment after 60 days. Additionally, a final payment is made on completion of the assignment to adjust for the actual compensation received by the executive hired. Out-of-pocket expenses are billed at the end of each month in which they are incurred. Searches cancelled within 60 days are prorated and a final statement, through the date of cancellation plus expenses related to the search is presented to the company for payment. If a recommended executive is employed in a position other than that called for by the assignment, a separate professional service charge of one-third of the annual starting compensation is payable upon employment.

Faced with costly services and the need to promote a successful search, the HR director should work closely with the search firm to ensure timely and effective results. A benchmark candidate should be identified early in the search to ensure that the search firm is on target with the company's needs. This permits early adjustments in screening procedures, avoids unnecessary out-of-pocket expenses, and expedites the delivery and hire of the best qualified executive.

A sample search agreement letter, designed to be representative of those used by executive search firms in general, is shown in Figure 2.5, Executive Search Agreement.

Personal and Confidential

Dear _____:

We are pleased to confirm our acceptance of your assignment to conduct a search for a (position title).

We understand your need for locating this executive as quickly as possible, and feel confident that we will be able to recommend several well qualified candidates within thirty to sixty days. Our Research Department already is working on this assignment; the search is under way.

Our charge for conducting a search is $33\frac{1}{3}$ percent of the anticipated first year's compensation, including base pay and any bonus or other incentive pay, plus out-of-pocket expenses. One-third of this professional service charge is payable upon commencement of this assignment. A bill in the amount of $_____ is enclosed for this nonrefundable initial retainer. An additional one-third, plus out-of-pocket expenses will be billed after 30 days and again after sixty days. When the candidate you select accepts your offer, a final bill will be provided to reconcile your company's account. It will include any balance due for expenses and an adjustment to compensate for the difference between estimated and actual negotiated compensation.

All out-of-pocket expenses, including travel expenses incurred by our associate or a candidate, will be itemized for your review.

Should you cancel the search within sixty days, we will provide a final statement for professional services which is prorated through the date of cancellation. This statement will include any expenses incurred in conducting the search.

If any executive we recommend is hired by your company or its affiliates for a position other than that called for by the assignment, a separate charge of one-third of annual compensation would be payable on the date of employment.

Enclosed for your review and approval are two copies of the candidate specifications that we developed during our recent meeting. Please initial and return one copy for our records. Should you wish to make any changes, please call me to discuss your revision requirements.

Please be assured that the identity of your company will be protected throughout this assignment. All correspondence and bills will be sent to your attention marked "personal and confidential."

When adequate information has been developed concerning a well qualified executive, we will send you a report that fully describes our assessment of the executive's overall qualifications. We will then contact you to arrange a suitable date and time for your preliminary interview with the candidate.

Should the executive you employ not remain with your company for one year, we agree to reinstate the search. Only approved out-of-pocket expenses would be charged.

(New client paragraph) It is understood that we will not solicit any employee of your company or its affiliates for a period of two years from the date of this agreement.

The confidence you have placed in (name of firm) is very much appreciated. If these standard terms and conditions are satisfactory, please indicate your acceptance by signing and returning the enclosed copy of this agreement.

Sincerely yours,

John T. Putnam
Executive Director

Agreed and Accepted:

Client's Representative _____ Date _____

Figure 2.5 Executive search agreement

2.6 INTERNAL JOB TO EMPLOYEE MATCHING: THE ESIS SEARCH REQUEST

As recommended in Section 2.1 on the personnel requisition process, the requisitioning manager should be required to routinely complete and attach an ESIS Search Request form to each Personnel Requisition. This form (Figure 2.6) provides the same structure of boxes at the top of the form that are used on the employee-completed Employee Skill Identification System form shown earlier in Figure 1.10. This one-for-one data relationship is designed to facilitate a manual search and retrieval technique, where position requirements are compared to employee qualifications as shown on forms or cards filed in the Employee Skill Identification System (see Section 1.10).

In setting up a manual file retrieval system, employee ESIS cards are grouped together by respective educational skill codes, which results in having all cards for mechanical engineers, accountants, and so on, filed together. Given a requirement for an accountant (code B100) with an MBA (code B100M), a minimum of eight years of recent auditing experience (code AC03), and a minimum of two years of supervisory experience to fill a managerial position at the headquarters in New York City, the requisitioner completes an ESIS Search Request as shown in Figure 2.6A. The information listed on the form results in a review of cards for accountants to compare requirements with employee qualifications. A sample is included of an employee's card that is retrieved through this process.

ESIS Search Request

1		2		3		4		5		6	7	8		9	10	11	

A	B	A	B	A	B	A	B	C	D

Job/Position Title _____

Organization _____ Location _____

Requirements: Please follow these instructions in providing the basis for the Human Resources Management Division to identify qualified employees.

Items 1 – 4 Designate respective Experience Category Code(s), in the order of their importance, to indicate the skill(s) needed for this position.

A How much experience is required? Enter the *minimum* number of years.

B How recent? If this is not a critical factor, omit the date. If recent experience is required, count back 5 years and enter that date.

5 C What primary type of education background is essential? Enter Educational Skill Code.

5 D What level is optimally required? Enter Educational Level Code.
If an alternate type of educational background and or level is acceptable, designate respective codes:

6 If supervisory experience is essential, specify the minimum number of years required.

7 Specify the minimum number of years of work experience to qualify for the position.

8 If fluency in a foreign language is *required or preferred*, enter code and check the appropriate box as follows:

☐ Required   ☐ Preferred

9 Enter the code for your company work location. *If candidates from other company locations are to be considered, complete items 10 and 11.*

10 Enter Y

11 Enter the code for your company work location.

Requested by (Name & Title) _____ Date _____

Figure 2.6   ESIS search request

ESIS Search Request

Sample of form completed by a requesting manager in 1987 to serve as the basis for identifying a qualified accountant:

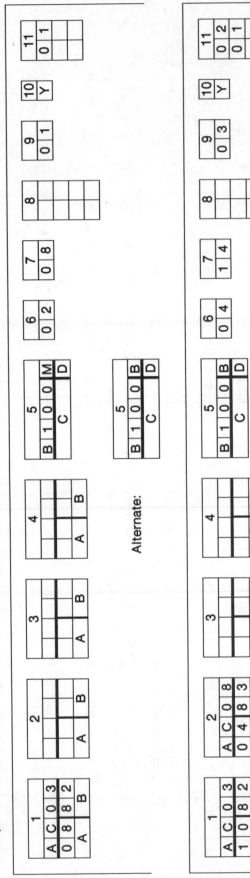

Employee Skill Identification System—This employee's card is retrieved as a possible candidate for the accounting position based on the following comparisons:

Item	Requirement	Candidate's Qualifications
1.	AC03—Experience in Auditing	AC03—Experience in Auditing
1A.	Minimum of 8 years of related experience	10 years of related experience
1B.	Recent related experience, i.e., not before 1982	Had related experience ending in 1982; therefore, meets requirement
5C.	B100—Education in accounting	B100
5D.	M = Educational level = Master Degree B = Alternate educational level = Bachelor Degree	B = Has alternate educational level
9.	New York work location	St. Louis work location
10.	Y = Yes; willing to relocate	Y = Yes; willing to relocate
11.	New York work location	New York work location is a secondary choice over Chicago work location

Figure 2.6A ESIS search request

2.7 HELP WANTED ADVERTISEMENT WORKSHEET

To plan an advertisement to be "pub-set"—that is, to be prepared according to your specifications by a newspaper or journal, the Help Wanted Advertisement Worksheet (Figure 2.7) is an essential tool. First draft your text. Then type it on the worksheet using 12-pitch characters. Using the 34-character grid provided, your typed draft provides the basis for estimating the number of lines needed for an ad with standard 8-point type. The grid includes provisions for designing a two-columnwide display advertisement.

Allow for white space at the top, on the sides, and at the bottom of the ad for visual impact. Also allow space for the headline, any subheadlines, the company name and/or logo and address, and the EEO statement.

Be prepared to specify the type size in points for the headline, subheadlines, company name, and so on. Examples of type sizes are shown on the right-hand side of the figure. A one-column ad drawn to scale (approximately $1\frac{1}{4}''$ wide) is shown with a 24-point headline for a "clerk typist" which provides the visual perspective needed to determine your requirements. Note that the size of this 24-point sample headline ("header") requires approximately thirteen lines.

The end product is a sample which may be shown to the requisitioning manager. The top of the worksheet includes provisions for designating proposed media, publication date(s), and estimated costs (based on the line rate charged by each publisher). The worksheet serves as an excellent tool for communicating your advertising plans to the manager, who participated in their formulation through suggestions which he or she included on the Personnel Requisition. This type of communication builds a service-oriented reputation and promotes understanding of the time-consuming complexities involved in the recruitment process.

Help Wanted Advertisement Worksheet

Proposed Media _____

Pub. Date (s) _____

Est. Cost $ _____ $ _____ $ _____

INSTRUCTIONS: Use a 12 pitch typewriter with this grid to estimate the number of lines for an ad with 8-point type. Check the width of the publication's columns and type accordingly; the grid provides a 34-character column. White space is needed at the left and right, top and bottom, to give ad visual impact. Count all intermediate spaces and punctuation marks. Leave space for headline, subheadlines, company logo and address, and the EEO line.

TYPE POINT SIZES:

8
10
12
14
18
24

Recommend using 14, 18, or 24 for headlines, and 18, 14, or 12 for correspondingly smaller subheadlines. For example, if the headline is 24 points, subheadings should not be more than 18 points. Be sure to provide adequate space in your design.

Single Column (34X)

Single Column (34X)

1.
2.
3.
4.
5.
6.
7.
8.
9.
10.
11.
12.
13.
14.
15.
16.
17.
18.
19.
20.
21.
22.
23.
24.
25.
26.
27.
28.
29.
30.
31.
32.
33.
34.

ACTUAL SIZE OF CLASSIFIED HELP WANTED COLUMN

1¼"

CLERK TYPIST

Approximately 13 lines!

Figure 2.7 Help wanted advertisement worksheet

2.8 HELP WANTED ADVERTISEMENT REQUEST LETTER

The request letter is printed on $8\frac{1}{2} \times 14$ inches stationery, and includes your company letterhead (Figure 2.8). The letter is designed to be completed legibly by hand. It is used to confirm the telephone placement of a help wanted advertisement, or mailed to order the placement of an ad. It is sent to the classified service representative of the newspaper that will print the advertisement.

This informal letter does a lot to avoid misunderstandings. It also serves as the basis for resolving problems that result when a service representative fails to place your ad as requested, runs the ad for a longer period than desired, erroneously transcribes your telephone-dictated wording, does not follow your instructions concerning format, and so on.

A copy is maintained in your help wanted advertisement file as supporting documentation for the related entry in the help wanted advertisement log.

(COMPANY LETTERHEAD)

Help Wanted Advertisement Request Letter

To: _____   Date: _____

Attention: _____

_____

_____

Please place the following ☐ Classified ☐ Classified Display Advertisement in your newspaper for the following dates: _____

☐ This confirms our telephone order of _____ .

☐ A glossy of this advertisement is enclosed for your use.

☐ Please repeat (re-run) our ad which appeared in your newspaper on _____ .

The following changes, if any, should be pub-set:

_____

_____

_____

_____

_____

☐ Please pub-set an advertisement as follows:

We would appreciate your ensuring that our advertisements are published with the required Equal Opportunity Employer designation.

Please call me at (   )   to confirm that the advertisement will run as requested, and to provide estimated cost information for our accounting records.

To ensure prompt payment, please be advised that our Accounts Payable Department requires tearsheets or affidavits of publication as supporting documents for invoices.

Many thanks for your assistance.

_____
Human Resources Director

Figure 2.8 Help wanted advertisement request letter

2.9 HELP WANTED ADVERTISEMENT LOG

The log shown in Figure 2.9 provides an accounting record of all help wanted advertisements. It includes details concerning:

- Ad Heading—the headline, for example, "executive secretary."
- Type of Ad—either IC (in column) or D (display).
- Media—name of publication.
- Placement Date and Method—telecon (placed by telephone and confirmed by letter) or letter (placed by mailed request).
- Date(s) of Publication—inclusion of the day of the week the ad begins is recommended.
- Estimated Size and Cost of the Ad—lines (number of lines), rate (cost per line), and total (cost for total number of lines).
- Invoice Approval—As invoices are received, reviewed, and approved for payment, the respective log entries are annotated to show the date of approval and the cost approved for payment. A copy of the advertisement is placed on file with the associated Recruitment Advertising Request form letter copy. *Copies of all recruitment advertisements must be maintained on file for EEO compliance inspections.*

Help Wanted Advertisement Log

| Ad Heading | Type | Media | Placement | | Date(s) of Publication | Estimated Size and Cost | | | Invoice Approval | |
			Date	Method		Lines	Rate	Cost	Date	Cost

Figure 2.9 Help wanted advertisement log

2.10 POSITION LISTING OF OPPORTUNITIES AT OTHER COMPANY LOCATIONS

Figure 2.10 shows a sample Internal Placement Program Bulletin which facilitates employee promotions and transfers among company locations. Employees who qualify for these promotion and transfer opportunities receive relocation expense reimbursements in accordance with company policy.

An interested employee is required to complete and submit a Request for Promotion and Transfer form (see Figure 2.12) to the internal placement program coordinator, who is a member of the Headquarters' HRM organization. Request for Promotion and Transfer forms must be received prior to the closing date specified in the heading of the Bulletin. A 15-day period is provided between the posting date and the closing date to allow ample time for responses. This relatively short time frame is essential for ensuring that the observance of Internal Placement Program procedures does not create unreasonable delays in the recruitment process. Qualified employees, if any, are required by this time frame to respond within a week of the posting date to ensure that their Request for Promotion and Transfer consideration will be received prior to the closing date.

Internal Placement Program

Bulletin No. _____

Posting Date _____
Closing Date _____

The following promotional opportunities are available for qualified employees at other company locations. Relocation costs are reimbursable in accordance with company policy. Interested employees are to submit a request for promotion and transfer form to the Human Resources Division at the NYC headquarters, ATTN: Internal Placement Program Coordinator.

No.	Position	Location
1026	*Senior Project Planning Analyst* Coordinates MIS projects. Develops and tracks progress of teams. Advises management regarding project milestones and overall accomplishments. Requires minimum of 3 years of company project planning experience including associated software skills. Requires detail-oriented individual with strong communications skills, both oral and written. Salary grade—11.	Princeton, NJ
1027	*Quality Assurance Manager* Reports to Division Manager. Overall projects assessment responsibility involves detailed evaluations of performance from inception through completion. Reviews quality assurance plans to ensure adequacy for meeting system development life cycles. Requires 5 + years of company experience in data system development, and thorough knowledge of quality assurance concepts. Salary grade—14.	Chicago, IL
1028	*Senior Systems Analyst* Plans office automation systems. Requires skill in effectively interfacing with users to identify interdivisional needs in terms of database design and programming specifications. Requires minimum of 5 years of company systems analysis and programming experience. COBOL and IBM mainframe knowledge are essential. Salary grade—12.	New York City, NY

Figure 2.10 Internal placement program

2.11 JOB POSTING FORM: INTERNAL PLACEMENT PROGRAM

In addition to advertising professional positions throughout all company locations by Internal Placement Program Bulletins, all professional positions and other positions open at each company location are advertised locally through listings of Current Position Opportunities (Figure 2.11). In addition to inviting qualified employees to apply for appropriate transfer and promotional opportunities, employees whose personal career development objectives merit consideration for within-grade transfers also are encouraged to apply. The application procedure requires completion and submission of a Request for Transfer and Promotion form to the local HRM organization prior to the closing date.

Internal Placement Program

<u>Current Position Opportunities</u>

The following positions are available for within-grade transfers to achieve personal career development objectives, or as transfer and promotional opportunities for employees who meet requisite qualifications. Apply by completing and submitting a Request for Promotion and Transfer form to (Local HR Office) on or before the closing date shown above.

Position No.	Description
101	Cost Estimator—BS and PE or certified cost engineer preferred, but will consider equivalent experience. Requires five years of construction estimating experience with knowledge of electrical, mechanical, structural, and HVAC systems. Thorough knowledge of construction materials and methods is essential. Work involves construction of new plant facility. Reports to Manager—Engineering Design. Salary Grade—9
102	Staff Accountant—Graduate accountant preferred but will accept equivalent experience. Requires three years of general accounting experience. Will prepare monthly financial statements, analyze accounts, and conduct special projects for Manager— General Accounting. (Will accept equivalent experience). Salary Grade—7
103	Senior Accounting Clerk—Requires 5 to 8 years of general accounting experience including at least one year of general ledger experience. Will process general ledger transactions and prepare monthly reports, reconcile accounts, and assist in preparing management reports. Salary Grade—6
104	Senior Clerk - Typist—3 to 5 years experience and excellent typing skills are required for report preparation functions. Requires knowledge of technical terminology. Salary Grade—3

Figure 2.11 Internal placement program

2.12 REQUEST FOR PROMOTION AND TRANSFER: INTERNAL PLACEMENT PROGRAM

This request form (Figure 2.12) is used by candidates to apply for transfer and promotion opportunities announced by the headquarter's HRM organization. These professional-level opportunities throughout the company are announced periodically by an Internal Placement Program Bulletin (refer to Figure 2.10). The bulletin is posted at all company locations on the same date, and interested candidates are instructed to submit a Request for Promotion and Transfer to the headquarter's HRM organization to the attention of the internal placement program coordinator, prior to the stipulated closing date.

The Request for Promotion and Transfer is submitted with the understanding that selection will result in the reimbursement of associated relocation costs in accordance with company policy. The candidate is required to provide basic details of how his or her experience, skills, and so on match the qualifications for the position, and explain his or her reason(s) for being interested in the opportunity. To further assist the internal placement coordinator in the screening process, the candidate also is required to give his or her date of hire and the number of years in the current position. The company's policy regarding the Internal Placement Program may stipulate that candidates must be with the company for more than one year, and on their current job for at least one year before being considered for relocation. This rationale ensures that the individual performs acceptably in his or her current work before being considered for an advancement opportunity. The last question on the form asks whether or not the individual's supervisor is aware of his or her interest in the advancement opportunity under consideration. Company policy should ensure *confidential* consideration for those individuals who do not want their supervisors to be aware of their interest in other opportunities until definite interest is established in their candidacy. When the top three candidates have been identified through assessing responses on the form and personnel records, the next step is for each candidate to be evaluated for the position by his or her present supervisor.

Internal Placement Program

REQUEST FOR PROMOTION AND TRANSFER

Name (Last, First, MI) _____

Position Title _____

Organization _____

Location _____

Supervisor (Name & Title) _____

Please consider my qualifications for the following Internal Placement Program promotion and transfer opportunity:

Position Number _____

Position Title _____

Location _____

My qualifications for this position (required experience, skills, etc.) are as follows:

My reason(s) for being interested in this position:

My date of hire was _____ . I have been in my current position for _____ years.

My supervisor ☐ is ☐ is not aware of my interest in this advancement opportunity.

_____   _____
Signature   Date

Figure 2.12 Internal placement program—request for promotion and transfer

2.13 SUPERVISORY EVALUATION OF CANDIDATE: INTERNAL PLACEMENT PROGRAM

This form (Figure 2.13) is provided to the candidate's current supervisor with a copy of the position description for the opportunity under consideration. It requires critical assessments of the following.

1. The degree of the individual's preparation to perform the duties and responsibilities of the new position as well as deficiencies which should be considered.
2. Prediction of future performance based on motivation and past performance.
3. Ability to effectively relate to and work with others.
4. Extent to which overall qualifications and interpersonal skills measure up to the requirements of the proposed supervisory role, or the degree of current managerial effectiveness.

Internal Placement Program

SUPERVISORY EVALUATION OF CANDIDATE

Supervisor (Name & Title) _____

Organization _____

Location _____

In accordance with the company's policy concerning the Internal Placement Program, your assistance would be appreciated in providing a brief assessment of your subordinate's qualifications for the position under consideration. A copy of the Position Description is attached for your reference.

Employee _____

Position _____

---

1. Based on your knowledge of the employee's skills and knowledge, how well prepared is he or she to meet the duties and responsibilities of this position? Are there any deficiencies which should be considered?

2. Considering the employee's degree of motivation and success in his or her present work, how effective do you predict his or her performance will be in the new position?

3. Please describe the employee in terms of the quality of his or her working relationships with others.

4. If a supervisory position is under consideration and the employee is not currently performing in a supervisory capacity, please predict whether or not his or her overall qualifications and interpersonal skills will meet associated requirements. If problems are anticipated, please provide details. If currently a supervisor, please describe his or her managerial effectiveness.

Signature _____ Date _____

Return Completed Form to the HRM Division, *ATTN:* Internal Placement Program Coordinator

Figure 2.13 Internal placement program—supervisory evaluation of candidate

2.14 CURRENT POSITION OPENINGS ANNOUNCEMENT

Figure 2.14 shows an example of a Current Recruitment Requirements Listing which is distributed to carefully selected employment agencies for candidate referrals. If the company has an equal employment opportunity commitment, the listing also can be used to meet legal requirements for advising the State Employment Service regarding all employment opportunities.

The procedure for referring candidates is through résumé referral only. A sheet is attached to the listing which provides the names and addresses of designated employment representatives at respective work locations. Candidates can review the position specifications, but the employment contact information is reserved for use only by agency representatives.

Résumés are annotated to indicate the referral code and the position title for which the candidate is to be considered. The candidate's salary requirement also is specified.

Agencies selected to receive these listings are ones which have demonstrated their effectiveness in only referring qualified candidates as an *associated agency*. By promoting understanding with these external recruitment partners, the telephone numbers of designated employment representatives also are provided. The intention is to provide clarifications concerning requirements, not to accept candidate referrals by telephone.

(Company Letterhead)

CURRENT RECRUITMENT REQUIREMENTS (Date)

This listing of our current professional recruitment requirements is provided to you for referring qualified employment candidates. Please refer résumés to the designated employment representatives at respective work locations; a listing is attached which provides their names, position titles, addresses, and telephone numbers. Please ensure that each résumé you refer is annotated to indicate the Referral Code–Position Title for the position and the candidate's salary requirement.

Position Specifications:

A1026—SENIOR PROJECT PLANNING ANALYST
Princeton, NJ
Starting Salary Range: $XX,XXX–$XX,XXX

Coordinates MIS projects through developing schedules and tracking the progress of teams in meeting associated objectives. Advises management regarding project milestones and overall accomplishments. Requires minimum of 3 years of project planning and related software experience with comparable company. Must have PERT and network diagramming skills. A detail-oriented individual with strong oral and written communication skills is needed.

A1027—QUALITY ASSURANCE MANAGER
Chicago, Illinois
Starting Salary Range: $XX,XXX–$XX,XXX

Reports to Manufacturing Division Manager. Will establish new overall assessment program to monitor projects from inception through completion. Reviews quality assurance plans to ensure their adequacy in meeting systems development life cycles. Requires 5 or more years of data system development experience and thorough knowledge of quality assurance concepts.

A1028—SENIOR SYSTEMS ANALYST
New York City, NY
Starting Salary Range: $XX,XXX–$XX,XXX

Plans office automation systems. Requires skills in effectively interfacing with users to identify interdivisional needs in terms of database design and programming specifications. Requires minimum of 5 years of systems analysis/programming experience. COBOL and IBM mainframe knowledge is essential.

AN EQUAL OPPORTUNITY EMPLOYER (M/F/H/V)

Figure 2.14 Current recruitment requirements listing

2.15 ASSOCIATED AGENCY POLICY

Figure 2.15 shows an example of a detailed letter of agreement, which establishes an associated agency working relationship with an employment agency.

The agreement provides the following benefits to a participating agency.

1. Receives periodic listings of Current Recruitment Requirements for use in referring résumés of qualified candidates. (See Figure 2.14.)
2. Opens communications with employment representatives to clarify requirements.
3. Company calls an agency when a candidate is of interest; the agency contacts the candidate, sells the opportunity, and has the candidate call the company *collect* to arrange an interview date.
4. The company provides feedback to the agency regarding interview findings on the day of the candidate's visit. The agency provides assistance in selling an offer when requested by the company.
5. Prompt payment of fees based on a standard company fee schedule. The company's fee schedule usually is below normal rates charged by agencies; this is based on a close working relationship where a high volume of placements is possible.
6. The company has a standard fee refund policy which promotes quality referrals by the agency.

ASSOCIATED AGENCY POLICY

Our company's policy provides for the development of close working relationships with carefully selected employment agencies. Those agencies which meet our criteria for Associated Agency status receive the following benefits:

1. Distribution of detailed information concerning our recruitment requirements in the format of periodic Current Position Openings listings. Each position is identified by a referral number which is used when referring applicant résumés. Résumés are time and date-stamped upon receipt to ensure that the first one received for a particular candidate receives credit for the referral.

2. Open communication regarding specific requirements is encouraged. We appreciate telephone calls to clarify our needs regarding any position shown in our listings. We do not want any résumé referred to us unless you are confident that it meets our requirements. We count on Associated Agencies to be highly selective in screening candidates prior to referring them for our consideration.

3. When we have an interest in one of your candidates, we will call you to arrange an interview. You, in turn, contact the candidate and have him/her call us COLLECT to arrange an interview date. This provides an opportunity for you to sell your candidate on the merits of our Company as a prospective employer.

4. We will provide feedback to you concerning the date established for the visit, and details concerning our findings on the day that the candidate visits. We will maintain this close communication throughout the process, and will encourage your assistance in "selling" our employment opportunities to those candidates who receive offers of employment.

5. We guarantee prompt fee payments within fifteen (15) working days of an individual's reporting for work date in accordance with the following schedule:

Insert Fee Schedule

6. In cases where an individual misrepresents his or her qualifications and termination action is taken, full refund of the fee payment will be required. If an individual does not meet normal performance standards within the first six (6) weeks of employment, or leaves the company of their his or her volition during this period, a full refund of the fee is required.

John L. Stewart
Human Resources Director

Agreed _____   Date _____
         Agency Representative

Please keep the copy for your records and return the original for our file.

Figure 2.15 Associated agency policy

2.16 FORM LETTERS FOR REJECTING UNSUITABLE CANDIDATES

All employment inquiries received by mail deserve a prompt and personalized reply. Although the majority of these reply letters involve candidates in whom the company has no current or future interest, responses should be phrased in a positive and encouraging manner so the applicant does not feel alienated. In addition to being employment candidates, applicants are customers of your company's products, clients for your company's services, and individuals whose good will is needed to promote the company's best interests.

A set of standard letters should be developed which will meet the majority of your overall needs. These standard form letters then should be stored in your computerized word processing data base for recall by assigned codes, which will provide the basis for annotating each "no-interest" résumé in the upper right-hand corner with computer-generated letter request codes such as "Send NIL/WRI" (send no interest letter/write-in).

Three examples of standard no-interest letters are provided as follows:

Figure 2.16A—NIL/WRI (write-in)
Figure 2.16B—NIL/WAI (walk-in)
Figure 2.16C—NIL/ADI (advertisement)

The practice of advertising without identifying your company (so called "blind ads") can be used to eliminate the need for responding to the flood of résumés which results when you advertise in publications with nationwide circulation. The publication provides a box number, which applicants are instructed to respond to at the publication's address. The effectiveness of a blind advertisement in reaching the best qualified candidates is debatable. Outstanding individuals who are doing very well with their present company, but who want to selectively and very confidentially explore the employment market to see if a better opportunity is available, may not respond to an anonymous advertiser. Their interest in not compromising their current employment situation makes them reluctant to respond to a blind ad unless it contains (1) wording which clearly distinguishes the company's business and product line(s)/service(s), and (2) a statement to the effect that the company's employees are aware of the employment opportunity listed.

Dear_____:

Many thanks for sending your résumé for our consideration regarding possible employment opportunities.

We have reviewed your excellent background with those managers who employ individuals with your qualifications and interests, but regret to advise you that they currently do not have a suitable opportunity for your consideration.

Although we cannot accommodate your association with our company at this time, we will place your résumé in our active candidate file in the hope than an appropriate employment opportunity will become available within the next few months.

Your interest in exploring career employment opportunities with (name of company) is very much appreciated.

Sincerely,

Mary T. Jackson
Director of Human Resources

Figure 2.16A No interest letter for a write-in candidate

Dear_____:

Many thanks for taking the time to bring your résumé to our receptionist. We are sorry that our busy schedule prevented us from meeting you during your visit, but are sure you understand our situation.

We forwarded your résumé for review by all these managers who might have a suitable employment opportunity for your consideration. Although they were very positive about your excellent qualifications, they regrettably do not have an appropriate position open for your consideration at this time. Accordingly, we have placed your résumé in our active candidate file in the hope that a position will become available in the near future.

Your interest in exploring the possibility of career employment with our company is very much appreciated. You have our best wishes for success in locating the opportunity you deserve.

Sincerely,

Mary T. Jackson
Director of Human Resources

Figure 2.16B No interest letter for a walk-in candidate

Dear_____:

Many thanks for submitting your résumé in response to our recent advertisement in (insert publication name) for a (insert position title).

We now have completed our review of the unusually large number of résumés received for this position. Although your background and qualifications are excellent, we regret to advise you that other candidates more closely meet the position's very specific requirements.

Although we do not have a suitable position for your consideration at this time, definite interest in your qualifications exists for future opportunities. We have placed your résumé in our active candidate file, and will not hesitate to contact you if a requirement for a professional with your qualifications becomes available within the next few months.

(Alternate paragraph for candidates in whom there is no future interest.) We have placed your résumé in our active candidate file, which will provide the basis for our contacting you if an appropriate opportunity develops in the near future.

Your interest in becoming associated with (name of company) is very much appreciated.

Sincerely,

Mary T. Jackson
Director of Human Resources

Figure 2.16C No interest letter for an advertisement response candidate

2.17 COMPANY DESCRIPTION SHEET

This sheet is a one-page synopsis of the company's products and/or services, future prospects, and employee benefits and is used as an enclosure for letters to prospective employees. An example is shown in Figure 2.17.

Electronix Corporation

One of the largest electronics companies in the world, we are leaders in the design, development, and production of advanced telecommunications systems and equipment for the industry. We also have a substantial role in promoting national defense through next-generation military information systems. We offer the security of 40 years of continuous growth, and sound prospects for continued advancement as we move into the next century. Our employee-oriented company provides a highly competitive compensation package which includes the following benefits:

- Annual Merit Reviews and Cash Awards for Special Achievements. Outstanding performance can result in a 10% salary increase after 6 months of employment. Cash awards start at 8% of annual salary.

- Employee and Dependent Life Insurance. Immediate coverage at the rate of 2 times your salary at company expense. A double indemnity provision for accidental death provides 4 times annual salary. Dependent coverage and additional employee insurance may be purchased at low group rates.

- Employee and Dependent Health and Dental Care Insurance. Comprehensive hospital, surgical, and medical expense coverage begins on first day of your employment. Employee coverage is paid by the company; dependent coverage is paid by the employee. The dental plan, also free for employees, provides up to 50% of major procedure costs.

- Accident Insurance for Business Travel. Company pays 5 times your annual salary with a maximum of $300,000.

- Income Protection Plan. Exempt employees receive full salary continuation, then $66\frac{2}{3}$% salary for a period of up to 6 months. Allowances are based on Company service.

- Savings Plan. Your contribution of up to 6% of salary is matched by 50%.

- Vacation Plan. 6 days after 6 months. Provides up to 25 days per year.

- Educational Assistance. Tuition and fees paid at 100%; book allowance of $100 per semester.

- Retirement Plan. Company-paid program offers early retirement at age 55 with 10 or more years of service.

- College Scholarship Awards for Dependent Children. To promote academic excellence, dependents who achieve Dean's List status receive $1,000 per semester.

AN EQUAL EMPLOYMENT OPPORTUNITY EMPLOYER (Male/Female/Handicapped)

Figure 2.17 Company description sheet

2.18 EMPLOYEE REFERRAL AWARD PROGRAM

As part of the internal placement program job-posting procedure, employees also should be encouraged to refer former associates and acquaintances who may qualify for the specific opportunities open for employment. This procedure must include the understanding that such referrals will be given consideration only after it is determined that qualified employees within the company are not available.

The employee is encouraged to have the applicant complete an employment application and, ideally, also provide a detailed résumé. These materials then are attached to the Employee Referral of Employment Candidate form (Figure 2.18) and submitted to the HR director.

The Employee Referral of Employment Candidate form also provides the basis for submitting a recommendation that a candidate receive "general consideration." The referral is forwarded to those managers who normally would have interest in the type of applicant under consideration. If the individual's qualifications are outstanding, then a Personnel Requisition is generated to initiate a formal recruitment process. Given no similarly well qualified employee applicants, the individual under consideration receives the position. Numerous situations will be encountered where it is known that there are no equally well qualified individuals among present employees. Initiating job posting routines and delaying the hiring of outstanding candidates would be definitely counterproductive. Accordingly, it is sound practice in setting up a job-posting policy to stipulate that all job/position opportunities are not subject to this action, for example, "job posting is subject to management's discretion based on an assessment of specific company requirements."

The Employee Referral of Employment Candidate form also requires background information to explain the basis for an employee's knowledge of a candidate. Comments regarding a former associate's qualifications are given more value than second-hand observations regarding a candidate who was referred to the employee by a mutual friend. The employee is asked to give a personal assessment of the candidate's potential for meeting position requirements—that is, statements concerning the individual's qualifications, interests, motivation, attitude, and so on. This promotes greater employee selectivity in making referrals because the employee must go on record as endorsing the individual.

The section at the bottom of the form offers provisions for giving feedback to the employee on whether or not the candidate was hired. If hired, the specific amount of the award (to be received after the new employee satisfactorily completes the probationary period) is specified. Concerning the amount of an award, the company's policy should offer two specified amounts—one for non-exempt and one for exempt employees—for example, $300 and $600 respectively. As with any award, the amounts selected should be sufficient to provide adequate recognition and incentive for participation in the program.

Employee Referral of Employment Candidate

To: HR Director

In accordance with the provisions of the Employee Referral Award Program, attached is the employment application and résumé of a candidate for employment consideration as follows:

Name _____

Recommended for either:

☐ The position announced as # _____ , for a (title) _____

☐ General consideration for employment opportunities which would effectively apply his or her background as a _____

My knowledge of this candidate is based on our prior work association, business working relationship, or referral and recommendation by a mutual friend, etc.

Explain: _____

_____

_____

_____

My personal assessment of this candidate's potential for meeting position requirements (qualifications, interests, motivation, etc.) is as follows:

_____

_____

_____

_____

Employee Name _____ Date _____ Organization _____
Attachments

To: _____ Organization _____

☐ Sorry! A thorough review of this candidate's qualifications has determined that other candidates are more suited to our specific/general requirements.

☐ Congratulations! Your candidate was hired and reported for work on _____ .
                                                    (Date)
Accordingly, you will receive a $_____ Employee Referral Award when this new employee successfully completes three months of employment on

_____ .
(Date)

_____ _____
HR Director   (Date)

Figure 2.18 Employee referral of employment candidate form

2.19 RÉSUMÉ REFERRAL CONTROL FORM

The Résumé Referral Form (Figure 2.19) provides a systematic basis for forwarding a résumé for managerial review. In cases where a particular position is under consideration, the position title and position number are indicated, and the box is marked in the section that specifies "the attached résumé and/or employment application is being referred to you for employment consideration regarding this employment opportunity." The recruiting manager's name, title, organization, and location are entered in the top box. The manager is required to check the appropriate response to indicate (1) no interest, (2) interest—please arrange interview—preferred date _____, or (3) future interest (within 3 months) and then sign and return the form and its attachments to the HR director by the specified date.

In cases where a résumé and/or employment application is circulated among a number of potentially interested managers for consideration, the candidate's name and the type of position of interest are specified. The box is marked for the section that specifies "the attached résumé and/or employment application is being referred to each manager indicated below to determine general interest regarding potential employment opportunities." Designated managers indicate (1) no interest, (2) interest—please arrange interview—preferred date _____, or (3) future interest (within 3 months) and then sign and return materials to the HR director prior to the specified date.

Résumé Referral Form　　　　　　　　　　　　Date _____

Candidate _____

Position _____ # _____

☐ The attached résumé and/or Employment Application is being referred to you for consideration regarding this employment opportunity.

☐ The attached résumé and/or Employment Application is being referred to each manager indicated below to determine general interest regarding potential employment opportunities.

To (Name & Title) _____

Organization _____ Location _____

☐ No Interest

☐ Interest—Please Arrange Interview—Preferred Date _____

☐ Future Interest (within 3 months)

Signature _____ Date _____

To (Name & Title) _____

Organization _____ Location _____

☐ No Interest

☐ Interest—Please Arrange Interview—Preferred Date _____

☐ Future Interest (within 3 months)

　Signature _____ Date _____

To (Name & Title) _____

Organization _____ Location _____

☐ No Interest

☐ Interest—Please Arrange Interview—Preferred Date _____

☐ Future Interest (within 3 months)

　Signature _____ Date _____

Please complete and return this form to me by _____

_____

HR Director

Figure 2.19 Résumé referral form

2.20 APPLICANT RESOURCE FILE

Résumés and/or applications of candidates for which there is possible "future interest" should be placed in an active file for a three-month period. The filing system should utilize educational skill inventory codes. The first step in setting up the overall filing system is to provide dividers for the five educational skill categories shown below.

B. Business
C. Computer Science
E. Engineering
S. Mathematics and Science
M. Miscellaneous

Next, behind each divider, file folders are provided for each of the codes within an educational skill category. For example, the B. Business divider is followed by sixteen folders for related educational skills such as B100—Accounting, B101—Administration (General), B102—Banking, and so on. An example is provided in Figure 2.20A.

If the volume of résumés and/or applications requires greater clarification, the next step would be to create folders for each of the experience skill categories within each educational skill category. For example, behind B101—Accounting would come AC01—Accounts Payable, AC02—Accounts Receivable, AC03—Auditing, and so on. An example is provided in Figure 2.20B.

Each applicant's paperwork is annotated to indicate the date filed and the date to be removed from the Applicant Resource File and placed in the Application for Employment File (see Figure 2.21). A rubber stamp containing the following information is recommended:

Active From _____ To _____
Educational Skill Code _____
Experience Skill Code _____
EEO Candidate Category _____

As paperwork is designated for the "active file," the date (month/year) is entered with a three-month suspense date (month/year). Respective skill codes also are entered to guide the filing process. The appropriate EEO candidate category code also is entered as follows:

1 = Officials and Managers
2 = Professionals
3 = Technicians
4 = Sales Workers
5 = Office & Clerical
6 = Crafts—Skilled
7 = Semi-Skilled Operatives
8 = Laborers—Unskilled
9 = Service Workers

At the end of each month, the active file is purged of paperwork that expired that month as shown by "to" dates. Purged paperwork is then placed in the Application for Employment File.

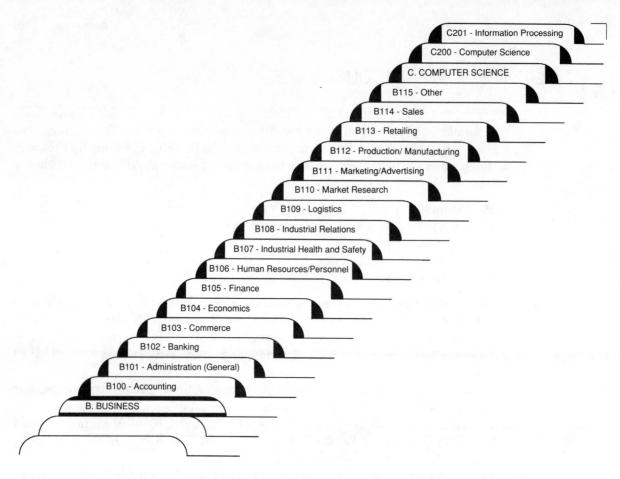

Figure 2.20A Applicant resource file—detailed educational skill categories

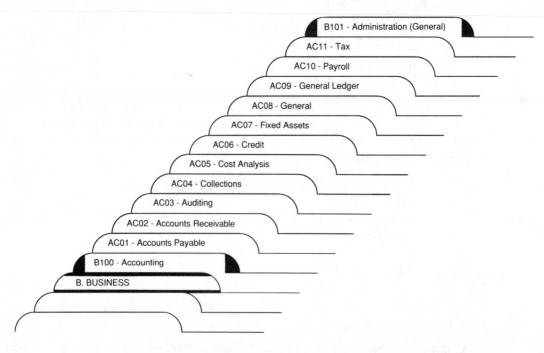

Figure 2.20B Applicant resource file—experience categories within educational skill categories

2.21 APPLICATION FOR EMPLOYMENT FILE

Materials are filed alphabetically by applicant name within respective EEO candidate category codes (refer to 2.20) for potential review by an EEO compliance inspector. If the initial review of an applicant's qualifications determines that there may be future interest, respective paperwork is stamped, coded, and filed in the Applicant Resource File for a three-month period. A Cross-Reference Information sheet (Figure 2.21) is completed and filed in lieu of the paperwork in the Application for Employment File. It remains on file until the paperwork is returned from the Applicant Resource File. Then it is discarded.

Cross-Reference   EEO Candidate Category _____

Employment application materials for this applicant have been placed in the applicant Resource File:

Applicant Name _____
(Last, First, MI)

Filed Under:

      Educational Skill Category Code _____

      Experience Skill Category Code _____

Return Date (Month/Year) _____

Figure 2.21 Cross-reference sheet—application for employment file

2.22 FORM LETTERS INVITING CANDIDATES TO INTERVIEWS

Successful recruitment efforts express and demonstrate personal concern for each applicant. A carefully planned and executed employment interview visit promotes the company's image as a well organized employer that cares about its employees. This positive sales-oriented approach does much to influence applicants to choose one company over others.

It is in the HR director's best interest to develop a set of standard letters for meeting typical requirements, and including them in his or her computerized word processing data base. This provides the capability to rapidly generate invitations to candidates who are of interest to your management.

Representative samples of such letters are shown in Figures 2.22 A, B, and C.

Interview Invitation for Campus Candidate (INV/CCI)

This letter (Figure 2.22A) establishes rapport by naming the recruiter who interviewed the individual on campus, sending his or her best regards, and indicating that he or she is looking forward to seeing the candidate again during the visit. It further promotes rapport by including information on the employee who will serve as the candidate's host, who has been matched to the candidate in terms of the same college, occupational interests, and so on.

Now that the individual is of definite interest to the company, it is appropriate to request that he or she arrange to have college transcripts sent to the company. Transcripts are needed to verify graduation and degree status; they also are required to assess the level of performance in coursework determined by the company to be critical for success in the position under consideration.

Interview Invitation for Advertisement Response Candidate (INV/ADR)

The use of the candidate host technique should be used for all individual contributor positions that involve peers performing the same or related types of work. The process is not encouraged for executive/managerial-level candidates, who should be hosted by a representative of the HRM organization (Figure 2.22B). For example, one of your key employment representatives would be assigned to the individual. Depending on the degree of interest in the candidate, as determined during the visit, appropriate members of management may decide to take the individual on an area tour, to the airport, for an early dinner, and so on. Accordingly, this letter omits the candidate host paragraph.

The requirement for transcripts is included to serve as the basis for verifying that the candidate has the degrees shown on his or her résumé.

Interview Invitation for Employment Agency Candidate (INV/EAC)

This letter (Figure 2.22C) assumes that the candidate is within driving distance. The question of when to encourage a candidate to use his or her personal automobile (or to rent an automobile at company expense) to visit the company's facility is highly judgmental. It is clearly appropriate to have the candidate use his or her own automobile when the candidate is located within commuting distance, but alternative means of transportation should be considered when driving time exceeds an hour.

When interest in an employment agency candidate is established, assuming that your close working relationship with the agency assures you that the candidate has been properly screened for the position in question, you have the agency contact the individual to advise him or her that an interview invitation letter is in the mail. The letter includes full details concerning the reimbursement of travel expenses, a map showing the route to the facility, an employment application for completion, a request for transcripts, and information concerning the company's products/services and employee benefits.

Dear_____:

Since your meeting at Cornell University with our Campus Relations Representative, John Smythe, we have reviewed your background and interests with the managers of those engineering organizations that can offer you appropriate professional challenges. It now would be mutually beneficial to have you meet with us to discuss these career employment opportunities. Accordingly, please call me COLLECT as soon as possible at (XXX) XXX-XXXX to arrange a convenient interview date.

We will reimburse you during your visit for air travel, local transportation, hotel, meal, and gratuity costs. An Employment Candidate Expense Report form is enclosed for this purpose. In planning your visit, please arrange air travel reservations to allow your arrival during the evening prior to our meeting date, and departure after 7:00 P.M. on the day of your visit. We will make a room reservation for you at the Executive Suites Hotel, 500 Somerset Avenue, Upland, New Jersey. They have an excellent shuttle service that meets guests at the airport every half hour at the US Airways entrance to the terminal.

Your host will be Bill Jones, who also is a recent alumnus of Cornell. He joined us two years ago and has been very successfully applying his electronics engineering background in work activities which are sure to be of interest to you. You two undoubtably have much in common. Bill will meet you in the hotel lobby at 8:00 A.M. for breakfast, explain the schedule of interviews that has been prepared for you, assist you in checking out, and bring you to our office. John Smythe, who sends his best regards, is looking forward to seeing you again; he will be taking you to lunch. At the conclusion of the day's interview activities, Bill will bring you on a brief tour of the area to offer suggestions concerning appropriate housing opportunities before taking you to the airport.

Please complete the enclosed Employment Application materials and bring them with you when you visit. I also would appreciate your arranging to have a transcript sent to me by each of your colleges; associated costs should be included on your Employment Candidate Expense Report.

Enclosed for your review is a one-page synopsis of our company's products, prospects, and employee benefits. Detailed information will be provided during your visit. We are looking forward to having you visit us in the near future to discuss the possibility of a rewarding career with our growing company.

Sincerely,

Mary C. Jackson
Human Resources Director

Enclosures

Figure 2.22A Interview invitation for campus candidate

Dear _____ :

Many thanks for responding to our recent advertisement in the *New York Times* for an Electronics Engineer—Advanced Computer Design. We have reviewed your résumé and cover letter with interest, and believe that it would be mutually beneficial to meet and discuss our career opportunity in detail. Accordingly, please call me COLLECT as soon as possible on (XXX) XXX-XXXX to arrange a convenient interview date.

We will reimburse you during your visit for air travel, local transportation, hotel, meal, and gratuity costs. An Employment Candidate Expense Report form is enclosed for this purpose. In planning your visit, please arrange air travel reservations to allow your arrival during the evening prior to our meeting date, and departure after 7:00 P.M. on the day of your visit. We will make a room reservation for you at the Executive Suites Hotel, 500 Somerset Avenue, Upland, New Jersey. They have an excellent shuttle service that meets guests at the airport every half hour at the US Airways entrance to the terminal.

I will meet you in the hotel lobby at 8:00 A.M. for breakfast. We can use that time to review the schedule of interviews that has been prepared for you, and for me to answer any questions you may have concerning our company. We then will go to the office, where interviews will begin at 9:30 A.M. Later in the day I will take you on a brief tour of the area to offer suggestions concerning appropriate housing opportunities, and then take you to the airport.

Please complete the enclosed Employment Application materials and bring them with you when you visit. I also would appreciate your arranging to have a transcript sent to me by each of your colleges; associated costs should be included on your Employment Candidate Expense Report.

Enclosed for your review is a one-page synopsis of our company's products, prospects, and employee benefits. Detailed information will be provided during your visit. We are looking forward to having you visit us in the near future to discuss the possibility of a rewarding career with our growing company.

Sincerely,

Mary C. Jackson
Human Resources Director

Enclosures

Figure 2.22B Interview invitation for advertisement response candidate

Dear_____:

Your résumé was called to our attention recently by Careers, Inc., an agency that assists us on a company fee-paid basis in identifying well qualified candidates for our current employment opportunities. We have reviewed your résumé with interest concerning a position as Senior Research Chemist—Polymer Development, and believe that it would be mutually beneficial to meet as soon as possible. Accordingly, please call me COLLECT at (XXX) XXX-XXXX to arrange a convenient interview date.

Because you reside reasonably near our facility, we assume that you will choose to use your personal automobile for the trip. We will reimburse you during your visit for mileage, tolls, and meal costs. An Employment Candidate Expense Report form is enclosed for this purpose. Also enclosed in a map for your use in planning your route. When you arrive, please park your car in the visitors parking area at the main entrance to the headquarters building. The receptionist located in the main entrance area will be expecting you.

You host for the day will be Mary Cortez. She also is an alumnus of Rutgers University. Mary became associated with us about four years ago, and has been very successfully applying her Doctorate in Chemistry in our polymer development program. You two undoubtably have much in common. She will greet you and join you for coffee at 9:00 A.M. Mary will have the schedule of interviews that has been prepared for you, and will answer any questions you have concerning our company. She also will take you for lunch and give you a brief tour of the area.

Please complete the enclosed Employment Application materials and bring them with you when you visit. I also would appreciate your arranging to have a transcript sent to me by each of your colleges; associated costs should be included on your Employment Candidate Expense Report.

Enclosed for your review is a one-page synopsis of our company's products, prospects, and employee benefits. Detailed information will be provided during your visit. We are looking forward to having you visit us in the near future to discuss the possibility of a rewarding career with our growing company.

Sincerely,

Mary C. Jackson
Human Resources Director

Enclosures

Figure 2.22C Interview invitation for employment agency candidate

2.23 COLLEGE RELATIONS/RECRUITMENT TRIP REPORT

The Campus Recruitment Report form (Figure 2.23) is completed by the member of the company's recruitment team who is designated as team captain. The primary function of a team captain is to do everything possible to promote effective college relations and successful recruiting efforts at a particular college or university. Such an individual usually is an alumnus with effective faculty and placement office contacts which promote the identification of candidates for career employment opportunities.

The Campus Recruitment Report is submitted to the HR director with the candidates' assessment and qualifications materials attached. It serves as a control device for ensuring candidate follow-up actions, and provides information necessary for promoting more effective future recruitment visits. The form becomes a permanent record in the file maintained on the college or university by the HRM organization. It also provides historical information that ensures continuity of efforts when new team members or a new team captain is appointed.

The structure of the form provides the following information: The top of the form includes provisions for identifying the team members for the visit date(s), and providing current placement office information (address, telephone number, and placement officer name and title).

Section 1, Interest Candidates—designates those individuals who potentially will visit for interviews with appropriate company units to explore career employment opportunities. Students designated as summer employment program prospects normally are not invited for employment interviews; managers review their qualifications and interests on paper to develop appropriate work assignments for candidates of interest. Faculty members who are potential summer employment program participants should be invited to obtain college relations benefits through promoting their understanding of company facilities, programs, and so on. They, in turn, can discuss their findings with student candidates for summer employment program work experience opportunities. This section also provides statistical data needed for initial assessments of recruitment effectiveness at the college or university under consideration.

Section 2, No Interest Candidates—provides a listing of those individuals who, after a suitable time lapse, are sent "no interest letters" which offer regrets that a review of their qualifications and interests with management did not identify suitable career/summer employment opportunities for their consideration. Such a letter is prepared by the HRM organization for signature by the team member who interviewed the candidate; this type of personal touch must be used in all college relations contacts for promoting the company's image as an employer. The date that the letter is sent is recorded on the form under the "no letter date" column.

Section 3, Placement Office Services Assessment—serves as a series of reminders to the team captain about his or her responsibilities for ensuring that up-to-date and adequate supplies of company information are available on campus, optimum recruitment date(s) are arranged, effective media are used to advertise recruitment visits, and so on. The assessment provides a uniform structure for providing feedback to the HR director for resolving problems.

Section 4, Campus Relations Contacts—gives details concerning the purpose and results of visits with professors and students while on campus. For example, a former summer employment program student participant who transferred to a college or university for graduate studies is contacted to meet for coffee, dinner, and so on. In addition to expressing continued interest in having the individual join the company after graduate studies are completed, the contact also can yield recommendations concerning other students who would be of interest to the company for career opportunities. Effective college relations activities such as this contact are essential for achieving campus recruitment objectives.

Section 5, General Comments—asks for the team captain's recommendations regarding travel arrangements and accommodations, problems encountered on campus, ways to enhance future success, and so on.

Campus Recruitment Report

College/University _____

Location _____ Dates _____

Team Members:

	Names	Representing (Company Unit)
Captain	_____	_____
Member	_____	_____
Member	_____	_____
Member	_____	_____

Placement Office Address & Tel. No.   Placement Officer/Representative
(Name & Title)

_____   _____

_____   _____

( ) _____   _____

1. Interest Candidates (Attach Campus Candidate Assessment forms)

Name	Emp. Code*	Degree	Grad. Date	Rating	Company Units

2. No Interest Candidates (Attach Campus Candidate Assessment forms)

Name	Emp. Code*	No Letter Date	Name	Emp. Code*	No Letter Date

*Emp. Codes: C = Career; S or F = Student or Faculty Candidate—Summer Employment Program

Figure 2.23 Campus recruitment report

continued

3. Placement Office Services Assessment:

   A. *Student Résumés/Data Sheets* —Provided with schedule, or by candidates when they report for interviews? Is a senior profile book or other data on student qualifications available for review prior to interviews?

   B. *Career Information Library* —Current company information on file? Was company's literature on-hand sufficient to meet needs? If not, recommended increase for future shipments?

   C. *Interview facilities* —Describe adequacy and suitability.

   D. *Interview Scheduling* —When do interviews begin and end each day? How much time is allotted for each interview? Between interviews?

   E. *Quality and Quantity of Sign-Ups* —Does Placement Office adequately screen sign-ups to ensure they meet company requirements?

   F. *Luncheon* —Is this an opportunity to meet professors? What faculty members were met by members of your team?

   G. *Transcript Request Arrangements* —Does the Placement Office have forms/procedures for expediting transcript requests?

   H. *Recommended Campus Advertising Media* —What publications are most effective in advertising company visits? Provide details regarding these publications, who they reach, and how we can contact them for rate information, etc.

   I. *Suitability of Current Interview Date(s)* —Describe any conflicts with examination schedules, etc. What date(s) would be more suitable? Date(s) reserved for next year?

   J. *Other (specify)* —

4. Campus Relations Contacts—Provide details concerning visits with professors and students, including follow-up contacts with former Summer Employment Program participants.

Name	Purpose and Result of Contact	Contacted by

5. General Comments—Recommendations regarding travel arrangements and accommodations, problems encountered on campus, ways to enhance future success, etc.

_____

_____

_____

Team Captain _____ Date _____

Figure 2.23 *(cont.)*

2.24 CAMPUS CANDIDATE ASSESSMENT FORM

The Campus Candidate Assessment form (Figure 2.24) provides the interviewer with a structured evaluation format. It also includes a procedural framework for the interviewer to invite career employment candidates to the company. The form is designed to accommodate a program in which the campus interviewer is the focal point for all candidate contacts. For example, the interviewer extends invitations while on campus, calls the candidate to establish the visit date and provide details, and confirms the invitation with a letter provided by the HRM organization for his or her signature. The HR director steps into the process after the visit to extend an offer by letter, or to send a "regrets" letter.

If the role of a campus interviewer in your company is to only screen candidates for subsequent decisions to invite the candidate for an interview by management, through invitation letters by the HR director, the Campus Candidate Assessment form can be adapted as shown in Figure 2.24A.

The heading of the Campus Candidate Assessment form requires specifying whether the individual is a career candidate or a summer employment candidate. The following information is then provided:

- Name (last, first, middle initial)
- Graduation date, degree (BSME, MBA, and so on), and school (business, engineering, and so on)
- Overall GPA (grade point average), honors (for example, Dean's list), and EEO (equal employment opportunity) Code. Codes to be used are:

   M   =   Male
   F   =   Female
   W   =   White
   B   =   Black
   S   =   Hispanic
   A   =   Asian
   H   =   Handicapped
   VV   =   Vietnam Veteran
   Example: MBHVV

Section 1, Assessments—provides a structure for quickly summarizing information about key factors. Basic questions are whether the candidate's personality and appearance, motivation, interests, and experience meet the company's expectations. Educational objectives are included to determine whether a senior-year student, or a summer employment candidate who desires work experience between his or her junior and senior years, will be seeking career employment after he or she receives the Bachelor's Degree. If the company's requirements are for Bachelor's Degree-level professionals only, it would be counterproductive and economically unsound to invite individuals who already have been accepted for Master's Degree programs. Such candidates should, if otherwise suitable for employment, receive an overall evaluation of "possible." The associated comments section would include a statement such as: "Solid candidate with excellent potential, but undoubtedly is going on for a Master's Degree. Send no-interest letter."

Section 2, Invite Data—The version of this form shown as Figure 2.24 indicates whether the candidate was "invited" by the interviewer on campus for specific opportunities with the organizations designated in Section 2A of the form, or is under consideration as a "potential invite—review." In the latter case, an "excellent" candidate has work interests which do not match specific requirements, but suitable opportunities may be developed through reviewing the individual's qualifications with management. This category also is used in situations where the interviewer is not sure of a match with existing requirements, and waits to review the candidate's background at the team member meeting. For both versions of this form, Figures 2.24 and 2.24A, this section also provides for specifying dates when the candidate will be available for an interview trip (for example, vacation periods). It also requires the date that the candidate will be available for employment thus ensuring that timely actions are initiated. Related comments are requested which recognize that some candidates will complete their college work in January instead of at the end of the school year, and that others must take summer courses before obtaining their degrees.

Section 3, Contact Information—recognizes that, in addition to campus contact information, the interviewer should have the details necessary to reach the individual at home during vacation periods. This information is essential for planning economically effective interview trips. If your company is located in Illinois and the candidate attends a university in Michigan, you do not want the candidate to visit you from his or her home in California during spring vacation, after completing all degree coursework in January.

Section 4, Interview Confirmation—For Figures 2.24 and 2.24A, respectively, this section of the form is used by the interviewer or the HR director for recording information on dates interview confirmation actions were completed. Details concerning the date(s) of the visit, the organizations to be visited (which may involve more than one company location), and any special arrangements are specified.

Campus Candidate Assessment

☐ Career Candidate
☐ Summer Employment
Program Candidate

Name (Last, First, MI) _____

Graduation Date _____ Degree _____ School _____

Overall GPA _____ / _____ Honors _____ EEO Code _____

1. Assessments:

   A. *Personality & Appearance* —Describe initial reaction and your overall perception after completing the interview.

   B. *Goal-Oriented Motivation* —Provide examples of past accomplishments and the candidate's achievement-oriented plans. Also provide examples of leadership roles.

   C. *Work Interests and Experience* —Define type of work desired and give examples of related work experience and/or related thesis topic and conclusion.

   D. *Educational Objectives* —If candidate is considering further education, provide details.

   E. *Overall Evaluation:* ☐ Not Suitable ☐ Possible ☐ Good ☐ Excellent
      Comments: _____
      _____
      _____

2. Invite Data: ☐ Invited—Date to Be Established   ☐ Potential Invite—Review

   A. Organizations to be visited: _____

   B. Dates candidate will be available for interviews _____

   C. Date candidate will be available for employment _____

      Comments: _____
      _____
      _____

3. Contact Information: At School Address Until (Date) _____
   School Address & Tel. No.   Home Address & Tel. No.

4. Interview Confirmation: Confirmation Letter Sent (Date) _____

                     Telephone Invite/Invite Confirmation (Date) _____
   Dates of Visit   Organization & Locations   Special Arrangements

Campus Interviewer _____ Date _____

Figure 2.24 Campus candidate assessment

Campus Candidate Assessment

☐ Career Candidate
☐ Summer Employment
Program Candidate

Name (Last, First, MI) _____

Graduation Date _____ Degree _____ School _____

Overall GPA ____ / ____ Honors _____ EEO Code _____

1. Assessments:

    A. *Personality & Appearance* —Describe initial reaction and your overall perception after completing the interview.

    B. *Goal-Oriented Motivation* —Provide examples of past accomplishments and the candidate's achievement-oriented plans. Also provide examples of leadership roles.

    C. *Work Interests and Experience* —Define type of work desired and give examples of related work experience and/or related thesis topic and conclusion.

    D. *Educational Objectives* —If candidate is considering further education, provide details.

    E. *Overall Evaluation:* ☐ Not Suitable ☐ Possible ☐ Good ☐ Excellent
    Comments: _____
    _____

2. Invite Data:

    A. Organizations to be visited: _____

    B. Dates candidate will be available for interviews_____

    C. Date candidate will be available for employment_____

    Comments: _____
    _____

3. Contact Information: At School Address Until (Date) _____

    School Address & Tel. No.   Home Address & Tel. No.

4. Interview Confirmation (HR Director):   Invitation Letter Sent (Date)_____

                                   Candidate Confirmation Telecon (Date)_____

    Dates of Visit   Organization & Locations   Special Arrangements

Campus Interviewer _____ Date _____

Figure 2.24A Campus candidate assessment

2.25 CANDIDATE TRANSCRIPT REQUEST LETTER

A transcript of a candidate's academic performance in a college or university is requested by a company to assess an individual's potential for meeting work requirements, and to verify that the degree required for the position under consideration was awarded. Typical transcript assessments consider the candidate's performance in courses perceived as critical for success in the position, and evaluate the impact of those courses in which the candidate had difficulty. For example, an individual who majored in mathematics and obtained very high grades in all related coursework, but who failed to perform well in English courses would be perceived as having potential problems. Such an individual, while technically sound, would have difficulty in effectively expressing concepts in writing. This would be a major impediment in a company where written reports represent the end product of a researcher's efforts. Unless the individual is a brilliant mathematician, a company would decide in favor of another candidate whose skills combine overall excellence in analytical and descriptive functions.

The Candidate Transcript Request Letter (Figure 2.25) provides a format which may be given to the candidate for arranging to have a transcript sent to the company. A separate form letter is provided for each transcript required. The section which states, "please send my transcript to:" is completed by the company representative to indicate the name and title of the company representative and the company address to which the transcript is to be sent. The balance of required information is completed by the candidate to authorize the release of the transcript. The candidate also provides his or her personal check for the required fee, which is then reimbursed by the company as part of the overall interview expenses.

To: Registrar   Date _____

    _____

    _____

    _____

I am under consideration for employment opportunities with the company indicated below, and would appreciate your forwarding a copy of my transcript to them as soon as possible. My personal check for the required fee is enclosed:

Please send my transcript to:

    _____

    _____

    _____

    _____

Signature _____

Name _____ Student I.D. # _____

School _____

Degree _____

Graduation Date _____

Enclosure

Figure 2.25 Candidate transcript request letter

2.26 TEMPORARY EMPLOYMENT AGENCY LOG

This log (Figure 2.26) is essential for maintaining the information necessary for controlling temporary employment agency services and costs. Its provisions include:

- *Agency and Name of Contact*—the name of the agency and the name of the placement representative who "fills" your order are indicated.
- *Position*—the agency's title for the position which best meets your needs is designated. For example, you may need an excellent typist and the agency uses the title "senior word processor."
- *Reports To*—enter the last name of the person who ordered the temporary employee and the organization's number.
- *Dates*—from and thru, as specified by the requisition.
- *Commitment*—the hours, rate per hour, and cost for the order are entered.
- *Employee Name and Performance*—a verification procedure is established to ensure that the temporary employee is performing satisfactorily within the first few hours of beginning an assignment. This permits the replacement of an unsatisfactory employee at no cost to the company under the terms of temporary employment agency working agreements. An additional follow-up is required to obtain a final performance rating for the temporary employee. When a similar temporary worker is needed in the future, the same employee is requested. Control over the payment of temporary employment agency charges also requires a procedure where the temporary employee is required to report to the HRM office to have his or her time record signed, which provides verification that the commitment for hours, as shown in the log, is not exceeded.
- *Invoice Processing*—the date that the invoice is approved for payment and the amount authorized are recorded in these columns. The amount authorized must equal the commitment cost entry.

Temporary Employment Agency Log _____ Year

Agency and Name of Contact	Position	Report to:		Dates		Commitment			Employee Name and Performance		Invoice Processing	
		Name	Org.	From	Thru	Hours	Rate	Cost	Name	P*	Date	Amt.

*P = *Performance Rating:* A = Outstanding, B = Above Average, C = Average, etc.

Figure 2.26 Temporary employment agency log

123

2.27 EMPLOYMENT AGENCY FEE LOG

The Employment Agency Fee Log (Figure 2.27) provides an accounting record of all employment agency fees. Entries are made as employees report for work. The log requires the following information:

- *Name*—name of an employee who was hired through the employment agency referral process.
- *Position Title*—the employee's position title.
- *Organization*—the designation of the company unit that hired the employee.
- *Agency*—name of the agency that receives credit for the referral, and which will bill the company for services rendered.
- *Annual Salary*—the employee's annual starting salary. The agency's invoice amount will be based on a percentage of the new employee's annual salary.
- *Fee %*—the percentage the agency will apply against the employee's annual starting salary in computing its fee.
- *Invoice Processed*—when the agency invoice is received, the computation of the fee percent versus the starting annual salary is compared with the amount of the fee charged. If correct, the invoice is approved and the amount and the date of approval are entered in respective columns.

Employment Agency Fee Log

Name	Position Title	Organization	Agency	Annual Salary	Fee %	Invoice Processed	
						Amount	Date

Figure 2.27   Employment agency fee log

CHAPTER 3

Selection

An effective selection process involves techniques created by the HR director for ensuring that only qualified applicants are offered employment. This quality control responsibility is met by designing tools and procedures for screening out unqualified and unsuitable candidates.

Well constructed Application for Employment forms (see Figures 3.1, 3.2, and 3.3) obtain the information needed for critical evaluations of candidate qualifications. Problem applicants are readily identified through legally permitted questions regarding convictions, medical impairments, citizenship/resident alien status (legal permission to work), and so on.

Structured interviews, based on worksheet guidance, are used to probe critical areas in determining a candidate's overall suitability for employment. The Applicant Interview Record (see Figure 3.7) is prepared by the HR representative, then provided to the hiring manager as the basis for using the Hiring Manager Interview Worksheet (see Figure 3.10) to obtain job-related assessments.

Telephone Reference Check formats (see Figures 3.11 and 3.13) and Reference Check Letters (see Figure 3.12) provide the basis for systematically verifying candidate qualifications.

A Pre-Employment Medical Questionnaire (see Figure 3.19) yields information needed to avoid hiring high-risk individuals who potentially will increase the cost of medical benefit programs while, through their absences, being responsible for a decrease in productivity.

3.1 APPLICATION FOR EMPLOYMENT FORM (NON-EXEMPT EMPLOYEES)

The Application for Employment form (Figure 3.1) is two-sided and contains questions designed to assess the following:

How long has the applicant lived in the area? People who have moved frequently in the past probably will continue to do so in the future. They typically do not make stable employees who can be counted on for long-term commitments.

Are the applicant's wage expectations in line with your company's compensation for the job under consideration?

If your company has multiple locations, the questions about prior applications or employment with the company can save time in obtaining assessment information. If the individual applied a few months ago at another company location, a phone call will provide interviewer assessment comments, and perhaps, information about an unfavorable reference check that precluded offering employment to the applicant.

Does the applicant have any physical problems that will affect his or her ability to perform job-related duties? If so, can accommodations be made to compensate for the handicap in question?

Is the applicant legally entitled to work? As a general rule, aliens without permanent residence status as proven by the so-called "green card," cannot legally be employed. Permanent residence status is verified by a blue I-151 Alien Registration Card.

Does the applicant's employment history show continuous work experience since the completion of his or her education? Are all gaps in employment fully and satisfactorily explained? Does work experience show growth and increased responsibilities?

Are the applicant's reasons for leaving prior employers logically sound? For example, "to accept an advancement opportunity" should be supported by data for the next employer which shows a higher level job title and/or wage. Suspicious responses should be targeted for telephone reference checks.

The form includes an all inclusive statement that the applicant signs to permit the company to fully investigate his or her background. The individual releases all sources of information from any loss or damage, and agrees that any information obtained by the company will be held confidential. This confidentiality agreement includes any demand made by the individual, except as required by law. False statements or omissions are understood to be sufficient grounds for discharge. This type of a release is an excellent device for promoting former employer cooperation in providing reference information. A copy of this page of the application may be attached to a letter requesting reference information. It provides assurance to the former employer that the individual has authorized release of the information, and will not hold the former employer liable for any resultant damages. This technique has the added advantage of showing the information that the individual provided in the employment history section concerning his or her record with the prior employer. A brief cover letter requesting verification and/or details concerning discrepancies, and calling the former employer's attention to the individual's signed release would be sufficient.

Application for Employment

ANSWER ALL QUESTIONS COMPLETELY. Please print. Use blue or black ink. If employed, this becomes a permanent record. Otherwise, this only will be retained for a thirty (30) day period. **XYZ Electronics, Inc.,** an equal opportunity employer who guarantees, pursuant to all applicable Federal and State laws, every applicant for employment and every employee the right to equal consideration without regard to race, color, religion, national origin, sex, age, marital status, or veteran status.

Personal Position Applied for _____

Date _____

Referred By: ☐ Ad ☐ Friend ☐ Relative ☐ Employment Agency ☐ Other

Name _____
    Last   First   Initial

Phone Number (_____) _____

Present Address _____
    Street   City   State   Zip Code

Social Security Number _____

Previous Address _____
    Street   City   State   Zip Code

How Long at Present Address? _____ How Long at Previous Address? _____

Have You Applied for Employment with XYZ Before? ☐ No ☐ Yes (Explain)
   Date _____
   Where _____

Have You Been Employed by XYZ Before? ☐ No ☐ Yes (Explain)
   Position _____
   Where _____
   Dates _____

Do Any of Your Friends or Relatives Work for XYZ? ☐ No ☐ Yes (Explain)

Date You Can Start to Work? _____ Available for Working ☐ Full Time ☐ Part Time ☐ Temporary ☐ Shifts Wage/Salary Desired

Have You Been Convicted of a Felony? ☐ No ☐ Yes (Explain)

Are You a Veteran of the U.S. Military Service? ☐ No ☐ Yes (Explain)

Do You Have Any Physical, Mental, or Medical Impairment or Disability Which Would Limit Your Ability to Perform Job Related Duties? ☐ No ☐ Yes (Explain)

Are You a Citizen of the U.S.? ☐ Yes ☐ No

Are You a Permanent Resident of the U.S.? ☐ Yes ☐ No

1-151 Alien Registration Card Number:
A- _____

Education	Elementary School	High School	College/University	College/University
Name of School and Location				
Circle Highest Year Completed	4 5 6 7 8	9 10 11 12	1 2 3 4	5 6 7 8
Type of Diploma/Degree		☐ Academic ☐ Commercial		
Describe Studies— Major, Minor, Etc.				
Grade Point Average				
Special Training— Courses, Seminars, Etc.			Office Skills (Secretary-Clerical)	☐ Type _____WPM ☐ Steno _____WPM ☐ 10 Key Adding Machine ☐ Dictaphone

Figure 3.1 Application for employment

continued

Employment History (List all positions, starting with most recent)

Dates	Names & Address of Employer	Wage/ Salary	Position Title— Duties Performed	Reason for Leaving
To		$ _____ To		
From	Supervisor—	$ _____ From		
To		$ _____ To		
From	Supervisor—	$ _____ From		
To		$ _____ To		
From	Supervisor—	$ _____ From		
To		$ _____ To		
From	Supervisor—	$ _____ From		
To		$ _____ To		
From	Supervisor—	$ _____ From		
To		$ _____ To		
From	Supervisor—	$ _____ From		

Special Skills or Qualifications (from employment or other experience):

Any Special Information You Want Us to Consider in Evaluating Your Qualifications?

In making this application, I realize that my character, reputation for honesty, habits, ability, records of convictions, if any, financial responsibility and reasons for leaving employment may be investigated and that persons who know me, now and/or in the past, may be contacted and questioned about me to which I hereby give my consent.

Anyone who may furnish any information concerning my character, habits, ability, criminal convictions, financial responsibility or any reason for leaving any employment shall not be responsible for any loss or damage that I may suffer in consequence thereof. I further agree that any information obtained by the Company from any source will be held confidential by the Company from all persons and even against any demand made by me, except as required by law. It is the policy of the Company to consider all the information supplied by the applicant in assessing his or her qualifications for employment. I understand that any false statements or omissions on this application will be sufficient grounds for discharge.

If hired, I understand and agree that I will be on a probationary period, not to exceed ninety (90) days duration. I understand that shift changes are a condition of employment.

Date _____ Signature _____

Figure 3.1 *(cont.)*

3.2 EMPLOYMENT APPLICATION (EXEMPT EMPLOYEES)

This four-page Employment Application form for exempt employees (Figure 3.2) contains an employment section which includes all of page 2 and part of page 3. Full details of employment with up to four employers may be entered. Instructions advise the applicant to "Use this section to supplement information provided in your résumé. Begin with most recent employer. List all employment, no matter how short the term." This list provides details for each former employer which normally are not provided in a résumé. If the applicant does not have a résumé to incorporate as part of his or her employment application, sufficient space is provided for detailed "description of duties" information.

The professional tone of the Employment Application includes questions such as "percent of college expenses earned" and "how earned." The basis for this question lies in the need to consider the applicant's scholastic average and class rank versus other demands on his or her time. The individual who worked in the college cafeteria 4 hours a day while maintaining a 3.2 grade point average demonstrated qualities of mature independence, application, persistence, and resourcefulness which will serve the company well. The question of college activities, including offices the applicant held, provides insight into the individual's interests and leadership abilities. An individual applying for a position as a writer would be a solid prospect if he or she had been the editor of the college newspaper. Similarly, the request that the applicant list any hobbies or special interests outside of business provides an excellent basis for predicting the experienced applicant's potential. For example, extensive leadership roles in community activities offers insight into managerial capabilities. If the applicant does not have business management experience, a history of successful community leadership may be projected as the foundation for assuming a supervisory role. Hobbies also provide excellent insight into the individual's personality and interests. If your company is engaged in electronics manufacturing, and an applicant for an accounting position indicates that he or she has an amateur radio license, then you may be assured that a commonality of work-related interests and understandings (terminology, functions of electronic parts, and so on) will promote the individual's success as an employee.

Although the form is designed principally for professionals, it also may be used to serve the universal employment needs of a company's headquarters where requirements include secretarial and clerical positions. An "applicants for secretarial/clerical positions" section is provided on page 3 of the form.

The potential employee is required to sign a statement to certify that statements made in the Employment Application are correct, to grant permission to solicit and investigate statements from any person or organization regarding his or her personal history and prior employment, and to indicate that he or she understands that false information may be the basis for disqualification or subsequent release from employment. The individual also agrees to conscientiously observe all rules and conditions of employment. This certification may be supplemented by an Addendum to Employment Application (Figure 3.2A) or a Release (Figure 3.2B) which expands the understanding of incorporating a release from liability/damage to those furnishing information about the applicant. A copy of either of these forms may be attached to a letter requesting reference information. It offers necessary reassurance to the former employer that providing negative information about the individual will not lead to legal entanglements. This technique will yield more candid and complete information about the applicant's prior employment.

Employment Application of _____

Date _____

| First Name | Middle | Last |

Applying for Position as _____ Date Available _____

Type of Employment: ☐ Permanent ☐ Temporary ☐ Part Time   Salary Requirement $ _____

Present Address _____
| Street | City | State | Zip Code | How Long? |

Previous Address _____
| Street | City | State | Zip Code | How Long? |

Home Telephone No. _____ Business Telephone No. _____
(Area Code)   (Area Code)

Have You Applied for Employment with Us in the Past? (If "Yes", explain) _____

Relatives or Friends Employed by Us? (If "Yes", identify) _____
(Names)

Who Referred You to Us?
(Check Appropriate Box and Name Source)

☐ Employment Agency ☐ Direct Contact ☐ School
☐ Advertisement ☐ Company Employee ☐ Other

Name _____

Education

Schools	Print Name, Number and Street, City, State, and Zip Code for Each School Listing	Dates (Mo./Yr.)	Type Course or Major	Graduated?	Degree Received
Grade School		From / To			
High School		From / To			
College		From / To			
Graduate School		From / To			
Trade, Bus. Night or Corres.		From / To			
Other		From / To			

Approximate Scholastic Average: High School _____ College _____ Class Rank: High School _____ College _____

Percent of College Expenses Earned _____ How Earned? _____

School and College Activities (Sports, Publications, Honors, Dramatics, Offices Held) _____

_____

FEDERAL LAW FORBIDS DISCRIMINATION BECAUSE OF RACE, COLOR, RELIGION, AGE, SEX OR NATIONAL ORIGIN.

Figure 3.2 Employment application

continued

Employment

Use this section to supplement information provided in your résumé.
Begin with most recent employer. List all employment, no matter how short the term.

Company
Name _____ Employed From __Mo–Yr__ To __Mo–Yr__

Street Address _____ Salary or Earnings Start _____ Finish _____

City _____ State _____ Zip Code _____ Tele. No. _____

Name and Title of
Immediate Supervisor _____ Your Title _____

Description of Duties

_____

Reasons for terminating or considering a change _____

Company
Name _____ Employed From __Mo–Yr__ To __Mo–Yr__

Street Address _____ Salary or Earnings Start _____ Finish _____

City _____ State _____ Zip Code _____ Tele. No. _____

Name and Title of
Immediate Supervisor _____ Your Title _____

Description of Duties

_____

Reasons for terminating _____

Company
Name _____ Employed From __Mo–Yr__ To __Mo–Yr__

Street Address _____ Salary or Earnings Start _____ Finish _____

City _____ State _____ Zip Code _____ Tele. No. _____

Name and Title of
Immediate Supervisor _____ Your Title _____

Description of Duties

_____

Reasons for terminating _____

Figure 3.2 *(cont.)*

Company Name _____	Employed From	Mo–Yr	Mo–Yr To

Street Address _____

Salary or Earnings	Start	Finish

City _____ State _____ Zip Code _____ Tele. No. _____

Name and Title of
Immediate Supervisor _____ Your Title _____

Description of Duties

_____

_____

Reasons for terminating _____

Military

Have you ever served in the Military Service of the United States? _____

Branch of Service _____ From _____ To _____ Rank _____

Give details of Service duties which might apply to civilian occupations _____

_____

_____

_____

_____

Skills

List any special skills you may have _____

_____

_____

List any hobbies or special
interests outside of business:

1. _____   4. _____
2. _____   5. _____
3. _____   6. _____

What Foreign Languages Do You Speak, Read, or Write? _____

☐ Speak   ☐ Speak
☐ Read   ☐ Read
☐ Write _____ ☐ Write

Applicants for Secretarial/Clerical Positions:

Business Machines you can operate _____

Typing Speed _____ words per minute ☐ Electric ☐ Manual

Steno Speed _____ words per minute Method _____

Figure 3.2 *(cont.)*

134

Personal

Have you ever been convicted of a felony?

☐ No ☐ Yes (Explain)

Are you a U.S. citizen or an alien immigrant? ☐ Yes ☐ No

Social Security No. _____

I-151 Alien Registration No. _____

Do you have any physical, mental, or medical impairment or disability which might limit your ability to perform job-related duties? ☐ No ☐ Yes (Explain) _____

_____

Have you had a serious or prolonged illness during the past five years?

☐ No ☐ Yes (Explain) _____

Person to be notified in case of emergency:

Name _____ Work Telephone _____ Home Telephone _____

May we contact your present employer at this time? ☐ Yes ☐ No

I HEREBY CERTIFY THAT ALL STATEMENTS MADE BY ME IN ANSWER TO THE QUESTIONS CONTAINED IN THIS APPLICATION ARE CORRECT TO THE BEST OF MY KNOWLEDGE AND RECOLLECTION. PERMISSION IS HEREBY GRANTED TO SOLICIT AND INVESTIGATE STATEMENTS FROM ANY PERSON OR ORGANIZATION WITH REGARD TO MY PERSONAL HISTORY AND PRIOR EMPLOYMENT.

I UNDERSTAND THAT INCLUSION OF ANY FALSE INFORMATION MAY BE CAUSE FOR DISQUALIFICATION OR SUBSEQUENT RELEASE FROM EMPLOYMENT. IF EMPLOYED, I WILL CONSCIENTIOUSLY ABIDE BY ALL THE RULES AND CONDITIONS OF EMPLOYMENT.

SIGNED _____

APPLICANT

SPACE BELOW FOR USE OF INTERVIEWERS

Figure 3.2 *(cont.)*

Addendum to Employment Application

I certify that all employment application information provided is true and complete, and hereby authorize the company or its representatives to investigate the accuracy of my statements. It is understood that false or significantly misleading information will disqualify me for employment, or will result in immediate dismissal if I am employed. I hereby authorize and release from any resultant liability, all individuals and organizations to supply information in complete confidence concerning my background, prior work performance, reputation, and character.

Name (First, MI, Last) _____

Social Security Number _____

Date of Birth _____

Signature _____ Date _____

Witness _____ Date _____

Figure 3.2A Addendum to employment application

Release

I, _____ , having made application for employment with (name of company), and desiring it to be informed as to my ability, reasons for leaving employment, character, reputation for honesty, financial responsibility, habits, and any records of convictions, I hereby authorize it to investigate and to ascertain any and all information which may concern any or all of the foregoing, whether same is of record or not. I hereby release my present and former employers, any city, county, or state law enforcement agencies, and all persons whomsoever from any damage resulting from furnishing said information.

Social Security Number _____

Date of Birth _____

Signature _____ Date _____

Witness _____ Date _____

Figure 3.2B Release

3.3 SHORT EMPLOYMENT APPLICATION FORM

When "walk-in" applicants flood your reception area, the ideal tool for expediting the applicant screening process is a one-page Employment Application (Figure 3.3). All applicants, including those who have résumés, are requested to complete this form. The application requires answers to critical questions which are used in eliminating undesirable or unqualified individuals, but does so without the extensive investment of time needed to provide full details concerning employment history. The applicant is required to only offer complete information regarding his or her current/ last employer, and, if needed to further demonstrate requisite background, notations concerning special skills or qualifications.

A well trained employment receptionist, whose next position in most companies probably will be that of an employment interviewer, is qualified to review the completed application and make sound judgments regarding applicant suitability. Only those individuals whose Employment Applications meet requisite criteria are referred to employment interviewers for further consideration.

Employment Application

XYZ COMPANY, INC. (an EEO Employer)

Position Applied for _____

Name _____ Referred By: ☐ Ad ☐ Friend ☐ Relative ☐ Employment Agency ☐ Other

Last   First   Initial

Present Address _____ Phone Number ( )

Have you applied for employment with XYZ before? ☐ No ☐ Yes (Explain)
Date _____
Where _____

Have you been employed by XYZ before? ☐ No ☐ Yes (Explain)
Position _____
Where _____
Dates _____

Do any of your friends or relatives work for XYZ? ☐ No ☐ Yes (Explain)
Social Security Number

Date you can start to work? _____ | Available for Working ☐ Full Time ☐ Part Time | ☐ Temporary ☐ Shifts | Wage/Salary Desired

Have you been convicted of a Felony? ☐ No ☐ Yes (Explain)

Are you a veteran of the U.S. Military Service? ☐ No ☐ Yes (Explain)

Do you have any physical, mental, or medical impairment or disability which would limit your ability to perform job related duties? ☐ No ☐ Yes (explain)

Are you a citizen of the U.S.? ☐ Yes ☐ No | Are you a permanent resident of the U.S.? ☐ Yes ☐ No | 1-151 Alien Registration Card Number: A-_____

Education	Elementary School	High School	College/University	College/University
Name of School and Location				
Circle Highest Year Completed	4 5 6 7 8	9 10 11 12	1 2 3 4	5 6 7 8
Type of Diploma/Degree		☐ Academic ☐ Commercial		
Describe Studies— Major, Minor, Etc.				
Grade Point Average				

Current/Last Employer

Dates	Names & Address of Employer	Wage/Salary	Position Title— Duties Performed	Reason for Leaving
To		$ To		
From	Supervisor—	$ From		

Special Skills or Qualifications: _____

Office Skills (Secretary-Clerical):
☐ Type _____WPM
☐ Steno _____WPM
☐ 10 Key Adding Machine
☐ Dictaphone

I swear or affirm the statements made by me are true and complete. Falsification of information can be cause for dismissal.

Date _____ Signature _____

Figure 3.3 Employment application

3.4 EEO DATA SHEET

An effective technique for uniformly and consistently obtaining legally required information concerning the Equal Employment Opportunity/Affirmative Action status of applicants is shown in Figure 3.4.

The form is designed to be completed voluntarily by each applicant for statistical purposes only. For example, normal practice designates the employment receptionist as responsible for maintaining applicant statistics. The form is issued with the Employment Application for completion, then separated for the exclusive use of the employment receptionist in compiling data. It is not provided to employment interviewers because the contents include information which cannot be legally considered in the selection process. An exception would be those cases where a handicapped applicant has suggested special equipment or physical environment accommodations needed to meet position requirements. Since this information is essential for employment consideration, the receptionist should extract such comments and provide an explanatory note to the interviewer.

EQUAL EMPLOYMENT OPPORTUNITY DATA

It is our company's policy to provide equal employment opportunity to all persons regardless of their race, sex, color, religion, national origin, age, or physical or mental handicap. We are an affirmative action employer with goals which include providing employment opportunities to disabled veterans and/or veterans of the Vietnam era. Your assistance in voluntarily completing this form will provide the information needed for us to comply with federal recordkeeping and reporting requirements.

Position Applied for: _____ Date _____

Name (Last, First, MI) _____

Social Security No. _____ Date of Birth _____ Age _____

Please check the appropriate box in each of the following sections

Sex
☐ Male
☐ Female

Race
☐ White (Caucasian)
☐ Black
☐ Hispanic/Spanish Surname
☐ Asian/Asian American/Pacific Islander
☐ American Indian/Alaskan Native

Citizen
☐ Yes
☐ No (I-151 Permanent Resident
   Registration # _____)

Handicapped
☐ No
☐ Yes
☐ Disabled Veteran

Handicapped Applicants

If your disability might affect your ability to perform the duties of this type of position, please explain these limitations and suggest special equipment or physical environment accommodations which will be needed:

_____

_____

_____

_____

_____

Vietnam Era Veteran
☐ Yes, I served honorably on active duty for more than 180 days, continuously, between August 5, 1964, and May 7, 1975.
☐ No

Figure 3.4 Equal employment opportunity data

3.5 EEO APPLICANT LOG

A long-standing approach to the collection of applicant EEO data, as recommended by the Equal Employment Opportunity Commission (EEOC), is to have the company's employment receptionist maintain a log. A visual identification process is used to determine respective applicant EEO codes.

The sample EEO Applicant Log (Figure 3.5) employs codes to designate the EEO "candidate category" (for example 5 = office and clerical), EEO status (for example B = Black), and source (for example H = help-wanted advertisement). These EEO Applicant Log Codes, as specified in Figure 3.5A, are printed for ready reference on the reverse side of the EEO Applicant Log. These data are used to generate reports on the company's effectiveness in attracting minority applicants.

The EEO Applicant Log also includes overall candidate data needed for a wide range of recruitment reports; for example, statistics on applicants for each position (based on aggregating data for respective personnel requisitions and associated position titles), statistics on applicants by types of recruitment sources to assess relative effectiveness, and so on.

The EEO Applicant Log also may be used in conjunction with the EEO data form (refer to Figure 3.4). Data from individual EEO DATA forms are transcribed to the log for facilitating report preparation. The log, in summarizing all applicant data, serves as the basis for compiling required statistics.

EEO Applicant Log

Dates: From _____ To _____

Date	Name	Position	Pers. Req. #	Cand. Cat. Code	Sex F	Sex M	EEO Code	Source Code	Action

Figure 3.5 EEO applicant log

EEO Applicant Log Codes

EEO CANDIDATE CATEGORY CODES

1. Official or manager
2. Professional
3. Technician
4. Sales worker
5. Office and clerical
6. Skilled craftsperson
7. Semi-skilled operator
8. Unskilled laborer

EEO CODES

W = White (Caucasian)
B = Black
S = Hispanic/Spanish surname
A = Asian/Asian American/Pacific Islander
I = American Indian/Alaskan native
H = Handicapped
V = Veteran of Vietnam era

SOURCE CODES

A = Employment agency
C = Campus recruitment
E = Employee referral
H = Help-wanted advertisement
I = Inquiry letter
M = Minority agency referral
P = Public employment service
S = Secondary school — high school vocational school
T = Technical school

Figure 3.5A EEO applicant log codes

3.6 INTERVIEW SCHEDULE

In a fast paced employment environment with extensive interviewing requirements, a system is needed for controlling applicant flow and maintaining records on the disposition of interviews. The Interview Schedule (Figure 3.6) meets these requirements.

Interviewers initially use these forms to schedule interviews. Interview schedules are set up in working file folders for each month. The day and date are entered on each form, and interview commitments are recorded as they are made. Provisions include designating the candidate's name, the title of the position under consideration, and the personnel requisition number for the position. Candidates interviewed without prior arrangements also are recorded on the Interview Schedule for the day they are considered.

As interviews are completed, entries are made for "rating" and "action." Rating information is taken from Section IV of the Applicant Interview Record (see Figure 3.7 in the next section). For example, a "D" rating means "not recommended." When an applicant receives a "D" rating, the action is to "send no further interest letter." At the conclusion of each day's interviewing activities, the employment interviewer provides the completed Interview Schedule with attached application materials to the clerical employee with responsibility for typing letters, filing, and so on. The request for a "no further interest letter" results in the preparation of a Rejecting Candidate After Interview letter (see Figure 3.14).

Interview Schedule

Interviewer _____

Day and Date _____

Time	Candidate	Position	Personnel Requisition #	Rating	Action
8:00					
9:00					
10:00					
11:00					
12:00					
1:00					
2:00					
3:00					
4:00					
5:00					
6:00					

Notes:

Figure 3.6 Interview schedule

3.7 APPLICANT INTERVIEW RECORD

The Applicant Interview Record (Figure 3.7) is an evaluation format used by the HR representative (employment interviewer, employment assistant, employment manager, and so on) in rating an applicant's suitability for employment. Evaluations center on the following three areas:

1. *Appearance and Personality*—how well the individual will be able to relate to others.
2. *Suitability of Overall Qualifications*—how well the individual's knowledge and skills meet position requirements.
3. *Predictors of Achievement-Oriented Work Performance*—how well the individual's achievements and goals relate to promoting success in the position.

An overall rating is designated based on these assessments. Comments are required to explain reservations, or to give reasons for not recommending the individual for employment consideration by the hiring manager.

The Selection Processing Checklist on the reverse side of the form (Figure 3.7A) is used for tracking the applicant through the selection process. The checklist provides a detailed record and control system for all actions that may potentially take place between the initial interview and the date of hire. The tracking process is visually enhanced by two vertical columns of boxes labeled "hire" and "no," respectively. A "no" entry stops the "hire" process.

The Selection Processing Checklist becomes a permanent EEO/AA record which serves as the basis for generating related reports. Its data also are used in analyses and reports on recruitment effectiveness.

APPLICANT INTERVIEW RECORD

EEO Coding _____

Date _____

Applicant Name (First, MI, Last) _____

Position _____ Personnel Requisition # _____

EVALUATION:

I. *Appearance and Personality* —Describe overall presentation, i.e., dress, grooming, poise, conversational ability, facility for relating effectively with others, etc.

II. *Suitability of Overall Qualifications* —Relate educational background, experience, skills, etc. to position requirements.

III. *Predictors of Achievement-Oriented Work Performance* —Obtain examples of past successes, and assess how well the applicant's current goals match those of the position.

IV. *Overall Rating*

☐ A. Highly Recommend—Outstanding Applicant

☐ B. Recommend—Well-Suited for the Position

☐ C. Recommend—Qualified, with Reservations!*

☐ D. Not Recommended*

* Comments: _____

_____

_____

Interviewer _____ Tel. No. _____

Figure 3.7 Applicant interview record

Selection Processing Checklist

Hire No

1. ☐   Expense Report Paid _____ Amt. $ _____

2. ☐   **No Further Consideration**—Letter Sent (Date) _____

3. ☐   **Referral for Hiring Manager (HM) Interview** (Date) _____

4. ☐   **No Interest** by HM—Reason: _____

5. ☐   **Future Interest** by HM—Letter Sent (Date) _____

6. ☐   **Interest** by HM—**Offer Consideration**

7. ☐   Favorable Telecon **Reference Check** by ☐HR ☐HM (Date) _____

8. ☐   Unfavorable Telecon **Reference Check** by ☐HR ☐HM (Date) _____

9. ☐   **Offer** ☐HR ☐HM Telecon (Date) _____ $ _____

10. ☐   Offer Confirmation Letter Sent (Date) _____

11. ☐   **Candidate Refusal** ☐Telecon ☐Letter

12. ☐   Refusal Regrets Letter and Questionnaire Sent (Date) _____

13. ☐   Refusal Questionnaire Received (Date) _____ Reason(s) for Refusal:

_____

14. ☐   Positive Pre-Employment Medical Exam Results Received (Date) _____
Limitations (If Any): _____

15. ☐   Advise Applicant—Medical Acceptance Telecon (Date) _____

16. ☐   Negative Pre-Employment Medical Exam Results Received (Date) _____
Problems: _____

17. ☐   Medical Rejection Letter Sent (Date) _____

18. ☐   **Offer Accepted** ☐Telecon ☐Letter (Date) _____

19. ☐   Acknowledgment of Acceptance Letter Sent (Date) _____

20. ☐   Failed to Report for Work on (Date) _____

21. ☐   **Reported for Work** on (Date) _____

HR Representative _____ Date _____

Figure 3.7A Selection processing checklist

3.8 SECRETARIAL-CLERICAL SKILL TESTING RECORD

Job-related testing of potential secretarial employees for assessing their typing, stenographic, and spelling skills are summarized in a Secretarial-Clerical Skill Testing Record (Figure 3.8). Typing tests and other skill-level tests are attached as supporting documentation. Similarly, typing and spelling skill tests for potential typists also are documented with this form. An additional feature is that the result of business machine operating skill tests (use of adding machine, IBM PC, and so on) involving these and other potential office employees may be recorded by using this form.

Failure to meet position skill requirements is discussed with the applicant by the test administrator. The completed Secretarial-Clerical Skill Testing Record is attached to the individual's employment application as the basis for disqualification or qualification. If the candidate is disqualified, an entry is made in the "Action" section of the EEO Applicant Log to indicate that the candidate was "Disqualified—Failed Typing Test," and so on. Successful performance leads to a "referred for interview" entry.

Some suggested words for setting up a spelling test are given in Figure 3.8A. Such a test must be validated by administering it to current employees. You must determine how predictive the test is for success in clerical positions that require writing skills. Acceptable test performance criteria result from this evaluation process.

Secretarial-Clerical Skill Testing Record

Applicant's Name (First, MI, Last) _____

Social Security No. _____ Date _____

Typing Skill Test   Requirement = _____ W.P.M.

	Test Version	No. Words Typed	Typing Errors	W.P.M.
Letter	_____	_____	_____	_____
Report Text	_____	_____	_____	_____
Statistical Table	_____	_____	_____	_____

Stenographic Skills Test   Requirement = _____ W.P.M.

	Speed	Errors	W.P.M.
Test Version A	_____	_____	_____
Test Version B	_____	_____	_____
Test Version C	_____	_____	_____
Test Version D	_____	_____	_____
Test Version E	_____	_____	_____
Test Version F	_____	_____	_____

Spelling Test

	Errors	Correct	Score
Test Version A	_____	_____	_____
Test Version B	_____	_____	_____

Business Machine Operating Skill Tests (Specify)

Administered by: _____

Figure 3.8 Secretarial-clerical skill testing record

The candidate for a secretarial or typing position should be given a short test to assess spelling skills. Words which are used in business correspondence, and which experience has proven to be problematic for members of your current staff should be selected in constructing the test. Two versions should be constructed and given at random. Test procedure involves dictating the words to the candidate, who transcribes them on a format provided. Scoring is determined based on results obtained through giving the test to valid samples of your current secretarial and typist populations. It is recognized that new computer word processing programs correct spelling mistakes, but spelling skills still are essential for effective work performance.

Here are forty words which are suggested for the construction of your Test A and Test B; select 20 for each:

acknowledgment	imminent
adherence	impracticable
aging	judgment
biased	license
caliber	likable
combating	maneuver
canceling	modeled
cancellation	offense
catalog	penciled
creditable	percent
defense	personnel
diagrammed	practice
disqualify	quantity
draft	referable
eligible	respectively
employee	skillful
enclosure	temporary
envelope	total
favor	visa
fulfill	willful

Figure 3.8A Spelling test

3.9 EMPLOYMENT CANDIDATE EXPENSE REPORT

A maximally efficient and economical procedure for processing employment candidate expenses is to have the individual arrange his or her own transportation, based on tourist or business class ticket purchase guidelines provided by the company, and to reimburse these costs during the visit. This procedure also applies to lodging costs, but the company is well advised to suggest a particular hotel or motel and make reservations for the candidate. Given the potential for a substantial number of reservations, a hotel manager is very receptive to offering a discount for the company's business.

The individual completes and submits an Employment Candidate Expense Report (Figure 3.9) during his or her visit. Payment is rendered by bank draft prior to the candidate's departure. The reimbursement amount is based on actual costs to date plus reasonable estimates for meals and other miscellaneous expenses that are to be incurred on the return trip home. Commercial transportation and lodging receipts are attached as supporting documentation.

The total amount of reimbursed expenses and the date paid are entered in item 1 of the Selection Processing Checklist (refer to Figure 3.7A) which provides the basis for compiling cost statistics for each recruitment requirement.

Employment Candidate Expense Report

Name (First, MI, Last) _____

Travel from _____ to _____

Date(s) _____

EXPENSES:

Air Transportation* $_____

Local Transportation (taxi, etc.)   _____

Use of Personal Automobile:

_____Miles @ _____/Mile   _____

    Tolls, Parking Fees, etc.   _____

Hotel/Motel Accommodations*   _____

Meals   _____

Miscellaneous (transcript fees, etc.)   _____

Total $_____

Signature _____ Date _____

Approved _____ Date _____

*Please attach receipt

Figure 3.9 Employment candidate expense report

3.10 HIRING MANAGER INTERVIEW WORKSHEET

As shown in Figure 3.10, the Hiring Manager Interview Worksheet, the manager receives a copy of the candidate's Employment Application and a copy of the Applicant Interview Record form for review. Given this information about the candidate's background and the HR organization's evaluation of his or her overall qualifications, the hiring manager uses the worksheet by:

1. Developing questions for assessing how well the candidate's background meets position requirements. For example, if a review of the Employment Application does not clearly indicate that a civil engineer has the required four years of in-depth structural design experience, with specific emphasis on petroleum refining process structures, then an appropriate question is entered in Section 2, "experience."

2. Using the worksheet as a reference source for asking questions, and for recording brief notes concerning responses and observations. Only absolutely essential notes are recorded during the interview to avoid detracting from the open flow of communication. Complete assessment notations are entered immediately following the interview before thoughts are lost.

3. Assessing overall findings regarding the candidate's suitability for the position, to arrive at an "evaluation" conclusion—that is, either "no interest," "possible future interest," or "interest—offer." The completed Hiring Manager Interview Worksheet and associated materials are returned to the HR representative for appropriate action.

Hiring Manager Interview Worksheet

Date _____

Applicant _____ Personnel Requisition # _____

Position _____

Attached for your review is a completed Applicant Interview Record form which provides information concerning the HRM division's evaluation of the applicant's overall qualifications. Please also review the attached copy of the applicant's Employment Application, then use this worksheet to develop interview questions for assessing how well the individual's background meets position requirements. The worksheet also is used for recording notes concerning the applicant's answers, your related assessments, etc.

---

1. Education?

2. Experience?

3. Skills?

4. Accomplishments?

5. Goals?

6. Personal Factors?

EVALUATION: Please indicate your interest and provide comments below, then return this form to _____ , HRM Division.

☐ No Interest   Comments: _____

☐ Possible Future Interest   _____

☐ Interest—Offer   _____

                    _____

Signature _____ Date _____

Figure 3.10 Hiring manager interview worksheet

3.11 TELEPHONE REFERENCE CHECK WORKSHEET

Company selection policies generally require obtaining at least one reference check of a recent employer before extending an offer of employment to a candidate. Two sample formats are provided for obtaining references by telephone; a Telephone Reference Check Worksheet (Figure 3.11) and a Telephone Reference Check (Figure 3.11A). Both are designed for use by HR representatives to obtain and verify information by contacting one of the candidate's former supervisors.

These structured formats promote the development of reference checking expertise through the use of standardized information-gathering techniques. They also provide assurance that all essential information will be requested.

Contacting a candidate's former supervisor for a reference can be very productive in terms of candid assessments, but many company policies require the referral of all such inquiries to the HR organization because of the legal liability associated with issuing damaging information about former employees. In protecting their companies, many HR organizations only release basic confirmation of employment data. Furthermore, they limit their responses to answering written inquiries.

Although such restrictive practices impede telephone reference checking techniques, being referred by the former supervisor to the HR organization still can yield results if the correct approach is used. For example, have your employment manager contact a mutual friend of the employment manager for the company in question (professional association contact, friend in that company, and so on) and have that individual act as an intermediary. The mutual friend calls the other employment manager to let him or her know that your company's management is interested in extending an offer to the former employee, and that your employment manager will be calling for some confidential feedback. This door-opening technique, including assurances regarding confidentiality, will permit your employment manager to personally obtain complete reference information from the other employment manager.

Telephone Reference Check Worksheet

_____   _____
Applicant's Name   Name and Title of Person Contacted

                                         (   )
_____   _____
Company   Telephone Number

1. (Introduce yourself by name, title, and company.) I would like to verify some information given to us by _____ , who has applied for
                                    (Applicant's name)
   employment with us as _____ .
                              (Position Title)

2. What were (his or her) dates of employment? From _____ 19_____ to
   _____ 19_____ .

3. What type of work was (he or she) doing for you? (Obtain position title and identify primary responsibilities.) _____
   _____
   _____

4. (He or she) said (his or her) salary was $_____ . Is this correct? (If "no" determine earnings $_____).

5. Was (he or she) a dependable, responsible employee? _____

6. Did (he or she) require close supervision? _____

7. What did you think of (him or her) as a person? _____
   _____

*8. Why did (he or she) leave?   _____

*9. What company did (he or she) join after leaving you?   _____

10. Would you rehire (him or her)?   Yes _____ No _____
    (If "no" why? _____
    _____)

11. What are (his or her) outstanding strong points? _____
    _____

12. What are (his or her) outstanding weak points? _____
    _____
    _____

*Not used if contacting present employer.

                              Checked By _____

                              Date _____

Figure 3.11 Telephone reference check worksheet

Telephone Reference Check

Name of Applicant _____ Date _____

Former Supervisor's Name _____

Company _____

Location _____ Tel. No. _____

Hello Mr./Ms. _____, this is (your name) of (company name). We are considering (applicant's name) _____ for an employment opportunity as a (job title) _____, and (he or she) suggested that we call you for a reference.

(Applicant's first name) _____ indicated that (he or she) worked for you during the period of (months and years) _____ to _____. Is this correct?

(He or she) also indicated that (his or her) earnings were $_____ (per hour, weekly, etc.) Is this also correct?

What kind of an employee was (applicant's first name)_____?

Did (he or she) get along well with others? How would you describe (his or her) personality? Performance? Integrity? Attendance?

Many thanks for your help. If I can ever be of assistance to you, don't hesitate to contact me.

Signature _____

Name and Title _____

Figure 3.11A Telephone reference check

3.12 REFERENCE CHECK LETTER TO PRIOR EMPLOYER

A sample Reference Check Letter to Prior Employer (Figure 3.12) is directed to the company's HR director to request verification of information provided by the designated applicant for employment. A copy of the applicant's Release (refer to Figure 3.2B) is enclosed as reassurance to the former employer that providing negative information will not lead to legal problems. This promotes candid and complete disclosures. Also enclosed, as a courtesy and convenience, is a stamped and addressed reply envelope.

The form letter includes all information that will be verified. The respondent is requested to only explain discrepancies, if any. Approaches where the respondent is asked to furnish the information are not recommended. To create additional work for another company's equally overworked HR staff slows down response time and reduces the amount of information they will provide.

The letter includes a unique approach to the usual "would you rehire?" inquiry. The typical response is that the company has a policy of not reemploying individuals. The answer you really want is whether the company has a reason for not wanting the person back. The question is phrased to ask for details about any problems with the individual's background, reputation, or character which precludes reemployment consideration.

Preparing a reply can be as simple as making two "no problems" notations, then signing and dating the letter. This promotes cooperation and expedites responses.

Date _____

Dear Human Resources Director:

We are considering the applicant indicated below for employment, and would appreciate your confidential assistance in verifying information provided by this individual concerning prior employment with your company. A copy of the applicant's Release is enclosed. Also enclosed for your convenience is a stamped business reply envelope.

Sincerely,

Mary R. Johnson
Human Resources Director

Enclosures

Applicant _____ Social Security No. _____

Company _____

Location _____

Employed from _____ to _____

Job/Position Title _____

Reason for Leaving _____

Final Wage/Salary Rate $_____ Per _____

If this is not an accurate representation of the individual's employment, please explain discrepancies:

If there are any problems regarding the applicant's background, reputation, or character which would preclude your considering this individual for re-employment, please provide details:

Signature _____ Date _____

Figure 3.12 Reference check letter to prior employer

3.13 PATTERNED TELEPHONE REFERENCE CHECK USED BY HIRING MANAGERS

The Telephone Reference Check (Figure 3.13) shows a patterned format used by managers and officers in contacting their counterparts at other companies for candidate reference information. This approach is recommended when candidates for high level professional or managerial positions are under consideration.

When a manager calls the candidate's former manager, rapport is established by:

1. Introducing himself or herself by name, title, and company name.
2. Explaining that he or she is considering (candidate's name) for a position on his or her staff, and that the individual has given the former manager's name as a reference.
3. Describing the duties and responsibilities of the position being considered.
4. Asking for advice about whether it is correct to conclude that the candidate is well qualified for the position. Since this finding is based on the candidate's representations about his or her experience while working for that manager, not responding openly would appear to be a negative reply. Accordingly, the former manager is inclined to provide valid feedback.

Advice-oriented questions follow which obtain specific details. For example, how well does the former manager think the individual will handle the new assignment? After this potential performance assessment is obtained, the former manager is asked to explain what kind of a performer the individual was for him or her.

Additional questions probe personality and interpersonal skills, the reason(s) why the candidate is leaving or has left the company, and "things to look out for" in working with this potential employee. Questions conclude with sharing proposed salary offer information, which is based on the candidate's representations about prior salary, and asking "is this the correct amount?". This places the former manager in a position where he or she is playing a part in developing an equitable salary offer. If the candidate significantly misrepresented former salary, guidance will be provided as needed to properly estimate the correct amount needed to attract the individual.

Telephone Reference Check

Candidate _____

Position _____

Manager Contacted _____

Company _____ Tel. No. (_____) _____

This patterned format is provided for contacting the candidate's former manager to obtain reference information in critical areas. Please probe all responses which require clarification or suggest additional information is needed.

I'm (name), the (your title) for (company name). My reason for contacting you is that (candidate's name _____), who I am considering for a position on my staff as a (title _____), gave me your name as a reference.

The position involves (give a brief synopsis of major duties and responsibilities). Since (candidate's first name) told me that (he or she) worked for you as a (position title _____) from (mo./yr. _____) to (mo./yr. _____), it appears that (he or she) is well suited for our position. Are we correct?

How well do you think (candidate's first name _____) will handle this assignment?

What kind of a performer was (he or she) for you?

(Candidate's first name _____) impressed us as being very personable. What kind of a person is (he or she) to work with day after day?

Tell me, confidentially, why did (he or she) leave (decide to leave) your company?

What things should I look out for in working with (candidate's first name _____)?

We are considering a starting salary offer of $_____ based on (his or her) having told us that you paid (him or her) $_____. Is this the correct amount?

Signature _____ Date _____

Name & Position Title _____

Organization _____

Figure 3.13 Telephone reference check by hiring manager

3.14 LETTER FOR REJECTING A CANDIDATE AFTER AN INTERVIEW

Figure 3.14 shows a sample of a typical "regrets" or "no" letter to an individual who is determined to be either unsuitable for employment with the company or unqualified for the position under consideration. The tone of the letter must be very positive. Do not forget that an employment candidate also is a stockholder, a customer of the company's goods and services, and a friend of current and prospective future employees. To alienate the individual with a harsh letter, which emphasizes shortcomings, is totally unproductive. Anyone can understand that another candidate may more closely match the company's requirements for the current opportunity but if the company expresses possible future interest, this type of rejection may pay dividends for the company. (A harsh rejection over 26 years ago by a company still keeps one of this author's friends from buying the company's well known cereal products. Given the fact that he raised three children during that time, a rough estimate is that the company lost at least $5,000 in sales. How much business have they lost over the years due to their obvious inability to apply basic human relations principles in their candidate rejection procedures?)

Dear _____:

Many thanks for giving us an opportunity to meet you and discuss your qualifications for the position as Manager of Project Accounting.

Although all who met you were very impressed with your excellent background and experience, we recently concluded that another candidate's qualifications more closely match position requirements. Accordingly, we sincerely regret that we cannot accommodate your joining our company at this time.

You have our best wishes for success in locating the career advancement opportunity you deserve. Be assured that we will not hesitate to contact you if a suitable position becomes available in the near future.

Very truly yours,

Mary E. Jones
Human Resources Director

Figure 3.14 Letter for rejecting candidate after interview

3.15 TELEPHONE WORKSHEET FOR EXTENDING AN OFFER OF EMPLOYMENT

Figure 3.15 shows a sample worksheet used by a line manager in extending an offer of employment. Having the line manager rather than the HR representative contact the candidate builds upon the rapport established during the interview visit, and provides the personal touch that encourages the individual to accept the offer.

The HR organization's responsibility in this process is to provide the basic framework of terminology necessary for a successful verbal offer—one in which the candidate is strongly encouraged to join the company. Using the worksheet ensures that all the considerations the candidate has in making his or her decision will be discussed.

The correct timing of a telephone call is critical in this process. Employed candidates who do not want to compromise their current positions while searching for other employment opportunities, are understandably reluctant to speak freely while at work. Preferably, the candidate should be contacted at home after hours. This more secure and relaxed approach is conducive for promoting discussions that enhance the possibility of acceptances. In planning the contact, remind the line manager about time zone differences if a long-distance call is involved. Consult the telephone directory to determine the time zone for the candidate's residence—that is, pacific, mountain, central, or eastern. When the line manager must make a late evening contact to reach the candidate at home, it is a good idea to alert the candidate to ensure that he or she will be available to receive the call. A low profile technique, which preserves confidentiality, is to have a secretary call the candidate and personally (leave no messages) advise him or her about the planned contact. This also permits arranging alternative contact plans as needed.

In a company with specific EEO/AA hiring objectives for officials and managers, policy requires final review and approval by top management prior to extending an offer to a candidate who is covered by this category. The line manager is required to prepare and submit an EEO Approval to Hire or Promote—Officials and Managers form memorandum (Figure 3.15A) to the company's president. The memorandum details the candidate's EEO status and written justification to support the proposed offer. The company's EEO officer reviews the proposal, provides employment statistics on how approval would impact minority hiring objectives, and then indicates his or her decision. Final review by the president determines whether or not the proposal is approved.

Candidate _____

Tel. No. (   ) _____

Hello, (candidate's first name) _____, this is (your name) of (company name). How are you?

It's really good to talk with you again. All of us at (company name) are very impressed with your background and enthusiasm, and are convinced that you will make a substantial contribution to our efforts. We want you to join us as (position title) _____ at an annual starting salary rate of $ _____.

You can look forward to a performance review after 6 months and a potential merit increase at that time. Your benefits include the following: (*Note:* format specifies names of programs, e.g., Thrift Plan, New Employee Relocation Policy, etc.) The details of these benefits are provided in the brochure you received during your visit. "Your Future Planning Guide." If you have any questions, please do not hesitate to contact our HR director, (name), by calling (him or her) collect at (   ) _____. By the way, (he or she) will be sending you a letter to confirm this offer.

Note: If company policy requires a pre-employment medical examination, the HR director advises the manager whether statement (1) or (2) applies to the candidate.

(1) You of course must meet routine pre-employment medical examination requirements, but I'm sure this will not be a problem for you.

(2) A review of your Pre-Employment Medical Questionnaire by our physician has determined that a physical examination will not be required.

How does this offer sound to you? Do you have any questions?

Note: If candidate accepts the offer, use statement (3); if a decision is postponed, use statement (4).

(3) I'm very pleased that you will be joining my staff. When can you report for work? (date) Monday, _____.

(4) I sincerely hope that you will decide to join my staff. When do you think you will be able to make a decision? (date) _____. Please call me collect at (   ) _____ with your answer; I'll be looking forward to hearing from you.

Figure 3.15 Telephone worksheet for extending an offer of employment

EEO Approval to Hire or Promote—Officials and Managers

Date: _____

To: Mr. Louis T. Peterson, President & Chief Executive Officer

From:

_____

Name _____ EEO Code _____ Sex (M/F) _____

Position Title _____

Justification: _____

_____

_____

_____

_____

_____

_____

EEO Office Analysis

This action will affect the officials and managers category as follows:

Current Statistics		Resultant Statistics	
Category	%	Category	%
Male _____	_____	Male _____	_____
Female _____	_____	Female _____	_____
Total _____	100	Total _____	100
Minority _____		Minority _____	

☐ Approved   ☐ Approved
☐ Not Approved   ☐ Not Approved

_____ Date _____   _____ Date _____
EEO Officer   President

Figure 3.15A EEO approval to hire or promote—officials and managers

3.16 LETTER FOR CONFIRMING OFFER OF EMPLOYMENT

After an offer is extended verbally by the line manager, the HR representative is responsible for providing a detailed confirmation letter (Figure 3.16) to the candidate.

The confirmation letter refers to the recent telephone contact by the line manager, then proceeds to confirm the specifics of the offer. The salary offer is stated in terms of an "annual starting salary rate." This wording is essential to avoid legal problems. Wording such as "your salary is $35,000" can be interpreted as a contractual obligation to pay the stipulated amount. Faced with legal action, the company could be required to pay $35,000 even if the individual is employed for only a few months. Recommended wording makes it clear that a "rate" of pay is being stipulated.

The letter is structured to remind the candidate that he or she has the potential for a merit increase after six months of employment, and that other specified compensation and benefit policies and programs also will increase overall rewards and personal security. *Note:* Two versions of this letter are offered based on pre-employment medical examination requirements. Figure 3.16 provides terminology for those cases where a physician's review of the candidate's completed Pre-Employment Medical Questionnaire (see Figure 3.19) determines that a medical examination will not be necessary. Figure 3.16A specifies that employment is contingent upon successfully meeting routine pre-employment medical examination standards. Procedural instructions are provided. An envelope containing a Pre-Employment Medical Examination form (see Figure 3.20) is enclosed for the individual's personal physician, who conducts the examination and forwards a report and an invoice for services rendered to the company. The individual is asked to encourage the physician to expedite forwarding the report.

Enclosures such as materials which provide details on employee benefits, the relocation policies and procedures for new employees, and so on, are referred to in the letter.

The letter concludes with words of encouragement, and a reminder that the manager is looking forward to hearing from the candidate concerning his or her decision. The HR director also offers assistance for answering questions about benefit programs.

(Letterhead)

Dear _____ :

Mr. William T. Smith, Manager of our Accounting Department, has asked me to confirm the terms of the employment offer he extended to you yesterday. As outlined during your telephone conversation, the position as a Senior Financial Analyst will involve the responsibility for reviewing the performance of all affiliated companies. You will report directly to Mr. Smith in this capacity.

Your annual starting salary rate will be $45,000, and you may look forward to a performance review and a potential merit increase after six months. You also are invited to immediately participate in our savings plan, which allows you to contribute 6% of your salary and receive company contributions of 3%. Your participation in our company-paid retirement plan also begins on your first day of employment. A company benefits brochure is enclosed for your information; please review the summary information provided concerning "Relocation Benefits for New Employees."

Our consulting physician's review of your Medical History Questionnaire has determined that a pre-employment medical examination will not be required. You may look forward to immediate life and medical insurance coverage when you report for work.

We are very enthused about having you join our company, and are sure that it will be a mutually rewarding relationship. Mr. Smith is looking forward to hearing from you concerning your decision. Meanwhile, if I can be of assistance to you in providing clarifications concerning benefit programs, etc., please call me COLLECT on (XXX) XXX-XXXX.

Sincerely,

Robert J. Abelson
Human Resources Director

Enclosures

cc: Mr. W.T. Smith

Figure 3.16 Letter for confirming offer of employment

(Letterhead)

Dear_____:

Mr. William T. Smith, Manager of our Accounting Department, has asked me to confirm the terms of the employment offer he extended to you yesterday. As outlined during your telephone conversation, the position as a Senior Financial Analyst will involve the responsibility for reviewing the performance of all affiliated companies. You will report directly to Mr. Smith in this capacity.

Your annual starting salary rate will be $45,000, and you may look forward to a performance review and a potential merit increase after six months. You also are invited to immediately participate in our savings plan, which allows you to contribute 6% of your salary and receive company contributions of 3%. Your participation in our company-paid retirement plan also begins on your first day of employment. A company benefits brochure is enclosed for your information; please review the summary information provided concerning "Relocation Benefits for New Employees."

As previously discussed, your employment is contingent upon meeting routine medical standards. An envelope containing pre-employment medical examination forms is enclosed for completion and return by your personal physician, who will bill us for services rendered. Please arrange to have this examination as soon as possible, and encourage your physician to expedite forwarding his or her report to us. We will contact you concerning the results as soon as they are received.

We are very enthused about having you join our company, and are sure that it will be a mutually rewarding relationship. Mr. Smith is looking forward to hearing from you concerning your decision. Meanwhile, if I can be of assistance to you in providing clarifications concerning benefit programs, etc., please call me COLLECT on (XXX) XXX-XXXX.

Sincerely,

Robert J. Abelson
Human Resources Director

Enclosures

cc: Mr. W.T. Smith

Figure 3.16A Letter for confirming offer of employment

3.17 LETTER FOR ACKNOWLEDGING THE CANDIDATE'S ACCEPTANCE AND EXPLAINING REPORTING-FOR-WORK PROCEDURES

The acknowledgment of offer acceptance letter (Figure 3.17) begins with confirming the date for reporting to work.

A personal touch for promoting an effective placement is confirmed: The hiring manager and his or her spouse will meet the new employee and employee's spouse for dinner on the Sunday evening they arrive in the area. Since the new employee's spouse also is there to go househunting, the group will have an opportunity to discuss schools, job opportunities for the spouse, and so on. The manager brings a package of information prepared by the company's real estate consultant on suitable homes for sale in the area. This package provides information on the relative merits of different areas of town and other aspects, which the new employee and the spouse can discuss.

Enclosed with the letter are specific details about the company's relocation policy and a supply of expense vouchers. Also enclosed are placement-on-payroll forms such as an enrollment card for group medical insurance, income tax withholding forms, and so on, for completion prior to an early Monday morning meeting with the HR director. Plans call for expediting processing procedures to permit the employee and spouse to begin househunting activities without delay.

(Letterhead)

Dear_____ :

We are very pleased that you have accepted the position as Senior Financial Analyst, and are looking forward to having you report for work on Monday, October 27.

Mr. Smith sends his best regards. As discussed during your telephone conversation, he and his wife will be joining you and your wife for dinner at the Hotel Upland on Sunday evening, October 26, at 7:30 P.M. Bill has some materials for you concerning suitable homes for sale in the area, and I am sure that your wives will have much to discuss.

Details concerning the company's relocation policy and a supply of relocation expense forms are enclosed. Should you have any questions, please do not hesitate to contact me.

To expedite your placement on the payroll, enclosed is a set of forms we would appreciate your completing and bringing with you on your first day of work. Please come directly to my office; I will be looking forward to joining you for coffee at 8:30 A.M. We promise to get you on your way by 10:00 A.M. to join your wife for househunting activities.

Sincerely,

Robert J. Abelson
Human Resources Director

Enclosures

cc: Mr. W.T. Smith

Figure 3.17 Letter for acknowledging candidate's acceptance and explaining reporting-for-work procedures

3.18 LETTER TO A CANDIDATE WHO REJECTS AN OFFER OF EMPLOYMENT

The sample letter (Figure 3.18) begins with congratulating the individual and expressing best wishes for success with the new employer. It then explains the company's interest in obtaining advice from an "excellent" candidate who refused an offer. The purpose is to obtain feedback on how the offer could have been more attractive. Accordingly, a "short" Offer Refusal Questionnaire (Figure 3.18A) is enclosed for completion along with a stamped and addressed reply envelope. The letter ends with a statement of continuing interest—that is, should the individual again want to be considered for employment sometime in the future, he or she should not hesitate to contact the HR director.

The Offer Refusal Questionnaire (Figure 3.18A) asks the following questions:

1. *Salary Offer*—was the offer competitive?
2. *Employee Benefits*—how competitive are the company's plans compared with those of the new employer?
3. *Work Assignment*—does the position that was accepted offer a comparably greater professional challenge, more responsibility, better opportunity for advancement, and so on?
4. *Personalities and Attitudes*—did the personality or attitude of prospective co-workers or the supervisor have an influence on the decision? Are there any negative reactions to the behavior or thoughts of these company employees?
5. *What Could Have Been Done Differently*—if the company "had done things differently," what kinds of "things" would have resulted in the individual's accepting the offer?

This information is of great value in making adjustments necessary for promoting future acceptances. If the salary offer was way off target, analysis is required to ensure that the company is sufficiently competitive in attracting top talent. Similarly, if the employee benefit package does not keep pace with the competition, specific revisions will be needed when patterns of deficiencies become evident. Feedback on work assignments is essential for evaluating the relative degree of challenges offered by the company; position enrichment may be required to attract and retain well qualified personnel. If abrasive personalities or negative attitudes about the company impact candidates, immediate corrective action is necessary to remove counterproductive influences from the selection process. The open ended question about "things" can yield a wide variety of insights into why the candidate chose not to accept the offer. All reasonable suggestions for improving the quality of interactions with candidates must be given full consideration; resultant revisions of selection procedures will promote the company's future successes.

Although an anonymous response is not encouraged, the questionnaire's format includes a request for the candidate's name in a section labeled "optional information." This section also includes requests for the title of the position accepted, the name of the company, and the specific work location.

Dear_____ :

I was very sorry to hear that you have decided not to join us. We sincerely believe that your future with us would have been excellent, but understand that employment decisions involve many complex comparisons. You have our best wishes for success with your new employer.

When an excellent candidate decides not to accept our offer of employment, we are very interested in obtaining advice on how the offer could have been more attractive. A short questionnaire and stamped reply envelope are enclosed. Please take a few minutes to give us the benefit of your thoughts.

Should the future bring you to a point where you again would be interested in a position with our company, please do not hesitate to contact me.

Sincerely,

Richard L. Thomas
Director of Human Resources

Enclosures

Figure 3.18 Letter to candidate who rejects an offer of employment

Offer Refusal Questionnaire

We are continuously searching for ways to improve our company's success in attracting excellent new employees. All of us sincerely regret your decision not to join us, and would appreciate your confidential comments on why you chose another opportunity.

1. Was our salary offer competitive? ☐ Yes ☐ No (please explain):

2. Are our employee benefits competitive with those offered by your new employer?
    ☐ Yes ☐ No (please explain):

3. Is your new work assignment comparable to the work we offered?
    ☐ Yes ☐ No (please explain):

4. Was your decision not to join us based, in any degree, on the incompatible personalities or attitudes of your prospective co-workers or supervisor?
    ☐ No ☐ Yes (please explain):

5. Please provide any suggestions concerning how, if we had done things differently in your case, you would have chosen to accept our employment offer:

Optional Information

Position Accepted _____

Company _____

Location _____

Name _____ Date _____

Figure 3.18A Offer refusal questionnaire

3.19 PRE-EMPLOYMENT HEALTH RISK QUESTIONNAIRE

Companies avoid hiring candidates with high medical risks in the interest of controlling health insurance benefit costs, minimizing costly and unproductive absences due to illnesses, and, ultimately, not incurring increased life insurance benefit costs. A typical company policy states:

> *Physical examination*—All candidates for employment are required to meet pre-employment medical standards; offers of employment to prospective employees are contingent upon satisfactory medical evaluations. Pre-employment medical examinations are required only for those candidates whose backgrounds show evidence of medical problems which require assessment. Satisfactory evaluations are necessary before offers may be extended in these cases.

The recommended approach is to have the candidate complete a comprehensive Pre-Employment Medical Questionnaire (Figure 3.19) for evaluation by the company's medical officer or a consulting physician. The two-sided questionnaire is designed to cite potential problem areas, and if applicable to the candidate, require full details. Past history of hospitalization and protracted absences from work due to illnesses or injuries also is probed. If the candidate currently is under a physician's care, an explanation including details of prescribed medications is requested. The candidate then is asked to describe his or her current health, including information about mental or physical impairments. The individual also is requested to provide information about any health problems in his or her immediate family. The completed questionnaire requires the applicant's certification that all information provided is complete and correct. This signed statement includes an understanding that misrepresentation will result in termination of employment.

The "physician's evaluation" section at the bottom of the second page is used for specifying whether or not the candidate should be employed, and providing details that support the conclusion. Note that the heading of the form contains contact information for the candidate's personal physician. In cases where consultation is needed to clarify the nature of a potential problem before making a decision, such contacts are strongly recommended.

Pre-Employment Medical Questionnaire

Name _____ Age _____ Sex (M/F) _____ Height _____ Weight _____

Position _____ Social Security No. _____

Personal Physician (Name, Address, Tel. No.) _____

_____

Please answer the following questions concerning your medical history:

1. Have you ever had any of the following medical problems? If "YES," please provide a complete explanation.

	No	Yes	Explanation
Allergies	☐	☐	_____
Anemia	☐	☐	_____
Arthritis	☐	☐	_____
Asthma	☐	☐	_____
Bleeding	☐	☐	_____
Breathing	☐	☐	_____
Convulsions	☐	☐	_____
Coughing	☐	☐	_____
Dizziness	☐	☐	_____
Epilepsy	☐	☐	_____
Fainting	☐	☐	_____
Hay Fever	☐	☐	_____
Headaches	☐	☐	_____
Hearing Impairments	☐	☐	_____
Heart Palpitations	☐	☐	_____
Hernia	☐	☐	_____
Nerves	☐	☐	_____
Rashes	☐	☐	_____
Ulcers	☐	☐	_____
Visual Difficulty	☐	☐	_____

Figure 3.19 Pre-employment medical questionnaire

continued

2. Have you ever had rheumatic fever, hepititis/jaundice, tuberculosis, cancer, or a venereal disease? If so, please provide full details:

3. Have you been hospitalized during the past 10 years? If so, please explain in detail.

4. How many days were you absent from work due to illness or injury during the past 12 months? Number of Days = _____ . Describe illnesses and injuries:

5. If you currently are under a physician's care, explain why and specify which medications were prescribed.

6. Describe your current health. Do you have any mental or physical impairments?

7. If there are any health problems in your immediate family, please explain:

8. <u>Women Only</u>: Provide details about menstrual or other female disorders:

I certify that this information is complete and correct. Misrepresentation will result in termination of employment.

Applicant's Signature _____ Date _____

Physician's Evaluation:

Signature _____ Date _____

Name _____

Address _____

Telephone No. ( ) _____

Figure 3.19 *(cont.)*

3.20 PRE-EMPLOYMENT MEDICAL EXAMINATION

The sample Pre-Employment Medical Examination form (Figure 3.20) is a modified version of the device designed by the federal government to define very specifically the functional requirements and environmental factors that are essential in performing the duties of a position. Before the examination is conducted, the HR director/representative provides the following information in Part B:

1. Type of work location
2. Position title
3. Brief description of what position requires employee to do
4. Circle the number preceding *each* functional requirement (Section A) and *each* environmental factor (Section B) which is essential to the duties of this position.

The applicant is asked to complete Part A, which includes the question: "Do you have any medical disorder or physical impairment which would interfere in any way with the full performance of the duties shown below?" If the answer is yes, the applicant is instructed to fully explain the impairments to the physician who performs the physical examination.

This form may be used in conjunction with the Pre-Employment Medical Questionnaire (refer to Figure 3.19) to ensure that the applicant gives full consideration to the specific functional and environmental factors of the position.

The reverse side of the Pre-Employment Medical Examination form is reserved for the examining physician, who uses the format provided to record examination findings. A note at the top of the page advises the physician that the applicant in question will have to cope with the functional requirements and environmental factors that have been circled on the other side of the form. The physician is asked to take them, and the brief description of position duties, into consideration when making the examination. Related findings are reported in the "conclusions" section, which instructs the physician to "summarize below any medical findings which, in your opinion, would limit this person's performance of the job duties and/or would make him a hazard to himself or others. If none, so indicate."

The physician also may be instructed to evaluate an applicant's handicap to make recommendations concerning possible accommodations. Representative categories of handicaps include:

- Amputation of major extremity and/or extremities
- Deformity or impaired function of upper or lower extremity or back
- Vision in one eye only
- No usable vision
- Hearing aid required
- No usable hearing
- No usable hearing and speech malfunction
- Normal hearing with speech malfunction
- Tuberculosis (inactive pulmonary)
- Organic heart disease (compensated)
- Diabetes (controlled)
- Epilepsy (adequately controlled)
- History of emotional behavioral problems requiring special placement efforts/mentally restored
- Mentally retarded

PRE-EMPLOYMENT MEDICAL EXAMINATION

Part A. TO BE COMPLETED BY APPLICANT

1. NAME *(last, first, middle)*	2. SOCIAL SECURITY ACCOUNT NO.		3. SEX ☐ MALE ☐ FEMALE	4. DATE OF BIRTH

5. DO YOU HAVE ANY MEDICAL DISOR-DER OR PHYSICAL IMPAIRMENT WHICH WOULD INTERFERE IN ANY WAY WITH THE FULL PERFORMANCE OF THE DUTIES SHOWN BELOW? ☐ YES ☐ NO *If your answer is YES, explain fully to the physician performing the examination)*	6. I CERTIFY THAT ALL THE INFORMATION GIVEN BY ME IN CONNEC-TION WITH THIS EXAMINATION IS CORRECT TO THE BEST OF MY KNOWLEDGE AND BELIEF _____ *(signature of applicant)*

Part B. TO BE COMPLETED BEFORE EXAMINATION BY HR REPRESENTATIVE

1. TYPE OF WORK LOCATION	2. POSITION TITLE

3. BRIEF DESCRIPTION OF WHAT POSITION REQUIRES EMPLOYEE TO DO

4. Circle the number preceding *each* functional requirement and *each* environmental factor essential to the duties of this position. List any additional essential factors in the blank spaces:

A. FUNCTIONAL REQUIREMENTS

1. Heaving lifting, 45 pounds and over
2. Moderate lifting, 15–44 pounds
3. Light lifting, under 15 pounds
4. Heavy carrying, 45 pounds and over
5. Moderate carrying, 15–44 pounds
6. Light carrying, under 15 pounds
7. Straight pulling (hours)
8. Pulling hand over hand (hours)
9. Pushing 9 hours)
10. Reaching above shoulder
11. Use of fingers
12. Both hands required
13. Walking (hours)
14. Standing (hours)
15. Crawling (hours)
16. Kneeling (hours)
17. Repeated bending (hours)
18. Climbing, legs only (hours)
19. Climbing, use of legs and arms
20. Both legs required
21. Operation of crane, truck, tractor or motor vehicle
22. Ability for rapid mental and muscular coordination simultaneously
23. Ability to use and desirability of using firearms
24. Near vision correctable at 13" to 16" to Jaeger 1 to 4
25. Far vision correctable in one eye to 20/20 and to 20/40 in the other
26. Far vision correctable in one eye to 20/50 and to 20/100 in the other
27. Specific visual requirement *(specify)*
28. Both eyes required
29. Depth perception
30. Ability to distinguish basic colors
31. Ability to distinguish shades of colors
32. Hearing *(aid permitted)*
33. Hearing without aid
34. Specific hearing requirements *(specify)*
35. Other *(specify)*

B. ENVIRONMENTAL FACTORS

1. Outside
2. Outside and inside
3. Excessive heat
4. Excessive cold
5. Excessive humidity
6. Excessive dampness or chilling
7. Dry atmospheric conditions
8. Excessive noise, intermittent
9. Constant noise
10. Dust
11. Sllica, asbestos, etc.
12. Fumes, smoke, or gases
13. Solvents *(degreasing agents)*
14. Grease and oils
15. Radiant energy
16. Electrical energy
17. Slippery or uneven walking surfaces
18. Working around machinery with moving parts
19. Working around moving objects or vehicles
20. Working on ladders or scaffolding
21. Working below ground
22. Unusual fatigue factors *(specify)*
23. Working with hands in water
24. Explosives
25. Vibration
26. Working closely with others
27. Working alone
28. Protracted or irregular hours of work
29. Other *(specify)*

Part C. TO BE COMPLETED BY EXAMINING PHYSICIAN

1. EXAMINING PHYSICIAN'S NAME *(type or print)*	3. SIGNATURE OF EXAMINING PHYSICIAN
2. ADDRESS *(including ZIP Code)*	_____ _____ *(signature)* *(date)*

Figure 3.20 Pre-employment medical examination

continued

NOTE TO EXAMINING PHYSICIAN: The person you are about to examine will have to cope with the functional requirements and environmental factors circled on the other side of this form. Please take them, and the brief description of job duties above them, into consideration as you make your examination and report your findings and conclusions.

1. HEIGHT: _____ FEET, _____ INCHES.   WEIGHT: _____ POUNDS.

2. EYES:

(A) Distant vision (Snellen): without glasses: right $\underline{20}$ left $\underline{20}$; with glasses, if worn: right $\underline{20}$ left $\underline{20}$

(B) What is the longest and shortest distance at which the following specimen of Jaeger No. 2 type can be read by the applicant? Test each eye separately.

_____ Jaeger No. 2 Type _____

employees in the Federal classified service as may be requested by the Civil Service Commission or its authorized representative. This order will supplement the Executive Orders of May 29 and June 18, 1923 (Executive Order, September 4, 1924).

without glasses: with glasses, if used:

R._____ in. to _____ in. R._____ in. to _____ in.

L._____ in. to _____ in. L._____ in. to _____ in.

(C) Color vision: Is color vision normal when Ishihara or other color plate test is used? ☐ YES ☐ NO

If not, can applicant pass lantern, yarn, or other comparable test? ☐ YES ☐ NO

3. EARS: (Consider denominators indicated here as normal. Record as numerators the greatest distance heard.)
Ordinary conversation: Audiometer (if given):

RIGHT EAR _____ ; LEFT EAR _____
                20 ft.   20 ft.

250	500	1000	2000	3000	4000	5000	6000	7000	8000

4. OTHER FINDINGS: In items a through l briefly describe any abnormality (including diseases, scars, and disfigurations). Include brief history, if pertinent. If normal, so indicate.

a. Eyes, ears, nose, and throat (including tooth and oral hygiene)

e. Abdomen

b. Head and back (including face, hair, and scalp)

f. Peripheral blood vessels

c. Speech (note any malfunction)

g. Extremities

d. Skin and lymph nodes (including thyroid gland)

h. Urinalysis (if indicated)

Sp. gr. _____ Sugar _____ Blood _____
Albumen _____ Casts _____ Pus _____

i. Respiratory tract (X-ray if indicated)

j. Heart (size, rate rhythm, function)
Blood pressure _____
Pulse _____
EKG (if indicated)

k. Back (special consideration for positions involving heavy lifting and other strenuous duties)

l. Neurological and mental health

CONCLUSIONS: Summarize below any medical findings which, in your opinion, would limit this person's performance of the job duties and/or would make him a hazard to himself or others. If none, so indicate.

☐ No limiting conditions for this job
☐ Limiting conditions as follows:

Figure 3.20 (cont.)

3.21 VERIFYING CANDIDATE CREDENTIALS

The information contained in this section was provided by the Honorable Claude Pepper, Chairman of the Subcommittee on Health and Long-Term Care, U.S. House of Representatives. Additional details may be obtained by reviewing Publication No. 99-550, which reports on the Joint Hearings held on fraudulent credentials before the Select Committee on Aging, U.S. House of Representatives, December 11, 1985.

A. Résumé Manipulation

The subcommittee found that résumé manipulation is commonplace. It is estimated that one in every three applicants embellishes his or her résumé in the following ways:

1. *Employment Dates*—stretching a short-term period of employment to make it more impressive, or extending dates to cover a period of unemployment.
2. *School Dates*—exaggerating attendance by additional months or years.
3. *Job Title*—creating titles which imply more responsibility.
4. *Academic Performance*—higher than actual grade point averages.
5. *Academic Major*—history major shows "computer science" to obtain programming position.
6. *College/University*—did not attend or graduate, but claims a degree from a particular institution.

In a job market that is increasingly credential-conscious, degrees bring greater social status and larger paychecks. As reported to the Committee by the U.S. Department of Commerce, based on salary offers to degree candidates in 1983, advanced degrees translate to significantly higher salaries. Masters and doctoral degree holders were offered from 18 to 57 percent more than those holding only undergraduate credentials. The motivation for misrepresenting one's degree status is clear.

B. Third-Party Consumer Reports: Candidate Background Investigations

As reported at the Joint Hearing by Mr. John C. Rahiya, Vice President, EQUIFAX Services, Inc., a firm that conducts background investigations for employment purposes, companies use their services for:

> (1) enhancing the value of their products and services by ensuring that they in fact employ the most qualified applicants; (2) controlling employee dishonesty, theft, or violation of trust or confidentiality; and (3) avoiding employer liability due to acts of unqualified employees, employees not suited to a particular position, or employees hindered by habitual substance abuse.

The consumer reports provided by companies such as EQUIFAX are subject to the Fair Credit Reporting Act (FCRA) and a number of similar state statutes. Costs range from $25.00 to several hundred dollars; the average is approximately $70.00. Reports are prepared by verifying and collecting information from numerous public and private sources, principally those listed on the individual's Employment Application and/or résumé. Included are former employers, educational institutions, and personal references. Public records to include criminal court records, motor vehicle records, litigation records, and bankruptcy records also may be checked. The resultant information is rechecked for its current status; no public record older than seven years is ever reported.

Prior employer contacts verify the exact dates of employment, the reason for termination, salary, performance, type of position, reliability, and eligibility for re-employment.

Personal references are used to obtain information on the applicant's interests, personality, reliability, and other factors relevant to the type of position under consideration.

College and university contacts generally only will verify attendance and graduation dates. This is because the Family Educational Rights and Privacy Act imposes confidentiality requirements on educational records. Accordingly, the candidate must provide a signed release form which authorizes the college to issue information.

Whether a company decides to use a third-party investigation service or not, there is no question that the failure to verify candidate backgrounds can lead to serious liabilities due to losses from employee dishonesty, incompetence, industrial espionage, drug or alcohol abuse in the workplace, and employer tort liability for negligent hiring. As the representative of EQUIFAX described:

> Employers have many legal responsibilities—to customers, shareholders, and employees. Product quality can suffer greatly through ineptness, reduced capacities due to substance abuse, or chronically poor work habits or attendance. Safety of all employees in the workplace can be jeopardized by a single employee who habitually uses drugs or has a history of violence or carelessness, or who claims to be trained or experienced in handling situations when he or she is not. The real economic costs of inefficiency, lack of professional education or training, carelessness, poor attitude, or dishonesty can cut deeply into the financial well being of a company. Some estimates place employee dishonesty alone as the primary cause of as many as 30 percent of business failures.

There is no question that employment background verification is a necessary and proper business practice.

C. Diploma Mills and Bogus Degrees

According to the subcommittee on Health and Long-Term Care, diploma mill schemes fit into five major categories:

1. *Official Look*—to promote an image of credibility, these mills use ads with official seals, crests, and so on, and information about how they have state approval or accreditation. (See Figure 3.21A which shows FBI-identified bogus accrediting agencies.)
2. *Sound Alikes*—prestigious sounding degrees from schools with names that are very close to those of well known, legitimate schools. For example, Cormell rather than Cornell. (See Figure 3.21B which shows sound-alike bogus institutions.)
3. *Life Experience*—mills that grant degrees for life experience as opposed to legitimate institutions which offer college credit for life experience.
4. *Good as New or Better: Replacement Degrees*—mills that purport to replace your stolen or lost degree regardless of whether you had one.
5. *No Strings Attached*—mills that offer degrees with no questions asked.

According to Anthony E. Daniels, Inspector-Deputy Assistant Director, Criminal Investigative Division, FBI, investigations conducted through December 1985 have identified more than 7,000 individuals in the United States who possess degrees from illegitimate scholastic institutions or counterfeit degrees. Mr. Daniels explained that

> degrees are awarded without regard to educational standards such as course attendance, classroom work, correspondence, examinations, or submission of written material. Recognition is for vague life experience, or equivalency evaluation, or résumé evaluation. In addition to degrees, these organizations produce fictitious transcripts, verification, and accreditation agencies.

(See Figure 3.21C which shows FBI-identified bogus educational institutions.)

The Council on Postsecondary Accreditation, known as COPA, has publications that list institutions that legitimately grant degrees.

D. Assuring the Authenticity of College Transcripts

A statement by Dr. Bruce T. Shutt, President, American Association of Collegiate Registrars and Admissions Officers, offers the following checklist for reviewing college records and/or transcripts to ensure they are official and accurate:

1. Was the document mailed directly from the registrar at the institution issuing the document?
2. Was the envelope postmarked in the city where the institution is located?
3. Did the envelope have an institutional meter mark rather than a postage stamp?
4. Does the document have a recent date of issuance?
5. Is there a registrar signature and university seal? Are they clear and authentic?
6. Is there consistency of type font, format, and so on?

Midwest Accrediting Association

Midwestern States Accrediting Agency

National Association of Open Campus Colleges and Universities

LEGITIMATE ACCREDITING AGENCIES:

It is understood that only six agencies are acknowledged and accepted as having the authority to accredit colleges. These accrediting bodies for post-secondary educational institutions work under an umbrella agency, i.e., the Council on Post-Secondary Accreditation (COPA):

Middle States Association of Colleges and Schools

New England Association of Colleges and Schools

North Central Association of Colleges and Schools

North West Association of Colleges and Schools

Southern Association of Colleges and Schools

Western Association of Colleges and Schools

FICTITIOUS ASSOCIATIONS

American Academy of Behavioral Science

American Board of Examiners in Psychotherapy

Arkansas Board of Natural Therapeutics, Batesville, Arkansas

Arkansas Naturopathic or Homeopathic Training Center

Board of Examiners—Homeopathic, Republic of Pakistan

Florida Psychoanalytics Institute

International Association of Homeopathic Physician and Surgeons, Ontario, Canada

International College of Physicians and Surgeons

Maryland Homeopathic Society

Nevada Association of Naturopathic Physicians, Blue Point, New York

Osteopathic, Naturopathic or Homeopathic Medical College

Palm Beach Psychotherapy Training Center or Institute

United American Medical College

World International Medical Association, Republic of Panama

Figure 3.21A FBI-Identified bogus accrediting agencies

AMERICAN NATIONAL UNIVERSITY OF PHOENIX, ARIZONA AND MIAMI, FLORIDA (legitimate—American University of Washington, D.C.)

BOSTON CITY COLLEGE (legitimate—Boston College)

CAMBRIDGE UNIVERSITY OF WASHINGTON, D.C. (legitimate—Cambridge University of Cambridge, England)

CORMELL UNIVERSITY (legitimate—Cornell University)

DARTHMOUTH (legitimate—Dartmouth)

LOYOLA UNIVERSITY OF PARIS, FRANCE (legitimate—Loyola University of New Orleans, Louisiana, and Loyola University of Chicago, Illinois)

NORTHWESTERN COLLEGE OF ALLIED SCIENCE OF TULSA, OKLAHOMA (legitimate—Northwestern College of Evanstown, Illinois)

SOUTHWESTERN UNIVERSITY OF TUCSON, ARIZONA AND COLUMBUS, OHIO (legitimate—Southwestern University of Georgetown, Texas)

STAMFORD UNIVERSITY (legitimate—Stanford University)

SOUTHEASTERN UNIVERSITY OF GREENVILLE, NORTH CAROLINA (legitimate—Southeastern University, Washington, D.C.)

THOMAS A. EDISON COLLEGE OF FLORIDA AND ARKANSAS (legitimate—Thomas A. Edison State College of Trenton, New Jersey)

Figure 3.21B Sound-alike bogus institutions

American Western University, Tulsa, Oklahoma and Springfield, Missouri

DePaul University, Advance Study Program, Paris, France

Johann Keppler School of Medicine, Toronto, Ontario, Canada and Zurich, Switzerland

Johann Keppler School of Medicine of Central America, Baja California, Mexico

Metropolitan Collegiate Institute, London, England

National College*

North American University, Hamilton, Ontario, Canada

Northwestern College of Allied Sciences (NCAS), Tulsa, Oklahoma and Springfield, Missouri

Pacific College, Beverly Hills, California

Roosevelt University, Brussels, Belgium

Sands University, Yuma, Arizona

Southeastern University and Preparatory School, Inc., Greenville, South Carolina

Southeastern University of Theological Seminary and Preparatory School, Inc., Greenville, South Carolina

Southeastern University of the Virgin Islands of the United States, Saint Croix, Virgin Islands

South Union Graduate School*

Southwestern University (SWU), Tucson, Arizona, St. George, Utah, and Salt Lake City, Utah

St. Paul Seminary*

Thomas A. Edison College (TAEC), West Palm Beach, Florida and Benton, Arizona**

United American Medical College, Metairie, Louisiana and Oakville, Ontario, Canada

University of East Georgia, Savannah, Georgia, Jacksonville, Florida, and Hendersonville, Tennessee

* Disciples of Truth, Inc., Tulsa, Oklahoma (Operated in Springfield, Missouri and Ohio)

** Not to be confused with Thomas A. Edison State College of Trenton, New Jersey, a legitimate and well respected institution.

Figure 3.21C FBI-Identified bogus educational institutions

Placement

Helping new employees to fully understand their duties and responsibilities, the standards for their conduct and performance, and how their roles support the company's objectives is essential for promoting their success. The HR director provides effective placement on payroll processes (see sections 4.2 through 4.10 in this chapter) and orientation techniques (see sections 4.12 through 4.15) to ensure that each new employee obtains a working knowledge of the terms and conditions of employment, and quickly feels comfortable in the work environment. The employee then is free to concentrate on job requirements and become productive in the least amount of time.

A unique Employment Agreement (see Figure 4.4) introduces the concept of "at will" employment, which avoids the costly legal problems that result from implied employment obligation interpretations. This concept is further reinforced in the content of the Work Rule Acknowledgment Statement (see Figure 4.6) and the related Employee Handbook Acknowledgment Statement (see Figure 4.7).

Company security interests are protected through new employees' completion of an Employee Conflict of Interest Statement (see Figure 4.8) and an Employee Confidentiality Agreement (see Figure 4.9).

A follow-up interview technique ensures productive placements (see Figure 4.17). An HR representative meets with the new employee to assess the individual's degree of satisfaction with his or her job and the work environment. In cases where unresolvable problems are apparent, but the individual is a promising employee, alternative placement opportunities can be explored.

Unproductive employees who do not meet the company's expectations, and for whom a corrective action plan is not feasible, can be identified and their employment terminated through a Probationary Performance Appraisal (see Figure 4.18).

4.1 COMPANY EEO POLICY STATEMENT: FOUNDATION FOR SUCCESSFUL PLACEMENTS

The company policy statement provides the foundation for successful placements by assuring all employees that personnel actions will be administered without discrimination, and that their work environment will be free of any employment discrimination or harassment.

Equal Employment Opportunity

To eliminate and avoid discrimination against any employee because of race, color, religion, sex, age, national origin, or handicap, the company's official policy:

1. Trains and promotes all persons in all job/position classifications without regard to race, color, religion, sex, age, national origin, or handicap.
2. Ensures that all promotion decisions are in accord with the principals of equal employment opportunity. Only valid criteria are to be used in selection processes.
3. Ensures that personnel actions such as those involving compensation, benefits, transfers, layoffs, return from layoff, company-sponsored training, educational assistance, and so on are administered in accordance with EEO principles and practices. This rule also applies to all company-sponsored employee recreational and social events.
4. Maintains a work environment which is free of any employment discrimination including sexual harassment in any form. Sexual advances, requests for sexual favors, and verbal or physical conduct of a sexual nature constitutes harassment when:
   (a) submission to such conduct is made a term or condition of employment either explicitly or implicitly, and/or
   (b) submission to or rejection of such conduct is used as the basis for decisions that affect employment status, and/or
   (c) such conduct has the effect of substantially interfering with work performance due to an intimidating, offensive, or hostile work environment.

Any problem involving discrimination or harassment is not tolerated. All such problems are reported to the HR director, who will investigate and report findings to the chief executive officer.

4.2 PLACEMENT-ON-PAYROLL CHECKLIST

To ensure that all required actions are completed when a new employee is placed on the payroll, a comprehensive checklist should be developed. The sample Placement-on-Payroll Checklist (Figure 4.2) covers all items normally included in processing new employees. Some items apply only to certain categories of employees. For example, the completion of a credit card application is limited to certain sales employees and members of management. Accordingly, the checklist first is used as the basis for designating which materials an employee will be required to complete for placement on payroll. Not applicable items, those not required for the employee's position, are marked "N/A." The checklist then is used to assemble a folder of essential materials. It is attached to the folder containing these selected materials, which are then filed in accordance with the sequence shown on the checklist, to facilitate processing. This well organized, systematic approach gives the new employee an excellent initial impression of the HR organization's administrative processes and their effectiveness in meeting employee needs.

Placement-on-Payroll Checklist

New Employee _____ Start Date _____

Position Title _____

—Employment Agreement

—Federal Income Tax Withholding

—State Income Tax Withholding

—Reporting for Work Expense Voucher

—Post-Employment Personal Data Form

—Life Insurance Enrollment

—Health and Dental Care Enrollment

—Savings Plan Enrollment

—Credit Card Application

—Employee Discount Card(s)

—U.S. Savings Bond Allotment Form

—Credit Union Membership Application

—Work Rules Acknowledgment Statement

—Employee Handbook Acknowledgment Statement

—Employee Conflict of Interest Statement

—Employee Confidentiality Statement

—Employee Identification Card/Badge

—Employee Automobile Parking Registration and Sticker

—Company Site Plan—Parking Areas, Entrances, etc.

—New Employee Orientation Invitation Memorandum

Figure 4.2 Placement on payroll checklist

4.3 NEW EMPLOYEE RELOCATION POLICY AND PLANNING FORM

A typical company policy for new employee relocations includes the following provisions.

I. Moving Expenses

A. The company shall assume the reasonable costs of moving a new employee's household goods and personal effects.

B. The company will arrange and pay directly for packing, in-transit storage, and insurance on the items covered in Section I.A.

C. The company will not assume the costs of moving pets, pianos, hobby equipment of unusual weight or size, boats, valuable jewelry, furs, antiques, firearms, and other such items.

D. Under unusual circumstances, such as when shipment is delayed for company convenience or when adequate housing is not yet available, short-term storage charges will be paid by the company for a period not to exceed ninety (90) days.

II. Transportation of New Employee and Immediate Family

A. The company will provide direct route, economy class-type air transportation to the work location.

B. The new employee has the option, in lieu of Section 11.A, of using his or her own automobile for transportation to the work location. It is expected that such travel will be by the most direct route with an average progress of three hundred (300) miles per day. A mileage allowance in accordance with the company's travel policy will be applied.

C. Reimbursable transportation costs shall include necessary in-transit meals and lodging if travel is by personal auto, or baggage handling fees and gratuities, and local ground transportation at departure and terminal points if traveling by air.

III. Temporary Living Expenses

A. If a new employee precedes his or her family to the new work location to begin employment and obtain suitable permanent housing, the company will reimburse his or her reasonable living expenses for a period not to exceed ninety (90) days.

B. The company will reimburse reasonable living expenses for a period not to exceed thirty (30) days if the new employee and his or her family arrive at the work location together.

C. In cases where furniture has not arrived, or housing is not available by the end of the thirty (30) day period specified in Section III.B., the company may reimburse temporary living expenses less normal estimated living costs.

IV. Relocation Allowance

The company will pay a relocation allowance in the amount of one-half of a month's pay for single employees, and one month's pay for married employees. This allowance, payable in lump sum, is intended to assist the new employee in meeting the costs of necessary alterations charges for refitting rugs and drapes, appliance connections, the moving costs of items specified in section I.C., and other miscellaneous expenses.

V. Income Tax Reimbursement

Most of the relocation expenses paid by the company are considered for tax purposes to be wages subject to withholding taxes. The company will calculate the additional tax consequences which result in order to provide a tax equalization payment to the new employee; such payment will be rendered during the year in which the additional tax obligation is incurred.

Relocation Planning Form

Figure 4.3 shows a sample of a New Employee Relocation Information form that has been designed for use by new employees in requesting company assistance. The first section, "housing requirements," provides the data needed to develop suitable housing opportunities for the new employee's consideration. The "moving requirements" section offers the information needed by the company to coordinate arrangements for the movement of household goods and personal effects. The "travel requirements" section gives the information necessary for arranging air travel tickets and temporary hotel/motel living accommodations for the new employee and his or her family. It also is used to request an advance needed for travel purposes.

New Employee Relocation Information

☐ Permanent
☐ Temporary (Summer Employment)

Name _____ Position _____

Organization _____ Location _____

Home Address _____

Home Tel. No. ( ) _____ Work Tel. No. ( ) _____ Reporting Date _____

Housing Requirements   Approximate Date Needed _____

Type of Housing Desired   Furnished/Unfurnished   Rent/Purchase

Single Unit House   ☐   ☐   ☐   ☐

Attached Row House   ☐   ☐   ☐   ☐

Apartment   ☐   ☐   ☐   ☐

Efficiency Apartment   ☐   ☐   ☐   ☐

Room   ☐

No. of Bedrooms _____ No. of Bathrooms _____ Garage? ☐ Yes ☐ No

Purchase Price Range: $ _____ to $ _____ Pets? ☐ Yes ☐ No

Monthly Rent Range (Not Including Utilities): $ _____ to $ _____

Moving Requirements   Approximate Move Date _____

If moving from campus location, provide college address and telephone numbers where mover can reach you to make arrangements:

Address: _____

_____

Daytime Tel. No.(_____) _____ Evening Tel. No.(_____) _____

How many rooms of furniture? _____

More than one pick-up location? ☐ No ☐ Yes (Explain) _____

_____

Travel Requirements

Do you need a travel expense advance? ☐ No ☐ Yes (amount needed = $ _____)

Date travel expense advance check is needed by? _____

Do you want us to arrange air travel tickets for you and your family? ☐ No ☐ Yes

Departure Airport Name/Location _____

Date of Departure _____ Preferred Time Range _____

Names of Family Members: _____

Do you want us to arrange hotel/motel accommodations? ☐ No ☐ Yes

No. of Rooms _____ Dates: from _____ to _____

Signature: _____ Date: _____

Figure 4.3 New employee relocation information

4.4 EMPLOYMENT AGREEMENT

Recent court rulings have reinforced the principle that in the absence of written employment agreements, the employee has an implied employment contract. Suits against employers for wrongful terminations, which place the burden on the employer to prove legitimate grounds for terminating employees, are resulting in extensive damage payments to former employees. Wording in company work rules or employee handbooks, which require "just cause" for terminations, must be avoided. Employers are well advised to adopt an employment agreement that requires all new employees to acknowledge that the employment relationship is "at will." This acknowledgment establishes the right of both parties to terminate the employment relationship at any time, for whatever reason(s) they, respectively, deem to be in their best interests.[*]

Figure 4.4, Employment Agreement, gives an example which can be used for developing your own company's agreement. The agreement begins with a general paragraph that specifies the employee's agreed upon starting position and rate of remuneration. An understanding regarding the "at will" nature of this employment relationship is established. Next, the complete terms and conditions of the probationary period are defined. A paragraph is included to specify the continuing role of performance appraisals, on an annual basis, in determining employee rewards and retention. An employee's failure to meet company-established performance standards again is cited as the basis for termination action, but compensatory compensation based on service-related separation allowances is payable under these circumstances. The final paragraph establishes an understanding that infringement of company policies concerning employee conduct will lead to disciplinary action, including possible termination, as determined by company management.

[*] David A. Bradshaw and Barbara C. Stikker, "Wrongful Termination: Keeping the Right to Fire At-Will," *Personnel Journal*, September 1986, pp. 45–47.

I, _____, hereby agree to perform the duties and responsibilities of the position as _____, and those of any subsequent positions, on behalf of my employer, _____ (herein referred to as "Company"). Initial remuneration shall be at the rate of $_____ per _____.

It is mutually understood and agreed that this employment relationship is at will. Accordingly, both parties to this Agreement are free to terminate the relationship at any time for any reasons which they, respectively, deem to be in their best interests.

Should this employment relationship continue throughout the ninety (90) day probationary period, the employee will be entitled to a formal performance appraisal and, if merited by the resultant rating, an appropriate adjustment in remuneration. If this probationary appraisal determines that the employee has failed to meet Company expectations, the employee will be terminated. If this appraisal determines that the employee can meet expectations by taking specific corrective actions, the Company will designate requisite standards and determine the period of time in which they must be achieved. Should the employee then fail to meet performance requirements, the employment relationship will be terminated.

The Company agrees to assess employee performance annually throughout the period of the employment relationship, and to take whatever action it deems appropriate to reward the employee for his or her contributions. Employee failure to meet performance standards, as determined by the Company, will lead to termination. Any and all compensatory compensation will be based on the Company's then existing policy concerning service-related separation allowances.

It is understood that infringement of Company policies regarding employee conduct will lead to appropriate disciplinary action, to include termination of the employment relationship, as determined by Company management.

Employee Signature _____   Date _____

WITNESSED BY   _____   Date _____

Typed Name   _____

Position Title   _____

Figure 4.4 Sample employment agreement

4.5 PATENT AND COPYRIGHT ASSIGNMENT AGREEMENT

A sample of a brief but effective Patent and Copyright Agreement is shown in Figure 4.5. As a new technical or scientific employee is placed on the payroll, this agreement is executed to assign to the company any patents or copyrights that may result from the individual's employment. Salary and any special awards that the individual may receive for his or her accomplishments are cited as the consideration which is received for potential assignments. The agreement further clarifies the company's right to use patents and copyrights in its own best interests, which may involve further assigning rights to other companies.

I, _____, in consideration for salary payments received during my employment, to include any outstanding achievement compensation which I may or may not be awarded, do hereby assign to _____ (hereafter referred to as "Company"), all rights to any and all patents and copyrights obtained as a result of my work for the Company. It is agreed that the Company has the exclusive right to use and or to assign such patents or copyrights and to establish related licensing agreements as deemed necessary for its best interests.

Employee Signature _____ Date _____

WITNESSED BY _____ Date _____

Typed Name _____

Position Title _____

Figure 4.5 Sample patent and copyright assignment agreement

4.6 WORK RULES AND REGULATIONS

Work rules and regulations may be published as a company policy statement, which the new employee is required to read and acknowledge by signing an appropriate statement. An example is shown in Figure 4.6, Work Rule Acknowledgment Statement. A traditional statement of company rules and regulations follows.

Work Rules and Regulations

It is the company's policy that certain rules and regulations be observed by each employee for the benefit of everyone in the organization. These guidelines are reasonable and necessary, and any infractions will be subject to disciplinary action. Disciplinary action will range from a written warning to immediate dismissal, depending on the severity of the infraction as assessed by company management. Examples of the types of conduct subject to disciplinary action are:

- Working under the influence of intoxicating beverages or nonprescribed drugs
- Possession of a "controlled substance" on company premises
- Fighting on company premises
- Malicious mischief
- Falsification of company records or documents
- Failure to observe company policies
- Insubordination
- Excessive absenteeism or tardiness
- Absence without proper authorization
- Dishonest or illegal acts
- Infractions of safety regulations
- Immoral conduct
- Discrimination or sexual harassment
- Improper behavior
- Neglect or carelessness in performing work
- Damage or destruction of company property
- Possession of firearms or other weapons on company premises
- Theft

I, _____, have read the company's Policy Statement on "Work Rules and Regulations," and have retained a copy for my reference.

It is clearly understood and agreed that adherence to the provisions and intent of this Company Policy Statement are a condition of my "at will" employment relationship with the company, and that infractions may lead to my immediate dismissal. Any resultant company-initiated termination of my employment shall be construed to be based on our mutual rights to terminate the employment relationship for any reason at any time.

It is acknowledged that the Policy Statement only includes examples of improper conduct. Any other conduct not specifically addressed by the examples provided, but deemed to be improper by company management, also shall be subject to disciplinary action. Appropriate disciplinary action will depend on the severity of the infraction as assessed by company management, and will range from a written warning to immediate dismissal.

Signature _____ Date _____

WITNESSED BY _____ Date _____

Typed Name _____

Position Title _____

Figure 4.6 Work rule acknowledgment statement

4.7 EMPLOYEE HANDBOOK ACKNOWLEDGMENT STATEMENT

Rather than issuing each new employee a copy of the policy statement regarding work rules and regulations, the company's employee handbook can be designed to include a section on rules and regulations or personal conduct. Wording can be structured in a positive, employee relations-oriented manner, for example:

(Name of company) employees fully support the principle that certain proper standards of behavior are essential for our effectiveness in working together. Any employee who engages in unacceptable types of conduct is subject to disciplinary action. Unacceptable practices such as the following can result in immediate discharge.

- Immoral, improper, dishonest, or illegal acts
- Working under the influence of intoxicating beverages or nonprescribed drugs
- Malicious mischief or fighting
- Insubordination

An added advantage of using the employee handbook for this purpose is to encourage the employee to use it as a general reference tool. A thorough understanding of all terms and conditions of employment does much to promote the success of new employees.

As part of the placement on payroll process, the new employee is required to sign an Employee Handbook Acknowledgment Statement (Figure 4.7). The statement is a permanent record of the employee's understandings regarding the consequences of improper conduct.

I, _____, hereby acknowledge receipt of a copy of the company's Employee Handbook. I have read the section entitled "Employee Conduct," and fully understand its contents. Accordingly, it is understood and agreed that my adherence to these guidelines are a condition of my "at will" employment relationship with the company, and that improper conduct, as defined by company management, may lead to my immediate dismissal. Any resultant company-initiated termination of my employment shall be construed to be based on our mutual rights to terminate the employment relationship for any reason at any time.

It further is acknowledged that the Employee Handbook contains references to company policies relating to the terms and conditions of employment. I hereby agree to diligently meet all such employee responsibilities to the best of my ability throughout the period of our employment relationship.

Signed_____ Date _____

WITNESSED BY _____ Date _____

Typed Name _____

Position Title _____

Figure 4.7 Employee handbook acknowledgment statement

4.8 EMPLOYEE CONFLICT OF INTEREST STATEMENT

A representative company policy on employee conflict of interest is as follows:

I. Objectives

To define appropriate standards and to state the position of the company on the matter of employee relationships with suppliers, distributors, customers, and other outside individuals or organizations in order to protect employees and the company from possible conflicts of interest. *Conflict of interest* as used herein shall mean a situation where interests other than those of the company's are being pursued.

II. Policy

The conduct of the company's relationships and transactions with individuals outside the company and with other business concerns in a businesslike and ethical manner is a matter of vital importance. The best interests of the company, not those of the employee or others, must be the only consideration. Therefore, the interests of any individual employee cannot be permitted to play a part in any decision relating to the choice of or terms of dealing with individuals or business concerns with whom the company may have a business relationship.

III. Application

To avoid conflicts of interest, each employee who is in a position to influence or control decisions concerning the choice of and terms of dealing with individuals or business concerns with whom the company may have business relationships must do the following:

A. To maintain constant awareness of the importance of ethical conduct, the employee should disqualify himself or herself from taking part in, or exerting any influence in, any transaction where personal interests may conflict with those of the company. Representative examples of activities that are considered to be detrimental to the company are:

1. Performing outside work or activities for a competitor.
2. Performing outside work or services for a vendor, which helps that vendor gain preferential treatment over other vendors with the company.
3. Performing outside technical services or other services, which are competitive with the company's activities.
4. Transmitting technical "know-how" or data to any outside interest, which the company has developed for its use or for the use of its clients.
5. Transmitting information on company business matters, which have not been publicly disclosed to any outside individual or interest.
6. Transacting personal business with outsiders under circumstances which might lead the outsider to believe that he or she is dealing with the

company rather than the individual, for example, transacting personal business using company letterhead stationery.

7. Using company business relationships with outside individuals or concerns for personal profit or advantage.

8. Competing with the company, directly or indirectly, in the development of a business opportunity, or in the purchase or sale of property, property rights, or interests.

B. Each employee must report any financial interest which he or she or a member of his or her immediate family has in an individual or business concern with which the company may have a business relationship; any connection he or she or a member of his or her immediate family has with any such individual or business concern as a result of which he or she or immediate relatives may receive remuneration as a director, officer, employee, or agent of the individual or business concern.

C. Each employee must comply with all provisions of the company's competitive bidding purchasing policy.

D. Neither an employee nor any member of his or her immediate family may accept gifts of more than token value, loans (other than routine loans from established financial institutions), excessive entertainment, or other substantial favors from any outside individual or concern which does or is seeking to do business with, or is a competitor of, the company.

IV. Responsibility

A. It is the responsibility of each employee to avoid potential conflicts of interests, to make such disclosures as the company may require from time to time, and to review with his or her management any questionable activities that might be construed to be a conflict of interest.

B. It is the responsibility of each employee's immediate supervisor to review and evaluate potential conflict-of-interest situations brought to their attention, and, when necessary, to refer such situations to higher levels of management as required to obtain decisions which protect employee and company interests.

V. Reporting

To ensure adherence to the provision of this policy, all new employees will be required to read its contents and execute an Employee Conflict of Interest Statement. All employees will be required to review the contents of this policy annually and execute an up-to-date Employee Conflict of Interest Statement. The statement will include disclosures regarding the following, if any:

A. Any contract, arrangement, understanding, practice, or circumstance in which the employee will be or might become entitled to a fee, commission, retainer, royalty, bonus, payment, deferred payment, compensation, loan, or any consideration whatsoever from a business, which is now or which may become a supplier, customer, or party to a contract with the company.

B.   Any situation in which the employee is a partner in a business enterprise, an owner either in whole or in part of a business, a consultant or advisor for compensation to a business enterprise or enterprises, or one who renders a professional or consulting service.

VI. Enforcement

Violation of this policy shall make the employee liable to disciplinary action, including possible dismissal, as deemed advisable by management. (A sample Employee Conflict of Interest Statement is provided as Figure 4.8.)

To: Chairperson, Corporate Ethics Committee

I, _____, have read the company's Policy Statement on "Employee Conflict of Interest," and have retained a copy for my future guidance. It is my understanding that this Policy Statement is only a guide to possible conflicts of interest, and that all potential conflicts and business ethics problems are to be reported whether or not they are of the type discussed in the Policy Statement.

I understand that I am to advise the Corporate Ethics Committee in writing immediately if any situation arises involving a possible conflict of interest or unethical business action.

I currently have no personal interests, nor does any member of my immediate family have personal interests, other than those set forth below, which may conflict with the interests of the company.

Disclosures:

Signature _____ Date _____

WITNESSED BY _____ Date _____

Typed Name _____

Position Title _____

Figure 4.8 Employee conflict of interest statement

4.9 EMPLOYEE CONFIDENTIALITY AGREEMENT

Where highly sensitive proprietary information may come into the possession of personnel at all levels, particularly at corporate headquarters locations, companies require all employees to execute a *confidentiality agreement* when they are placed on the payroll. A sample Employee Confidentiality Agreement (Figure 4.9) is provided for your guidance. All such agreements should be prepared by company attorneys who are competent to ensure that applicable and appropriate provisions of state laws are incorporated within the wording.

The general objective of this agreement, as a condition of employment, is to prohibit the unauthorized disclosure or utilization of company secrets or confidential information obtained as a result of employment. Employees who fail to comply with the terms of the confidentiality agreement are subject to such management action as may be deemed appropriate under the circumstances.

The agreement prohibits the following actions both during employment and after termination of employment:

1. Disclosure of company confidential information to others or for one's own personal business gains.
2. Use of company confidential information for personal profit, either directly or indirectly.
3. Buying or selling securities or other interests based on company confidential information pertaining to acquisitions or divestments.

The agreement broadly defines company confidential information to include methods of conducting or obtaining business; inventions, discoveries, improvements, formulae, practices, processes, and methods (whether patentable or not); and "other information or confidences" acquired in the course of employment.

The employee agrees to surrender all documents, papers, records, notes, and so on in the event of termination for any reason. Wording ensures that if part of the agreement is found to be invalid or unenforceable by a court judgment, the remainder of the agreement remains intact. Furthermore, the employee also agrees that the company has the right to obtain an injunction to restrain him or her from doing or continuing to do any act in violation of the agreement.

In consideration of my continued employment with _____, I, _____, agree that I will not, with respect to the Company, its affiliates, and subsidiaries (collectively referred to herein as "Company"), directly or indirectly during the term of my employment except as required in the normal course of the performance of my duties, or at any time after my employment is terminated for any reason:

(a) disclose or furnish to any person, corporation, or other entity, or use in my own personal business, any confidential information obtained by me as an employee which has not previously been disclosed to the public; or

(b) utilize any such confidential information or my affiliation with the Company for the gain, advantage, or profit of any entity other than the Company; or

(c) buy or sell, directly or indirectly, any security or other interest, or take advantage of any investment or other business opportunity which, because of confidential information obtained in my employment capacity, I know the Company may be considering to acquire or divest either in whole or in part.

Confidential information, which involves both secret and confidential classifications, includes the following, without limitation:

(a) methods of conducting or obtaining business to include know-how and trade secrets;

(b) inventions, discoveries, improvements, formulae, practices, processes, methods of processes, whether patentable or not, directly or indirectly related to the Company;

(c) any other information or confidences I may acquire in the course of my employment, no matter from where or in what manner such information may have been acquired.

Upon termination of my employment for any reason, regardless of whether initiated by the Company or myself, I shall surrender all papers, records, memoranda, notes, or other documents of any kind which have come into my control or possession, and any and all copies thereof, whether prepared by myself or others, which relate directly or indirectly to the business of the Company. The confidentiality obligation assumed hereunder shall survive the termination of my employment.

If any provision, or part thereof, of this Agreement shall, for any reason, be adjudged by any court of competent jurisdiction to be invalid or unenforceable, such judgment shall not affect, impair, or invalidate the remainder of the Agreement. It shall be confined in its operation to the provision, or part thereof, of this Agreement directly involved in the controversy in which such judgment shall have been rendered.

I agree that there is no adequate remedy at law for the breach by me of any of the covenants or agreements herein contained, and that the Company will suffer irreparable harm from such breach. Therefore, in the event of a breach or a threatened breach of any of the covenants or agreements herein contained, the Company shall be entitled, in addition to any other rights and remedies it may have, to an injunction restraining me from doing or continuing to do any such act in violation of this Agreement.

This Agreement shall be construed and enforced in accordance with and governed by the laws of the State of _____. This Agreement may not be modified or amended, nor may any provision thereof be waived or discharged, except in writing signed by both parties or their duly constituted representatives. All of the terms of this Agreement, whether so expressed or not, shall be binding on the personal representatives, successors, or assigns of the parties hereto.

Employee Signature _____ Date _____

ACCEPTED FOR THE COMPANY

BY _____ Date _____

Typed Name _____

Title _____

Figure 4.9 Employee confidentiality agreement

4.10 POST-EMPLOYMENT PERSONAL INFORMATION FORM

Nondiscrimination guidelines make it illegal to request information concerning marital status and dependents during the pre-employment process. However, this information may be obtained when an employment commitment is established. The Post-Employment Personal Information form (Figure 4.10) provides the structure for having the new employee, as part of placement on payroll procedures, give details for employee benefits and services purposes. The form includes three sections:

Personal Data—the need for age data centers on retirement planning purposes. The new employee's current address and telephone number are particularly useful in contacting individuals living in temporary quarters pending their relocation to a permanent address at the new work location; such information is not available in the new employee's Employment Application, which shows the former permanent address.

Emergency Contact Information—knowing the relationship of the person to be contacted in the case of an emergency is essential for determining how to best provide information. If a wife is called about her husband, who has been severely injured on the job, the approach will be considerably more moderated than if a friend were contacted.

Insurance Information—the new employee's marital status is clarified to determine whether the spouse will participate in health benefits coverage. Eligible dependents who will participate in the health insurance program are assessed through the data given in the "members of the immediate family" section. Duplicate insurance considerations are clarified through the inclusion of a section about "data for coordination of health insurance benefits."

Post-Employment Personal Information

Personal Data

Name (Last, First, MI) _____ Social Security # _____

Date of Birth (Mo./Day/Yr.) _____ Age _____ Employee I.D. # _____

Current Address _____

_____ Telephone No. (_____) _____

Emergency Contact Information

Contact Name _____ Relationship _____

Daytime Telephone No. (_____) _____
Evening Telephone No. (_____) _____

Home Address _____

_____

Insurance Information   Marital Status: ☐ Married ☐ Divorced ☐ Separated

Members of Immediate Family

Name	Relationship	Social Security No.	Date of Birth	Age
_____	_____	_____	_____	___
_____	_____	_____	_____	___
_____	_____	_____	_____	___
_____	_____	_____	_____	___
_____	_____	_____	_____	___

Data for Coordination of Health Insurance Benefits

If your spouse has health insurance coverage with his or her employer, please provide the following information:

Employer Name & Address _____

Insuring Company Name & Address _____

_____

Coverage Effective Date _____ Identification # _____

Who is covered? ☐ Spouse Only ☐ Spouse & Family

Signature _____ Date _____

Figure 4.10 Post-employment personal information

4.11 STORE EMPLOYEE PERSONNEL FOLDER AND RECORD

An employee personnel folder can be designed to serve as a complete and vital employment record in addition to being a repository for employment-related forms. The simplicity and efficiency of this approach is well suited for small companies. The example provided in Figure 4.11, the Store Employee Personnel Folder, has been designed to facilitate employee recordkeeping processes by the store managers of a chain of convenience stores.

A. *Employee Name, Address, Telephone Number, and Emergency Contact Information*—The front cover of the Store Employee Personnel Folder contains the employee's home address and telephone number and emergency contact information. Because this information is subject to change, entries are made in pencil. All other entries within the folder are required to be written in ink. Other sections on the front cover require information about employee name, social security number, and employee identification number. An entry is made in the "A. Inter-Store Transfer Record" section each time a district-level manager authorizes the transfer of an employee to another store. If a change of position title is involved, an entry also is required in "G. Reclassifications" (located inside the folder). In such cases, the folder is transmitted to the employee's new store manager by the district manager for that store. The inside left-hand portion of the folder contains sections for maintaining a permanent record of the following information:

B. *Absence Record*—The date and code for each type of occurrence are entered in chronological order. Dates are shown as month-day-year. Codes include S = sick, L = late, J = jury duty, P = personal, and A = unauthorized absence. This section also includes provisions for recording leaves of absence. The inclusive dates and the reason are specified.

C. *Accident Record*—Each on-the-job accident is described and the date of occurrence and the amount of lost time also are specified.

D. *Quarterly Employee Performance Appraisals*—The date of each appraisal and the overall rating obtained from completion of an Employee Performance Appraisal form are entered. Overall rating codes include: U = unsatisfactory, S = satisfactory, G = good, and E = excellent.

E. *Verbal/Written Warnings*—Notations are recorded concerning each infraction of work rules—that is, the date of occurrence, the type of infraction, and the corrective action. This is the only record of verbal warnings. Written warnings, which are documented by copies of disciplinary action forms or memoranda in the employee's folder, also are summarized in this section.

F. *Cash Register Overages/Shortages*—Frequent problems with overages/shortages are indicative of careless work procedures which should be reflected in performance appraisals.

G. *Reclassifications*—Any change of position classification or rate of compensation is entered.

The "store copy" of each multiple-part personnel form is filed on the inside right-hand portion of the folder.

CONFIDENTIAL

MUST BE MAINTAINED IN LOCKED FILE

EMPLOYEE NAME: _____

Last   First   Initial

STORE EMPLOYEE PERSONNEL FOLDER

* HOME ADDRESS & TELEPHONE #:

_____

Street   Apt. No.

_____

City   State   Zip Code

Telephone No. ( ) _____

SOCIAL SECURITY NUMBER ____ ‑ ____ ‑ ____

EMPLOYEE NUMBER _____

* EMERGENCY CONTACT INFORMATION:

_____

Name   Relationship

Work Telephone No. ( ) _____

Home Telephone No. ( ) _____

* PLEASE MAKE THESE ENTRIES IN PENCIL AS THEY ARE SUBJECT TO CHANGE. ALL OTHER ENTRIES ARE TO BE MADE IN INK AS A PERMANENT RECORD

A. INTER–STORE TRANSFER RECORD (Please insert information required for Section G – RECLASSIFICATIONS)

STORE # _____ DATE OF HIRE _____ AUTHORIZED BY _____

STORE # _____ DATE OF TRANSFER _____ AUTHORIZED BY _____

STORE # _____ DATE OF TRANSFER _____ AUTHORIZED BY _____

STORE # _____ DATE OF TRANSFER _____ AUTHORIZED BY _____

STORE # _____ DATE OF TRANSFER _____ AUTHORIZED BY _____

Figure 4.11 Store employee personnel folder

continued

213

B. ABSENCE RECORD: (Show Date and Code, e.g., ⌈S⌉, in Chronological Order, top to bottom, left to right.

<u>DATE</u>: Mo.–Day– Yr.   <u>CODES</u>: ⌈S⌉= Sick ⌈L⌉= Late   ⌈J⌉= Jury Duty   ⌈P⌉= Personal   ⌈A⌉= Unauthorized Absence

LEAVES OF ABSENCE: Dates: _____ to _____ Reason: _____

Dates: _____ to _____ Reason: _____

C. ACCIDENT RECORD: (Describe on-the-job accident, date of occurrence, and amount of lost time.)

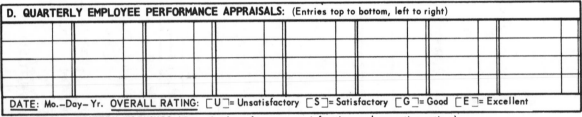

D. QUARTERLY EMPLOYEE PERFORMANCE APPRAISALS: (Entries top to bottom, left to right)

<u>DATE</u>: Mo.–Day– Yr. <u>OVERALL RATING</u>: ⌈U⌉= Unsatisfactory ⌈S⌉= Satisfactory ⌈G⌉= Good ⌈E⌉= Excellent

E. VERBAL – WRITTEN WARNINGS: (Describe date of occurrence, infraction, and corrective action.)

F. CASH REGISTER OVERAGES/SHORTAGES: (Indicate date, amount, and appropriate CODE: ⌈O⌉= Over ⌈S⌉= Short

	$			$			$			$	
	$			$			$			$	
	$			$			$			$	

G. RECLASSIFICATIONS: (Promotions/Demotions and New Hourly/Salary Rates)

EFF.DATE	POSITION	$	EFF.DATE	POSITION	$

$ – If no change, show prior hourly/weekly salary rate)

Figure 4.11 *(cont.)*

4.12 NEW EMPLOYEE ORIENTATION SCHEDULE

A sample New Employee Orientation Agenda (Figure 4.12) begins with a session first thing in the morning on "placement on the payroll." A representative of the human resources management organization provides step-by-step guidance to the group as needed for completing required paperwork, and answers questions concerning the associated terms and conditions of employment. Each new employee receives a folder of materials concerning employee benefits and other company information; a copy of the employee handbook is included.

The formal "orientation program" is next. The leader in organizing and conducting the program is the manager of employee development. The vice president of human resources management begins the program by providing "welcoming remarks." He or she then introduces the company president, who presents information on the company's history, current prospects, and future potential. The compensation manager then provides guidance concerning the employees' rewards and career advancement opportunities. Next, the employee benefits and services manager discusses employee benefits. A break for refreshments is provided to encourage individuals to meet other new employees. The focal point for the remainder of this training session is the employee development manager who conducts sessions on employee responsibilities as listed in the employee handbook, and the employee's future success on the job. He or she then guides the evaluation process. Each participant is requested to complete a questionnaire which assesses the critical aspects of the program in the interest of continuously improving its content. Figure 4.15 offers a sample New Employee Orientation Questionnaire. After the concluding remarks, employees report to their respective work locations.

The placement-on-the-payroll session takes one hour. One and one-half hours are allocated for the orientation program. A full morning of effective activities is provided to inform, acclimate, and motivate new employees. It is time well spent because it also offers the efficiency and economy of processing individuals as a group.

XYZ Corporation
New Employee Orientation Agenda—Monday, October 18, 19XX

Placement on the Payroll   (9:00–10:00 a.m.)

A representative of the Human Resources Management Division will provide guidance required for your completion of all necessary paperwork. All questions you may have regarding the terms and conditions of your employment will be answered by the HR representative. You also will receive a folder of materials concerning employee benefits, company information, and a copy of the Employee Handbook.

Orientation Program   (10:00–11:30 a.m.)

   I. Welcoming Remarks
      Ms. Louise T. Markham, Vice President—Human Resources Management

  II. The Company's History, Current Prospects, and Future Potential
      Mr. Thomas J. Putnam, President

  III. Your Rewards and Career Advancement Opportunities
      Mr. Thomas J. Smith, Manager—Compensation

  IV. Your Employee Benefits
      Ms. Barbara T. Bowen, Manager—Employee Benefits and Service

  V. Refreshments

  VI. Employee Responsibilities—The Employee Handbook
      Mr. Robert Barinsky, Manager—Employee Development

  VII. Success on the Job
      Mr. Barinsky

  VIII. Evaluation
      Mr. Barinsky

  IX. Concluding Remarks
      Mr. Barinsky

Figure 4.12 New employee orientation agenda

4.13 NEW EMPLOYEE ORIENTATION CHECKLIST

Whether your company already has a formal New Employee Orientation Program or is engaged in developing one, use of the New Employee Orientation Checklist (Figure 4.13) ensures that all essential subject matter is covered.

Checklist topics are grouped within seven categories:

- Introduction to company
- Physical facilities
- Time and attendance
- Rewards
- Benefits
- Work rules
- Safety

The guiding principle for developing the content of your program is to provide all the information needed for understanding the terms and conditions of employment. Information about the company fosters new employee identification with and commitment to related goals. Physical facility descriptions, which include the locations and functions performed by respective organizations and services, help the individual to feel at ease. Time, attendance, and payroll procedures information is a high priority for the new employee, who is very concerned about how and when he or she will be paid. Similarly, reward-related information on how to improve the new employee's rate of pay through on-the-job performance and advancement opportunities also is of vital interest. Employee responsibilities for personal conduct and safety in the workplace also deserve emphasis; these obligations are fundamental to the employment relationship.

INTRODUCTION TO COMPANY

—Historical Perspective
—Today's Challenges—Commitment to
  Excellence
—Tomorrow's Opportunities—Company and
  Employee Growth
—Our Commitment to EEO
—Employee Communications

PHYSICAL FACILITIES

—Medical Clinic
—Security Office
—Supply Rooms/Tool Rooms
—Cafeteria/Food Service/Vending Machines
—Smoking Areas
—Restrooms/Lounge Areas/Showers
—Employee Entrances
—Parking Areas

TIME AND ATTENDANCE

—Working Hours
—Breaks
—Lunch Periods/Other Meal Periods
—Overtime Pay
—Shift Differential Payments
—Attendance
—Reporting Absences/Tardiness
—Reporting Time Worked
—Paydays
—Paycheck Cashing Procedures

REWARDS

—Performance Standards and Reviews
—Merit Increases and Performance Awards
—Internal Placement Program—Advancement
  Opportunities

BENEFITS

—Compensation
—Performance Appraisals
—Life Insurance
—Health and Dental Care Insurance
—Business Travel Accident Insurance
—Income Protection/Sick Leave

—Personal Days
—Savings Plan
—Paid Vacation
—Paid Holidays
—Leaves of Absence
—Civic Responsibility Leaves—Jury Duty and
  Military Duty
—Bereavement Leave
—Employee Discounts
—Credit Union Loans
—Retirement Plan
—Employee Assistance Program
—Employee Recreational and Social Programs
—Workmen's Compensation
—Educational Assistance
—Relocation Assistance

WORK RULES

—Personal Telephone Calls and Personal Mail
—Physical Examinations
—Personal Conduct
  Substance Abuse
  Malicious Mischief, Neglect, or
    Carelessness
  Fighting
  Dishonesty
  Safety Infractions
  Insubordination
  Extensive Absences; Unauthorized Absence
  Improper Actions
  Immoral Actions
—Solicitations
—Confidential Company Information
—Sickness/Lateness Reporting
—Grievance Procedures
—Disciplinary Procedures

SAFETY

—Personal Safety Equipment
—First Aid
—Emergencies
—Fire Alarms/Fire Drills
—Accident Prevention
—Reporting Safety Hazards
—Fire Prevention
—OSHA Considerations

Figure 4.13 New employee orientation checklist

4.14 SELF-STUDY NEW EMPLOYEE ORIENTATION MANUAL

An effective technique for promoting new employee understanding of the company and its policies, and how the individual's role relates to the objectives and functions of the company, is to develop a self-study orientation manual. This approach may be used either as a substitute for or as a supplement to a formal new employee orientation program. This technique allows the new employee to study at his or her own pace and the individual is encouraged to invest that amount of time needed to fully comprehend the materials provided.

The flexibility of a loose-leaf notebook format is recommended over a bound manual, which becomes obsolete each time policies change. The appropriate pages of a loose-leaf notebook can be revised and inserted. The format also facilitates personalizing copies of the manual—that is, the individual's position description and information on his or her department may be inserted readily. Recommended subject matter for sections of the manual follows.

1. *Your Company*—historical perspective, current activities, and future prospects.
2. *Your Organization*—the functions performed by the employee's organization, and how that organization fits into the company's overall structure.
3. *Your Role*—how the duties and responsibilities of the employee's job/position relate to organizational objectives.
4. *Your Rewards*—compensation and incentives for excellence.
5. *Your Employee Benefits*—employee benefit program and employee services.
6. *Your Responsibilities*—conduct and performance.
7. *Your Future*—employee development and advancement opportunities.

The structure of a critically important section, "your role," should include the following types of materials:

- *Your Job/Position Description*—the employee's specific duties and responsibilities, and related standards for assessing performance in achieving objectives.
- *Functions of Your Organization*—the role performed by the employee's organization in supporting company goals and objectives, and how the organization is organized to achieve assigned responsibilities.
- *Company Organization Chart*—how the employee's organization fits into the company's overall structure.
- *Company Floor Plan*—helping the employee to find his or her way to essential areas; the locations and functions of the human resources department, the safety office, the medical clinic, and so on.

To the maximum extent possible, the company's employee handbook should be used as the principle source of orientation-related information. This avoids needless duplication of information in the Self-Study New Employee Orientation Manual. It also serves to emphasize the importance of the employee handbook as the focal point for basic information on the terms and conditions of employment. Accordingly, the format of the section on "your employee benefits" (Figure 4.14) should cite the employee handbook as its reference material source.

5. YOUR EMPLOYEE BENEFITS

OBJECTIVE: This section gives you an opportunity to study the basic provisions of the comprehensive and competitive benefits program which is provided by the company to all permanent employees who work 30 or more hours per week.

REFERENCE MATERIALS: Employee Handbook, pages 7 through 12

(*Note:* If you require more detailed information concerning your benefits in the future, please refer to the respective plan description booklets which were provided to you by the Human Resources Department. Any questions should be referred to your HR representative.)

REVIEW QUESTIONS: Now that you have studied the information provided in the Employee Handbook, please test your knowledge by answering the following questions:

1. When are you eligible for life insurance coverage? _____
   _____

2. What is the dollar amount of the life insurance you receive at company expense? $ _____

3. What is the dollar amount of the life insurance benefit which would be received by your survivors in the event of your accidental death? $ _____

4. How much optional life insurance may you purchase? _____
   _____

5. When are you eligible for comprehensive hospital, surgical, and medical coverage? _____

6. When are you eligible for dental care insurance? _____
   _____

7. How many days of hospital confinement are payable annually under the provisions of the basic health care benefit? _____ days

8. What is the annual deductible amount per person which you must pay before major medical expenses are reimbursed? $ _____

**Figure 4.14 Sample page from self-study new
employee orientation manual**

4.15 NEW EMPLOYEE ORIENTATION EVALUATION QUESTIONNAIRE

At the conclusion of a formal New Employee Orientation Program training session, participants should be invited to offer feedback on the effectiveness of the activity in meeting their informational needs. The New Employee Orientation Questionnaire (Figure 4.15) is designed to obtain the critical assessments needed for improving the program.

The new employee is asked to critically assess and candidly comment on how well the program met his or her needs in each of the subject matter areas covered. Specific questions include:

1. What information was unnecessary?
2. What information should have been included?
3. What could have been explained more effectively?
4. How useful was the information to you?

The new employee then is asked to provide "general comments (overall evaluation)." In addition to providing a summary of overall findings, these comments open up the discussion to any and all other comments which were not elicited in response to the questions asked.

The individual has the option of submitting the completed questionnaire anonymously, which promotes more critical and valuable assessments while dispelling concerns about jeopardizing his or her position.

New Employee Orientation Questionnaire

We would appreciate your assistance in evaluating our New Employee Orientation Program. Your critical assessments and candid remarks are needed for improving the program's effectiveness; we want to meet new employee information requirements optimally.

PLEASE COMMENT ON HOW EFFECTIVELY EACH OF THE FOLLOWING PORTIONS OF THE PROGRAM MET YOUR NEEDS FOR INFORMATION. WHAT WAS UNNECESSARY? WHAT SHOULD HAVE BEEN INCLUDED? WHAT COULD HAVE BEEN EXPLAINED MORE EFFECTIVELY? HOW USEFUL WAS THE INFORMATION TO YOU?

1. The company's history, current prospects, and future potential:

2. Your rewards and career advancement opportunities:

3. Your employee benefits:

4. Employee responsibilities—the Employee Handbook:

5. Success on the job:

General Comments (Overall Evaluation):

Name (Optional) _____ Orientation Date _____

Figure 4.15 New employee orientation questionnaire

4.16 NEW EMPLOYEE ANNOUNCEMENT MEMORANDUM

In addition to providing information concerning new employees in the company's "house organ," the practice of issuing a New Employee Announcement Memorandum (Figure 4.16) is recommended. As soon as the new employee is placed on the payroll, the memorandum is prepared and distributed to all employees. This memorandum provides an immediate introduction of the individual to his or her co-workers throughout the company, who later will see a photograph and more informal details about this new employee in the company newspaper.

The procedure promotes recognition and acceptance of the new employee as a valuable member of the company with an essential role and the credentials needed for success. It provides the data needed by employees to answer the inevitable question of why the company chose an outsider rather than promoting someone from within. It also helps the new employee feel that he or she belongs, and promotes the development of interpersonal relationships with co-workers who also went to the same college, previously worked for the same company, and so on.

Memorandum

TO: ALL EMPLOYEES   DATE: 01/15/88

FROM: Mary L. Victor, Director—Human Resources Management

SUBJECT: NEW EMPLOYEE ANNOUNCEMENT—Mr. T. J. Rutson

We are pleased to announce that Mr. Thomas J. Rutson has joined our company as a Senior Financial Analyst reporting to Mr. R. J. Smith, Manager of the Financial Planning Department. His assignment will concentrate on the evaluation of companies under consideration for acquisition.

Tom joins us from International Electronics, Inc., where he has been engaged as Financial Analyst for the past three years. A graduate of Rutgers University, Tom has a B.S. degree in Economics and an MBA in Finance.

Please welcome Tom and extend your best wishes for much success.

Figure 4.16 New employee announcement memorandum

4.17 PLACEMENT FOLLOW-UP INTERVIEW REPORT

To identify placement problems before they cause unnecessary, unproductive, and costly turnover, a follow-up interview technique is recommended. The Placement Follow-Up Interview Report (Figure 4.17) provides a structured format for probing the degree of the new employee's satisfaction with his or her job and work environment. An HR representative conducts this interview after the new employee has been with the company for approximately thirty days. This interview report provides adequate time to recommend appropriate corrective action well before the end of the normal ninety-day probationary employment period.

The structure of the Placement Follow-Up Interview Report form includes four key evaluation areas plus an overall evaluation. The following types of assessments are requested:

1. How effective was the orientation conducted by the employee's supervisor? Did it result in employee understanding of the duties, responsibilities, and performance standards for his or her job?
2. Is the employee making a satisfactory adjustment in meeting position requirements? What problem areas has the employee identified, and what special efforts are needed?
3. Have pre-employment promises been kept? Have pre-employment perceptions and expectations been met by the realities of the job?
4. Are there any personal problems, such as conflicts with the immediate supervisor or co-workers?
5. In general, how satisfied is the new employee with the job? If problems cannot be resolved, what other type of placement is recommended?

The HR representative is required to specify "overall findings." When the section on "placement problems—discuss with immediate supervisor" is checked, the interviewer has determined that problems may be resolved potentially through the encouragement of appropriate supervisory action. If necessary understanding and cooperation is not received from the new employee's supervisor, transfer possibilities should be considered. In those cases where the interviewer determines that unresolvable problems are in evidence, the section for "placement problems—review transfer possibilities" is checked. The results of these actions are summarized in the "final disposition" section.

Placement Follow-up Interview Report

New Employee Name _____ I.D. No. _____

Job/Position Title _____ Organization _____

Hire Date _____ Interview Date _____

1. How effective were the supervisor's orientation procedures in helping the new employee to feel at ease, and to understand job/position requirements? Is the incumbent thoroughly familiar with the contents of his or her position description and the associated performance standards?

2. Is the new employee adjusting satisfactorily to the overall requirements of the job/position? Any difficulty in meeting productivity or quality standards? Are there any areas where the employee feels that insufficient prior experience requires special efforts to obtain necessary knowledge and skills?

3. Have pre-employment promises been kept? How do the new employee's pre-employment perceptions of the job/position and the company measure up to post-employment realities?

4. Are there any personal problems with the immediate supervisor or co-workers?

5. In general, how satisfied is the new employee with the job/position? If apparently unresolvable problems are in evidence, what other type of placement would be more suitable?

Overall Findings:

☐ Satisfactory Placement
☐ Placement Problems—Discuss with Immediate Supervisor
☐ Placement Problems—Review Transfer Possibilities

Final Disposition: _____

_____

_____

Interviewer _____ Date _____

Figure 4.17 Placement follow-up interview report

4.18 PROBATIONARY EMPLOYEE PERFORMANCE APPRAISAL

A formal evaluation of the new employee's performance is required immediately prior to the expiration of the ninety-day probationary employment period. The primary purpose of this assessment is to determine whether the individual has met the requisite performance standards. If he or she has not, the assessment then concentrates on determining whether specific corrective actions are possible, or if termination action should be initiated. The Probationary Employee Performance Appraisal form (Figure 4.18) provides a uniform framework for the evaluation of new employees.

The structure of the Probationary Employee Performance Appraisal form includes five standards which cover the broad spectrum of factors that determine on-the-job effectiveness:

I.   Quantity of work
II.   Quality of work
III. Knowledge of work
IV.   Initiative
V.   Reliability

For each of these standards, the probationary employee's immediate supervisor is required to evaluate performance in terms of whether or not the individual "meets standard" or "exceeds standard." If a standard is not met, and specific corrective action is possible within an additional ninety-day period, then an explanation of proposed actions and the time frame the action is to be completed is required. An explanation also is required when the individual's performance exceeds the requirements for meeting a standard.

The evaluation process includes specifying "overall evaluation results," which requires carefully reviewing all the findings in order to make a decision to retain the new employee. If an employee does not meet most standards, and if corrective action potentially will solve only some of the performance problems, then termination action is recommended. If specified corrective actions will potentially resolve performance problems within a reasonable time frame, then the individual is given a "deferred probationary employee evaluation date." The key consideration is to provide the basis for retaining a potentially effective performer who, given additional guidance and on-the-job training, can meet or exceed requirements. Every reasonable effort should be made to avoid costly turnover.

A merit increase is recommended when a new employee's performance exceeds the standards. Meaningful wage/salary adjustments are necessary for properly rewarding these exceptional contributors. Proper recognition is essential for encouraging their continued high level of effectiveness and productivity and to retain them as employees.

The form also includes an "employee acknowledgment." Procedures should require the immediate supervisor to review the findings with the employee. The excellent employee deserves a detailed commendation. The employee whose performance requires corrective action must understand and agree with the need for specific changes if successful outcomes are to be achieved within a specified time frame. The employee who fails to meet expectations deserves a final accounting of the unsolved problems that are leading to termination action.

Probationary Employee Performance Appraisal

Employee Name _____ I.D. No. _____ Job/Position Title _____

Department _____ Hire Date _____ Probationary Period Ends (Date) _____

Please evaluate this probationary employee's work performance to determine whether the following standards have been met. An explanation is required for each deficiency. If specific corrective actions are possible within a ninety (90) day period, explain proposed actions and time frames. An explanation also is required when the employee's performance exceeds a standard.

Standard	Meets Standard?	Exceeds Standard?	Explanation
I. Quantity of Work Does employee consistently meet productivity expectations and output requirements?	☐ Yes ☐ No	☐ Yes ☐ No	
II. Quality of Work Does employee consistently meet accuracy, thoroughness, and effectiveness requirements? Does employee consistently work effectively with others?	☐ Yes ☐ No	☐ Yes ☐ No	
III. Knowledge of Work Does employee consistently apply and demonstrate requisite skill and understanding of requirements?	☐ Yes ☐ No	☐ Yes ☐ No	
IV. Initiative Does employee consistently apply creativity and resourcefulness in analyzing problems to make sound decisions?	☐ Yes ☐ No	☐ Yes ☐ No	
V. Reliability Does employee consistently meet objectives in a timely manner? Does employee meet expectations regarding minimal or no absences or latenesses?	☐ Yes ☐ No	☐ Yes ☐ No	

Overall Evaluation Results:

☐ Employee's performance does not meet standards; termination action is recommended.

☐ Employee's performance requires the specified corrective actions by _____, the deferred probationary employee evaluation date.
(date)

☐ Employee's performance *meets standards.*

☐ Employee's performance *exceeds standards;* a merit increase is recommended.

Approvals:

_____ Employee acknowledgment:
Supervisor   _____
                                        Signature
_____   _____
Date   Date

_____
Manager

_____
Date

Figure 4.18 Probationary employee performance appraisal

CHAPTER 5

Human Resources

Continuously promoting the more effective utilization of the company's human resources is a major responsibility of the HR director. If company growth objectives are to be achieved, requisite employee knowledge and skills must be developed through appropriate training opportunities.

Representative types of developmental programs include:

- On-the-job training
- Company-conducted courses, workshops, and seminars
- Temporary work assignments—rotational and exchange programs
- Undergraduate college coursework—tuition refund program
- Graduate college coursework for masters degrees
- Management development programs—courses, seminars, understudy assignments
- Professional association meetings, conferences, and conventions

This chapter provides a framework for administering the employee development process, in which individual responsibilities are emphasized. For example, the employee is responsible for assessing skill requirements to identify training needs. Consideration is given to the needs of the current position and those required for advancement so that results are obtained for both on-the-job and formal coursework proposals. These conclusions are obtained through the Individual Development Plan (see Figure 5.1).

Individuals are required to submit an Employee Training Request form (see Figure 5.2) to obtain approval for participating in each course not offered by the company.

Certain college coursework is considered to be mutually beneficial to the company and the employee. The Educational Assistance Application—Tuition Refund Plan (see Figure 5.3) provides the basis for this subsidized training.

The skills required of supervisory and managerial personnel require special consideration. As part of the management development program, a Requirements Assessment form (see Figure 5.4) provides a listing of representative skill requirements. The individual and his or her manager use this tool to assess developmental requirements, which are translated into critically needed and prioritized training objectives in the Individual Development Plan (see Figure 5.5).

An employee exchange program based on the identification of assignment-related knowledge and abilities is possible through the use of the Professional Exchange Program Application (see Figure 5.6).

A format for developing units of instruction, the Instruction Plan, is explained in Section 5.7. A schedule planning matrix and guidelines also are provided for use in properly structuring a meaningful training program.

The Employee Development Summary form, which serves as a résumé of developmental growth on each job/position within the company, is discussed in Section 5.8.

A variety of sample student evaluation of training forms are offered in Section 5.9.

The Employee Training Record (see Figure 5.10) and Certificate of Training (see Figure 5.11) offer effective approaches for documenting training activities.

5.1 INDIVIDUAL DEVELOPMENT PLAN

Figure 5.1 shows a format for use by employees in preparing their Individual Development Plan. This approach places the responsibility for training needs assessment on the employee, who begins by identifying the types of skills needed to improve performance in his or her current position. The employee is asked to consider skill requirements for his or her future position—the one personally targeted as a potential advancement opportunity. This consideration requires an estimate of the time needed to qualify for the position, and details of the specific skills that are necessary.

After completing Section I, "Skill Requirements Assessment," the employee must identify specific courses or other types of training opportunities needed to meet skill requirements. Completion of Section II, "Training Needs," includes specifying on-the-job training possibilities and company/outside training courses which will meet overall developmental objectives.

The individual development plan is reviewed by the employee's immediate supervisor, who implements requisite on-the-job training and provides tentative approval for proposed company/outside training course attendance. Final approval is reserved until the employee submits the requisite Employee Training Request forms (see Figure 5.2).

Individual Development Plan

Date _____

Employee _____ Social Security No. _____

Job/Position Title _____

Organization _____

I. SKILL REQUIREMENTS ASSESSMENT

    A.   Current Position—What skills are needed to improve your performance?

        _____

        _____

        _____

    B.   Future Position

        1. What is the title of the position that you are considering as an advancement opportunity?

          _____

        2. How much time will be needed for you to meet required qualifications?

          _____

        3. What specific skills must you develop in order to qualify?

          _____

II. TRAINING NEEDS

What specific courses or other training opportunities are needed to meet your skill requirements?

        1. On-the-Job Training: _____

          _____

          _____

        2. Company/Outside Training Courses: _____

          _____

          _____

          _____

Employee Signature _____

Supervisory Review _____

Figure 5.1 Individual development plan

5.2 EMPLOYEE TRAINING REQUEST FORM

When an employee submits an Individual Development Plan for review by his or her immediate supervisor, the process includes preliminary review and/or approval of courses proposed to meet skill-related developmental requirements. Final approval for courses not offered by the company is reserved until the employee submits an Employee Training Request (Figure 5.2).

The heading of the Employee Training Request (Figure 5.2) form asks for specific details concerning the course: course name and identification number, the name and address of the training institution, and the proposed dates of attendance. A statement of justification, which explains how the course will meet the employee's training objective, also is required. A separate form is required for each course.

An "estimated cost data" section is included for management's use in making potential benefit versus expense assessments, and for allocating associated budgetary resources.

Required "approvals" include the immediate supervisor, the manager (next higher level of management), and the human resources development manager.

The final section of the form is used by the human resources development department in certifying that the employee has completed training requirements. A copy of the form and supporting documentation is given to the accounting department for substantiating related purchase order (tuition, books and materials, and so on), and travel expense costs.

Employee Training Request

Employee _____ Social Security No. _____

Job/Position Title _____

Organization _____

_____

Course _____ No. _____

Name & Address of Training Institution _____

Dates: From _____ To _____   No. of Days _____

Purpose (Training Objective): _____

_____

ESTIMATED COST DATA

1. Tuition $_____

2. Books & Materials $_____

3. Other—Specify: _____ $_____

4. Travel Expenses $_____

                              TOTAL: $_____

_____

APPROVALS

Immediate Supervisor _____ Date _____

Manager   _____ Date _____

HRD Manager   _____ Date _____

_____

TO: Accounting Department   Date _____

As indicated by the attached supporting documentation, subject employee has satisfactorily completed this course.

Signature (HRD Representative) _____

Figure 5.2 Employee training request

5.3 EDUCATIONAL ASSISTANCE APPLICATION (TUITION REFUND)

A representative company policy statement regarding an educational assistance—tuition refund plan follows.

It is not the intention of the company to underwrite a general education which an employee may be taking for his or her own personal satisfaction, or to prepare himself or herself for work that is not available in the company. Should a particular degree or specific college coursework be a prerequisite for advancement to a higher position in the employee's vocational field, and if this action is consistent with the company's needs, then subsidized training will be provided.

Educational assistance will be limited to no more than three (3) courses per college quarter/semester. The company will reimburse the cost of tuition, fees, textbooks, and materials for courses successfully completed by the employee, providing that the following requirements are satisfied:

1. The employee must certify that he or she will not be receiving training allowances for the coursework from other sources.

2. The immediate supervisor must ensure that the proposed coursework relates directly to the requirements of the employee's current position, or is consistent with the company's future plans for the employee.

3. Within ninety (90) days of completion of the course(s), the employee must submit documentation of successful completion to the human resources development Department.

This policy and associated procedures are implemented through the use of an Educational Assistance Application (Figure 5.3). The form is prepared in duplicate and submitted through the immediate supervisor to the human resources development Manager. The "supervisor's evaluation" section provides the certification needed for ensuring that course(s) are consistent with the company's educational assistance—Tuition Refund policy. The "reply to employee" section, which is completed by the human resources development manager, provides information on whether the application has been approved. The duplicate copy is returned to the employee, who uses it to initiate reimbursement action when approved courses are completed successfully. Receipts for payments and certification of passing grade(s) documentation are attached to the copy and forwarded to the HR manager, who approves special salary payment action (payment is subject to withholding deductions for income tax and Social Security).

EDUCATIONAL ASSISTANCE APPLICATION

Prepare in duplicate and submit to your immediate supervisor. He will evaluate your application and forward both copies to the HRD Manager Duplicate copy will be returned to you. Upon completion of course(s), receipts for payments and certification of passing grades must be attached to duplicate application and sent to the HRD Manager for refund processing.

NAME (Last, First, Initial)		POSITION		DEPARTMENT		
LOCATION		ROOM	TELEPHONE EXT.	IMMEDIATE SUPERVISOR		

COURSE TITLE	SUBJECT (English, etc.)	CREDITS	CLASS MEETS		GRADE	TUITION
			DAYS	HOURS		
1.						
2.						
3.						

School _____ TOTAL [____]

Total Tuition	$
Registration Fee	
Books	
Materials	
TOTAL	$

Address _____

Date Courses Start _____ End _____

Type of Degree _____ Major _____ Estimated Graduation Date _____

Relationship of course(s) to company work; current or long-range benefits:

Will you receive training allowances for this coursework from another source such as a scholarship or fellowship? ☐ No   ☐ Yes
(If Yes, explain) _____

I understand that if the above course(s) is approved under the Educational Assistance Program that payment initially will be made at my personal expense. I also understand that I will be entitled to 100% reimbursement less Social Security and Withholding Tax upon the submission of receipt(s) and proof of satisfactory completion, attached to a duplicate copy of this application.

SIGNATURE _____ DATE _____

SUPERVISOR'S EVALUATION:

☐   I recommend this application for approval.

☐   I do not recommend this application for approval because:

SIGNATURE _____ DATE _____

REPLY TO EMPLOYEE:

☐   Application is approved. Refund request must be made within 3 months of course completion.

☐   Application has not been approved because:

☐   Application is being returned for additional information as follows:

SIGNATURE _____ DATE _____

REFUND REQUEST: TO: **ATTN.:** Payroll

Please arrange salary payment to reimburse the above employee for $ _____ less Social Security and Withholding Tax.

This amount was expended for approved educational assistance as itemized above; expenditures are documental by the attached receipts. Charge to _____

SIGNATURE _____ DATE _____

Figure 5.3 Educational assistance application

5.4 MANAGEMENT DEVELOPMENT PROGRAM—REQUIREMENTS ASSESSMENT FORM

For maximum effectiveness in assessing the developmental needs of supervisory and managerial personnel, both the individual and his or her manager should participate in the process. The Management Development Program—Requirements Assessment form (Figure 5.4) provides the structure needed to achieve this objective.

The form lists eighteen categories of functions performed by supervisory and managerial employees. For example, the first category is "A. Helping Workers with Problems." Each category is divided into specific types of related skills which are assessed in terms of the individual's needs. Accordingly, the first category includes six skills: (1) help employees with job adjustment problems, (2) help subordinates improve performance, (3) help employees solve personal problems, (4) listening skill development, (5) conflict resolution, and (6) employee assistance referral techniques.

The employee reviews each "supervisory/managerial function" to assess his or her need for associated developmental opportunities. Each need is assessed by placing a code in the box provided under the "employee" column of the "developmental requirement" section. "O" signifies no need, "S" signifies some need, and "N" signifies need. The completed form is reviewed by the immediate supervisor, who enters assessment codes in the "manager" column. Although most managers concur with their employees' self-evaluations, some evaluations are perceived quite differently by the manager and employee. For example, a manager may believe that a degree of need exists where the employee has not indicated any, or the employee has identified a requirement that the manager may believe is unnecessary. In the event that the employee and manager cannot concur on the evaluation through subsequent discussions, the manager's ratings will receive priority in the planning implementation actions used in the Management Development Program—Individual Development Plan form (see Figure 5.5).

**Management Development Program
Requirements Assessment**

Employee _____ Social Security No. _____

Position Title _____

Organization _____ Location _____

Supervisor (Name & Title) _____

Employee: Please review each "Supervisory/Managerial Function" to assess your need for improving related skills through appropriate developmental opportunities. Your evaluations are to be shown in the "Employee" portion of the "Developmental Requirement" section. One of the following codes should be entered in each box: O = No Need, S = Some Need, or N = Need. **Immediate Supervisor:** Please review the employee's assessment's to indicate your findings in respective boxes ("Manager" portion of the "Developmental Requirement" section).

	Developmental Requirement	
Supervisory/Managerial Function	Employee	Manager

A. Helping Workers with Problems

  1. Help employees with job adjustment problems ☐ ☐
  2. Help subordinates improve performance ☐ ☐
  3. Help employees solve personal problems ☐ ☐
  4. Listening skill development ☐ ☐
  5. Conflict resolution ☐ ☐
  6. Employee assistance referral techniques ☐ ☐

B. Giving Information to Employees

  1. Keeping employees informed ☐ ☐
  2. Conducting effective meetings ☐ ☐
  3. Responding to employee suggestions ☐ ☐

C. Receiving Information from Employees

  1. Responding to productivity concepts ☐ ☐
  2. Encouraging employee participation ☐ ☐
  3. Consulting with employee concerning
     work procedures and activities to
     improve working conditions ☐ ☐

D. Labor-Management Relations

  1. Employee rights under agreement ☐ ☐
  2. Handling employee grievances ☐ ☐

Figure 5.4 Management development program—requirements assessment

continued

237

Supervisory/Managerial Function	Developmental Requirement	
	Employee	Manager

E. Leadership

1. Participative management concepts	☐	☐
2. Encouraging employees to assume personal responsibility for work performance	☐	☐
3. Promoting employee cooperation	☐	☐

F. Safety and Health

1. Promoting employee understanding of health services and occupational health hazards	☐	☐
2. Promoting adherence to safety regulations	☐	☐

G. Representing Company Management

1. Defining and defending company goals and objectives	☐	☐
2. Communicating employee view to company management	☐	☐
3. Assuming responsibility for work group's problems	☐	☐

H. Employee Development

1. Providing detailed work instruction	☐	☐
2. Introducing change	☐	☐
3. Teaching and coaching skills	☐	☐
4. Encouraging employee skill development	☐	☐

I. Employee Utilization

1. Assessing individual abilities to more effectively assign work	☐	☐
2. Matching individuals with jobs	☐	☐
3. Considering individual interests	☐	☐
4. Understanding employee feelings about their assignments	☐	☐

J. Planning, Scheduling, and Organizing

1. Division of labor assignments	☐	☐
2. Planning strategies and policies	☐	☐
3. Time management	☐	☐
4. Setting priorities	☐	☐
5. Following up to ensure work completion	☐	☐

K. Controlling Work Progress

1. Assessing daily developments and progress	☐	☐
2. Reviewing individual progress in carrying out orders	☐	☐
3. Correcting employee work problems	☐	☐
4. Early detection of productivity problems	☐	☐

Figure 5.4 *(cont.)*

| | Developmental Requirement | |
Supervisory/Managerial Function	Employee	Manager
5. Employee participation in setting goals and associated deadlines	☐	☐
L. Appraising Performance		
1. Establishing job performance standards	☐	☐
2. Effective employee discussion techniques; feedback on good or poor performance	☐	☐
3. Constructive criticism	☐	☐
M. Cooperation		
1. Ensuring that employees have required equipment and materials through obtaining cooperation from other company units	☐	☐
2. Effective coordination with other members of management to resolve problems	☐	☐
N. Resource Utilization		
1. Effective budgeting techniques	☐	☐
2. Financial management	☐	☐
O. Administration		
1. Properly prepare paperwork in a timely manner	☐	☐
2. Administrative policies and procedures	☐	☐
3. Preparation and maintenance of records	☐	☐
4. New employee interviewing techniques and selection criteria	☐	☐
P. Equal Employment Opportunity and Affirmative Action Plan Implementation		
1. Equal treatment of employees in work	☐	☐
2. Equal treatment of employees in advancement decisions	☐	☐
Q. Disciplinary Actions		
1. Verbal and written disciplinary actions	☐	☐
2. Resolving employee conduct problems	☐	☐
R. Personal		
1. Psychological concepts—understanding human behavior	☐	☐
2. Self-analysis for improving effectiveness	☐	☐
3. Coping with stress	☐	☐
4. Improving communications skills (oral and written)	☐	☐

Signature _____ Date _____

Supervisor _____ Date _____

Figure 5.4 *(cont.)*

5.5 MANAGEMENT DEVELOPMENT PROGRAM–INDIVIDUAL DEVELOPMENT PLAN

The Individual Development Plan form (Figure 5.5) is used by the supervisory/ managerial employee to assign priorities to his or her Management Development Program—Requirements Assessment (refer to Figure 5.4) findings.

The first section, "critical developmental requirements," identifies the seven most essential objectives. The individual is instructed to give particular emphasis to "N" (need) ratings which received the manager's concurrence. After listing the seven most critical "developmental requirement objectives," the individual shows the relative importance of the objectives in the "ranking" column. The form is given to the manager, who assigns ranking data in the column provided. If significant discrepancies exist among these rankings, discussions and negotiations ensue. The employee then is prepared to complete the second section of the form, "training plan proposal."

For each critical developmental requirement objective that has been identified, the supervisory/managerial employee coordinates with the human resources development manager to obtain information on related courses. Courses included in the Training Plan Proposal are listed in their relative order of importance, which are based on the ratings shown in the "manager's ranking" column for the respective developmental requirement objectives.

The completed Individual Development Plan is reviewed and approved by the individual's manager, who uses it as a basis for authorizing subsequent implementation actions.

Although seven proposed courses are listed, company policies generally limit the number of management development courses that may be taken each year. Management authorizes the number of courses the employee may take based on the following considerations:

1. *Cost*—direct costs (training course costs and travel expenses) and indirect costs (time away from work).
2. *Benefit*—value of training in improved performance versus loss of productivity associated with absence.
3. *Critical Need*—absolutely essential for meeting company-oriented objectives.

The company pays all direct costs for courses, seminars, workshops, and so on based on an approved Employee Training Request form (refer to Figure 5.2). Approvals are required from two levels of management and the human resources development manager. The company's travel expense policy governs the payment of costs incurred for transportation, meals, accommodations, and so on.

Upon completion of a course, the supervisory/managerial employee submits a written evaluation through his or her manager to the human resources development manager. This evaluation provides the following information:

1. An appraisal of course content, quality of instruction, and so on, for use by the HRD department in determining whether other company employees should attend future sessions.
2. A technique for the individual to analyze and describe the benefits to the company that have resulted from his or her attendance.

Sample Student Evaluation of Training forms are provided in Section 5.9 of this chapter. These forms may be adapted to meet your company's need for feedback, or your company may opt for a Memorandum for Record format.

Management Development Program
Individual Development Plan

Employee _____ Social Security No. _____

I. Critical Developmental Requirements

This section is for use in extracting data from your **Requirements Assessment** worksheet to identify the 7 most critical objectives. Emphasis is placed on those "Supervisory/Managerial Function" items your Manager also has rated as "N = Need". List the 7 most critical objectives, show their relative importance in the "ranking" column, and then review findings with your Manager. "Manager's Ranking" data are need for preparing Section II., Training Plan Proposal.

Developmental Requirement Objective	Item No.	Ranking	Manager's Ranking
_____	_____	_____	_____
_____	_____	_____	_____
_____	_____	_____	_____
_____	_____	_____	_____
_____	_____	_____	_____
_____	_____	_____	_____

II. Training Plan Proposal

Suggest specific types of training opportunities which will meet each of the Developmental Requirement Objectives you identified in Section I. Please coordinate with the Human Resource Development Manager as needed to obtain information on related courses. Each item should be listed in its relative order of importance; the item which received a "Manager's Ranking'" of 1 should be shown first, etc. Your completed Individual Development Plan is to be reviewed and approved by your manager.

Item No.	Type of Course/Seminar/Workshop/On-The-Job Training	Start Date	End Date
_____	_____	____	____
_____	_____	____	____
_____	_____	____	____
_____	_____	____	____
_____	_____	____	____
_____	_____	____	____

Approved _____ Date _____

Figure 5.5 Management development program—individual development plan

5.6 PROFESSIONAL EXCHANGE PROGRAM APPLICATION

The U.S. Department of Transportation, which is organizationally analogous to a highly diversified company, has designed an excellent professional exchange program for promoting employee development. The program provides employees with temporary transfer opportunities to:

1. Broaden their experience.
2. Gain new knowledge and abilities; demonstrate current knowledge and abilities.
3. Observe different management styles.
4. Work for another organization.

The length of developmental assignments ranges from one to twelve months. Types of assignments include temporary replacement positions and positions as members or leaders of work groups brought together to perform special studies or projects.

Employees apply for the exchange program by submitting a form that is similar to the Professional Exchange Program Application (Figure 5.6), providing information on their personal qualifications, and including a copy of their most recent performance appraisal.

To arrange exchange assignments, knowledge and abilities are required in various combinations. The Professional Exchange Program Application provides this information. The employee completes the "knowledge of" and "ability to" sections of the form by designating the following categories: H = has the knowledge or ability, and D = wants to develop the knowledge or ability.

Depending on the position's requirements and priorities, two types of selections are possible:

1. The candidate has all or most of the knowledge and abilities required for the assignment.
2. The candidate wants to obtain the specified knowledge, and has all or most of the abilities required for the assignment.

Professional Exchange Program

APPLICATION OF _____

Social Security No. _____ Job/Position Title _____

Organization _____ Location _____

Please review the "Knowledge of" and "Ability to" listings to designate those you have (use letter "H") or want to develop (use letter "D").

KNOWLEDGE OF

_____ 1. Accounting procedures

_____ 2. Administrative procedures

_____ 3. Administrative support services (printing, records management, etc.)

_____ 4. Artistic design and display

_____ 5. Auditing

_____ 6. Behavioral science techniques and procedures

_____ 7. Budgeting methods and techniques

_____ 8. Business law and practices

_____ 9. Computer requirements and techniques

_____ 10. Economics

_____ 11. Electronics theories

_____ 12. Engineering

_____ 13. Environmental planning and protection

_____ 14. Equal employment opportunity policies and practices

_____ 15. Experimental design and research

_____ 16. Financial transactions and operations

_____ 17. Governmental relations

_____ 18. Human resources management policies and practices

_____ 19. International business

_____ 20. Investigative techniques

_____ 21. Legal documents and procedures

_____ 22. Library functions and services

_____ 23. Logistical support techniques

_____ 24. Management planning and processes

_____ 25. Mathematics

_____ 26. Office automation

_____ 27. Physical science techniques and procedures

_____ 28. Procurement methods

Figure 5.6 Professional exchange program application

continued

_____ 29. Public relations

_____ 30. Safety and occupational health

_____ 31. Statistics

_____ 32. Supply systems

_____ 33. Systems analysis and design

_____ 34. Training program design and development

ABILITY TO

_____101. Assign or delegate work

_____102. Brief or instruct large groups

_____103. Communicate orally to explain, advise, or persuade others in one-on-one or small group situations

_____104. Determine the quality of programs and projects by comparing performance with standards and objectives

_____105. Develop new ideas and approaches to solve problems

_____106. Establish requirements and priorities for meeting objectives

_____107. Express ideas in written reports, papers, memoranda, etc.

_____108. Function under pressure, e.g., severe time limitations

_____109. Independently originate action; a "self-starter"

_____110. Effective team player; interacts with sound tact and diplomacy in one-on-one and group situations

_____111. Monitor and evaluate the work of others

_____112. Define problems, obtain information, identify relationships, evaluate quality, assess impact, arrive at conclusions, and make recommendations

_____113. Write technical reports and manuals

Figure 5.6 *(cont.)*

5.7 FORMAT FOR DEVELOPING A TRAINING PROGRAM—THE INSTRUCTION PLAN

The Instruction Plan format (Figure 5.7) develops each unit of instruction for a training program. The process identifies the subject matter topic, briefly outlines the content, designates the specific types of training aids, and indicates what type of test and/or practical work will be used. The information contained in "sequence," "day," and "hours" is not filled in until all the units of instruction have been arranged in a tentative schedule. Developing a tentative schedule requires the use of a matrix such as is shown in Figure 5.7A, Assistant Store Manager Training Program—Tentative Schedule and Course Content Outline. Each unit of instruction, as described on respective Instruction Plan pages, is placed in an optimal sequence based on considerations such as:

1. Promoting a logical flow and development of information.
2. Grouping of related topics to foster an understanding of connections.
3. Maintaining participant interest through the placement of activities such as tours and demonstrations between formal classroom instruction.

Based on these types of considerations, the first day's schedule incorporates the following units of instruction:

1. Introduction to Company—Program Summary (Figure 5.7B)
2. Sales/Merchandising and Customer Relations (Figure 5.7C)
3. Advertising and Sales Promotion (Figure 5.7D)
4. Stocking-Pricing-Displaying-Signing (Figure 5.7E)
5. Stock Control-Inventory and Ordering (Figure 5.7F)
6. Buying—Hardlines (Figure 5.7G)
7. Buying—Softlines (Figure 5.7H)

INSTRUCTION PLAN

Training Program _____

Unit of Instruction _____

Sequence _____ Day _____ Hours _____

Instructor _____

CONTENT OUTLINE

TRAINING AIDS

TEST/PRACTICAL WORK

Figure 5.7 Instruction plan

Assistant Store Manager Training Program—Tentative Schedule and Course Content Outline

Schedule	Monday	Tuesday	Wednesday	Thursday	Friday
		XXXX	XXXX	XXXX	XXXX
8:00– 8:15	Registration				
8:30– 9:30	Introduction to Company—Program Summary	Receiving Controls	Cashiering Operations	Recruitment, Training, and Devt. of Employees	Review
9:30– 9:45	Break	Break	Break	Break	Break
9:45–10:45	Sales/Merchandising and Customer Relations	Warehouse Tour	Bookkeeping—Sales Reports	Tour of Main Office Functional Areas	Review
10:45–11:45	Advertising and Sales Promotion	Expense Control	Work Planning/Scheduling: The Store Payroll	Housekeeping	Test
11:45–12:45	Lunch	Lunch	Lunch	Lunch	Lunch
12:45– 1:45	Stocking—Pricing—Displaying—Signing	Security Procedures (Shrinkage)	Packing Operations Tour	Sales Planning	Critique and Discussion
1:45– 2:45	Stock Control—Inventory and Ordering	Safety and Accident Prevention	Store Timekeeping Procedures	Implementing Sales Programs	Sales = Key to Success
2:45– 3:00	Break	Break	Break	Break	Break
3:00– 4:00	Buying—Hardlines	Store Design—Training Store Tour	District Store Manager Inspections	Employee Appraisal Workshop	Your "P&L Statement"—the Bottom Line
4:00– 5:00	Buying—Softlines	Cash Register Demonstration	Personnel Policies—Procedures	Personal Development	Your Future—Promotions

Figure 5.7A Assistant store manager training program—tentative schedule and course content outline

INSTRUCTION PLAN

Training Program   Assistant Manager

Unit of Instruction   Introduction to Company—Program Summary

Sequence   1   Day   Monday   Hours   8:30-9:30

Instructor   HR Director/President/HR Development Manager

CONTENT OUTLINE

I. Introduction—HR Director

II. Welcoming Remarks—President

Growing Company with Advancement Opportunities for Highly Motivated and Hard-
working Individuals with Management Potential
Our Company: Historical, Present, and Future Perspectives

III. How to Fully Benefit from Participating in this Training Program—HR Development
Manager

An Overview of the Week's Activities and Objectives . . . Outlining Program Objectives . . . Previewing the Schedule . . . Administrative Details

TRAINING AIDS

Overhead Projector—Presenting Slides to Explain the Schedule
Question and Answer Period

TEST/PRACTICAL WORK

Figure 5.7B Introduction to company-program summary

INSTRUCTION PLAN

Training Program ___Assistant Manager___

Unit of Instruction ___Sales/Merchandising & Customer Relations___

Sequence ___2___ Day ___Monday___ Hours ___9:45–10:45___

Instructor ___Vice President—Merchandising___

CONTENT OUTLINE

I. Public Image—Public Contact = Opportunities for Selling the Company. Each Employee Is an Advertisement, Good or Bad, for Selling the Company

II. Welcoming Customers—The Personal Touch Pays Off . . . Giving Customers Friendly, Courteous, Individual Attention

III. Helping Customers—Offering Assistance . . . A Positive Approach Is Essential . . . Suggesting Alternative Merchandise Selections . . . Promoting Related Accessory and Timely Merchandise (raingear during a storm, etc.) . . . Pointers Concerning The Optimum Positioning of Sale Items

IV. Sincerity—The Value of Offering Sincere Thanks to Shoppers . . . The Route to Ensuring Repeat Business and Shopper Referrals of Other Customers

TRAINING AIDS

Training Booklet—"Promoting Sales Through Effective Customer Relations"

TEST/PRACTICAL WORK

Role Playing—A very dissatisfied customer is helped by an effective customer relations-oriented Assistant Store Manager

Figure 5.7C Sales merchandising and customer relations

INSTRUCTION PLAN

Training Program   Assistant Manager

Unit of Instruction   Advertising & Sales Promotion

Sequence   3   Day   Monday   Hours   10:45–11:45

Instructor   Director—Advertising

CONTENT OUTLINE

I. The Need for Advertising—General Approaches and Their Respective Benefits . . . The Role of The Advertising Agency

II. Media Coverage—TV/Radio/Newspapers—Review Samples and Discuss Their Relative Effectiveness . . . Explain How Each Store Benefits from Overall Program and Pays A "Fair Share" Cost

III. Special Campaigns—Seasonal Promotions . . . The Major Role of the Christmas Season in Achieving Annual Sales Objectives

IV. In Store Advertising Materials—The Store "Signing" Program . . . Techniques for Emphasizing Brand Names . . . Window Signs . . . Copies of Current Ads and Circulars on Display

TRAINING AIDS

- Sample TV Advertisement
- Sample Newspaper Insert
- Sample Newspaper Advertisement

TEST/PRACTICAL WORK

Figure 5.7D Advertising and sales promotion

INSTRUCTION PLAN

Training Program   Assistant Manager

Unit of Instruction   Stocking–Pricing–Displaying–Signing

Sequence   4   Day   Monday   Hours   12:45–1:45

Instructor   Guest District Manager

CONTENT OUTLINE

I. How to Face, Front, and Sign—Basic Principles and Practices for Displaying Merchandise

II. How to Display Ad Merchandise—Procedures for Setting Up Merchandise Displays for Advertised Merchandise . . . Timely Preparation . . . Maintenance During Sale . . . Taking Down Ads

TRAINING AIDS

Training Booklets—"Store Operational Procedures" & "Store Signing Program"

TEST/PRACTICAL WORK

Practical Work in Training Store

Figure 5.7E Stocking–Pricing–Displaying–Signing

INSTRUCTION PLAN

Training Program   Assistant Manager

Unit of Instruction   Stock Control—Inventory and Ordering

Sequence   5   Day   Monday   Hours   1:45–2:45

Instructor   Guest District Store Manager

CONTENT OUTLINE

I. Store Order Catalog—Ordering Regular Stock Requirements . . . Special Approaches for Ordering Items for Planned Advertisements . . . "Open-to-Buy $" versus Inventory . . . Effective Techniques for Ensuring Proper "Mix" of Merchandise . . . Knowing Customer Needs Provides Basis for More Effective Ordering and Increased Sales . . . Optimally Balancing Inventory to Maximize Basics and Other Highly Saleable Items . . . Handling Buyer Merchandise Distributions

II. Step-by-Step Procedures for Making Up an Order (Show Videotape)

TRAINING AIDS

- Sample Store Ordering Catalog
- Videotape—"Ordering" (Time = 15 Minutes)

TEST/PRACTICAL WORK

Practical Work in Training Store

Figure 5.7F Stock control—inventory and ordering

INSTRUCTION PLAN

Training Program ___Assistant Manager___

Unit of Instruction ___Buying—Hardlines___

Sequence ___6___ Day ___Monday___ Hours ___3:00–4:00___

Instructor ___General Merchandising Manager—Hardlines/Buyers___

CONTENT OUTLINE

I. <u>Introduction to Company Hardlines</u>—General Merchandising Manager-Hardlines
Product Mix . . . Seasonal Lines . . . Quality . . . Company Brands and Brand Names
. . . Future Lines . . . Tips for Successfully Merchandising Hardlines

II. <u>Introduce Buyers</u>—(Each shows new goods and/or samples of their best selling items)

- Smoking Accessories, Household Paper Goods, Cookware, Giftware, Christmas Items

- Photo, Electronics, Watches, Appliances, Personal Care Items

- Auto, Garden, Hardware, Electrical, Lamps, & Paint

- Toys

TRAINING AIDS

Samples of Products . . . New Goods That Will Be Available Soon . . . Examples of Best
Selling Items

TEST/PRACTICAL WORK

Figure 5.7G Buying—hardlines

INSTRUCTION PLAN

Training Program   Assistant Manager

Unit of Instruction   Buying—Softlines

Sequence   7   Day   Monday   Hours   4:00–5:00

Instructor   General Merchandising Manager—Softlines/Buyers

CONTENT OUTLINE

I. <u>Introduction to Company Softlines</u>—General Merchandising—Manager—Softlines
Product Mix . . . Seasonal Lines . . . Quality . . . Company Brands and Brand Names
. . . Future Lines . . . Tips for Successfully Merchandising Softlines

II. <u>Introduce Buyers</u>—(Each shows new goods and/or samples of their best selling items)

- Menswear & Boyswear

- Ladieswear & Girlswear

- Shoes

- Domestics

TRAINING AIDS

Samples of Products . . . New Goods Which Will Soon Be Available . . . Examples of
Best Selling Items

TEST/PRACTICAL WORK

Figure 5.7H Buying—softlines

5.8 EMPLOYEE DEVELOPMENT SUMMARY FORM

To compete for advancement opportunities based on company experience, an employee needs a format for summarizing the developmental growth he or she achieved in each of his or her positions. The Employee Development Summary form (Figure 5.8) is designed to meet this need.

A separate Employee Development Summary form is completed for each job/position. The initial portion of the form details the following categories:

- Dates
- Job/position title
- Organization and location
- Immediate supervisor's name and title
- Wage/salary progression
- Summary of principle duties and responsibilities
- Significant accomplishments and awards

The employee provides the following information on his or her training accomplishments:

- *Training Record*—list of course/seminar/workshop titles with respective completion dates and grades and ratings.
- *On-the-Job Training Record*—goals obtained and associated accomplishments and completion dates.

Maintenance of Employee Development Summary forms is a continuing employee responsibility. As the employee progresses through his or her career, a form is started for each new job/position. Copies of all forms are maintained in the employee's personnel record as a summary of his or her experience. The individual's forms serve as a résumé of company experience, which can be used in the company's internal placement program advancement decisions.

Employee Development Summary

Job/Position No. _____

Name _____   Social Security No. _____

An Employee Development Summary page is completed for each job/position you have held since joining the company. Please indicate the chronological sequence of each page by providing a job/position number in the upper right-hand corner (1 = your first job/position, etc.).

Dates: From _____ To _____

Job/Position Title _____

Organization _____ Location _____

Immediate Supervisor _____

Wage/Salary Progression: From $_____ per _____ To $_____ per _____

Summary of Principle Duties & Responsibilities

Significant Accomplishments and Awards

Training Record

Course/Seminar/Workshop Title	Completion Date	Grade/Rating
_____	_____	_____
_____	_____	_____
_____	_____	_____
_____	_____	_____

On-the-Job Training Record

Goals	Accomplishments	Completion Date

I certify that this information is correct and complete.

Signature _____ Date _____

Figure 5.8 Employee development summary

5.9 STUDENT EVALUATION OF TRAINING FORMS

The Company Training Course Evaluation form (Figure 5.9A) is structured to obtain anonymous ratings and comments in order to evaluate the effectiveness of a course. Anonymity promotes more candid and critical assessments. Constructive evaluations are encouraged by requesting comments. The employee is asked to explain problem areas identified in the rating process, and then suggest improvements to resolve these shortcomings.

Company Training Course Evaluation feedback is used by the instructor to modify the course appropriately. It also serves as the basis for instructor performance evaluations by the human resources development manager.

The Outside Training Course Assessment form (Figure 5.9B) requires the employee to go "on record" with an assessment of the value of the training. The employee initially rates the overall effectiveness of the course based on the following considerations.

1. Quality of instruction
2. Course content
3. Participation
4. Facilities

Each of these factors is rated either as excellent, satisfactory, or unsatisfactory. Explanations are requested for unsatisfactory ratings.

The employee then is asked to answer the following three questions ("no" responses require explanations).

1. Did the training meet your expectations by adequately providing the information outlined in the course announcement?
2. Would you recommend this course for other employees?
3. What changes, if any, would you recommend for improving this course?

This information is critically important to the human resources development department for determining whether the course is a worthwhile training experience for other employees.

The Outside Training Course Assessment form concludes with an employee statement that the course has been satisfactorily completed, and that supporting documentation is attached for his or her training record.

The Seminar Evaluation form (Figure 5.9C) is designed for assessing an in-house program. The form requires thoughtful consideration of eight evaluation factors and written responses. Participants in the seminar are advised that they do not have to identify themselves on the completed form.

The Seminar Evaluation forms provide essential feedback to the seminar leader(s) for improving future sessions. The human resources development manager also has the resultant data summarized to evaluate the seminar's overall effectiveness. If corrective action is needed, steps are taken to ensure that any problems are resolved before the next session is conducted.

Company Training Course Evaluation

Course Title _____

Evaluation Date _____

Your anonymous assessments and comments are needed to evaluate the effectiveness of this course. Please answer the following questions by circling the appropriate responses:

1. Organization of subject matter?	Well Organized	Adequate	Poorly Organized
2. Suitability of instructional materials?	Excellent	Acceptable	Poor
3. Level of difficulty?	Too Advanced	Appropriate	Too Basic
4. Length of course?	Too Long	Appropriate	Too Short
5. Coverage of subject matter?	Excellent	Acceptable	Poor
6. Instructor's effectiveness?	Excellent	Good	Poor
7. Were objectives accomplished?	Yes	Partially	No

Please provide comments to explain problems. Suggestions for improvements also would be appreciated. _____

_____

_____

_____

_____

_____

_____

Thank you for your assistance.

Figure 5.9A Company training course evaluation

Outside Training Course Assessment

Employee _____ Social Security No. _____

Job/Position Title _____

Organization _____

Name & Address of Training Organization _____

_____

Course Title _____ No. _____

Course Dates: From _____ To _____ No. of Days _____

Please rate the overall effectiveness of the course as follows:

	Excellent	Satisfactory	Unsatisfactory
1. Quality of Instruction	_____	_____	_____
2. Course Content	_____	_____	_____
3. Participation	_____	_____	_____
4. Facilities	_____	_____	_____

Please explain "unsatisfactory" ratings:

Did this training meet your expectations by adequately providing the information outlined in the course announcement?

_____Yes _____No (please explain)

Would you recommend this course for other employees?

_____Yes _____No (please explain)

What changes, if any, would you recommend for improving this course?

To: Manager—Human Resources Development

I have satisfactorily completed this course. Supporting documentation is attached for my training record.

Signature _____ Date _____

Figure 5.9B Outside training course assessment

Seminar Evaluation

Seminar Title _____

Evaluation Date _____

_____

1. Why did you attend this seminar?

2. Did the seminar meet your expectations and needs? Did it deliver what was promised? Were objectives met?

3. How dynamic, informative, and well organized were the seminar leaders?

4. What could have been done differently to increase the value of the seminar for you?

5. What topics could have been shortened or eliminated? What topics should have been given more time?

6. Did you have sufficient time to participate in discussions? Were you able to obtain answers for your questions?

7. How would you describe the overall quality and value of the seminar?

8. Will you recommend this seminar to your associates?

Figure 5.9C Seminar evaluation

5.10 EMPLOYEE TRAINING RECORD

A sample of an Employee Training Record format is shown in Figure 5.10. This form summarizes the individual's developmental experiences during his or her employment with the company. It is a key to the documentation filed in the employee's training record—that is, copies of Employee Training Request forms (refer to Figure 5.2) and supporting documentation relating to proof of course completion and expenses incurred.

Headings recommended in the construction of an Employee Training Record form include:

- Subject/title
- No. (Course number)
- Conducted by (company, name of institution, and so on)
- Type of training (seminar/course/workshop/on-the-job, and so on)
- Dates: from–to
- Days/Hours/Credits
- Rating/grade
- Cost

Employee Training Record of _____

Subject Title	No.	Conducted by	Type of Training	Dates		Days/Hours Credits	Rating	Cost
				From	To			

Figure 5.10 Employee training record

5.11 CERTIFICATE OF TRAINING

A sample Certificate of Training is shown in Figure 5.11. Suitable for framing, this form of recognition reinforces the positive benefits participation in training courses can provide. The certificate also serves as documentation of successful course completion. A copy is placed in the employee's personnel file as a permanent record of this developmental achievement.

Certificate of Training

_____

has satisfactorily completed a _____ hour course

_____

given at _____

Dated this_____day of_____19_____

_____   _____

Figure 5.11 Certificate of training

CHAPTER 6

Employee Performance and Conduct

A detailed procedure is offered for the annual performance appraisal process in Section 6.1. It maximizes interactions between the immediate supervisor and the employee for promoting understanding and commitment to valid performance objectives. In Section 6.2, guidelines are given for use in developing valid performance objectives. A highly personalized performance appraisal approach, which rates actual performance against a number of performance standards, is facilitated by use of the Performance Standard Appraisal form (see Figure 6.3). For designing more traditional performance appraisal systems, guidance is provided on performance appraisal factors in Section 6.4 and performance assessment ratings in Section 6.5. A sample Non-Exempt Employee Evaluation form (Figure 6.6) is provided for assessing hourly employee performance. An example of how to tailor performance appraisal forms to meet specialized requirements is shown in Figure 6.7, an Employee Performance Appraisal (Store Employees) form. A technique is outlined in Section 6.8 for eliminating biased performance appraisal problems. A sample company policy statement on performance appraisals is provided in Section 6.9. Highlights of procedures for assessing performance through a management by objectives program are offered in Section 6.10. A sample performance appraisal form for managerial and professional personnel is shown as Figure 6.11. Guidelines are included in Section 6.12 for effective employee disciplinary actions; the Disciplinary Action Report form (Figure 6.13A) and the Employee Conduct Inquiry Statement (Figure 6.13B) are used in documenting this process. Employee innovations are promoted through an Employee Suggestion Program (Section 6.14). An Employee of the Month Program and awards for excellence are explained in Section 6.15.

6.1 THE ANNUAL PERFORMANCE APPRAISAL PROCESS

A recommended approach to the performance appraisal process, which maximizes interactions between the immediate supervisor and the employee in the interest of promoting understanding of and commitment to objectives, involves the five-step procedure shown in Figure 6.1:

Plan Performance Objectives (Step 1)

A. *Reviewing Job/Position Description.* The employee and immediate supervisor meet at the beginning of each appraisal period to ensure that the employee's job/position description is accurate. Changes are made as required to adequately describe all current duties and responsibilities. Agreement is reached concerning the validity of the revised job/position description.

B. *Establishing Performance Requirements.* After the job/position description has been reviewed and modified as required to define all duties and responsibilities, it can serve as a valid basis for judging performance. The immediate supervisor and the employee are able to identify specific elements of the job that will be used to assess performance. Their goal is to translate supervisory expectations concerning employee performance into objective understandings. To the extent possible, quantifiable objectives are established.

Review Progress and Take Corrective Action (Steps 2, 3, and 4)

Periodic counseling sessions are used to evaluate progress and provide the feedback needed to correct or improve employee performance. These informal meetings take place every three months. Critical performance problems are discussed and appropriate corrective actions are taken as they occur. Revised understandings and commitments are documented.

Conduct Annual Performance Appraisal Conference (Step 5)

Conducted during the eleventh month of the annual appraisal period, this conference is the employee's opportunity to offer data which may affect the final performance rating. The immediate supervisor reviews preliminary findings for each rating factor with the employee. The employee is encouraged to provide any information that should be considered in arriving at his or her final performance ratings, and to ask any questions that will promote understanding and improve future performance. At the conclusion of this conference, the immediate supervisor prepares the final performance appraisal document, and forwards it to the next higher level of management for review and approval. Higher management may, based on this review process, revise the employee's overall performance appraisal rating.

Plan Performance Objectives (Repeat Step 1)

During the twelfth month of the annual performance appraisal period, the employee reviews and signs the final performance appraisal document to indicate his or her understanding of the findings and related performance improvement objectives. The annual performance appraisal process begins again at this time with a review of the job/position description to ensure that it is still valid, and the revision or addition of performance objectives as needed to properly evaluate future accomplishments.

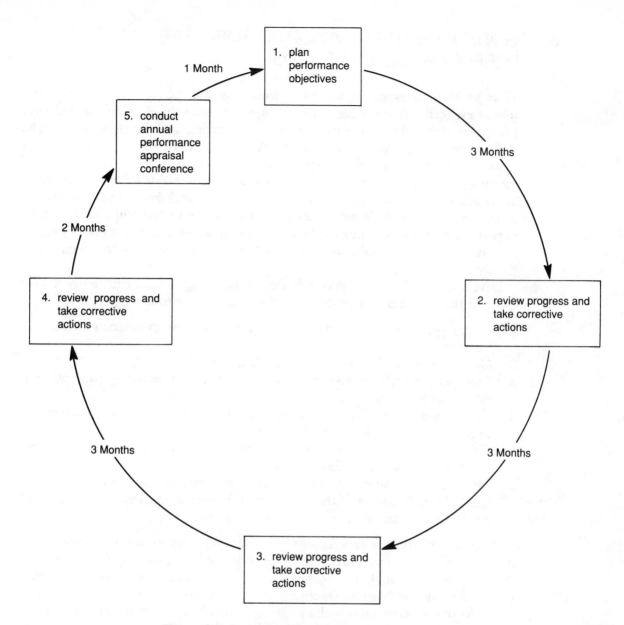

Figure 6.1 Annual performance appraisal process

6.2 GUIDELINES FOR DEVELOPING EMPLOYEE PERFORMANCE STANDARDS

To objectively assess an employee's performance, well defined statements of job-related expectations are needed. For example, consider an electronic technician's job description, which primarily involves the testing and certification of radio transmitters at a manufacturing facility. A major performance standard for this individual might be stated as, "satisfactory performance requires setting up and running the three-step certification testing sequence on HF-101E transmitter units in an average of 15 minutes per unit (28 units per workday)." The standard accounts for the employee's two fifteen-minute breaks and a one-half hour luncheon period during the eight hour workday; therefore, seven productive hours yielding four units per hour results in a performance requirement of twenty eight units per day.

Developing performance standards that quantify expectations in terms of how many or the rate of productivity should be based on the following criteria:

1. *Timing*—an average yield per specific unit of time, or an outcome by a particular date.
2. *Quantity*—number of units per specific unit of time.
3. *Cost*—effectiveness in meeting cost limitations, or in reducing costs per unit or outcome.
4. *Comparisons Versus Past*—improvement by specified quantity or percentage over prior measurement period.
5. *Comparison Versus Others*—improvement by amount or percentage as compared with average for other organizational units.
6. *Absolutes*—stipulated achievements for new activities, for example, specific quotas by each quarter of the year for a new product line; expressed in units of production, dollar value of sales orders, and so on.

Because performance expectations for many jobs and positions cannot be reduced to numbers, you must find other reasonable approaches for assessment. Processes involving subjective opinions are a poor substitute for reasonably objective, observable, and assessable criteria. Definitive wording should be chosen to avoid the use of generalities such as "timely," "well," "as much as possible," and so on, in describing requirements. For example, an element for assessing the performance of an electronics engineer may be stated as, "satisfactory performance requires consistent accuracy in calculations required for reducing test data to yield statistically sound conclusions."

6.3 PERFORMANCE APPRAISAL BY JOB-RELATED PERFORMANCE STANDARDS

A highly personalized system for performance appraisal involves the following process:

1. The employee and supervisor review the individual's job/position description to identify those elements that will be used for assessing performance—that is, work tasks, duties, functions, responsibilities and/or activities of the job.
2. Performance standards are written by the supervisor, who determines the relative importance of each for arriving at an overall performance evaluation. Each of these standards specifies measurements of satisfactory achievement defined in terms of quantity, quality, or timeliness.
3. Actual performance is compared with the performance standards to determine whether an acceptable overall level of performance has been achieved. The evaluation serves as a basis for appropriate rewards and corrective actions.

A sample Performance Standard Appraisal form, which provides the basis for implementing this type of an appraisal process, is shown in Figure 6.3.

Performance Standard Appraisal

Page _____ of _____ Pages

Evaluation Period: From _____ To _____

Employee _____ Job/Position Title _____ Social Security No. _____

Organization _____ Location _____ Supervisor _____

Performance Standard—Describe the results that will be achieved when the employee satisfactorily performs each major function/task of the job/position. Show the relative value of each performance standard by specifying the % of the overall rating (100%) which it represents. *Description of Actual Performance*—Compare results achieved versus each performance standard to determine the appropriate rating as follows: Failed to Meet Requirements = 0, Meets Requirements = 1, and Exceeds Requirements = 2. The overall rating is calculated by using the table on the reverse side of this form.

Performance Standard	%	Description of Actual Performance	Rating

Figure 6.3 Performance standard appraisal

continued

Performance Standard Appraisal Results

#	(1) %		(2) Rating		(3) Score
1	_._____	×	_____	=	___.___
2	_._____	×	_____	=	___.___
3	_._____	×	_____	=	___.___
4	_._____	×	_____	=	___.___
5	_._____	×	_____	=	___.___
6	_._____	×	_____	=	___.___
7	_._____	×	_____	=	___.___
8	_._____	×	_____	=	___.___
9	_._____	×	_____	=	___.___
10	_._____	×	_____	=	___.___
11	_._____	×	_____	=	___.___
12	_._____	×	_____	=	___.___
13	_._____	×	_____	=	___.___
14	_._____	×	_____	=	___.___
15	_._____	×	_____	=	___.___
			(4) Total	=	___.___

\# = PERFORMANCE STANDARD number

(1) = % (expressed as decimal) of the overall performance appraisal represented by the PERFORMANCE STANDARD

(2) = RATING for actual performance achieved versus the PERFORMANCE STANDARD, e.g., "Exceeds Requirements = 2"

(3) = Multiplying (1) × (2) yields the score

(4) = The TOTAL for column (3), the SCORE, is converted into an OVERALL RATING as follows:

Total Score		Overall Rating
0–0.74	=	Unsatisfactory
.75–1.74	=	Satisfactory
1.75–2.00	=	Exceptional

Approvals:

Supervisor _____

Date _____

Manager _____

Date _____

Employee acknowledgment

_____ Date _____

Figure 6.3 *(cont.)*

271

6.4 PERFORMANCE APPRAISAL FACTORS

To build a performance appraisal system that meets your company's needs, consider the following:

1. *Quantity.* The volume (output) of work regularly and consistently produced. The degree of productivity represented by a specific amount or measurement. The effective use of time; speed versus time limits. Meeting schedules.

2. *Quality.* The degree of excellence that characterizes the individual's contributions. The acceptability of products or results; how well the individual meets requirements for accuracy, effectiveness, thoroughness, neatness, and dependability. Accuracy versus errors; freedom from errors, or a specified expectation regarding the number of errors.

3. *Job Knowledge and Skills.* The adequacy and thoroughness of information gained through education (general and specialized) for providing mastery of job-related duties and responsibilities. Understanding job requirements; the interrelationships among operational functions; the company's operations, policies, and procedures. Promotes the ability to act independently with minimal supervision.

4. *Dependability/Reliability.* The degree to which the individual may be counted upon or entrusted to carry out instructions and assignments, to be present at work (versus absenteeism and tardiness), and to generally fulfill responsibilities. Reliably and consistently meets work schedules and other deadlines.

5. *Initiative/Innovation.* The degree of resourcefulness, originality, and independent action in performing tasks and assignments. Special contributions and efforts involve developing and introducing new ideas and methods that improve work processes. Seeks additional responsibilities.

6. *Attitude.* The degree of application and enthusiasm that characterizes the individual's efforts to promote the company's best interests. Responsiveness and willingness to help co-workers, to perform special and emergency work assignments, to learn new skills, and so on.

7. *Communication.* The degree of effectiveness for giving and exchanging information through written and oral expressions. Clear, concise, persuasive, and articulate skills. Includes the individual's effectiveness in listening to others and benefitting from other viewpoints.

8. *Adaptability.* The degree of versatility/flexibility in readily adapting behavior to adjust to changing conditions; and to learn new ideas, procedures, duties, and so on. Using skill and judgment to place priorities in proper perspective.

9. *Judgment.* The degree of facility for selecting among alternative courses of action to arrive at sound decisions. Using intelligence and common sense to arrive at logical and reasonable conclusions based on objective analyses of data.

10. *Interpersonal/Human Relations.* The degree of effectiveness in influencing and cooperating with other individuals in work-related relationships (other employees, co-workers, supervisor, management, customers, other company representatives, and so on).

11. *Supervision.* The degree of effectiveness in planning, organizing, delegating, directing, and controlling the work of others. Achieves objectives through the maximally efficient and timely utilization of resources.

6.5 PERFORMANCE ASSESSMENT RATINGS

A five-level system ranging from excellent to unsatisfactory offers the spectrum needed to thoroughly distinguish relative degrees of performance and determine ratings. The following guidelines are offered for constructing rating categories that will meet your company's requirements:

1. *Excellent/Outstanding/Distinguished/Exceptional/Superior.* Far exceeds position requirements. Exceptional contributions and accomplishments. Performance consistently exceeds standards in all aspects of work.
2. *Very Good/Commendable.* Generally and consistently exceeds position requirements. Excels by exceeding standards for many aspects of work.
3. *Good/Competent/Fully Acceptable/Satisfactory.* Regularly meets normal position requirements. Fully and adequately meets standards. No major problems with performance.
4. *Fair/Adequate/Marginally Acceptable/Provisional/Poor.* Does not consistently meet position requirements. Specific improvements are needed for achieving a satisfactory overall performance rating.
5. *Unsatisfactory/Unacceptable.* Consistently fails to meet position requirements. Unacceptable performance does not merit retention unless relatively immediate corrective actions are possible.

6.6 NON-EXEMPT EMPLOYEE EVALUATION FORM

This sample performance evaluation form (Figure 6.6) has been designed to meet the assessment requirements of factory workers, service industry workers, and clerical personnel.

Section 6.4, Performance Appraisal Factors, was used as the basis for developing the following appropriate factors:

I.   Quantity and Quality were combined into an assessment of "work performance"
II.   Job Knowledge and Skills
III. Initiative/Innovation
IV.   Dependability/Reliability
V.   Attitude and Interpersonal/Human Relations were combined into an assessment of "cooperation"

Quantity was not selected as a separate rating factor because of its exclusive ties to traditional assessments of productivity. Although the assembly line jobs of factory workers lend themselves to quantifiable output standards, assessments of productivity based on specific amounts become very difficult as the worker moves into the varied work requirements of an office environment or the somewhat intangible results expected from service workers. *Quality*—the degree of results-oriented excellence that characterizes the worker's contributions—becomes a more viable evaluation tool. Accordingly, a combined factor, "I. Work Performance," considers accuracy, speed, quantity, and quality of work products. Another very important factor for assessing productivity in jobs that do not involve specific volumes of output is "III. Initiative." The worker's enthusiasm and demonstrated resourcefulness in developing and introducing new and improved work methods is an excellent index of effectiveness.

The Non-Exempt Employee Evaluation form includes performance rating categories and a point-scoring technique which promote greater objectivity. The stigma associated with rating an individual as unsatisfactory, which suggests a decision to terminate the employee, is avoided by using "poor" as the lowest rating category. An explanation is required when an employee receives this overall rating. The immediate supervisor must describe why the employee should be retained, and provide details regarding immediate corrective actions which will be taken to achieve an acceptable level of performance. Similarly, a "fair" overall rating also requires an explanation of planned corrective actions. The expected level of performance is realistically reflected by "fair" and "good" rating categories. Those rare individuals who do not need to increase their efforts in certain areas of performance to fully meet all expectations would receive a "good" (fully satisfactory/meets all job requirements) rating under this system. To be rated as "outstanding," a perfect point score is required. Also required are examples of significant accomplishments, contributions, and so on, which merit this unique recognition.

The form includes provisions for the employee to acknowledge understanding of the evaluation and any required corrective actions.

Non-Exempt Employee Evaluation

Name _____ Job Title _____ Social Security No. _____

Organization _____ Location _____ Supervisor _____

Date of Hire _____ Date Started in Present Position _____ Appraisal Period: From _____ To _____

Instructions: For each of the following factors, rate the employee's performance by considering job requirements and the comparable performance of other employees in the same type of job. Performance ratings yield point scores as follows: POOR = 1 point; FAIR = 2 points; GOOD = 3 points; and OUTSTANDING = 4 points. The total of these points provides an overall rating: 5–9 = POOR; 10–14 = FAIR; 15–19 = GOOD; and 20 = OUTSTANDING.

Factors	Performance Ratings (Points)				Points
	Poor (1)	Fair (2)	Good (3)	Outstanding (4)	
I. *Work Performance*—Meets requirements for accuracy, speed, quantity, and quality of work products	____	____	____	____	____
II. *Job Knowledge*—Demonstrates understanding of duties and mastery of required skills	____	____	____	____	____
III. *Initiative*—Displays resourcefulness and energy in carrying out work assignments	____	____	____	____	____
IV. *Reliability*—Performs work dependably in a consistent manner; no absence or lateness problems	____	____	____	____	____
V. *Cooperation*—Works harmoniously and effectively with co-workers and supervisors	____	____	____	____	____

Total Points = _____

Overall Rating = _____

Approvals _____ Date _____

_____ Date _____

Figure 6.6 Non-exempt employee evaluation

continued

275

Non-exempt Employee Evaluation for _____

Explanation: If the employee receives a POOR overall rating, explain why he or she should be retained. A program of immediate corrective actions should be specified. If the employee receives a FAIR overall rating, explain the corrective actions that are planned to accomplish required performance improvements. If the employee achieves an OUTSTANDING overall rating, provide examples of significant accomplishments, contributions, etc., which merit this recognition.

_____

_____

_____

_____

_____

_____

_____

_____

_____

_____

_____

Employee Comments and Acknowledgment:

_____   _____
Employee Signature   Date

Figure 6.6 *(cont.)*

6.7 SPECIALIZED EMPLOYEE PERFORMANCE APPRAISAL FORM—RETAIL STORE EMPLOYEES

This performance appraisal form is designed to illustrate how specialized needs can be met by the addition of evaluation factors. The Employee Performance Appraisal (Store Employees) form shown in Figure 6.7 serves the needs of a small convenience-type store where employees perform the wide variety of duties involved in all phases of daily operations. The high level of turnover experienced in these types of stores dictates frequent assessments and definitions of training requirements to correct performance deficiencies of new employees. Accordingly, the introduction to the form states: "The purpose of this performance appraisal is to inventory a store employee's strengths and weaknesses every 3 months to ensure mutual understanding of problem areas, and to develop practical plans for improvement."

The twenty appraisal factors include several that are unique to store operations. These considerations are listed below.

Merchandising (9)*—understanding of marketing techniques.
Cash Control (11)—effectiveness in properly handling cash, credit cards, checks, and so on.
Customer Service (12)—skill in promoting sales through effective customer relations.
Selling Ability (14)—degree of aggressiveness in improving sales.

Other unique factors that have broader application include:

Ability to Learn (4)—degree of comprehension and retention of information.
Safety (8)—compliance with safety rules, and reduction of hazards.
Housekeeping (10)—effectiveness in maintaining a clean and sanitary work environment.
Appearance (13)—well groomed, properly dressed, and good personal hygiene.
Emotional Stability (15)—degree of self-control as evidenced by steadiness and well balanced behavior under pressure.
Motivation (16)—degree of drive for achieving realistic goals; improving one's position.
Responsibility (17)—ability to assume responsibilities and accept the consequences of one's actions.
Administration (18)—effectiveness in preparing reports, maintaining records, and so on.
Potential (20)—degree of willingness and ability to train for promotional opportunities.

The reverse side of the form contains sections for detailing the employee's performance in terms of strengths and weaknesses. Specific goals are specified for improving weaknesses. The "employee acknowledgment" section includes a statement that the individual fully understands the plans that have been made for specific improvements—that is, his/her goals.

---

* Numbers in parentheses correspond to numbered entries in Figure 6–7.

EMPLOYEE PERFORMANCE APPRAISAL

STORE EMPLOYEES   NAME _____

Last   First   Initial

THE PURPOSE OF THIS PERFORMANCE APPRAISAL IS TO INVENTORY A STORE EMPLOYEE'S STRENGTHS AND WEAKNESSES EVERY 3 MONTHS TO ENSURE MUTUAL UNDERSTANDING OF PROBLEM AREAS AND TO DEVELOP PRACTICAL PLANS FOR IMPROVEMENT: EACH OF 20 FACTORS IS TO BE EVALUATED WITH RATINGS SHOWN IN RESPECTIVE BOXES: 0=UNSATISFACTORY; 1=SATISFACTORY; 2=GOOD; 3=OUTSTANDING.

1. QUALITY OF WORK   ☐
How precise, accurate, complete and neat?

2. QUANTITY OF WORK   ☐
Amount of output? Degree of productivity?

3. COOPERATION   ☐
How well does employee work with co-workers?

4. ABILITY TO LEARN   ☐
Degree of comprehension and retention of information?

5. KNOWLEDGE OF WORK   ☐
How efficient, thorough, and detailed is employee's understanding of job requirements?

6. DEPENDABILITY   ☐
Can be counted on to reliably perform? Attendance and lateness record?

7. INITIATIVE   ☐
Self-starter? Degree of supervision required?

8. SAFETY   ☐
Compliance with safety rules? Reduction of hazards?

9. MERCHANDISING   ☐
Degree of understanding of marketing techniques, i.e., proper displaying, signing, etc.?

10. HOUSEKEEPING   ☐
Maintains clean and sanitary environment?

11. CASH CONTROL   ☐
Properly safeguards and handles cash? Asset protection effectiveness?

12. CUSTOMER SERVICE   ☐
How skillful in dealing with customers to promote sales and repeat business?

13. APPEARANCE   ☐
Well groomed, properly dressed, and good personal hygiene?

14. SELLING ABILITY   ☐
Aggressively improves sales? Awareness of profit objectives?

15. EMOTIONAL STABILITY   ☐
Steady and well balanced under pressure? Self-control?

16. MOTIVATION   ☐
Drive to achieve goals? Realistically ambitious? Seeks to improve position?

17. RESPONSIBILITY   ☐
Willing to accept consequences of actions? Does not evade duties?

18. ADMINISTRATION   ☐
Effectively conducts inventories, maintains records, prepares reports, keeps personal time record in accordance with company policy, etc.?

19. ATTITUDE   ☐
Positive attitude towards company, its objectives, its management, etc.?

20. POTENTIAL   ☐
Willing and able to train for promotional opportunities?

| 1–10 TOTAL POINTS | | | 11–20 TOTAL POINTS | |

Figure 6.7 Employee performance appraisal

continued

TOTAL POINTS _____

  1 – 10 TOTAL POINTS = _____

11 – 20 TOTAL POINTS = _____

            TOTAL POINTS = _____

**OVERALL PERFORMANCE
APPRAISAL RATING** _____

TOTAL POINTS = OVERALL RATING

Less than 10 POINTS = UNSATISFACTORY

10 to   30   POINTS = SATISFACTORY

30 to 50   POINTS = GOOD

50 POINTS and ABOVE = OUTSTANDING

EMPLOYEE'S OVERALL PERFORMANCE RATING _____ Date Reviewed _____

COMMENTS: What explanatory details, both positive and negative, should be provided in explaining this employee's performance? Provide detailed explanations in this section.

STRENGTHS:

WEAKNESSES:

GOALS:

RECOMMENDATIONS & GENERAL COMMENTS:

PERFORMANCE APPRAISAL CONDUCTED BY:

Store Manager Signature _____ **Date** _____

EMPLOYEE ACKNOWLEDGEMENT: My Store Manager and I have discussed the contents of this performance appraisal. I fully understand the plans which have been made for specific improvements, i.e., my "GOALS".

Employee Signature _____ **Date** _____

Figure 6.7 *(cont.)*

6.8 DEALING WITH BIASED PERFORMANCE RATINGS

Personal experience as a human resources director convinced this author that it is futile to use conventional appraisal techniques in rating the performance of secretaries and administrative assistants. Predictably, all these employees were rated as outstanding by managers who depended on the continued good will and support of these individuals for their own survival.

Because merit salary increase percentages are tied to performance ratings, unmerited outstanding ratings are problematic. The solution lies in not using conventional performance appraisal approaches, but in opting for a system which offers the following features.

1. *Accomplishment Summary Memorandum.* Each manager prepares a memorandum that provides examples of specific accomplishments, special contributions, and so on of the secretary/executive secretary/administrative assistant during the rating period. Each example is assigned a relative percentage of its impact on the overall performance, that is, 100 percent. Incumbents are encouraged to participate in and identify with this rating process by preparing a *draft* version of this memorandum.

   A sample special accomplishment paragraph in a memorandum for an administrative assistant to the vice president of marketing may include the following information:

   > (75%) Conducted special study of relative effectiveness of prospective advertising agencies in meeting promotional goals.

   > Requested data from 3 agencies under consideration regarding their top 10 client activities. Compared client dollar investments for services versus sales increases which were potentially attributable to advertising programs. Developed relative cost effectiveness assessments, which demonstrated that Smith & Smith clearly evidenced outstanding performance by yielding 12% level annual sales gains; the nearest competitor was in the 8% range. Recommendations led to contracting with this effective agency. Their creative approaches during the past six months already have yielded a 7% improvement in sales with no increase in advertising costs. The projected annual bottom-line yield for an estimated sales increase of 14% is estimated at $1,200,000.

2. *Rating Panels.* For each type of comparable position classification, for example the same level of executive secretaries, a *rating panel* reviews the accomplishment summary memorandum to classify each individual's performance. Three levels of performance are defined as follows:

   III. Fully Meets Position Requirements—accomplishments demonstrate that position requirements are very adequately and resourcefully achieved. Accomplishments include some significant contributions.

   II. Exceeds Position Requirements—accomplishments include a substantial amount of significant achievements.

   I. Far Exceeds Position Requirements—accomplishments primarily are highly significant achievements.

The rating panel, which is composed of a representative sample of management representatives and the HR director, attempts to achieve the following statistical distribution of ratings:

$$
\begin{aligned}
\text{III} &= 70\% \\
\text{II} &= 20\% \\
\text{I} &= \underline{10\%} \\
&\ 100\%
\end{aligned}
$$

This distribution permits the translation of these ratings for merit increase purposes to the percentages prescribed for average (III), above average (II), and outstanding (I) performance.

3. *Employee Communication.* Managers communicate the rating panel findings to their respective subordinates, who are encouraged to understand that excellence also has its relative degrees.

6.9 SAMPLE COMPANY POLICY STATEMENT FOR PERFORMANCE APPRAISALS

A typical company policy statement and procedure for the administration of the performance appraisal, using the form shown as Figure 6.11, follows:

I. *Objective*

The performance of all managerial and professional personnel will be appraised annually to determine the extent of their contributions to the company. Evaluations of overall performance will reflect the degree to which employee-established performance objectives have been achieved.

II. *Procedures*

A. The Performance Appraisal (managerial and professional personnel) form is used by an employee for specifying performance objectives, results to be accomplished, and associated completion dates. Proposed objectives are developed by the employee and reviewed with the immediate supervisor to obtain agreement and approval. This action is required at the beginning of each twelve-month evaluation period.

B. The employee is required to define at least two major performance objectives. Definitions are subject to review and revision based on agreements reached between the employee and supervisor during a required goal-setting conference.

C. A *probationary review* will be held for new managerial and professional employees immediately prior to their completion of six months of employment. Progress in meeting planned objectives is assessed.

D. An *interim review* may be scheduled at the time performance objectives are established; scheduling can be for three, six, or nine months after the beginning of the evaluation period. An interim review is required to assess progress toward complex objectives which may require redirection or revision of planned actions. An interim review also is required in those cases where an employee must demonstrate significantly improved performance, as stipulated during the individual's annual review, in less than the normal twelve-month evaluation period.

E. At the end of an evaluation period, the employee and the immediate supervisor will meet to review accomplishments. This is the employee's opportunity to present written and verbal information on his or her self-assessment of achievements.

F. The supervisor assesses the individual's performance to determine appropriate ratings, establish an overall rating, and develop recommendations concerning necessary improvements and related development program activities. This process is recorded in the appropriate portions of the Performance Appraisal—Managerial and Professional Personnel form.

G. The completed Performance Appraisal form is reviewed and approved by the immediate supervisor's superior, who may revise ratings and developmental plans based on personal observations concerning the employee's contributions and needs.

H. Performance Appraisal results are discussed in detail with the employee by the immediate supervisor. This appraisal conference should yield an agreement regarding "development program" objectives, which may include specific work assignments, educational courses, and other developmental experiences designed to improve the individual's work performance.

I. The Performance Appraisal form is annotated to indicate whether the results have been reviewed with the employee, then forwarded to the human resources management division for inclusion in the employee's personnel record.

6.10 MANAGEMENT DEVELOPMENT NEWSLETTERS—INTRODUCING AN MBO PROGRAM

To assist in explaining a new management by objectives program, and its results-oriented appraisal process, two Management Development Newsletters may be issued in successive weeks to all managerial and professional employees. Recommended samples follow.

Management by Objectives Program (Part I)

This Management Development Newsletter introduces a new objective-centered performance and review process for all professional and managerial personnel. The "management by objectives" process calls for specific performance objectives to be established for each position. These objectives must be consistent with overall corporate goals as well as the related goals of each division, and must identify well defined results to be achieved over a given period of time, usually a year. At the end of this period, actual achieved results are measured against planned goals.

The process of measuring results against planned goals is derived from the sound principle that managers and other professionals should be measured by their accomplishments. Their value to the company is not based on what they do, but on what they get done.

Management by objectives calls upon participants to define their jobs in terms of what should be accomplished and specific results that should be achieved. Each individual writes down personal performance objectives for the coming year, and specifies plans and timing for their achievement. Objectives then are submitted to the immediate supervisor for review. The employee and the supervisor discuss plans and arrive at a mutually agreeable set of objectives. Depending on the timing of the proposed accomplishments, they get together to discuss the individual's progress on an interim basis. Objectives and plans are revised and updated as needed during these conferences. At the end of the year, results actually achieved are compared with the results expected to be achieved. Reasons why goals are not met are explored, and a new set of objectives is developed for the twelve-month period.

This objective-centered approach to performance appraisal is based on mutual planning and problem solving. It goes well beyond the traditional approach where the immediate supervisor makes an independent judgment regarding the individual's performance. Now, the amount and direction of individual growth and job performance improvement largely are controlled by the quality of the objectives that the employee has established.

Quantitative Performance Objectives: Here are a few basic examples of managerial performance objectives which specifically and realistically state what must be accomplished. To the maximum extent possible, they are quantified in terms of revenue, cost, sales volume, return on investment, units of production, or other specific measures.

   Construction Manager—complete construction of Michigan plant addition within estimated cost of $750,000.

Human Resources Director—reduce unit cost of clerical personnel recruitment from $3,000 to $2,500 (17 percent), without sacrificing quality, through increased advertising and employment staff interviewing activity.

Controller—reduce clerical accounting labor costs by $300,000 through acquiring improved PC software.

Sales Director—increase sales of condominium apartments by 25 percent at Baltimore development.

General Counsel—reduce outside legal counsel costs by 15 percent.

Management by Objectives Program (Part II)

Early next month, all managerial and professional personnel will receive a copy of the new Performance Appraisal form for setting their performance objectives. A sample copy of this form is attached for your information. (NOTE: Sample provided in Figure 6.11.)

Each manager and professional employee will be required to develop at least two major goals and four or more minor goals. These goals are summarized in the "objectives" section of the form. They are defined in terms of the specific results to be achieved, how results are to be measured, and respective completion dates. These proposed objectives are reviewed by the employee with his or her immediate supervisor. This review conference will ensure that objectives are consistent with overall company/division/department/action plans. The supervisor also will ensure that each goal is realistically attainable by the employee. Objective statements and completion dates are revised accordingly, then both the employee and the immediate supervisor sign the form to indicate their agreement.

Interim review date(s) may be scheduled and shown in the space provided in the heading of the form. These interim conferences generally are required in those cases where extremely complex planned actions may require redirection or revision before the end of the usual twelve-month period. The timing of these interim evaluations may be on a three-month, six-month, or nine-month basis.

The employee maintains an approved copy of his or her objectives as the basis for self-assessment of progress. At the end of the evaluation period, the employee and supervisor will meet to review the accomplishments. This meeting is the employee's opportunity to present written and verbal information on his or her self-assessment of achievements. The supervisor will use this conference to determine how closely the employee's performance approximates anticipated results. These supervisory assessments are shown in the "evaluation" section of the form. Each "rating" will play a part in evaluating the employee's "accomplishment" (see second part of form). The employee also is evaluated from the standpoints of "thinking," "administration," "relationships," and "knowledge." Each of these rating factors involves a basic question which is answered for both managerial and professional personnel; associated questions are rated only for managers.

In each case, an "overall appraisal of performance" is developed by considering ratings on all the factors. This consideration involves weighing those factors heavily which have the greatest bearing on the requirement's of the individual's present position. This assessment yields the rating that most accurately characterizes the individual's overall performance.

A development program may be proposed as needed to assist the individual in improving work performance. Such actions may involve special work assignments, educational courses, or other developmental experiences.

The supervisor will review ratings and development program recommendations with his or her superior, who may revise assessments or plans based on personal evaluations of the individual's contributions and needs.

The appraisal should be discussed in detail with the employee. This appraisal conference should yield an agreed-upon development program which is summarized on the form.

When this process is completed, the Performance Appraisal form is forwarded to the human resources management division for inclusion in the employee's personnel record.

6.11 PERFORMANCE APPRAISAL FORM

To evaluate the performance of managerial and professional employees in a company, which emphasizes management by objectives program results (see Section 6.10), assessments may focus solely on the individual's achievements. For example, the performance appraisal process could be limited to the information shown on the front of the sample form provided in Figure 6.11, Performance Appraisal (Managerial and Professional Personnel). Each of the individual's objectives are specified in terms of describing the action, what is to be achieved, how it is to be measured, and the planned completion date. At the time when the immediate supervisor assesses the individual's performance, the overall question is, "how effective has the individual been during the past year in producing tangible, measurable results?" Achievements for each specified objective are evaluated, and qualitative ratings are assigned as follows:

A = Outstanding—rarely equaled
B = Excellent—clearly exceeds job requirements
C = Average—meets job requirements
D = Below Average—meets minimum job requirements
E = Unsatisfactory—fails to meet job requirements

To arrive at an overall rating of performance, consideration is given to the relative importance of major versus minor goals. If this relationship is established to be 2:1, then individual ratings for each objective would be translated into the following numerical values:

Major Goal	Minor Goal
A = 12	A = 6
B = 8	B = 4
C = 4	C = 2
D = 2	D = 1
E = 0	E = 0

Given a system in which the individual was required to set two major and four minor goals, an overall rating of outstanding would require 48 points.

Overall Ratings

Rating	Points Required
A	48
B	32
C	16
D	8

Although using this type of an approach to evaluate only the individual's accomplishments serves pragmatic objectives, much is lost in the process. A hybrid evaluation approach, which includes traditional assessment factors, offers increased benefits. For example, consider the factors included on the back of the sample Performance Appraisal form. A particularly relevant example is "relationships"—that is, how effective is the individual in dealing with others? Although an individual may have been very successful in meeting objectives as evidenced by tangible results, you must consider whether others paid a price for this individual's apparent successes. If the individual is the type of person who generates conflicts through inept and inappropriate interpersonal relationships, the effectiveness of others in meeting overall

288 • CHAPTER 6

organizational objectives is adversely affected. Accordingly, the individual's accomplishments are weighed against the negative impact that his or her behavior had on the ability of others to achieve their objectives, which collectively represent the best interests of the company.

This approach requires sound assessments of the individual's overall performance by weighing his or her accomplishments as well as the following factors:

Thinking. What caliber of thinking does the individual apply in the performance of work?

Administration. How effective is the individual in performing duties?

Relationships. How effective is the individual in dealing with others?

Knowledge. What is the level of the individual's understanding of functional and environmental matters pertaining to the position, and how effective is the individual in applying this knowledge?

To arrive at an overall rating, the immediate supervisor gives primary emphasis to those factors that have the greatest bearing on the requirements of the employee's position. The rating that results from these judgments should accurately characterize the individual's overall performance. The intent is not to diminish the value of accomplishments, but to give credit to the employee for personal effectiveness factors which promote the present and future interests of the company. Accordingly, an individual whose objectives-related accomplishments are rated as average (meets job requirements) has the potential for an excellent (clearly exceeds job requirements) rating when other factors are considered.

Performance Appraisal
(Managerial and Professional Personnel)

Personal and Confidential

Name _____ Position _____

Immediate Supervisor (Name and Position) _____

Division _____ Department _____ Location _____

Evaluation Period: Beginning _____ Probationary or Interim Review _____ Ending _____

INSTRUCTIONS: Supervisor will provide this form to employee for "Objectives" information. Employee will define at least two major performance objectives for the Evaluation Period. Each objective is to be stated in terms of specific results to be attained; a target completion date is to be designated. Goals then are to be reviewed with supervisor. Both will sign below to indicate approval. Employee is to keep a copy of approved objectives to serve as basis for self-assessment of progress. Employee and supervisor again meet on Interim Review Date, if one is planned, and at end of Evaluation Period to review accomplishments. Supervisor will review accomplishments with employee, and determine appropriate ratings. Rating process will include an analysis of details of performance to arrive at an overall rating. Recommendations for necessary improvements and development program activities are to be discussed with employee and summarized on this form.

THE FOLLOWING RATINGS APPLY: A = OUTSTANDING: rarely equaled; B = EXCELLENT: clearly exceeds job requirements; C = AVERAGE: meets job requirements; D = BELOW AVERAGE: meets minimum job requirements; E = UNSATISFACTORY: fails to meet job requirements; ? = UNDETERMINED: insufficient knowledge; N = NOT APPLICABLE.

	Objectives (Prepared by Employee)	Completion Date	Evaluation (by Supervisor)	
No.	Definition—What is to be achieved? How is it measured?		Comments	Rating
1.				
2.				
3.				
4.				
5.				
6.				

Attach additional pages (use white bond) for listing more than 6 objectives.

Employee _____ Supervisor _____

Figure 6.11 Performance appraisal (managerial and professional personnel)

continued

Accomplishment: How effective has the individual been during the past year in producing tangible, measurable results?		☐
Profit: Effectiveness in meeting profit objectives; in generating and implementing money-making ideas.	☐	
Operating: Effectiveness in meeting other established operating objectives such as sales, production, manufacture, transportation, maintenance, or construction.	☐	
Staff Service: Effectiveness in meeting staff service objectives, considering quantity, quality, and timeliness of work.	☐	
Cost: Effectiveness in meeting cost objectives; in operating at lowest cost, with minimum manpower, by most efficient methods.	☐	
Thinking: What caliber of thinking does the individual apply in the performance of work?		☐
Vision: Effectiveness in perceiving needs and opportunities and in conceiving alternative courses of action to meet them.	☐	
Creativity: Effectiveness of original thinking.	☐	
Analysis: Effectiveness in grasping problems and in recognizing, securing, and evaluating relevant facts.	☐	
Judgment: Soundness of recommendations, decisions, and actions.	☐	
Administration: How effective is the individual in performing duties?		☐
Planning: Effectiveness in anticipating needs; establishing objectives and policies, goals and procedures, budgets and schedules.	☐	
Organizing and Delegating: Effectiveness in subdividing, distributing, and assigning the work load; in granting authority and freedom to manage.	☐	
Leading: Effectiveness in securing the full and willing response of all members of his team in working towards common objectives; synchronizing and integrating actions of subordinate units and personnel.	☐	
Developing People: Effectiveness in the selection, appraisal, coaching, and development of personnel.	☐	
Controlling: Effectiveness in working toward objectives; measuring performance, interpreting results, and initiating corrective action.	☐	
Relationships: How effective is the individual in dealing with others?		☐
Cooperation: Effectiveness in working with associates in the Company's best interest.	☐	
Public Relations: Effectiveness in relationships with contacts outside of the Company.	☐	
Self-Control: Ability to handle problems rationally under adverse conditions.	☐	
Communication: Effectiveness in giving advice, in shaping up and presenting matters, both orally and in writing; giving regard to appropriate methods and timing.	☐	
Knowledge: What is the level of the individual's understanding of functional and environmental matters pertaining to his position, and how effective is the individual in applying this knowledge?		☐
Function: Knowledge of particular function for which the individual is responsible	☐	
Related Functions: Knowledge of related functions, the understanding of which contributes to effectiveness of performance.	☐	
Area: Understanding of the people and the social, economic, and political conditions in area of responsibility.	☐	
Application: Effectiveness in applying functional and environmental knowledge.	☐	
Over-All Appraisal of Performance: After considering above factors and performance and weighing heavily those factors which have greatest bearing on the requirements of the individual's present position, indicate the rating which most accurately characterizes the over-all performance.		☐

*For non-managerial personnel, only answer basic question by providing rating in far right-hand column.

DISCUSSION OF PERFORMANCE: Have you discussed this appraisal with the individual?   ☐ Yes   ☐ No
If not, why? _____

DEVELOPMENT PROGRAM: Summarize specific work assignments, educational courses, or other developmental experiences designed to assist the individual in improving his performance on his present job.

ACTIONS PLANNED	DATE TO BE INITIATED	DATE TO BE COMPLETED

Completed Appraisal is to be approved by Supervisor and Supervisor's superior, then forwarded to the HRM Division

Supervisor: _____   Supervisor's Superior: _____

Figure 6.11 *(cont.)*

6.12 GUIDELINES FOR EFFECTIVE EMPLOYEE DISCIPLINARY ACTION

Employment begins with orientation procedures which fully explain acceptable standards of performance and conduct. The immediate supervisor provides continuing guidance to the employee, and takes appropriate action for promptly correcting any deviations from acceptable standards. To the maximum extent possible, informal approaches are employed to correct behavioral problems through timely advice and closer supervision. Oral warnings, which point out deficiencies and specify required behavior, are used before formal actions are initiated.

The following principles should be applied in correcting employee conduct problems effectively:

1. Informal corrective actions are maximized; every opportunity should be provided for encouraging self-improvement.
2. Potential corrective actions should be evaluated to select the optimal solution— that is, one involving the minimum degree required to solve the problem appropriately.
3. Corrective actions should be graduated to suit the severity of the problem. Progressively more severe actions are required as the same problem continues, or as other infractions are encountered. All actions must be weighed in terms of the employee's overall history of conduct problems.
4. Corrective actions must be consistently fair and equitable. The system must be perceived by employees as providing uniform treatment to all.

The following types of formal disciplinary action are required in cases where informal procedures fail to solve a problem, or where the severity of the problem precludes informal approaches:

Written Warnings. A memorandum or disciplinary action report form defines precisely what the employee has done wrong, and the corrective actions required. The employee is advised that more severe disciplinary action will be taken if the problem is not corrected, if the problem is repeated in the future, or if other conduct problems are encountered.

Suspensions. Continued infractions or certain severe infractions, which because of mitigating circumstances do not lead to discharge, are subject to suspension. This disciplinary action places the employee in a non-pay status for an appropriate number of workdays, for example, 10 days. It is a last resort before discharge action is taken.

6.13 ASSESSING EMPLOYEE CONDUCT INCIDENTS

With the exception of minor and routine corrective guidance provided to the employee by the immediate supervisor, all other incidents involving questionable employee conduct should be documented. It is essential to have a complete written record of the employee's conduct problems to effectively protect the company's interests. Well documented histories of work rule infractions and other conduct problems, warnings, suspensions, and so on, promote a legal victory should the company be faced with litigation by former employees who claim wrongful termination.

The Disciplinary Action Report form (Figure 6.13A) provides the framework for properly documenting and processing each incident involving questionable employee conduct in the following manner.

1. *Supervisor's Description of Incident.* The immediate supervisor initiates the form by providing employee information, specifying the date and time that the incident occurred, and fully describing the incident.

2. *Employee's Description of Incident.* The employee reviews the supervisor's description of the incident to provide written comments. This is the employee's opportunity to provide details concerning his or her version of the incident, reasons for actions, names of witnesses, and so on.

3. *Statements from Witnesses.* Based on the supervisor's knowledge of individuals who witnessed the incident, to include any witnesses mentioned in the "employee's comments" section of the Disciplinary Action Report, action is taken to obtain written statements. The Employee Conduct Inquiry Statement format (Figure 6.13B) serves this purpose. These statements are attached to the Disciplinary Action Report, and are used in the evaluation process to ensure that all factors are considered in arriving at appropriate findings.

4. *Prior Disciplinary Record Assessment Considered in Preparing Findings.* The supervisor is required to summarize the employee's "prior disciplinary record," if any, to place the incident in proper context. Similar past incidents or other conduct problems must be thoroughly considered in arriving at "findings" and a decision concerning "action."

5. *Review and Approval Process.* If the action requires more than a warning, a proposed suspension or discharge must be reviewed with and approved by the immediate supervisor's manager and the HR director, who ensure that personnel records include sufficient Disciplinary Action Report documentation from prior incidents to support the planned action. Similarly, in cases where a severe conduct infraction dictates discharge action, but no prior disciplinary records exist, the HR director ensures that adequate Disciplinary Action Report documentation has been provided to support the planned actions.

6. *Employee Acknowledgment Requirement.* An "employee acknowledgment" section is signed by the employee who is subject to warning or suspension action to indicate his or her understanding of the consequences of continued unacceptable conduct. The employee faced with suspension action also acknowledges the number of workdays and the dates of the planned suspension period. A discharge requires employee acknowledgment of the "effective date." Provision is included for the employee's "comments."

7. *Recordkeeping Considerations.* Should a thorough review of an incident determine that the employee did not commit an infraction, the employee is advised accordingly and all associated paperwork is discarded. Paperwork for incidents which result in disciplinary action are filed as a permanent record in the employee's personnel file. Company policy may include a provision for removing an isolated warning from an employee's personnel file after one or two years of meeting expectations for proper conduct.

Disciplinary Action Report

Employee _____ Social Security No. _____

Job/Position Title _____

Organization _____ Location _____

Date of Incident _____ Time of Incident _____ A.M. / P.M.

Description of Incident: _____

_____

_____

_____

Employee's Comments (your version of incident, the reason for your actions, names of witnesses, etc): _____

_____

_____

_____

Prior Disciplinary Record (similar past incidents? other conduct problems?): _____

_____

_____

_____

Findings: _____

_____

_____

_____

Action:

__ **Warning** — Employee has been advised that continued employment is contingent upon not repeating this type of unacceptable conduct.

__ **Suspension** for _____ work days (Dates: from _____ to _____) Employee has been advised that repetition of this conduct or other conduct problems will lead to discharge.

__ **Discharge** — (Effective Date _____)

Approvals:

Supervisor _____ Date _____

Manager _____ Date _____

HR Director _____ Date _____

Employee Acknowledgment:

Comments: _____

_____

_____

Signature _____ Date _____

Figure 6.13A Disciplinary action report

Employee Conduct Inquiry

<u>STATEMENT</u>

The following statement is provided concerning my personal observations regarding an incident involving questionable employee conduct:

Date of Incident _____ Time of Incident _____ A.M. / P.M.

Individual(s) Involved: _____

_____

Other Witnesses: _____

_____

Description of Incident: _____

_____

_____

_____

_____

_____

_____

_____

_____

_____

_____

_____

_____

_____

_____

_____

Prepared By _____ Title _____

Organization _____ Location _____

I certify that this information is an accurate and complete description of my personal observations.

Signature _____ Date _____

Figure 6.13B Employee conduct inquiry statement

6.14 EMPLOYEE SUGGESTION PROGRAMS: PROMOTING EMPLOYEE EXCELLENCE

Employee participation in improving the efficiency and effectiveness of company operations is essential for survival in the ever-increasing competitive marketplace. A vital *employee suggestion program*, one which actively encourages and adequately rewards productive innovations, is an excellent vehicle for encouraging employee identification with company profitability. This type of employee suggestion program encourages employees to offer suggestions which:

- Eliminate useless operations and duplication of effort.
- Improve methods and procedures to increase effectiveness.
- Increase productivity through improved efficiency of operations.
- Yield increased quality of work products.
- Reduce costs.
- Save time and materials.

All employees should be encouraged to participate. Although managers and certain higher-level professional employees are expected to be innovative within their respective areas of responsibility, their participation in suggesting innovations elsewhere in the company should be encouraged strongly. If all employees participate, the support and enthusiasm generated by their collective efforts can yield very successful results on a sustained basis.

To ensure the success of the program, three vital ingredients are needed.

1. *Confidential Processing of Suggestions: Promoting Objective Assessments.* The Employee Suggestion form (Figure 6.14) is designed for *confidential* submission to the HR director, who preserves the employee's identity during the review process in the interest of obtaining objective assessments. The upper portion of the form, which describes the suggestion fully, includes a section where the HR director assigns a "suggestion number." The lower portion of the form, which includes the employee's name, is masked over when a copy is made and forwarded to the respective functional manager with a cover memorandum requesting assessment. The manager reviews the suggestion and prepares a memorandum to the HR director concerning its merits. An estimate of potential first-year savings also is provided.

2. *Top Management Review of All Suggestions.* The final decision concerning the merits of each suggestion must come from a review board comprised of representatives of top management. Suggestion assessment materials are provided by functional managers to the HR director, who continues to preserve the employee identities in referring suggestions for review board consideration at monthly meetings.

3. *Adequate Rewards and Recognition.* A significant reward should be given to each employee who takes the time to offer a constructive suggestion, whether or not it is adopted. A $200 after-tax payment is recommended. Those suggestions which are adopted should receive significant compensation payments based on estimated first-year savings; a 50 percent cash award is appropriate. Consideration may be given to further promoting employee identification with the company's interests by offering common stock in lieu of cash.

The lower portion of the Employee Suggestion form includes a "reply to employee" section which is used by the HR director to advise the employee of the results of top management's review. The specific amount of the award is stipulated in a letter of congratulations to the employee from the company's chief executive officer.

Recognition should be given by arranging a presentation for the check award by those top management officials who are responsible for the functions that will be impacted by the suggestion. Publicity, through photographic and written coverage of these ceremonies, should appear in the company's newspapers and newsletters to reward participants properly, and to sustain employee interest in participating in the program.

The importance of top management's support cannot be overemphasized. Periodic letters addressed to all employees from the chief executive officer should provide details about the many successes of the program and further acknowledge the contributions of those employees whose suggestions have made significant contributions. This type of periodic reinforcement, coupled with the employees' belief that substantial rewards can be theirs for offering productive ideas, will maintain the viability of the program.

Employee Suggestion

<table>
<tr><td>Suggestion
Number:</td></tr>
</table>

WHAT is the present condition, method, or procedure? (Attach explanatory materials, sample forms, etc.)

HOW do you think it can be improved? (Attach explanatory materials)

WHY should the change be made? What benefits or savings in time or money will result?

Name (Last, First, Initial)	Position	
Department	Location	Suggestion Number:

Reply to Employee   From _____   Date _____

☐ While your suggestion is very much appreciated, we regret that it cannot be adopted for the following reasons:

☐ Congratulations, your suggestion is being adopted. You will be contacted in the near future concerning the details of your award.

Figure 6.14 Employee suggestion

6.15 ENCOURAGING EMPLOYEE EXCELLENCE— SPECIAL AWARD PROGRAMS

Recognition of special efforts, contributions, and accomplishments by employees enhances morale, promotes identification with the company, and encourages excellence. In addition to a merit-based wage/salary adjustment process and a viable employee suggestion program, a company is well advised to recognize employees through the following creative programs.

Employee(s) of the Month Program. This program provides each organization throughout the company with nomination forms for employees to suggest candidates for recognition as an employee of the month. A sample Employee of the Month Nomination Form is shown in Figure 6.15.

Depending on the size of the company, a number of such individuals may be cited each month. Criteria for nomination should include:

- Superior performance
- Respect of other employees and management for personal qualities and competence
- Excellent personality and appearance
- Demonstrated effectiveness in promoting the achievement of company objectives; excellence in working with other employees, relating to customers, and so on.

Nominations are referred to the HR director, who ensures that the employee meets requisite performance and conduct standards by reviewing personnel records and contacting the employee's immediate supervisor for current references. Qualified individuals receive the following:

- A letter of congratulations from the chief executive officer, which includes a check for $200.
- If a number of individuals are selected each month, then a special luncheon should be held to honor their selection. Representative members of top management host the employees of the month at the luncheon.
- An employee of the month receives a special pin which symbolizes his or her achievement. A framed award certificate or plaque also is provided. Public recognition involves extensive coverage in company newspapers or newsletters and in local newspapers. Photos of the employee receiving these rewards from members of top management provides well deserved recognition, and encourages others to aspire for similar recognition. A viable program does much to encourage current employees, and promotes an image of the company as one which appreciates its employees in the eyes of outsiders who may be prospective candidates for employment.

Awards for Excellence. The special contributions of a few employees go well beyond the scope of normal reward and recognition programs. These unique performers deserve significant recognition in the form of an outstanding award payment and a letter citing the achievement from the chief executive officer of the company. The letter should become part of the individual's personnel record, and further recognition should be provided through extensive publicity concerning the employee's accomplishments.

To implement this type of program, managers throughout the company should be encouraged to submit recommendation memoranda through the proper channels leading up to the chief executive officer whenever necessary in order to recognize the outstanding contributions of their subordinates.

Management must decide on a reward system which will adequately compensate outstanding performers. Special salary adjustments are not recommended for the following reasons.

- They artificially distort individual salaries, which are inequitable when compared with peer salaries. The greater the percentage of increase needed to provide a suitable reward, the greater the distortion.
- They unnecessarily inflate the individual's salary for a one-time accomplishment. Future salary increase percentages will be applied against this larger-than-normal amount; therefore, the company inadvertently pays over and over again for the award.

It is undoubtedly more economical for the company to provide a substantial one-time award in recognizing an outstanding achievement. The amount of the award should be tied to a percentage of the employee's annual compensation, not an arbitrarily established dollar amount, which has no meaningful relationship to the requirement for adequately rewarding recipients. For example, a universal $1,500 award may be very good for the individual earning $20,000 per year, but it would have relatively little significance for the individual who earns $50,000 per year. The company must be prepared to offer substantial rewards which adequately recognize excellence; 10 percent of annual salary (before taxes) is the minimum price for success.

**Employee of the Month
Nomination Form**

I nominate _____ as a candidate for **Employee of the Month**. This employee deserves to be recognized for overall excellence as follows:

- Superior performance
- Respected by all for personal qualities and competence
- Excellent personality and appearance

Recommended by _____ Date _____

Job/Position Title _____

Organization _____ Location _____

PLEASE FORWARD THIS COMPLETED FORM TO THE HR DIRECTOR IN A SEALED ENVELOPE MARKED "CONFIDENTIAL."

_____

TO BE COMPLETED BY THE HRM DIVISION:

Nominee _____ Social Security No. _____

Job/Position Title _____

Organization _____ Location _____

Hire Date _____ Supervisor _____

Eligibility Determination: _____ YES _____ NO

COMMENTS: _____

_____

Management Review & Approval for Month of _____

APPROVED: _____ Date _____

Figure 6.15 Employee of the month nomination form

CHAPTER 7

Wage and Salary Administration

This chapter provides the policy and procedural guidelines needed for the development of an effective wage and salary administration program, one which provides the basis for attracting and retaining qualified employees through competitive and equitable compensation practices. This developmental process involves five steps.

Step 1. Job Analysis—determining the Duties and Responsibilities of Each Job/Position

This is the most important step in the developmental process because it serves as the foundation for a valid program. Each job is thoroughly reviewed through the use of tools such as the Position Design Workbook (refer to Section 1.6), to define its overall purpose, duties, and responsibilities. The Position Design Workbook includes detailed Instructions, a Position Design Worksheet, Factor Level Definitions for each of the seven principal criteria used in determining the salary grade for a position, and a sample of a completed Position Design Worksheet for a mechanical engineer position. Employee participation in providing information concerning the duties and responsibilities of their positions is provided through the structure of the Position Analysis Questionnaire (Figure 7.2). A sample Position Specification Format, which results from this process, is given in Section 7.3.

Step 2. Job Evaluation—establishing the Relative Worth of All Jobs

A point factor evaluation technique, which compares Position Design Worksheet data with respective Factor Level Definitions, is used to prepare a Position Evaluation Worksheet (see Figure 7.4). The Position Evaluation Plan (see Figure 7.5) is used to convert the *total rating points* obtained on the Position Evaluation Worksheet into an appropriate *salary grade*.

Step 3. Job Pricing—translating Relative Job Worth into Money Values

To validate the tentative salary grade for a position, current salary survey data are reviewed to determine the average (mean) earned salary rate that the local labor market commands for a fully qualified incumbent. A sample company-initiated Salary Survey Questionnaire is given in Section 7.11. The questionnaire yields competitive salary data which provide the average paid rate (mean) for each benchmark position. Salary ranges are then constructed around each of these "midpoints" in accordance with the Guidelines for Establishing a Wage/Salary Structure given in Section 7.6. A Matrix for Validating Job/Position Evaluations is explained in Section 7.8.

Step 4. Merit Rating—rewarding Employees for Higher Productivity and Better Job Performance

As detailed in Chapter 6, each employee's level of performance should determine his or her amount of merit compensation. Employees in the same type of job should receive pay increases which are proportional to their relative accomplishments. To provide the basis for merit increases, all employees are reviewed annually to assess their performance compared with all individuals in similar jobs. Resultant ratings should approximate a normal distribution.

Step 5. Administration—providing Policy and Procedural Guidance to Managers as Required to Carry Out the Program

An employees merit rating and the positioning of his or her current salary within the salary range determine the amount and time interval for the increase. Sample Merit Increase Guidelines are offered in Section 7.9. An annual salary review procedure, as part of the administrative budget preparation process, is recommended in Section 7.12.

7.1 POSITION DESIGN WORKSHEET

The Position Design Worksheet with Factor Level Definitions serves two purposes: First, it is used by supervisors and line managers to define the duties and responsibilities of a new position, or to define the scope of an existing position. Second, it is used by human resource managers to determine the salary grade of a position. Although the Position Design Worksheet and the factor level definitions are also part of the Position Design Workbook (see Figure 1.6), they are reproduced here in Figures 7.1A–7.1G to facilitate understanding of the point-factor position classification process. Numerous references are made to their contents throughout this chapter. The 7 Factor Level Definitions are:

Figure 7.1A   Knowledge
Figure 7.1B   Mental Application
Figure 7.1C   Programs and Projects
Figure 7.1D   Supervision
Figure 7.1E   Accountability
Figure 7.1F   Policies and Methods
Figure 7.1G   Relationships

A. KNOWLEDGE

Factor Level	Definitions
1.	Ordinarily requires the education acquired by graduation from high school, related experience of up to one or two years, and only those skills acquired through such education and limited experience.
2.	Requires two years of college or the equivalent, related experience of two or three years, and skill and proficiency in a semi-professional occupation or specialized business function.
3.	Requires the equivalent of a college degree in skills acquired either academically or through specialized business experience.
4.	Requires the equivalent of a college degree with business or academic training in applicable subjects; three or four years related experience; and skills in a professional or advanced business function having a direct bearing on the products or services of the Company.
5.	Requires the equivalent of a college degree; four or five years of related business experience; and managerial or administrative skills at department head level or equivalent in administrative, professional or scientific functions.
6.	Requires broad and intensive knowledge acquired by full academic training; five to seven years of applicable experience; and skills in planning, organizing, controlling, and administering in a management position.
7.	Requires intensive knowledge of a broad field of business enterprise acquired by sufficient academic training; seven to ten years applicable experience; skill in planning, organizing, integrating viewpoints of people, motivating department heads; and experience in administering an important business function at the officer level.

Figure 7.1A Factor level definitions

B. MENTAL APPLICATION

Factor Level	Definitions
1.	Work is well organized and supervised. Offers some opportunity for ingenuity in applying accepted methods, with concentrated attention to the examination of details, to make logical decisions from limited alternatives.
2.	Work requires individual to devise own methods under close supervision; to make choices from knowledge of accepted methods; to examine details of specialized subjects; to make decisions within scope of own assignments; and to compose reports and correspondence.
3.	Work requires ingenuity in planning and implementing projects under general supervision. Examines advanced subjects, and uses independent judgment to make decisions under established policies. Prepares reports requiring technical concepts.
4.	Work requires individual to devise own methods; to assist in the development of methods used by others; to exercise ingenuity; to analyze situations and apply judgment required to make decisions of an administrative nature; and to prepare and edit reports and other materials involving technical concepts.
5.	Work requires originality, initiative, and ingenuity to devise departmental methods; to solve problems not covered by procedures; and to make administrative or supervisory decisions.
6.	Work requires the high degree of originality, initiative, and ingenuity needed for operating a department or major function under general direction; to analyze situations of a highly complex nature; and to make major policy decisions subject only to officer approval.
7.	Work requires the highest degree of originality, initiative, and ingenuity as required to manage an important major function involving a number of departmental activities. Analyzes interdepartmental or functional situations to make decisions in situations requiring policy formulation, and approves actions of subordinates within broad limits of authority.

Figure 7.1B Factor level definitions

C. PROGRAMS AND PROJECTS

Factor Level	Definitions
1.	Projects are on an assigned basis involving well defined tasks, approved methods, and standard procedures.
2.	Projects have a relation to product or services, but are not complex in nature. The possibility for errors is slight. Requires interpretation and application of known facts by using approved methods or following precedents.
3.	Projects are complex in nature. Requires originality and the application of related knowledge within accepted standard practice.
4.	Projects are diversified or specialized in nature. Requires selections from a broad range of procedures, and the analysis of facts to determine appropriate actions. Creative ability to improve or develop a product or service for an established program is essential.
5.	Projects are diversified and highly technical with direct effect on products or services. Requires extensive subject matter knowledge and the ability to adapt and modify procedures to meet new situations and conditions.
6.	Work involves the planning, direction, and supervision of numerous projects which are part of an overall program. Applies extensive subject matter and policy and procedural knowledge in devising new methods. Accomplishes objectives independently.
7.	Work requires the development and administration of programs at the departmental level based on an appraisal of facts, trends, and anticipated results which relate to overall Company objectives.
8.	Work requires the development, implementation, and administration of programs of an important division-level function of the Company. Incumbent usually is an Officer of the Company.

Figure 7.1C Factor level definitions

D. SUPERVISION

Factor Level	Definition
1.	Works under direct supervision. Receives detailed instructions and guidance. Does not supervise others, but may assist with the instruction and training of new employees.
2.	Works under general instructions. May supervise and train a small unit of semi-skilled or clerical employees as a group leader.
3.	Works under general instructions of a department manager. Responsible for a small group of employees assigned to a project.
4.	Works under general supervision of a major Department Manager. While usually responsible for a Section, could be the Manager of a small Staff Function or Department.
5.	Works under the general direction of a Division Manager with responsibility for the supervision of a major department under defined limits of authority.
6.	Works under direction of an officer or top functional executive. Directs a major corporate staff function or division-level organization, or serves as a key assistant to a corporate officer.
7.	Works under direction of an officer or a top functional executive. Directs a major activity that may involve operations at more than one location.
8.	Works under the direction of a Chief Executive Officer. Responsible for the direction of a major function through managers who are directly responsible for their activities. Incumbent is an officer and/or top functional executive of the Company.

Figure 7.1D Factor level definitions

E.   ACCOUNTABILITY

Factor Level	Description
1.	Responsible for the proper use and care of assigned equipment and materials. Influences costs only through the degree of personal efficiency.
2.	Responsible for the proper use and care of highly valuable equipment and supplies. Nature of work may indirectly affect company costs and profitability.
3.	Work involves direct responsibility for the control, preservation, and efficient utilization of equipment and/or facilities. Effectiveness results in controlling expenses.
4.	As a supervisor, incumbent is responsible for the control, protection and efficient use of equipment and/or facilities. Efforts have an important influence on the production of income and the control of costs.
5.	Responsible and accountable as a department-level manager for the control, protection, and efficient use of the equipment and facilities of a department. Efforts directly affect the production of income and the control of costs.
6.	Responsible and directly accountable to a corporate officer for the control and efficient utilization of equipment and facilities of a major function or division. Responsible for the production of income and the control of costs by the organizational unit(s) managed.
7.	Responsible as a key executive for the effective control and efficient use of equipment company-wide, or for a group of major company organizations. Directly responsible for the production of income and the control of costs.
8.	Responsible as an officer for the acquisition, maintenance, and efficient use of all equipment and facilities. Full responsibility for the production of income and the control of expenditures in meeting operating plan profitability objectives.

Figure 7.1E Factor level definitions

F. POLICIES AND METHODS

Factor Level	Definitions
1.	Performs work according to well-defined policies, procedures, and methods, which apply to a particular activity.
2.	Responsible for interpreting policies and applying associated procedures and methods to a particular activity.
3.	Responsible for interpreting and applying methods and procedures. Ensures that policies are maintained and that interpretations by others are in accordance with established standards.
4.	Responsible for formulating policies and/or recommending modifications of policies and procedures to meet changing conditions and generally improve operations.
5.	As a manager, is responsible for initiating and developing major policies. Interprets Company policy as required by complex requirements.
6.	As an officer, responsible for promoting and contributing to the formulation of organization-wide policies. Ensures that policies and procedures are properly interpreted and applied throughout the functions for which the position is held accountable.

Figure 7.1F Factor level definitions

G. RELATIONSHIPS

Factor Level	Definition
1.	Few and irregular external relationships. Internal relationships largely are with individuals in own immediate organization.
2.	Limited external contacts with customers, vendors, staff, and other company representatives. Department-wide and occasional inter-departmental contacts.
3.	Extensive external contacts involve significant importance. For example, meetings with management level personnel of other companies regarding customer relations issues. Requires extensive inter-departmental contacts, and occasional contacts with company management.
4.	Extensive external contacts on a management level regarding company projects. Internal relationships on all levels are primarily at the division level in scope and purpose.
5.	Direct and regular external contacts with the top management of other companies, with important representatives of the community, government agencies, etc. Internal contacts are Company-wide and primarily at the officer level.

Figure 7.1G Factor level definitions

7.2 POSITION ANALYSIS QUESTIONNAIRE

In those cases where a position with an incumbent requires evaluation, either as part of introducing a new wage and salary administration program or for assessing the impact of changes which have occurred in the individual's duties and responsibilities, the employee is called upon to provide essential information. The Position Analysis Questionnaire (Figure 7.2) provides a systematic framework for this purpose. It elicits the details needed to fully describe each of the seven position requirements which must be defined to complete a Position Design Worksheet (see Figure 7.1). To facilitate this process, each section of the Position Analysis Questionnaire is correlated with Position Design Worksheet items as follows:

1. Your Job-Related Qualifications (relates to Section II, A. Knowledge)
2. Originality Required (relates to Section II, B. Mental Application)
3. Nature and Variety of Your Work (relates to Section II, C. Programs and Projects)
4. Nature of Supervision Received and Exercised over Other Employees (relates to Section II, D. Supervision)
5. Nature and Scope of Your Recommendations, Decisions, Commitments, and Conclusions (relates to Section II, E. Accountability)
6. Nature of Guidelines for Performing Your Work (relates to Section II, F. Policies and Methods)
7. Purpose and Nature of Your Person-to-Person Contacts (relates to Section II, G. Relationships)
8. Overall Duties and Responsibilities of Your Position (relates to Section I, General Function)

Position Analysis Questionnaire (Administrative)

Employee Name _____

Position Title _____

Organization _____

Immediate Supervisor (Name & Title) _____

_____

Please complete this Questionnaire to provide information needed by the HRM Division for assessing the relative value of your position to the Company. Should additional space be needed for answering a question, please continue on the reverse side of that page. Your immediate supervisor will review your answers; if clarifications or revisions are needed, he/she will review these requirements with you prior to forwarding the completed Questionnaire to the Compensation Manager.

1. YOUR JOB-RELATED QUALIFICATIONS

    a. What knowledge is essential for performing your job? Consider policies, procedures, work processes, etc.

    b. What abilities are essential in order to perform your duties? Consider job-related competence and personal characteristics.

    c. What skills are essential? Consider expertise, proficiency, physical and mental attributes, etc.

    d. What type of educational background is needed to perform your duties and responsibilities?

    e. How many years of on-the-job or equivalent specialized experience is needed to fully perform your duties and responsibilities?

2. ORIGINALITY REQUIRED

    a. What parts of your work are not covered by rules, procedures, precedents, etc.?

    b. Give examples of times when you must use your imagination and inventiveness for creating and improvising in your work.

Figure 7.2 Position analysis questionnaire (administrative)

continued

314

    c.   To what extent does your work require the development of new or revised techniques, or the adaptation of old methods to new problems?

    d.   Describe the extent to which you must plan work projects or establish policies.

3.   NATURE AND VARIETY OF YOUR WORK

    a.   What equipment, if any, is required in performing your duties?

    b.   If some of your work is part of an overall process, describe what has been done to it before it reaches you, what steps you take, and what happens to it after you forward it to the next step in the process.

    c.   To what extent are you responsible for planning your work and the methods used?

    d.   What errors are possible in your work? What are the consequences?

    e.   What problems arise when you are performing your duties?

    f.   If you review the work of others, describe the purpose of your review activities.

    g.   Describe a typical project. How complex is it? What must you do? What is needed in terms of creativity and originality to achieve desired results?

4.   NATURE OF SUPERVISION RECEIVED AND EXERCISED OVER OTHER EMPLOYEES

    a.   Describe the manner in which you receive assignments. For example, do you receive detailed step-by-step instructions, or are you told what is wanted and given general procedures to be followed? Provide an example.

    b.   How difficult are your work assignments as compared to others in your organization?

    c.   What types of problems do you refer to your immediate supervisor for assistance?

    d.   Who reviews your work? Provide the position title of this individual, and explain the purpose of this review.

Figure 7.2 *(cont.)*

e. What final actions are you permitted to take without review?

f. Do your supervise/lead the work of others? If so, what are the position titles of these employees?

g. Describe your responsibility for setting policies; establishing objectives; planning and organizing work; making assignments; and reviewing accomplishments.

h. Explain the nature of your supervisory responsibilities by describing the level of difficulty of the work performed by your subordinates, and the degree of independence and responsibility they have in accomplishing representative functions.

i. Describe the size and complexity of the organization that you supervise.

5. NATURE AND SCOPE OF YOUR RECOMMENDATIONS, DECISIONS, COMMITMENTS, AND CONCLUSIONS

a. What actions can you take that are binding on your organization and/or the Company? How extensive is the effect of these actions or decisions?

b. Do your actions only affect a given case, or do they affect future action in similar cases?

c. What are the limits of your authority in making commitments?

d. Are your commitments subject to review? If so, by whom? Provide the position title(s) of any individual(s) who review your commitments.

e. What is the extent of your accountability for the utilization of Company equipment, materials, facilities, supplies, etc.?

6. NATURE OF GUIDELINES FOR PERFORMING YOUR WORK

a. What policies, procedures, manuals, precedents, or other guides do you use in your work?

b. Do you receive well-defined instructions, or must you frequently use guidelines to make interpretations? Give examples.

c. If you have a problem that is not covered by guidelines, how do you solve it?

Figure 7.2 *(cont.)*

7. PURPOSE AND NATURE OF YOUR PERSON-TO-PERSON CONTACTS

   a. Characterize the general nature of your person-to-person contacts. Are they primarily to give information, to obtain information, to explain policies and procedures, to persuade others concerning the benefits of a program, to settle problems, etc.?

   b. Who must you contact for what specific purpose? Provide position titles and information on the affiliations of these individuals (other employees within the Company, customers, vendors, representatives of other companies, governmental representatives, etc.).

8. OVERALL DUTIES AND RESPONSIBILITIES OF YOUR POSITION

   a. Describe the overall purpose of your position.

   b. Explain the most important duties that you perform, and specify the percentage of your total time that is spent on each.

      Duties   % of Time

_____

Signature _____ Date _____

REVIEWED BY:

Supervisor's Signature _____ Date _____

Figure 7.2 *(cont.)*

7.3 POSITION SPECIFICATION FORMAT

As discussed in Chapter 1, Section 1.7, Job/Position Description Formats, the Position Design Workbook (refer to Section 1.6) serves as the basis for preparing a special position description format—that is, a Position Specification (Figure 7.3). This type of format is used by companies that elect to have HRM professionals prepare final versions of position descriptions in a uniform structure and style which facilitates the classification process. The "general function" section of the Position Specification includes a statement of the specific qualifications which must be met in the recruitment process.

Position Specification

Position Title Mechanical Engineer - III

Division Engineering Services   Department Design Engineering

Location Philadelphia, PA   Reports To Manager, Design Engineering

GENERAL FUNCTION:

Performs design engineering assignments involving the preparation of layouts and detail drawings for elements of office building mechanical systems (heating, ventilating, air conditioning, plumbing, and steam distribution). *Requires a college degree in Mechanical Engineering or its equivalent in terms of professional knowledge obtained through specialized work experience. Working knowledge of related engineering disciplines, particularly structural and electrical, is essential.*

DUTIES AND RESPONSIBILITIES:

Receives assignments with specific instructions concerning objectives and procedures to be used, and detailed guidance needed to solve problems; however, repetitive work is performed independently. Some ingenuity is required in selecting appropriate guidelines and deciding between alternative problem-solving approaches.

Performs assignments, as assigned by supervision, which require applying standard engineering principles, methods, and practices for solving well-defined problems through specified standard procedures. Prepares layout and detail drawings for routine projects or portions of larger and more complex projects. Performs calculations. Reviews contractor drawings to ensure adherence to specifications.

Works under the direct supervision of the Supervisor or higher-level engineers. Receives detailed instructions and guidance. Requires effective application of professional skills in providing adequate designs while relieving higher-level engineers from performing routine work. Performs duties in accordance with well-defined established methods and procedures.

Requires personal contacts with other engineers and technicians within the immediate office, and limited external contacts with Company construction engineering personnel and design engineering contractor personnel. Obtains advice, assistance, or information regarding the condition of existing facilities. Reports on status or results of work.

Figure 7.3 Sample position specification format

7.4 POSITION EVALUATION WORKSHEET

Given the information provided by a manager in a Position Design Worksheet—Professional/Administrative/Managerial and/or a Position Analysis Questionnaire (see Section 7.2) prepared by an incumbent, a compensation analyst evaluates the position by assessing each of the following factors (refer to Section 7.1):

A. Knowledge
B. Mental Application
C. Programs and Projects
D. Supervision
E. Accountability
F. Policy and Methods
G. Relationships

This process reviews the Factor Level Definitions for each factor to determine which one best describes position requirements. For example, seven Factor Level Definitions are provided for "A. Knowledge." If the position requires the equivalent of a college degree in skills acquired either academically or through specialized business experience, then the appropriate factor level (sometimes referred to as "degree") is number 3. Accordingly, the analyst enters "FL#3" in the column provided on the Position Evaluation Worksheet (Figure 7.4).

When all the factors have been evaluated and the resultant factor levels have been entered on the Position Evaluation Worksheet, the analyst then uses the "position evaluation plan" (see Section 7.5) to determine the tentative grade level for the position.

POSITION EVALUATION WORKSHEET

Confidential

Position Title _____

FACTOR	NOTES	FACTOR LEVEL (DEGREE)	POINTS
A. KNOWLEDGE			
B. MENTAL APPLICATION			
C. PROGRAMS AND PROJECTS			
D. SUPERVISION			
E. ACCOUNTABILITY			
F. POLICY AND METHODS			
G. RELATIONSHIPS			
GRADE	SALARY RANGE	TOTAL POINTS	

Figure 7.4 Sample position evaluation worksheet

7.5 POSITION EVALUATION PLAN

After a compensation analyst determines the appropriate factor levels for a position, the Position Evaluation Worksheet (refer to Figure 7.4) then is used in conjunction with the Position Evaluation Plan to determine the appropriate grade level. The analyst first uses the Position Evaluation Plan: Table of Factor Levels and Point Values (Figure 7.5A) to convert factor levels into *points*. The total points yielded on the worksheet then are converted through the use of the Position Evaluation Plan: Table for Converting Total Points to Grade Level (Figure 7.5B). For example, if an evaluation yields total points of 145, then the total point range of 130–150 is selected. The corresponding grade level is 11. This is a tentative evaluation of the position subject to validation provided through the matrix comparison of relative position values process described in Section 7.8.

| Factor | Factor Levels and Point Values | | | | | | | |
	1	2	3	4	5	6	7	8
A. Knowledge	15	20	30	40	50	66	80	-
B. Mental Application	10	15	20	30	40	50	65	-
C. Programs & Projects	5	10	15	20	30	40	50	65
D. Supervision	0	5	10	15	20	30	40	50
E. Accountability	0	5	10	15	20	30	40	50
F. Policies & Methods	0	5	10	15	20	30	-	
G. Relationships	5	10	15	20	30	-	-	-

Figure 7.5A Position evaluation plan: table of factor levels and point values

Total Point Range	Grade Level
90–110	9
110–130	10
130–150	11
150–170	12
170–190	13
190–210	14
210–230	15
230–250	16
250–270	17
270–290	18
290–310	19
310–330	20
330–350	21
350–370	22
370 +	23

Figure 7.5B Position evaluation plan: table for converting total points to grade level

7.6 GUIDELINES FOR ESTABLISHING A WAGE/SALARY STRUCTURE

The flexibility offered by wage/salary ranges is preferable to alternative techniques such as specified pay rate structures, which designate by grade level the amount payable as a hiring rate and subsequent step increase amounts for longevity. A representative wage/salary range structure which has met the test of real-world requirements involves twenty-three grade levels. The range of compensation assigned to each of these grades is based on the relative contribution of associated jobs/positions to the successful operations of the company. These dollar values also reflect the competitive levels paid by other companies for similar work. A wage/salary range involves a minimum, midpoint, and maximum for each grade level as defined below.

Minimum—the lowest rate paid to an individual who is hired for or promoted to a job/position that has been classified in the grade level.

Midpoint—competitive rate for the particular grade level which represents the worth of the job/position to the company–that is, the amount of compensation considered to be fair and equitable for an employee who is fully qualified in terms of training and experience.

Maximum—highest rate which may be paid to an incumbent in the grade level. It is based on the company's assessment of the extent to which it wants to recognize the value of company experience and related performance for the job/position in question.

To design an appropriate wage and salary structure for your company, the percentage of the spread between the minimum and the maximum of each grade level should be competitive with other employers while ensuring that economical controls are established. As shown in Figure 7.6A, A Twenty-Three Grade Level Wage/Salary Structure, ranges are built with a constant relationship between midpoints and increased range spreads as the positions increase in importance to the company.

Given a company policy of annually adjusting ranges by a uniform percentage factor to compensate for inflationary trends and ensure competitive midpoints based on current wage and salary data, conservative range spreads of 35 percent from minimum to maximum (± 17.5 percent on either side of the midpoint) are adequate for factory (production) jobs, office (clerical) positions, and lower-level professional positions. As shown in Figure 7.6B, Designing a Wage/Salary Range Structure, this same range spread is used from Grade 1 through Grade 9. Beginning with Grade 10, each range spread increases uniformly by 1.5 percent from 36 percent to 75 percent at Grade 23. As depicted in Figure 7.6A, each midpoint value is structured to be 10 percent above the preceding midpoint.

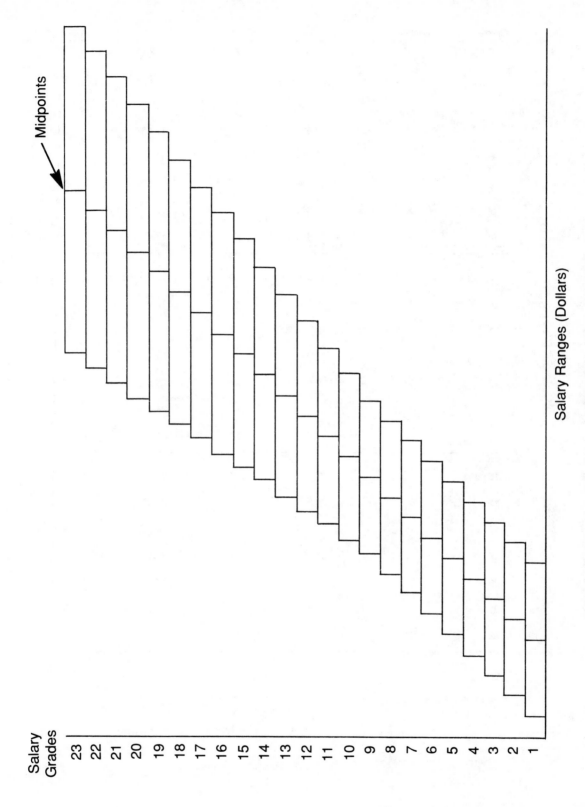

Salary Grades

Midpoints

Salary Ranges (Dollars)

23
22
21
20
19
18
17
16
15
14
13
12
11
10
9
8
7
6
5
4
3
2
1

Figure 7.6A A twenty-three grade level wage/salary structure

Grade	Minimum		Midpoint		Maximum
1	X	17.5%	X	17.5%	X
			*		
2	X	17.5%	X	17.5%	X
			*		
3	X	17.5%	X	17.5%	X
			*		
4	X	17.5%	X	17.5%	X
			*		
5	X	17.5%	X	17.5%	X
			*		
6	X	17.5%	X	17.5%	X
			*		
7	X	17.5%	X	17.5%	X
			*		
8	X	17.5%	X	17.5%	X
			*		
9	X	17.5%	X	17.5%	X
			*		
10	X	18.0%	X	18.0%	X
			*		
11	X	19.5%	X	19.5%	X
			*		
12	X	21.0%	X	21.0%	X
			*		
13	X	22.5%	X	22.5%	X
			*		
14	X	24.0%	X	24.0%	X
			*		
15	X	25.5%	X	25.5%	X
			*		
16	X	27.0%	X	27.0%	X
			*		
17	X	28.5%	X	28.5%	X
			*		
18	X	30.0%	X	30.0%	X
			*		
19	X	31.5%	X	31.5%	X
			*		
20	X	33.0%	X	33.0%	X
			*		
21	X	34.5%	X	34.5%	X
			*		
22	X	36.0%	X	36.0%	X
			*		
23	X	37.5%	X	37.5%	X

* = + 10.0% between midpoints

Figure 7.6B Designing a wage/salary range structure

7.7 MATURITY CURVES—A SALARY RANGE ALTERNATIVE

High technology companies employing scientific and engineering professionals use statistical analysis to advantage in summarizing salary survey data for categories of positions, for example, electronics engineers. Considerations such as grouping only data for nonsupervisory positions and then doing so by highest degree held (B.S., M.S., or Ph.D.) ensure comparability. The end product is a chart which plots salary data versus years of experience in percentile curves (10th, 25th, 50th, 75th, and 90th) for nonsupervisory B.S. degree-level electronics engineers. Sample Maturity Curves are provided in Figure 7.7.

This very detailed approach to establishing compensation guidelines provides the following benefits:

- As compared to salary ranges for each grade level that involve discrete midpoints (the equivalent of 50th percentile data), minimums (the equivalent of 25 percent data), and maximums (the 75th percentile data), this approach also identifies extremes beyond normal range considerations, i.e., 90th percentile and 10th percentile data.

- In recruiting candidates for employment with varied levels of experience, maturity curve data provides a basis for qualitative analysis of candidate qualifications based on assessing the performance level represented by their current salaries. Data also is used to establish competitive salary offers for employment candidates.

- If tied to performance standards, the data may be used to determine appropriate levels of compensation and associated merit salary adjustments. This is particularly important in providing the highly competitive rewards needed to retain outstanding professionals in the early years of their career development. Outstanding performance may require recognition beyond the 75th percentile level, which is not possible under the constraints of typical salary range systems and their associated administrative procedures.

- The approach provides a statistical basis for identifying individuals whose relatively low level of performance, as reflected in compensation below the 25th percentile, could merit separation action. Company policy may require separation action if the employee fails to move up to an acceptable level of performance and associated compensation within a specified period of time.

- In the event that economic conditions require a major reduction-of-force, employees whose salaries are below the 25th percentile are the first to be considered for separation action.

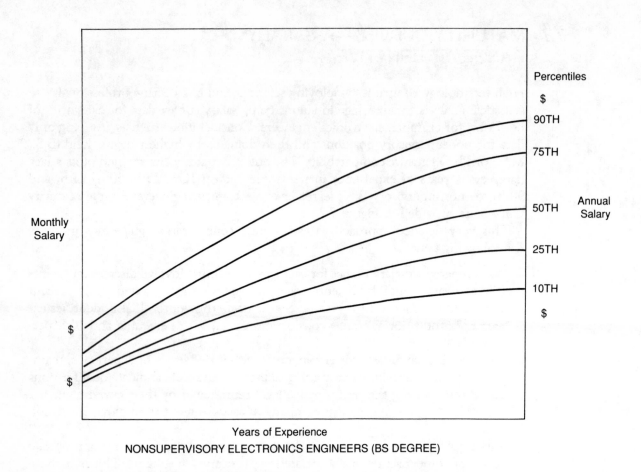

Monthly
Salary

Percentiles
$
90TH
75TH
50TH
25TH
10TH
$

Annual
Salary

$
$

Years of Experience
NONSUPERVISORY ELECTRONICS ENGINEERS (BS DEGREE)

Figure 7.7 Sample maturity curves

7.8 MATRIX FOR VALIDATING JOB/POSITION EVALUATIONS

The point-factor evaluation of a position yields a tentative grade level, which then must be validated by the following process.

1. The midpoint of the proposed grade level is compared with the mean value reported in current salary survey data for the position. If not sufficiently comparable, then a more representative midpoint is tentatively selected.
2. The position is compared with other positions already assigned to the grade level represented by the tentative midpoint. If the position is judged to be comparable in value to these other positions, then it is assigned to this grade level as a final evaluation.

A matrix is used to facilitate the comparisons involved in this process (see Figure 7.8). The vertical axis provides wage/salary range data for each grade level—from 1 up to 23. The horizontal axis provides columns for each organizational unit. Each job/position is listed in the appropriate box for its grade level and organization. Notations are included regarding salary survey data which confirms the evaluation—that is, the name of the survey and mean value reported for this type of position.

This matrix serves as the framework for periodic analyses to ensure that job/position evaluations remain competitive. As proposed annual wage/salary range increases are assessed, the associated midpoint revisions are compared with current survey data for representative jobs/positions. If suitably comparable, the range structures are revised accordingly. Representative positions, often referred to as *benchmark* positions, are used to test the suitability of proposed midpoint adjustments. For example, typical benchmark office positions include:

Position	Grade Level
Senior bookkeeper	7
Senior accounting clerk	6
Senior audit clerk	6
Secretary	6
Stenographer	5
Senior clerk-typist	5
Senior file clerk	4

Grade & Range Min.–Midpoint–Max.	Production	Engineering	All
23 $XXXXX–$XXXXX–$XXXXX			
22 XXXXX–$XXXXX–$XXXXX			
21 XXXXX–$XXXXX–$XXXXX			
20 XXXXX–$XXXXX–$XXXXX			
19 XXXXX–$XXXXX–$XXXXX			
18 XXXXX–$XXXXX–$XXXXX			
17 XXXXX–$XXXXX–$XXXXX			
16 XXXXX–$XXXXX–$XXXXX			
15 XXXXX–$XXXXX–$XXXXX			
14 XXXXX–$XXXXX–$XXXXX			
13 XXXXX–$XXXXX–$XXXXX			
12 XXXXX–$XXXXX–$XXXXX			
11 XXXXX–$XXXXX–$XXXXX			
10 XXXXX–$XXXXX–$XXXXX			
9 XXXXX–$XXXXX–$XXXXX			
8 XXXXX–$XXXXX–$XXXXX			
7 XXXXX–$XXXXX–$XXXXX			
6 XXXXX–$XXXXX–$XXXXX			Secretary AMA–$XXXXX
5 XXXXX–$XXXXX–$XXXXX			Stenographer AMA–$XXXXX
4 XXXXX–$XXXXX–$XXXXX			Sr. Clerk-Typist AMA–$XXXXX
3 XXXXX–$XXXXX–$XXXXX			
2 XXXXX–$XXXXX–$XXXXX			
1 XXXXX–$XXXXX–$XXXXX			

Figure 7.8 Matrix for validating job/position evaluations

7.9 SAMPLE MERIT INCREASE GUIDELINES

By adjusting wage/salary ranges annually to account for inflationary factors, a company includes inflationary cost-of-living adjustments (COLA) within the structure of so-called merit increase payments. This technique is used in lieu of across-the-board general increases to account for annual changes in the Consumer Price Index (CPI). Although this wage/salary range adjustment approach is recommended, two associated problems must be considered.

1. All employees do not receive annual merit increases. Those employees in the upper portion of their wage/salary ranges whose performance is not exceptional, generally will have waiting periods of more than 12 months for merit increases which include their cost-of-living adjustments.
2. While the annual CPI remains in the 3–4 percent range, inclusion of cost-of-living adjustments within wage/salary range adjustments still provides sufficient salary budget resources at the 6 percent level to provide meaningful recognition of merit. If the CPI rises to double-digit levels, as it did in 1979 and 1980, salary budgets are stretched to the 10 percent level. Faced with a CPI in the 12–14 percent range, employee compensation failed to keep pace with inflation and, in effect, merit increases no longer were economically feasible. A so-called merit increase was, in reality, only a partial COLA.

In outlining your company policy, a merit increase would be defined as in-grade adjustment of wage/salary based on management's evaluation of an employee's performance. The frequency and amount of a merit increase is based on the employee's performance level and the positioning of the employee's current wage/salary within the rate range for the job/position. Merit increases normally range from 5 to 10 percent of current compensation. For those few cases involving outstanding performance as demonstrated by significant accomplishments and contributions, increases of 11–12 percent may be granted. The amounts and intervals of merit increases for nonmanagement personnel must be consistent with the following guidelines.

As shown in Figure 7.9A, Sample Merit Increase Guidelines, the "amount of increase" is based on the employee's performance rating. For example, a "B" rating permits either 9 percent or 10 percent. Similarly, the "increase interval" for the employee's performance rating provides guidelines based on whether current wage/salary is below or above the range midpoint. For example, if the wage/salary of this B-rated employee is below the range midpoint, a minimum of 12 months, an average of 15 months, or a maximum of 18 months may be selected. If a minimum interval of 12 months is selected, then 9 percent rather than 10 percent generally should be designated as the increase percentage. The 10 percent is reserved for longer increase intervals such as the 18 month waiting period required for the B-rated employee whose current compensation is above the midpoint.

Merit increases for employees whose current compensation is below the minimum of their rate ranges may be granted increases at 6-month intervals until the minimum is reached.

An alternative approach is outlined in Figure 7.9B, Sample Merit Increase Guidelines. This concept provides annual increases for all employees whose performance is satisfactory. Although range maximums are observed, increased intervals for employees who have exceeded midpoints are eliminated. The result is a requirement for a more extensive salary budget, one which is approximately double that needed in the other approach. It also should be noted that these guidelines require more discretion in determining appropriate merit increase percentages. For example, a "marginally satisfactory" employee can receive a raise of from 3 to 5 percent while a "satisfactory" employee can receive 5 to 7 percent.

Another alternative approach, which provides annual increases for all satisfactory performers, is outlined in Figure 7.9C, Sample Merit Increase Guidelines. Two additional performance rating categories are provided. Specified percentage of increase amounts are shown for each performance rating based on the positioning of current salary in the rate range for the employee's position–that is, "below minimum," "lower $\frac{1}{3}$," "middle $\frac{1}{3}$," and "upper $\frac{1}{3}$." As a range position moves upward, increase percentages decrease. While virtually all employees are granted an annual increase under these guidelines, many receive a relatively small percentage of increase amounts ranging from 1.7 to 4.5 percent. It might be psychologically better to offer larger minimum adjustments of 5 to 6 percent and specify a 15-month waiting period for the lower $\frac{1}{3}$, 18 months for the middle $\frac{1}{3}$, and 21 months for the upper $\frac{1}{3}$.

Promotional Increases. Company policy should include a statement to the effect that a promotional increase will be in addition to any merit increase which would have been granted under normal in-grade administration. A promotion is defined as the advancement of an employee to a job/position in a higher rate range. If increase percentage guidelines permit, the employee's new wage/salary rate should be placed at the minimum of the new rate range. A minimal promotional increase of 8 percent is combined with the individual's planned merit increase percentage (or a pro rata share thereof in cases where the increase is scheduled for more than 6 months in the future); the resultant overall increase normally should not exceed 20 percent.

Rating	Amount of Increase — % of Annual Salary	Increase Interval (in Months) Currently Below Range Midpoint			Currently Above Range Midpoint		
		Min.	Av.	Max.	Min.	Av.	Max.
A	11–12	6	9	12	12	15	18
B	9–10	12	15	18	18	21	24
C	7– 8	12	15	18	18	21	24
D	5– 6	12	15	18	18	21	24
E	None	—	—	—	—	—	—

Figure 7.9A Sample merit increase guidelines

Performance Level	Merit Increase (Percent)
Outstanding	10–12
Very Satisfactory	7–10
Satisfactory	5– 7
Marginally Satisfactory	3– 5
Unsatisfactory	0

Figure 7.9B Sample merit increase guidelines

Performance Rating	Below Minimum	Lower 1/3	Middle 1/3	Upper 1/3	Above Maximum
6	15.8%	14.0%	8.8%	7.6%	0.0%
5	13.2	10.8	7.4	5.7	0.0
4	10.8	8.6	6.3	4.3	0.0
3	9.7	7.7	5.4	3.0	0.0
2	6.4	4.5	3.9	2.4	0.0
1	3.6	3.2	1.7	0.0	0.0
0*	0.0	0.0	0.0	0.0	0.0

*Unacceptable Performance—employee is about to be terminated.

Figure 7.9C Sample merit increase guidelines

7.10 INCENTIVE COMPENSATION

A number of factors are combining to require a new approach to employee compensation which emphasizes special incentives.

- Government initiatives, which are requiring companies to provide uniformly equal benefits to all of their employees, are causing reassessments of programs to arrive at economically feasible, but lower overall levels of company-sponsored benefits. This will result in increased employee pressure for more substantial wage and salary increases.
- The ever-increasing need to achieve significant gains in product quality and higher productivity levels to surpass foreign competition. Existing merit pay and other compensation schemes have not fostered these objectives.
- Inflationary pressures, while abated to a degree, continue to erode employee buying power. So-called annual merit increase budgets are approximating the 6 percent level at a time when the reported inflationary rate is approximately 4 percent. The net result is that very few employees receive annual adjustments which adequately reflect the merit of their contributions.

The time has come to consider the development of an integrated reward system based on employee ownership of company common stock. All achievements that deserve recognition should be rewarded with shares. Employee suggestions, service anniversaries, outstanding performance recognition awards, and so on would receive appropriate numbers of shares. Beyond pay and benefits, the entire employee reward system would emphasize building ownership in the company. Employees who have an ever-increasing piece of the action will closely identify with the needs and objectives of their company.

7.11 SALARY SURVEY QUESTIONNAIRE

A competitive compensation program requires periodic assessments of the pay practices of other comparable employers within your company's geographical area. The Bureau of Labor Statistics of the U.S. Department of Labor periodically issues wage and salary data for representative occupations by type of industry and geographical areas. The American Management Association is a prominent source of survey information which provides national norms on professional, technical, and managerial positions. The College Placement Council is the authoritative source of information on current starting salaries of graduates by degree levels and majors.

Although there are numerous sources of survey data, many companies choose to supplement this information by conducting or participating in surveys conducted by cooperating companies within a specific geographical area. A representative example of a questionnaire used in this type of approach is the Non-Exempt Clerical Compensation Survey (Figure 7.11). In addition to obtaining information regarding starting rates and average rates paid, salary range data are requested for each type of position. The questionnaire also requests information concerning *incentive compensation*, which when added to a basic salary can significantly increase actual paid rates. Data regarding the "non-exempt personnel salary budget" also is requested; the continued competitiveness of a company's compensation program is dependent on adequate budgetary commitments.

Non-Exempt Clerical Compensation Survey

Company Name _____

Address _____

Name and Title of Respondent _____

Telephone (_____) _____

_____

Please provide the data requested for the following clerical and secretarial positions:

1. Entry-Level Clerical Position (Non-Keyboard)

    Recent high school graduate without business experience to perform the lowest level of work, e.g., filing and distributing mail.

    Typical starting rate . . . . $ _____

    Salary range minimum . . . . . . $ _____

    Salary range maximum . . . . . $ _____

    Number of incumbents. . . . . .   _____

2. Intermediate Clerical Position (Non-Keyboard)

    High school graduate hired to perform clerical work involving specific instructions, e.g., records processing or service functions such as receptionist duties. May occasionally use basic office machines to perform assigned duties.

    A. Recent graduate without business experience.

    B. Up to 2 years of specialized job-related training and/or experience.

	A	B
Typical starting rate	$ _____	$ _____
Salary range minimum	$ _____	$ _____
Salary range maximum	$ _____	$ _____
Average rate paid.	$ _____	$ _____
Number of incumbents.	_____	_____

3. Keyboard Positions

    A. Typist without business experience for straight typing from clear copy. Works under close supervision.

    B. Typist with up to 2 years of job-related experience to prepare final copy of average difficulty. May also perform basic clerical duties.

    C. Word processing specialist with up to 2 years of directly related experience. Uses word processing equipment to prepare final copy of average difficulty from handwritten copy. Performs routine clerical tasks such as answering telephones, filing, duplicating materials, etc.

	A	B	C
Typical starting rating	$ _____	$ _____	$ _____
Salary range minimum	$ _____	$ _____	$ _____
Salary range maximum	$ _____	$ _____	$ _____
Average rate paid.	$ _____	$ _____	$ _____
Number of incumbents.	_____	_____	_____

Figure 7.11 Salary survey questionnaire

continued

4. Secretarial Positions

    A. What is the typical starting rate for an individual hired without business experience for an entry level secretarial position?

    High School graduate . . . . . . $ _____

    Secretarial school graduate . . . . $ _____

    B. What is the typical starting rate for an individual with up to 2 years of experience?

    Typical starting rate . . . . $ _____

    Salary range minimum . . . . . . $ _____

    Salary range maximum . . . . . $ _____

    Average paid rate . . . . $ _____

    Number of incumbents . . . . . .   _____

5. Incentive Compensation

    Do these non-exempt clerical and secretarial employees receive incentive compensation?

    ☐ No   ☐ Yes

    If YES, please describe the type of award granted, how these awards are calculated, and the form of payment:

    _____

    _____

    _____

    _____

6. Non-Exempt Personnel Salary Budget

    A. What is the percentage of payroll represented by your current salary increase budget for non-exempt clerical personnel?

    _____%

    B. What is your best estimate of next year's salary increase budget percentage for non-exempt clerical personnel?

    _____%

    C. Please indicate which of the following are included in your salary increase budget:

    Promotional increases   _____No   _____Yes

    Merit increases   _____No   _____Yes

    Cost-of-living increases   _____No   _____Yes

    Longevity (length of
    service) increases   _____No   _____Yes

    Other (specify)_____

    _____

    _____

Figure 7.11 *(cont.)*

7.12 ANNUAL SALARY REVIEW WORKSHEET

On or about September 15 of each year, the annual salary and staffing planning budget is prepared in conjunction with the next year's annual administrative budget. The HR division initiates this process by preparing and distributing Salary Review Worksheet materials (see Figure 7.12) to the management of each organization. An organization's Salary Review Worksheet lists all assigned employees by name, position title, salary grade, salary range midpoint (based on new salary schedules to be effective on January 1), last merit increase data, last performance rating, and current salary.

Each manager examines the data shown in the "current" section to reflect planned changes, if any, for the balance of the current year. Managers then project merit increases and anticipated additions and reductions to staff for the coming year in the "proposed" section of the Salary Review Worksheet in accordance with the following guidelines:

1. The total for proposed merit increases should not exceed 8 percent* of the total for current year-end salaries (including estimated annual salaries for proposed additions to staff).
2. Due to required time intervals between merit increases, many employees will not be eligible for merit increases in the coming year. Strict adherence to established time interval guidelines, which are based on whether salaries are below or above midpoints, is required.
3. Performance ratings should approximate a normal distribution as follows:

Rating	Percentage
A	5
B	15
C	60
D	15
E	5

Completed Salary Review Worksheets are reviewed and approved through the top management level. The HR director's review prior to top management approval is required to ensure that performance ratings approximate a normal distribution, that increase amounts and timing are consistent with company policy, and that 8 percent budgetary constraints are met by planned actions. In cases where planned additions to the staff are listed, the HR director ensures that adequate estimated salary projections are included for the positions in question. Top management approval is then obtained for overall staffing and compensation plans.

The approved Salary Review Worksheets are used by the HR division for initiating scheduled salary changes throughout the next calendar year.

---

* Requires a 4 percent budget based on merit increase guidelines specified in Figure 7.9A.

Salary Review Worksheet

Organization _____

Employee	Position	G*	Range Midpoint	Current (Last Increase)					Proposed (Planned Increase)					Monthly Salary Budget													Annual Total
				Amt.	%	Month Eff.	P*	Salary	Amt.	%	Month Eff.	P*	Salary	Jan	Feb	Mar	April	May	June	July	Aug	Sept	Oct	Nov	Dec	

Totals:

*Key G = Wage/Salary Grade
      P = Performance Rating

Approvals: _____ _____ _____
           Date   Date   Date

Figure 7.12 Salary review worksheet

339

CHAPTER 8

Employee Benefits

This chapter highlights some approaches that facilitate and enhance the employee benefits process. Emphasis is placed on improved administrative procedures and more effective techniques for communicating benefits information to employees.

Section 8.1 offers a sample of a personalized annual benefits report by a company to an employee. This Employee Benefits Summary Statement also provides insights concerning typical benefit programs. In elaborating on the types of health benefits, the coverage offered by traditional group health insurance is compared with the benefits of a health maintenance organization in Section 8.2. Administrative simplicity and reduced paperwork is promoted by introducing a unified health and life insurance enrollment form in Section 8.3. The Beneficiary Designation Form in Section 8.4, offers guidance needed by employees concerning the types of special designations that promote estate planning objectives. Some thoughts about employee problems associated with having to provide "medical evidence of insurability" before being permitted to enroll in group life and medical benefit programs are discussed in Section 8.5. A novel approach to hospital cost containment is explained in Section 8.6 and a sample Hospital Diary and employee review of services versus billing process is described. No matter what time of the year an employee joins a company, the Equitable Vacation Policy described in Section 8.7 provides a uniform basis for vacation accrual. The details of A Matching Gifts Plan and a sample form used in all phases of administering a gift are offered in Section 8.8. Highlights of an Employee Child Care Program (Section 8.9) and The Employee Assistance Program Concept (Section 8.10) give valuable insights concerning these types of employee services. Samples of required annual benefit plan reports, as mandated by the Employee Retirement Income Security Act of 1974 (ERISA), are shown in Section 8.11. The need for planning in order to promote successful retirements is emphasized in Section 8.12, which provides a sample, Your Retirement Planning Checklist (Figure 8.12). To supplement this information further for planning retirements, a variety of guidance regarding Social Security benefits is provided in Section 8.13.

8.1 EMPLOYEE BENEFITS SUMMARY STATEMENT— THE EMPLOYEE'S ANNUAL REPORT

This section provides a sample of a 1986 Personal Statement of Employee Benefits booklet, a technique used by companies in providing a computer-generated personalized annual report of benefits to each of their employees. This approach offers an excellent vehicle for promoting each employee's understanding of the wide variety of benefits the company provides, reinforcing comprehension of the dollar value of benefits in terms of the employee's overall compensation, and emphasizing the need for cost containment in the interest of maximizing benefits at minimal cost to the company and the employee.

The 1986 Personal Statement of Employee Benefits for: MR. JOSEPH J. DOE (shown in Figure 8.1) includes the following:

Chairman of the Board's Message (Figure 8.1A)

This message from the chief executive officer reinforces the company's ongoing commitment to review and update its benefit program to ensure that it provides quality, comprehensive protection.

Health Care Benefits (Figure 8.1B)

The company offers a group medical plan which promotes many outpatient services with 100 percent coverage (no required deductible). More costly outpatient services, hospital emergency room services, and hospital confinements require deductibles before 100 percent of covered charges are paid by the plan.

The employee is reminded of his or her personal responsibility for managing health care benefits and medical expenses to obtain the best possible care and value for expenditures. To promote the concept that elective surgery requires a second opinion, a toll-free number is provided for obtaining the names of specialists who are prepared to offer this service. Similarly, the employee is encouraged to question doctors and dentists so that each diagnosis is clearly understood, and that all possible treatment plans and alternatives to hospital confinement are fully explored. The need to carefully review resultant medical bills for accuracy also is emphasized.

Disability Benefits (Figure 8.1C)

The company's short-term and long-term disability insurance policies pay the stated benefits subject to reductions for other related types of income, for example, Social Security disability benefits, Worker's Compensation benefits, and so on.

A provision concerning total and permanent disability provides continued group life insurance and medical insurance coverage. Basic life insurance remains in effect at no cost to the employee. Medical insurance for the employee and eligible dependents continues at special rates set by the company.

Survivor Benefits (Figure 8.1D)

A notation is provided to the effect that if the employee dies while on the payroll, eligible dependents may continue coverage under the group medical plan for 90 days at no cost. Additionally, federal law now provides a surviving spouse and other eligible dependents with eligibility for continued group coverage, at their own expense, for up to 3 years. The employer is required to notify the health insurance company regarding the employee's death, and to offer the survivor this continued group coverage. The survivor has 60 days to accept.

Beneficiary Data (Figure 8.1E)

Legal requirements relating to sole beneficiary rights of a spouse to assets in the employee's savings and investment plan and the employee stock ownership plan (ESOP) are specified. Unless a spouse signs a waiver and consent form allowing the designation of someone else as the primary beneficiary, the spouse remains the primary beneficiary under law.

The need for ensuring that "primary beneficiary" designations are current is emphasized, and the estate planning value of designating "contingent beneficiaries" is explained.

Retirement Benefits (Figure 8.1F)

Revised federal law, effective in 1989, will require corporate pension plans either to fully vest employees after 5 years of service, or to progressively vest employees according to the following schedule:

Years of Service	Amount of Vesting (%)
3	20
4	40
5	60
6	80
7	100

Concerning the lump sum settlement from the retirement annuity plan, tax law changes now have reduced a 10-year forward averaging provision to 5 years. While the employee still is not required to include the entire amount as income during the year it is received, now it only can be spread out over a 5-year period. A provision of the law allows individuals who reached age 50 by January 1, 1986, to use either the 10-year or 5-year averaging techniques. As a general rule for most employees, it appears that 10-year averaging will offer the most favorable tax treatment.

Savings and Investment Plan (Figure 8.1G)

Recent tax law changes limit the total annual employee and company contributions to profit sharing, stock ownership, and other investment accounts to 25 percent of the employee's pay, or $30,000, whichever is less. All after-tax dollars count against the $30,000 ceiling; a $7,000 maximum applies to 401K investments.

New withdrawal limitations are more stringent. The employee is now only able to withdraw his or her own contributions from a 401K. Unless the withdrawal is used for the payment of medical expenses which exceed $7\frac{1}{2}$ percent of adjusted gross income, income tax plus a 10 percent penalty is payable. Similarly, a 10 percent tax penalty also applies to early withdrawals from other company-sponsored plans unless the funds are applied to paying tax deductible medical bills.

Withdrawals from tax-deferred savings plans can no longer involve only withdrawing nontaxable employee contributions. Each withdrawal now must include employee contributions, company contributions, and account earnings. Accordingly, only 10 percent of the withdrawal now qualifies as a tax-free return of employee principle; the balance of the withdrawal is subject to income tax plus a 10 percent penalty for early withdrawal.

Other Benefits (Figure 8.1H)

The employee is reminded that principal additional benefits include days off with pay for holidays and vacations, participation in the employee stock ownership plan, and the matching gifts plan. Procedural details are provided to assist the employee in exercising options to purchase company stock. Additional "other benefits" that are cited include educational assistance, adoption benefits, paid funeral leave, paid jury duty leave, service awards, and college scholarships and international exchange scholarships for eligible dependent children.

Check Your Benefits (Figure 8.1I)

This section includes a vitally important disclaimer that the booklet is not a "contract," and is not intended to impose "contractual liability" on the company. Official copies of company benefit plans are designated as the authoritative source of information in the event of inconsistencies. Furthermore, the company reserves the right to change or terminate benefit plans described in the booklet.

About This Report (Figure 8.1J)

The assumptions used in preparing the statement included "fully insured" as defined by the Social Security Administration. For verifying that prior year earnings meet associated requirements, the employee is provided with a special postcard ("request for statement of earnings") for obtaining this information from the Social Security Administration. A sample of this postcard and an explanation of the process is provided in Section 8.13, Social Security Benefits.

Cost of Benefits (Figure 8.1K)

In view of the major expense to the company for providing comprehensive employee benefits, the inappropriateness of the term "fringe benefits" is shown by specific examples of representative costs. To personalize this point, the employee's personal benefits account is specified in terms of total cost, employee's cost, and dollar value added to employee's annual compensation.

An Overview (Figure 8.1L)

A fundamental estate planning framework is provided. The "personal net worth statement" provides a rudimentary analysis of the current financial condition, and points to areas where remedial action may be appropriate. The basic question is, "Could my spouse and dependents meet their needs with company-provided benefits and other resources?" If not, alternatives such as acquiring additional life insurance protection should be explored.

The HR director includes a transmittal letter addressed to "Dear Company Employee" (Figure 8.1M) which highlights the points necessary for promoting the understanding of the statement and its functions. An Employee Benefits Questionnaire (Figure 8.1N) is enclosed for soliciting employee comments about the statement and the company's benefit program.

TO ████ EMPLOYEES:

This personalized summary of your benefits has been designed to show the extent to which you and your family are currently participating in the ████ benefit program. In some cases, it also provides you with projections of certain benefits that you may be entitled to in the future.

Only through understanding how the ████ benefit program works will you be able to use your ████ benefits to your own — and your family's — best advantage. You will note that your benefit program has been designed to meet a wide range of needs and situations, both while you're working and after you retire. The benefit program is reviewed and updated on an ongoing basis to ensure that it continues to provide quality, comprehensive protection.

If you have any questions about this benefits statement, or about ████ benefits in general, please ask your supervisor or Personnel representative.

Chairman of the Board

TABLE OF CONTENTS

Figure 8.1A Chairman of the board's message and Table of contents

HEALTH CARE BENEFITS

GROUP MEDICAL PLAN

Our records show that you and your eligible dependents **are covered under the** ▮▮▮ **Group Medical Plan.**

The ▮▮ Medical Plan pays **100%** for many outpatient services with no deductible required. Most other covered services are paid at **80%** or **100%** after the deductibles outlined below are met:

- Calendar year Plan deductible of **$200** per individual or **$500** per family;
- Per confinement hospital deductible of **$100** (plus the calendar year Plan deductible, if not previously met); this deductible will be limited to three per person per calendar year.
- Per visit hospital emergency room deductible of **$25** for treatment received within **72** hours of an accident or for hospital expenses when outpatient surgery is performed. For all other covered services performed in the emergency room, the **$200** calendar year Plan deductible will also apply if not previously satisfied.

An out-of-pocket calendar year maximum of **$2,000** per family applies to most covered expenses not reimbursed by the Plan. Thereafter, the Plan pays **100%** of additional covered charges incurred during the remainder of that calendar year. (Expenses for the treatment of alcohol or drug abuse cannot be applied toward the out-of-pocket maximum.)

For the names of appropriate specialists for a second opinion for elective surgery, call toll-free **(800)527-0764.**

For most covered expenses, there are no dollar limits. However, there is a **$50,000** per person maximum for hospice care and a **$50,000** per person lifetime maximum for outpatient treatment of mental illness, alcoholism or drug abuse.

GROUP DENTAL PLAN

In addition, you and your eligible dependents **are** covered by the ▮▮ Group Dental Plan.

The Plan pays **50%**
of reasonable and customary charges
for corrective work, plus **100%**
of reasonable and customary charges
for diagnostic work, up to **$1,000**
per covered member of your
family per year, and **$5,000**
maximum lifetime benefits for you and
each covered dependent.
In addition, the Dental Plan pays. **50%**
of reasonable and customary
orthodontic charges, up to. **$1,000**
per person per lifetime.

Your Employee Assistance Plan phone number is ▮▮▮▮▮.

As a health care Company, we are interested in ensuring that you and your family receive quality health care in a cost effective manner.

Understanding your health care benefits and managing your medical expenses puts you in control when it comes to getting the care you need and the best value for the dollars you spend. To help you make wise health care choices you should:

- Carefully read your Plan booklets.

- Ask your doctor or dentist questions so that you clearly understand the diagnosis and treatment for your condition, as well as alternative treatments.

- Inquire about alternatives to hospital confinement.

- Ask about the cost of services before the treatment begins.

- Obtain a second opinion before proceeding with elective surgery.

- Carefully review all of your bills.

You should also know that, under current law, an active employee age 65-69 must receive all medical benefits payable under the ▮▮ Medical Plan (or, if applicable, the Health Maintenance Organization in which he or she has chosen to participate) before Medicare will make any payments, unless the employee elects Medicare as the "primary" payor. This provision also applies to an employee's spouse if he or she is age 65-69, as long as the employee is less than age 70.

When you or an eligible dependent require health care services, the medical identification card(s) on page 24 may prove useful. The card(s) should be signed immediately and carried at all times.

Figure 8.1B Health care benefits

DISABILITY BENEFITS

WORK-RELATED ("OCCUPATIONAL") DISABILITY
If you become hurt or sick **due to a work-related cause,**
you would receive $3,583 a month
starting on the first day and continuing for
as long as 6 months.

Then your benefits would be
paid at the rate of $2,150
a month beginning after
6 months and continuing while
totally disabled, up to age 65.

IF YOU'RE PERMANENTLY AND TOTALLY DISABLED WHILE ACTIVELY EMPLOYED, YOU WOULD ALSO HAVE BENEFITS OF:
The value of your Savings and Investment Plan account. (As of Apr. 30 1986 your account was valued at $43,990 .)

Annual Income of ****** from the ▓▓▓ Retirement Annuity Plan at age 65.

NON-WORK-RELATED ("NON-OCCUPATIONAL") DISABILITY
If you become hurt or sick for **reasons unrelated to your work,** you would receive $3,583 a month
starting on the first day and continuing for as long as 6 months.

Then your benefits would be
paid at the rate of $2,150
a month beginning after
6 months and continuing while
totally disabled, up to age 65.

DEPENDING ON THE CIRCUMSTANCES OF YOUR DISABILITY, YOU COULD ALSO RECEIVE:
$107,500 or more from your ▓▓▓ Accidental Death and Dismemberment Insurance
$129,000 or more under your ▓▓▓ Business Travel Accident Insurance.

In preparing this report, we have attempted to give you an idea of the minimum benefits payable from all disability income sources ▓▓▓ plans together with government plans) thereby, perhaps understating the value of your benefits in some cases. It is important for you to know that benefits payable under the ▓▓▓ Short-Term Disability Policy and the ▓▓▓ Long-Term Disability Plan are reduced by the amount of certain other income benefits you may be entitled to receive. Examples of such other income benefits include your ▓▓▓ retirement annuity, Social Security disability benefits, Workers' Compensation benefits, No-fault insurance benefits and benefits from other statutory disability income programs.

If you become totally and permanently disabled prior to your Normal Retirement date, but have credit for ten or more years in the ▓▓▓ Retirement Annuity Plan, you will continue earning credits toward a retirement annuity by being placed on Disability Leave Status. By so doing, dollar credits will be added to your ▓▓▓ retirement annuity account based on your annual earnings for the calendar year preceding the year in which the disability occurred. You may elect to receive this annuity at your Normal Retirement date or at an earlier time, if eligible for retirement. The same provisions for choosing optional forms of payment and for early retirement apply as for active employees. Disability Leave Status does not affect receipt of ▓▓▓ Long-Term Disability benefits. You may also withdraw all or a portion of your account under the Savings and Investment Plan.

In addition, you should know, if you become totally and permanently disabled prior to your Normal Retirement date, your current amount of Basic Group Life Insurance would remain in effect until your Normal Retirement date at no cost to you. Also, Medical Insurance for you and your eligible dependents may be continued for as long as your disability lasts, at a rate set by the Company depending on your length of service.

Figure 8.1C Disability benefits

SURVIVOR BENEFITS

SINGLE-SUM PAYMENTS

If you were to die from any cause, your ▮ Group Life Insurance would pay the designated beneficiary . . . . **$ 86,000**

plus Supplemental Life Insurance of **129,000**

If you die due to an accident, as defined in the plan, the designated beneficiary would receive an additional **215,000**

If death occurs while you're covered under the ▮ Business Travel Accident Policy, an additional payment of . . . . **258,000** would be made.

Total **$688,000**

At death, the total value of your ▮ Savings and Investment Plan account would be paid to your designated beneficiary. As of **Apr. 30 1986** your account was valued at . . . . **$ 43,990**

At your death, Social Security will pay . . . . . **$ 255** to your eligible spouse for funeral expenses.

If death is due to a work-related cause, Workers' Compensation benefits would also pay your dependent survivors ▪

CONTINUING INCOME PAYMENTS

If your surviving dependent spouse is caring for a child at the time of your death, they will be eligible for continuing Social Security payments of . . . . **$1,400** a month for as long as the child retains dependent status, or . . . . **$1,634** if caring for **more than one** dependent child.

If death is due to a work-related cause, Workers' Compensation benefits would also provide weekly payments to your dependent survivors ▪

If you die while on our payroll, your dependents, if eligible, may continue coverage under the Group Medical Plan for 90 days at no cost.

The value of insurance protection is adjusted in terms of your annualized compensation whenever your pay is adjusted during the year.

An assumption was made in showing death benefits under Workers' Compensation, that is, we assumed that you will be survived only by a dependent spouse. Additional benefits exist, which vary by state depending on number and degree of dependency of children.

Figure 8.1D Survivor benefits

BENEFICIARY DATA

Our records show that you have designated the following beneficiaries for your Pfizer group benefits programs.

```
          BASIC GROUP LIFE INSURANCE
PRIMARY        JANICE M DOE
CONTINGENT     JOSEPH J DOE JR

          SUPPLEMENTAL LIFE INSURANCE
PRIMARY        JANICE M DOE
CONTINGENT     JOSEPH J DOE JR

          BUSINESS TRAVEL ACCIDENT INSURANCE
OUR RECORDS INDICATE THAT YOU HAVE ASSIGNED THIS POLICY TO
JANICE M DOE
YOUR ASSIGNEE HAS MADE THE FOLLOWING BENEFICIARY DESIGNATIONS
PRIMARY        JANICE M DOE
CONTINGENT     ESTATE OF JANICE M DOE

          SAVINGS AND INVESTMENT PLAN *
PRIMARY        JOSEPH J DOE JR

          EMPLOYEE STOCK OWNERSHIP PLAN
PRIMARY        YOUR SPOUSE

* A CONSENT AND WAIVER FORM ALLOWING YOU TO NAME A PRIMARY
BENEFICIARY OTHER THAN YOUR SPOUSE WAS SIGNED ON AUG.  6 1985
BY YOUR SPOUSE JANICE DOE
```

Remember, for the ▆▆ Savings and Investment Plan and the ▆▆ Employee Stock Ownership Plan, the law states that if you are married your spouse is your sole primary beneficiary, regardless of your designation, unless your spouse signs a waiver and consent form permitting you to designate someone else as the primary beneficiary. If you have any questions about the beneficiary data shown on the preceding page, please contact your Personnel representative.

Too often, we forget whom we have designated as our beneficiaries. Many times there is no reason to change these intended recipients of certain benefits. In other instances, events in our lives suggest change—for example, a beneficiary may have died. That is why some employees have named "contingent" beneficiaries, specific persons they would like to receive the survivor benefits if all the "primary" beneficiaries predecease the employee. Of course, if all the beneficiaries predecease you, the benefits become part of your estate.

Although we have made every effort to include on our computerized files the names of your beneficiaries, your most recent changes may not have been recorded. In any case, it is not our computerized files, but the original documents signed by you as well as the requirements of the law that determine the recipient of these benefits.

We recommend that you contact your Personnel representative to verify that the record reflects your wishes and is consistent with this statement. Should you wish to make any changes in your beneficiaries, your Personnel representative will be happy to provide you with the necessary forms.

Figure 8.1E Beneficiary data

RETIREMENT BENEFITS

HEALTH CARE BENEFITS
Group Medical coverage could continue under normal, late, and some forms of early retirement, although payments would be reduced by benefits available under Medicare.

SURVIVOR BENEFITS
If eligible, your ▇ Group Life Insurance upon retirement, based on your **current** compensation, will be **$43,000 (assuming early or normal retirement).**
Thereafter, it will be reduced **$4,050** per year with a minimum coverage of $2,500 for life.

SOCIAL SECURITY
As you know, you may begin receiving your Social Security retirement annuity after reaching age 65, or earlier at a reduced level. In addition, if your spouse received Social Security annuity payments based on your account, after reaching age 65, they would be 50% of your annuity during your lifetime and 100% of your annuity as your survivor. Payment to your spouse could begin earlier at a reduced level.

RETIREMENT ANNUITIES
The annuities available from the ▇ Retirement Annuity Plan discussed on this page and the facing page are some of the options available to you. If you are married, election of some of the options will require the consent of your spouse. A description of available options is contained in the Summary Plan Description in the Plan Booklet, which is available through your Personnel representative.
You **will be** vested in your ▇ Retirement Annuity Plan benefits **in May 1989.**

Shown below are possible dates for you to begin receiving payments as a vested annuitant (plus Social Security at age 65)

Examples of your current entitlement as a vested annuitant (assuming no future earnings)

. . . if payments begin . . .   . . . when you are age:

No current entitlement, as you are not now vested.

YOUR ANNUAL ANNUITY	
excluding Social Security:	including Social Security at age 65 and after:

235-83-1474

Shown below are possible retirement dates and projected annuities (plus Social Security at or after age 65) assuming **continued earnings at your present level until retirement and a 50% benefit to your surviving spouse.**

Type of Retirement . . .	. . . and date of retirement . . .	. . . when you are age:	YOUR ANNUAL ANNUITY excluding Social Security:	including Social Security at or after 65:
Normal	Mar. 1 2018	65	$18,402	$29,574
90 Combination				
(no discount)	Mar. 1 2013	60	$17,710	$28,690
(discounted)	July 1 2011	58	$15,830	$26,690
65 Combination	Mar. 1 2003	50	$5,108	$16,280

With the appropriate approvals, you could receive at age **65** —with no further Company obligation—a Lump Sum settlement from the Retirement Annuity Plan of **$164,167** based on current rates (subject to change).

THE SAVINGS AND INVESTMENT PLAN If you **continue with** contributions to the Plan at the rate of **8%,** **$124,494** will be contributed by age **65** and the Company will have matched that with **$62,533** for a total of **$187,027** —without considering any investment gain or loss. Based on current rates (subject to change) an account of this value at age **65** would provide the annuities described below.

TOTAL ESTIMATED INCOME AT 65 (based on the stated assumptions)	. . . WITHOUT PROVISION FOR A SURVIVOR . . . Your annual annuity:	. . . OR WITH 50% PAYMENTS TO A SURVIVOR	
		Your annual annuity:	Surviving spouse's annual annuity:
from the ▇ Retirement Annuity Plan	$20,881	$18,402	$ 9,201
from Social Security	$11,172	$11,172	$11,172
from the ▇ Savings and Investment Plan	$20,755	$19,333	$ 9,666
ANNUAL TOTAL	$ 52,808	$ 48,907	$ 30,039

Adding together the lump sums from the Retirement Annuity Plan and the Savings and Investment Plan would give a total lump sum of **$351,194** and an annual annuity from Social Security of **$11,172.**

Figure 8.1F Retirement benefits

SAVINGS AND INVESTMENT PLAN

Saving for tomorrow is something we all try to do. If you currently participate in the ▮▮▮ Savings and Investment Plan you already know its advantages—through it you build savings for the future with substantial help from the Company.

Contributions from 2% to 15% of your regular earnings, up to the maximum permitted by current laws and regulations, may be made to the Plan. Contributions may be made on a before-tax basis, after-tax basis or a combination of both.

In addition, the Company matches these contributions dollar for dollar on the first 2% of your pay that is contributed to the Plan and 50¢ for every dollar on the next 4% of your pay that is contributed. All Company matching contributions are invested in ▮▮▮ common stock, which gives you an important stake in the success of the Company.

You may withdraw up to 100% of the market value of both your own after-tax contributions and your vested portion of the Company's matching contributions. You may not make such withdrawals, called Non-Hardship Withdrawals, more than once in a 12-month period without first obtaining the consent of the Savings and Investment Plan Committee. In addition, you will incur a mandatory 6-month suspension of Plan contributions if you take a Non-Hardship Withdrawal within 24 months of a previous Non-Hardship Withdrawal.

If your Plan benefits become payable because you terminate employment, whether as a result of retirement, death or otherwise, there are several payment options available. If you are married, the election of some of these options may require your spouse's consent. You must choose a payment option within 13 months following your termination or your funds will remain in the Plan until you attain age 65, become disabled or die, whichever occurs first. Please refer to your Savings and Investment Plan booklet for details of the payment options and what happens upon termination of employment.

If you have not participated in the Plan, now is the time to reconsider. To enroll in the Plan, you simply complete and return the enrollment and beneficiary forms which are available from Payroll or your Personnel representative. Your participation will start on the first day of the calendar month—or on the first day of your first payroll period within that calendar month— after you enroll.

Displayed below is the status of your account as of **Apr. 30 1986** . In accordance with your election and the terms of the Plan, **8%** of your earnings were contributed to the ▮▮▮ Savings and Investment Plan. **This 8% is the sum of 8% before-tax and 0% after-tax.**

Allocation of Contributions:			Contributions to date:	Market value:
FUND A	**15%**	Before-tax	$ 1,578.50	$ 1,759.35
		After-tax	$ 0.00	$ 0.00
		Total	$ 1,578.50	$ 1,759.35
FUND B	**0%**	Before-tax	$ 0.00	$ 0.00
		After-tax	$ 0.00	$ 0.00
		Total	$ 0.00	$ 0.00
FUND C	**85%**	Before-tax	$ 8,242.00	$ 15,029.60
		After-tax	$ 5,167.00	$ 11,329.08
		Total	$ 13,409.00	$ 26,358.68
CONTRIBUTION TOTAL			$ 14,987.50	$ 28,118.03
▮▮▮ **MATCHING CONTRIBUTION***			$ 7,780.45	$ 15,872.12
COMBINED TOTAL			$ 22,767.95	$ 43,990.15

*You were **100%** vested in the market value of the ▮▮▮ Matching Contribution shown above.

235-83-1474

Figure 8.1G Savings and investment plan

The preceding pages have covered a lot of ground in showing how you stand in terms of your major ▮ benefits. Of course, some aspects of our benefits program don't fit into the categories we've discussed so far. But they do add value to your total compensation and they do help make ▮ a better place to work. On page 17 you will see additional information about paid holidays and vacations, the Employee Stock Ownership Plan, the Matching Gifts Plan and the Stock Option Plan.

Please be aware that the date of your retirement or termination may affect the last permissible date of exercise for some of your stock options. In order to exercise your stock option(s), you must complete a Stock Option Transaction Request form which is available from the payroll department which issues your paycheck.

You do not have to purchase all the shares of an option at one time, however, you must buy at least 10 shares or such lesser number as may remain under the option. Your option will be exercised as of the day your payroll department receives the signed Stock Option Transaction Request form and payment for the shares. Payment may be made by check or, if you have authorized payroll deductions, from your stock option account.

In addition to the plans mentioned above, you are eligible for a number of other benefits, including: educational assistance; adoption benefits; paid funeral leave; paid jury duty leave; service awards; college scholarships and international exchange scholarships for eligible dependent children; and other items. Your Personnel representative can tell you more about these benefits.

DAYS OFF WITH PAY

You are eligible for **12** paid holidays and **3 weeks** of vacation in **1986.**

That makes a total of **27** days off with pay in **1986.**

You will be eligible for 4 weeks of vacation in 1989. This vacation combined with 12 paid holidays will give you 32 days off with pay in 1989.

THE EMPLOYEE STOCK OWNERSHIP PLAN

Your ▮ Employee Stock Ownership Plan account contained **19.39588** shares, as of **May 31 1986** with a market value on that date of **$1,219.51.**

THE MATCHING GIFTS PLAN

According to our records as of **May 31 1986** the Company matched **$0** of the contributions you made to eligible institutions through the Plan during **1985.**

Your ▮ STOCK OPTION account contained **$0** as of **May 31 1986** and your status was as follows:

Grant date	Shares	Type	Price	Exercise on or after…	…and on or before…
June 26 1980	49	NQ	$20.63	June 26 1981	June 25 1990
Aug. 16 1982	31	ISO	$28.00	Aug. 16 1983	Aug. 15 1992
May 22 1986	53	ISO	$60.50	May 22 1987	May 21 1996

Based on the May 31 1986 market price ($62.875), the potential gain on your options would be $3,277.

235-83-1474

Figure 8.1H Other benefits

CHECK YOUR BENEFITS

This booklet is not a contract and is not intended to impose contractual liability on ▮▮▮ It is a brief outline of some of the highlights of the various benefit plans described herein which may be available to you. In the event that there is an inconsistency between this booklet and the actual plans themselves, the terms of the plans will control. Copies of the plans may be obtained from your Personnel representative upon request.

The Company expects and intends to continue the benefit plans outlined in this booklet, but reserves the right to change or terminate them in the future. Any such action would be taken only after careful consideration.

Although every effort has been made to report carefully and accurately, it is possible for errors to occur. Please be sure your Social Security number appears correctly on pages 1, 12, 15, 17, 19 and 21 and also examine the information included on the facing page. If you see what seems to be an error—either there or elsewhere in this report—please contact your Personnel representative.

The information presented in this booklet is based on your status as of the following dates as indicated on our computerized files:

"As of" date for payroll information	May	31 1986
"As of" date for savings and investment plan information	Apr.	30 1986
"As of" date for stock option information	May	31 1986
"As of" date for retirement information	Dec.	31 1985
"As of" date for employee stock ownership plan information	May	31 1986
"As of" date for beneficiary information	May	31 1986
"As of" date for group life, long-term disability and business travel accident insurance earnings determination	May	31 1986

According to our records:

You were born on	Feb.	19 1953
Your employment date is	Nov.	1 1979
Your marital status is		Married
Your spouse's name is		Janice
Your spouse was born on	Jan.	23 1953
Your work location is	New York Office	

Our records show that you have had no
break in employment since joining ▮▮▮▮▮

Ref. No. 15800   235-83-1474

Figure 8.1l Check your benefits

ABOUT THIS REPORT

In preparing this report, we have assumed continuous future employment on your part and that your earnings and the plans themselves will remain unchanged. If there is any difference between the benefits stated in this report and those to which you are entitled under the terms of a plan (and applicable laws and regulations) at the time you become eligible to receive them, the latter would, of course, govern.

Furthermore, Social Security benefits were estimated based on current benefit provisions and reasonable assumptions of your past earnings, and assume you are "fully insured" as defined by the Social Security Administration and that you have been participating in Social Security throughout your career. Because of these assumptions, the benefits reflected in this statement may vary from those you would actually receive. The enclosed

postcard will enable you to receive a current statement of your Social Security earnings directly from the Social Security Administration, if you are interested.

Annuity benefits from the ████ Retirement Annuity Plan are provided on a joint and survivor basis to married employees, unless the employee's spouse signs a waiver and consent form permitting the employee to choose a payment option other than a joint and survivor annuity.

Also, ████ Savings and Investment Plan projections and statements of current value do not take into account future investment gains or losses, which are risks assumed by Plan participants, and therefore, are not guarantees as to the amounts which will be paid.

Figure 8.1J About this report

COST OF BENEFITS

FOR THE COMPANY AS A WHOLE

Not too many years ago, benefits such as those discussed in this booklet were referred to as "fringe benefits." The phrase is hardly appropriate today since the scope of our programs is comprehensive and the cost to the Company to provide these benefits is quite significant. In 1985, benefit programs for ████ and its subsidiaries in the United States cost over $200 million. Shown below are some of the major expense categories.

Life & Health Care Insurance	$42.4 million
Pension Plans	30.1 million
Savings and Investment Plan	15.3 million
Time Off With Pay	46.0 million
Social Security, Workers' Compensation, etc.	48.2 million

FOR YOU AS AN INDIVIDUAL

Based on your level of benefits participation, current compensation, and years of service with the Company, the annual cost of the benefits covered in this report . . . including Social Security benefits . . . is approximately **$21,470** per year.
Of that amount your annual contribution to your benefits program . . . including your half of Social Security taxes . . . is about **$6,710**
This leaves a dollar value added to your annual compensation by the Company of **$14,760**

The information on this page is being provided so that you will be aware of the cost impact of our benefit program on the Company as a whole and also so that you will have a way of interpreting its value to you.

Figure 8.1K Cost of benefits

AN OVERVIEW

You probably have other significant items adding to your financial net worth—your home, car, stocks, bonds, savings account, furniture, clothes, or other items.

For those interested in highlighting the current market value of these items we have included an abbreviated net worth financial statement. You can make it as brief as the one shown or more elaborate by adding additional categories.

As you write down the current value of what you own, you may want to look at the other side of the ledger—namely what you owe. If you have a home and a car you probably have a mortgage and a loan. Maybe you have a balance on your credit cards which extends beyond a 30-day repayment period. Write them down, add them up and subtract the total from your total assets, the result is your net worth.

Space has also been provided for highlighting your various insurance plans (e.g., life, homeowners, automobile, disability, liability, etc.). In addition, there is room for any "other information" you believe important (e.g., name of your attorney, location of will, or other important papers, credit card name and number, etc.).

Spending a few minutes completing this section may not only be interesting, but worthwhile as well.

PERSONAL NET WORTH STATEMENT

ASSETS

Home/Real Estate . . . . $ _____

Automobile/Furniture/Clothes . . . . _____

Bonds/Stocks (including ▮▮▮) . . . . _____

Savings Account . . . . _____

▮▮▮ Savings & Investment Plan . . . . _____

Other:_____ _____

   TOTAL ASSETS $ _____

LIABILITIES

Mortgage . . . . $ _____

Loan — Car . . . . _____

Credit Cards . . . . _____

Other:_____ _____

   TOTAL LIABILITIES $ _____

NET WORTH (Assets Minus Liabilities) $ _____

INSURANCE HIGHLIGHTS

What is insured?	Name of the Insurance Company?	What is the Policy Number?	Amount of Insurance?	Annual Cost of Insurance?	Who Receives Benefits?	Where is the Policy Located?
			$	$		

OTHER INFORMATION

Figure 8.1L An overview

Date

Dear Company Employee:

We are pleased to provide you with the enclosed Employee Benefits Statement. Although you may have received this statement in previous years, and are familiar with its contents, it is helpful to highlight the following points:

- The statement was prepared using data taken from your personnel record; therefore, the information provided applies specifically to you and your family.

- Please check the accuracy of your personnel records data by reviewing the information on page 19. If you believe there is an error, contact your HRM division representative immediately to arrange corrective action.

- Wherever asterisks (********) are printed, it means that the information was not available for you or your family at the time this summary was prepared.

- The projections for the Retirement Annuity Plan and the Savings and Investment Plan are based on your earnings as of the date indicated on page 19. They do not take into account any changes of pay you may receive in the future.

- The "cost of benefits" section on page 21 shows the annual cost of your benefits. As you can see, these benefits represent a substantial addition to your base pay.

- Medical Identification Cards are provided for you (and your spouse, if applicable) on page 24.

Please take this opportunity to thoroughly review your statement. We would appreciate your comments about the statement and the company's benefit program; an Employee Benefits Questionnaire is enclosed for your convenience. Your completed questionnaire should be forwarded to my attention by (date).

Sincerely,

John T. Hall
Vice President—Human Resources

Figure 8.1M HR director transmittal letter to company employee

Employee Benefits Questionnaire

We would appreciate your comments and suggestions about this benefit statement and our benefit program in general.

1. Is the personal information on page 19 accurate and up-to-date?

    ☐ YES ☐ NO

    If not, please describe necessary corrections: _____

    _____

2. If you could change one benefit plan, which would it be?

    ☐ Disability ☐ Dental Insurance ☐ Medical Insurance

    ☐ Retirement ☐ Life Insurance ☐ Savings and Investment Plan

    ☐ Vacations and Holidays

    ☐ OTHER (Please specify in "COMMENTS")

    COMMENTS (Describe the proposed change): _____

    _____

    _____

    _____

3. Do you have any suggestions for improving the benefit statement? For example, what additional information should be included, what clarifications are needed, etc.?

    _____

    _____

    _____

    _____

    _____

4. Do you want a reply to your comments?

    ☐ YES ☐ NO

    If you indicated "Yes," please provide your name and your home mailing address:

    _____

    _____

Figure 8.1N Employee benefits questionnaire

8.2 COMPARISON OF HEALTH CARE PLAN ALTERNATIVES

Company-sponsored health insurance plans generally offer the following types of coverage for employees and their families:

- Hospitalization and surgical procedure expenses
- Supplemental major medical expenses such as outpatient medical care by physicians

Many plans also provide dental, prescription, and vision care benefits.

As a general rule, employees should be eligible immediately for health insurance benefits at the time they are hired. Coverage costs for the employee should be paid fully by the company, but dependent coverage costs should be shared by the employee.

Cost containment is achieved by requiring the employee to pay an annual deductible amount before major medical benefits are paid by the insurance plan.

Some companies offer employees the option of participating in a health maintenance organization (HMO), which provides prepaid medical services through designated physicians.

A comparison of the benefits offered by a health insurance plan and an HMO is shown in Figure 8.2, Comparison Chart—Health Care Plan Alternatives.

Comparison of Health Insurance Plan vs. Health Maintenance Organization Benefits

Health Insurance Plan	Health Maintenance Organization
Coverage protects the employee and eligible dependents from major out-of-pocket medical expenses. Any physician, specialist, or hospital may be selected to provide service.	Coverage provides the employee and eligible dependents with complete health care through participating physicians, specialists, and hospitals.
Insurance company payments begin after an annual deductible is satisfied. Both an individual and a family deductible amount are specified. A special deductible applies to each hospitalization. Costs are shared for most services until the employee, in addition to meeting the deductible requirements, reaches specified contribution limits; costs thereafter are fully paid by the insurance company. An individual lifetime maximum benefit may be specified.	No deductibles or lifetime maximum benefits apply; 100% coverage is provided. Individuals receiving certain services from their primary physicians are required to make a small "co-payment."
Hospitalization (including maternity) involves a special deductible, costs are shared until a specified dollar limit is reached, then the insurance company provides 100% payment. Similarly, Convalescent Facility care is provided subject to these provisions; however, a specified number of days limits this coverage.	100% coverage is provided.
Coverage subject to annual deductibles and shared costs to a specified dollar limit are provided for the following:	**100% coverage is provided unless otherwise noted below:**

- Physician and surgeon fees
- Diagnostic laboratory and X-ray services
- Pre-operative laboratory testing
- Anesthesia
- Birthing centers
- Private duty nursing
- Hospice facilities

Figure 8.2 Comparison chart: health care plan alternatives

continued

Health Insurance Plan	Health Maintenance Organization
• Doctor visits	(Co-payments are required. A minimum amount applies to an office visit, and about $2\frac{1}{2}$ times that amount is charged for a home visit.)
• Home health care (up to 120 visits per year)	(As an alternative to hospitalization)
• Ambulance	(With special approval)
• Prescription drugs	Not covered
• Durable medical/surgical equipment, prosthetic devices	(If implanted)
• Blood and plasma	Not covered
• Chiropractic services for full treatment plus monthly maintenance visits	Not covered
• Alcoholism treatment program	
• Bi-annual vision examinations	
• Vision lenses and frames (specified dollar maximum payable once every two years)	(Specified dollar maximum)
• General dentistry (calendar year dollar maximum)	Not covered
• Dental crowns, inlays, and fixed bridgework (50% limitation and calendar year dollar maximum)	Not covered
Other Coverage Provisions:	
• Dental X-rays, oral exams, and cleanings (100% coverage)	Not covered
• Immunizations and inoculations (not covered)	100% coverage
• Mental health hospitalization (subject to annual and lifetime maximums)	100% coverage with period of less than 1 month specified as an annual maximum
• Outpatient mental health (subject to a dollar limit for each visit, and a maximum annual dollar payment which limits the number of visits to 20)	Co-payment provisions for each visit, and maximum of 20 visits. (Focus is on crisis intervention and short-term evaluation, not therapy)

Figure 8.2 *(cont.)*

8.3 UNIFIED HEALTH AND LIFE INSURANCE ENROLLMENT FORM

In the interest of reducing paperwork and simplifying benefits enrollment procedures, a model Insurance Enrollment Form is shown in Figure 8.3. This model offers provisions for all types of administrative actions relating to the overall insurance programs of a representative company. For example, it accounts for varied transactions such as the

- Initial enrollment of a new hire
- Enrollment of a transferred employee in plans not offered by a previous company unit
- Enrollment of a reinstated employee
- Waiver of coverages for which a new, transferred, or reinstated employee is eligible
- Notification of dependent changes for medical insurance purposes, for example, the birth or adoption of a child (to be included in coverage), or the marriage of a child who would be eligible (removal from coverage)
- Basis for the company to advise the insurance company regarding an employee name change
- Dependent benefit cancellation of personal accident insurance

The form also is structured to serve as a worksheet by HRM division and payroll representatives. The right-hand column is used by the HRM division representative to designate effective dates for elected types of coverage; the payroll representative designates associated payroll deductions.

Insurance Enrollment Form

		For HRM Division/ Payroll Use Only
Employee Name (Last, First, MI)	**Social Security No.**	**Effective Date**
		_____
Date of Birth **Sex**	**Marital Status**	
_____ □ M □ F	□ Single □ Married	
ACTION:		
□ New Hire	□ Name Change	**Employee Number**
□ Transfer	□ Dependent Change	
□ Reinstatement	□ Dependent Benefit Cancellation	_____

Medical & Dental Insurance

Do you want dependent benefits? □ Yes □ No

LIST YOUR ELIGIBLE DEPENDENTS:

Last Name (if different), First Name	Date of Birth Mo. Day Year	Effective Date
_____	_____	_____
_____	_____	**Monthly Deduction**
_____	_____	$ _____
_____	_____	
_____	_____	

I accept the company-paid Medical Insurance and Dental Insurance for myself. It is my understanding that Medical Insurance and Dental Insurance for my eligible dependents require deductions from my earning for their benefits. It also is understood that if I decline to enroll my eligible dependents at the time of their initial entitlement, their future enrollment will be subject to the submission of evidence of satisfactory medical and dental health to the insurance company.

Employee Signature _____ Date _____

Figure 8.3 Insurance enrollment form

continued

	For HRM Division/ Payroll Use Only
Life Insurance	
BASIC LIFE INSURANCE—Two times annual salary to the next higher $1,000, to a maximum of $200,000. Amount = $ _____	Effective Date _____
OPTIONAL LIFE INSURANCE IN ADDITION TO BASIC LIFE INSURANCE: ☐ Optional Life Insurance—1 × Annual Salary ☐ Optional Life Insurance—2 × Annual Salary Amount = $ _____ ☐ If I waive Optional Life Insurance, proof of insurability will be required to purchase this insurance coverage in the future. It is with this understanding that I waive Optional Life Insurance coverage at this time. Employee Signature _____ Date _____	Effective Date _____ Monthly Deduction $ _____
ACCIDENTAL DEATH AND DISMEMBERMENT INSURANCE— Two times annual salary to the next higher $1,000, to a maximum of $200,000. Amount = $ _____	Effective Date _____
PERSONAL ACCIDENT INSURANCE: ☐ Employee Only ☐ Employee and Family Benefit Payable By: ☐ Lump Sum ☐ For _____ Years Amount = $ _____ ☐ I waive Personal Accident Insurance for myself and my family. Employee Signature _____ Date _____	Effective Date _____ Monthly Deduction $ _____

Figure 8.3 *(cont.)*

8.4   BENEFICIARY DESIGNATION FORM

Figure 8.4 shows a sample Beneficiary Designation Form which is initially completed when the employee enrolls in company benefits such as group life insurance and a savings plan. If varied designations apply to these benefit plans, separate forms are initiated as needed. When revisions become necessary due to changed estate planning requirements, appropriately revised forms are prepared to cancel previous designations.

Traditional forms only require specifying the name of an individual to whom benefits are payable, but sound estate planning principles dictate more extensive designations to avoid legal problems. For example, one of the options provided is: "Jane Smith, wife, if living, otherwise to John Smith, son, and Mary Smith, daughter, equally, or the survivor."

The form also is used to designate the method for payment of benefits—that is, a choice between a lump-sum payment, a partial lump-sum payment with the balance in installments over a specified period of years, payment in installments during a specified period of years, or payment in the form of an annuity. The employee also may elect to have the beneficiary select the method of payment.

Due to the rights of a spouse to life insurance proceeds, the signature of the employee's spouse is obtained in lieu of a witness. This acknowledges the understanding and agreement of the spouse concerning the alternative beneficiary designation.

Beneficiary Designation Form

Employee Name ——————————————————————————————
                           First   Middle   Last

Social Security No. ————————————————

I hereby cancel any previous beneficiary designation and designate the beneficiary or beneficiaries named below to receive payments relating to survivor benefits from the following specified company benefit plan or plans:

——
——
——

Beneficiary Designation *: ——————————————————————————
——

I further direct that the distribution of amounts credited to me from specified company benefit plan or plans shall be paid to my beneficiary or beneficiaries as follows:

☐ A lump-sum distribution.

☐ $———— as a lump-sum distribution, with the balance paid in equal monthly install-ments for a period of ———— years.

☐ In equal monthly installments for a period of ———— years.

☐ As an annuity to be selected by my beneficiary or beneficiaries.

☐ Any one of the above options as selected by my beneficiary or beneficiaries. If agreement concerning an option cannot be achieved by my beneficiaries, payment will be in the form of a lump-sum distribution.

Signature of Employee ———————————————————— Date ————————
Signature of Witness/Spouse —————————————————— Date ————————
Name and Address of Witness ————————————————————————
——

---

*Sample Beneficiary Designations:

- Jane Smith, wife, if living, otherwise to John Smith, son, and Mary Smith, daughter, equally, or the survivor.
- Jane Smith, wife, if living, otherwise to John Smith, son.
- Jane Smith, wife, if living, otherwise to my children, equally, or the survivor.
- John Smith, son, and Mary Smith, daughter, equally, or the survivor.

Figure 8.4 Beneficiary designation form

8.5 EVIDENCE OF INSURABILITY STATEMENTS

In cases where a new employee elects not to enroll in company group life insurance and/or medical plans at the time of employment, medical evidence of insurability will be required by the insurance company in the event that the employee subsequently requests individual and/or dependent coverage.

A typical insurance company form for providing evidence of insurability probes for problem areas such as an existing pregnancy; a dental condition requiring treatment; an operation recommended or contemplated; consultations with physicians, associated findings, and medical confinements during the past 5 years; and any denial of benefits due to medical problems during the past 10 years. Specific details are required for the employee and all dependents.

The employee certifies that all health statements are complete and true to the best of his or her knowledge and belief. In addition to this certification, a detailed *authorization* is signed which permits the insurance company and its agents to investigate the medical history of all individuals covered by the application for determining their eligibility. Understanding of the terms and conditions of the insurance company's privacy notice also is acknowledged.

The insurance company's privacy notice includes an explanation that while reliance on the health information furnished is primary in determining eligibility, it may request additional information from the employee or any of the sources specified in the authorization, for example, physicians, other health professionals, hospitals, and so on. It is further stipulated that the insurance company may require physical examinations. While assurances are given to the effect that all resultant information will be treated as confidential and not disclosed to others, certain exceptions are specified. Of primary concern is the exception which involves furnishing information to the Medical Information Bureau, a nonprofit membership organization of life insurance companies which operates an information exchange on behalf of its members. This exception has potentially significant consequences in those cases where a medical problem affects insurability. By reporting findings to the Medical Information Bureau, all potential insurers have access to information which negatively impacts the individual's ability to obtain medical and life insurance. Faced with these considerations, the best interests of employees and their dependents dictates encouraging enrollments at the time of employment.

8.6 COST CONTAINMENT OF HOSPITAL BILLS— AN EMPLOYEE REVIEW PROCESS

Faced with the reality that hospital-related medical expenses account for the major portion of health insurance plan costs, companies should enlist the assistance of employees in reviewing the accuracy of their hospital bills. Effective controls ensure that insurance cost increases are minimized; employees have a vital interest in keeping their share of insurance costs at the lowest possible level.

One suggestion is to provide a Hospital Diary (Figure 8.6) to the employee for maintaining a record of services received. Particular emphasis is placed on recording the following types of information:

- Date and time of admission
- Type of room provided (private, semi-private, and so on)
- Dates of visits by personal physician, consulting physicians, and other health professionals (log the name and the purpose of the visit)
- Medications received; dates and times provided
- Special equipment or materials (cane, walker, and so on)
- Therapy, X-rays, and so on (specify and indicate dates received)
- Date and time of discharge

The employee should request a copy of the final bill from the hospital's accounting department, and compare all the charges with his or her Hospital Diary notes to verify that the services billed were provided. Any apparent discrepancies are annotated with explanations. Whether or not discrepancies are identified, the employee then signs the bill, attaches a copy of the Hospital Diary, and forwards these materials to the health insurance program coordinator in the HRM division. Employee annotations then serve as the basis for a letter of inquiry to the hospital's accounting department to request a review of the problem(s) and appropriate corrective action(s).

Resultant savings are acknowledged by a letter of appreciation from the HR director to the employee, with copies to the employee's management, which cites the individual's special efforts in promoting a cost-effective medical insurance program.

Hospital Diary of _____

Page _____ of _____ Pages

_____
Employee

at _____
Hospital

Reason for Hospitalization _____

Type of Room Provided _____

Date _____ Time _____

Date of Discharge _____ Time _____

Health insurance costs continue to rise due to hospitalization costs! All employees have a personal interest in helping to keep these costs down so that the company may continue to provide insurance coverage at the current level of benefits. Employees can help by voluntarily reviewing the accuracy of their hospital bills. This Hospital Diary will help you keep a record of services provided. When you are discharged from the hospital, obtain a copy of your bill and review it for accuracy. Annotate discrepancies, if any, then sign the bill and forward it with a copy of your Hospital Diary to the health insurance program coordinator in the HRM division.

Day	Surgery/ Treatment (Specify)	Surgeon & Anesthesia (Names)	Service Health Pros (Specify)	Visit by Consulting Physician (Name)	Visit by Personal Physician	Lab Tests (Specify)	X-Rays	Medications (Times Provided)	Therapy (Specify)	Special Equipment & Supplies (Specify)
1										
2										
3										
4										
5										
6										
7										

Figure 8.6 Hospital diary

8.7 AN EQUITABLE VACATION POLICY

This vacation policy statement is unique in its equitable approach to the accrual of vacation days. Although many vacation plans stipulate that an employee must be on the payroll by a particular date to qualify for a first year vacation allowance (for example, before June 1) this approach provides uniformly equitable allowances. Regardless of the month that the employee is hired, eligibility for 5 days of vacation begins after 6 months of service are completed. During the balance of the first year of employment, the employee accrues an additional day of vacation as each of the next 5 months of service are completed. The next 10 days of vacation allowance is granted as of the date of the employee's second service anniversary. A graphic explanation is provided as Figure 8.7, Vacation Allowance Table.

The suggested wording for this type of vacation policy follows.

Vacations

I. *Objectives.* To provide employees with periodic rest from their duties and responsibilities in the interest of promoting sound health, improved morale, and increased productivity.

II. *General Principles*

A. *Annual Vacation Period.* The annual vacation period coincides with the calendar year. Employees are able to schedule vacation periods in accordance with their needs and obligations throughout each year.

B. *Vacation Allowances.* Permanent, full-time employees are eligible for vacation allowances as follows:

1. *First 12 Months of Employment.* As shown by the Vacation Allowance Table (refer to Figure 8.7) an employee is eligible for 5 days of vacation after completing 6 months of service. An additional day of vacation allowance is accrued for each of the following 5 months; eligibility for each vacation day is as of the date that the employee was employed. For example, an employment date of January 16 yields a day of vacation allowance effective August 16, another day effective September 16, and so on.

2. *Second through Fourth Service Anniversaries.* The employee is eligible for 10 days (2 business weeks) of vacation allowance as of each service anniversary date.

3. *Fifth through Fourteenth Service Anniversaries.* The employee is eligible for 15 days (3 business weeks) of vacation allowance as of each service anniversary date.

4. *Fifteenth or More Service Anniversaries.* The employee is eligible for 20 days (4 business weeks) of vacation allowance as of each service anniversary date.

C. *Vacation Scheduling.* A Vacation Schedule Worksheet (Figure 8.7A) is used to plan vacations. Scheduling must be arranged to minimize disruption to the efficient operation of each organization. Vacations normally are scheduled in full week units (5 successive working days). Employee preferences are observed whenever possible; conflicts in scheduling choices generally are resolved in favor of longer-service employees.

D. *Vacation Paycheck Advances.* Employees who will be on vacation during a payday may request advance payment. An advance payment will be made on the payday before the vacation providing that the payroll department is given one month of prior notification.

E. *Pay in Lieu of Vacation.* Employees are encouraged to take their full vacation allowance within the 12 month period following their service anniversary. Payment in lieu of vacation may be authorized when emergency work requirements require the cancellation of vacation plans and suitable rescheduling is not possible. Payment also may be granted to employees who elect not to take their third and/or fourth weeks of vacation allowance.

F. *Termination of Employment.* Employees who resign with proper notice, or who are released from employment in good standing, shall receive payment for their remaining vacation allowance. An employee with less than 6 months of employment is not eligible for vacation pay.

Vacation Allowance Table

Based on the *month employed*, the employee becomes eligible for vacation allowances in accordance with the designated number of vacation days shown for the respective *months of employment*:

Vacation Allowance Table

Month Employed

Month Employed	First Year												Second Year												Third Year											
	Jan	Feb	Mar	Apr	May	June	July	Aug	Sept	Oct	Nov	Dec	Jan	Feb	Mar	Apr	May	June	July	Aug	Sept	Oct	Nov	Dec	Jan	Feb	Mar	Apr	May	June	July	Aug	Sept	Oct	Nov	Dec
January	E	X	X	X	X	X	5	6	7	8	9	10	Y												10											
February		E	X	X	X	X	X	5	6	7	8	9	10	Y												10										
March			E	X	X	X	X	X	5	6	7	8	9	10	Y												10									
April				E	X	X	X	X	X	5	6	7	8	9	10	Y												10								
May					E	X	X	X	X	X	5	6	7	8	9	10	Y												10							
June						E	X	X	X	X	X	5	6	7	8	9	10	Y												10						
July							E	X	X	X	X	X	5	6	7	8	9	10	Y												10					
August								E	X	X	X	X	X	5	6	7	8	9	10	Y												10				
September									E	X	X	X	X	X	5	6	7	8	9	10	Y												10			
October										E	X	X	X	X	X	5	6	7	8	9	10	Y												10		
November											E	X	X	X	X	X	5	6	7	8	9	10	Y												10	
December												E	X	X	X	X	X	5	6	7	8	9	10	Y												10

Key: E = Employed during this month (service begins)
Y = Year of service completed during this month (service anniversary)

Figure 8.7 Vacation allowance table

Vacation Schedule Worksheet - _____ Department _____ Location _____

Employee Name	Service Record Date*	Number of Days Vacation	January	February	March	April	May
1							
2							
3							
4							
6							
7							
8							
9							
10							
11							
12							
13							
14							
15							
16							
17							
18							
19							
20							
21							
22							
23							
24							
25							
26							
27							
28							
29							
30							

* Usually coincides with date of employment.

Figure 8.7A Vacation schedule worksheet

continued

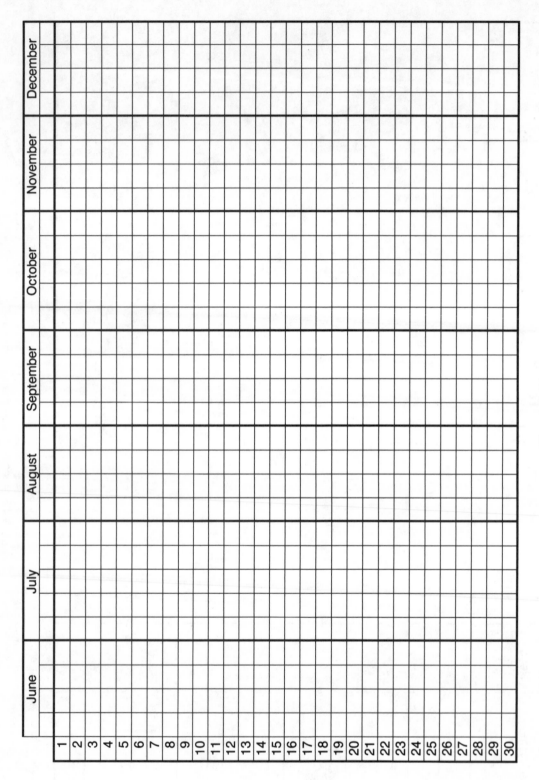

Figure 8.7A *(cont.)*

8.8 MATCHING GIFTS PLAN

I. Policy

The Matching Gifts Plan is part of the company's continuing effort to support educational, health care, civic, and cultural institutions which provide services to its employees and the community at large. The plan provides for contributions by the company to eligible institutions, which are equal to amounts contributed voluntarily by eligible employees.

II. Program

The company will match any gift of at least $20.00 not to exceed a total of $10,000 for gifts per employee during each calendar year. Gifts must be made to eligible institutions—that is, those located in the United States and recognized as tax-exempt organizations under Section 501(c3) of the Internal Revenue Code.

III. Eligible Institutions

Types of institutions eligible for the Matching Gifts Plan include the following.

EDUCATION — graduate and professional schools; four-year colleges and universities; two-year junior and community colleges; private secondary, elementary, and pre-elementary schools; theological seminaries; and the range of national and local education-related organizations.

HEALTH CARE — hospitals, hospices, psychiatric/mental health institutions, ambulatory care facilities, long-term/convalescent facilities, and so on, and the range of national and local health-related organizations including those that relate to specific diseases such as diabetes, cancer, birth defects, and so on.

CIVIC AFFAIRS — a wide range of national and local civic and social service groups such as community recreation centers, programs for the elderly, drug/alcohol rehabilitation projects, youth programs, vocational/technical training programs, and so on.

CULTURE — aquariums, art galleries, botanical gardens, performing arts centers, libraries, museums, zoos, orchestras, public broadcasting television and radio stations, and so on.

IV. Ineligible Institutions

Religious, fraternal, partisan political, labor, and veterans organizations are ineligible for support through the Matching Gifts Plan. Any educational, health care, civic or cultural programs that operate under the sponsorship of a religious organization and are not incorporated as independent nonreligious tax-exempt organizations also are excluded from the plan.

Also excluded are in-kind donations of any type; payments for tuition, books, or other student fees by the donor; dues to alumni groups; subscription fees for publications; insurance premiums; unitrust or charitable remainder trusts; payments for hospital, hospice, physician, therapy, surgical, or laboratory fees; payments for memberships in health maintenance organizations or health care corporations; contributions to individual research projects; individual, family, or group memberships in educational, health care, civic, or cultural organizations; contributions to individual artistic projects; and any gifts not intended to further the general program of the recipient educational, health care, civic or cultural institution, as defined by this plan.

V. Plan Administration

The employee, as donor, completes Part I of the Matching Gifts Plan form and forwards it with the contribution to the financial officer of the eligible educational, health care, civic or cultural institution (or its affiliated fund, foundation, or association).

The financial officer of the receiving institution completes Part II of the form and returns it to the HR director for processing.

The administrator of the Matching Gifts Plan verifies the eligibility of the receiving institution and the donor, and authorizes a check for the matching gift donation.

When the check is issued to the institution, the employee is notified by a copy of the Matching Gifts Plan form (Figure 8.8).

Part I—Employee completes this information, then sends this form and a personal donation to the financial officer of the eligible educational, health care, civic, or cultural institution or its affiliated fund, foundation, or association.

Name of Institution _____

Address _____

Amount of Contribution (In Words) _____

My check for $ _____ is enclosed as a personal gift. I hereby certify that this is entirely my personal contribution; it is not in whole or in part the gift of another individual, the sum of gifts of other individuals, or the gift of any group or organization. I also certify that this contribution does not represent payment of or payment in lieu of tuition or other educational fees. I hereby authorize the above named institution to report this gift to my company for the purpose of attempting to qualify for a contribution under the provisions of the Matching Gifts Plan.

Employee Signature _____ Date _____

Part II—Financial officer of receiving organization completes this information, encloses a copy of the organization's tax-exemption status per IRS 501 (c) (3), and sends this form to the HR Director, ATTN: Administrator, Matching Gifts Plan, NTC, 1207 Newport Avenue, Greenwich, CT 21098.

I hereby certify that a contribution of $ _____, as described above, was received on (date) _____.

I further certify that this organization is recognized as an independent, nonreligious, tax-exempt organization under Section 501 (c) (3) of the Internal Revenue Code. I also certify that this donation represents a charitable contribution to this organization, and that the donor does not derive any material benefit (tuition, gift, dues credit, magazine subscription, etc.) as a result of this gift.

Financial Officer Signature _____ Date _____

Financial Officer Name   _____
(Printed)

Title _____ Telno (_____) _____

Eligibility Verification: ☐ Individual ☐ Institution

Previous Calendar Year Total of Matched Gifts = $ _____

Check Authorization Approved $ _____

New Calendar Year Total of Matched Gifts = $ _____

Approved: _____   _____
              Administrator, Matching Gifts Plan   Date

Figure 8.8 Matching gifts plan

8.9 HIGHLIGHTS OF AN EMPLOYEE CHILD CARE PROGRAM

Here is an example of an advertisement which promotes an independent contractor's child care center, one where working mothers are assured of proper supervision and concern for their children in an environment that promotes healthy play and learning experiences. The facility is recommended by area companies, which subsidize employee costs on a 50/50 shared basis.

****

The xyz child care center offers you more . . .
- A tradition of fine child care since 1974
- A safe and healthy environment
- Promotes social, emotional, physical, and cognitive growth
- Licensed by the State Department of Human Services
- Open to periodic, unannounced inspections to verify that operational standards are being met fully
- Parents may visit at any time
- Open Monday through Friday, 7:30 A.M. to 5:30 P.M.
- Cares for children from age 2 through $5\frac{1}{2}$ years of age
- During school holidays we care for children up to 11 years of age
- Qualified, experienced child care specialists care for your child
- Regular special activities and field trips
- Visits from Smokey the Bear, the Easter Bunny, and Santa
- Lessons from police and fire department representatives
- Breakfast, lunch, and afternoon snack served daily
- Fully enclosed outdoor play area
- Indoor activity center
- Two-way observation mirror in staff offices
- Full-time nurse available
- Scheduled parent/teacher meetings
- Newsletter of activities and events
- Only $50 per week or $1.75 by the hour
- Special rates for each additional child

FOR A TOUR OF OUR FACILITIES AND MORE INFORMATION, CALL XXX-XXXX.

8.10 EMPLOYEE ASSISTANCE PROGRAM CONCEPT

In recognition of the fact that a healthy bottom line is dependent on healthy employees, companies are investing resources in *Wellness Programs*. These programs are based on the premise that a physically and mentally sound employee is a productive contributor.

Companies are promoting healthy lifestyles through educational programs and counseling assistance which focus on a wide range of problems such as:

- Substance abuse (alcohol and nonprescription drugs)
- Emotional disorders
- Ineffective interpersonal relations
- Marital discord/separation/divorce
- Coping with death of loved one
- Behavioral irregularities (failure to follow work rules)
- Healthier lifestyles (smoking cessation, control of hypertension, stress reduction, and so on).

These "wellness" or "employee assistance programs" designate individuals whom employees and their families may call, in complete confidence, regarding these types of problems. The employee assistance program (EAP) counselor is an objective third-party who assesses each problem and makes appropriate referrals to outside agencies and resources in the community, ones that offer the specialized counseling and/or treatment needed. Follow-up is provided to assure successful conclusions.

Another way in which an employee becomes involved with the employee assistance program is if a supervisor, who has observed a decline in the individual's work performance, suggests that the EAP counselor should be contacted. This is an alternative to disciplinary action in more serious cases; however, employees who fail to obtain and benefit from necessary assistance, and whose problems continue, are subject to appropriate disciplinary action. Fortunately, EAP program experience has demonstrated that most employees who are advised to seek help do so and are successful in returning to acceptable levels of performance.

An effective EAP requires supervisors who are prepared to step in when they think an employee has a problem which is becoming serious—that is, one which has not yet critically affected job performance but may in the near future. The nature of the problem or its symptoms should be documented (performance, attendance, conduct, and so on), and the EAP counselor should be consulted to develop employee referral strategies. Using good judgment regarding timing, an informal talk with the employee generally is used as the basis for expressing concerns and assessing the problem. If appropriate, after reviewing an employee's excuses for behavioral problems, referral to the EAP counselor is suggested.

8.11   ERISA SUMMARY ANNUAL REPORTS

The Employee Retirement Income Security Act of 1974 (ERISA) requires companies to give their employees specific types of information concerning benefit plans. For example, employees must receive a summarized annual report within nine months after the end of each plan year. This type of annual report must be prepared for the retirement plan and each type of welfare benefit plan, that is, those which provide employee benefits for sickness, hospitalization, surgery, accidents, death, disability, unemployment, vacation, holidays, day care, scholarship, legal services, and so on. As shown in Figure 8.11, Sample ERISA Annual Benefits Report, a consolidated report on all plans provides an excellent technique for simplifying this employee communications requirement.

SOURCE: WHAT YOU SHOULD KNOW ABOUT THE PENSION LAW, A Guide to the Employee Retirement Income Security Act of 1974, as Amended by the Retirement Equity Act of 1984, U.S. Department of Labor, Office of Pension and Welfare Benefit Programs, December 1985. pp 6–8

Summary Annual Reports

These Summary Annual Reports are designed to provide plan members and their beneficiaries with financial information concerning the costs incurred by the company for the following benefit plans. Annual reports for these benefit plans have been filed with the Internal Revenue Service as required under the Employee Retirement Income Security Act of 1974 (ERISA).

Group Life and Medical Plan

This is a summary of the annual report of the Group Life and Medical Plan for the plan year beginning January 1, 1987 and ending December 31, 1987.

The company has committed itself to pay a portion of the medical claims incurred under the terms of the plan. This is accomplished by depositing a specified amount of money in a special account for the payment of medical claims. The plan has a contract with the XYZ Life Insurance Company to pay all claims, other than the portion of medical claims paid from the special account, which are incurred under the terms of the plan.
The total amount paid for the plan year ending December 31, 1987 was $31,235,165.

Group Dental Plan

This is a summary of the annual report of the Group Dental Plan for the plan year beginning January 1, 1987 and ending December 31, 1987.

The company has committed itself to pay a portion of the dental claims incurred under the terms of the plan. This is accomplished by depositing a specified amount of money in a special account for the payment of dental claims. The plan has a contract with XYZ Life Insurance Company to pay all dental claims not paid from this special account.

The total amount paid for the plan year ending December 31, 1987 was $4,632,821.

Long-Term Disability Insurance Plan

This is a summary of the annual report of the Long-Term Disability Insurance Plan for the plan year beginning July 1, l986 and ending June 30, 1987.

The plan has a contract with the XYZ Life Insurance Company to pay all long-term disability claims incurred under the terms of the Plan. The total amount of premiums paid for the plan year ending June 30, 1987 was $1,863,757.

Business Travel Accident Insurance Plan

This is a summary of the annual report of the Business Travel Accident Insurance Plan for the plan year beginning January 1, 1987 and ending December 31, 1987.

The plan has a contract with the XYZ Life Insurance Company to pay all claims incurred under the terms of the plan. The total amount of premiums paid for the plan year ending December 31, 1987 was $91,365.

Educational Assistance Plan

This is a summary of the annual report of the Educational Assistance Plan for the plan year beginning January 1, 1987 and ending December 31, 1987.

The company has committed itself to reimburse certain tuition claims incurred under the terms of the plan. Expenses for the plan year ending December 31, 1987, which represent tuition reimbursements paid to participants, were $872,346.

Figure 8.11 Sample ERISA annual benefits report

continued

Rights to Additional Information

Plan members have the right to receive a copy of the full reports filed for these benefit plans, or any part thereof, on request. To obtain a copy of a full annual report, or any part thereof, write to the Employee Benefits Director, Progressive Corporation, 1206 6th Ave., New York, NY 10019, or telephone (212) 573-3197.

Plan members also have the right to examine these annual reports at the company headquarters, at their work location, and at the U.S. Department of Labor in Washington, D.C. To obtain a copy from the U.S. Department of Labor, upon payment of copying costs, requests should be addressed to: Public Disclosure Room, N4677, Pension and Welfare Benefit Programs, U.S. Department of Labor, 200 Constitution Avenue, N.W. Washington, D.C. 20216. Our company's identification number is 13-5925873.

Additional Financial Information

To Participants and Beneficiaries

In addition to the summary annual reports required by the U.S. Department of Labor, the following charts are designed to provide additional information on the following benefit plans. Descriptions of plan benefits are contained in the plan booklets, which have previously been distributed to you and are available at your work location.

Group Life and Medical Plan Statement of Financial Operations For Plan Year Ending December 31, 1987		
Company Contribution to Plan	$29,872,673	
Employee Payroll Deductions	1,362,492	
Total Cost		$31,235,165
Claims Paid	27,634,689	
Retention by Insurance Company	1,762,436	
Total		29,397,125
Change in Claim Reserves		$ 1,838,040
Claim Reserves at End of Plan Year		$12,789,132

Group Dental Plan Statement of Financial Operations For Year Ending December 31, 1987		
Company Contribution to Plan	$ 4,263,197	
Retiree Contributions	369,624	
Employee Payroll Deductions	0	
Total Cost		$ 4,632,821
Claims Paid	3,872,633	
Retention by Insurance Company	559,689	
Total		4,432,322
Change in Claims Reserves		$ 200,499
Claim Reserves at End of Plan Year		$ 879,968

Figure 8.11 *(cont.)*

Long-Term Disability Insurance Plan Statement of Financial Operations For Year Ending June 30, 1987		
Company Contribution to Plan	$1,863,757	
Employee Payroll Deductions	0	
Total Cost		$ 1,863,757

Business Travel Accident Insurance Plan Statement of Financial Operations For Year Ending December 31, 1987		
Company Contribution to Plan	$91,635	
Employee Payroll Deductions	0	
Total Cost		$ 91,635

Educational Assistance Plan Statement of Financial Operations For Year Ending December 31, 1987		
Plan Expenses Paid by Company	$872,346	
Employee Payroll Deductions	0	
Total Cost		$ 872,346

Figure 8.11 *(cont.)*

8.12 PREPARATION FOR RETIREMENT CHECKLIST

A preparation for retirement checklist is provided in Figure 8.12, "Your Retirement Planning Checklist," for use as a model in preparing a self-help device for employees who are planning to retire.

The focus of a maximally effective preretirement planning program is to develop a positive perception of retirement as a new beginning, and to reinforce the need for sound planning and effective choices. Your Retirement Planning Checklist encourages a responsible and meaningful assessment of the many considerations which lead to a successful retirement.

The potential retiree needs to realistically assess financial resources and make a commitment to a reasonable budget and associated modifications of spending levels. An activity-oriented commitment to sound mental and physical health is essential. Ways to achieve a productive and rewarding post-retirement lifestyle, one which promotes self-esteem, must be explored. Group-oriented activities involving task-oriented objectives are analogous to those that are left behind when an employee retires. Through this type of participation, the individual finds purpose, receives the affirmations of others, and reinforces feelings of self-worth. The importance of remaining independent and in control of one's life must be emphasized; this is particularly relevant in perpetuating parent-child relationships with children. Abdicating control over one's own life by becoming dependent on children must be avoided. Improved communication, increased understanding, and compromises are needed with one's spouse. One must continue to promote a satisfying social life with sound interpersonal relationships and mutual benefits. Questions about suitable housing and transportation must be resolved. Issues regarding safety and security require commonsense solutions. All the potential benefits of retirement must be explored. The legal aspects of doing everything possible to protect one's survivors require action.

Your Retirement Planning Checklist

1. FINANCIAL PLANNING FOR ECONOMIC SECURITY—Assessing the amount of your post-retirement income, then making required budgetary adjustments.
   — Calculate company pension income
   — Determine amount of Social Security income
   — Do you have other sources of income such as interest, dividends, rent for owned properties, etc.?
   — What is your net worth? (Assets minus liabilities = net worth.) Do you have resources that can be used in a financial emergency?
   — Prepare a realistic monthly budget based on your income assessment.

2. PROMOTING PHYSICAL AND MENTAL HEALTH
   — Physical conditioning? Exercise as if your life depends on it—it does!
   — Develop nutritional skills. A sound diet is essential for physical and mental health.
   — Prepare yourself emotionally for the transitional period that leads to a successful retirement. Think young!
   — Reduce stress; practice a caring but relaxed approach to living effectively.
   — Schedule the first of future periodic health examinations. The sooner a problem is identified, the greater the probability of successful medical solutions.

3. ESTABLISHING A PRODUCTIVE AND REWARDING LIFESTYLE
   — Set goals and plan your use of time. Establish routines; develop daily schedules.
   — Be active! If you engage in useful and productive activities, you will be and will feel like a useful and worthwhile individual.
   — Avoid perpetual loafing. A sedentary, passive, and unproductive lifestyle leads to boredom, emptiness, depression, and untimely death.
   — Capitalize on your interests, e.g., rededicate yourself to hobbies, participation in sports, etc.
   — Develop new interests. Try a new hobby, make your dream of being an artist come true, etc.
   — Participate in community service projects.
   — Become an active member of civic, religious, and service organizations.
   — Evaluate possibilities for applying your work experience in a new career or business venture.
   — Consider taking college courses or engaging in other educational experiences.
   — Provide consulting assistance to small businesses that need your expertise.

4. DEALING WITH YOUR CHILDREN
   — Remain independent! Do not plan your retirement around your children or grandchildren. Mutual independence rather than dependence promotes sound relationships.
   — Maintain control of your assets. Do not make the mistake of giving a major share of your assets to your children, allowing them to take control of a family business, or to sign an agreement that allows them to exercise control over your personal affairs. This is essential to maintain the position of dominance that engenders continued respect and proper treatment as an independent adult.

Figure 8.12 Preparation for retirement checklist

continued

5. A NEW RELATIONSHIP WITH YOUR SPOUSE
   — Improve communications to yield mutual understanding of your post-retirement relationship. Each partner's needs and unique problems must be considered in developing sound guidelines for this new relationship.
   — Define each partner's responsibilities for issues involving the home, shopping, travel, etc., to avoid conflict based on territorial disputes.
   — Plan to offer each partner space and time alone; excessive exposure on a daily basis will severely strain the best of relationships.

6. A SATISFYING SOCIAL LIFE
   — Live near your good friends who have shared experiences and mutual interests. It feels good to have good friends who affirm your feelings of self-worth, provide encouragement, and offer worthwhile advice based on sound perceptions of your personality and needs.
   — Do things that make you feel good; go dancing, take a hike in the mountain, take that ski vacation in Colorado, do some deep water fishing. The possibilities are limited only by your imagination and enthusiasm. Wherever you go, commit yourself to making new friends with these shared interests.
   — Build and maintain sound interpersonal relationships on a foundation of mutual respect. Each new acquaintance has the potential to enrich your life. The key is to be a good listener, and to express interest in the things that are important to them.

7. YOUR RETIREMENT HOME
   — Is it suited to your needs? If you are rattling around in a house that is much too spacious now that the children have left home, consider alternatives such as purchasing a smaller home or a condominium in the same area.
   — Is it important for your well being to remain close to your roots? If so, do not go rushing off to an adult community in the Sun Belt. Many have made this mistake, one which most were financially unable to correct.
   — If you are confident that you need the adventure of a different lifestyle and a new location, make sure that you can live with your choice. If you have reservations, consider a compromise such as a condominium in the area where your roots are established, and a second seasonal residence in a recreational area. This provides the variety and stimulation of winter/summer transitions.

8. TRANSPORTATION FOR PERSONAL FREEDOM
   — A reliable and safe new automobile is a sound investment for promoting a successful retirement. You must have the ability to go where you want to go whenever you want to go.
   — Place practicality over the urge to buy an impressive luxury car to boost your sagging ego. It's better to use the money saved by purchasing a reasonably priced automobile to have some fun and feel good about yourself and your new lifestyle.
   — Think very carefully before committing yourself to a motor home or other expensive recreational vehicle. If you think this is your "thing" for a fun retirement, try renting a vehicle to test the reality before purchasing your dream vehicle.

Figure 8.12 *(cont.)*

9. SAFETY AND SECURITY
   — Review your home to eliminate safety hazards
   — Make your home theft-proof; travel will be more rewarding if you have the assurance that your home and possessions are secure.
   — If you do not already have a safe deposit box, consider the security of protecting valuables and documents which cannot readily be replaced.
   — Inventory the contents of your home, obtain appraisals as needed, and arrange to increase your homeowners insurance policy accordingly. Similarly, make sure that the current market value of your home is adequately protected by the fire insurance portion of your homeowners policy. If necessary, call upon a real estate appraiser and pay for a current appraisal.

10. ARRANGING YOUR BENEFITS
   — Contact the Social Security Administration to arrange Medicare hospital and medical insurance coverage and retirement benefit payments.
   — Review federal and state income tax laws for provisions that apply to retirees.
   — Contact your community tax assessor regarding special tax rates for retired homeowners.
   — Explore so-called "senior citizen discounts."
   — Review how the company's medical insurance plan supplements your Medicare coverages.
   — If your spouse is covered by company medical insurance, but is not yet eligible for Medicare (not age 65), arrange to continue adequate coverage.
   — Consider the advantages provided through membership in organizations such as the American Association of Retired Persons (AARP). Representative benefits include low rate prescription drug services, economical group insurance plans, group travel opportunities, and publications with advice for promoting a more productive and economically sound retirement.

11. LEGAL CONSIDERATIONS
   — Make sure you and your spouse have current wills that adequately protect the survivor, then consider provisions for children, relatives, etc.
   — Set up an estate planning file of insurance policies; deeds for owned properties; information on savings accounts, stocks, etc. Military records should be included so that Veterans benefits may be obtained. This should be a complete repository of all essential information needed by the survivor in settling an estate.

Figure 8.12 *(cont.)*

8.13 SOCIAL SECURITY BENEFITS

Here are some basic facts about Social Security benefits which will be useful in counseling employees who are contemplating retirement.

To be eligible for Social Security benefits, an individual must have a specific number of years of work covered by Social Security as shown in the following table:

Year Individual Reaches Age 62	Total Years Needed
1984	$8\frac{1}{4}$
1985	$8\frac{1}{2}$
1986	$8\frac{3}{4}$
1987	9
1988	$9\frac{1}{4}$
1989	$9\frac{1}{2}$
1991 (and beyond)	10

To determine the number of years of work for which an individual is to receive Social Security credit, information concerning the amount of earnings credited to the individual's account for each year of covered employment is needed. This information may be obtained by submitting a Request for Statement of Earnings postcard (Figure 8.13A) to the Social Security Administration.

An individual is credited with a year of coverage if earnings, as shown on his or her statement of earnings provided by the Social Security Administration, equals or exceeds the figure shown for each year in the following worksheet:

Year	Required Amount of Earnings	Years of Coverage
1937–50[a]	$ 900	
1951	900	
1952	900	
1953	900	
1954	900	
1955	1,050	
1956	1,050	
1957	1,050	
1958	1,050	
1959	1,200	
1960	1,200	
1961	1,200	
1962	1,200	
1963	1,200	
1964	1,200	
1965	1,200	
1966	1,650	
1967	1,650	
1968	1,950	
1969	1,950	
1970	1,950	
1971	1,950	
1972	2,250	
1973	2,700	
1974	3,300	
1975	3,525	
1976	3,825	
1977	4,125	
1978	4,425	
1979	4,725	
1980	5,100	
1981	5,550	

Year	Required Amount of Earnings	Years of Coverage
1982	6,075	
1983	6,675	
1984	7,050	
1985	7,425	
Total Years of Coverage		

[a] Total credited earnings from 1937 through 1950 are divided by $900 to obtain the number of years of coverage (maximum of 14 years).

To plan the time for retirement, a benefit increase provision of the Social Security law should be considered. If an employee works past the full benefit retirement age, which currently is age 65, future monthly benefits are increased by 3 percent for each year ($\frac{1}{4}$ of 1 percent for each month) that employment continues. This credit will be increased gradually to 8 percent during the period of 1990 to 2008.

Early retirement at age 62 is possible with reduced benefits in order to compensate for the longer period that benefits will be paid. Representative reductions are 20 percent at age 62; $13\frac{1}{3}$ percent at age 63, and $6\frac{2}{3}$ percent at age 64.

Starting in the year 2000, the full benefit retirement age will gradually be increased until it reaches 67 in 2027.

How much can you receive in monthly benefits? The maximum amount payable to a 65-year old worker who retired in 1986 was $760 per month. Similarly, a 62-year old retiree received as much as $630 a month. With eligible dependents, total maximum payments could have amounted to $1,330 and $1,222 per month, respectively.

You may work after becoming eligible for Social Security payments, but there are limits on earnings. For example, individuals from age 65 to age 70 could earn $7,800 during 1986 and still receive full benefits. Similarly, those under age 65 could earn $5,760. If earnings exceed specified limits, $1 in benefits is withheld for each $2 of earnings which exceed the exempted amount. Beginning in 1990, this rate will change to $1 for each $3 for individuals who are age 65 or more. A special rule applies during the year an individual retires. The individual's annual earnings may exceed the exempt amount, but monthly earnings limits are imposed. For example, limits for 1986 were $650 for individuals age 65 or over, and $480 for those under 65.

A portion of Social Security benefits may be subject to income tax for higher income retirees. The amount which may have to be considered as taxable income could equal one-half of the benefits paid during the year. Individuals should consult with an income tax specialist to assess potential liability.

Full details are provided in a helpful pamphlet entitled "Thinking about Retiring?", which is available from the Social Security Administration. A copy of this pamphlet should be included in the materials your company provides in pre-retirement counseling sessions.

The following materials are recommended for facilitating employee applications for Social Security benefits: When to Apply for Social Security Retirement/Medicare Benefits (Figure 8.13B) and a Social Security Pre-Retirement Checklist (Figure 8.13C).

YOUR SOCIAL SECURITY
RECORD

If you want a statement of your
social security earnings, please fill in
the other side of this card.

In the space marked "Social Security
Number," show your number *exactly*
as it is shown on your social security
card. We need your correct number
to identify your record. If you have
more than one social security number,
give all of them.

You do not need to pay anyone to
help you get a statement of your
earnings. There is no charge for this
service.

Be sure to put a stamp on this card
before mailing it.

FORM OAR-7004 (3-74)

SOCIAL SECURITY ADMINISTRATION

P.O. BOX 57

BALTIMORE, MARYLAND 21203

REQUEST FOR

STATEMENT

OF EARNINGS

SOCIAL
SECURITY →
NUMBER

DATE OF →
BIRTH

MONTH	DAY	YEAR

Please send a statement of my social security earnings to:

NAME _____

STREET & NUMBER _____

CITY & STATE _____ ZIP CODE _____

Print
Name
and
Address
In Ink
Or Use
Type-
writer

SIGN YOUR NAME HERE
(DO NOT PRINT) _____

Sign your own name only. Under the law, information in your social security record
is confidential and anyone who signs another person's name can be prosecuted.

If you have changed your name from that shown on your social security card, please
copy your name below exactly as it appears on your card.

Figure 8.13A Request for statement of earnings

Contact the nearest office of the Social Security Administration to arrange benefits if either you or your spouse is:

- Age 62 or older and planning to retire
- Within 3 months of age 65

Whether or not retirement is planned at age 65, this contact is necessary for arranging to have MEDICARE protection begin during the month age 65 is reached.

Note: Medicare consists of two parts, i.e., Hospital Insurance (Part A) and Medical Insurance (Part B). The Hospital Insurance portion pays the cost of in-patient hospital care and certain types of follow-up care. Medical Insurance helps pay for the cost of physicians' services, outpatient hospital services, and certain other medical items and services not covered by the Hospital Insurance. The cost of the Hospital Insurance portion of Medicare is paid from Social Security taxes you have paid throughout your employment. You may elect to purchase Medical Insurance protection for a monthly premium which is approximately one-third of its cost; the balance is paid for from general revenues of the federal government. Unless you specifically decline this option, Medical Insurance enrollment is automatic when you enroll in the Hospital Insurance portion of Medicare. You will undoubtably want both coverages due to the fact that your existing company health insurance becomes subject to coordination of benefits with Medicare when you reach age 65. Should you continue working after age 65, company hospitalization and medical insurance remains your primary coverage, but Medicare will become your secondary insurance. This means that through coordination of benefits, the combination of these two plans generally will fully cover your personal medical costs. Should your spouse not yet be covered by Medicare, his or her company health insurance coverage will continue as before. In the event that you retire at age 65, Medicare then will become your primary health insurance and the company will provide supplemental health insurance benefits which generally will fully cover the payment of normal and customary costs.

Prompt Social Security benefit applications ensure that payments will be provided on the following basis:

- Benefits between age 62 and 65 are effective beginning the month of application. You must apply for benefits no later than the last day of the month for which the first payment is desired. The check for that first month is payable early during the following month.
- If you apply for benefits months or years after reaching age 65, back payments may be made for up to 6 months.

As a general rule, you should apply for benefits 3 months before your month of retirement. This will provide sufficient time to obtain additional documentation that may be required for eligibility determinations, and ample administrative processing time for ensuring that your first benefit check will be received early during the month following your month of retirement

For details and clarifications, look in the "U.S. Government" section of your telephone directory for the number of your nearest Social Security Administration office. A representative will give you the advice you need, and will be pleased to send helpful pamphlets such as: "Your Social Security," "Thinking About Retiring?," "A Brief Explanation of Medicare."

Figure 8.13B When to apply for social security retirement/medicare benefits

Social Security Pre-Retirement Checklist

Before you apply for Social Security or Medicare, get ready by rounding up the following information, then call your nearest Social Security office and learn how easy it is to apply by phone. Do not delay applying because you do not have all required proofs; other alternative proofs will be specified by your Social Security office representative.

Listed below are necessary proofs or information you will have to supply up to 3 months before the month you want benefits to start. Before calling or visiting your Social Security office, please fill in the following blocks:

Needed Information	Suggestions and Proofs
Your Full Name _____ _____ Other Names Used _____ _____	If You have used other names, please list them also.
Your Full Address _____ _____	Don't forget your zip code.
Best Time to Call Your Telephone Work _____ Number(s) Home _____ Other _____	Where and when can we call you during working hours?
Your Social Security Number _____	Copy directly from your card. Bring your card or an official record of your number with you if you apply in person.
Your Date of Birth _____ Your Place of Birth (County & State) _____ _____	You will need proof of your age: an original birth certificate or baptismal record before you were age 5.
Your F.I.C.A. Earnings for this Year and the Last Two Years. Estimated F.I.C.A. Earnings for this Year _____ F.I.C.A. Earnings for Last Year _____ F.I.C.A. Earnings for Year before Last _____	You will need your W-2 forms for the last year of your Federal Income Tax Returns if you are self employed. Proof of filing, such as canceled checks, also are required.
Active Military Services From To Dates: _____ _____	Note: Only active duty counts. Copy from discharge or form DD-214.

Figure 8.13C Social security pre-retirement checklist

continued

Needed Information	Suggestions and Proofs
Marriage Information (If applying for wife/widow/widower benefits) Date of marriage _____ Place of marriage _____ Name of spouse _____ Date of birth of spouse _____	If you have had more than one marriage, list all on the back of this form and explain when and where each prior marriage began and ended. You may need your marriage certificate.
Social Security Number of Current Spouse _____ Social Security Number of Prior Spouses _____ _____ _____	If you know the social security numbers of prior spouses, please list them in addition to providing the number for current spouse.
Number of Unmarried Children under age 19 (Or disabled before age 22) Names Social Security No. Disabled? _____ _____ ☐ Yes ☐ No _____ _____ ☐ Yes ☐ No _____ _____ ☐ Yes ☐ No	You will need an original birth or baptism record and social security number for each listed child.

Notes:

Figure 8.13C *(cont.)*

CHAPTER 9

Personnel Administration

Section 9.1 defines employee classifications in terms of hours worked, periods of employment, and the provisions of the Fair Labor Standards Act (FLSA). Background information needed to establish exemptions from the paid overtime provisions of the FLSA for executive, administrative, and professional employees, is provided in Section 9.2. Sample FLSA Exemption Questionnaire forms for use in gathering background information are shown in Sections 9.3, 9.4, and 9.5, respectively. Examples of representative jobs/positions which are non-exempt, ones covered by the provisions of FLSA, are listed in Section 9.6. A typical company policy on overtime, in Section 9.7, outlines the terms and conditions for the payment of overtime compensation to both non-exempt and exempt employees.

Section 9.8, Sample Company Policy on Employee Absences, provides guidelines for reporting and administering employee absences for sickness and disability, personal leave, maternity leave, military leave, and jury duty. An approach which may be used to reduce controllable employee absences and latenesses is offered in Section 9.9, Attendance Award Program. Guidance for formulating a policy on promotions and transfers is provided in Section 9.10. A Personnel Change Notice Authorization form, which may be used to process all types of personnel status changes, is introduced in Section 9.11; samples of typical applications demonstrate the versatility of this form.

9.1 DEFINITIONS OF EMPLOYEE CLASSIFICATIONS

The following guidelines define different employee classifications:

A. *Full-Time Employee.* An employee who normally is scheduled to work a 40-hour work week.

B. *Part-Time Employee.* An employee who normally is scheduled to work less than a 40-hour work week.

C. *Temporary Employee.* A full or part-time employee who is hired for a pre-determined period of employment.

D. *Probationary Employee.* A full or part-time employee is considered to be a probationary employee during the first 6 months of employment, a mutual trial period during which either the employee or the company may immediately terminate the working relationship.

E. *Permanent ("Regular") Employee.* A full or part-time employee hired with the expectation that the working relationship will continue as long as it is mutually satisfactory.

F. *Non-Exempt Employee.* An employee whose job duties and rate of pay meet requirements for paid overtime as defined by the provisions of the FLSA.

G. *Exempt Employee.* An executive, administrative, or professional employee whose duties and rate of pay meet requirements for exemption from the paid overtime provisions of the FLSA.

9.2 U.S. DEPARTMENT OF LABOR GUIDELINES FOR FAIR LABOR STANDARDS ACT EXEMPTIONS

In accordance with the provisions of the Fair Labor Standards Act (FLSA), employers are not required to pay overtime to those salaried employees who qualify for executive, administrative, or professional exemption. Current guidelines specify that executive and administrative employees must be paid a salary of at least $155 per week, and professional employees must be paid at least $170 per week in salary or fees. If an executive, administrative, or professional employee is paid $250 per week or more, a "short test" of duties and responsibilities must be met. A "long test" is required for those who are paid less than $250 per week.

The following information will assist you in determining whether positions meet the criteria for exemption from the provisions of the FLSA.

I. FLSA Exemption—Administrative

Qualifications for exempt employee status require a primary duty of office or nonmanual work directly related to management policies or general business operations of the employer or the customers of the employer. The employee also must regularly and customarily exercise discretion and independent judgment in one or all of the following:

1. Directly assisting an executive, administrator, or proprietor
2. Performing specialized work, under general supervision, which requires special training, experience, or knowledge
3. Conducting special assignments and tasks only under general supervision

If the employee receives a salary of $250 or more per week, the following short test is applied:

1. The employee must have a primary duty which involves office or nonmanual work that is directly related to management policies, or to the general business operations of the employer or customers of the employer.
2. The employee's work must involve tasks which require exercising discretion and independent judgment.

II. FLSA Exemption—Professional

A professional employee must be paid a salary or fee of at least $170 per week. Professionals are defined by the types of positions that require specialized academic training, for example, lawyers, physicians, nurses, accountants, scientists, and teachers. Such individuals must perform work which requires:

1. Consistent application of discretion and judgment
2. Predominately intellectual and varied duties rather than manual, mechanical, or physical duties
3. Spending less than 20 percent of his or her time during the work week performing non-exempt work

SOURCE: Fair Labor Standards Act 13(a)(1), 29 USC 213(a)(1).

Those employees who earn $250 or more per week in salary or fees are required to meet only the following criteria for exempt status:

1. The employee must perform work which primarily requires knowledge of an advanced field of learning
2. The employee's work must require the regular and consistent application of discretion and judgment

III. FLSA Exemption—Executive

If the salary is at least $250 per week, only two requirements must be met to be classified as exempt:

1. Management is the primary duty of the employee.
2. The employee must regularly direct the work of two or more employees.

If the salary ranges from $155 to $249 per week, a long test is necessary for determining if the employee meets the following five requirements:

1. Management must be the primary duty of the employee.
2. The employee must regularly direct the work of two or more employees.
3. The employee must have the authority to hire and fire or to otherwise affect the job status of other employees.
4. The employee must customarily and regularly exercise discretionary powers.
5. The employee must not spend more than 20 percent of the normal work-week hours performing nonexecutive duties (40 percent in a retail or service establishment).

IV. Guideline Revisions

The Department of Labor is considering a number of revisions to salary and duties tests which would potentially simplify this evaluation process. It appears that executive and administrative positions would be considered to be exempt regardless of duties and responsibilities providing that new salary tests are met. Respective salary test amounts have not yet been defined. Professional positions will continue to involve complex assessments with new salary test amounts; however, it appears that professional status will be accorded to a number of additional occupations such as those involving computer science and related training.

9.3 FLSA EXEMPTION QUESTIONNAIRE—ADMINISTRATIVE

FLSA EXEMPTION QUESTIONNAIRE

• ADMINISTRATIVE •

STAFF JOB TITLE

DATE

STAFF JOB CODE NO.

SUPERVISOR'S TITLE

DEPARTMENT

DIVISION/SUBSIDIARY

LOCATION

INSTRUCTIONS:
1. If proposed salary is $8,060 or more but less than $13,000, the Long Test is used. If proposed salary is $13,000 or more, the Short Test may be used.
2. This questionnaire should be completed by a personnel representative in an interview with the employee's staff supervisor.
3. Specific statements, not broad generalizations should be noted in the space provided for explanations.
4. The questionnaire should be signed by the supervisor, and the interviewer should complete the section provided for him.

I **LONG TEST**

Is the employee's proposed salary $8,060 or more a year?
If answer to question II is no, answer questions III through VI.

☐ YES ☐ NO

II **SHORT TEST**

Is the employee's proposed salary $13,000 or more a year?
If yes, answer questions III and V only.

☐ YES ☐ NO

III Does the primary duty relate directly to administrative or general business operations of substantial importance to the Company?

☐ YES ☐ NO

IF "YES", DESCRIBE THE WORKING CONDITIONS AND EXTENT OF PHYSICAL EXERTION REQUIRED.

_____

_____

_____

_____

IV a. Do the duties performed involve directly assisting someone employed in either a bona fide executive or administrative capacity?

☐ YES ☐ NO

IF "YES", EXPLAIN THE EXTENT OF SUCH ASSISTANCE. _____

_____

_____

_____

_____

b. Do the duties performed involve only general supervision in a specialized or technical line requiring special training, experience or knowledge?

☐ YES ☐ NO

IF "YES", SPECIFY THE TYPE, EXTENT, AND WHY SUCH TRAINING, EXPERIENCE OR KNOWLEDGE IS REQUIRED. _____

_____

_____

_____

c. Do the duties performed involve only general supervision, work consisting almost exclusively of special assignments or tasks?

☐ YES ☐ NO

IF "YES", GIVE EXAMPLES. _____

_____

_____

_____

V Do the duties performed require customary and regular exercise of discretion and independent judgement in evaluating alternatives and making decisions in significant matters without direction from others (exclude skill in applying techniques, procedures or specific standards)? ☐ YES ☐ NO

IF THE ANSWER IS "YES", GIVE EXAMPLES. _____

_____

_____

_____

_____

_____

_____

_____

_____

_____

_____

_____

_____

_____

_____

_____

_____

_____

_____

_____

VI What percent of time is spent performing non-exempt duties (i.e. work of the same nature as that performed by non-exempt subordinates; but not to include the time spent on non-exempt work necessary for the accomplishment of exempt duties because of its direct or close relationship)? ____%

GIVE EXAMPLES OF THE TYPE OF NON-EXEMPT WORK INCLUDED IN THIS PERCENTAGE. _____

_____

_____

_____

_____

TO BE COMPLETED BY INTERVIEWER	TO BE COMPLETED BY WAGE & SALARY ADMINISTRATION
DOES THIS POSITION MEET FLSA REQUIREMENTS? ☐ YES ☐ NO	DOES THIS POSITION MEET FLSA REQUIREMENTS? ☐ YES ☐ NO
BRIEFLY EXPLAIN DECISION _____	BRIEFLY EXPLAIN DECISION _____

INTERVIEWER'S SIGNATURE	DATE	WAGE & SALARY ADMINISTRATION REP.	DATE
DIVISIONAL PERSONNEL REP. SIGNATURE	DATE	SIGNATURE	DATE

9.4 FLSA EXEMPTION QUESTIONNAIRE—PROFESSIONAL

FLSA EXEMPTION QUESTIONNAIRE

• PROFESSIONAL •

STAFF JOB TITLE

DATE | STAFF JOB CODE NO.

SUPERVISOR'S TITLE | DEPARTMENT

DIVISION/SUBSIDIARY | LOCATION

INSTRUCTIONS:

1. If proposed salary is $8,840 or more but less than $13,000, the Long Test is used. If proposed salary is $13,000 or more, the Short Test may be used.
2. This questionnaire should be completed by a personnel representative in an interview with the employee's staff supervisor.
3. Specific statements, not broad generalizations should be noted in the space provided for explanations.
4. The questionnaire should be signed by the supervisor, and the interviewer should complete the section provided for him.

I   **LONG TEST**

Is the employee's proposed salary $8,840 or more a year?
If answer to question II is no, answer questions III through VII.   ☐ YES   ☐ NO

II   **SHORT TEST**

Is the employee's proposed salary $13,000 or more a year?
If yes, answer question III (a or b) and VI.   ☐ YES   ☐ NO

III   a. Does the primary duty require knowledge of an advanced type in a field of science or learning customarily acquired by a prolonged course of specialized intellectual instruction and study?   ☐ YES   ☐ NO

IF "YES", INDICATE SPECIFICALLY THE COLLEGE COURSES REQUIRED AND HOW THE EMPLOYEE HAS MET THESE REQUIREMENTS. _____

_____

_____

_____

_____

  b. Does the primary duty involve original and creative work in a recognized field of artistic endeavor depending on the invention, imagination and talent of the employee?   ☐ YES   ☐ NO

IF "YES", INDICATE THE ARTISTIC FIELD AND THE EXTENT OF THE EMPLOYEE'S TRAINING IN THIS AREA. _____

_____

_____

_____

_____

IV   Are the duties performed predominately intellectual and varied in character, not routinely mental, manual, mechanical or physical in nature?   ☐ YES   ☐ NO

IF "YES", GIVE EXAMPLES. _____

_____

_____

_____

_____

V   Are the duties performed of such a nature that the output or the results cannot be standardized in relation to a given period of time?   ☐ YES   ☐ NO

IF "YES", GIVE EXAMPLES. _____

_____

_____

_____

_____

VI Do the duties performed require customary and regular exercise of discretion and independent judgement in evaluating alternatives and making decisions in significant matters without direction from others (exclude skill in applying techniques, procedures or specific standards)?   ☐ YES   ☐ NO

IF THE ANSWER IS "YES", GIVE EXAMPLES. _____

_____

_____

_____

_____

_____

_____

_____

_____

_____

_____

_____

_____

_____

_____

_____

_____

_____

_____

_____

_____

_____

VII What percent of time is spent performing non-exempt duties (i.e. work of the same nature as that performed by non-exempt subordinates; but not to include the time spent on non-exempt work necessary for the accomplishment of exempt duties because of its direct or close relationship)?   [%]

GIVE EXAMPLES OF THE TYPE OF NON-EXEMPT WORK INCLUDED IN THIS PERCENTAGE. _____

_____

_____

_____

_____

_____

TO BE COMPLETED BY INTERVIEWER	TO BE COMPLETED BY WAGE & SALARY ADMINISTRATION
DOES THIS POSITION MEET FLSA REQUIREMENTS? ☐YES ☐NO	DOES THIS POSITION MEET FLSA REQUIREMENTS? ☐YES ☐NO
BRIEFLY EXPLAIN DECISION _____	BRIEFLY EXPLAIN DECISION _____

INTERVIEWER'S SIGNATURE	DATE	WAGE & SALARY ADMINISTRATION REP.	DATE
DIVISIONAL PERSONNEL REP. SIGNATURE	DATE	SIGNATURE	DATE

9.5 FLSA EXEMPTION QUESTIONNAIRE—EXECUTIVE

<table>
<tr><td rowspan="4">
FLSA EXEMPTION QUESTIONNAIRE

• EXECUTIVE •
</td><td colspan="2">**FOR CORPORATE PERSONNEL USE ONLY**</td></tr>
<tr><td colspan="2">STAFF JOB TITLE</td></tr>
<tr><td>DATE</td><td>STAFF JOB CODE NO.</td></tr>
<tr><td>SUPERVISOR'S TITLE</td><td>DEPARTMENT</td></tr>
</table>

Note: DIVISION/SUBSIDIARY | LOCATION

INSTRUCTIONS:
1. If proposed salary is $8,060 or more but less than $13,000 the Long Test is used. If proposed salary is $13,000 or more, the Short Test may be used.
2. This questionnaire should be completed by a personnel representative in an interview with the employee's staff supervisor.
3. Specific statements, not broad generalizations should be noted in the space provided for explanations.
4. The questionnaire should be signed by the supervisor, and the interviewer should complete the section provided for him.

I LONG TEST

Is the employee's proposed salary $8,060 or more a year?
If answer to question II is no, answer questions III through VII.   ☐ YES ☐ NO

II SHORT TEST

Is the employee's proposed salary $13,000 or more a year?
If yes, answer questions III and IV only.   ☐ YES ☐ NO

III Does the primary duty consist of managing or supervising a subdivision of the company such as a Section, Department or Division? If yes, please indicate the percentage of time spent managing or supervising this subdivision. ____%   ☐ YES ☐ NO

IF "YES", DESCRIBE THIS SUBDIVISION'S FUNCTION IN DETAIL. _____

_____

_____

_____

_____

_____

_____

IV Does the position require the direction of at least two full-time employees?   ☐ YES ☐ NO

IF THE ANSWER IS "YES", LIST THE JOB TITLES AND NUMBER OF SUBORDINATES ALONG WITH AN "E" OR "NE" TO INDICATE WHETHER THEY ARE EXEMPT OR NON-EXEMPT EMPLOYEES.

JOB TITLE	NO.	JOB TITLE	NO.	JOB TITLE	NO.

V Do the duties performed include the authority to hire and fire or make recommendations to which particular weight is given concerning the hiring or firing, and the promotion or changing of status of other employees?   ☐ YES ☐ NO

IF "YES", DESCRIBE THE EXTENT OF SUCH AUTHORITY AS WELL AS THE RESPONSIBILITY FOR INITIATING WAGE ADJUSTMENTS AND COUNSELING SUBORDINATES ON THEIR PERFORMANCE.

_____

_____

_____

_____

VI Do the duties performed require customary and regular exercise of discretion and independent judgement in evaluating alternatives and making decisions in significant matters without direction from others (exclude skill in applying techniques, procedures or specific standards)? ☐ **YES** ☐ **NO**

IF THE ANSWER IS "YES", GIVE EXAMPLES. _____

_____

_____

_____

_____

_____

_____

_____

_____

_____

_____

_____

_____

_____

_____

_____

_____

_____

_____

_____

_____

_____

VII What percent of time is spent performing non-exempt duties (i.e. work of the same nature as that performed by non-exempt subordinates; but not to include the time spent on non-exempt work necessary for the accomplishment of exempt duties because of its direct or close relationship)? ☐ **%**

GIVE EXAMPLES OF THE TYPE OF NON-EXEMPT WORK INCLUDED IN THIS PERCENTAGE. _____

_____

_____

_____

_____

_____

TO BE COMPLETED BY INTERVIEWER	TO BE COMPLETED BY WAGE & SALARY ADMINISTRATION
DOES THIS POSITION MEET FLSA REQUIREMENTS? ☐ YES ☐ NO	DOES THIS POSITION MEET FLSA REQUIREMENTS? ☐ YES ☐ NO
BRIEFLY EXPLAIN DECISION _____	BRIEFLY EXPLAIN DECISION _____

INTERVIEWER'S SIGNATURE	DATE	WAGE & SALARY ADMINISTRATION REP.	DATE
DIVISIONAL PERSONNEL REP. SIGNATURE	DATE	SIGNATURE	DATE

404

9.6 SAMPLE NON-EXEMPT POSITION CLASSIFICATIONS

It is recommended that the HRM organization issue a listing of all positions classified as non-exempt—that is, ones classified as being covered by the overtime pay eligibility provisions of the Fair Labor Standards Act (Wage and Hour Law). The following sample Overtime Authorizations listing shows each covered position title and classification, which designates non-exempt ("NE") status and the wage/salary grade for the job/position.

Overtime Authorizations

Position Title	Classification
Bookkeeper-Cashier	NE-7
Bookkeeper-II	NE-6
Bookkeeper-I	NE-7
Clerk-Accounting-II	NE-4
Clerk-Accounting-I	NE-6
Clerk, Audit-II	NE-4
Clerk, Audit-I	NE-6
Clerk, File-II	NE-2
Clerk, File-I	NE-4
Clerk, Office Services-II	NE-3
Clerk, Office Services-I	NE-5
Clerk Typist-II	NE-4
Clerk Typist-I	NE-5
Expediter-II	NE-6
Expediter-I	NE-8
Operator, Data Entry-II	NE-5
Operator, Data Entry-I	NE-8
Operator, Telephone-II	NE-4
Operator, Telephone-I	NE-6
Operator, Teletype	NE-6
Secretary	NE-6
Stenographer	NE-5
Typist, Statistical	NE-6

9.7 SAMPLE COMPANY POLICY ON OVERTIME

Overtime

I. Objectives

This policy provides uniform and equitable guidelines for the administration of overtime pay.

II. General Principle

The company will pay overtime to non-exempt employees in accordance with the applicable provisions of the Fair Labor Standards Act (Wage and Hour Law).

III. Non-Exempt Employees

All employees whose jobs/positions are classified as being subject to the overtime pay provisions of the Fair Labor Standards Act (FLSA) shall be eligible for overtime compensation on the following basis:

A. Time and one-half shall be paid for time worked in excess of eight (8) hours in one day (except Sundays), or in excess of forty (40) hours in one week.

B. Double time shall be paid for all hours worked on any Sunday.

C. Double time shall be paid for all hours worked on a day observed by the company as a holiday.

D. Any time during which an employee is absent with pay shall be considered as time worked in computing overtime.

E. Overtime is to be credited in minimal units of one-quarter hour.

IV. Exempt Employees

A. Employees whose positions are exempt from the provisions of the FLSA normally shall not be eligible for overtime compensation.

B. In cases involving special project activities and emergency situations deemed by management to necessitate the scheduled overtime of exempt employees, such employees will be authorized to receive overtime compensation. The payment of these additional working hours will be based on straight time compensation—that is, the computed hourly rate represented by the employee's annual salary. This hourly rate of pay shall be calculated by dividing an employee's annual salary by 2080 hours.

C. Exempt employees are required to complete a weekly time report form to specify overtime hours worked and obtain requisite managerial approvals.

V. Additional Provisions

A. Employees at the New York City corporate headquarters who are scheduled to work overtime past 7:00 P.M. must take a thirty (30) minute unpaid break between 5:00 P.M. and 7:00 P.M.

B. Any employee who works two (2) or more hours of paid or unpaid overtime to at least 7:00 P.M. is authorized to submit a petty cash voucher for a $6.00 supper allowance.

9.8 SAMPLE COMPANY POLICY ON EMPLOYEE ABSENCES

Absences

I. Objectives

This policy describes a uniform time and absence reporting system and provides guidelines for the administration of employee absences.

II. Weekly Time Report

A. All non-exempt employees are required to maintain a personal weekly time report form. Exempt employees only will be required to prepare a weekly time report form for the purpose of reporting authorized overtime.

B. The Weekly Time Report form (see Figure 9.8A) is the official company record for use by non-exempt employees in meeting the time worked recording requirements of the Fair Labor Standards Act. It is maintained by individual employees on an "honor system" basis.

III. Weekly Absence Report

A. Each department manager will ensure that an accurate and complete record of all employee latenesses and absences is maintained on a weekly basis for all assigned employees. The Weekly Absence Report form (see Figure 9.8B) is used for this purpose.

B. Weekly Absence Report forms for a department provide cumulative data for management review of employee performance.

C. A copy of each Weekly Absence Report is due at the HRM organization by noon of each Friday; it serves as the basis for necessary payroll adjustments and provides the data needed for statistical assessments.

D. Employees shall have access to Weekly Absence Report records as needed to obtain information required for income tax reporting purposes.

IV. Sickness and Disability Absences

A. Permanent full-time employees with six (6) or more months of service may be granted a leave of absence with pay due to sickness or injury as follows:

Length of Service at Beginning of Disability	Working Days of Benefits for any Service Year*
Less than 6 months	None
6 months, but less than 1 year	5 working days
1 year, but less than 2 years	10 working days
2 years, but less than 3 years	15 working days
3 years, but less than 4 years	20 working days
4 years, but less than 5 years	25 working days
5 years and over	5 working days for each additional year of service to a maximum of 130 working days of full pay for 25 or more years of service

* An employee's "service year" consists of the 12-month period beginning with the date of employment, or subsequently, the employment anniversary date.

B. It is the responsibility of the department manager to notify the HRM organization when an assigned employee is disabled for a period of at least one (1) week. This notice will provide the basis for initiating forms required for medical and disability benefits.

C. Any employee who becomes ill while on the job and is sent home shall receive pay for the entire day. Such pay will not be charged against sick pay entitlement.

D. Benefits paid for all covered absences throughout an employee's service year shall not exceed the number of days authorized by the schedule listed in paragraph A. If an absence extends into a new service year, days of continued benefits are limited to the entitlement remaining from the employee's prior service year. The benefit entitlement for the new service year does not apply to the preexisting condition.

E. Benefit entitlements do not accumulate from year to year. Unused working days of benefits expire at the end of each service year. The only exception shall be for cases involving a continuing disability; carryover and use of remaining benefits during a new service year is authorized under these circumstances.

F. An employee's sick pay entitlement is to be applied against all sickness and injury absences of one or more days which occur during a service year. Excess absences beyond the number of authorized working days of benefits will be without pay.

G. In a case where an employee is not able to return to work prior to the expiration of authorized benefit entitlements, the individual must be placed in an unpaid leave of absence status. Such a leave of absence will begin on the date following the date that paid benefits expire, and may continue for a period equal to the paid benefits entitlement. During this period of unpaid leave of absence the company will continue the employee's coverage under group insurance programs.

V. Personal Leave of Absence

A. An employee may be granted a personal leave of absence without pay for compelling personal reasons. Approval shall be at the discretion of the department manager based on an assessment of mutual needs. Such leaves normally shall be limited to a maximum period of thirty (30) calendar days.

B. The HRM organization must be contacted prior to authorizing an employee request for a personal leave of absence for guidance concerning the suitability of granting the leave based on precedents. This coordination also is required to assess the potential need for a temporary employee to cover the vacant position.

VI. Maternity Leave of Absence

A. Maternity leave may be requested by an employee based on a date specified by the individual's personal physician. A medical certificate that specifies the last day of permitted employment shall be required in each such case.

B. The employee shall be granted up to six (6) months of unpaid leave based on the individual's assessment of personal need. The company will continue the employee's group insurance plan benefits throughout this leave of absence period.

C. The company shall provide the same position or a similar position to the employee at the time the leave of absence expires. Should the employee elect not to return to work at that time, employment shall be considered to be terminated due to resignation.

VII. Military Leave of Absence

A. The company shall grant a military leave of absence to permanent full-time employees who are called into military service for active duty with an organized reserve unit of the Armed Forces of the United States or a state National Guard Unit.

B. Employees with over six (6) months of service with the company will receive the difference between their government pay (exclusive of all allowances) and their regular straight-time salary for a maximum of two (2) weeks in any one calendar year. This payment will be made upon return to work after completion of such service, and upon presentation of government pay vouchers covering the period of absence.

C. Time off and pay for such compulsory annual active duty military training duty will be in addition to regular vacation time and pay.

VIII. Jury Duty

A. In the event that an employee is required to be absent from work to serve on a jury, no deduction from pay shall be made for related absences or fees received.

B. To obtain salary payment for such an absence, an employee must obtain certification of jury service by the clerk of the court. This documentation shall be provided to the HR organization at the time the employee returns to work.

Weekly Time Report

Last Name		First Name		Middle Initial

Social Sec. No.	Department		Week Ending

Remarks

SEE REVERSE SIDE FOR INSTRUCTIONS AND ABSENCE CODES

Day	Time In	Lunch Out	Lunch In	Time Out	Total Hours Regular	Total Hours Absent	OT
Mon							
Tue							
Wed							
Thu							
Fri							
Sat							
Sun							
					TOTALS		

I hereby certify that the time recorded is correct.

Employee's Signature	Date

For Payroll Use

Approval Section

Pay For	Do Not Pay For
☐ Regular Hours	
☐ Overtime Hours	☐ Hours

Department Mgr. or Spvsr.	Date

Instructions

<u>Print in ink.</u>

Record the exact time (hour and minute) of arrival and departure. If you arrive later, or leave earlier than your assigned schedule, record the date and reason in the remarks section.

Record all absent hours and minutes and the explanatory absence code (listed below) in the total hours absent column.

Record the hours and minutes (to the nearest 15 minutes) of <u>approved</u> overtime worked in the total hours OT column.

Review the data recorded during the week for accuracy, sign the certification section, and give the weekly time report to your supervisor prior to departure on the last day of the week.

Absence Codes

A—Attendance Award Day
C—Compensatory Day
D—Death in Family
F—Family Illness

H—Holiday/Official Closing
*I —Accident (Injury at work)
J—Jury Duty
*L—Leave of Absence

*O—Other
P—Personal Absence
R—Religious Observance
S—Sick (personal illness)
V—Vacation

* = Explain in Remarks Section.

Figure 9.8A Weekly time report

Weekly Absence Report

Page ____ of ____ Pages

Department _____ Location _____ Week of _____

Name (Last, Initials)	Type of Absence					Total Days Absent	Comments	Cum. Total Days Absent
	Mon.	Tue.	Wed.	Thu.	Fri.			

Note: Immediately advise the Personnel department of serious illnesses or injuries

Signature: _____

Instructions: Form is prepared daily by Department Manager to provide weekly record of employee latenesses and absences. All employees are to be listed in alphabetical order. "TYPE OF ABSENCE" is to be designated by using codes (see below); explanations are to be provided in "COMMENTS" column.

* A—Attendance Award Day   * I —Accident (Injury at Work)   *R—Religious Observance
* B—Company Business   * J —Jury Duty   S—Sick (Personal Illness)
* C—Compensatory Day   L —Leave of Absence   *T—Late (Tardiness)
* D—Death in Family   O —Other   *V—Vacation
  F—Family Illness   P —Personal Absence

* = Exclude from "TOTAL DAYS ABSENT" column and "CUM. Total Days Absent" column.

Figure 9.8B Weekly absence report form

9.9 ATTENDANCE AWARD PROGRAM: REWARDING NON-EXEMPT EMPLOYEES FOR PERFECT ATTENDANCE

A unique approach which will reduce controllable absences and latenesses very successfully is to offer non-exempt employees an Attendance Award Program. This employee-oriented, positive approach provides the incentive of earning a company-sanctioned personal day off with pay every four months. Experience has demonstrated that a company's absence statistics, adjusted for additional days awarded, still fall well below prior experience levels.

Attendance Award Program

A. One (1) day off with pay will be granted for perfect attendance during an attendance period. The maximum award for any employee will be three (3) days per calendar year.

B. An award day normally will be taken in conjunction with a weekend, and must be taken during the attendance period following the attendance period for which it was earned.

C. The following attendance periods will be used to determine attendance awards in any given year:

January 1 through April 30
May 1 through August 31
September 1 through December 31

D. All full-time, non-exempt employees with six (6) or more months of continuous service with the company are eligible to participate. New employees shall be eligible to participate on the first day of May, September, or January immediately following their completion of this service requirement.

E. An award day will be earned for perfect attendance during an attendance period. On-the-job absences and certain personal absences, such as those for a death in the immediate family, will not count against the employee's perfect attendance record.

F. Excessive or unexcused lateness during an attendance period will preclude an attendance award.

G. Excessive absenteeism or lateness in an attendance period may preclude attendance award consideration during the next attendance period.

9.10 SAMPLE COMPANY POLICY ON PROMOTIONS AND TRANSFERS

Promotions and Transfers

I. Objectives

To define and provide uniform guidelines for the administration of promotions and transfers.

II. Promotions

A promotion involves a marked increase in the complexity of duties and/or the addition of increased responsibilities which merit the assignment of a new job/position title in a higher wage/salary grade level.

A. All eligible company employees shall be considered for each advancement opportunity before consideration may be given to candidates outside the company.
B. Promotional increases shall be in addition to any merit increases which would have been granted under normal in-grade administration.
C. The compensation of an employee who is promoted normally shall be increased to a wage/salary rate at or above the minimum rate for the new grade level.
D. In the event a promoted employee's compensation is below the minimum rate for the new grade level, then special salary reviews may be scheduled at six (6) month intervals until compensation falls within the rate range for the position.
E. The amount of a promotional increase normally should be at least 8 percent and not more than 20 percent.

III. Transfers

A transfer without a promotion involves a move to a comparable position at the same rate of compensation. Duties, working conditions, and supervision change; and the employee receives an opportunity to increase knowledge and skills through a new assignment.

A. All transfer proposals are to be coordinated with the HRM organization to assess the suitability of candidates for proposed assignments, and the laborpower planning implications of such actions.
B. Special review and approval by the chief executive officer will be required in cases where transfers without promotion involve employee relocation at company expense to another work location.

9.11 PERSONNEL CHANGE AUTHORIZATION FORM: ONE FORM FOR PROCESSING ALL EMPLOYEE STATUS CHANGES

This multiple part, color coded form may be typed or generated by a computer system to implement all types of personnel status changes. The form includes the following pages:

1. White (original)—HRM organization copy

When the form is approved and implemented, to include arranging appropriate payroll action, this copy is placed in the employee's personnel record folder as a permanent record of the change.

2. Yellow (first copy)—payroll organization copy
3. Green (second copy)—originating organization copy
4. Blue (third copy)—employee copy

A sample copy of the form is shown in Figure 9.11. The following examples of the versatility of the form include:

Figure 9.11A   Personal Data Change (New Emergency Contact Information)
Figure 9.11B   Termination (Release)
Figure 9.11C   Employment and Placement on the Payroll
Figure 9.11D   Promotion
Figure 9.11E   Personal Data Change (New Address)
Figure 9.11F   Salary Adjustment
Figure 9.11G   Transfer and Reclassification
Figure 9.11H   Leave of Absence (Personal)
Figure 9.11I   Return from Leave of Absence (Re-employment)
Figure 9.11J   Termination (Resignation)

A fundamental concept for effectively using the Personnel Change Notice Authorization form is to enter the minimal amount of information needed to accomplish the specific type of personnel action by indicating the following:

- Employee Name
- Social Security Number
- Dates: Prepared and Effective
- Type of Change—the specific type of change(s) are designated within the appropriate heading:

—EMPLOYMENT

   Addition
   Replacement
   Re-employment

—PERSONNEL

   Transfer
   Promotion

Reclassification
Salary

—LEAVE OF ABSENCE

Jury Duty
Maternity
Personal
Sickness-disability

—TERMINATION OF EMPLOYMENT

Resignation
Release
Retirement
Reduction of staff

—PERSONAL

Name change
Address/telephone change
New emergency contact
Other

When a personnel action involves changes of grade, position title, organization, work location, annual salary rate, or performance rating, these sections are used to show current information versus proposed changes. Provisions for obtaining required approval signatures are included in the "approvals" portions of these sections.

- Other Changes—special sections of the form are used in providing details needed for processing the following types of personnel actions:

  — Leave of absence
  — Termination
  — Clearance and benefit conversion (for termination)
  — Personal data

The form includes a "classification codes" section in the heading. These codes are defined in the listing provided in the lower right-hand portion of the form, which also includes a line for inserting EEO code data as follows:

- Employee Categories
  1. Manager
  2. Professional
  3. Technician
  4. Sales worker
  5. Office-clerical worker
  6. Skilled craftsperson
  7. Semi-skilled operator
  8. Unskilled laborer
  9. Service worker
- Male or Female = M/F
- White/Black/Hispanic/Asian = W/B/S/A
- Handicapped = H
- Vietnam Era Veteran = VV

EXAMPLE: A Black, female, mechanical engineer who is neither handicapped nor a Vietnam era veteran would be coded as 2FB.

Personal Data Change (New Emergency Contact Information)(Figure 9.11A)

Consistent with the concept of entering the minimal amount of information needed to accomplish a specific type of personnel action, this employee-initiated action includes only:

- Employee Name
- Social Security Number
- Dates: Prepared and Effective
- Type of Change—Personal—New Emergency Contact
- Employee Authorization Signature and Date

Termination (Release)(Figure 9.11B)

To implement this termination (release) action, which involves a company-initiated separation of an employee, the following information is required:

- Employee Name
- Social Security Number
- Dates: Prepared and Effective
- Type of Change—Termination—Release
- Approval Signatures in "TO" Section
- Termination
  — Date for last day in office
  — Date for last day on Payroll
  — Notice, if any, given to employee
  — Code that designates the reason for the release
  — Re-employment eligibility? Yes or No
  — Allowance (workdays) for termination pay—that is, the number of days of pay for unused vacation in lieu of notice, and severance pay based on a service-related formula. For example, the employee was entitled to 10 days of vacation pay, 10 days in lieu of notice, and 10 days of separation pay for 2 years of service with the company. The total of 30 days is specified as being payable through "payroll continuation," but the employee will have the option of electing a lump-sum payment during the exit interview with the HRM department. Payroll continuation includes company-paid benefits for an additional 30 days, but serves to postpone the date the employee will apply for unemployment benefits. This trade-off is highly advantageous to the company in helping to minimize unemployment experience and associated increases of the overall contribution rate required by a state unemployment insurance (UI) fund. The higher the company's experience rating, the higher the percentage of overall employee salaries that a company must pay into a state UI fund. By retaining an employee on the payroll, the employee has the option of telling prospective employers that he or she is on "vacation" and looking for a better opportunity, which provides a positive basis for facilitating a new employment opportunity. From the company's viewpoint, most employees will hopefully secure new employment before their period of payroll continuation expires.

- Clearance is a record that shows the employee has returned all company property, settled expense accounts, and turned in company I.D. and credit cards. Checkmarks are placed on the form by the HRM department representative who conducts the exit interview, which includes verification that company clearance procedures have been completed before the HRM director approves payroll release action for the employee. Figure 9.11B shows that during the exit interview the employee opted for payroll continuation (selected in lieu of the lump-sum payment option), and that the employee intends to exercise his rights to benefit conversion at the end of the payroll continuation period—that is, the "last on payroll" date specified in the termination section.
- Employee Authorization Signature and Date is required for indicating the employee's understanding of the terms and conditions of the termination.

Employment and Placement on the Payroll (Figure 9.11C)

The following detailed data is required for placing an individual on the payroll as well as providing information for personnel records:

- Employee Name
- Social Security Number
- Dates: Prepared and Effective
- Classification Codes—As shown by the listing of "employee classification codes" provided in the lower right-hand corner of the form, the individual is a full-time employee (A), a probationary employee (D) serving an initial 6-month trial period, and an exempt employee (G) whose position is not covered by the paid overtime provisions of the FLSA.
- Type of Change—Employment—Replacement
- From (present status)—Full details are provided such as the employee's position classification, organization, work location, starting salary rate, effective date, budgetary impact of the change, and the name of the former employee for whom the new employee is a "replacement." The "approvals" portion of this section is used for obtaining required authorization signatures.
- Employment Agreement—A special agreement/commitment with the new employee is to provide a salary review after 6 months of employment. While the company's policy is to review the performance of all new employees just prior to their completion of 6 months of employment to assess the desirability of their retention, this definitive commitment assures the individual that his or her review will include a salary adjustment based on his or her degree of successful performance. Such commitments are made in cases where the new employee agrees to come on board at a rate that is lower than anticipated with a negotiated agreement for adjusting the rate based on demonstrated merit.
- Personal Data—The new employee provides his or her home address and telephone number and emergency contact information for personnel records purposes.

The HRM department designates the individual's EEO code for statistical reporting purposes. The code shown in the figure indicates that the employee is "professional-male-white-handicapped."

- Employee Authorization Signature and Date—The employee acknowledges acceptance of the terms and conditions of employment.

Promotion (Figure 9.11D)

A personnel change to effect a promotion, which includes both reclassification and salary adjustment action, requires the following data:

- Employee Name
- Social Security Number
- Dates: Prepared and Effective
- Classification Codes—The employee has successfully completed the 6-month probationary period; therefore, the "D" probationary employee code no longer is applicable. He is now designated as an "E" permanent (regular) employee.
- Type of Change—Personnel—Promotion
- From and To—Full data on the employee's current status is provided in the "from" section for comparison with "to" data, which only reflects proposed changes. Approvals for the proposed action are shown by signatures in the "to" (new status) section.

The employee's outstanding performance is shown by an "A" performance rating. The proposed increase percentage, according to the company's policy guidelines for promotions, combines a percentage for promotional purposes with a pro-rata percentage which compensates for merit. The fact that this special increase is related to an Employment Agreement commitment is specified in the "other information/changes" portion of this section.

Personal Data Change (Figure 9.11E)

The employee provides the following information in notifying the company that his personnel record should be revised to reflect a new home address and telephone number:

- Employee Name
- Social Security Number
- Dates: Prepared and Effective—Some advance notice is given in the example.
- Type of Change—Personal—Address/Telephone Change
- Personal Data—Specifics of new home address and telephone number are entered.
- Employee Authorization Signature and Date—Employee authorizes the personnel record change based on the information provided.

Salary Adjustment (Figure 9.11F)

The information required for salary adjustments includes:

- Employee Name
- Social Security Number
- Dates: Prepared and Effective
- Type of Change—Personnel—Salary
- From and To—Full details regarding the status of the employee are provided in the "from" section, and proposed changes are shown in the "to" section. Based on a performance rating of "B," Excellent, a 9 percent merit increase is specified. While the resultant dollar amount is shown as being budgeted, the actual

amount planned for the employee during the annual salary review and salary budget planning process exceeded the dollars shown for the proposed increase. This is because the individual previously was rated "A," an outstanding contributor who would have been entitled to an 11 percent increase if that level of performance was maintained.

Transfer and Reclassification (Figure 9.11G)

The employee has been designated for a transfer from the general accounting department, where he was an accountant, to the auditing department for a developmental assignment as an auditor. No change of salary grade or salary is proposed. This lateral transfer is accomplished by providing the following data:

- Employee Name
- Social Security Number
- Type of Change—Personnel—Transfer and Reclassification—Both categories apply; therefore, both are specified.
- From and To—Full data are provided for the employee in the "from" section, which also includes the approvals of the management of the division that is losing the employee. The "to" section only designates the new position code, position title, department code, and department name. The effective date is indicated, and the fact that required budgetary resources are available is specified. The management of the division gaining the employee indicates its approvals in the "to" section.

Leave of Absence (Figure 9.11H)

The employee is not happy with the developmental assignment, and makes this known to management, which decides that the employee would be well advised to take some time off without pay and look for another opportunity. This mutually agreed upon action is accomplished by the following entries:

- Employee Name
- Social Security Number
- Type of Change—Leave of Absence—Personal
- To Section—Used by management to indicate approvals.
- Leave of Absence Section—Completed to designate the overall dates, the duration in terms of workdays, "yes" to "benefit continuation?", and a notation to the effect that time off will be without pay.
- Employee Authorization Signature and Date—Individual indicates agreement with the terms and conditions of this personal leave of absence.

Return from Leave of Absence (Re-employment)(Figure 9.11I)

If the employment of the individual is considered to have been interrupted by this type of personal leave of absence (LOA), and company service record credit is to be revised accordingly, then a "re-employment" action is completed as follows:

- Employee Name
- Social Security Number

- Dates: Prepared and Effective
- Type of Change—Employment—Re-employment
- From Section—Used to specify "return from personal LOA" and the effective date. Management approvals are indicated.
- Employment Agreement—Re-employment includes a provision for a "revised service record date of 2/18/87," which adjusts the individual's overall service to exclude the period represented by the leave of absence.
- Employee Authorization Signature and Date—Employee signs the form to indicate his understanding of the terms of re-employment.

Termination (Resignation)(Figure 9.11J)

The employee's job hunting activities during the leave of absence were successful. The individual submits his resignation, which requires completion of the following:

- Employee Name
- Social Security Number
- Dates: Prepared and Completed
- Type of Change—Termination—Resignation
- To Section—Used by management to indicate approvals of provisions shown in the "termination" section.
- Termination Section—Specifies dates for last (day) in office and last (day) on payroll. Employee has given the required 10 days of notice, which results in a last day in the office date of 12/16/88. Since the employee has elected to take 10 days of vacation after that date, he will continue on the payroll through 12/30/88.
- Clearance—The employee meets clearance requirements during his last day in the office.
- Employee Authorization Signature and Date—Employee signs the form during the exit interview on his last day in the office.

PERSONNEL CHANGE NOTICE AUTHORIZATION   CONFIDENTIAL

EMPLOYEE NAME _____ SOCIAL SECURITY NO. _____
LAST   FIRST   INITIAL

DATES: PREPARED _____ EFFECTIVE _____

CLASSIFICATION
CODES □A □B □C □D □E □F □G

TYPE OF CHANGE	PERSONNEL	LEAVE OF ABSENCE	TERMINATION	PERSONAL
EMPLOYMENT	□TRANSFER	□JURY DUTY	□RESIGNATION	□NAME CHANGE
□ADDITION	□PROMOTION	□MATERNITY	□RELEASE	□ADDRESS/TELE. CHANGE
□REPLACEMENT	□RECLASSIFICATION	□PERSONAL	□RETIREMENT	□NEW EMERGENCY CONTACT
□REEMPLOYMENT	□SALARY	□SICKNESS-DISABILITY	□REDUCTION OF STAFF	□OTHER _____

FROM (PRESENT STATUS)			TO (NEW STATUS)		
GRADE	POS. CODE	POSITION TITLE	GRADE	POS. CODE	POSITION TITLE
DEPT. CODE	DEPARTMENT	LOCATION	DEPT. CODE	DEPARTMENT	LOCATION

LAST INCREASE	ANNUAL SALARY RATE	EFFECTIVE DATE	PROPOSED INCREASE	ANNUAL SALARY RATE	EFFECTIVE DATE
$ %	$		$ %	$	

PERFORMANCE RATING	BUDGETED	PERFORMANCE RATING	BUDGETED
□A □B □C □D □E	□YES □NO	□A □B □C □D □E	□YES □NO

OTHER INFORMATION/CHANGES: OTHER INFORMATION/CHANGES:

APPROVALS: APPROVALS:
_____ DATE _____   _____ DATE _____
_____ DATE _____   _____ DATE _____
_____ DATE _____   _____ DATE _____

EMPLOYMENT AGREEMENT:
THE UNDERSIGNED AGREES TO "AT WILL" EMPLOYMENT IN THE ABOVE INDICATED POSITION, AT SPECIFIED STARTING SALARY RATE, SUBJECT TO THE FOLLOWING AGREEMENTS OR COMMITMENTS, IF ANY:

LEAVE OF ABSENCE	DATES	DURATION (WORKDAYS)	BENEFIT CONTINUATION?
	FIRST_____ LAST_____		□YES □NO

DETAILS:

TERMINATION	DATES	NOTICE (WORKDAYS)	CODE	REEMPLOYMENT ELIGIBILITY?
	LAST IN OFFICE _____ LAST ON PAYROLL _____			□YES □NO

DETAILS:

ALLOWANCE (WORKDAYS)   □PAYROLL   □LUMP-SUM
                                                                    CONTINUATION   PAYMENT
VACATION _____ NOTICE _____ SEVERANCE _____ OTHER _____ TOTAL _____

CLEARANCE	□BOOKS		BENEFIT CONVERSION
	□PERSONAL PHONE BILL	□EXIT INTERVIEW	INSURANCE: □LIFE □MEDICAL
□KEYS	□T & E EXPENSE STATEMENT	CLEARED BY _____	SPECIAL INSTRUCTIONS:
□DOCUMENTS	□I.D. CARD		
□EQUIPMENT	□CREDIT CARDS	□PAYROLL RELEASE _____	

PERSONAL DATA

EMPLOYEE'S HOME ADDRESS └_____┘   EEO CODE:_____

CITY/STATE/ZIP CODE └_____┘   EMPLOYEE CLASSIFICATION CODES:

HOME TELEPHONE NO. └____┘ └____ — _____┘

EMERGENCY CONTACT INFORMATION   A. FULL-TIME EMPLOYEE

                                                              B. PART-TIME EMPLOYEE
NAME (RELATIONSHIP) └_____┘
                                                              C. TEMPORARY EMPLOYEE
STREET ADDRESS (APT.) └_____┘
                                                              D. PROBATIONARY EMPLOYEE
CITY/STATE/ZIP CODE └_____┘
                                                              E. PERMANENT EMPLOYEE
TELEPHONE NUMBER DURING
WORKING HOURS └____┘ └____ — _____┘ └_____┘ EXTENSION   F. NON-EXEMPT EMPLOYEE

                                                              G. EXEMPT EMPLOYEE

EMPLOYEE AUTHORIZATION _____
                              SIGNATURE   DATE

Figure 9.11 Personnel change notice authorization

421

PERSONNEL CHANGE NOTICE AUTHORIZATION   CONFIDENTIAL

EMPLOYEE NAME Smith, Thomas J.   SOCIAL SECURITY NO. 472-93-1846
                 LAST   FIRST   INITIAL

DATES: PREPARED 5/14/86   EFFECTIVE 5/14/86   CLASSIFICATION
                                                CODES □A □B □C □D □E □F □G

TYPE OF CHANGE	PERSONNEL	LEAVE OF ABSENCE	TERMINATION	PERSONAL
EMPLOYMENT	□TRANSFER	□JURY DUTY	□RESIGNATION	□NAME CHANGE
□ADDITION	□PROMOTION	□MATERNITY	□RELEASE	□ADDRESS/TELE. CHANGE
□REPLACEMENT	□RECLASSIFICATION	□PERSONAL	□RETIREMENT	☒NEW EMERGENCY CONTACT
□REEMPLOYMENT	□SALARY	□SICKNESS-DISABILITY	□REDUCTION OF STAFF	□OTHER _____

FROM (PRESENT STATUS)				TO (NEW STATUS)			
GRADE	POS. CODE	POSITION TITLE		GRADE	POS. CODE	POSITION TITLE	
DEPT. CODE	DEPARTMENT		LOCATION	DEPT. CODE	DEPARTMENT		LOCATION

LAST INCREASE	ANNUAL SALARY RATE	EFFECTIVE DATE	PROPOSED INCREASE	ANNUAL SALARY RATE	EFFECTIVE DATE
$ %	$		$ %	$	

PERFORMANCE RATING	BUDGETED	PERFORMANCE RATING	BUDGETED
□A □B □C □D □E	□YES □NO	□A □B □C □D □E	□YES □NO

OTHER INFORMATION/CHANGES: OTHER INFORMATION CHANGES:

APPROVALS: APPROVALS:

_____ DATE _____   _____ DATE _____

_____ DATE _____   _____ DATE _____

_____ DATE _____   _____ DATE _____

EMPLOYMENT AGREEMENT:
THE UNDERSIGNED AGREES TO "AT WILL" EMPLOYMENT IN THE ABOVE INDICATED POSITION, AT SPECIFIED STARTING SALARY RATE, SUBJECT TO THE FOLLOWING AGREEMENTS OR COMMITMENTS, IF ANY:

LEAVE OF ABSENCE	DATES	DURATION (WORKDAYS)	BENEFIT CONTINUATION?
	FIRST_____ LAST_____		□YES □NO

DETAILS:

TERMINATION	DATES	NOTICE (WORKDAYS)	CODE	REEMPLOYMENT ELIGIBILITY?
	LAST IN OFFICE _____ LAST ON PAYROLL_____			□YES □NO

DETAILS:

ALLOWANCE (WORKDAYS)   □PAYROLL   □LUMP-SUM
                                                CONTINUATION   PAYMENT
  VACATION _____ NOTICE _____ SEVERANCE _____ OTHER _____ TOTAL _____

CLEARANCE	□BOOKS		BENEFIT CONVERSION		
	□PERSONAL PHONE BILL	□EXIT INTERVIEW	INSURANCE:	□LIFE	□MEDICAL
□KEYS	□T & E EXPENSE STATEMENT	CLEARED BY _____	SPECIAL INSTRUCTIONS:		
□DOCUMENTS	□I.D. CARD				
□EQUIPMENT	□CREDIT CARDS	□PAYROLL RELEASE _____			

PERSONAL DATA

EMPLOYEE'S HOME ADDRESS ⌐_____⌐   EEO CODE:_____

CITY/STATE/ZIP CODE ⌐_____⌐   EMPLOYEE CLASSIFICATION CODES:

HOME TELEPHONE NO. ⌐____⌐ ⌐____ — ____⌐   A. FULL-TIME EMPLOYEE

                                            B. PART-TIME EMPLOYEE

EMERGENCY CONTACT INFORMATION

                                          C. TEMPORARY EMPLOYEE

NAME (RELATIONSHIP) ⌐ Mary L. Smith (Mother) ⌐   D. PROBATIONARY EMPLOYEE

STREET ADDRESS (APT.) ⌐ 1742 Pine Street ⌐   E. PERMANENT EMPLOYEE

CITY/STATE/ZIP CODE ⌐ Woodbridge   NJ   08244 ⌐   F. NON-EXEMPT EMPLOYEE

TELEPHONE NUMBER DURING WORKING HOURS ⌐ 201 ⌐ ⌐ 629 — 7413 ⌐ ⌐_____⌐ EXTENSION   G. EXEMPT EMPLOYEE

EMPLOYEE AUTHORIZATION _Thomas J. Smith_   5/14/86
                              SIGNATURE   DATE

Figure 9.11A Personnel change notice authorization—personal data change

PERSONNEL CHANGE NOTICE AUTHORIZATION   CONFIDENTIAL

EMPLOYEE NAME Smith, Thomas J.   SOCIAL SECURITY NO. 472-93-1846
LAST   FIRST   INITIAL

DATES: PREPARED 10/6/86   EFFECTIVE 10/10/86   CLASSIFICATION
CODES □A □B □C □D □E □F □G

TYPE OF CHANGE	PERSONNEL	LEAVE OF ABSENCE	TERMINATION	PERSONAL
EMPLOYMENT	□ TRANSFER	□ JURY DUTY	□ RESIGNATION	□ NAME CHANGE
□ ADDITION	□ PROMOTION	□ MATERNITY	☒ RELEASE	□ ADDRESS/TELE. CHANGE
□ REPLACEMENT	□ RECLASSIFICATION	□ PERSONAL	□ RETIREMENT	□ NEW EMERGENCY CONTACT
□ REEMPLOYMENT	□ SALARY	□ SICKNESS-DISABILITY	□ REDUCTION OF STAFF	□ OTHER _____

FROM (PRESENT STATUS)				TO (NEW STATUS)			
GRADE	POS. CODE	POSITION TITLE		GRADE	POS. CODE	POSITION TITLE	
DEPT. CODE	DEPARTMENT		LOCATION	DEPT. CODE	DEPARTMENT		LOCATION

LAST INCREASE		ANNUAL SALARY RATE	EFFECTIVE DATE	PROPOSED INCREASE		ANNUAL SALARY RATE	EFFECTIVE DATE
$	%	$		$	%	$	

PERFORMANCE RATING		BUDGETED	PERFORMANCE RATING		BUDGETED
□A □B □C □D □E		□ YES □ NO	□A □B □C □D □E		□ YES □ NO

OTHER INFORMATION/CHANGES: OTHER INFORMATION CHANGES:

APPROVALS: _____ DATE _____   APPROVALS: _a.a. Jones_ DATE 10/7/86
_____ DATE _____   _F.P. Greene_ DATE 10/8/86
_____ DATE _____   _J.T. Thomas_ DATE 10/8/86

EMPLOYMENT AGREEMENT:
THE UNDERSIGNED AGREES TO "AT WILL" EMPLOYMENT IN THE ABOVE INDICATED POSITION, AT SPECIFIED STARTING SALARY RATE, SUBJECT TO THE FOLLOWING AGREEMENTS OR COMMITMENTS, IF ANY:

LEAVE OF ABSENCE	DATES		DURATION (WORKDAYS)	BENEFIT CONTINUATION?
	FIRST _____ LAST _____			□ YES □ NO

DETAILS:

TERMINATION	DATES		NOTICE (WORKDAYS)	CODE	REEMPLOYMENT ELIGIBILITY?
	LAST IN OFFICE 10/10/86 LAST ON PAYROLL 11/21/86		0	V	□ YES ☒ NO

DETAILS:

ALLOWANCE (WORKDAYS)
VACATION 10 NOTICE 10 SEVERANCE 10 OTHER — TOTAL 30   ☒ PAYROLL CONTINUATION   □ LUMP-SUM PAYMENT

CLEARANCE	☒ BOOKS		BENEFIT CONVERSION	
	☒ PERSONAL PHONE BILL	☒ EXIT INTERVIEW	INSURANCE: ☒ LIFE	☒ MEDICAL
☒ KEYS	☒ T & E EXPENSE STATEMENT	CLEARED BY FTS	SPECIAL INSTRUCTIONS:	
☒ DOCUMENTS	☒ I.D. CARD			
☒ EQUIPMENT	☒ CREDIT CARDS	☒ PAYROLL RELEASE aas		

PERSONAL DATA

EMPLOYEE'S HOME ADDRESS

CITY/STATE/ZIP CODE

HOME TELEPHONE NO.

EMERGENCY CONTACT INFORMATION

NAME (RELATIONSHIP)

STREET ADDRESS (APT.)

CITY/STATE/ZIP CODE

TELEPHONE NUMBER DURING WORKING HOURS _____ EXTENSION

EEO CODE: _____

EMPLOYEE CLASSIFICATION CODES:

A. FULL-TIME EMPLOYEE

B. PART-TIME EMPLOYEE

C. TEMPORARY EMPLOYEE

D. PROBATIONARY EMPLOYEE

E. PERMANENT EMPLOYEE

F. NON-EXEMPT EMPLOYEE

G. EXEMPT EMPLOYEE

EMPLOYEE AUTHORIZATION _Thomas J. Smith_   10/10/86
SIGNATURE   DATE

Figure 9.11B Personnel change notice authorization—termination (release)

PERSONNEL CHANGE NOTICE AUTHORIZATION   CONFIDENTIAL

EMPLOYEE NAME __Jones, William F.__   SOCIAL SECURITY NO. __276-42-1087__
LAST   FIRST   INITIAL

DATES: PREPARED __1/19/87__   EFFECTIVE __1/19/87__   CLASSIFICATION CODES ☒A ☐B ☐C ☒D ☐E ☐F ☒G

TYPE OF CHANGE	PERSONNEL	LEAVE OF ABSENCE	TERMINATION	PERSONAL
EMPLOYMENT	☐TRANSFER	☐JURY DUTY	☐RESIGNATION	☐NAME CHANGE
☐ADDITION	☐PROMOTION	☐MATERNITY	☐RELEASE	☐ADDRESS/TELE. CHANGE
☒REPLACEMENT	☐RECLASSIFICATION	☐PERSONAL	☐RETIREMENT	☐NEW EMERGENCY CONTACT
☐REEMPLOYMENT	☐SALARY	☐SICKNESS-DISABILITY	☐REDUCTION OF STAFF	☐OTHER _____

FROM (PRESENT STATUS)				TO (NEW STATUS)			
GRADE	POS. CODE	POSITION TITLE		GRADE	POS. CODE	POSITION TITLE	
9	A405	Accountant - III					

DEPT. CODE	DEPARTMENT	LOCATION	DEPT. CODE	DEPARTMENT	LOCATION
413	General Accounting	NYC			

LAST INCREASE	ANNUAL SALARY RATE	EFFECTIVE DATE	PROPOSED INCREASE		ANNUAL SALARY RATE	EFFECTIVE DATE
$ %	$ 27,500	1/19/87	$ %	$		

PERFORMANCE RATING	BUDGETED	PERFORMANCE RATING	BUDGETED
☐A ☐B ☐C ☐D ☐E	☒YES ☐NO	☐A ☐B ☐C ☐D ☐E	☐YES ☐NO

OTHER INFORMATION/CHANGES:
Replace T. J. Smith

OTHER INFORMATION/CHANGES:

APPROVALS:
John F. Pettingham DATE 1/19/87
ST Formento DATE 1/19/87
R Smith DATE 1/19/87

APPROVALS:
_____ DATE _____
_____ DATE _____
_____ DATE _____

EMPLOYMENT AGREEMENT:
THE UNDERSIGNED AGREES TO "AT WILL" EMPLOYMENT IN THE ABOVE INDICATED POSITION, AT SPECIFIED STARTING SALARY RATE, SUBJECT TO THE FOLLOWING AGREEMENTS OR COMMITMENTS, IF ANY:

Salary review after 6 months of employment.

LEAVE OF ABSENCE	DATES	DURATION (WORKDAYS)	BENEFIT CONTINUATION?
	FIRST_____ LAST_____		☐YES ☐NO

DETAILS:

TERMINATION	DATES	NOTICE (WORKDAYS)	CODE	REEMPLOYMENT ELIGIBILITY?
	LAST IN OFFICE _____ LAST ON PAYROLL_____			☐YES ☐NO

DETAILS:

ALLOWANCE (WORKDAYS)   ☐PAYROLL CONTINUATION   ☐LUMP-SUM PAYMENT

VACATION _____ NOTICE _____ SEVERANCE _____ OTHER _____ TOTAL _____

CLEARANCE	☐BOOKS		BENEFIT CONVERSION
	☐PERSONAL PHONE BILL	☐EXIT INTERVIEW	INSURANCE: ☐LIFE ☐MEDICAL
☐KEYS	☐T & E EXPENSE STATEMENT	CLEARED BY _____	SPECIAL INSTRUCTIONS:
☐DOCUMENTS	☐I.D. CARD		
☐EQUIPMENT	☐CREDIT CARDS	☐PAYROLL RELEASE _____	

PERSONAL DATA

EMPLOYEE'S HOME ADDRESS   174 Potamkin Place

CITY/STATE/ZIP CODE   Oakcrest   NY   27904

HOME TELEPHONE NO.   205   731 - 6240

EEO CODE: 2MWH

EMPLOYEE CLASSIFICATION CODES:

A. FULL-TIME EMPLOYEE

B. PART-TIME EMPLOYEE

EMERGENCY CONTACT INFORMATION

NAME (RELATIONSHIP)   Mary M. Jones (Wife)

C. TEMPORARY EMPLOYEE

STREET ADDRESS (APT.)   (Same as Above)

D. PROBATIONARY EMPLOYEE

CITY/STATE/ZIP CODE

E. PERMANENT EMPLOYEE

TELEPHONE NUMBER DURING WORKING HOURS   202   397 - 2167   EXTENSION

F. NON-EXEMPT EMPLOYEE

G. EXEMPT EMPLOYEE

EMPLOYEE AUTHORIZATION   _William F. Jones_   1/19/87
SIGNATURE   DATE

Figure 9.11C Personnel change notice authorization—employment & placement on payroll

PERSONNEL CHANGE NOTICE AUTHORIZATION   CONFIDENTIAL

EMPLOYEE NAME __Jones, William F.__   SOCIAL SECURITY NO. __276-42-1087__

       LAST   FIRST   INITIAL

DATES: PREPARED __7/20/87__   EFFECTIVE __7/27/87__   CLASSIFICATION CODES □A □B □C □D ☒E □F □G

TYPE OF CHANGE.	PERSONNEL	LEAVE OF ABSENCE	TERMINATION	PERSONAL
EMPLOYMENT	□ TRANSFER	□ JURY DUTY	□ RESIGNATION	□ NAME CHANGE
□ ADDITION	☒ PROMOTION	□ MATERNITY	□ RELEASE	□ ADDRESS/TELE. CHANGE
□ REPLACEMENT	□ RECLASSIFICATION	□ PERSONAL	□ RETIREMENT	□ NEW EMERGENCY CONTACT
□ REEMPLOYMENT	□ SALARY	□ SICKNESS-DISABILITY	□ REDUCTION OF STAFF	□ OTHER _____

FROM (PRESENT STATUS)				TO (NEW STATUS)			
GRADE	POS. CODE	POSITION TITLE		GRADE	POS. CODE	POSITION TITLE	
9	A405	Accountant - III		11	A407	Accountant - II	

DEPT. CODE	DEPARTMENT		LOCATION	DEPT. CODE	DEPARTMENT		LOCATION
413	General Accounting		NYC				

LAST INCREASE		ANNUAL SALARY RATE	EFFECTIVE DATE	PROPOSED INCREASE		ANNUAL SALARY RATE	EFFECTIVE DATE
$ N/A	%	$ 27,500	1/19/87	$ 3,850	14 %	$ 31,350	7/27/87

PERFORMANCE RATING	BUDGETED	PERFORMANCE RATING	BUDGETED
□A □B □C □D □E	□ YES ☒ NO	☒A □B □C □D □E	□ YES ☒ NO

OTHER INFORMATION/CHANGES:

OTHER INFORMATION CHANGES:
Employment Agreement-6 Month Salary Review

APPROVALS:		APPROVALS:	
_____ DATE _____		_John F. Pettingham_ DATE 7/20/87	
_____ DATE _____		_J Forment_ DATE 7/20/87	
_____ DATE _____		_R Smith_ DATE 7/20/87	

EMPLOYMENT AGREEMENT:
THE UNDERSIGNED AGREES TO "AT WILL" EMPLOYMENT IN THE ABOVE INDICATED POSITION, AT SPECIFIED STARTING SALARY RATE, SUBJECT TO THE FOLLOWING AGREEMENTS OR COMMITMENTS, IF ANY:

LEAVE OF ABSENCE	DATES		DURATION (WORKDAYS)	BENEFIT CONTINUATION?
	FIRST _____ LAST _____			□ YES □ NO

DETAILS:

TERMINATION	DATES		NOTICE (WORKDAYS)	CODE	REEMPLOYMENT ELIGIBILITY?
	LAST IN OFFICE _____	LAST ON PAYROLL _____			□ YES □ NO

DETAILS:

ALLOWANCE (WORKDAYS)   □ PAYROLL CONTINUATION   □ LUMP-SUM PAYMENT

VACATION _____ NOTICE _____ SEVERANCE _____ OTHER _____ TOTAL _____

CLEARANCE	□ BOOKS		BENEFIT CONVERSION	
	□ PERSONAL PHONE BILL	□ EXIT INTERVIEW	INSURANCE: □ LIFE	□ MEDICAL
□ KEYS	□ T & E EXPENSE STATEMENT	CLEARED BY _____	SPECIAL INSTRUCTIONS:	
□ DOCUMENTS	□ I.D. CARD			
□ EQUIPMENT	□ CREDIT CARDS	□ PAYROLL RELEASE _____		

PERSONAL DATA

EMPLOYEE'S HOME ADDRESS

CITY/STATE/ZIP CODE

HOME TELEPHONE NO.

EMERGENCY CONTACT INFORMATION

NAME (RELATIONSHIP)

STREET ADDRESS (APT.)

CITY/STATE/ZIP CODE

TELEPHONE NUMBER DURING WORKING HOURS _____ EXTENSION

EEO CODE: _____

EMPLOYEE CLASSIFICATION CODES:

A. FULL-TIME EMPLOYEE

B. PART-TIME EMPLOYEE

C. TEMPORARY EMPLOYEE

D. PROBATIONARY EMPLOYEE

E. PERMANENT EMPLOYEE

F NON-EXEMPT EMPLOYEE

G. EXEMPT EMPLOYEE

EMPLOYEE AUTHORIZATION _____
      SIGNATURE   DATE

Figure 9.11D Personnel change notice authorization—promotion

PERSONNEL CHANGE NOTICE AUTHORIZATION   CONFIDENTIAL

EMPLOYEE NAME __Jones, William F.__   SOCIAL SECURITY NO. __276-42-1087__
                   LAST   FIRST   INITIAL

DATES: PREPARED __10/19/87__   EFFECTIVE __11/2/87__   CLASSIFICATION
CODES □A □B □C □D □E □F □G

TYPE OF CHANGE	PERSONNEL	LEAVE OF ABSENCE	TERMINATION	PERSONAL
EMPLOYMENT	□TRANSFER	□JURY DUTY	□RESIGNATION	□NAME CHANGE
□ADDITION	□PROMOTION	□MATERNITY	□RELEASE	X ADDRESS/TELE. CHANGE
□REPLACEMENT	□RECLASSIFICATION	□PERSONAL	□RETIREMENT	□NEW EMERGENCY CONTACT
□REEMPLOYMENT	□SALARY	□SICKNESS-DISABILITY	□REDUCTION OF STAFF	□OTHER _____

FROM (PRESENT STATUS)				TO (NEW STATUS)			
GRADE	POS. CODE	POSITION TITLE		GRADE	POS. CODE	POSITION TITLE	
DEPT. CODE	DEPARTMENT		LOCATION	DEPT. CODE	DEPARTMENT		LOCATION

LAST INCREASE		ANNUAL SALARY RATE	EFFECTIVE DATE	PROPOSED INCREASE		ANNUAL SALARY RATE	EFFECTIVE DATE
$	%	$		$	%	$	

PERFORMANCE RATING	BUDGETED	PERFORMANCE RATING	BUDGETED
□A □B □C □D □E	□YES □NO	□A □B □C □D □E	□YES □NO

OTHER INFORMATION/CHANGES: OTHER INFORMATION/CHANGES:

APPROVALS: APPROVALS:

_____ DATE _____   _____ DATE _____
_____ DATE _____   _____ DATE _____
_____ DATE _____   _____ DATE _____

EMPLOYMENT AGREEMENT:
THE UNDERSIGNED AGREES TO "AT WILL" EMPLOYMENT IN THE ABOVE INDICATED POSITION, AT SPECIFIED STARTING SALARY RATE, SUBJECT TO THE FOLLOWING AGREEMENTS OR COMMITMENTS, IF ANY:

LEAVE OF ABSENCE	DATES	DURATION (WORKDAYS)	BENEFIT CONTINUATION?
	FIRST _____ LAST _____		□YES □NO

DETAILS:

TERMINATION	DATES	NOTICE (WORKDAYS)	CODE	REEMPLOYMENT ELIGIBILITY?
	LAST IN OFFICE _____ LAST ON PAYROLL _____			□YES □NO

DETAILS:

ALLOWANCE (WORKDAYS)   □PAYROLL CONTINUATION   □LUMP-SUM PAYMENT

VACATION _____ NOTICE _____ SEVERANCE _____ OTHER _____ TOTAL _____

CLEARANCE	□BOOKS		BENEFIT CONVERSION		
	□PERSONAL PHONE BILL	□EXIT INTERVIEW	INSURANCE:	□LIFE	□MEDICAL
□KEYS	□T & E EXPENSE STATEMENT	CLEARED BY _____	SPECIAL INSTRUCTIONS:		
□DOCUMENTS	□I.D. CARD				
□EQUIPMENT	□CREDIT CARDS	□PAYROLL RELEASE _____			

PERSONAL DATA

EMPLOYEE'S HOME ADDRESS | 1206 South Maple Drive |

CITY/STATE/ZIP CODE | Middletown | NJ | 08305 |

HOME TELEPHONE NO. | 203 | 624 - 1297 |

EMERGENCY CONTACT INFORMATION

NAME (RELATIONSHIP) |_____|

STREET ADDRESS (APT.) |_____|

CITY/STATE/ZIP CODE |_____|

TELEPHONE NUMBER DURING WORKING HOURS |___|___-___| |___| EXTENSION

EEO CODE:_____

EMPLOYEE CLASSIFICATION CODES:

A. FULL-TIME EMPLOYEE

B. PART-TIME EMPLOYEE

C. TEMPORARY EMPLOYEE

D. PROBATIONARY EMPLOYEE

E. PERMANENT EMPLOYEE

F. NON-EXEMPT EMPLOYEE

G. EXEMPT EMPLOYEE

EMPLOYEE AUTHORIZATION __William F. Jones__   __10/19/87__
                                     SIGNATURE   DATE

Figure 9.11E Personnel change notice authorization—personal data change

PERSONNEL CHANGE NOTICE AUTHORIZATION   CONFIDENTIAL

EMPLOYEE NAME __Jones, William F.__   SOCIAL SECURITY NO. __276-42-1087__

      LAST   FIRST   INITIAL

DATES: PREPARED __7/13/88__   EFFECTIVE __8/1/88__   CLASSIFICATION CODES □A □B □C □D □E □F □G

TYPE OF CHANGE	PERSONNEL	LEAVE OF ABSENCE	TERMINATION	PERSONAL
EMPLOYMENT	□TRANSFER	□JURY DUTY	□RESIGNATION	□NAME CHANGE
□ADDITION	□PROMOTION	□MATERNITY	□RELEASE	□ADDRESS/TELE. CHANGE
□REPLACEMENT	□RECLASSIFICATION	□PERSONAL	□RETIREMENT	□NEW EMERGENCY CONTACT
□REEMPLOYMENT	☒SALARY	□SICKNESS-DISABILITY	□REDUCTION OF STAFF	□OTHER _____

FROM (PRESENT STATUS)

GRADE	POS. CODE	POSITION TITLE
11	A407	Accountant - II

DEPT. CODE	DEPARTMENT	LOCATION
413	General Accounting	NYC

LAST INCREASE		ANNUAL SALARY RATE	EFFECTIVE DATE
$ 3,850	14 %	$ 31,350	1/19/87

PERFORMANCE RATING: ☒A □B □C □D □E   BUDGETED: □YES ☒NO

TO (NEW STATUS)

GRADE	POS. CODE	POSITION TITLE

DEPT. CODE	DEPARTMENT	LOCATION

PROPOSED INCREASE		ANNUAL SALARY RATE	EFFECTIVE DATE
$ 2,820	9 %	$ 34,170	8/1/88

PERFORMANCE RATING: □A ☒B □C □D □E   BUDGETED: ☒YES □NO

OTHER INFORMATION/CHANGES:

OTHER INFORMATION CHANGES:

APPROVALS: _____ DATE ____   _____ DATE ____   _____ DATE ____

APPROVALS: _John F. Pellingham_ DATE __7/13/88__   _J. Formento_ DATE __7/15/87__   _R. Smith_ DATE __7/19/87__

EMPLOYMENT AGREEMENT:
THE UNDERSIGNED AGREES TO "AT WILL" EMPLOYMENT IN THE ABOVE INDICATED POSITION, AT SPECIFIED STARTING SALARY RATE, SUBJECT TO THE FOLLOWING AGREEMENTS OR COMMITMENTS, IF ANY:

LEAVE OF ABSENCE	DATES FIRST_____ LAST_____	DURATION (WORKDAYS)	BENEFIT CONTINUATION? □YES □NO

DETAILS:

TERMINATION	DATES LAST IN OFFICE_____ LAST ON PAYROLL_____	NOTICE (WORKDAYS)	CODE	REEMPLOYMENT ELIGIBILITY? □YES □NO

DETAILS:

ALLOWANCE (WORKDAYS)

VACATION ____ NOTICE ____ SEVERANCE ____ OTHER ____ TOTAL ____   □PAYROLL CONTINUATION   □LUMP-SUM PAYMENT

CLEARANCE	□BOOKS		BENEFIT CONVERSION
	□PERSONAL PHONE BILL	□EXIT INTERVIEW	INSURANCE: □LIFE □MEDICAL
□KEYS	□T & E EXPENSE STATEMENT	CLEARED BY _____	SPECIAL INSTRUCTIONS:
□DOCUMENTS	□I.D. CARD		
□EQUIPMENT	□CREDIT CARDS	□PAYROLL RELEASE _____	

PERSONAL DATA

EMPLOYEE'S HOME ADDRESS _____

CITY/STATE/ZIP CODE _____

HOME TELEPHONE NO. _____

EMERGENCY CONTACT INFORMATION

NAME (RELATIONSHIP) _____

STREET ADDRESS (APT.) _____

CITY/STATE/ZIP CODE _____

TELEPHONE NUMBER DURING WORKING HOURS _____ EXTENSION

EEO CODE: _____

EMPLOYEE CLASSIFICATION CODES:

A. FULL-TIME EMPLOYEE

B. PART-TIME EMPLOYEE

C. TEMPORARY EMPLOYEE

D. PROBATIONARY EMPLOYEE

E. PERMANENT EMPLOYEE

F. NON-EXEMPT EMPLOYEE

G. EXEMPT EMPLOYEE

EMPLOYEE AUTHORIZATION _____   SIGNATURE   DATE

Figure 9.11F Personnel change notice authorization—salary adjustment

PERSONNEL CHANGE NOTICE AUTHORIZATION   CONFIDENTIAL

EMPLOYEE NAME __Jones, William F.__   SOCIAL SECURITY NO. __276-42-1087__
    LAST   FIRST   INITIAL

DATES: PREPARED __10/3/88__   EFFECTIVE __10/17/88__   CLASSIFICATION CODES ☐A ☐B ☐C ☐D ☐E ☐F ☐G

TYPE OF CHANGE	PERSONNEL	LEAVE OF ABSENCE	TERMINATION	PERSONAL
EMPLOYMENT	☒TRANSFER	☐JURY DUTY	☐RESIGNATION	☐NAME CHANGE
☐ADDITION	☐PROMOTION	☐MATERNITY	☐RELEASE	☐ADDRESS/TELE. CHANGE
☐REPLACEMENT	☒RECLASSIFICATION	☐PERSONAL	☐RETIREMENT	☐NEW EMERGENCY CONTACT
☐REEMPLOYMENT	☐SALARY	☐SICKNESS-DISABILITY	☐REDUCTION OF STAFF	☐OTHER _____

FROM (PRESENT STATUS)					TO (NEW STATUS)			
GRADE	POS. CODE	POSITION TITLE			GRADE	POS. CODE	POSITION TITLE	
11	A407	Accountant - II				A607	Auditor - II	
DEPT. CODE	DEPARTMENT		LOCATION	DEPT. CODE	DEPARTMENT			LOCATION
413	General Accounting		NYC	417	Auditing			

LAST INCREASE		ANNUAL SALARY RATE	EFFECTIVE DATE	PROPOSED INCREASE		ANNUAL SALARY RATE	EFFECTIVE DATE
$ 2,820	9 %	$ 34,170	8/1/88	$	% $		10/17/87
PERFORMANCE RATING			BUDGETED	PERFORMANCE RATING			BUDGETED
☐A ☒B ☐C ☐D ☐E			☒YES ☐NO	☐A ☐B ☐C ☐D ☐E			☒YES ☐NO

OTHER INFORMATION/CHANGES: OTHER INFORMATION/CHANGES:

APPROVALS: _John F. Fettingham_ DATE 10/4/88   APPROVALS: _Richard Von Meter_ DATE 10/5/88
Formento DATE 10/5/88   _S. Thompson_ DATE 10/5/88
R. Smith DATE 10/5/88   DATE 10/5/88

EMPLOYMENT AGREEMENT:
THE UNDERSIGNED AGREES TO "AT WILL" EMPLOYMENT IN THE ABOVE INDICATED POSITION. AT SPECIFIED STARTING SALARY RATE. SUBJECT TO THE FOLLOWING AGREEMENTS OR COMMITMENTS. IF ANY:

LEAVE OF ABSENCE	DATES		DURATION (WORKDAYS)	BENEFIT CONTINUATION?
	FIRST_____	LAST_____		☐YES ☐NO

DETAILS:

TERMINATION	DATES		NOTICE (WORKDAYS)	CODE	REEMPLOYMENT ELIGIBILITY?
	LAST IN OFFICE_____	LAST ON PAYROLL_____			☐YES ☐NO

DETAILS:

ALLOWANCE (WORKDAYS)   ☐PAYROLL CONTINUATION   ☐LUMP-SUM PAYMENT

VACATION ____ NOTICE ____ SEVERANCE ____ OTHER ____ TOTAL ____

CLEARANCE	☐BOOKS		BENEFIT CONVERSION		
	☐PERSONAL PHONE BILL	☐EXIT INTERVIEW	INSURANCE:	☐LIFE	☐MEDICAL
☐KEYS	☐T & E EXPENSE STATEMENT	CLEARED BY ____	SPECIAL INSTRUCTIONS:		
☐DOCUMENTS	☐I.D. CARD				
☐EQUIPMENT	☐CREDIT CARDS	☐PAYROLL RELEASE ____			

PERSONAL DATA

EMPLOYEE'S HOME ADDRESS ____

CITY/STATE/ZIP CODE ____

HOME TELEPHONE NO. ____

EMERGENCY CONTACT INFORMATION

NAME (RELATIONSHIP) ____

STREET ADDRESS (APT.) ____

CITY/STATE/ZIP CODE ____

TELEPHONE NUMBER DURING WORKING HOURS ____ EXTENSION

EEO CODE: ____

EMPLOYEE CLASSIFICATION CODES:

A. FULL-TIME EMPLOYEE

B. PART-TIME EMPLOYEE

C. TEMPORARY EMPLOYEE

D. PROBATIONARY EMPLOYEE

E. PERMANENT EMPLOYEE

F. NON-EXEMPT EMPLOYEE

G. EXEMPT EMPLOYEE

EMPLOYEE AUTHORIZATION ____
    SIGNATURE   DATE

Figure 9.11G Personnel change notice authorization—transfer & reclassification

PERSONNEL CHANGE NOTICE AUTHORIZATION   CONFIDENTIAL

EMPLOYEE NAME ___Jones, William F.___   SOCIAL SECURITY NO. ___276-42-1087___
LAST   FIRST   INITIAL

DATES: PREPARED ___10/24/88___   EFFECTIVE ___11/1/88___   CLASSIFICATION
CODES □A □B □C □D □E □F □G

TYPE OF CHANGE	PERSONNEL	LEAVE OF ABSENCE	TERMINATION	PERSONAL
EMPLOYMENT	□TRANSFER	□JURY DUTY	□RESIGNATION	□NAME CHANGE
□ADDITION	□PROMOTION	□MATERNITY	□RELEASE	□ADDRESS/TELE. CHANGE
□REPLACEMENT	□RECLASSIFICATION	☒PERSONAL	□RETIREMENT	□NEW EMERGENCY CONTACT
□REEMPLOYMENT	□SALARY	□SICKNESS-DISABILITY	□REDUCTION OF STAFF	□OTHER _____

FROM (PRESENT STATUS)			TO (NEW STATUS)		
GRADE	POS. CODE	POSITION TITLE	GRADE	POS. CODE	POSITION TITLE
DEPT. CODE	DEPARTMENT	LOCATION	DEPT. CODE	DEPARTMENT	LOCATION

LAST INCREASE	ANNUAL SALARY RATE	EFFECTIVE DATE	PROPOSED INCREASE	ANNUAL SALARY RATE	EFFECTIVE DATE
$ %	$		$ %	$	

PERFORMANCE RATING   □A □B □C □D □E   BUDGETED □YES □NO   PERFORMANCE RATING   □A □B □C □D □E   BUDGETED □YES □NO

OTHER INFORMATION/CHANGES: OTHER INFORMATION/CHANGES:

APPROVALS:
_____ DATE _____
_____ DATE _____
_____ DATE _____

APPROVALS:
Richard Von Meter DATE 10/24/88
S. Thompson DATE 10/X/88
W. Slupl DATE 10/26/88

EMPLOYMENT AGREEMENT:
THE UNDERSIGNED AGREES TO "AT WILL" EMPLOYMENT IN THE ABOVE INDICATED POSITION, AT SPECIFIED STARTING SALARY RATE, SUBJECT TO THE FOLLOWING AGREEMENTS OR COMMITMENTS, IF ANY:

LEAVE OF ABSENCE	DATES FIRST ___11/1/88___ LAST ___11/30/88___	DURATION (WORKDAYS) 22	BENEFIT CONTINUATION? ☒YES □NO

DETAILS:
Mutual agreement - time off without pay to resolve personal problems.

TERMINATION	DATES LAST IN OFFICE _____ LAST ON PAYROLL _____	NOTICE (WORKDAYS)	CODE	REEMPLOYMENT ELIGIBILITY? □YES □NO

DETAILS:

ALLOWANCE (WORKDAYS)   □PAYROLL CONTINUATION   □LUMP-SUM PAYMENT
VACATION _____ NOTICE _____ SEVERANCE _____ OTHER _____ TOTAL _____

CLEARANCE	□BOOKS		BENEFIT CONVERSION
	□PERSONAL PHONE BILL	□EXIT INTERVIEW	INSURANCE: □LIFE □MEDICAL
□KEYS	□T & E EXPENSE STATEMENT	CLEARED BY _____	SPECIAL INSTRUCTIONS:
□DOCUMENTS	□I.D. CARD		
□EQUIPMENT	□CREDIT CARDS	□PAYROLL RELEASE _____	

PERSONAL DATA

EMPLOYEE'S HOME ADDRESS |_____| EEO CODE:_____

CITY/STATE/ZIP CODE |_____| EMPLOYEE CLASSIFICATION CODES:

HOME TELEPHONE NO. |___| |___ — ___| A. FULL-TIME EMPLOYEE

B. PART-TIME EMPLOYEE

EMERGENCY CONTACT INFORMATION

C. TEMPORARY EMPLOYEE

NAME (RELATIONSHIP) |_____|

D. PROBATIONARY EMPLOYEE

STREET ADDRESS (APT.) |_____|

E. PERMANENT EMPLOYEE

CITY/STATE/ZIP CODE |_____|

F. NON-EXEMPT EMPLOYEE

TELEPHONE NUMBER DURING WORKING HOURS |___|___ — ___| |_____| EXTENSION

G. EXEMPT EMPLOYEE

EMPLOYEE AUTHORIZATION ___William F. Jones___   ___11/30/88___
SIGNATURE   DATE

Figure 9.11H Personnel change notice authorization—leave of absence

PERSONNEL CHANGE NOTICE AUTHORIZATION   CONFIDENTIAL

EMPLOYEE NAME ___Jones, William F.___   SOCIAL SECURITY NO. 276-42-1087
LAST   FIRST   INITIAL

DATES: PREPARED ___12/1/88___   EFFECTIVE ___12/1/88___   CLASSIFICATION
CODES □A □B □C □D □E □F □G

TYPE OF CHANGE	PERSONNEL	LEAVE OF ABSENCE	TERMINATION	PERSONAL
EMPLOYMENT	□TRANSFER	□JURY DUTY	□RESIGNATION	□NAME CHANGE
□ADDITION	□PROMOTION	□MATERNITY	□RELEASE	□ADDRESS/TELE. CHANGE
□REPLACEMENT	□RECLASSIFICATION	□PERSONAL	□RETIREMENT	□NEW EMERGENCY CONTACT
☒REEMPLOYMENT	□SALARY	□SICKNESS-DISABILITY	□REDUCTION OF STAFF	□OTHER _____

FROM (PRESENT STATUS)				TO (NEW STATUS)			
GRADE	POS. CODE	POSITION TITLE		GRADE	POS. CODE	POSITION TITLE	
DEPT. CODE	DEPARTMENT		LOCATION	DEPT. CODE	DEPARTMENT		LOCATION

LAST INCREASE		ANNUAL SALARY RATE	EFFECTIVE DATE	PROPOSED INCREASE		ANNUAL SALARY RATE	EFFECTIVE DATE
$	% $		12/1/88	$	% $		
PERFORMANCE RATING			BUDGETED	PERFORMANCE RATING			BUDGETED
□A □B □C □D □E			□YES □NO	□A □B □C □D □E			□YES □NO

OTHER INFORMATION/CHANGES: OTHER INFORMATION CHANGES:

    Return from Personal LOA.

APPROVALS: APPROVALS:
Richard Von Meter DATE 12/1/88   _____ DATE ____
TS Thompson DATE 12/1/88   _____ DATE ____
W Stepha DATE 12/1/88   _____ DATE ____

EMPLOYMENT AGREEMENT:
THE UNDERSIGNED AGREES TO "AT WILL" EMPLOYMENT IN THE ABOVE INDICATED POSITION, AT SPECIFIED STARTING SALARY RATE, SUBJECT TO THE FOLLOWING AGREEMENTS OR COMMITMENTS, IF ANY:

    Revised Service Record Date of 2/18/87.

LEAVE OF ABSENCE	DATES		DURATION (WORKDAYS)	BENEFIT CONTINUATION?
	FIRST_____ LAST_____			□YES □NO

DETAILS:

TERMINATION	DATES		NOTICE (WORKDAYS)	CODE	REEMPLOYMENT ELIGIBILITY?
	LAST IN OFFICE _____	LAST ON PAYROLL _____			□YES □NO

DETAILS:

ALLOWANCE (WORKDAYS)   □PAYROLL CONTINUATION   □LUMP-SUM PAYMENT
VACATION ____ NOTICE ____ SEVERANCE ____ OTHER ____ TOTAL ____

CLEARANCE	□BOOKS		BENEFIT CONVERSION
	□PERSONAL PHONE BILL	□EXIT INTERVIEW	INSURANCE: □LIFE □MEDICAL
□KEYS	□T & E EXPENSE STATEMENT	CLEARED BY _____	SPECIAL INSTRUCTIONS:
□DOCUMENTS	□I.D. CARD		
□EQUIPMENT	□CREDIT CARDS	□PAYROLL RELEASE ____	

PERSONAL DATA   EEO CODE: _____

EMPLOYEE'S HOME ADDRESS   EMPLOYEE CLASSIFICATION CODES:

CITY/STATE/ZIP CODE   A. FULL-TIME EMPLOYEE

HOME TELEPHONE NO.   B. PART-TIME EMPLOYEE

EMERGENCY CONTACT INFORMATION   C. TEMPORARY EMPLOYEE

NAME (RELATIONSHIP)   D. PROBATIONARY EMPLOYEE

STREET ADDRESS (APT.)   E. PERMANENT EMPLOYEE

CITY/STATE/ZIP CODE   F. NON-EXEMPT EMPLOYEE

TELEPHONE NUMBER DURING WORKING HOURS   EXTENSION   G. EXEMPT EMPLOYEE

EMPLOYEE AUTHORIZATION _William F. Jones_   12/1/88
SIGNATURE   DATE

Figure 9.11I Personnel change notice authorization—return from leave of absence

430

PERSONNEL CHANGE NOTICE AUTHORIZATION   CONFIDENTIAL

EMPLOYEE NAME __Jones, William F.__   SOCIAL SECURITY NO. __276-42-1087__
LAST   FIRST   INITIAL

DATES: PREPARED __12/5/88__   EFFECTIVE __12/16/88__   CLASSIFICATION
CODES □A □B □C □D □E □F □G

TYPE OF CHANGE	PERSONNEL	LEAVE OF ABSENCE	TERMINATION	PERSONAL
EMPLOYMENT	□TRANSFER	□JURY DUTY	☒RESIGNATION	□NAME CHANGE
□ADDITION	□PROMOTION	□MATERNITY	□RELEASE	□ADDRESS/TELE. CHANGE
□REPLACEMENT	□RECLASSIFICATION	□PERSONAL	□RETIREMENT	□NEW EMERGENCY CONTACT
□REEMPLOYMENT	□SALARY	□SICKNESS-DISABILITY	□REDUCTION OF STAFF	□OTHER _____

FROM (PRESENT STATUS)			TO (NEW STATUS)		
GRADE	POS. CODE	POSITION TITLE	GRADE	POS. CODE	POSITION TITLE

DEPT. CODE	DEPARTMENT	LOCATION	DEPT. CODE	DEPARTMENT	LOCATION

LAST INCREASE	ANNUAL SALARY RATE	EFFECTIVE DATE	PROPOSED INCREASE	ANNUAL SALARY RATE	EFFECTIVE DATE
$ %	$		$ %	$	

PERFORMANCE RATING □A □B □C □D □E   BUDGETED □YES □NO   PERFORMANCE RATING □A □B □C □D □E   BUDGETED □YES □NO

OTHER INFORMATION/CHANGES: OTHER INFORMATION/CHANGES:

APPROVALS: APPROVALS:
_____ DATE _____   _Richard Von Meter_ DATE 12/5/88
_____ DATE _____   _J S Thompson_ DATE 12/5/88
_____ DATE _____   _W Sui_ DATE 12/6/88

EMPLOYMENT AGREEMENT:
THE UNDERSIGNED AGREES TO "AT WILL" EMPLOYMENT IN THE ABOVE INDICATED POSITION, AT SPECIFIED STARTING SALARY RATE, SUBJECT TO THE FOLLOWING AGREEMENTS OR COMMITMENTS, IF ANY:

LEAVE OF ABSENCE	DATES FIRST_____ LAST_____	DURATION (WORKDAYS)	BENEFIT CONTINUATION? □YES □NO
DETAILS:			

TERMINATION	DATES LAST IN OFFICE __12/16/88__ LAST ON PAYROLL __12/30/88__	NOTICE (WORKDAYS) 10	CODE 0	REEMPLOYMENT ELIGIBILITY? □YES ☒NO

DETAILS:
  Accepted position with XYZ Company as a Sr. General Accountant.

ALLOWANCE (WORKDAYS)
VACATION __10__ NOTICE __-__ SEVERANCE __-__ OTHER __-__ TOTAL __10__   ☒PAYROLL CONTINUATION   □LUMP-SUM PAYMENT

CLEARANCE	☒BOOKS		BENEFIT CONVERSION	
☒KEYS	☒PERSONAL PHONE BILL	☒EXIT INTERVIEW CLEARED BY	INSURANCE: □LIFE □MEDICAL	
☒DOCUMENTS	☒T & E EXPENSE STATEMENT		SPECIAL INSTRUCTIONS:	
☒EQUIPMENT	☒I.D. CARD ☒CREDIT CARDS	☒PAYROLL RELEASE	Not requested.	

PERSONAL DATA

EMPLOYEE'S HOME ADDRESS _____

CITY/STATE/ZIP CODE _____

HOME TELEPHONE NO. _____

EMERGENCY CONTACT INFORMATION

NAME (RELATIONSHIP) _____

STREET ADDRESS (APT.) _____

CITY/STATE/ZIP CODE _____

TELEPHONE NUMBER DURING WORKING HOURS _____ EXTENSION

EEO CODE: _____

EMPLOYEE CLASSIFICATION CODES:

A. FULL-TIME EMPLOYEE

B. PART-TIME EMPLOYEE

C. TEMPORARY EMPLOYEE

D. PROBATIONARY EMPLOYEE

E. PERMANENT EMPLOYEE

F. NON-EXEMPT EMPLOYEE

G. EXEMPT EMPLOYEE

EMPLOYEE AUTHORIZATION __William F Jones__   __12/16/88__
SIGNATURE   DATE

Figure 9.11J Personnel change notice authorization—termination (resignation)

CHAPTER 10

Relocation

A sample of an equitable and competitive employee relocation policy is presented in Section 10.1. This Employee Relocation Plan offers the guidelines needed for preparing or revising your company's program for providing financial assistance to transferred employees and new employees who must relocate. As new employee relocation entitlements are less than those offered to current employees, misunderstandings regarding applicable benefits should be avoided by having a separate New Employee Relocation Policy statement (see Chapter 4, Section 4.3).

Section 10.2 contains a sample of the Relocation Expense Report which is referred to in these policies. Through following the detailed instructions provided on its reverse side, the employee uses this form to account for all authorized relocation expenditures. A Relocation Questionnaire in Section 10.3, is designed to obtain the information needed for planning overall relocation assistance. Structured responses yield complete details of employee relocation plans, which serve as the basis for authorizing appropriate benefits.

Section 10.4, Relocation Service Summary, describes special services provided to transferred employees of companies that elect to contract with relocation management companies rather than self-administer home sale and home acquisition activities. Guaranteed home sale, home marketing, mortgage placement, and home-finding assistance are explained.

Next, a What Are Your Housing Requirements? questionnaire is shown in Section 10.5. Designed to systematically assist the transferred employee in identifying specific requirements, the completed form offers the information needed to communicate needs effectively to real estate or rental agents. Section 10.6, How to Finance Your Home?, is a self-help device for use by relocated homeowners who intend to purchase a home in the new area. It provides basic descriptions of numerous mortgage financing alternatives in the interest of promoting employee understanding of innovative approaches. Similarly, in Section 10.7, a self-help Mortgage Application Checklist offers additional employee assistance. It prepares the employee to provide the varied types of financial information and documentation needed for completing a mortgage application. Samples of Mortgage Application Forms are shown in Section 10.8. Included are representative types of forms used in obtaining verification of employee assets, liabilities, credit payment history, and employment status. Section 10.9 contains Home Purchase Closing Cost Guidelines for use in providing guidance to employees regarding allowable expenses, and in subsequently reviewing and approving employee home acquisition cost reimbursement claims.

In the interest of promoting well planned and properly implemented relocations, an employee checklist entitled, Preparing for a Successful Move is offered in Section 10.10. Helpful employee guidance for arranging and accomplishing trouble-free household goods moves is incorporated in How to Select and Contract with Your Moving Company in Section 10.11, and How to Make Your Move in Section 10.12. A sample Household Goods Shipment Services Report, shown in Section 10.13, is structured for use by the HRM organization in obtaining employee feedback on the quality of moving company (carrier) performance. In addition to using this information to avoid contracting with problem carriers in the future, it also serves as the basis for providing assistance to employees in resolving specific carrier performance problems. Representative actions include resolving paperwork deficiencies or discrepancies, disputed claims, or employee inconvenience compensation issues. Employee information on What Are My Income Tax Liabilities? in Section 10.14, explains the tax consequences of an employee relocation.

10.1 SAMPLE COMPANY RELOCATION POLICY

Employee Relocation Plan

I. Objectives

This policy provides a uniformly equitable basis for providing financial assistance to employees who relocate their principal residence as a result of being transferred to another company work location. The distance between an employee's old principal residence and the new work location, as compared with the distance between the old principal residence and the old work location, must be at least thirty-five (35) miles more to qualify for relocation assistance.

II. Moving Expenses

A. The company will assume the reasonable costs of moving an employee's household goods and personal effects.

B. The company will arrange and directly pay packing and crating, in-transit storage, and insurance costs for authorized household goods and personal effects.

C. The company will not assume the costs of moving pets, pianos, hobby equipment of unusual weight or size, boats, valuable jewelry, furs, antiques, firearms, and other such items.

D. Under unusual circumstances not under the employee's control, such as when a shipment is delayed or housing is not yet ready at the new work location, the director of human resources may authorize company-paid short-term storage for a period not to exceed 90 days.

III. Home Sale

A. At the request of an employee who has been scheduled for relocation, the company shall obtain a minimum of two real estate appraisals and calculate the fair market value of the employee's owned residence. This calculation is based on an average of two appraisals with less than 10 percent variation. The company guarantees that the employee will realize the "fair market value" that results from this calculation, but the employee is encouraged to find a buyer at a higher price. To qualify for this guarantee, the property must be multiple-listed for sale at a mutually agreed upon "selling price" for a period of at least thirty (30) days. A selling price at or below the fair market value then may be authorized by the company to expedite the sale of the property.

B. The company will reimburse an employee for a competitive real estate broker commission incurred in selling the property.

C. The company will reimburse an employee for reasonable mortgage pre-payment penalties and normal and customary selling costs.

D. The costs to be reimbursed by the company will be limited to those incurred in the sale of a principal residence. To qualify for these reimbursements, the employee must apply for home sale assistance within three (3) months of accepting a transfer to a new work location.

IV. Lease Cancellation

A. The company will reimburse an employee who is leasing a principal residence for the reasonable costs of cancelling the lease. Such assistance to a relocated employee includes deposit forfeiture, additional rental payments needed to effect cancellation, and any required legal fees.

B. If an employee elects to sub-lease, providing such action is permitted by the terms of the lease, the company will reimburse costs incurred for a reasonable rental agent fee or advertising costs, and any necessary legal fees.

V. Exploratory Trip

An employee and spouse may be authorized a seven (7) day exploratory trip to secure permanent housing in the vicinity of the new work location. Reimbursable expenses are limited to round trip transportation (economy air fares), local transportation, lodging, and meals.

VI. Transportation of Employee and Family

A. The company will provide direct route, economy air transportation for the employee and members of the employee's immediate family to the area of the new work location.

B. The employee will have the option of using a personal automobile for transportation to the area of the new work location. It is expected that such travel will be by the most direct route with average daily progress of at least three hundred (300) miles per day. The current company travel policy mileage rate will apply to these reimbursements. Tolls also will be reimbursed.

C. Reimbursable transportation costs also will include in-transit meals and lodging costs if travel is by personal automobile, or baggage handling fees, gratuities, and local ground transportation at departure and terminal points if traveling by air.

VII. Temporary Living Expenses

A. If an employee precedes his or her family to a new work location to begin work and obtain suitable permanent housing, the company will reimburse reasonable living expenses for a period not to exceed ninety (90) days.

B. The company will reimburse reasonable living expenses for a period not to exceed thirty (30) days if the employee and family relocate to the new area prior to the availability of permanent housing.

C. The company may, depending on the circumstances, elect to continue the reimbursement of temporary living expenses beyond the initial thirty (30) day period in cases such as those involving the delay of household goods, delay in closing on a new home, and so on. Any such authorization by the director of human resources will be subject to reimbursement of temporary living expenses less a "differential" for estimated normal living costs.

D. An employee who occupies temporary living quarters while awaiting the relocation of his or her immediate family may be authorized a reasonable number of trips home at company expense. The number of such trips will be determined by assessing the duration of absence, the distance to home, and compelling personal factors.

VIII. New Accommodations

    A.   An employee who sells a principal residence in accordance with the provisions of Section III will be reimbursed for reasonable and customary closing costs incurred in purchasing a new principal residence.

    B.   An employee who leased a principal residence previously will be reimbursed by the company for the customary rental agent fee and reasonable legal fees incurred for leasing a principal residence in the new area.

IX. Relocation Allowance

The company will pay a relocation allowance in the amount of one-half of a month's pay for single employees, and one month's pay for married employees. This allowance is paid in lump sum at the time when an employee relocates his or her principal residence to the area of a new work location. It is intended to assist the employee in meeting the cost of necessary alterations for refitting rugs and draperies, appliance disconnection and reconnection, the costs of moving items excluded in Section II C, and other incidental expenses.

X. Home Acquisition Loan

The company will provide an interest-free equity loan to an employee who participates in the "home sale" provisions of this plan. The loan, as required for the purchase of a home in the area of the new work location, is to be repaid when the employee transfers title on the former residence.

XI. New Employees

New employees may be granted authorization for participation in the following provisions of this plan: Sections II, VI, VII (A, B, and C), IX, and XII.

XII. Treatment of Taxable Relocation Expenses

Since some of the relocation expenses that are reimbursed by the company are considered to be wages for income tax purposes, such payments are subject to withholding taxes. Accordingly, the company will "gross up" the employee's base earnings to offset this tax liability during the year that it is incurred.

XIII. Administration

These policies and procedures will be administered by the director of human resources. Employees will be required to prepare Relocation Expense Report forms (see Figure 10.2) for all reimbursable expenses, and to submit them to their management for review and approval. Final review and approval will be by the director of human resources.

10.2 RELOCATION EXPENSE REPORT

As stipulated in the Employee Relocation Plan, Section 10.1, the Relocation Expense Report form is used by employees for vouchering authorized costs. This form includes sections designed to meet the specific requirements of each type of relocation expense, from top to bottom, as follows:

- Home/Lease Disposal Expenses
- Home/Lease Acquisition Expenses
- Exploratory Trip Expense
- Transportation of Employee and Family
- Temporary Living Expense
- Relocation Allowance
- Pre-Departure Living Expenses
- Other Relocation Expenses

An "instructions" section contains the detailed guidance needed for completing each section of the form. Conveniently located on the reverse side of the form, where it always is available for user reference, this information is presented in the same sequence that associated sections appear on the form.

Relocation Expense Report

Name	Old Loc.	New Loc.	Date

☐ Domestic	☐ International Indefinite	☐ International Temporary	Effective Date of Change _____

Company	Position	Department

Home/Lease Disposal Expenses	Amount	Home/Lease Acquisition Expenses	Amount	Totals

Exploratory Trip Expense

		Dates	Location	Mileage	Tolls	Cash Fares	Meals	Lodging
Exploratory Trip Expense	Going to							
	At							
	Return to							
	Totals							

		Dates	Location	Mileage	Tolls	Cash Fares	Meals	Lodging
Trans-portation of Employee and Family	Employee							
	Family							
	Totals							

	Dates From	To	Location	Lodging	Utilities	Laundry-Valet	Meals
Temporary Living Expense							
			Differential	( )	( )	( )	( )
	Totals						

Relocation Allowance	☐ Single	☐ Married

	Dates From	To	Location	Lodging	Telephone	Laundry-Valet	Meals	Travel	Misc.
Pre-depart. Living Exp.									

	Description	Amount
Other Relocation Expenses		

		Grand Total	

Signed _____ Employee _____ Date

Approvals: _____ Date
_____ Date
_____ Date

Date	Advanced by	Amount
Balance Due Company/Employee		

Figure 10.2 Relocation expense report

continued

General

1. <u>Use This Report</u> to account for <u>all</u> expenditures incurred in relocating your principal residence in accordance with the Employee Relocation Plan.
2. <u>Keep A Written Record</u> of your expenditures. Use this form to claim expenses for "Exploratory Trip," "Transportation," "Temporary Living Expense," and "Pre-Departure Living Expense."
3. <u>Report Only Those Expenses</u> which have been authorized.
4. <u>Attach Receipt of Other Documentation</u> of your expenses. The documentation required in the case of home disposal expenses, home acquisition costs, loan interest, etc., shall be as prescribed by the Director of Human Resources.
5. <u>If You Receive An Expense Money Advance</u> to defray relocation expenses, you should report your expenses promptly upon completion of an exploratory trip, or monthly in the case of temporary living expenditures.
6. <u>Be Sure That The Proper Section</u> of this report is used for the type of expenses you are recording.

Home/Lease Disposal Expenses

7. Enter expenses incurred in disposing of your principal residence at your former location. Show the type of expenses incurred (i.e., real estate broker's commission, legal fees, etc.) and the amount for each item. Show the total in the right-hand column. Attach a copy of the closing statement for the sale of your home to substantiate these expenses.

Home/Lease Acquisition Expenses

8. Enter costs incurred in taking title to a principal residence at your new base location. Enter the item and amount for expenses incurred. Show the total in the right-hand column. Attach a copy of the closing statement on your new home to substantiate the expenses shown.

Exploratory Trip Expenses

9. Enter all expenses incurred on exploratory trips as authorized by the Director of Human Resources. Show separately the expenses incurred in going to the new area, while at the new area, and in returning home. Use the "Cash Fares" column to enter the cost of renting an automobile <u>for cash</u> while seeking housing in the vicinity of the new location.

Total each column of exploratory trip expenses on the "Totals" line, add the totals to the right, and enter their sum in the right-hand column in the box.

Transportation of Employee and Family Expense

10. Reimbursable transportation costs shall include direct route economy class air transportation to new work location and other miscellaneous expenses as prescribed in the Employee Relocation Plan.

Temporary Living Expense

11. Enter living expenses incurred during an interim expense period authorized by the Director of Human Resources. Show the period covered and indicate the location (city, town) in which the expenses were incurred. If an additional period is authorized, enter dates on the "Differential" line and show any amount by which normal lodging, meal, and laundry expenses have been increased because you are occupying temporary quarters. Deduct amounts shown on the "Differential" line, if any, from amounts shown for lodging, utilities, laundry/valet, and meals, and enter the results on the "Totals" line.

   Add the amounts shown on the "Totals" line to the right and enter the sum in the right-hand column in the box.

Relocation Allowance

12. Enter allowances as stated in the Employee Relocation Plan.

Pre-Departure Living Expenses

13. If an employee must vacate regular housing prior to overseas departure, the company will reimburse reasonable living expenses for a period not exceeding seven (7) days.

Other Relocation Expenses

14. Enter other expenses incurred in connection with your relocation which are prescribed in the Employee Relocation Plan and authorized in advance by the Director of Human Resources for which no headings are provided in other sections of the Relocation Expense Report.

For Payroll Accounting Use:

1. Amount reported on reverse side which is subject to withholding tax $ _____
2. Estimated Tax   _____
3. Tax Equalization Adjustment   _____
4. Payment to employee (2 + 3)   _____

Figure 10.2 *(cont.)*

10.3 RELOCATION PLANNING QUESTIONNAIRE

The Relocation Planning Questionnaire provides a uniform structure for obtaining the information needed for planning relocation assistance. An employee completes its six sections to designate requirements for the following types of relocation benefits:

1. Family Data—transportation of family and temporary living expenses (see items 4B and 5B below).
2. Exploratory Trip
   A. Employee expenses
   B. Spouse expenses
3. Residential Change
   A. Home disposal expenses
   B. Home acquisition expenses
   C. Lease disposal expenses
4. Reporting for Work Travel
   A. Employee transportation expenses
   B. Family transportation expenses
5. Temporary Living Expenses
   A. Employee expenses
   B. Family expenses
6. Transportation of Household Goods—estimate cost of household move based on weight of shipment and storage requirements.

Relocation Planning Questionnaire

This questionnaire has been prepared to assist you in providing information needed by the HRM division for expediting your relocation.

Employee Name _____ Social Security No. _____

Present Work Location _____

New Work Location _____

Effective Date of Transfer _____

Address of Present Residence _____

_____

1. Family Data

List the members of your immediate family who will be relocating to the area of your new work location.

Names	Relationship
_____	_____
_____	_____
_____	_____
_____	_____
_____	_____

2. Exploratory Trip to Obtain Housing

   A. Will you be taking an exploratory trip?

      ☐ Yes   ☐ No

   B. Will your spouse join you for this trip?

      ☐ Yes   ☐ No

   C. Dates planned for trip:

      From _____   To _____

   D. Mode of Travel:

      ☐ Air & Rented Auto   ☐ Personal Auto

      ☐ Other (Specify) _____

3. Residential Change

   A. Will you sell your present home?

      ☐ No   ☐ Yes   Estimated Sale Price $ _____

   B. Will you purchase a house at the new work location?

      ☐ No   ☐ Yes   Estimated Price $ _____

   C. Do you have an unexpired lease which will require settlement?

      ☐ No   ☐ Yes   Estimated Cost $ _____

Figure 10.3 Relocation planning questionnaire

continued

4. Reporting for Work Travel

    A. What mode of transportation will you use in reporting for work?

        ☐ Air ☐ Personal Auto ☐ Other (Specify) _____

    B. What mode of transportation will your family use in relocating to the new area?

        ☐ Air ☐ Personal Auto ☐ Other (Specify) _____

5. Temporary Living Expenses

    A. Will you incur temporary living expenses at the new location?

        ☐ No ☐ Yes, for this period: From _____ To _____

    B. Will your family incur temporary living expenses at the new location?

        ☐ No ☐ Yes, for this period: From _____ To _____

6. Transportation of Household Goods and Personal Effects

    A. Estimated weight of materials to be shipped: _____ pounds. (Use estimate of 1,000 pounds per room.)

    B. Proposed Shipping Schedule:

    Mover Assessment Date _____ Packing Date(s) _____

    Loading Date _____ Unloading Date _____

    In-Transit Date(s) From _____ To _____

    Storage Date(s) From _____ To _____

Employee Signature _____ Date _____

Figure 10.3 *(cont.)*

10.4 RELOCATION SERVICE SUMMARY

Although companies, such as the one whose Employee Relocation Plan was described in Section 10.1, self-administer all phases of employee relocations, others choose to contract with employee relocation service companies for this purpose. The following descriptions of typical relocation management company services is provided for your guidance.

I. Guaranteed Homesale

An offer to purchase the employee's home is made based on the average of two independent market value appraisals. The employee receives 100 percent of equity upon acceptance of this offer. The relocation management firm is responsible for selling the home, and for paying all carrying costs after the employee vacates the home. The company pays a flat rate fee for this purpose; employees are not required to submit vouchers for the reimbursement of associated costs.

A. The Home Sale Process. The employee is required to choose three appraisers from a listing of qualified appraisers provided by the relocation management company. Two of these appraisers, based on the employee's preferences, will immediately appraise the home. If their appraised valuations are not within 10 percent of each other, a third appraisal will be required.

During the time required to obtain appraisals, the relocation management company arranges a title search, necessary inspections (termites, well, septic, and so on), and a local real estate broker's market evaluation of the marketability of the property.

The employee is encouraged to market the home during this period by listing it with a qualified multiple listing broker. The listing agreement must include an exclusion clause that protects the right of the employee to sell the home to the relocation company without payment of a commission or other fee to the broker.

B. Purchase Offer. The relocation management company extends an offer to the employee as soon as valid appraisals are obtained and inspections are completed. The offer is made by telephone and confirmed in writing. It is valid for a 60-day period, and may be accepted by signing and returning a notarized contract of sale and other required documents to the relocation management firm. The employee receives 100 percent of equity within five (5) days of the receipt of the signed documents.

If the employee feels that the offer does not adequately reflect the market value of the property, an appeal may be filed with the relocation management firm.

C. Assignment of Sale. Should the employee receive an offer to purchase from another buyer, which would net more than the relocation management firm's offer, the employee assigns the contract to the relocation management firm. The employee receives 100 percent of equity based on the relocation company's offer, and additional equity after the settlement of this "assigned sale." In reviewing an assigned sale, the relocation company deducts expenses such as discount points, repairs, and so on that are not reimbursable in accordance with company policy. Contracts that are contingent upon the buyer's sale of a present home are not acceptable for an "assigned sale."

D. Vacating the Home. When the employee accepts the relocation management firm's offer or receives approval for an assigned sale, a period of up to 45 days is given to vacate the property. The employee is responsible for the maintenance and carrying costs of the home until the day it is vacated.

II. Home Marketing Assistance

The relocation management company also is prepared to offer assistance for selling the former home. Such assistance involves providing an employee with real estate broker advice concerning the preparation of the home for sale, recommended listing and probable selling prices, information on real estate market conditions which could affect the sale, and effective working relationship techniques for achieving a sale.

III. Home-finding Assistance

The relocation management company also can refer an employee to a real estate broker in the new area for home-finding assistance. By thoroughly defining employee housing needs, the broker prepares an effective agenda which maximizes the individual's prospects for quickly locating suitable housing.

IV. Mortgage Placement Assistance

The relocation management company also is able to provide mortgage counseling assistance through referring the employee to reliable and competitive home financing firms. The employee is encouraged to obtain full information regarding mortgage rates and requirements, and to determine his or her ability to qualify for a mortgage before taking a househunting trip. This information provides the basis for more effective home search activities that focus on properties within the employee's price range.

V. Rental Property Management

The relocation management firm is prepared to offer professional assistance for the leasing and rental of the employee's former home. This assistance is accomplished for a management fee which is paid by the company for up to a 3-year period. The employee is responsible for costs associated with maintenance of the property and any costs that exceed the rental income. This type of option, in lieu of home sale assistance, is used by employees who will return to their former work location.

VI. Spouse Employment Counseling Assistance

The relocation management company has contacts with employment counselors, who are able to provide employee-paid counseling assistance to a spouse for the purpose of obtaining employment in the new area.

Notes

All relocation management company services for an employee must be completed within 3 years of that individual's transfer date.

Home sale assistance also applies to an owned condominium or cooperative.

To qualify for home sale assistance, the title of the property must be in the name of the employee and/or spouse as of the date of the employee's transfer.

10.5 HOUSING REQUIREMENTS QUESTIONNAIRE

What Are Your Housing Requirements?

This questionnaire has been designed to help you define your housing requirements so that you can communicate your needs to real estate agents more effectively.

Name _____

Present address _____
_____

Home telephone number ( ) _____

Office telephone number (current location) ( ) _____

Office telephone number (new location) ( ) _____

Temporary Quarters Needed?

☐ Yes ☐ No

Type (Specify): _____

I will occupy temporary quarters as of this date _____

I am planning to ☐ Buy ☐ Rent

I am able to make monthly payments of $_____

Type of House/Condo/Apartment Desired:

☐ Split Level ☐ Rambler (Ranch) ☐ Contemporary

☐ Colonial ☐ Townhouse ☐ Duplex

☐ Low-Rise Condo/Apartment ☐ High-Rise Condo/Apartment

☐ Garden Apartment ☐ Other (Specify) _____

Age of House Preferred:

☐ New ☐ Resale (Approximate Age _____)

Type of Heating Preferred:

☐ Gas ☐ Electric ☐ Oil

Is Air Conditioning Required?

☐ Yes ☐ No

Is a Garage Needed?

☐ Yes ☐ No

How many bedrooms are required? _____

How many bathrooms? _____

Specify other required features (fireplace, recreation room, basement, etc.):
_____

What type of an area is preferred?

☐ Rural ☐ Semi-Rural ☐ Suburban ☐ Urban

How will you commute to work?

☐ Car ☐ Public Transportation

☐ Maximum Commuting Time = _____ Minutes

What types of schools will your children attend?

☐ Public ☐ Private ☐ Church-Affiliated

☐ Elementary ☐ Intermediate ☐ High

(Church School Denomination = _____)

Particular areas and neighborhoods of interest:
_____
_____
_____

10.6 HOME MORTGAGE OPTIONS AND FINANCING ALTERNATIVES

The following information is used by transferred employees for considering the variety of mortgages and financing alternatives that may be applied in purchasing a home.

How to Finance Your Home?

Conventional Mortgages. This traditional financing arrangement involves an interest rate that remains the same throughout the life of the loan, which can be 15, 25, or 30 years. This arrangement permits monthly payments that do not change. Normal down payment requirements are 20 to 25 percent. If the buyer purchases private mortgage insurance, which covers the top 20 to 25 percent of the loan against default, down payment requirements may be reduced to 5, 10, or 15 percent.

Adjustable Mortgage Loans (AMLs). Federally chartered savings and loan associations offer mortgages where the interest rate moves up or down depending on market conditions. Interest rate changes typically are made at the lender's discretion in 6 month-to-a-year intervals based on independent rate indexes such as treasury bills. Interest rate decreases are mandatory when the interest rate changes. Since interest rate increases typically result in an increase of the monthly payment amount, a home buyer can end up with a payment that he or she cannot afford. If such increases are applied against the loan balance, the buyer runs the risk of having an unpaid balance which exceeds the amount owed when the mortgage began. The primary advantage of this type of loan is that the loans typically start at 1 to $1\frac{1}{2}$ percentage points below the rate for a fixed rate mortgage.

Adjustable Rate Mortgages (ARMs). National banks are authorized to offer this type of loan, which is very similar to an AML loan. Many ARMs set an annual maximum adjustment for interest rate changes, and an overall maximum and minimum interest rate for the life of the loan.

Balloon and Rollover Mortgages. The interest rate remains fixed and monthly payments are made as if the loan was granted for 25 or 30 years, but at the end of a specified period the mortgage matures and the unpaid balance is due. This final payment, which could become due as early as 5 years after the mortgage is granted, requires the buyer to refinance the loan and pay loan origination and other fees. Furthermore, the lender may not be committed to refinancing the loan. This large, one-time payment requirement is referred to as a "balloon." If the lending institution is committed to renewing the loan, then it is referred to as a "rollover" mortgage.

FHA-Insured Loans. The Federal Housing Administration (FHA) insures mortgage loans so that down payments may be as low as 3 percent of the first $25,000 of the appraised home value and 5 percent of the value over $25,000. The FHA also charges an advanced Mortgage Insurance Premium (MIP) fee, which may be either financed with the loan or paid in cash at the settlement. The fee is 3.8 percent of the loan amount. The lender may charge prepaid interest, referred to as "points," but the borrower is free to negotiate points and the loan interest rate. The FHA appraises a home to determine its fair market value and inspects it to make sure that it meets structural standards. Subject to meeting these requirements, the FHA will insure a home mortgage loan for up to $90,000 throughout either a 15- or 30-year term.

Veterans Administration (VA) Guaranteed Loans.   Certain veterans and active duty military personnel may qualify for a VA home loan guarantee as follows:

> At least 90 days of active duty from September 16, 1940 to July 25, 1947, or from June 27, 1950 to January 31, 1955.
> At least 180 days of active duty since January 1, 1955.
> At least 90 days of active duty between August 5, 1964 and May 7, 1975.
> At least 24 months of active duty since September 7, 1980.
> Current service personnel who have served at least 180 days on active duty.

The current VA benefit allows a total entitlement of $27,500, which means that qualified veterans may obtain a home loan of $110,000 or less with no down payment. The usual term is 30 years, but 15-year VA loans also may be obtained. Should the veteran wish to purchase a home involving a loan that exceeds $110,000, a down payment will be required. The veteran is required to pay the lending institution 1 point plus a 1 percent funding fee; the seller pays all other points.

Interest rates for VA loans generally are lower than the market rate. VA loans are fully assumable. The VA, as is the case with FHA loans, also has the home appraised and inspected.

Graduated Payment Mortgages.   This type of mortgage starts with low monthly payments that gradually increase up to a fixed level after 5 or 10 years. For example, under a 5-year schedule the annual mortgage payment increase would be 7.5 percent. This type of plan is attractive to younger homeowners who anticipate income increases.

Graduated Payment Adjustable Mortgages.   This type of mortgage combines the features of a Graduated Payment Mortgage with those of an Adjustable Rate Mortgage. In addition to graduated payment schedule increases, the buyer also is subject to adjustments based on interest rate increases.

"Buy-Down" Mortgage Plans.   A builder agrees to pay the lender an amount needed to cover the differential between the normal interest rate and a much lower rate for the first to fifth years of the mortgage. This agreement provides some temporary relief until the interest rate and the monthly payment amount return to the mortgage-specified amounts at the end of the "buy-down" period.

Developer Financing.   Some developers provide attractive financing rates to encourage home buyers. Some developers have negotiated lower rates with lending institutions; others have their own sources of funds they use to offer special terms.

Government Subsidized Mortgages.   Many cities and states subsidize mortgages by offering lower-than-market rates to residents with specified qualifications. For example, these special-rate loans through savings institutions may be restricted to first-time buyers whose income does not exceed a designated limit.

Wraparound Mortgages. This type of mortgage takes an existing mortgage, which is not sufficient to meet loan requirements, and "wraps" additional financing around it to meet needs. One, all-inclusive monthly mortgage payment is the result.

Second Mortgages. In assuming a mortgage (to take advantage of a low interest rate) without sufficient cash to purchase the seller's equity, the seller might be willing to personally offer a second mortgage. If not, the buyer arranges to obtain a second mortgage from an outside lender and uses these funds to pay money due the seller. While second mortgage rates are higher than normal mortgage rates, their combination with a low rate on an existing mortgage should place the overall rate below the market rate to make this approach economically sound.

Seller Financing. Depending on how an existing mortgage interest rate compares with rates yielded by investing money elsewhere, the seller might be willing to hold on to the mortgage and have the buyer make payments to him or her. This is an excellent alternative for a buyer if a better-than-market interest rate is yielded in the process. Should interest rates fall to a lower level, the buyer can finance the home and pay off the seller.

Shared Appreciation Mortgages. In exchange for a share of the profits when a home is sold, or a share of equity participation after a specified period of years, the lender provides the buyer with a significantly lower mortgage interest rate.

Lease-Purchase Agreements. Rather than purchasing a home at a time when mortgage interest rates are temporarily high, a lease–purchase agreement may be used to defer the sale until a more favorable time. A formal agreement is made in which the buyer leases the home with an option to purchase it for a specified price by a designated date, which usually is within 12–18 months. A deposit is placed with the seller; the amount is used as a down payment in the event of a purchase. A portion of monthly lease payments may be applied toward the established purchase price.

10.7 MORTGAGE APPLICATION CHECKLIST

This checklist is provided to transferred employees who are purchasing a residence in the area of their new work location. It offers helpful reminders concerning the information needed by a mortgage company representative in preparing the employee's mortgage application.

Mortgage Application Checklist

This checklist offers you reminders concerning the information you will need to complete a mortgage application. If you are married, you also must have this information for your spouse. The mortgage company wants full details of your personal finances to assess your ability to finance and carry the proposed loan.

Assets

_____ Name, address, account number, and current balance for each financial institution where you have a checking or savings account.

_____ Name, address, and account number for the company that holds the mortgage on your currently owned residence. Data on the current balance of the mortgage and the Fair Market Value of the property as evidenced by recent tax assessment appraisals or other appraisals are needed to assess your equity.

_____ Listing of bonds, stocks, and other investments with company names, number of shares, and recent valuations.

_____ If a life insurance loan will be used to make a down payment, have details regarding the company name and address, the policy number, the face value of the policy, and the cash value.

_____ An estimate of the value of furniture and personal effects. Include jewelry, coin collections, art and antiques, and so on.

_____ W-2 forms for the past 3 years plus a current pay stub to show earnings history required to meet the potential mortgage commitment. If self-employed, either Federal Income Tax returns or profit and loss statements certified by a public accountant are needed; 3 years of recent information must be provided.

_____ Documentation regarding other income such as an annuity, inheritance, disability payment from the Veterans Administration, and so on.

Liabilities

_____ Financial institution name and address, and the account number, outstanding balance, and monthly payment for personal loan(s).

_____ Information concerning any liens against your currently owned property, for example, details of a second mortgage (name and address of mortgage company, account number, current balance due, and monthly payment amount).

_____ Details of automobile loan(s); name and address of financial institution, current value of automobile and balance of account, and the monthly payment amount.

_____ Names, addresses, current balance, and monthly payment for each charge account and bank card (department stores, VISA, MASTER CARD, and so on).

_____ Estimated annual amounts to be paid for Federal Income Tax, state and local income/property taxes, Social Security, and child care fees.

_____ Bring a copy of your separation or divorce decree if your financial obligations include the payment of child support or alimony. These documents are needed to verify your specific payment requirements.

10.8 MORTGAGE APPLICATION FORMS

After an employee provides a mortgage company representative with detailed credit information as needed to process and approve a mortgage application, a variety of reference-checking forms must be signed to obtain detailed credit information. Representative samples include:

Rating Request (Figure 10.8A)

This form is used to obtain information from the employee's present mortgage company and other lending institutions to verify the extent of the individual's obligations, monthly payments, and past performance in making timely payments.

Request for Verification of Deposit (Figure 10.8B)

This form is used for loans involving federal mortgage insurance programs (principally VA and FHA mortgages). It provides the basis for verifying information provided by the employee concerning deposits and loans. Resultant information from financial institutions concerning assets and "credit worthiness," as assessed by a record of timely loan payments and paid-in-full loans, plays a major role in determining whether the mortgage loan should be approved.

Request for Verification of Employment (Figure 10.8C)

In addition to forwarding Request for Verification of Deposit forms to financial institutions for assessing the employee's assets, liabilities, and payment record, the mortgage company representative will forward a Request for Verification of Employment form to your company to verify the employee's employment status.

This form, which is required for federally insured mortgages, requests full details of the individual's compensation, a statement regarding the probability of continued employment, and verification of data provided concerning previous employment.

As the director of human resources, you will want to encourage your personnel to be thoroughly familiar with this form, its purpose, and its completion requirements. Your procedures should consider the potential liability involved in providing negative information concerning the "probability of continued employment" which leads to an employee being refused a mortgage loan. For example, although providing this information is not problematic for an outstanding employee whom the company is transferring, it would be problematic for a marginal performer who decides to purchase a home at a time when the company is seriously considering termination of employment action.

Another example of the many forms that must be completed in the mortgage application process is shown in Figure 10.8D, an Earnest Money Deposit Certification. This certificate is required from the employee, as purchaser, and contains the amount of the deposit placed on the home being purchased, to whom the payment was made, and identification of the exact source of these funds. The employee also certifies that no indebtedness other than that stipulated in the mortgage application exists or is intended to be incurred. The co-purchaser spouse of an employee also is required to sign this certification.

Rating Request

Name:

Address:

Account No.:

Mortgage Loan Address:

To Whom It May Concern:

We are processing a mortgage loan application for the referenced individual who has given us authorization to secure a loan rating from your institution.

We would appreciate your forwarding, for our confidential use, a verification of the applicant's credit as authorized by the applicant, below.

Please return this completed form in the self-addressed envelope enclosed for your convenience. Thank you for your assistance.

Cordially,

Residential Mortgage Origination Department

_____
(Applicant's signature authorizing disclosure of information)

Telephone No. _____

For assistance in completing form, see reverse side   Date _____

Origination Date	Type of Loan (if mortgage: Please indicate if Conv., FHA, FHA 221-D2, VA)		
Original Amount	Present Balance	Term	Monthly Payment

Is Escrow Maintained (for Mortgage loan only). Please answer Yes or No — for taxes _____ for insurance _____
Has this loan been sold to FHLMC _____ Yes _____ No   FNMA _____ Yes _____ No

Payment History/Remarks (Please indicate number of times late per category)

_____ 30 days _____ 60 days _____ 90 days   Next payment due date _____

Authorized Signature and Title	Date

Figure 10.8A Rating request

HUD COMMUNITY PLANNING AND DEVELOPMENT
HUD HOUSING - FEDERAL HOUSING COMMISSIONER

REQUEST FOR VERIFICATION OF DEPOSIT

PRIVACY ACT NOTICE STATEMENT - This information is to be used by the agency collecting it in determining whether you qualify as a prospective mortgagor for mortgage insurance or guaranty or as a borrower for a rehabilitation loan under the agency's program. It will not be disclosed outside the agency without your consent except to financial institutions for verification of your deposits and as required and permitted by law. You do not have to give us this information, but, if you do not, your application for approval as a prospective mortgagor for mortgage insurance or guaranty or as a borrower for a rehabilitation loan may be delayed or rejected. This information request is authorized by Title 38, U.S.C., Chapter 37 *(if VA)*; by 12 U.S.C., Section 1701 et seq., *(if HUD/FHA)*; and by 42 U.S.C., Section 1452b *(if Hud/CPD)*.

INSTRUCTIONS

LENDER OR LOCAL PROCESSING AGENCY: Complete Items 1 through 8. Have applicant(s) complete Item 9. Forward directly to the Depository named in Item 1. DEPOSITORY: Please complete Items 10 through 15 and return DIRECTLY to Lender or Local Processing Agency named in Item 2.

PART I - REQUEST

1. TO *(Name and Address of Depository)*	2. FROM *(Name and Address of Lender or Local Processing Agency)*

I certify that this verification has been sent directly to the bank or depository and has not passed through the hands of the applicant or any other party.

3. Signature of Lender or Official of Local Processing Agency	4. Title	5. Date	6. Lender's Number *(Optional)*

7. INFORMATION TO BE VERIFIED:

Type of Account and/or Loan	Account/Loan in Name of	Account/Loan Number	Balance
			$
			$
			$
			$

TO DEPOSITORY: I have applied for mortgage insurance or guaranty or for a rehabilitation loan and stated that the balance on deposit and/or outstanding loans with you are as shown above. You are authorized to verify this information and to supply the lender or the local processing agency identified above with the information requested in Items 10 through 12. Your response is solely a matter of courtesy for which no responsibility is attached to your institution or any of your officers.

8. NAME AND ADDRESS OF APPLICANT(S)	9. SIGNATURE OF APPLICANT(S)

TO BE COMPLETED BY DEPOSITORY

PART II - VERIFICATION OF DEPOSITORY

10. DEPOSIT ACCOUNTS OF APPLICANT(S)

Type of Account	Account Number	Current Balance	Average Balance for Previous Two Months	Date Opened
		$	$	
		$	$	
		$	$	
		$	$	

11. LOANS OUTSTANDING TO APPLICANT(S)

Loan Number	Date of Loan	Original Amount	Current Balance	Installments *(Monthly/Quarterly)*	Secured by	Number of Late Payments within Last 12 Months
		$	$	$ per		
		$	$	$ per		
		$	$	$ per		

12. ADDITIONAL INFORMATION WHICH MAY BE OF ASSISTANCE IN DETERMINATION OF CREDIT WORTHINESS: *Please include information on loans paid-in-full as in Item 11 above)*

13. Signature of Depository Official	14. Title	15. Date

The confidentiality of the information you have furnished will be preserved except where disclosure of this information is required by applicable law. The completed form is to be transmitted directly to the lender or local processing agency and is not to be transmitted through the applicant or any other party.

Figure 10.8B Request for verification of deposit

VETERANS ADMINISTRATION,
U.S.D.A., FARMERS HOME ADMINISTRATION, AND
U.S. DEPARTMENT OF HOUSING AND URBAN DEVELOPMENT.
(Community Planning and Development, and
Housing - Federal Housing Commissioner)

**REQUEST FOR VERIFICATION
OF EMPLOYMENT**

INSTRUCTIONS

LENDER OR LOCAL PROCESSING AGENCY (LPA): Complete Items 1 through 7. Have the applicant complete Item 8. Forward the completed form directly to the employer named in Item 1. EMPLOYER: Complete either Parts II and IV or Parts III and IV. Return form directly to the Lender or Local Processing Agency named in Item 2 of Part I.

PART I - REQUEST

1. TO: (Name and Address of Employer)

2. FROM: (Name and Address of Lender or Local Processing Agency)

3. I certify that this verification has been sent directly to the employer and has not passed through the hands of the applicant or any other interested party.

4. TITLE OF LENDER, OFFICIAL OF LPA, OR FmHA LOAN PACKAGER

5. DATE

6. HUD/FHA/CPD, VA, OR FmHA NO.

(Signature of Lender, Official of LPA, or FmHA Loan Packager)

I have applied for a mortgage loan or a rehabilitation loan and stated that I am/was employed by you. My signature in the block below authorizes verification of my employment information.

7. NAME AND ADDRESS OF APPLICANT

8. EMPLOYEE'S IDENTIFICATION

SIGNATURE OF APPLICANT

PART II - VERIFICATION OF PRESENT EMPLOYMENT

EMPLOYMENT DATA

9. APPLICANT'S DATE OF EMPLOYMENT

10. PRESENT POSITION

11. PROBABILITY OF CONTINUED EMPLOYMENT

13. IF OVERTIME OR BONUS IS APPLICABLE, IS ITS CONTINUANCE LIKELY?

OVERTIME ☐ Yes ☐ No

BONUS ☐ Yes ☐ No

PAY DATA

12A. BASE PAY (Current)

$_____ ☐ Annual $_____ ☐ Hourly

$_____ ☐ Monthly $_____ ☐ Weekly

$_____ ☐ Other (Specify)

12B. EARNINGS

Type	Year to Date	Past Year
BASE PAY	$	$
OVERTIME	$	$
COMMISSIONS	$	$
BONUS	$	$

FOR MILITARY PERSONNEL ONLY

Type	Monthly Amount
BASE PAY	$
RATIONS	$
FLIGHT OR HAZARD	$
CLOTHING	$
QUARTERS	$
PRO PAY	$
OVERSEAS OR COMBAT	$

14. REMARKS (If paid hourly, please indicate average hours worked each week during current and past year)

PART III - VERIFICATION OF PREVIOUS EMPLOYMENT

15. DATES OF EMPLOYMENT

16. SALARY/WAGE AT TERMINATION PER ☐ YEAR ☐ MONTH ☐ WEEK

BASE PAY	OVERTIME	COMMISSIONS	BONUS
$	$	$	$

17. REASONS FOR LEAVING

18. POSITION HELD

PART IV - CERTIFICATION

Federal statutes provide severe penalties for any fraud, intentional misrepresentation, or criminal connivance or conspiracy purposed to influence the issuance of any guaranty or insurance by the VA Administrator, the U.S.D.A., FmHA Administrator, the HUD/FHA Commissioner, or the HUD/CPD Assistant Secretary.

19. SIGNATURE

20. TITLE OF EMPLOYER

21. DATE

Figure 10.8C Request for verification of employment

Earnest Money Deposit Certification

RE:

This is to certify that I (we) have made payment(s) of $ ________________ to date for the purchase of the above property.

These payment(s) were made to ____.

Funds for these payments were derived from the following source(s):

______ Cash from savings.

______ Sale of Savings Bonds.

______ Withdrawal from Bank Account at (Bank) ________________________.

______ Other (Specify) ____.

Further, I (we) have not incurred, and do not intend to incur any indebtedness, secured or unsecured, other than that of the mortgage loan applied for, for any purpose connected with this transaction.

____

Signature

____

Signature

Date: ____________________

Figure 10.8D Earnest money deposit certification

10.9 HOME PURCHASE CLOSING COST GUIDELINES

Transferred employees being counseled about home purchase costs, should be advised to obtain full details from their real estate broker concerning "closing" or "settlement" costs for the area where they are purchasing a residence. These types of costs are divided into two general categories: (1) charges for title examinations and document preparation, and (2) charges for prepaid real estate taxes and homeowners insurance.

Here are some estimated costs for representative closing/settlement expenses:

- Title Charges, which include items such as a settlement closing fee, title exam, binder fee, notary fees, and document preparation costs, can range up to $300.
- Recording Fee—up to $40.
- Recordation Tax—$2 per thousand up to 1 percent of sale price.
- Transfer Tax—$1 per thousand up to 2 percent of sale price.
- Survey—up to $150.
- Appraisal—up to $150.
- Loan Origination Fee—a percentage of the sale price, for example, $2\frac{1}{2}$ percent.
- Discount Point—1 percent of the sale price for each "point."

The purchaser also will be required to place funds in escrow accounts held by the lender for the payment of real estate taxes and fire insurance.

Depending on the type of mortgage financing, other types of fees and insurance costs are added to the employee's closing/settlement costs.

10.10 RELOCATION CHECKLIST

This checklist is used by transferred employees for arranging their relocations.

Relocation Checklist—"Preparing for a Successful Move"

Use this checklist to effectively plan and accomplish your relocation. There are many details to remember, and lots to do before life returns to normal in your new home.

_____ Discuss the relocation with your family. Review the schedule of events, the features of the new area, and so on.

_____ If your company requires you to select a mover, arrange to have three moving company representatives provide estimates. Obtain full details regarding services and procedures. Ensure that the movers can meet your proposed schedule.

_____ Inventory your household goods. Identify items that are not worth shipping; get rid of these unwanted items by donating them to charity, holding a garage sale, and so on.

_____ Define your housing requirements for the new area, then discuss your needs with a real estate broker in preparation for your househunting trip. Request maps of the new area, information and pictures, and details concerning representative housing.

_____ Arrange your househunting trip. Will your spouse accompany you? If so, will child care arrangements be needed? Obtain air travel, hotel, and auto rental reservations. Arrange a cash advance for the trip; purchase travelers checks.

_____ Use canned goods and frozen foods.

_____ Begin your home sale/lease cancellation procedures.

_____ Make a list of change of address notification requirements. As soon as the new address and effective date are known, use a kit of postcards available from your postmaster to notify publishers, business accounts, professional and alumni associations, friends and relatives, and so on.

_____ Arrange a bank account in the new area.

_____ Contact utility companies to arrange to have services disconnected at the former residence and connected in time for your occupancy of the new residence.

_____ Review your renters/homeowners insurance policy to assess move-related coverage. Arrange policy for your residence in the new area.

_____ Contact the moving company you and/or the company selected, regarding inventory date, planned moving dates, the destination, and how you may be reached in temporary quarters in the new area while household goods are in transit.

_____ Obtain school records and other documents such as physician reports as required for transferring children to their new schools.

_____ Arrange for service workers to have appliances, such as your washer and dryer, disconnected and prepared for shipment. Also arrange for connection service at your new residence.

_____ Make plans for moving delicate plants, paints, inflammable or explosive items, and so on, which the mover will not transport.

_____ Cancel newspaper deliveries.

_____ Arrange your relocation trip to the new area. Have your automobile serviced in preparation for the trip. Make motel reservations.

_____ Pack clothes, items for personal hygiene, and a kit of items you will need at your new residence until your household goods are unpacked (cleaning materials, instant coffee, a manual can opener, and so on).

_____ How are you planning to transport your pets? Contact the veterinarian in your new area to arrange temporary kennel facilities. Arrange air transportation, or plan for equipment needed to transport your pet by personal auto (water, food, dish, and so on).

_____ Prepare for the packers by sorting materials so that items for specific rooms will be grouped together. Remove pictures and mirrors from walls. Disconnect stereo, TV, VCR, and so on. Personally pack all jewelry and other valuables you will carry with you.

_____ Be available to advise moving company packers on how to label each box to ensure that they will be placed in the correct rooms and storage areas in the new residence. Call their attention to items that should be labeled "fragile."

_____ Defrost and clean your refrigerator-freezer to prepare it for loading.

_____ On the day your household goods are loaded, carefully review the mover's inventory of your goods to make sure that their condition is as indicated (existing damage, scratches, and so on), and that all items are included in this accounting. The movers will disassemble beds, place mattresses in cartons, roll up carpets, and so on. Make sure that all items have been loaded by making an inspection of closets, storage areas, and so on, before giving the movers a tip and signing their documents (bill of lading).

_____ Before you leave the residence, make sure that windows and doors are locked, lights are turned off, water is shut off, and so on.

_____ Stay in touch with the moving company agent while your household goods are in transit; if the delivery date slips, you will be prepared to extend temporary living accommodation arrangements.

_____ If the company has authorized you to pay the mover directly for services (moving companies require payment before unloading), make sure that you have sufficient travelers checks to meet this requirement.

_____ Make sure that you inventory all your household goods when they are delivered. Note all damage on the mover's documents. Any damaged boxes that have not been unpacked also should be documented as the basis for potential claim.

10.11 POINTERS FOR SELECTING AND CONTRACTING WITH A MOVING COMPANY

If your company requires employees to select their own moving company, these helpful suggestions will promote more effective choices.

How to Select and Contract with Your Moving Company

Careful review of the moving company's services and understanding of its practices can do much to prevent the aggravation and additional expense you will incur if the mover fails to pick up or deliver your household goods on the dates promised, or if some of your household goods arrive damaged.

First, make it a point to obtain estimates from at least three moving companies before making your selection. A mover is prepared to make either a binding or a nonbinding estimate. Moving companies charge by the amount of weight and the distance the goods are to be transported. If you obtain a binding estimate, the amount quoted will be your final cost. While a moving company normally weighs household goods to determine the weight of the truck before and after loading, this will not be the case if you obtain a binding estimate. Whatever rate was quoted is the amount to be charged for services. Binding estimates are recommended over nonbinding estimates, which generally understate the actual cost of the move. Although moving companies are not permitted by Interstate Commerce Commission (ICC) regulations to charge for nonbinding estimates, they are allowed to charge for binding estimates. However, in actual practice, moving companies generally will not charge you for providing a binding estimate.

When you have obtained your binding estimates, which also include promises regarding the move dates, make your selection. The best company may not be the one with the lowest estimate. The key is to ask a lot of questions. For example, ask the moving company agents about the percentage of their customers who must file damage claims, and the average number of days it takes to settle those claims. Ask about their record for on-time pickups and deliveries. If you are involved in an interstate move, ICC regulations require the mover to provide a copy of the ICC pamphlet entitled, "Your Rights and Responsibilities When You Move" and a copy of the moving company's annual performance record. If an intrastate move is involved, check with your state's agency for regulating moving company operations, such as a public utility commission, for information on the performance records of the companies you are considering. You local Better Business Bureau also can be helpful in providing information on the reputation of moving company agents.

The moving company you select will prepare an "Order for Service." Because this order is not a contract, it may be canceled if your plans change or if you decide to work with another mover. The Order for Service completion process includes your being asked to select several consecutive days as loading dates, and another set of dates as unloading days, in the interest of giving the mover maximum scheduling flexibility. This uncertainty regarding dates can be very problematic if you must vacate your residence by a date the mover may not be able to accommodate. Do not depend on a range of dates or a verbal promise for meeting specific pickup and delivery dates. Have the mover commit to your dates by incorporating them in the Order for Service and the Bill of Lading, which is the formal contract for the move. (The Bill of Lading is signed at the time your household goods are packed; make sure that it specifies the loading date and the delivery date. Should the mover fail to meet a designated date, you then have the basis for a claim against the moving company for any additional expenses that result from associated inconveniences.)

Even if the mover you select has an excellent record in providing damage-free moves, you should adequately insure your household goods for possible losses. Moving companies offer three types of insurance coverage:

(1) *Limited Liability.* There is no additional charge for this coverage, which provides 60 cents of insurance for each pound of household goods and personal effects. This means that if a mover breaks a mirror that is worth $400, but only weighs 10 pounds, you would collect only $6.00.

(2) *Added Valuation.* The amount collected for loss or damage is based on the current replacement value of the item minus depreciation. You will be required to provide a "declared valuation" amount for your household goods, and to pay about 50 cents for each $100 of this amount. This coverage is subject to specified limits for claims, for example, no more than $1.25 times the number of pounds in the shipment.

(3) *Full Value Protection.* This protection covers the full cost of repairing or replacing household goods without any deduction for depreciation. This protection plan may involve a deductible or a minimum amount of coverage requirement. The approximate cost is 75 cents per $100 of declared valuation with no deductible. Because deductibles are included, costs are reduced: approximately 30 cents per $100 with a $250 deductible, 15 cents per hundred with a $500 deductible, and 5 cents per $100 with a $1,000 deductible.

When you complete these carefully planned arrangements for moving your household goods and personal effects, you will have done everything possible to ensure a trouble-free relocation.

10.12 TIPS FOR MAKING A HOUSEHOLD GOODS MOVE

The information contained in this section is designed for companies to provide guidance to employees for implementing successful household goods moves.

How to Make Your Move

The mover will arrive at your residence after 8:00 A.M. on the moving date. You should be there to personally supervise the move, and to answer any questions that may arise.

Do not leave money or other valuables around your residence; although moving company personnel are usually carefully selected, you may have the misfortune of encountering an employee who cannot resist temptation.

The mover is committed to using new, clean packing materials for linens, clothing, bedding, and so on; wrapping pictures and mirrors and placing them in special cartons; wrapping and protecting finished surfaces of furniture as needed to prevent marring or scratching; properly rolling and protecting rugs and rug pads; and placing all nuts, bolts, and so on from disassembled items into bags that are securely tied to their respective items.

When the packing is completed, all boxes and items will be numbered. The name (boxes are identified in most cases by the name of the destination room or area) and number of each item is placed on an inventory listing with an indication of its condition. (For example, Item # 35 is a coffee table. The condition of the table is shown as "M" and "SC"; "M" means marred and "SC" means scratched.) Make sure all entries are correct, and all of your items are accounted for on the inventory listing. Should you and the mover not agree on the condition of an item, make a notation concerning this exception on the inventory listing before signing. Each sheet of the inventory has a section at the bottom for your comments regarding exceptions. Remember, unless exceptions are noted, your signature on this inventory or Bill of Lading indicates full agreement with the mover's listing. Be sure to get a copy; you will need it to verify the receipt of items at your destination.

If the company advises you that payment must be made to the mover at the time your household goods are delivered, make arrangements with the moving company agent for determining the exact amount that will be needed at that time. If the cost of the move will be based on weighing the loaded truck to determine the weight of your household goods, then make sure that the driver arranges to coordinate with the agent regarding the resultant certified weight. As soon as you are advised of the amount due, obtain a cash advance.

The mover should deliver your household goods after 8:00 A.M. on the agreed upon date. If you cannot be at your residence to accept the shipment, make sure that your representative is there when the truck arrives. Although the movers will wait for a reasonable period of time, they have the right to place your goods into temporary storage if nobody is available to accept the delivery.

If you do your homework, you will be prepared to tell the movers where each piece of furniture is to be placed, and to clarify where boxes are to be taken for unpacking. The movers only are required to make one placement of each piece of furniture, so make sure your choice of locations for heavy pieces will be correct. The mover will remove all packing materials and other clutter from the premises. The mover also will record losses and damage. You are responsible for ensuring that all damages and losses are noted by the mover on the inventory listing; if the mover refuses, then you should make the notations yourself before signing the inventory or delivery receipt. Watch what you are signing; the proper wording is that your shipment arrived in "apparent" good condition except as noted on the shipping documents. Make sure that you get a copy of all documents.

Be prepared to pay the mover's bill before your household goods are unloaded. Either cash, a certified check, or a money order will be required.

Do not refuse to sign any papers because of losses or damage. There is no problem as long as they have been noted. In fact, even subsequently discovered losses and damage will be covered. You must notify the moving company immediately by telephone and provide written confirmation within 15 days from the delivery date.

Keep your copy of the inventory. The notations regarding lost and damaged items are legal proof for claim purposes. To file a claim for these documented items, write to the moving company about the problem, and request claim forms and a visit by their representative to verify the loss or damage. Your letter must be postmarked no later than 5 days after the date your household goods were delivered. Should you discover damage or loss while doing your own unpacking, the same type of letter should be sent to the moving company no later than 15 days after your goods were delivered.

If the mover verifies the loss and/or damage, a copy of the mover's verification and comments regarding any exceptions to the mover's findings also should be submitted with the claim form. A copy of the inventory should be included.

If the mover fails to have a representative visit you, and does not send the requested claim forms, then you should prepare a detailed explanation of the lost and damaged items which provides the following information:

- Inventory item number
- Description of item
- Description of loss/damage
- Estimated purchase date
- Cost at time of purchase
- Repair/replacement cost
- Estimated weight

This written claim must include a statement to the effect that the mover has refused to verify the loss and/or damage at the residence.

If you cannot obtain a satisfactory settlement from the moving company, the matter may be referred to the ICC to determine whether arbitration is possible through the mover's participation in a dispute resolution program. Inquiries should be directed to:

Director, Office of Compliance and Consumer Assistance
Interstate Commerce Commission
12th Street and Constitution Avenue, N.W.
Washington, D.C. 20433

Do not hesitate to contact the director of human resources for advice or assistance in resolving any move-related problems.

Source: "Shipping Your Household Goods," May 1985, Office of Transportation/Office of Federal Supply and Services/U.S. General Services Administration, National Stock Number 7610-00-058-7938, pp. 14–16.

10.13 EVALUATION OF HOUSEHOLD GOODS MOVE SERVICES

Household Goods Shipment Services Report

The company would appreciate your assessments and comments concerning the services provided to you by the moving company (carrier) during the recent relocation. This information is needed to evaluate the quality of overall carrier performance, and to correct specific performance problems.

Employee Name _____ Date _____

Name of Carrier _____

Please rate the carrier's performance in providing the following services:

Service	Evaluation
1. Pre-Move Survey: Did agent discuss the details of the move and give useful advice? Comments: _____ _____	☐ Excellent ☐ Good ☐ Fair ☐ Poor
2. Packing: Were clean materials and containers used? Were containers marked properly? Was packing debris cleaned up and removed? Comments: _____ _____	☐ Excellent ☐ Good ☐ Fair ☐ Poor
3. Loading: Were household goods loaded carefully? Were beds and other items disassembled properly? Did special items receive proper handling? Was inventory documentation correct and complete? Comments: _____ _____	☐ Excellent ☐ Good ☐ Fair ☐ Poor
4. Unloading and Unpacking: Were household goods unloaded carefully? Were items properly reassembled, placed where requested, etc.? Were goods unpacked by carrier personnel? Was there any damage or breakage? Were all packing materials removed from the premises? Comments: _____ _____	☐ Excellent ☐ Good ☐ Fair ☐ Poor

Service	Evaluation	
5. Did carrier furnish a copy of the inventory/condition of goods list?	☐ Yes	☐ No
6. Did carrier use enough competent and efficient personnel?	☐ Yes	☐ No
Comments: _____ _____		
7. Were carrier personnel courteous and professional in their conduct?	☐ Yes	☐ No
Comments: _____ _____		
8. Did the carrier settle your claims promptly and satisfactorily?	☐ Yes	☐ No
Comments: _____ _____		
9. Would you want to use this carrier again in the future?	☐ Yes	☐ No
Comments: _____ _____		

10.14 INCOME TAX LIABILITIES

The following information is used to explain relocation-related income tax liabilities to employees.

What Are My Income Tax Liabilities?

When an employee is relocated by the company, reimbursements for some of his or her expenses will be taxable as income and subject to 20 percent withholding for federal income tax purposes. the reimbursed expenses that are subject to withholding are:

1. The combined amount reimbursed for an exploratory trip for househunting purposes and temporary living expenses in excess of $1,500.
2. The amount reimbursed for an exploratory trip and temporary living expenses up to $1,500 is deducted from $3,000, the combined allowance for these reimbursements and those for the sale/purchase of a residence or the settlement of an unexpired lease. Reimbursements for the sale/purchase of a residence or the settlement of an unexpired lease which exceed the remaining portion of this allowance are subject to withholding. (For example: If you are reimbursed $1,200 for househunting and temporary quarters, any amount reimbursed over $1,800 for the sale/purchase of a residence is taxable.)
3. The full amount of the lump-sum relocation allowance you receive for incidental relocation expenses is subject to withholding.

Other Considerations

4. Reimbursements will be reported as gross income on your W-2, Wage and Tax Statement, that you receive for the calendar year in which these payments are received.
5. If your relocation involves a real estate transaction, it is recommended that you become familiar with the applicable provisions of Internal Revenue Service rules. For example, capital gains taxes realized through the sale of your home may be postponed through the reinvestment of funds in another principal residence.
6. The following moving expenses are deductible from your federal income tax even though you are reimbursed for them by the company:

    (a) Meals and lodging for you and your family while you are traveling between residences
    (b) Transportation of household goods and personal effects
    (c) Transportation, meals, and lodging incurred for a househunting trip
    (d) Temporary quarters for thirty (30) days after reporting for work
    (e) The cost of selling your owned residence

7. You will be required to file IRS Form 3903 with your income tax return to report moving expense deductions.

CHAPTER 11

Safety and Security

This chapter begins with a sample company policy on Safety and Security in Section 11.1. Emphasis is placed on the need for accident prevention and fire precautions. A safe work environment is promoted through frequent inspections to identify and eliminate safety hazards, and periodic fire drills to familiarize employees with effective fire emergency procedures.

In addition to these procedures for preventing employee injuries, the policy fosters employee security through visitor control and loss prevention guidelines. The security of confidential company information also is covered. Control processes are defined for assigning security classifications to documents, and special handling procedures are outlined to preserve confidentiality through controlled access.

Section 11.2 offers a sample policy statement on Medical Emergencies–Accident Reporting. These guidelines focus on emergency medical treatment procedures and injury reporting requirements. Next, in Section 11.3, some valuable insights are provided on how to obtain the information and assistance needed to develop or enhance a safety program. This OSHA Safety Management Resources section includes an order form and instructions for obtaining free safety publications from the U.S. Department of Labor.

A Safety Hazard/Violation Citation is introduced in Section 11.4. This multipurpose form provides the basis for administering an aggressive program for correcting safety hazards and eliminating unsafe working practices.

A comprehensive Employee Accident Report form is introduced in Section 11.5. The report is initiated by an employee and completed by an immediate supervisor. The completed form provides the essential information needed for disability insurance claims and OSHA reporting purposes.

Next, in Section 11.6, the complexities involved in providing adequate fire safety procedures are illustrated by a sample Fire Command Post Instructions and Action Record form. An excellent example of a State Disability Insurance Claim form is provided in Section 11.7. It combines three forms into one—that is, the employee's statement, a medical certificate, and the employer's statement.

A sample Application for Sick Leave form is shown in Section 11.8. It provides the basis for having employees request and obtain advance approval for planned medical absences such as those for surgery, dental work, optical examinations, physical examinations or medical treatments, and pregnancy-related absences. The form also provides documentation on long-term disability absences, which have been certified by the employee's physician.

The Security Incident Report, shown in Section 11.9, provides a framework for systematically and thoroughly reporting, investigating, and proposing corrective actions for breaches of security.

Section 11.10 contains a Personal or Company Property Loss Report. Designed for use by employees in documenting the theft of their personal or company-assigned property, it effectively summarizes the information needed for security investigation purposes.

11.1 SAMPLE COMPANY POLICY ON SAFETY AND SECURITY

Safety and Security

I. Objective

To provide guidelines for ensuring safety and security at the corporate headquarters office.

II. Fire Precautions

Periodic fire drills are held to familiarize employees with the procedures to be followed in a fire emergency. Associated instruction includes the location of alarm boxes and fire exits on each floor, and the correct method of evacuating the building.

III. Injury Prevention

A safe place to work is an essential condition of employment. Every effort must be made to eliminate safety hazards and prevent employee injuries. Each manager is responsible for ensuring that:

1. Employees are fully informed of fire drill regulations and procedures.
2. Periodic inspections are conducted to identify and eliminate safety hazards promptly.
3. All injuries, no matter how slight, are reported to the human resources management division through the completion of an Employee Accident Report form.

IV. Office Security

Each manager is responsible for ensuring that assigned employees understand and take the following loss prevention precautions:

1. Money and other employee valuables must not be kept in unlocked desks, file drawers, or in outer garments which are hung in clothing closets. Handbags should be either secured in a locked drawer or taken with the employee when leaving the work area.
2. Portable office equipment must be secured in a locked cabinet or drawer when not in use.
3. Company papers and other valuable documents must be secured in locked desks or filing cabinets during the lunch period and at the end of each work day.
4. Unauthorized sales personnel or solicitors must be reported to the human resources division. Solicitations for charity or other purposes must be approved in advance by the director of human resources.
5. Visitors are required to register with the receptionist, who notifies respective employees regarding their arrival. The receptionist maintains a daily record of

all visitor activities, which includes the following data: visitor name, organization represented, employee visited, and time in and out. Visitors must be escorted by employees at all times.

V. Building Security

The human resources management division administers a company identification card system for employee identification purposes. The receptionist is required to have employees present their card as needed to verify employment status. The loss of a company identification card must be reported immediately to the director of human resources.

VI. Secrecy Agreements

Certain designated employees are required to enter into secrecy agreements with the company as a condition of their employment. These agreements are reaffirmed upon termination of employment.

VII. Information Control

A. *Security Classifications.* To ensure the confidentiality of company information, the following safeguarding classifications are assigned to documents based on their degree of sensitivity:
   1. *Secret.* The unauthorized disclosure of this type of information could result in major loss or damage to the company.
   2. *Confidential.* The unauthorized disclosure of this information could result in loss or damage to the company.
   3. *Personal.* The unauthorized disclosure of this information could be detrimental to a person or persons within the organization.
B. *Security of Classified Documents.* Classified documents with secret, confidential, or personal security classifications must receive the following special handling:
   1. Properly marked documents showing the overall security classification on each page.
   2. Documents must be stored in a secure place after working hours and whenever the work area is left unattended during working hours.
   3. Documents should not be released to individuals, regardless of their organizational level, who do not have a "need to know."
   4. Internal transmittals must be in sealed envelopes marked with respective security classifications and the wording, "to be opened only by (name of recipient)." An unmarked envelope is addressed to the recipient when documents are transmitted by mail. An inner envelope is used to designate the security classification and the wording, "to be opened only by (name of recipient)."
   5. Disposal of used documents is to be by shredding or any other technique that ensures complete destruction.
C. *Release of Company Information.* Any public request for the release of company information requires the review and approval of the director of human

resources, who coordinates with top management as needed to define security requirements. Representative types of information include, but are not limited to, details of contract negotiations, plans for facility expansions, production methods and techniques, and sources of supply.

D. *Removal of Information.* The advance approval of an employee's division director is needed to authorize the temporary removal of a "secret" document from the office.

E. *Discussion of Information.* Company classified information cannot be discussed with unauthorized personnel. It should not be discussed in public places, on public conveyances, or at home. It should not be transmitted by telephone, TWX or other commercial telegraph, or by radio (including auto and portable telephones).

11.2 SAMPLE COMPANY POLICY ON MEDICAL EMERGENCIES–ACCIDENT REPORTING

Medical Emergencies–Accident Reporting

I. Objective

To provide guidelines for emergency medical treatment and accident reporting at the corporate headquarters office.

II. First Aid–Medical Assistance

A. The human resource management division is responsible for making arrangements for first aid and/or other emergency medical treatment in the event an employee is injured or becomes ill while at work, or if a visitor is injured or becomes ill while on the premises.

B. The human resources management division clinic should be contacted immediately in cases that require either or all of the following services:

   1. First aid treatment and assistance by the company nurse or another qualified employee. Oxygen, blankets, bandages, and other first aid supplies are maintained for this purpose.

   2. Treatment by paramedics and transfer by ambulance to a nearby hospital.

III. Injury or Illness Reporting

To ensure that disability insurance and other types of claim requirements are met, all injuries and illnesses that occur at the corporate headquarters office must be reported to the human resources management division as follows:

A. Regardless of how minor an employee's injury may appear to be, all such incidents must be reported through the preparation of an Employee Accident Report form.

B. An illness that requires medical treatment at the work site is to be documented by the employee's manager in a Memorandum for File. The memorandum must specify the date and time of the occurrence, and explain the condition and treatment provided. All such memoranda are to be provided to the company nurse for incorporation in the employee medical files.

C. In the event a visitor to the company is injured or becomes ill while on the premises, the employee who was responsible for the visitor must prepare a Memorandum for File, which specifies the date and time of the incident, and describes the condition and type of first aid and/or medical treatment received. All such memoranda are provided to the director of human resources, who coordinates with the company legal department about potential liabilities.

11.3 OSHA SAFETY MANAGEMENT RESOURCES*

If you are developing a safety and health program for implementation, determine whether your state has its own occupational safety and health program in lieu of the Federal OSHA program. You can accomplish this by contacting the nearest federal OSHA office to determine which level of government has jurisdiction. Next, make sure that you have all current information for complying with the mandatory minimum standards that are subject to workplace inspections. Should you be under the jurisdiction of the Occupational Safety and Health Administration of the U.S. Department of Labor, you will need certain OSHA publications for use in developing your safety and health activities. As listed in Figure 11.3, OSHA Will Send You One Complimentary Copy of Any Publication Checked Below, free guidance is available on general, management, programs and policy, safe work practices, and job health hazards subjects.

Publications that introduce an OSHA program include:

OSHA Workplace Poster

This poster (or a state OSHA poster) must be displayed in your workplace. The ordering information provided for the OSHA poster is "Job Protection and Health Protection (OSHA 2203), 1976."

OSHA Standards for Your Type of Business

Most businesses come under the provisions of the General Industry Standards. These standards may be ordered by requesting the "General Industry: OSHA Safety & Health Standards Digest (OSHA 2254), June 1975."

Occupational Health and Safety Act

For your information and reference, you should have a copy of the Occupational Health and Safety Act. The copy may be ordered by requesting "The Occupational Safety and Health Act of 1970 (OSHA 2001), December 1970."

Your request should include the full name and address of your company, and your name and telephone number (for contacting you as needed to clarify your requirements). The request is forwarded to:

> U.S. Department of Labor
> Occupational Safety and Health Administration
> Room N–3641
> 3rd & Constitution Avenue, NW
> Washington, D.C. 20210
>
> ATTN: Office of Public and Consumer Affairs

SOURCE: "OSHA Handbook for Small Businesses, Safety Management Series," U.S. Department of Labor, Occupational Safety and Health Administration, revised 1979, OSHA 2209.

Other Sources of Guidance

Worker's Compensation Insurance Companies and Other Carriers. Many worker's compensation insurance companies as well as liability and fire insurance companies conduct periodic inspections of insured companies to evaluate safety and health hazards.

Trade Unions. If your employees are organized, many trade unions have safety and health expertise they are willing to share in a coordinated program for action on hazards.

National Safety Council. The NSC offers a broad variety of information services. If there is no local chapter in your area to call or visit for assistance, you can write to:

National Safety Council
444 North Michigan Avenue
Chicago, Illinois 60611

Red Cross. For assistance in first-aid training for your employees, contact your local chapter of the Red Cross. If there is none in your area, write to:

American National Red Cross
National Headquarters
18th and E Streets, NW
Washington, D. C. 20006

OSHA WILL SEND YOU ONE COMPLIMENTARY COPY OF ANY PUBLICATION CHECKED BELOW

General

☐ THE OCCUPATIONAL SAFETY AND HEALTH ACT OF 1970 (OSHA 2001) *Dec. 1970*
Full text of the Act.

☐ JOB SAFETY AND HEALTH PROTECTION (OSHA 2203) *1976*
Official OSHA poster required by law to be prominently posted in the workplace.

☐ GENERAL INDUSTRY: OSHA SAFETY & HEALTH STANDARDS DIGEST (OSHA 2201) *June 1975*
Alphabetical digest of OSHA standards for General Industry in nontechnical language, covering 90% of the basic applicable standards.

☐ CONSTRUCTION INDUSTRY: OSHA SAFETY & HEALTH STANDARDS DIGEST (OSHA 2202) *June 1975*
Alphabetical digest of OSHA standards for construction in nontechnical language, covering approximately 90% of the basic applicable standards.

☐ TRAINING REQUIREMENTS OF OSHA STANDARDS (OSHA 2254) *Feb. 1976*
Publication is designed to assist employers in identifying those standards requiring the training of employees.

Management

☐ ORGANIZING A SAFETY COMMITTEE (OSHA 2231) *June 1975*
Booklet of guidelines for the employers in any size business on setting up safety and health committees in their establishments.

☐ OSHA HANDBOOK FOR SMALL BUSINESSES (OSHA 2209) *Nov. 1976*
Handbook to assist small business employers to meet their legal requirements under the Occupational Safety and Health Act, and to achieve an "in-compliance" status voluntarily and prior to any OSHA inspection.

Programs & Policy

☐ ALL ABOUT OSHA (OSHA 2056) *Apr. 1976*
Booklet which explains in broad terms the provisions of the Occupational Safety and Health Act of 1970 and the policies of OSHA.

☐ OSHA INSPECTIONS (OSHA 2098) *June 1975*
Booklet explaining to the employer what to expect when an OSHA compliance officer comes to inspect his or her establishment.

☐ WORKERS RIGHTS UNDER OSHA (OSHA 2253) *Oct. 1975*
Booklet explaining the rights and responsibilities of workers under the Occupational Safety and Health Act.

☐ SBA LOANS FOR OSHA COMPLIANCE (OSHA 2005) *Jan. 1975*
Booklet outlining small business procedures in obtaining OSHA assistance in applying for Small Business Administration (SBA) loans to help meet OSHA requirements.

☐ PROTECTION FOR WORKERS IN IMMINENT DANGER (OSHA 2205) *Apr. 1975*
Booklet providing employees with an interpretation of imminent danger, with guidance in reporting such situations, and with related personal rights.

Safe Work Practices

☐ EXCAVATION AND TRENCHING OPERATIONS (OSHA 2226) *June 1975*
Booklet of safe work practices and common sense procedures for those responsible for developing and maintaining an accident prevention program for excavating, trenching, and backfilling operations.

☐ ESSENTIALS OF MACHINE GUARDING (OSHA 2227) *Aug. 1975*
Booklet on the basic methods of machine guarding that involve relatively simple machinery found frequently in industry.

☐ ESSENTIALS OF MATERIALS HANDLING (OSHA 2236) *Oct. 1975*
Booklet alerting employees and vocational students to the basic safety procedures in materials handling. Also useful to employers as part of their safety training program.

☐ HANDLING HAZARDOUS MATERIALS (OSHA 2237) *Sept. 1975*
Booklet on important safety precautions in handling and storing hazardous materials which are widely used throughout industry.

Job Health Hazards

☐ HOT ENVIRONMENTS (OSHA 2277) *1976*
Pamphlet giving employers and employees an overview of the hazards of work in hot environments, and to alert them to the precautions which should be taken to avoid excessive heat stress.

☐ CARBON MONOXIDE (OSHA 2224) *June 1975*
Booklet presenting an overview of the dangers of carbon monoxide and the OSHA standards that apply to workplaces where it is present.

☐ LEAD (OSHA 2230) *June 1975*
Booklet presenting an overview of the dangers involved in working with lead and explaining applicable OSHA standards.

☐ MERCURY (OSHA 2234) *Aug. 1975*
Booklet presenting an overview of the dangers of working with mercury and explaining applicable OSHA standards.

Figure 11.3 OSHA will send you one complimentary copy of any publication checked below

11.4 SAFETY HAZARD/VIOLATION CITATION

The sample Safety Hazard/Violation Citation (Figure 11.4) is a multi-purpose form designed to perform all of the following functions:

1. Serve notice that a safety hazard has been identified in a supervisor's area of responsibility. Immediate corrective action is requested.
2. Cite an employee who is observed violating a safety regulation. The individual is required to explain the possible consequences of the unsafe practice, and to explain what will be done in the future to ensure the infraction is not repeated.
3. A full description of the hazard or violation is provided by the safety representative who prepares the citation.
4. Suggested corrective action(s) are provided in detail by the safety representatives to explain how a hazard should be eliminated. If a violation is being cited, wording such as "employee is required to explain the type of injury which may result from this unsafe practice."
5. The director of human resources signs the citation to show his or her personal concern, and to demonstrate a commitment to employee safety and health program objectives.
6. The individual who is cited is required to complete a section of the form to explain completed corrective actions. Quick response time is required in the interest of emphasizing the importance of eliminating safety hazards or unsafe work practices. Replies must be returned to the director of human resources within 2 working days.
7. A copy of the completed form is placed in the individual's personnel record for work performance assessment purposes.

Safety Hazard/Violation Citation

Date _____

Time _____ A. M.
                        P. M.

Issued To _____ Position _____

Organization _____ Location _____

☐ The following safety HAZARD has been identified. Your immediate corrective action is required.

☐ The following VIOLATION of safety regulations has been observed. Your immediate action is required to ensure that this infraction is not repeated.

DESCRIPTION OF SAFETY HAZARD/VIOLATION:

SUGGESTED CORRECTION ACTION(s):

_____   _____
Director of Human Resources   Date

Explain completed corrective actions below, and return this citation to the Director of Human Resources by _____
                               Date

Signature _____ Date _____

Figure 11.4 Safety hazard/violation citation

11.5 EMPLOYEE ACCIDENT REPORT

Completion of the comprehensive Employee Accident Report form (Figure 11.5) involves the following process:

> The upper portion of the form is completed by the employee or by an individual who assists a disabled employee.
>
> The immediate supervisor is responsible for having the employee complete the upper portion of the form, preparing the "to be completed by immediate supervisor" portion of the form, and returning the form to the human resources management division to serve as the basis for completing disability insurance forms, and for maintaining records used for OSHA inspections and statistical reporting purposes.
>
> The time frame for the completion and return of an Employee Accident Report is 72 hours from the time that the accident occurred.

To complete the form, the employee provides personnel data, home address and telephone number (so that the employee or the family of a hospitalized employee may be readily contacted regarding disability procedures), and full details of the accident and injury.

The immediate supervisor completes the form to indicate when he or she learned of the accident, provide opinions regarding the factors that contributed to the accident, and to explain actions taken to eliminate associated safety hazards.

Employee Accident Report

Employee _____ Social Security No. _____

Position Title _____

Organization _____ Location _____

Home Address: _____

_____ Telephone No. (_____) _____

Date of Accident _____ Time of Accident _____ A.M. P.M.

Location of Accident _____

Description of Accident _____

_____

_____

Injury: _____

Return to Work Date: _____

Signature: _____ Date: _____

_____

TO BE COMPLETED BY IMMEDIATE SUPERVISOR

When did you learn of this accident? _____

In your opinion, what factors contributed to this accident? _____

_____

Actions taken to eliminate safety hazards? _____

_____

_____

Name _____ Position Title _____

Signature _____ Date _____

Due in HRM Division within 72 Hours of an Accident!

Figure 11.5 Employee accident report

11.6 FIRE COMMAND POST INSTRUCTIONS AND ACTION RECORD

To plan procedures that meet the complex personnel evacuation and control requirements of a fire, companies with high-rise or other multiple-story buildings face unique problems. An illustration of these complexities is shown in Figure 11.6, Fire Command Post Instructions and Action Record.

The company fire marshal and the fire wardens on each floor of the building are trained to interact with the Fire Department and provide data on trapped and endangered occupants, the details of evacuation routes and progress, and the location and extent of fire and smoke conditions.

This form provides a set of instructions and required actions in a checklist format. In the confusion of an emergency situation, this step-by-step procedure ensures that all required actions are taken in preparation for the arrival of the Fire Department.

Fire Command Post Instructions and Action Record

1. Has alarm been transmitted to the Fire Department?   Yes _____   No _____

2. Have all elevators been recalled to the street floor?   Yes _____   No _____

3. Which floor is alarm coming from? _____

4. Contact fire warden on alarm floor and determine:

   Exact location of fire _____

   Extent of fire _____

   Smoke conditions _____

   Approximate number of occupants _____

   Status of occupants: Any endangered?   Yes _____   No _____

                                 Any trapped?   Yes _____   No _____

   Is evacuation underway?   Yes _____   No _____

   What stairs are being used for evacuation? _____

5. Contact fire warden on floor above fire floor and determine:

   Any fire?   Yes _____   No _____

   If "Yes", specify location and extent _____

   Smoke conditions? _____

   Approximate number of occupants _____

   Status of occupants: Any endangered?   Yes _____   No _____

                                 Any trapped?   Yes _____   No _____

   Is evacuation under way?   Yes _____   No _____

   What stairs are being used for evacuation? _____

6. Identification of elevators serving alarm floor:

   Bank identification _____

   Elevator numbers _____

7. Sprinklers operating?   Yes _____   No _____

   Number of heads _____   Location _____

8. Smoke detectors activated?

   Number _____   Location _____

9. HVAC System shut down?   Yes _____   No _____

10. Any access stairs connecting alarm floor with floors:

   Above   Yes _____   No _____   Location _____

   Below   Yes _____   No _____   Location _____

Fire Marshall Signature _____ Date _____

Time Actions Initiated _____A.M. P.M.

Figure 11.6 Fire command post instructions and action record

11.7 PROOF OF CLAIM FOR DISABILITY BENEFITS: SAMPLE STATE FORM

With special thanks to Mr. George M. Krause, the Deputy Commissioner of Labor of the state of New Jersey, this section offers an excellent example of a state plan disability insurance benefits claim form. This Proof and Claim for Disability Benefits State Plan form, as shown in Figure 11.7, combines three forms into one. It includes provisions for the "claimant's statement" in Part A, a "medical certificate" by the claimant's doctor in Part B, and an "employer's statement" in Part 3. In addition, the form also is designed to serve as its own envelope; it is folded to reveal the address and is self-sealed with a pre-glued and perforated flap.

The form includes instructions for the employee, as claimant, to complete and submit it to the Department of Labor as soon as possible after the commencement of a disability. A statement is included which indicates that the law requires an employee to file within 30 days of the start of the disability, and that late submission may result in the denial or reduction of benefits. A claim for an individual who is pregnant must be filed as soon as the pregnancy reaches that stage where the employee no longer is able to continue working. To obtain all the information necessary to process the claim, the employee is encouraged to bring the claim form to his or her physician and employer and wait while they complete their respective portions. In view of the time limit for filing, each claimant should be advised by the human resources management organization that it is his or her personal responsibility to see that the state plan disability claim form is filed promptly. Leaving a claim form with a doctor who does not complete and forward it in time to meet the filing deadline is not a valid excuse for late filing. Accordingly, to avoid a denial or reduction of benefits, the employee must make completion arrangements with the HRM organization and his or her physician as needed to ensure that the completed claim form is submitted in time.

Courtesy of: Department of Labor, State of New Jersey.

PROOF AND CLAIM FOR DISABILITY BENEFITS STATE PLAN

D. D.

N.J. DEPARTMENT OF LABOR - DISABILITY INSURANCE SERVICE

DS-1 (R-1-85)

PART A — CLAIMANT'S STATEMENT

READ INSTRUCTIONS ON REVERSE SIDE

PRINT ANSWERS TO QUESTIONS 1 THROUGH 18

SOCIAL SECURITY NUMBER

COPY FROM YOUR SOCIAL SECURITY CARD

1. Your Name (print): _____

2. Your Home
   Address: _____
   (Street) _____ (Apt. #)
   _____ _____ _____
   (City) (State) (Zip Code)

3. Your Mailing
   Address if _____
   Different: (Street) _____ (Apt. #)
   _____ _____ _____
   (City) (State) (Zip Code)

4. [_____]

4.a. Are you a citizen of the United States? ☐ Yes ☐ No

4.b. If "NO" Alien Registration No. _____

5. Male ☐ Female ☐   Birth Date No. of Dependents
   M   D   Y

6. Your Occupation: _____

7. Dates of Hospitalization: From _____ Through _____

8. What was the last day you worked before this present disability began?.......... _____ (Month) (Day) (Year)

9. What was the first day you were unable to work because of this disability,
   even if this is a Saturday, Sunday, holiday or regular day off?.......... _____ (Month) (Day) (Year)

10. If now recovered, what was the first day on which you were able to work?.......... _____ (Month) (Day) (Year)

11. Describe your disability and state HOW and WHERE it happened. _____

12. Was this disability caused by your work? ☐ No ☐ Yes If yes, explain _____

13. What is the name, address and telephone number of the doctor who is treating you for this disability?

    _____
    (Name and Street Address) _____ _____
    (City and State) (Phone Number)

14. Have you filed a claim for unemployment benefits AGAINST THE STATE OF NEW JERSEY during the past year? If yes, what date? _____

15. Are you receiving disability benefits under Private Plan of your employer? ☐ No ☐ Yes

16. Are you performing work for wages or profit? ☐ No ☐ Yes

17. Are you receiving pension/Social Security benefits? ☐ No ☐ Yes

18. NAME YOUR EMPLOYER OR EMPLOYERS DURING THE PAST TWELVE (12) MONTHS.
    Give business names and addresses as they appear on your pay envelopes, your employer's stationery or the telephone book listing.

Emp.
No. LAST EMPLOYER FOR WHOM YOU WORKED WHEN DISABLED OR BEFORE YOU BECAME UNEMPLOYED

(1) Name _____ EMP. REG. # _____

    Street Address _____

    City, State and Zip Code _____ worked from _____ _____ _____ to _____ _____ _____
    (Mo.) (Day) (Yr.) (Mo.) (Day) (Yr.)

    Address of your work location _____ Union Local No. _____

OTHER EMPLOYERS FOR WHOM YOU WORKED DURING THE PAST TWELVE (12) MONTHS.

(2) Name _____ EMP. REG. # _____

    Street Address _____

    City, State and Zip Code _____ worked from _____ _____ _____ to _____ _____ _____
    (Mo.) (Day) (Yr.) (Mo.) (Day) (Yr.)

    Address of your work location _____

(3) Name _____

Street Address _____

City, State and Zip Code _____

Address of your work location _____ worked from _____ to _____

(Mo.) (Day) (Yr.) (Mo.) (Day) (Yr.)

EMP.	
REG. #	

IF YOU HAD MORE THAN 3 EMPLOYERS, LIST OTHERS WITH DATES WORKED, ON A SEPARATE SHEET OF PAPER AND ATTACH TO THIS FORM

SIGNATURE AND CERTIFICATION:

19. I was unable to work during the period for which benefits are claimed and hereby certify that all the statements made by me on this form are true. I know that the law provides penalties for false statements made to obtain benefits. You are hereby authorized to obtain such information as is necessary to determine the eligibility of this claim.

Date _____ Claimant's Signature _____ Phone No. _____

Witness Signature (Required if claimant is unable to sign and writes an "X") _____

PART B ## MEDICAL CERTIFICATE

GET YOUR DOCTOR TO FILL IN THE MEDICAL CERTIFICATE. If this cannot be done without delay, mail the claim without the medical certificate, so your claim will be filed on time.

1. Patient has been under my care for **this period of disability** *(See item 8 above)* from _____ to _____

(Date) (Date)

and has been seen every _____

(Frequency)

2. Patient has been unable to perform all the duties of his/her regular or usual job (or unable to work) from _____

(Date)

Prognosis: Approximate date claimant will be able to return to work. Please give estimated date _____

If now recovered, what was the first day on which claimant was able to work? _____

Diagnosis: Nature and cause of this disability which prevents claimant from working _____

3. In your opinion, was this disability: ☐ Due to an accident at work?   ☐ Not related to his employment.

☐ Due to a condition which developed because of the nature of the work?

4. Dates of Hospitalization: From _____ Through _____ .

5. Surgery performed _____ Surgery contemplated _____

(Month) (Day) (Year) (Month) (Day) (Year)

6. If this disability is due to pregnancy, give expected date of delivery: _____

If pregnancy terminated, give date _____ ☐ Birth   ☐ Miscarriage   ☐ Abortion

7. I hereby certify that the above statements, in my opinion, truly describe the claimant's disability and the estimated duration thereof.

_____

(Doctor's Signature)

_____

(Print Doctor's Name, and Indicate Degree)

_____ _____ _____

(Street Address) (City and State) (Phone) (Certificate License No.)

_____

(Mailing Address, If Different) (Date Signed)

DO NOT WRITE IN THIS SPACE

Figure 11.7 Proof and claim for disability benefits state plan

PART C — EMPLOYER'S STATEMENT - ANSWER ALL QUESTIONS ACCURATELY

Not required if claimant was unemployed more than 14 days before this disability commenced.

Fold forward on this line last →

Fold back on this line first →

1 EMPLOYER STATUS

Are you subject to the New Jersey Unemployment Compensation Law? [ ] Yes [ ] No

If "Yes", give N. J. Employment Security Registration No. _____

2 PRIVATE PLAN COVERAGE

(a) Do You have a New Jersey approved Private Plan? [ ] Yes [ ] No

(b) If "Yes", is claimant covered under this approved Private Plan? [ ] Yes [ ] No

3 DATA REGARDING LAST DAY WORKED

(a) Claimant's actual last day worked immediately before this disability: _____

(b) Reason for separation from work on above date _____

(c) Has claimant returned to work? [ ] Yes [ ] No   If "Yes", give date: _____

If intermittent, give dates worked after disability began _____

4 CONTINUED PAY

(a) Have you paid the claimant any money since the last day of work? [ ] Yes [ ] No

(b) If "Yes", how much per week $ _____

(c) These moneys represent pay from _____

through _____

(Month) _____ _(Day)_ _____ _(Year)_

(Month) _____ _(day)_ _____ _(Year)_

(d) What do these payments represent?

1. [ ] Regular Weekly wage   3. [ ] Supplemental benefits or gratuities

2. [ ] Difference between regular weekly wage and disability benefits to be received.   4. [ ] Regular vacation   5. [ ] Pension

NOTE: Items (d) 1, 4 and 5 may reduce benefits to claimant.

5 GOVERNMENT EMPLOYEES

If claimant is employed by a government entity, complete this section.

(a) Payroll number (For N. J. State Employees) _____

(b) Number of unused accumulated sick days as of the last day worked. _____

6 WORKERS' COMPENSATION LIABILITY

(a) Did claimant's disability happen in connection with his/her work or while on your premises, or was the disability due in any way to his/her occupation? [ ] Yes [ ] No

(b) If "Yes", have you filed or do you intend to file a workers' compensation claim on behalf of this claimant? [ ] Yes [ ] No

(c) If "Yes", give name and address of workers' compensation insurance carrier and phone number.

Name _____   Phone No. _____

Address _____

7 BASE WEEKS AND BASE YEAR WAGES

In how many calendar weeks did this claimant earn $54.00 or more with you in NEW JERSEY EMPLOYMENT during his/her base year, which is 52 weeks immediately preceding the week in which the disability began? _(See Item 8 on front of claim for date)_ _____

Total number of base weeks _____

Total wages in base year $ _____

8 REGULAR WEEKLY WAGE immediately prior to disability: $ _____

9 WEEKLY WAGES

Show in the spaces below; dates and claimant's GROSS earnings in New Jersey employment during last eight calendar weeks prior to week in which disability began.

	Calendar Week Ending Date	Gross Wages
Calendar Week in Which Disability Began		(Omit This Week)
Prior Week Before Disability		$
2nd Week Before Disability		$
3rd Week Before Disability		$
4th Week Before Disability		$
5th Week Before Disability		$
6th Week Before Disability		$
7th Week Before Disability		$
8th Week Before Disability		$
TOTAL		$

Are you exempt from FICA tax? [ ] Yes [ ] No

10

Firm Name _____   Phone No. _____

Address _____   Signed _____

City, State and Zip Code _____   Official Title _____   Date _____

Mailing Address If Different _____

INSTRUCTIONS FOR PREPARING CLAIM

MAIL THIS CLAIM FORM AS SOON AS POSSIBLE AFTER DISABILITY COMMENCES. No action may be taken toward payments to you, until this claim form is received at the address shown below.

TRY TO GET YOUR PHYSICIAN AND EMPLOYER to complete their portion of the claim while you wait. A great deal of time will be saved in this manner. If this cannot be done, **MAIL THE CLAIM FORM IMMEDIATELY.**

A pregnant woman should file her claim as soon as her pregnancy reaches a stage in which she is unable to continue working.

WARNING

THE LAW REQUIRES **YOU** TO FILE THE CLAIM WITHIN THIRTY DAYS OF THE BEGINNING OF THE DISABILITY. IF THIS CLAIM IS FILED MORE THAN THIRTY (30) DAYS AFTER THE BEGINNING OF THE DISABILITY, BENE-FITS MAY BE DENIED OR REDUCED.

Ignorance of the Law or leaving your claim with your doctor or employer to be mailed in your behalf, are NOT valid excuses for late filing. IT IS YOUR OWN DIRECT PERSONAL RESPONSIBILITY to see that your claim is filed promptly.

RETURN ADDRESS

PLACE
STAMP
HERE

DISABILITY INSURANCE SERVICE
DEPARTMENT OF LABOR
C N 387
TRENTON, N. J.   08625-0387

Figure 11.7 *(cont.)*

487

11.8 APPLICATION FOR SICK LEAVE

The Application for Sick Leave form, shown in Figure 11.8, has been adapted from the Federal government's Application for Leave, Standard Form 71, Office of Personnel Management.

The Application for Sick Leave form, which you might want to consider calling an "Application for Medical Absence," provides the administrative basis for having employees request and obtain advance approval for planned medical absences. For example, an employee who must have surgery faces an extensive period of hospitalization and recuperation. Such an employee requests approval for the planned period of sick leave by designating the dates and hours "from" and "to" in the time block at the top of the form, which also requires specifying the total working hours represented by this proposed absence. The "reason" is shown by checking the box provided for "medical treatment or examination (medical, dental, or optical)." Similarly, short-term absences for medical, dental, or optical examinations or treatments also are approved in advance through this procedure. The employee who is planning to take an afternoon off for an optical examination completes and submits the form to obtain approval for the proposed absence.

The Application for Sick Leave form also is used for "after-the-fact" documentation of absences that result from an "on-the-job injury" or an "off-the-job injury." The form is used initially in these cases to obtain an estimate of the duration of the absence and details concerning the severity of the employee's condition. The form is given to the recently disabled employee, who coordinates completion of the "certification of physician" section by his or her personal physician, and then completes and returns the form to the HRM organization.

The "certification of physician" section is used primarily to verify that an employee was under professional care during the period of an absence, and that a medical condition existed that made it inadvisable for that employee to report for work. Completion of this section by an employee's personal physician or other practitioner is recommended for any absence of three or more working days; this should be a standard requirement which is incorporated in your policy and procedures for paid absences due to employee medical requirements. Absences of less than 3 days under questionable circumstances also may require medical certification, particularly those involving employees who appear to be abusing the company's paid health leave policy with a pattern of extensive short-term absences.

For all cases involving long-term absences, the employee must have his or her personal physician complete the "certification of physician" section of the Application for Sick Leave form. Associated information provides the basis for the employee to return to work, and serves as documentation for the validity of the absence. It specifies the medical basis for the absence, and provides professional assurance that the employee is able to return and resume normal work requirements. Should there be related medical limitations for the returning employee, such as temporary constraints on physical activities or a need for part-time working hours during further recuperation, details are included in the "remarks" portion of this section.

Application for Sick Leave

Name (Last, First, M.I.) _____

Employee I.D. Number _____

Organization _____ Location _____

I hereby request approval for sick leave during the period shown below for the following reason:

	Month	Day	Hour	Total Hours of Absence
From:			A.M.	
			P.M.	
To:			A.M.	
			P.M.	

☐ Illness

☐ Medical Treatment or Examination (Medical, Dental, or Optical)

☐ On-the-Job-Injury

☐ Off-the-Job-Injury

☐ Pregnancy and Confinement

Employee Signature _____ Date _____

☐ Approved ☐ Disapproved

Supervisor Signature _____ Date _____

CERTIFICATION OF PHYSICIAN

Period under professional care (indicate month, day, and year):

From _____ To _____

Remarks:

I certify that this employee was under my professional care for the period indicated above, and that a medical condition during this period made it inadvisable for the employee to report for work.

Signature _____ Date _____

Figure 11.8 Application for sick leave

11.9 SECURITY INCIDENT REPORT

This worksheet offers a structured format for providing the details of a breach of security, and documenting findings and recommendations concerning remedial and strategic corrective actions. The Security Incident Report, (Figure 11.9) is initiated by the employee who identifies the problem, and completed by the individual designated by management to conduct an investigation. This type of investigation assesses immediate action requirements and implications for improved security controls and procedures, and recommends initiatives for management consideration. If your company places responsibility for security with the HRM organization, you will want to take an active role in promoting thorough investigations and sound proposals for corrective action. Use of this Security Incident Report will encourage a systematic approach to this problem-solving process.

Security Incident Report

Reported By: _____ Date: _____ Time: _____ A.M. P.M.

Organization: _____ Phone: Office _____

Location: _____ Home _____

Details   (persons involved, dates, quantity, value, law enforcement agency involved, etc.).

_____

_____

_____

_____

_____

_____

_____

_____

_____

_____

_____

_____

Investigated By: _____ Date: _____

Findings and Recommendations: _____

_____

_____

_____

_____

_____

_____

_____

Figure 11.9 Security incident report

11.10 PERSONAL OR COMPANY PROPERTY LOSS REPORT

The Personal or Company Property Loss Report form (Figure 11.10) offers a standard structure for reporting the theft of employee or company property. Completed by the employee whose personal or company-assigned property is involved, or by a manager who determines that company property assigned to his or her functional area is missing, it fully documents the details of the loss. A full description of the item is provided; serial number and/or other positive identification data is included. Details concerning the time of the loss, value, suspects, and so on are offered. The completed form is given to the HRM organization, where a full security investigation of the incident is initiated. Findings and recommendations are reported to management through the Security Incident Report (refer to Figure 11.9).

An aggressive program of investigating and solving thefts, and providing improved security measures to avoid similar occurrences in the future, is essential for preserving and reinforcing employee morale. The belief that some co-workers are thieves is highly detrimental to positive team efforts. Employees who take all company-recommended steps for safeguarding personal property, yet suffer losses due to inadequate company security measures, will undoubtably expect compensation from the company.

The theft of company property assigned to employees is highly disruptive to morale and productivity. The accounting clerk whose assigned calculator is stolen and the secretary whose typewriter disappears have a common problem. They both face the disruption of not having their principal office machine available to perform their duties, but they also have lost a familiar and comfortable device that, in their eyes, can never be replaced. When the replacement arrives, although it is exactly the same model, things will never be the same again. An "old friend" has been taken away, and the thought that someone has invaded their work area and disrupted their feelings of personal security and comfort is unsettling. Investigations that yield improved office security are essential.

Personal or Company Property Loss Report

Date _____

Name of Complainant _____

Location _____ Organization _____

Telephone Extension _____ Name of Supervisor _____

Description of Item _____

_____

_____

_____

Serial Number _____

   Time last seen _____ A.M. P.M.

   Time discovered missing _____ A.M. P.M.

   Approximate value $ _____

Suspects _____

_____

_____

Additional Information _____

_____

_____

_____

Received By _____ Date _____ Time _____ A.M. P.M.

   Signatures

   Employee _____

   Supervisor _____

Figure 11.10 Personal or company property loss report

CHAPTER 12

Expatriate Employees

This chapter begins with complete guidelines for an expatriate compensation policy that equitably supplements a base salary with a variety of overseas allowances, and provides income tax equalization techniques for ensuring that the overseas employee is not penalized financially. A Sample Company Policy for Expatriate Compensation is given in Section 12.1. Similarly, in Section 12.2, a Sample Company Relocation Policy for Expatriate Employees offers relocation assistance guidelines, which include consideration of special employee needs such as the shipment or purchase of a personal automobile overseas.

To provide a framework for reviewing overall compensation for expatriate employees, an Expatriate Compensation Worksheet is given in Section 12.3. The Tax Reconciliation Worksheet provided in Section 12.4 serves as the basis for comparing company-generated hypothetical tax information versus actual obligations to provide expatriates with "tax equalization" reimbursements.

An Automobile Shipment/Purchase Agreement shown in Section 12.5, provides a record of the company's proportionate equity in an expatriate's personal automobile. When the automobile is sold, the expatriate pays the company a percentage based on the original equity represented by shipment or purchase assistance costs.

A Social Club Membership Proposal form is introduced in Section 12.6 as part of a company policy for providing reimbursement for business-related membership expenses. A related form, the Annual Social Club Dues Claim voucher, is discussed in Section 12.7. It provides the structure for data and calculations that lead to expatriate reimbursement of proportionate overall costs for annual business uses.

Section 12.8 includes a sample Expatriate Home Leave Request form. It is used to administer a policy on providing company-paid vacation travel home for expatriates and their dependents.

12.1 SAMPLE COMPANY POLICY FOR EXPATRIATE COMPENSATION

Expatriate Compensation

I. Objectives

This policy provides uniform guidelines for the compensation of employees who perform services at the company's overseas work locations.

II. Salary Administration

An expatriate employee receives a base salary in accordance with the duties and responsibilities of the assigned position. Excluded from base salary are bonuses and overseas allowances.

III. Tax Equalization

In the interest of equity, the company applies a balance sheet approach to expatriate compensation. This technique ensures that the individual's tax liability neither exceeds nor is less than the amount that would have been incurred if the employee had remained in the United States. The company will, in accordance with this approach, reimburse the expatriate for excess tax liabilities that result from an overseas assignment.

IV. Expatriate Responsibilities

Although the expatriate is personally liable for the submission and payment of foreign and domestic income tax returns, the company will pay the reasonable fees charged by a company-recommended tax consultant for the preparation of employee tax returns. The company will not pay any fines, penalties, or interest for which the expatriate may become liable as a result of such services.

V. Procedures

A. *Estimated Overall Compensation.* The company will provide an expatriate with a detailed estimate of overall compensation, which includes salary, overseas compensation allowances, and a standard withholding amount for taxes and insurance. An Expatriate Compensation Worksheet (see Figure 12.3) provides these data to an expatriate for assessing the amount of total compensation required to meet overseas obligations.

B. *Foreign Tax Payment.* The company recognizes that foreign tax payment obligations do not generally coincide with the U.S. income tax filing schedule. Accordingly, the company will provide assistance to the expatriate in meeting foreign tax payment liabilities through the immediate reimbursement of associated costs.

C. *Annual Tax Reconciliation*
  1. *Employee and Company Prepared Tax Returns.* The expatriate is responsible for providing the company with copies of federal, state, and foreign tax returns. The company will prepare hypothetical federal and state tax returns which estimate the tax liabilities that would have been experienced if the individual was employed in the United States; coordination with the employee will result in the inclusion of data for other income, dividends, interest, and so on.
  2. *Tax Reconciliation Calculations.* The tax reconciliation procedure compares the employee's hypothetical tax with actual expenditures minus any refunds received. When the actual tax exceeds the hypothetical tax, the company reimburses the difference to the expatriate with a "tax equalization" payment. If the actual tax is less than the hypothetical tax, then the employee reimburses the company for the difference. Foreign taxes previously reimbursed to the employee will be accounted for in this process. The Tax Reconciliation Worksheet (see Figure 12.4) computes expatriate/company liability.

VI. Overseas Compensation Allowances

Employees hired for or transferred to a foreign assignment from the United States are eligible for the following overseas compensation allowances:

A. *Incentive Allowance.* The incentive allowance is intended to compensate an employee for working outside of the United States in a foreign environment. The payment recognizes that the expatriate must make extensive adjustments in adapting to new and different customs, laws, working schedules, and so on. The amount of this allowance is equal to 15 percent of the expatriate's annual base salary; the maximum annual base salary amount to be used for computational purposes is $40,000.
B. *Cost-of-Living Allowance.* The cost-of-living allowance is based on a percentage of an employee's annual base salary as determined by the most recent U.S. Department of State "living cost" index for the city and country of assignment. Employees assigned to a country with a negative or par value living cost index value will not receive a cost-of-living allowance. The amount of this allowance will be reviewed each January and adjusted in accordance with living cost index changes.
C. *Housing Allowance.* The housing allowance is computed by deducting an amount equal to 15 percent of the employee's annual base salary from the annual rent incurred at the foreign location. The rental amount may include charges for utilities, trash disposal, garage, property taxes, building maintenance, and, if required by the landlord, the cost of fire and property damage insurance. The following types of housing-related expenses are not reimburseable as rent: decorating or painting, gardening services, maid services, pool maintenance, and insurance for public liability or personal property. A housing allowance will be reviewed and adjusted each January based on changes in annual base salary and rent charges.
D. *Dependent Education Allowance.* This allowance is for the reasonable cost of tuition, books, fees, necessary supplies, and local transportation for dependent

children in grades 1 through 12, or their equivalent. If an adequate school is not within commuting distance, the educational allowance also will include room and board and two round-trip economy fares per year to the nearest adequate school. Dependents who are undergraduate college students are eligible for one (1) round-trip air fare between the foreign assignment location and their college in non-home leave years.

VI. Other Provisions

A. *Home Leave.* Employees on foreign assignment will be eligible for a thirty (30) day home leave upon completion of each twenty-four (24) months of overseas service. Home leave entitlement will accrue at the rate of $1\frac{1}{4}$ days per month, and will take the place of normal vacation entitlement in the home leave year. The company will pay the actual cost of transportation for the employee and authorized dependents to and from their country of origin by direct route, economy class air transportation. The company also will reimburse reasonable incidental expenses incurred while in transit. Time spent in conducting company business during a home leave will be credited toward the home leave entitlement.

B. *Third-Country Nationals.* In cases where an individual is hired in one foreign country for employment in another, that employee will be eligible to receive overseas compensation allowances. In computing a cost-of-living allowance, it will be based on the difference between the living cost indexes for the country of origin and the country of assignment.

C. *Local Conditions.* Managers of foreign company operations must be given maximum flexibility to meet the needs of local laws, practices, customs, and changing conditions. Accordingly, should any provisions of this policy require modification to meet local requirements, implementation of proposed exceptions should be coordinated with the director of human resources.

D. *Other Agreements.* The content of this policy statement is not intended to require the review of existing employment agreements with other provisions.

12.2 SAMPLE COMPANY RELOCATION POLICY FOR EXPATRIATE EMPLOYEES

Expatriate Employee Relocation Plan

I. Objectives

This policy provides a uniformly equitable basis for providing financial assistance to employees who relocate their principal residence overseas as a result of being transferred to another company work location.

II. Moving Expenses

A. The company will assume the reasonable costs of moving an employee's household goods and personal effects.

B. The company will arrange and directly pay packing and crating, in-transit storage, and insurance costs for authorized household goods and personal effects.

C. The company will not assume the costs of moving pets, pianos, hobby equipment of unusual weight or size, boats, valuable jewelry, furs, antiques, firearms, and other such items. Items subject to excessively high customs duties or import restrictions also are excluded.

D. The employee may elect to ship only part of his or her authorized household goods and receive a cash payment in the amount of the saved shipping costs. This amount will be applied toward the purchase of furnishings at the new location.

E. Under unusual circumstances not under the employee's control, such as when a shipment is delayed or housing is not yet ready at the new work location, the director of human resources may authorize company-paid short-term storage for a period not to exceed ninety (90) days.

III. Home Sale

A. At the request of an employee who has been scheduled for relocation, the company shall obtain a minimum of two (2) real estate appraisals and calculate the fair market value of the employee's owned residence. This calculation is based on an average of two appraisals with less than 10 percent variation. The company guarantees that the employee will realize the fair market value that results from this calculation, but the employee is encouraged to find a buyer at a higher price. To qualify for this guarantee the property must be multiple-listed for sale at a mutually agreed upon selling price for a period of at least thirty (30) days. A selling price at or below the fair market value may be authorized by the company to expedite the sale of the property.

B. The company will reimburse an employee for a competitive real estate broker commission incurred in selling the property.

C. The company will reimburse an employee for reasonable mortgage prepayment penalties and normal and customary selling costs.

D. The costs to be reimbursed by the company will be limited to those incurred in the sale of a principal residence. To qualify for these reimbursements, the employee must apply for home sale assistance within three (3) months of accepting a transfer to an overseas work location.

IV. Lease Cancellation

A. The company will reimburse an employee who is leasing a principal residence for the reasonable costs of canceling the lease. Such assistance to a relocated employee includes deposit forfeiture, additional rental payments needed to effect cancellation, and any required legal fees.

B. If an employee elects to sub-lease, providing such action is permitted by the terms of the lease, the company will reimburse costs incurred for a reasonable rental agent fee or advertising costs, and any necessary legal fees.

V. Transportation of Employee and Family

A. For flights not exceeding ten (10) hours, the company will provide direct route, economy air transportation for the employee and members of the employee's immediate family to the area of the new work location. For flights exceeding ten (10) hours scheduled flying time with no overnight stopovers en route, first-class air travel may be provided. Alternatively, the company will reimburse overnight stopover costs for flights where an overnight stopover or plane change is required after ten (10) hours of flying time.

B. Reimburseable transportation costs will include local transportation, meals, and lodging costs incurred during an authorized overnight stopover. The company also will reimburse the cost of incidental travel expenses such as the cost of passports and visas; health and immunization certificates; baggage handling fees and gratuities; and local ground transportation at departure and terminal points. For economy class travel, the Company will reimburse excess baggage charges of up to forty-four (44) pounds for each passenger.

VI. Temporary Living Expenses

A. If an employee precedes his or her family to the overseas work location to begin work and obtain suitable permanent housing, the Company will reimburse reasonable living expenses for a period not to exceed ninety (90) days.

B. The company will reimburse reasonable living expenses for a period not to exceed thirty (30) days if the employee and family relocate to the foreign location prior to the availability of permanent housing.

C. The company may, depending on the circumstances, elect to continue the reimbursement of temporary living expenses beyond the initial thirty (30) day period in cases such as those involving a delay in the shipment of household goods. Any such authorization by the director of human resources will be subject to reimbursement of temporary living expenses less a "differential" for estimated normal living costs.

VII. Overseas Accommodations

A. The company normally discourages the purchase of homes at overseas locations; however, assistance may be provided in cases where the scarcity and high cost of rentals warrant this action. Such assistance shall include the reimbursement of closing costs and associated legal fees. The company will not assume responsibility for employee home disposal costs at the conclusion of an overseas assignment.

B. The company will reimburse employees for legal fees incurred in connection with the leasing of suitable housing at the overseas location. In addition, cash advances may be made to cover rental deposits, "key money," and advance payments. Such cash advances are to be repaid to the company through scheduled deductions.

VIII. Relocation Allowance

A. The company will pay a relocation allowance in the amount of one-half ($\frac{1}{2}$) of a month's pay for single employees, and one (1) month's pay for married employees. This allowance is paid in lump sum at the time when an employee relocates his or her principal residence to the area of the overseas work location. It is intended to assist the employee in meeting the cost of necessary alterations for refitting rugs and draperies, appliance disconnection and reconnection, the costs of moving items excluded in Section II C., and other incidental expenses.

B. The company may supplement the relocation allowance by providing an interest-free loan of up to one (1) month's salary to assist in the purchase of expensive appliances or equipment. Such loans will be repaid within one (1) year of their being granted.

IX. Automobile Assistance

A. The company recognizes that employees transferred overseas may need an automobile for personal transportation, and that the costs of such locally purchased vehicles may be higher than comparable vehicles in the United States. Considering the numerous variables involved—that is, import restrictions, high customs duties, and the prices of local cars for any given country, the company will decide appropriate assistance to be provided on a case-by-case basis.

B. By comparing the total cost of shipping and customs duties with the combined costs of a "forced sale" loss reimbursement and assistance for the purchase of a comparable car overseas, the company may find it more economical to ship an employee's car. In such cases, the company will assume all charges for preparation, handling, and documents; freight; loading; unloading; pick-up and delivery; shipping insurance; customs duties and other direct expenses of importation.

C. When local purchase at the foreign location is authorized, the company will reimburse the employee for the amount by which the purchase price exceeds the normal retail price of a comparable car in the United States.

D. The company will reimburse the employee for any forced sale loss incurred in selling the car prior to relocating overseas. The amount of such loss will be determined by taking the difference between the price actually received and the retail price value of the "NADA Official Used Car Guide." The maximum limit for forced sale reimbursement will be 20 percent of the NADA retail/value.

E. The company will maintain an equity in any car for which shipping or purchase assistance is granted. When the employee sells such a car at the foreign location, he or she must reimburse the company for its proportionate equity in the car. The amount of this reimbursement will not exceed the amount originally paid by the company for shipping or purchase assistance costs.

F. The company will provide such assistance on a one-time basis, and only for one automobile per employee.

X. Termination of Employment

A. Should the company terminate the employment of an expatriate, or if an expatriate who has been on assignment for at least one (1) year resigns with proper notice, Sections II, IV, V, and IX E of this policy will apply. Such expense reimbursements are intended to promptly return the employee, dependents, and personal possessions to their original departure point in the United States.

B. If the company terminates the employment of an expatriate for cause, or if the expatriate resigns before serving a minimum of one (1) year or without proper notice, Sections II A, II B, V, and IX E will apply. Return transportation to the original point of departure in the United States will be by direct route, economy class air transportation.

XI. Treatment of Taxable Relocation Expenses

Because some of the relocation expenses reimbursed by the company are considered to be wages for U.S. income tax purposes, such payments are subject to withholding taxes. Accordingly, the company will 'gross up" the employee's base earnings to offset this tax liability.

XII. Administration

These policies and procedures will be administered by the director of human resources. Employees will be required to prepare Relocation Expense Report forms (refer to Figure 10.2) for all reimburseable expenses, and to submit them to their management for review and approval. Final review and approval will be made by the director of human resources.

12.3 EXPATRIATE COMPENSATION WORKSHEET: PLANNING OVERSEAS COMPENSATION

An Expatriate Compensation Worksheet (Figure 12.3) is used by the HRM organization for developing an estimate of the expatriate employee's overall compensation. The worksheet is used initially to explain the benefits yielded by overseas compensation allowances to a prospective expatriate employee. It subsequently serves as the basis for providing the expatriate employee with an annual update of estimated benefits.

The worksheet also offers the data needed by an expatriate for planning overseas salary payment requirements. To meet tax and insurance deduction requirements through withholding an appropriate amount of salary, a company stipulates a minimum ratio for U.S. versus overseas salary payments. For example, the salary payment ratio may be designated as 25 percent U.S. and 75 percent overseas. Any flexibility provided by company policy, concerning an appropriate proportion for overseas salary payments, is used by the expatriate in increasing the amount of U.S. salary payment to include some or all of the compensation not needed to meet overseas expenses.

The sample Expatriate Compensation Worksheet provides a rudimentary framework for demonstrating the impact of overseas compensation allowances on overall compensation. In the case of a prospective expatriate employee, the "base salary" shown on the worksheet includes any proposed increase that is being offered as part of the inducements to accept the transfer. Accordingly, exact incentive allowance and cost-of-living allowance calculations are possible. The calculation of the amount shown for housing allowance either is based on an "estimated rent" which is obtained by analyzing the monthly payments authorized for other expatriates at that location, or by obtaining an estimate from local management concerning the price for suitable accommodations. Similarly, information on the educational requirements of the expatriate's dependent children is provided to local management for preparation of cost estimate data needed for determining dependent education allowance(s). The estimated cost of college student transportation for an expatriate's dependent is prepared by the HRM organization. Worksheet entries are summarized in the "total base salary and allowances" amount, which is reduced by a 25 percent deduction for "standard estimated withholding" to account for tax and insurance payment requirements. The result is "total net pay." The lower portion of the form is used to show the payment ratio and associated amounts of U.S. and overseas compensation.

Expatriate Compensation Worksheet

Name _____ Social Security No. _____

Position Title _____

Organization _____ Location _____

	ANNUAL	MONTHLY
1. BASE SALARY	$_____	$_____

2. OVERSEAS COMPENSATION ALLOWANCES:

Incentive Allowance
(15% of Annual Base Salary to $40,000) _____ _____

Cost-of-Living Allowance _____ % Index
(Living Cost Index % × Annual Base Salary) _____ _____

Housing Allowance $_____ Estimated Rent
(Annual Rent—15% of Annual Base Salary) _____ _____

Dependent Education Allowance(s)
(Tuition, Fees, Books & Supplies, and
Transportation and/or Room and Board) _____ _____

College Student Transportation
(Annual Trip Overseas) _____ _____

Automobile Assistance
(Forced Sale and Purchase Allowances) _____ _____

3. TOTAL BASE SALARY & ALLOWANCES (1 + 2 = 3) _____ _____

4. DEDUCTIONS
Standard Estimated Withholding
(25% of Annual Base Salary for Taxes and Insurance) _____ _____

5. TOTAL NET PAY (3 – 4 = 5) _____ _____

_____ % PAYABLE IN U.S.
(U.S. $) $_____ $_____

_____ % PAYABLE OVERSEAS
(LOCAL CURRENCY) $_____ $_____

100 % TOTAL $_____ $_____

Figure 12.3 Expatriate compensation worksheet

12.4 TAX RECONCILIATION WORKSHEET: THE BASIS FOR A TAX EQUALIZATION PAYMENT

The sample Tax Reconciliation Worksheet (Figure 12.4) offers a framework for comparing actual versus hypothetical taxes. Because the structures of federal and state income tax return forms change from year to year, a review of this format should be made by tax accounting professionals to determine necessary enhancements. Use this sample as a departure point for creating a current and complete worksheet.

The basic concept demonstrated by the worksheet is a systematic comparison of the hypothetical tax obligation that the expatriate would have had if he or she had not accepted the overseas assignment versus the actual tax obligations that resulted. The worksheet is prepared in April of each year, or sooner if the expatriate is able to file a U.S. tax return early, to assess and reimburse the consequences of actual tax payment obligations.

The worksheet is structured to provide a hypothetical tax calculation which excludes overseas compensation allowances and includes consideration of state income tax. The actual data include consideration of the economic impact of overseas compensation allowances and relocation expense reimbursements on U.S. federal income tax; the amount of foreign taxes paid also is included.

If the hypothetical tax amount is less than the actual tax obligation, the company reimburses the employee for the difference. This "tax equalization" amount, which is subject to deduction for previously reimbursed foreign tax payments, is paid to the employee with a 20 percent "gross up" to compensate for associated tax consequences. The full amount of this additional salary payment is considered in the next Tax Reconciliation Worksheet.

Tax Reconciliation Worksheet

Expatriate _____ Tax Year _____

FEDERAL INCOME TAX	Actual	Hypothetical
A. Base Annual Salary	$_____	$_____
B. Overseas Compensation Allowances	_____	_____
C. Other Income	_____	_____
D. TOTAL INCOME (A + B + C = D)	_____	_____
E. Adjustments to Income	(_____)	(_____)
F. ADJUSTED GROSS INCOME D – E = F)	_____	_____
G. Less Itemized Deductions	(_____)	(_____)
H. Less Exemptions	(_____)	(_____)
I. TAXABLE INCOME (F – G – H = I)	_____	_____
J. Federal Tax	_____	_____
K. Tax Credits	_____	_____
L. Other Taxes	_____	_____
M. TOTAL FEDERAL TAX (J – K + L = M)	_____	_____

STATE INCOME TAX

A. Federal Adjusted Gross Income		_____
B. Less Itemized Deductions		(_____)
C. Less Exemptions		(_____)
D. TAXABLE INCOME (A – B – C = D)		_____
E. STATE TAX		_____
F. Tax Credits		(_____)
G. Other Taxes		_____
H. TOTAL STATE TAX (E – F + G = H)		_____

FOREIGN TAX

_____

TOTALS _____ _____

AMOUNT DUE EXPATRIATE/COMPANY $_____

Figure 12.4 Tax reconciliation worksheet

12.5 AUTOMOBILE SHIPMENT/PURCHASE AGREEMENT (DEFINING COMPANY EQUITY RIGHTS)

This sample Automobile Shipment/Purchase Agreement, as shown in Figure 12.5, is designed for confirming expatriate employee understanding and agreement of the terms and conditions for company-sponsored automobile shipment or purchase assistance.

The agreement begins with a confirmation of the type of assistance which the company has authorized. Full descriptions of shipment and purchase options are provided. The expatriate then agrees, in consideration for the specified type of assistance, that the company has proportionate equity in the personal automobile. The method to be used in computing the "equity percentage" is defined. When the automobile is sold in the future, the employee pays the company a portion of the sale price which corresponds to this equity percentage. To allow the expatriate to fully benefit from any appreciation of value, it is stipulated that this amount will not exceed the dollar value of the company's assistance.

Although the company has financial interest in the automobile, the employee agrees to pay all required costs for insurance coverage. It is stipulated that minimum coverage amounts will be specified by the company.

Federal income tax treatment of this type of assistance and its implications for the company and the expatriate should be reviewed with tax accounting professionals. The tax consequences of company-sponsored automobile shipment costs and cash payments for employee purchases of automobiles, payments which might be defined as loans in view of the pay back provision, should be thoroughly explored.

Automobile Shipment/Purchase Agreement

In accordance with the provisions of the "automobile assistance" portion of the Expatriate Employee Relocation Plan, the company has authorized me to (check appropriate section):

☐ Have my personal automobile shipped at the company's expense to my overseas residence. It is my understanding that the company will pay all costs for preparation, handling, and documents; freight; loading; unloading; pick-up and delivery; shipping insurance; customs duties and other direct expenses of importation.

☐ Purchase a personal automobile in the vicinity of my overseas residence, and receive reimbursement from the company for the amount by which the purchase price exceeds the normal retail price of a comparable car in the United States.

In consideration of this assistance, I hereby acknowledge and agree that the company has proportionate equity in my personal automobile. Such equity shall be based either on the percentage yielded by comparing the overall cost of shipping the automobile with the U.S. retail value of the automobile at the time of shipment, or the amount represented by the company's reimbursement to me with the purchase price of the automobile, whichever is appropriate to the assistance provided.

It is understood and agreed that when I sell this automobile, I will promptly remit to the company that portion of the sale price that corresponds to the company's equity percentage. It is further understood that the amount to be repaid to the company shall not exceed the amount originally paid on my behalf for shipment costs or paid to me for purchase assistance.

I hereby agree to maintain and pay all costs for automobile insurance, which includes adequate collision, comprehensive, theft, and liability coverage. Appropriate minimum amounts of coverage shall be prescribed by the company.

By: _____   _____
                        Employee   Date

Accepted By: _____   _____
                     Director of Human Resources   Date

Figure 12.5 Automobile shipment/purchase agreement

12.6 SOCIAL CLUB MEMBERSHIP PROPOSAL

In recognition that it is customary for professionals and managers to participate in social clubs at many overseas locations, companies may reimburse expatriate employees for membership costs. Such reimbursements include social club membership initiation fees, dues, and assessments.

The Social Club membership Proposal form (Figure 12.6) is completed by an expatriate employee to request company approval of membership in a particular social club. Full particulars of costs are specified, and a detailed explanation of the benefits realized by the company is provided. The director of human resources has the responsibility for coordinating with the expatriate's management to review the proposal, to assess the proposal in comparison with membership assistance being provided to other expatriates, and to make a decision concerning the suitability of this request.

In addition to stipulating that the business efforts of a company be promoted through the employee's affiliation, policies may include a provision that reimbursements be proportionate to the amount of business use.

Social Club Membership Proposal

Expatriate _____ Date _____

Position Title _____

Organization _____ Location _____

Name of Club _____

Location _____

Membership Fee (Initial Charge) _____ (U.S. $)

Monthly Dues/Assessments _____ (U.S. $)

Do members have equity? ☐ No ☐ Yes Explain: _____

_____

Describe the benefits that the company will realize through your membership. Give specifics concerning business contacts and potential business contacts who are members of this club (specify names, their business affiliations, and their titles). What prestige and reputation does the club have in the community? Is it the type of site that promotes acceptances of invitations for luncheon/dinner meetings?

_____

_____

_____

_____

_____

_____

_____

_____

_____

This proposal ☐ is ☐ is not approved for employee reimbursement of proportionate annual membership costs based on business usage.

_____   _____
Director of Human Resources   Date

Figure 12.6 Social club membership proposal

12.7 ANNUAL SOCIAL CLUB DUES CLAIM

The Social Club Dues Claim form (Figure 12.7) offers an annual accounting technique for expatriates who are authorized to be reimbursed for social club membership costs in proportion to business use. The structure of this sample form requires the expatriate employee to provide data for calculating the appropriate reimbursement.

The expatriate specifies the number of times during the year the club was used for "business" and "personal" reasons. The resultant "total times used" is compared with the number of business uses to calculate the "percentage of business use." This percentage is applied toward a "total dues and assessments paid" amount to calculate the "business portion of dues and assessments." To support this reimbursement request, the expatriate reports the details of each business use ("date," "persons entertained," and "business purpose").

Additional pages of the Social Club Dues Claim form are used as needed for a complete accounting of all business uses throughout the year. Receipts for payments are attached. Monthly overseas payments shown on receipts are converted by the expatriate into equivalent U.S. dollars by using exchange rates in effect on respective dates.

Social Club Dues Claim— _____
                            Year

Page _____ of _____ Pages

Date _____

Expatriate _____   Social Security No. _____

Name and Location of Club _____

Number of Times Club Used During Year	Business Use Calculation
A. Business _____	D. Percentage of Business Use _____
B. Personal _____	E. Total Dues and Assessments Paid $ _____
C. Total Times Used _____	F. Business Portion of Dues and Assessments $ _____
$\frac{A}{C}$ = % of Business Use = D	D × E = F

Date	Persons Entertained	Business Purpose

I certify that this information is correct and complete.

_____   _____
            Signature   Date

Approved: _____   _____
        Director of Human Resources   Date

Figure 12.7 Social club dues claim

12.8 EXPATRIATE HOME LEAVE REQUEST

As part of planning a home leave, which is provided every other year in 24-month intervals, the overseas employee prepares an Expatriate Home Leave Request form (Figure 12.8). The form should be provided to management for review and approval at least 45 days prior to the proposed departure date.

To complete the form, the expatriate provides the dates needed by management in order to verify his or her eligibility for the proposed company-paid home leave. Information also is provided on the dependents who will accompany the expatriate employee. Approval of the form serves as an authorization for company-paid economy class airfares and incidental travel expense reimbursements for these members of the employee's immediate family.

The expatriate also provides details of proposed travel plans in the "itinerary" section of the form. Time designated for visiting company work locations to conduct business is not charged against the 30-day home leave authorization. This detailed information on travel plans is essential for contacting the employee if an emergency situation develops at the work location during this period of extended absence. If the employee's planned itinerary changes, a revised copy of the form is provided to management.

Expatriate Home Leave Request

Name _____ Position _____

Organization _____ Location _____

Month previous home leave completed _____, 19_____

Month eligible for home leave _____, 19_____

Dates of proposed home leave   From _____ To _____

Names of dependents who will accompany you (specify ages of children)

_____   _____

_____   _____

_____   _____

_____   _____

ITINERARY—Show your planned schedule. If changes occur, please prepare and provide a revised itinerary to your management.

| Dates | | Destination | Mode of Travel |
Arrival	Departure	City and Country	

Approvals: Dates:

_____ - _____

_____ - _____

Figure 12.8 Expatriate home leave request

CHAPTER 13

Termination of Employment

This chapter provides suggested approaches for processing both company and employee-initiated termination of employment actions, conducting exit interviews, and providing outplacement assistance. Detailed guidance begins with a sample company policy on Termination of Employment in Section 13.1. Its procedures require detailed written warnings to employees whose performance is unsatisfactory. They are given every reasonable opportunity to achieve specified improvements within designated time frames before being faced with company-initiated termination action. The policy also provides an example of how termination allowances may be calculated, and outlines termination clearance procedures which include an exit interview by a representative of the HRM organization.

The Separation Questionnaire referred to in this policy is explained in Section 13.2. Completed by employees who resign of their own volition to accept other employment opportunities, it offers the data needed for identifying problem areas and developing initiatives for reducing controllable turnover. Associated comments and suggestions are explored in depth during the exit interviews that subsequently are conducted with each of these employees.

Sample exit interview instructions are provided in Section 13.3, the Structured Exit Interview Format. The format specifies required actions in a logical sequence to ensure that all actions are completed in the exit interview process. For example, the HRM representative begins by verifying termination allowance provisions, then determines that all clearance requirements have been satisfied, and concludes the exit interview by offering appropriate outplacement assistance such as résumé review or development. Helping terminated executives, managers, and professionals to prepare effective résumés is discussed in Section 13.4, Sample Resume Format: Outplacement Assistance. Suggestions about how résumés should be written and formatted are demonstrated with a sample résumé; the recommended approach is carefully calculated to generate employer interest and interviews.

To further assist these terminated key employees in obtaining other employment, they should be given a copy of the current Executive Search Consultants listing shown in Figure 13.5, which includes the names and addresses of all members of the Association of Executive Search Consultants, Inc. As explained in Section 13.5, this listing is used by the terminated executive as the basis for a direct mail campaign to some of these executive search firms. Appropriate cover letters that incorporate suggested wording are used to send résumés to develop employment opportunities. For those lower-level professionals whose backgrounds are not of interest to executive search firms, referral to "professional employment agency" firms is recommended. To provide more effective outplacement counseling to these individuals, they should be made fully aware of the distinctions that exist among the varied types of firms that provide employment assistance. The basis for providing this type of guidance is offered in Section 13.6, Sample Professional Employment Agency Agreement: Professionals Place Professionals.

13.1 SAMPLE COMPANY POLICY FOR TERMINATION OF EMPLOYMENT

Termination of Employment

I. Objectives

This policy provides procedural guidance for processing termination of employment actions at the company headquarters office.

II. Definitions

Termination of employment actions are defined as follows:

1. *Resignation*—an employee decides, of his or her own volition, to terminate company employment.
2. *Release*—the company decides to terminate the employment of an individual due to unsatisfactory work performance or improper conduct.
3. *Retirement*—an employee decides to exercise annuitant rights accrued in the company pension plan.
4. *Reduction of Staff*—the company decides to terminate the employment of an individual whose services no longer are required due to changed workloads or organizational realignments.

III. Termination Action

The "termination" section of a Personnel Change Notice Authorization Form (see Figure 9.11) is used to process these actions. The form should be initiated as far as possible in advance of the employee's last day in the office in order to facilitate timely processing and payroll actions.

IV. Warning Notice

A. To the maximum extent possible, employees are to be advised of their unsatisfactory performance, specific types of improvements that are required, and the time in which specified improvements must be demonstrated.
B. Company performance appraisal forms and "warning notice" memoranda to the employee (with a copy to the director of human resources for the employee's personnel file) are used for documenting required performance improvements.
C. Provided that a written warning is provided to the employee, continued failure to meet performance requirements will lead to termination-of-employment action.

V. Termination Allowances

A. In cases where circumstances warrant the granting of a termination allowance, such as when organizational realignments require reduction-of-staff action, the following guidelines shall apply:

1. An allowance of two (2) weeks pay in lieu of notice for immediate separation.
2. Severance allowance based on one (1) week of pay for each full year of company service.

B. Employees eligible for early retirement at the time of company-initiated termination will not receive a severance allowance.

VI. Vacation Pay

Employees who resign and employees whose services are terminated by the company due to reduction of staff or unsatisfactory work performance will be entitled to pay for any unused vacation allowance.

VII. Termination Clearance

A. An employee must report to the HRM division to obtain final clearance during the last day in the office. A final paycheck may not be released until clearance requirements have been met.

B. The "clearance" portion of the employee's Personal Change Notice Authorization is used for recording the completion of clearance actions as follows:
1. The employee's immediate supervisor is responsible for collecting office equipment, keys, and company documents.
2. The accounting department will ensure that the employee has submitted all travel vouchers and reimbursed the company for any outstanding balances, returned all company credit cards, and made settlement for any obligations such as personal telephone bills.
3. The HRM division will ensure that all required clearances have been obtained as part of the exit interview process.

C. The HRM division will conduct an exit interview with the employee to provide detailed information on any pay in lieu of notice, severance pay, and vacation pay allowances; to discuss payroll continuation versus lump-sum payment options where appropriate; and to review unemployment compensation procedures with employees whose services are terminated by the company.

D. For each employee who resigns, the exit interview process will be preceded by the employee's completion of a Separation Questionnaire (see Figure 13.2). The completed questionnaire is used in the exit interview for discussing problem areas within the company. This Structured Exit Interview Format (see Figure 13.3) yields recommended management actions for retaining those highly productive employees who are necessary for ensuring the continued success of the company.

13.2 SEPARATION QUESTIONNAIRE: PROBING THE REASONS FOR VOLUNTARY SEPARATIONS

Separation Questionnaire

We are sorry that you have decided to leave the company for another employment opportunity, but wish you every success in your new position. It would be very helpful to us if you would take a few minutes to complete this Separation Questionnaire. Your candid assessments of company working conditions and problem areas are needed. The information you provide will be used to propose changes needed to encourage other highly skilled and productive employees to remain with the company. Please bring your completed questionnaire to your exit interview with the HRM division. You need not identify yourself on this form; whether or not you provide your name, your responses are CONFIDENTIAL information for use only by the HRM division.

1. Why did you decide to leave the company?

2. What factors contributed to your decision to leave the company?

3. What types of improvements are offered by your new position?

4. Please describe your immediate supervisor's leadership abilities. If problems are in evidence, what kind of solutions are needed?

5. Did the company provide you with adequate opportunities for personal development? Consider new and challenging assignments, educational experiences, formal education, etc.

6. Consider the good and bad aspects of your job. What were its strong and weak points?

7. Do you feel that you made some significant contributions to the company? Please summarize your major accomplishments.

8. Please describe the feelings of your fellow employees about the Company. What major changes do they want to improve working conditions and their career prospects?

9. Considering the types of changes that are needed by the company, what specific changes would have encouraged you to stay with the company?

10. Are company benefits and compensation competitive compared with those offered by your new company? If not, please explain how the company should improve these programs.

11. What company policies require improvement to make them more competitive? What changes would you recommend?

Many thanks for your comments and advice. You may be assured that your CONFIDENTIAL responses will be used to improve the company's human relations activities.

Name (Optional) _____ Date _____

Organization _____ Location _____

Figure 13.2 Separation questionnaire

13.3 STRUCTURED EXIT INTERVIEW FORMAT

Exit Interview

Employee _____ Social Security No. _____

Position Title _____

Organization _____ Location _____

Immediate Supervisor
(Name & Title) _____

Last date in office   _____

Pay in lieu of notice   _____   Workdays

Severance allowance   _____   Workdays

Vacation pay   _____   Workdays
                 _____

        Total   _____   Workdays

Last Date on Payroll   _____

---

1. Review terms and conditions shown in the TERMINATION section of the Personnel Change Notice Authorization form. Ensure that termination allowance (workdays) for pay in lieu of notice, severance pay, and vacation pay are correct by entering data above and using the calendar to compute "last date on payroll." Determine whether any vacation days have been taken since the allowance was computed; if so, make corrections. If circumstances permit retention of the employee on "payroll continuation" status, and unless the employee requests a "lump-sum payment," indicate this action on the form. After all revisions have been made in the termination section of the form, and after the clearance section is completed, provide a copy to payroll for implementing appropriate action.

2. Use the clearance section of the Personnel Change Notice Authorization form as a checklist for ensuring that all required actions have been completed. Contact the employee's immediate supervisor to verify that keys, documents, office equipment, and books have been returned. Contact the accounting department to verify that the employee has made settlement for obligations such as a personal phone bill, has submitted all travel and expense vouchers and reimbursed the company for any outstanding balances, and has returned all company credit cards. Collect the employee's I.D. card and any other items that were not provided to the immediate supervisor or the accounting department.

3. For Resignations—Review the completed Separation Questionnaire with the individual. Go through the questionnaire on a question-by-question basis, and comment on each response. Build rapport with statements such as "I understand what led to your

Figure 13.3 Structured exit interview format

continued

decision . . . ," "That was a difficult choice . . . ," "I know how you felt . . . ," etc., but also use statements such as "What do you mean by . . . ," "Were there any other factors . . . ," etc., as needed to clarify or expand answers. To fully benefit from the individual's comments and suggestions, we must invest the time to fully understand the individual's intentions. Based on your evaluation of the employee's overall responses, summarize the reasons why this individual decided to resign:

A. Problems with company employment

B. Solutions offered by new employment

4. In all cases, make sure that you represent the company in the most favorable manner possible under the circumstances. When appropriate to the type of termination, offer outplacement services such as reviewing the individual's résumé to suggest improved format and content, suggesting the names of your employment agency contacts that might be able to provide placement assistance, etc. Make sure that you do all that is professionally and humanly possible to make the best of these difficult circumstances.

HRM Representative _____ Date _____

_____

Note: See Figure 9.11 for a sample Personnel Change Notice Authorization form.

Figure 13.3 *(cont.)*

13.4 SAMPLE RÉSUMÉ FORMAT: OUTPLACEMENT ASSISTANCE

A valuable outplacement service to executives, managers, and professionals provides assistance in the development of an effective résumé or reviews an existing résumé to suggest revisions of format and content. There are undoubtably many successful approaches to résumé formatting and writing techniques, but the perspective offered in this section is that of the author who has screened hundreds of thousands of different types of résumés during the past 28 years.

As demonstrated in the sample résumé shown in Figure 13.4, here are some pointers for effective résumé development:

- Place yourself in the role of the individual who is "screening" résumés to identify qualified candidates. The magic words have to jump off the page within seconds or the résumé is disqualified.
- A résumé should be ideally limited to one page. If the individual has extensive experience, then a two-page résumé may be justified. If an individual's experience cannot be contained within two pages, it is not worth recording.
- The heading of the résumé should include complete contact information—that is, home address, home telephone number, and office telephone number. Job-hunting reality dictates that it is easier to acquire a new position if an individual is still employed in another. An office telephone number on a résumé connotes employment. Accordingly, an HRM division office telephone number should be used on résumés of former employees who received outplacement assistance. As calls are received at this number, which is identified by using the company's name rather than an organizational designation, messages are taken for individuals who are "out of the office." This type of outplacement assistance includes calling former employees at their homes regarding such messages.
- A "career objective" should be specified. This objective should be short and sweet—the position title is usually sufficient. If the individual is interested in a variety of positions, two or three job titles may be shown, for example, general accountant/internal auditor/financial analyst. A preferred alternative would be to leave the space for the title blank, then, as a specific position is applied for, the individual inserts the exact title.
- Information concerning education is placed either after the "background" section, or in the beginning of the résumé after the "objective" section. This decision depends on how important a certain education is for certain types of positions. Education is a high priority on a résumé for an individual with minimal experience. This also may be the case for an individual with extensive experience who is applying for management positions; graduate degree credentials and graduation from the "right" colleges and universities can play a major role in the executive selection process. When these types of considerations are encountered, "education" should be placed after the "objective" section. In all other cases, one is well advised to place "education" after the section on "background". This sequence serves to assure the interested reader that the individual has the requisite academic background.
- Experience should be presented by the years in which it was acquired (months and days are details appropriate for Employment Applications). The name of the company, city, and state are sufficient identification. Make sure that the

position title is at the beginning of each experience statement for providing focus, then identify major duties, responsibilities, and achievements. Emphasize the last or the most important position held with each employer; complete details of all the positions held are usually counterproductive. An exception would be where the individual performed in a wide variety of developmental positions as a participant in a management development program. Mentioning this type of participation and giving the position titles emphasizes the individual's versatility. To describe duties and responsibilities, use action words such as directed, formulated, designed, established, and conducted. Use the present tense to describe the current position. Show budgetary and assigned staff statistics as needed to emphasize managerial capabilities.

It is in the best interests of all concerned for the company to type and provide about 100 copies of the résumé to an individual who receives this type of outplacement assistance. If the individual obtains other employment in time, costly impact on the company's unemployment insurance experience ratio may be avoided.

John T. Richards
186 Birch Street
Edison, N.J. 08832
Telephone: (201) 549-8319—Home
                       (201) 548-7230—Office

OBJECTIVE: Manufacturing Manager—Packaging Machinery

BACKGROUND:

1979–Present   MAREX INCORPORATED, Piscataway, N.J.

As Manufacturing Manager, responsible for production of special purpose machinery for packaging consumer goods. Expertise in blister packing technology. Direct workforce of 176 engaged in producing heat seal and trimming machines to support annual sales of $52 million. Designer of innovative production line improvements which yielded savings of $475,000 during past year. Serve as Co-Chairperson of marketing strategy task force. Prior responsibilities for 4 years as Production Engineering Superintendent.

1974–1979   PLASTIX TECHNOLOGY, INC., Cleveland, Ohio

As Manager—Automation Design Department, responsible for team of 10 machine design engineers engaged in developing state-of-the-art blister packaging technology. Efforts were responsible for the introduction of the PLASTICON 6400, an automated device that reduced human resource requirements by 80 percent while increasing productivity by 50 percent. Moved to MAREX Incorporated to accept production-oriented engineering management position.

EDUCATION:

Ohio State University, Cleveland, Ohio

B.S. in Mechanical Engineering—1974
(Graduated with Highest Honors)

PERSONAL:

- Excellent health

- Willing to relocate

- Active in community as Chairperson of Exchange Club and Vice Chairperson for Fund Raising—Edison Council, Boy Scouts of America

- Hobbies include sailing, restoring vintage automobiles, and amateur radio (W2IUX)

Figure 13.4 Sample résumé format

13.5 LISTING OF EXECUTIVE SEARCH FIRMS: ASSISTING DISPLACED EXECUTIVES

A listing of current executive search consultant members is provided in Figure 13.5 courtesy of the Association of Executive Search Consultants, Inc. To provide outplacement assistance to displaced executives and high-level professionals, a copy of this listing should be given to them for their reference.

Executive search consulting firms assist client companies in the identification, evaluation, and selection of executives. They only work for client companies on a fee-paid basis; they do not work on behalf of individuals who are seeking employment. The Association of Executive Search Consultants, Inc. was founded in 1959. Its goals are to (1) define and communicate the role of the professional search consultant, (2) establish and uphold a code of ethics for appropriate professional conduct, and (3) expand and share the body of knowledge accumulated through the professional development of member firms.

Although executive search consulting firms do not solicit résumés, an approach for contacting them is to encourage the executive to prepare a special résumé cover letter. The letter should include terminology such as: I am considering new challenges that will capitalize on my major accomplishments as (position title) of (name of company). Representative achievements include (bullets and short descriptions). If one of your current search requirements offers this type of growth opportunity, please do not hesitate to contact me. My résumé is enclosed for your confidential consideration."

BARGER & SARGEANT, INC.
One Bicentennial Square
Concord, NH 03301

Industries served:

    Financial Services
    Health Care
    High Technology
    Manufacturing
    Retailing
    Service Business

BATTALIA & ASSOCIATES, INC./EURAM CONSULTANTS
    GROUP, LTD.
275 Madison Avenue
New York, NY 10016

Industries served: most, with emphasis in:

    Apparel
    Chemicals
    Computer Manufacturing
    Consumer Products
    Financial Services
    Paper and Packaging
    Pharmaceuticals
    Retail
    Telecommunications and Electronics

MARTIN H. BAUMAN ASSOCIATES, INC.
410 Park Avenue, Suite 1600
New York, NY 10022

Industries served:

    Consumer Products
    Cosmetics
    Distribution
    Financial Services
    High Technology
    Textiles
    Transportation

BIESTEK & PASINI, INC.
1011 East Touhy Avenue
Des Plaines, IL 60018

Industries served:

    Chemicals
    Consumer Products
    Defense/Military
    Electronics
    Financial Services
    Health Care
    Telecommunications
    Utilities

BOWDEN & COMPANY, INC.
5000 Rockside Road
Cleveland, OH 44131

Industries served: most, with emphasis in:

    Banking
    High Technology

    Hospital and Health
    Industrial and Consumer Manufacturing
    Insurance

BOYDEN INTERNATIONAL
260 Madison Avenue, Suite 2000
New York, NY 10016

Industries served: all

THE BRAND COMPANY, INC.
12740 North River Road
Mequon, WI 53092

Industries served:

    Automotive, Agricultural and Construction
        Machinery
    Chemical
    Consumer Products
    Electrical Utilities and Electronics
    Financial and Banking
    Fluid Power
    Food and Beverage
    Graphic Arts, Printing, and Publishing
    Heavy and Light Machinery
    Legal
    Metal Fabrication
    Primary Metals
    Pulp and Paper

CHRISTENSON & MONTGOMERY
466 Southern Boulevard
Chatham, NJ 07928

Industries served: various, including the following
    concentrations:

    Financial Services
    Health Care
    Manufacturing
    Real Estate

CONSULTANTS FOR CORPORATE MANAGEMENT, INC.
P.O. Box 4649
210 West Stone Avenue
Greenville, SC 29608

Industries served:

    Banking
    High Tech Electronics
    Industrial, Commercial, and Residential
        Construction
    Manufacturing
    Resort/Land Development

DEVINE, BALDWIN & PETERS, INC.
250 Park Avenue
New York, NY 10177

Industries served:

    Banking
    Consumer Products Manufacturing
    Industrial Products Manufacturing
    Law
    Public Sector (Foundations, etc.)

Figure 13.5 Executive search consultants

continued

ROBERT W. DINGMAN COMPANY, INC.
32131 West Lindero Canyon Road
Westlake Village, CA 91361

Industries served:

Aerospace
Construction and Engineering
Consumer Products
Electronics
Financial Services
Manufacturing
Non-Profit (charitable, religious, etc.)
Transportation

LEON A. FARLEY ASSOCIATES
468 Jackson Street
San Francisco, CA 94111

Industries served: all, with particular strengths in:

Distribution
Energy
Financial Services
Health Care
Professional Services (Law, General Management Consulting, Public Accounting, etc.)
Technology Based Industries (Communications, Computers, Biotechnology, Instrumentation, etc.)
Transportation

FLEMING ASSOCIATES, INC.
1428 Franklin Street
P.O. Box 604
Columbus, IN 47202

Industries served: all with emphasis on:

Advertising and Publishing
Colleges and Universities
Consumer Products
Electronics and Metals Manufacturing
Energy
Financial Services
Health Care
Pharmaceuticals
Venture Capital

FOSTER & ASSOCIATES, INC.
601 California Street
San Francisco, CA 94108

Industries served:

Consumer Products
Distribution
Engineering—Technology
Financial Services
Forest Products
Resource Recovery—Energy
Transportation
Utility

JAY GAINES & COMPANY
598 Madison Avenue
New York, NY 10022

Industries served:

Commercial Banking
Financial Services
Information and Technology
Investment Banking
Management Consulting
Telecommunications

GAROFOLO, CURTISS & COMPANY
326 W. Lancaster Avenue
Ardmore, PA 19003

Industries served:

Banks
Consulting Firms
HMOs
Hospitals
Insurance Companies
Medical Schools
Physician Groups
Rehabilitation Centers
Universities
Utility Companies

GOULD & MCCOY, INC.
551 Madison Avenue
New York, NY 10022

Industries served:

Apparel
Bioengineering
Consumer Packaged Goods
Energy
Financial Services (Commercial Banking, Insurance, Real Estate, Consumer Finance, etc.)
High Technology
Industrial
Non-Profit Organizations
Pharmaceutical/Health Care
Research and Development
Telecommunications

HALBRECHT ASSOCIATES, INC.
1200 Summer Street
Stamford, CT 06905

Industries served:

Artificial Intelligence
Computer Software
Financial Services
High Technology (Robotics, Automation, etc.)
Manufacturing
Telecommunications

Figure 13.5 *(cont.)*

HALEY ASSOCIATES, INC.
375 Park Avenue
New York, NY 10152

Industries served:

Advertising—Direct Mail
Commercial Banking
Consumer Products
Financial Services
Health Care
High Technology
Insurance
Investment Banking
Manufacturing
Non-Profit Organizations
Process Industries
Public Relations
Real Estate
Resort—Hospitality
Telecommunications
Venture Capital

HARRIS & U'REN, INC.
1976 Arizona Bank Building
101 North First Avenue
Phoenix, AZ 85003

Industries served: most, with emphasis in:

Automotive
Banking/Finance
Distribution/Retail
Engineering/Construction
Health Care
High Technology
Manufacturing
Real Estate
Utilities

HASKELL & STERN ASSOCIATES, INC.
529 Fifth Avenue
New York, NY 10017

Industries served:

Banking
Consumer Products
Emerging Business
Financial Services
Food Service
Manufacturing
Utilities

THE HEIDRICK PARTNERS, INC.
20 North Wacker Drive, Suite 4000
Chicago, IL 60606

Industries served: all with emphasis in:

Aerospace
Chemical
Construction and Engineering
Consulting
Consumer and Industrial Manufacturing

Distribution
Electronics
Energy
Financial Services (Banking, Insurance, Real
    Estate, etc.)
Forest Products
Health Care
High Technology
Non-Profit Organizations
Retailing
Telecommunications
Transportation
Utilities

HODGE-CRONIN AND ASSOCIATES, INC.
9575 West Higgins Road, Suite 904
Rosemont, IL 60018

Industries served:

Business Equipment
Chemical
Direct Mail
Electronics
Engineering/Construction
Food and Beverage
Floor Tile
Insurance
Pharmaceuticals
Plastics
Pressure Sensitive Tape
Public Sector
Publishing
Store Fixtures
Toys and Sporting Goods

WILLIAM C. HOUZE & COMPANY
Del Amo Financial Center
21535 Hawthorne Boulevard, Suite 250
Torrance, CA 90503

Industries served:

Aerospace and Defense Electronics
Consumer Products and Services
Telephone, Computers, and Related Electronics

HOUZE, SHOURDS & MONTGOMERY, INC.
Peninsula Point, Suite 190
27520 Hawthorne Boulevard
Rolling Hills Estates, CA 90274

Industries served: most, with emphasis in:

Aerospace
Commercial and Military Electronics
Computers
Financial Services
Information
Manufacturing
Telecommunications

Figure 13.5 *(cont.)*

WARD HOWELL INTERNATIONAL, INC.
99 Park Avenue
New York, NY 10016

Industries served:

Aerospace
Automotive and Related
Construction
Consumer Products
Drugs and Cosmetics
Electronics
Energy
High Technology
Hospital and Health Care
Industrial Chemicals and Fibers
Instrumentation
Insurance and Financial Services
Leisure Products
Machinery and Equipment
Metals and Mining
Non-Profit Organizations
Pharmaceutical
Printing, Publishing, and Communications
Professional Services
Real Estate and Building Products
Service Industries
Textiles and Apparel
Transportation and Distribution
Utilities
Wood, Paper, and Forest Products
Wholesale and Retail

HUMAN RESOURCES, INC.
7 James Street
Providence, RI 02903

Industries served:

Computer Systems
Data Communications/Telecommunications
Defense Electronics
Printer and Graphic Arts
Software and Artificial Intelligence

INTERNATIONAL MANAGEMENT ADVISORS, INC.
767 Third Avenue
New York, NY 10017

Industries served:

Chemicals
Consumer Goods
Data Processing Equipment
Equipment Industry
Financial Services
Hospitals
Industrial Companies
Pharmaceutical Products
Publishing
Textile, Apparel
Transportation

CHARLES IRISH COMPANY, INC.
420 Lexington Avenue
New York, NY 10170

Industries served: all

JOHNSON, SMITH & KNISELY, INC.
475 Fifth Avenue, Suite 1402
New York, NY 10017

Industries served: all, with special practice groups in:

Communications and Entertainment
Consumer Markets
Financial Services
Information Technology Management

KEARNEY EXECUTIVE SEARCH
222 South Riverside Plaza
Chicago, IL 60606

Industries served:

Financial Services
Foods and Other Consumer Goods
Health Care
Manufacturing
Non-Profit Organizations
Pharmaceutical
Telecommunications

KREMPLE & MEADE
1900 Avenue of the Stars
Los Angeles, CA 90067

Industries served: most, with special emphasis in:

Aerospace
Computer Systems and Peripherals
Electronic Equipment and Components
Financial Services
Lighting and Electronic Products
Semiconductor Devices

KUNZER ASSOCIATES, LTD.
298 South LaSalle Street
Chicago, IL 60604

Industries served:

Chemicals
Consumer Products
Energy
Financial Services
Health Care
High Technology
Instrumentation
Machinery and Equipment
Pharmaceuticals

LAWRENCE L. LAPHAM, INC.
80 Park Avenue, Suite 3-K
New York, NY 10016

Industries served:

Consumer Products
Direct Marketing

Figure 13.5 *(cont.)*

Financial Services
Food
Hi-Tech (Marketing and General Management)
Light Manufacturing
Retail

LAUER, SBARBARO ASSOCIATES, INC.
3 First National Plaza, Suite 650
Chicago, IL 60602

Industries served:

Banking
Communications
Consumer Products
Data Processing
Direct Market
Financial Services
Health Care
Higher Education
Industrial Products
Insurance
Machine Tools
Manufacturing
Office Furniture and Remodeling
Packaging
Venture Capital

LOCKE & ASSOCIATES
Charlotte Plaza—Suite 2160
201 South College Street
Charlotte, NC 28244

Industries served:

Engineering and Construction
Financial
Manufacturing
Service

THE LOCKRIDGE GROUP, INC.
Post Office Box 2658
Des Plaines, IL 60017

Industries served: practice limited to manufacturing
and distributing companies:

THE JOHN LUCHT CONSULTANCY, INC.
The Olympic Tower
645 Fifth Avenue
New York, NY 10022

Industries served: most, with emphasis in:

Agribusiness
Basic Industries
Broadcasting
Communications
Consumer Products
Direct Marketing
Electronics
Fashion
Financial Services
Health Care

Industrial Components
Management Consulting
Public Sector
Publishing
Real Estate
Retailing

MCBRIDE ASSOCIATES, INC.
1151 K Street, NW
Washington, D.C. 20005

Industries served: most

MCFEELY WACKERLE ASSOCIATES
20 North Wacker Drive
Chicago, IL 60606

Industries served:

Aerospace/Defense
Conglomerates
Entertainment
Financial Services
Health Care/Biotechnology
High Technology

JON MCRAE & ASSOCIATES, INC.
2260 First Union Plaza
Charlotte, NC 28282

Industries served:

Financial Services
Health Care
Higher Education

HAROLD A. MILLER ASSOCIATES
Box 9006
Winnetka, IL 60093

Industries served:

Aerospace and Ordinance
Consumer Products
Electrical and Electronic Products and
    Components
Engines and Turbines
Household Appliances
Housing and Components
Land Development/Construction/Property
    Management
Metal and Woodworking Machinery
Motor Vehicles and Equipment
Oil Field, Construction, Mining and Material
    Handling Machinery and Equipment
Pharmaceuticals
Recreation and Camping Vehicles
Retailing (Department and Specialty Stores)
Transportation
Wholesaling, Food

Figure 13.5 *(cont.)*

OLIVER & ROZNER ASSOCIATES, INC.
598 Madison Avenue
New York, NY 10022

Industries served:

>Chemicals
>Consumer Products and Packaged Goods
>Direct Selling
>Furniture
>Hospital Administration
>Pharmaceuticals and Health Care Products
>Textiles and Apparel

PINSKER & SHATTUCK, INC.
100 Bush Street
San Francisco, CA 94104

Industries served: all, with special emphasis in:

>Aerospace
>Bio-Technology
>Consumer Products
>Electronics
>General Manufacturing
>High Technology
>Plastics
>Specialty Chemicals and Materials
>Telecommunications
>Venture Capital

DAVID POWELL, INC.
3000 Sand Hill Road
Building 3—Suite 230
Menlo Park, CA 94025

Industries served:

>Biotechnology
>Energy and Natural Resources
>Financial Services
>Health Care
>Medical (Pharmaceutical and Medical Devices)

BRUCE ROBINSON ASSOCIATES
250 West 57th Street, Suite 417
New York, NY 10019

Industries served:

>Advertising
>Chemical
>Communications
>Consulting Firms
>Consumer Packaged Goods
>Engineering
>Financial Services
>Insurance
>Petrochemical

ROBINSON & MCAULAY
3100 NCNB Plaza
Charlotte, NC 28280

Industries served: all

ROPES ASSOCIATES, INC.
One Financial Plaza, Suite 1404
Fort Lauderdale, FL 33394

Industries served:

>Financial Institutions
>Real Estate

SCHWARZKOPF CONSULTANTS, INC.
21005 Gumina Road
Pewaukee, WI 53072-2932

Industries served: most, with emphasis in:

>Capital Goods
>Consumer Hard Goods
>Consumer Packaged Goods
>Financial Services

SILER & ASSOCIATES, INC.
P.O. Box 17526
5261 North Port Washington Road
Milwaukee, WI 53217

Industries served: all with some concentration in:

>Brewing
>Chemicals
>Fabricated Metals
>Financial Services
>Food Processing
>Graphic Arts
>Hardware Housewares
>Heavy Machinery
>Paper Conversion

SKOTT/EDWARDS CONSULTANTS, INC.
230 Park Avenue
New York, NY 10169

Industries served:

>Consumer Products
>Financial Services
>Health Care
>High-Tech
>Venture Capital

SMITH, GOERSS & FERNEBORG, INC.
25 Ecker Street, Suite 600
San Francisco, CA 94105

Industries served:

>Banking/Financial Services
>Biotechnology
>Consumer Products
>Forest Products
>Health Care
>High Technology
>Real Estate
>Retailing
>Telecommunications
>Transportation

Figure 13.5 *(cont.)*

SOCKWELL& HENDRIX
One Tryon Center, Suite 1420
Charlotte, NC 28284

Industries served: most with some emphasis in:
    Banking and Related Financial Institutions
    Emerging Growth companies
    Graphic Arts
    Real Estate

WILLIAM STACK ASSOCIATES, INC.
230 Park Avenue
New York, NY 10169

Industries served: all

PAUL STAFFORD ASSOCIATES, LTD.
45 Rockefeller Plaza
New York, NY 10111

Industries served:
    Consumer Products
    Data Processing
    Financial Services
    Medical and Health
    Natural Resources
    Non-Profit Organizations
    Professional Services
    Telecommunications

S.K. STEWART & ASSOCIATES
The Executive Building
P.O. Box 40110
Cincinnati, OH 45240

Industries served:
    Computer
    Feed and Food
    Health Care
    High-Tech

TASA
875 Third Avenue, Suite 1501
New York, NY 10022

Industries served: all

TAYLOR, JOHNSTON INC.
240 Crandon Boulevard
Key Biscayne, FL 33149

Industries served: all

WILKINS & THOMAS, INC.
100 S. Wacker Drive, Suite 1506
Chicago, IL 60606

Industries served:
    Chemicals
    Consumer Products

Consumer Services
Pharmaceutical

WILKINSON & IVES
601 California Street, Suite 1809
San Francisco, CA 94108

Industries served: most, with emphasis in:
    Agribusiness
    Computer Technologies
    Electronics
    Energy
    Financial Services
    Health Care
    Insurance
    Transportation

WILLIAM H. WILLIS, INC.
445 Park Avenue
New York, NY 10022

Industries served: all, with emphasis in:
    Consumer Products
    Emerging Growth Companies
    Financial Services
    Health Care and Pharmaceuticals
    High Technology
    Telecommunications and Broadcasting

WITT ASSOCIATES INC.
724 Enterprise Drive
Oak Brook, IL 60521

Industries served:
    Health Care Providers
    Health Care Service Companies
    Insurers Providing Alternative Health Care
        Delivery (HMOs, PPOs, etc.)

YELVERTON & COMPANY
353 Sacramento Street
San Francisco, CA 94111

Industries served:
    Communication
    Computers and Peripheral Devices
    Instrumentation
    Machinery and Equipment
    Process
    Semiconductor Devices
    Software
    Technical Materials
    Wine

Figure 13.5 *(cont.)*

BATTALIA/EURAM CONSULTANTS GROUP, LTD.
  INTERNATIONAL OFFICES:

Industries served: most, with emphasis in:

Pharmaceuticals
Telecommunications and Electronics

Battalia/Euram Consultants Group, Ltd.
14 Sandyford Place
Glasgow G3 7NB, Scotland

Battalia/Euram Consultants Group, Ltd.
115 Mount Street
London W1Y 5HD, England

Battalia/Euram Consultants Group, Ltd.
Biebricher Allee 3
D-6200 Wiesbaden, Germany

Battalia/Euram Consultants Group, Ltd.
1200 Bay Street
Toronto, Ontario M5R 2A5, Canada

Battalia/Euram Consultants Group, Ltd.
Jose Abascal, 55
Madrid 3, Spain

BERNDTSON INTERNATIONAL S.A.
8, Rue Bovy-Lysberg
CH-1204 Geneva, Switzerland

Industries served: all

Other offices:

Berndtson International S.A.
200 av Franklin Roosevelt
B-1050 Brussels, Belgium

Berndtson International A/S
Bodums Gaard, Nyhavn 63
DK-1051 Copenhagen, Denmark

Berndtson International Ltd.
6 Westminster Palace Gardens, Artillery Row
GB-London SW1P 1RL, England

Berndtson International Sarl
10 rue Cambaceres
F-75008 Paris, France

Berndtson International GmbH
Hamburger Allee 1
D-6000 Frankfurt/Main, Germany

Berndtson International Srl
22 via Conservatorio
1-20122 Milan, Italy

Berndtson International SA
Fortuny 37
E-28010 Madrid, Spain

BOYDEN INTERNATIONAL OFFICES:

Industries served: all industries and institutions

Boyden Associates International
Marland House, 570 Bourke Street
Melbourne, Victoria 3000, Australia

Byoden Associates International
Suite 1004-1005, The Cliveden
4 Bridge Street
Sydney, N.S.W., 2000, Australia

Boyden International, S.A.
Avenue de la Toison d'Or 1, Bte. 6
B-1060 Brussels, Belgium

Boyden do Brasil, Ltda.
Rua Bento de Andrade, 421, Jardim Paulista
04503 Sao Paulo, Brasil

Boyden/Consultores Ejecutivos Ltda.
Executive Tower
Carrera 7a, No. 67-02 Piso 8
Bogota, Colombia, S.A.

Boyden International, Ltd.
148 Buckingham Palace Road
London SW1W 9TR, England

Boyden International S.A.R.L.
13 Rue Madeleine Michelis
92522 Neuilly Cedex, France

Boyden International GmbH
Postfach 1724, Schoene Aussicht 20
D-6380 Bad Homburg v.d.H., Germany

Boyden Associates, Ltd.
Suite 3403, Bank of America Tower
12 Harcourt Road
Hong Kong

Boyden International S.R.L.
Via Lazzaro, Palazzi 2/A
Milan, Italy

Boyden International, S.R.L.
Via Parigi 11
00185 Rome, Italy

Boyden Associates Japan Ltd.
Suite 1307 Aoyama Building, 1-2-3 Kita Aoyama
Minato-ku Tokyo 107, Japan

Boyden Associates SDN. BHD.
23rd Floor, Menara Kewangan
Jalan Sultan Ismail
50250 Kuala Lumpur, Malaysia

Boyden Latin America, S.A. de C.V.
Apartado Postal M8566
06000 Mexico, D.F.

Boyden Associates Ltd.
P.O. Box 28-297 REMUERA
Auckland 5, New Zealand

Boyden International
Av. Eng. Duarte Pacheco
Torre 2 Das Amoreiras, 10-N.R.5
1000 Lisbon, Portugal

Boyden Associates Pte. Ltd.
50 Raffles Place 19-02
Shell Tower
Singapore 0104, Republic of Singapore

Figure 13.5A International executive search consultants

continued

Boyden/Executive Services
Hampstead House, 5th Floor
46 Biccard Street
Braamfontein, 2001, Johannesburg, South Africa

Boyden/Ceuve, S.A.
Balmes, 195, 6
08006 Barcelona, Spain

Boyden/V.S. International, S.A.
P. de la Castellana-141-P.22
28046 Madrid, Spain

Boyden International, S.A.
Jorge Juan, 10
46004 Valencia, Spain

Boyden International AB
Wahrendorffsgatan 8, Box 7023
S-103 86 Stockholm, Sweden

Boyden International S.A.
4, rue de la Scie
1207 Geneva, Switzerland

Boyden Associates Ltd.
142/21 Soi Suksavittaya
North Sathorn Road
Bangkok 10500, Thailand

Boyden/Investec Ltd.
14/F Ever Spring Building
147 Chien Kuo North Road, Section 2
Republic of China, Taipei, Taiwan

THE CALDWELL PARTNERS INTERNATIONAL
64 Prince Arthur Avenue
Toronto, Ontario M5R 1B4
Canada

Industries served:

> Automotive
> Building
> Consumer Products
> Electronics and Telecommunications
> Energy
> Finance and Insurance
> Health Care
> High Tech
> Leisure and Entertainment
> Metal and Mining
> Non-Profit Organizations
> Publishing
> Service
> Transportation
> Wholesale and Retail

Other offices:

> The Caldwell Partners International
> 700 Fourth Avenue, SW, Suite 1260
> Calgary, Alberta T2P 3J4
> Canada

The Caldwell Partners International
1115 Sherbrooke Street, West, Suite 2201
Montreal, Quebec H3A 1H3
Canada

The Caldwell Partners International
280 Albert Street, 6th Floor
Ottawa, Ontario K1P 5G8
Canada

The Caldwell Partners International
999 West Hastings Street, Suite 750
Vancouver, British Columbia V6C 2W2
Canada

The Caldwell Partners International
29 Buckingham Gate
London, FW1 6NF, England

J-B INTERNATIONAL A-S
Vester Sogade 10
DK-1601 Copenhagen, Denmark

Industries served: all

Other offices:

> J-B International S-A
> Mannerheimintie 16TL676
> SF 00101 Helsinki 10, Finland

> J-B International S-A
> P.O. Box 1952 Vika
> 0125 Oslo 1, Norway

> J-B International S-A
> Box 1612
> S 11186 Stockholm, Sweden

KEARNEY EXECUTIVE SEARCH INTERNATIONAL OFFICES:

Industries served: all

> Kearney Executive Search
> Avenue des Arts 46
> 1040 Brussels, Belgium

> Kearney Executive Search
> 134 Picadilly
> London W1V 9FJ, England

> Kearney Executive Search
> Jan Wellem Platz 3
> 4000 Dusseldorf, Germany

> Kearney Executive Search
> Herengract 499
> 1017 BT Amsterdam, The Netherlands

JIM MCCROHAN ASSOCIATES
1, Stillorgan Park Avenue
Blackrock, Co. Dublin, Ireland

Industries served:

> Chemicals
> Electronics

Figure 13.5A *(cont.)*

Food Processing
Health Care
Manufacturing
Mechanical and Electrical Engineering
Pharmaceuticals
Textiles

CHRISTOPHER MILL & PARTNERS
Russell Chambers, Covent Garden
London, WC2 E8AA, England

Industries served:

Advanced Technology
Computing
Consumer Goods
Electronics
Engineering and Construction
Financial and Professional Services
Manufacturing
Oil and Gas

HERMAN SMITH INTERNATIONAL, INC.
P.O. Box 255
Toronto-Dominion Centre
Toronto, Ontario M5K 1J5
Canada

Industries served:

Consumer Products
Financial Services
Health Science
Information Science
Parts Manufacturing
Retail and Distribution

JOHN STORK & PARTNERS INTERNATIONAL LTD.
10 Haymarket
London SW1Y 4BP, England

Industries served:

Business and Professional Services
Consumer Goods and Services
Financial Services
Information Technology
Manufacturing

JOHN STORK & PARTNERS INTERNATIONAL OFFICES:

Industries served:

Business and Professional Services
Consumer Goods and Services
Financial Services
Government and Non-Profit Organizations
Information Technology
Manufacturing Industries
Other Technology

John Stork & Partners BV
14 Grand' Place
1000 Brussels, Belgium

John Stork & Partners Sarl
10 rue des Saussaies
75008 Paris, France

John Stork & Partners International GmbH
Steinweg 1
6000 Frankfurt am Main 1, Germany

John Stork & Partners BV
Herengracht 329
1016 AW Amsterdam, Holland

John Stork & Partners A/S
Bygdoy Alle 15
0257 Oslo 2, Norway

John Stork & Partners A/S
Hinnavegen 32
4030 Hinna/Stavanger, Norway

John Stork & Partners/Personalinvest AB
Kunsgatan 56
S-111 22 Stockholm, Sweden

John Stork & Partners/Personalinvest AB
Engelbrektsgatan 7
S-211 33 Malmo, Sweden

TASA INTERNATIONAL OFFICES:

Industries served: all

TASA de Argentina, S.A.
San Martin No. 1143
Buenos Aires, Argentina

TASA
National Bank Centre, 20th Level
500 Bourke Street, G.P.O. Box 1518N
Melbourne, Victoria, Australia

TASA
Level 21, 83 Clarence Street
Sydney, New South Wales 2000, Australia

TASA Austria
Reisnerstrasse 29
1030 Wein, Austria

TASA S.A.
327, Avenue Louise-Bte. 10
B-1050 Brussels, Belgium

TASA do Brasil S.C. Ltda.
Rua Guilherme Moura, 234
05449 Sao Paulo, SP, Brasil

Woods Gordon Executive Search
1300 Iveagh House
707-7th Avenue, S.W.
Calgary, Alberta T2P 3H6, Canada

Woods Gordon Executive Search
1700 Continental Bank Building
10250-101 Street
Edmonton, Alberta T5J 3P4, Canada

Figure 13.5A *(cont.)*

Woods Gordon Executive Search
Suite 2000
630 Dorchester Blvd., West
Montreal, Quebec H3B 1T9, Canada

Woods Gordon Executive Search
Royal Trust Tower
P.O. Box 251, Toronto Dominion Centre
Toronto, Ontario M5K 1J7, Canada

Woods Gordon Executive Search
P.O. Box 10101, Pacific Centre
700 West Georgia Street
Vancouver, British Columbia V7Y 1C7, Canada

TASA de Columbia S.A.
Calle 80 No. 9-65
Bogota 8, D.E., Columbia

TASA
17-18 Old Bond Street
London W1X 3DA, England

TASA SARL
6, Avenue Marceau
F-75008, Paris, France

TASA/Consulting Partners GmbH
Mendelssohnstrasse 79
D-6000 Frankfurt/Main 1, Germany

TASA Consultants, Ltd.
Great Eagle Center, 27th Floor
23 Harbour Road
Wanchai, Hong Kong

TASA s.r.l.
Via Boccaccio 39
1-20123, Milano, Italy

TASA de Mexico S.A.
Paseo de las Palmas 731
11010 Mexico, D.F., Mexico

TASA LTD.
Ristone Office Park/East Wing
Sherborne Road-Parktown
2193 Johannesburg, South Africa

TASA AG
Plaza Francesc Macia 2
08021 Barcelona 2, Spain

TASA AG
Velazquez 31
28001 Madrid, Spain

TASA International AG
Dufourstrasse 101, Postfach
CH-8034, Zurich, Switzerland

TASA de Venezuela S.A.
Edificio RNV-Planta Baja, Local B
Avenida Romula Gallegos
Urb. Montecristo
Caracas 107, Venezuela

Figure 13.5A *(cont.)*

13.6 SAMPLE PROFESSIONAL EMPLOYMENT AGENCY AGREEMENT: PROFESSIONALS PLACE PROFESSIONALS

To provide outplacement assistance to professionals, guidance concerning the distinction among employment counseling firms, general employment agencies, and professional employment agencies is essential. The employment counseling firm charges the individual a fee for assistance, which includes résumé preparation, employment interview skill training sessions, and so on. Résumé mailing campaigns are used to obtain interviews. The general employment agency is a state-licensed broker, which, under the provisions of associated regulatory statutes, requires the individual to contract for a fee payment when a position is obtained as a result of their services. Such contracts usually stipulate that no fee payment will be required in a company fee-paid situation, but associated conditions require payments by the individual to the agency in cases where the individual terminates the employment relationship before a specified period of time has elapsed. The definition of a professional employment agency is one that, although it may be licensed as an employment agency, does not require the professional to sign a financial contract. It is understood that the firm works for client companies who pay all fees associated with their services. Such a firm may be a fledgling executive search firm that is still engaged in "contingency" placement assignments—that is, it only receives payment when a professional is placed with a company. Its approach is marked by a high degree of professionalism in terms of the the types of questions asked about employment objectives, and its understanding of the educational and experience requirements associated with the positions for which it is recruiting. Often the firm's representatives are specialists in the fields it represents, for example, a former engineer who places engineers, a computer scientist who places computer professionals, and so on.

A sample Professional Employment Agency Qualifications and Employment Objectives form is shown in Figure 13.6. It is helpful to discuss with the professional receiving outplacement assistance the types of questions included under the "employment objectives" section of this form. A review of these questions will help the individual to focus on the types of information needed by a professional employment agency to provide meaningful and productive assistance. For example, the first question deals with the issue of defining why new employment is being considered. A definition of basic motives is requested, for example, "improve salary position, more professional challenge, increase opportunity for advancement," and so on. The individual must candidly explain why he or she no longer is employed, but the explanation should be given in the most positive terms possible, for example, "Due to adverse business conditions and the need to curtail operating expenses, my company found it necessary to eliminate the market research function. I am currently available for a new opportunity, one where my productive hotel market research background can lead to a sales management position."

The wording of the agreement the professional must sign to be represented by the professional employment agency includes the following:

- Confidential placement assistance.
- No cost to professionals selected for placement assistance; only obligation of professional is that of professional conduct.

- Professional agrees not to disclose the identities of client companies and the details of their positions to other professionals.
- Professional agrees to keep the firm informed of employment status and immediately advise the firm of any change that affects the working relationship.
- Professional agrees to contact the firm after each interview with feedback concerning impressions.
- Professional conduct also includes providing accurate and complete information on background and employment objectives so that the firm is able to represent qualifications to client companies correctly.

SUITE 100, 540 MIDDLESEX AVENUE (201) 494-0611
METUCHEN, N. J. 08840

QUALIFICATIONS & EMPLOYMENT OBJECTIVES OF: _____

FIRST NAME   INITIAL   LAST NAME   CALL NAME

If you have a resume, please attach a copy. Print or type information on this form.

ADDRESS: _____
STREET   CITY   STATE   ZIP CODE

TELEPHONE: _____
AREA CODE   NO.

REFERRED TO US BY: _____

Call After _____ p.m.

HEIGHT _____ WEIGHT _____ MEDICAL (Describe
CONDITION Problems) _____

MARITAL STATUS _____ AGES OF CHILDREN _____ SECURITY CLEARANCE (Type)? _____ U. S. CITIZEN? _____

MILITARY SERVICE _____ GEOGRAPHICAL (State, area, etc.) PREFERENCES _____

EDUCATION: College or University and Location	DATE (Mo./Yr.)		FIELDS OF STUDY		GRADUATION		OVERALL CLASS STANDING	OVERALL GRADE POINT AVERAGE
	FROM	TO	MAJOR	MINOR	DEGREE	DATE (MO./YR.)	QUARTER? TOP = 1ST	EXAMPLE: 3.0/4.0

ACADEMIC HONORS, HONOR SOCIETIES, ETC.

EXPERIENCE: Show most recent experience first. Attach additional page if necessary.

FROM (Mo./Yr.) _____ TO (Mo./Yr.) _____ COMPANY NAME AND LOCATION _____

POSITION TITLE _____ ANNUAL SALARY _____ REPORTED TO (Name & Title) _____

RESPONSIBILITIES & ACCOMPLISHMENTS _____

REASON(S) FOR NEW EMPLOYMENT _____

FROM (Mo./Yr.) _____ TO (Mo./Yr.) _____ COMPANY NAME AND LOCATION _____

POSITION TITLE _____ ANNUAL SALARY _____ REPORTED TO (Name & Title) _____

RESPONSIBILITIES & ACCOMPLISHMENTS _____

REASON(S) FOR NEW EMPLOYMENT _____

FROM (Mo.Yr.) _____ TO (Mo./Yr.) _____ COMPANY NAME AND LOCATION _____

POSITION TITLE _____ ANNUAL SALARY _____ REPORTED TO (Name & Title) _____

RESPONSIBILITIES & ACCOMPLISHMENTS _____

REASON(S) FOR NEW EMPLOYMENT _____

FROM (Mo./Yr.) _____ TO (Mo./Yr.) _____ COMPANY NAME AND LOCATION _____

POSITION TITLE _____ ANNUAL SALARY _____ REPORTED TO (Name & Title) _____

RESPONSIBILITIES & ACCOMPLISHMENTS _____

REASON(S) FOR NEW EMPLOYMENT _____

EMPLOYMENT OBJECTIVES: Briefly describe the position you are seeking by giving a probable title and summarizing its duties, responsibilities, and opportunities for accomplishment. Relate this position to your career objectives.

Figure 13.6 Qualifications and employment objectives form

continued

EMPLOYMENT OBJECTIVES (Continued): This information will allow us to provide truly professional service

WHY ARE YOU CONSIDERING NEW EMPLOYMENT? What are your basic motives, e.g., improve salary position, more professional challenge, increase opportunity for advancement, etc.?

COMPENSATION: What annual compensation do you believe to be appropriate for your next position? Explain in terms of base salary plus incentive and deferred compensation payments. How does this compare to your present compensation package?

EMPLOYMENT CAMPAIGN: What steps have you taken to obtain new employment?

COMPANIES WHICH SHOULD OR SHOULD NOT BE CONTACTED ON MY BEHALF:

_____   _____
                   Contact   Do Not Contact

Is your present employer aware of your interest in obtaining another position? _____

AVAILABILITY FOR EMPLOYMENT: Explain contractual arrangements with your present employer which affect your availability for employment (amount of notice required for termination, restrictions concerning nature of new employment, etc.)

RELOCATION AND TRAVEL: Willing to relocate? _____ Stipulations for relocation (if any) _____

Own home? _____ Wife employed? (If "Yes", explain) _____

Willing to travel (explain limitations, if any) _____

SOCIAL AND PROFESSIONAL ACHIEVEMENTS: Beginning with your college years, what offices of responsibility have you held, what professional recognition have you received, etc.

REFERENCES: Exclude relatives and former employers

Name and Address _____ Profession _____ Years of Acquaintance _____

GRANHOLM ASSOCIATES provide confidential placement assistance to carefully-selected professionals at no cost to these individuals. We are Professional Employment Consultants to a number of client companies who pay for our services. Your only obligation to GRANHOLM ASSOCIATES is that of professional conduct: to not disclose the identities of our client companies and the details of their positions to other professionals, to keep us informed of your employment status and to advise us immediately of any change which affects our working relationship, to contact us after an interview which we have arranged with feedback concerning your impressions, and to provide accurate and complete information on your background and employment objectives so that we will not misrepresent your qualifications to our client companies.

DATE	SIGNATURE	CONFIDENTIAL

Figure 13.6 *(cont.)*

CHAPTER 14

Computerized HRM Records and Reports

This chapter begins with an example of a full scale HRM information system. The system shows how computerization can maintain personnel records and automatically use the data to generate a wide variety of human resources management reports. For example, the system's features include the automatic accrual of employee vacation, personal leave, and sick leave based on user formulas. Readers also may model proposed wage and salary range structures to develop optimum configurations, then allow the system to calculate each employee's salary range position.

This chapter also provides samples of other human resource management reports generated by different systems. The samples chosen are highly diverse to show how reporting requirements may be addressed by computerized techniques.

SAMPLE HUMAN RESOURCES MANAGEMENT SOFTWARE SYSTEM

The following information is provided as an example of a full-scale HRM information system through the courtesy of KOPP COMPANY, KOPP Information Systems for HRM, Summit Two, Suite 300, 4700 Rockside Road, Cleveland, OH 44131.

The KOPP HRM Software System Expanded Main Module™

The Expanded Main Module is a complete human resource information management center that features maintenance; tracking; and standard and ad-hoc reporting of employee and organization data dealing with compensation, benefits, EEO/AAP, education/training/career development, performance appraisal, succession planning, and time-off management. This menu-driven program includes standard features such as full screen input and editing capabilities (including easy editing of extensive history files); an automatic editor that monitors information input and alerts you to possible errors; an English language, menu-driven, ad-hoc report writer that allows you to design and create customized reports; a mass update capability; user-defined tables such as benefits, vacation/personal leave/sick time accrual and salary structure design (automatic update and editing of all employee records with table information); user-defined code screens accessible at all coded fields; security features such as password protection and audit trail; menu-driven interfaces to popular spreadsheets, word processors, and graphics packages; and optional payroll interface and mainframe up/down loading.

All activity of the HRMSS modules is initiated through a directory (or menu) similar to the following:

Figure 14.1—Main Directory
Figure 14.2—Standard Report Directory

To perform an activity, you simply choose the number of the action and the system automatically prompts you through all the steps needed to successfully complete the chosen action. This is known as a *menu-driven* system.

The Expanded Main Module allows the user to maintain, access, and report on twenty-eight different code/table screens. All table screens are interactive with the employee data base, which allows quick and easy input of common data between employee records. Table screens also allow the user to complete global changes (which affect many employee records) with the press of a function key. All code screens allow the user to see the actual uncoded version of any specific code while querying or correcting an employee record. This too is completed by simply pressing a function key. Two unique features of the Expanded Main Module include tables that automatically accrue employee vacation, personal leave, and sick time based on user input formulas for accrual. In the Model and Define Salary Structure table the user has the ability to model various wage/salary structures (based on differing percentages in salary range and between salary midpoints) before deciding on the optimal structure. Once the structure is saved, the system automatically calculates position in salary range and the compa-ratio for all employees with the press of a button.

Expanded Main Module Employee Record

The Expanded Main Module Employee Record contains six pages of current employee information and six pages of historical employee information. Information is entered or updated quickly and easily through a full record input/edit procedure that allows you to instantly access either the entire employee record or only specific pages. Input of information is monitored through an automatic editor which alerts the user to information that may not be accurate. Input and editing of employee records is completed on your microcomputer screen. As you add, change, or delete data about employees, the system automatically updates the record. This includes automatic updating of current information from the history files (no need to input data twice). Through the query record feature, you are able to see the updated information immediately. An audit trail is developed that lists the identification code and date of the most current user accessing the employee record. The system also allows you to transfer terminated employee records into a special terminated file.

Samples of the six current employee information and six historical employee information record formats follow.

Figure 14.3—Basic Employee Data
Figure 14.4—Organizational/Incumbent Data
Figure 14.5—Vacation/Personal Leave/Sick Time Summary
Figure 14.6—Benefit/Payroll Data
Figure 14.7—Previous Education/Foreign Languages/Skills
Figure 14.8—In-House Education and Training
Figure 14.9—History File: Positions/Performance Ratings
Figure 14.10—History File: Salary Information
Figure 14.11—History File: Status Information
Figure 14.12—History File: Vacation Time
Figure 14.13—History File: Personal Leave Time
Figure 14.14—History File: Employee Sick Time

Report Generation Capabilities—Sample Report Formats

Figure 14.15—Position/Grade Analysis by Department
Figure 14.16—Position/Grade Analysis by Salary
Figure 14.17—Grade Summary

These reports are designed to assist the user in obtaining information such as:

- Reporting relationships
- Organizational charts
- Types of positions within department
- Salary/grade discrepancies between subordinates and supervisors and/or among peers
- Labor expense for salary budgeting
- Average salary per grade

Figure 14.18—Seniority Summary
Figure 14.19—Specific Hire Date Analysis
Figure 14.20—Birthdate Summary
Figure 14.21—Specific Birthdate Analysis

These reports provide the user with data on:

- Which employees were born or hired in a specific year (used for determining eligibility for pension plans, profit sharing or stock option plans, service awards, birthday cards, and so on)
- Where problems may exist concerning seniority and promotions

Specific Employee Status Analysis (Figure 14.22)

This report allows the user to list employees that have a certain employee status code. For example, the user may want to know all employees who currently are "active" (status code 1), those on medical leave of absence (status code 2), those on educational leave of absence (status code 3), and so on. All such status codes are user-defined based on company needs. This report also includes data on the change of status dates and the departments of these employees, which provides the basis for readily verifying information by contacting respective supervisors.

Specific Deduction Analysis (Figure 14.23)

This report lists all employees who have specific types of payroll deductions. This report facilitates making payroll deduction revisions and advising affected employees.

Summary of Employee Vacation/Personal Leave/Sick Time by Department (Figure 14.24)

This report for each department shows the amount of vacation, personal leave, and sick time accrued, taken, and remaining for each assigned employee.

Figure 14.25—Summary of Basic EEO Data
Figure 14.26—Summary of Job Group and Workforce Data
Figure 14.27—Specific EEO Code Analysis

These reports listed above are designed to assist the user in completing reports required by the government, for example, the EEO-1 form, the workforce analysis report, and the job group analysis report. The following code structure is employed:

1. Officials and managers
2. Professionals
3. Technicians
4. Sales workers
5. Office clerical
6. Craft workers (skilled)
7. Operatives (semi-skilled)
8. Laborers (unskilled)
9. Service workers

	Male	Female
White	B	G
Black	C	H
Hispanic	D	I
Asian	E	J
American Indian	F	K

The number in the EEO code refers to EEO-1 job category, and the letter refers to the race and sex of the incumbent.

Figure 14.28—Summary of Individual Employee Benefits
Figure 14.29—Benefit Summary Statement by Department

The reports alone allow the user to obtain information on each employee's benefits. The Summary of Individual Employee Benefits allows the user to create a "benefits statement," which is sent to employees; a custom tailored letter is developed to meet company needs. The system automatically interacts to obtain data needed for each employee benefits statement. The Benefit Summary Statement by Department report analyzes the various benefits of each employee, including the cost to the employee and the company, to create departmental listings. This is an effective tool for developing cost containment or reduction strategies.

Figure 14.30—Review Date Summary
Figure 14.31—Specific Position Code Analysis
Figure 14.32—Specific Reason for Change in Position Analysis

The Review Date Summary report allows the user to quickly determine which employees are due for a performance review during a particular month so that required actions may be scheduled. The Specific Position Code Analysis report offers the capability of listing all employees who currently hold a particular type of position. This listing identifies individuals who may be qualified for transfer and promotional opportunities. The Specific Reason for Change in Position Analysis provides the basis for calling up data on all employees who have had a particular type of salary change. For example, if information is needed on all employees who have received a salary change due to promotion, a "PR" salary change code yields the required data.

Figure 14.33—Salary Range Analysis by Grade
Figure 14.34—Salary Range Analysis by Department
Figure 14.35—Merit Rating and Place in Range Matrix

These reports assist in simplifying budget preparation tasks through providing information on:

• Employees currently below minimum, in the first quarter, in the second quarter, in the third quarter, in the fourth quarter, or above the maximum of their salary range
• Compa-ratio for each employee
• Total number of employees and average salaries

This information assists the user in determining equitable merit increase percentages based on the employee's performance rating, placement in salary range, and so on.

Figure 14.36—Salary and Dollar Increase by Department
Figure 14.37—Salary and Dollar Increase by EEO Code

These reports provide assistance in controlling the merit increase budget. Information includes:

- Total salaries
- Total merit increase amounts
- Average merit increase amount
- Average merit increase percentage

Data are reviewed to ensure that merit increase percentages and associated amounts are consistent with employee performance ratings. The Salary and Dollar Increase by EEO Code report facilitates monitoring minority employee data to ensure equitable compensation.

The system also is capable of generating internal telephone listings and employee mailing labels. A Report Writer capability also is provided.

```
                           MAIN DIRECTORY
********************************************************************************

THE FOLLOWING HUMAN RESOURCES OPTIONS ARE AVAILABLE:

    HUMAN RESOURCES DATABASE
        1...ADDING NEW EMPLOYEE RECORDS
        2...CORRECTING/CHANGING/DELETING EMPLOYEE RECORDS
        3...QUERYING EMPLOYEE RECORDS

    CODE SCREENS
        4...ADDING/CORRECTING/CHANGING/DELETING TABLES/CODES
        5...QUERYING TABLES/CODES

    ADDITIONAL FEATURES
        SR..STANDARD REPORTS
        RW..REPORT WRITER
        MS..MODEL AND DEFINE SALARY STRUCTURE
        PC..PROCESSING COMPLETE


********************************************************************************

ENTER OPTION DESIRED AND PRESS RETURN: __
```

Figure 14.1 Main directory

```
                    STANDARD REPORT DIRECTORY
********************************************************************************
        1..ALPHABETICAL EMPLOYEE LISTING
        2..PRINTOUT OF EMPLOYEE RECORD(S)
        3..POSITION/GRADE ANALYSIS BY DEPARTMENT
        4..POSITION/GRADE ANALYSIS BY SALARY
        5..GRADE SUMMARY
        6..SENIORITY SUMMARY
        7..SPECIFIC HIREDATE ANALYSIS
        8..BIRTHDATE SUMMARY
        9..SPECIFIC BIRTHDATE ANALYSIS
       10..SPECIFIC EMPLOYEE STATUS ANALYSIS
       11..SPECIFIC DEDUCTION ANALYSIS
       12..SUMMARY OF EMPLOYEE VACATION/PERSONAL LEAVE/SICK TIME
       13..SUMMARY OF BASIC EEO DATA
       14..SUMMARY OF JOB GROUP AND WORK FORCE DATA
       15..SPECIFIC EEO CODE ANALYSIS
       16..ADDITIONAL STANDARD REPORT DIRECTORY

********************************************************************************

                ADDITIONAL STANDARD REPORT DIRECTORY
********************************************************************************
       17..SUMMARY OF INDIVIDUAL EMPLOYEE BENEFITS
       18..BENEFITS SUMMARY STATEMENT BY DEPARTMENT
       19..SPECIFIC REVIEW DATE SUMMARY
       20..SPECIFIC POSITION CODE ANALYSIS
       21..SPECIFIC REASON FOR CHANGE IN POSITION ANALYSIS
       22..SALARY RANGE ANALYSIS BY GRADE
       23..SALARY RANGE ANALYSIS BY DEPARTMENT
       24..MERIT RATING AND PLACE IN RANGE MATRIX (ORGANIZATION-WIDE)
       25..SALARY INCREASE ANALYSIS BY DEPARTMENT
       26..SALARY INCREASE ANALYSIS BY EEO CODE
       27..INTERNAL PHONE LISTING
       28..MAILING LABELS
       29..RETURN TO MAIN DIRECTORY
       30..RETURN TO STANDARD REPORT DIRECTORY
       31..PROCESSING COMPLETE

********************************************************************************
```

Figure 14.2 Standard report directory

```
                                              Update:        860804
Employee Name:          DOE_JOHN_M_____   User ID:     AJC
Internal Phone:         x3351                    Room #:      111

First Address Line:     3864_SCENIC_AVE_____
Second Address Line:    APT1C_____
City/State/Zip:         CHICAGO_____, IL 60606   County:    DUPAGE____
Telephone Number:       (312) 123-3456

Social Security:        111-11-1111              Sex (M/F):   M
                                                 Birthdate:   53/01/01
                                                 Age:           33

Marital Status (M/S):   M
Name of Spouse:         JANE_____               Handicap:    N
Spouse's Social Sec:    122-22-2222              Veteran:     N
Spouse's Birthdate:     54/02/02                 Military:    N

Emergency Contact:      JANE_DOE_____
Emergency Phone:        (312) 123-4677

                                              F10-CANCEL AND EXIT
```

Figure 14.3 Basic employee data

```
Employee Number:    1111111        Status Code:          A
Employee Type:      __             Status Change Date:   78/09/01
                                   Officer Status:       __

EEO Code:           2B             Citizenship:          US
FLSA Code:          E_             Security Code:        __
Hiredate:           77/02/01
Anniversary Date:   77/02/01       Wage/Salary:          16000.00
                                   Place in Range:       2ND    QTR
Position:           ACCT           Compa-ratio:          .993  %
Grade:              06
Location:           CHIC_          WAGE/SALARY RANGE:
Division:           NIF__            Minimum    Midpoint    Maximum
Department:         FIN             $ 12723.    $ 16105.    $ 19487.
Section:            B____
Supv Pos Code:      CONTR

                                              F10-CANCEL AND EXIT
```

Figure 14.4 Organizational/incumbent data

```
Vacation Calc Date:     77/02/01      Vacation Allowed:     10
Vacation Schedule:      A             Vacation Taken:        5
                                      Vacation Avail:        5


Pers Leave Calc Date:   77/02/01      Pers Leave Allowed:   24
Pers Leave Schedule:    A             Pers Leave Taken:     14.5
                                      Pers Leave Avail:      9.5


Sick Time Calc Date:    77/02/01      Sick Time Allowed:    32
Sick Time Schedule:     A             Sick Time Taken:      24
                                      Sick Time Avail:       8



                                            F10-CANCEL AND EXIT
```

Figure 14.5 Vacation/personal leave/sick time summary

SCREEN 4 OF 6 - BENEFIT/PAYROLL DATA

```
                            Employee Benefit Dollars Available: $260.00__
BENEFITS                                             Wage/Salary: $16000.00
        Type        Effect Date  EE Amount   ER Amount  Covered Dependents
 1 : MEDICAL_FAM_    77/02/01    $135.00     $70.00_     1 2 3 4 _ _ _ _
 2 : DENTAL_FAM__    78/02/01    $20.00_     $10.00_     1 2 3 4 _ _ _ _
 3 : PEN_PLAN____    78/02/01    $16____     $32____     1 _ _ _ _ _ _ _
 4 : PROFIT_B____    78/06/01    $8_____     $9.6___     _ _ _ _ _ _ _ _
 5 : _____     __/__/__    $_____      $_____      _ _ _ _ _ _ _ _
 6 : _____     __/__/__    $_____      $_____      _ _ _ _ _ _ _ _
 7 : _____     __/__/__    $_____      $_____      _ _ _ _ _ _ _ _
 8 : _____     __/__/__    $_____      $_____      _ _ _ _ _ _ _ _
 9 : _____     __/__/__    $_____      $_____      _ _ _ _ _ _ _ _
10 : _____     __/__/__    $_____      $_____      _ _ _ _ _ _ _ _
                    Totals:    $    179   $.    121.6    _ _ _ _ _ _ _ _
Dependents
1. JANE_DOE__W_____   5. _____   Life Ins Beneficiary:
2. SUSAN.DOE__D_____   6. _____   JANE_DOE_____
3. GEORGE_DOE__S_____   7. _____   Relation:  WIFE_____
4. CAROL_SMITH__MIL_____  8. _____   SS Number: 122-22-2222


                                            F10-CANCEL AND EXIT
```

Figure 14.6 Benefit/payroll data

```
OUTSIDE EDUCATION
         School         Date    Degree    Major        Minor        GPA
1 : NORTH_CEN_     75/06      BS_     ACCT_____   BUSINESS__   4.0
2 : _____     __/__      ___     _____   _____   ___
3 : _____     __/__      ___     _____   _____   ___

SPECIAL SKILLS INVENTORY
     Skill Code    Level      How/Where Acquired      Yr Acqrd    Last Used
1 :CPA_____      __     BOARD_CERTIFIED_____    75/07        __/__
2 :COMP_MICRO      C_     ON_JOB_EXP_____    76/01        77/02
3 :_____      __     _____     __/__        __/__
4 :_____      __     _____     __/__        __/__
5 :_____      __     _____     __/__        __/__

FOREIGN LANGUAGE SKILLS
    Language   Speaking   Reading   Writing
1:   40          C          B         C
2:   __          -          -         -
```

                                                F10-CANCEL AND EXIT

Figure 14.7 Previous education/foreign languages/skills

```
IN-HOUSE EDUCATION AND TRAINING
         School      Date     Course     Cost       GPA        Comment
1 : FIN_____     77/12    ACCT_____   $50.00__   P__    SEND_TO_AUDIT_____
2 : FIN_____     78/02    AUDIT_____  $50.00__   P__    _____
3 : UAW_____     78/06    AUDIT_____  $150.00_   4.0    _____
4 : _____     __/__    _____   $_____   ___    _____
5 : _____     __/__    _____   $_____   ___    _____
6 : _____     __/__    _____   $_____   ___    _____
7 : _____     __/__    _____   $_____   ___    _____
8 : _____     __/__    _____   $_____   ___    _____
9 : _____     __/__    _____   $_____   ___    _____
10 :_____     __/__    _____   $_____   ___    _____
11 :_____     __/__    _____   $_____   ___    _____
12 :_____     __/__    _____   $_____   ___    _____
13 :_____     __/__    _____   $_____   ___    _____
14 :_____     __/__    _____   $_____   ___    _____
15 :_____     __/__    _____   $_____   ___    _____
                           Totals    $ 250
```

                                                F10-CANCEL AND EXIT

Figure 14.8 In-house education and training

HISTORY FILE - POSITIONS/PERFORMANCE RATINGS

DOE JOHN M

```
       Position     Date      Grade     Dept     Perf Rating    Perf Review Date
 1 : JACCT       77/02/01     04       FIN__                        __/__/__
 2 : _____       __/__/__     --       _____         E             78/01/01
 3 : _____       __/__/__     --       _____         E             79/01/01
 4 : ACCT_       80/03/04     06       _____                        __/__/__
 5 : _____       __/__/__     --       _____         E             81/01/01
 6 : _____       __/__/__     --       _____         _              __/__/__
 7 : _____       __/__/__     --       _____         _              __/__/__
 8 : _____       __/__/__     --       _____         _              __/__/__
 9 : _____       __/__/__     --       _____         _              __/__/__
10 :_____       __/__/__     --       _____         _              __/__/__
11 :_____       __/__/__     --       _____         _              __/__/__
12 :_____       __/__/__     --       _____         _              __/__/__
13 :_____       __/__/__     --       _____         _              __/__/__
14 :_____       __/__/__     --       _____         _              __/__/__
15 :_____       __/__/__     --       _____         _              __/__/__
```

F10-CANCEL AND EXIT

Figure 14.9 History file—positions/performance ratings

HISTORY FILE - SALARY INFORMATION

DOE JOHN M

```
       Salary        Date Effective    Reason for Change   $ Increase      % Increase
 1 : $10000.00_        77/02/01              NH            $_____      _____%
 2 : $11000.00_        78/02/01              MI            $1000.00__       _10__%
 3 : $13000.00_        79/02/01              MI            $1000.00__       _9.09%
 4 : $14000.00_        80/04/04              MI            $1000.00__       _7.69%
 5 : $16000.00_        81/02/01              MI            $1000.00__       _7.14%
 6 : $_____       __/__/__             --            $_____      _____%
 7 : $_____       __/__/__             --            $_____      _____%
 8 : $_____       __/__/__             --            $_____      _____%
 9 : $_____       __/__/__             --            $_____      _____%
10 :$_____       __/__/__             --            $_____      _____%
11 :$_____       __/__/__             --            $_____      _____%
12 :$_____       __/__/__             --            $_____      _____%
13 :$_____       __/__/__             --            $_____      _____%
14 :$_____       __/__/__             --            $_____      _____%
15 :$_____       __/__/__             --            $_____      _____%
```

F10-CANCEL AND EXIT

Figure 14.10 History file—salary information

```
DOE JOHN M

            Status      Date
    1 :     A___        77/02/01
    2 :     EL__        78/06/15
    3 :     A___        78/09/01
    4 :     ____        __/__/__
    5 :     ____        __/__/__
    6 :     ____        __/__/__
    7 :     ____        __/__/__
    8 :     ____        __/__/__
    9 :     ____        __/__/__
   10 :     ____        __/__/__
   11 :     ____        __/__/__
   12 :     ____        __/__/__
   13 :     ____        __/__/__
   14 :     ____        __/__/__
   15 :     ____        __/__/__


                                    F10-CANCEL AND EXIT
```

Figure 14.11 History file—status information

```
DOE JOHN M

            Date      Time                    Date      Time
    1 :    81/03/15   1____      16 :     __/__/__    _____
    2 :    81/04/16   1____      17 :     __/__/__    _____
    3 :    81/04/17   1____      18 :     __/__/__    _____
    4 :    81/06/12   .5___      19 :     __/__/__    _____
    5 :    81/06/13   .5___      20 :     __/__/__    _____
    6 :    81/07/23   1____
    7 :    __/__/__   _____      Vacation Calc Date:   77/02/01
    8 :    __/__/__   _____      Vacation Schedule:    A
    9 :    __/__/__   _____
   10 :    __/__/__   _____      Vacation Allowed:     10___
   11 :    __/__/__   _____      Vacation Taken:        5
   12 :    __/__/__   _____      Vacation Available:    5
   13 :    __/__/__   _____
   14 :    __/__/__   _____
   15 :    __/__/__   _____

                                    F10-CANCEL AND EXIT
```

Figure 14.12 History file—vacation time

```
                HISTORY FILE - PERSONAL LEAVE TIME

DOE JOHN M

             Date      Time                  Date      Time
   1 :    81/08/22     2.5__       16 :    __/__/__    _____
   2 :    81/08/23     4____       17 :    __/__/__    _____
   3 :    81/10/01     8____       18 :    __/__/__    _____
   4 :    __/__/__     _____       19 :    __/__/__    _____
   5 :    __/__/__     _____       20 :    __/__/__    _____
   6 :    __/__/__     _____
   7 :    __/__/__     _____       Leave Calc Date:    77/02/01
   8 :    __/__/__     _____       Leave Schedule:     A
   9 :    __/__/__     _____
  10 :    __/__/__     _____       Leave Allowed:      24___
  11 :    __/__/__     _____       Leave Taken:        14.5
  12 :    __/__/__     _____       Leave Available:    9.5
  13 :    __/__/__     _____
  14 :    __/__/__     _____
  15 :    __/__/__     _____


                                              F10-CANCEL AND EXIT
```

Figure 14.13 History file—personal leave time

```
                HISTORY FILE - EMPLOYEE SICK TIME

DOE JOHN M

             Date    Time    Reason              Date    Time    Reason
   1 :    81/02/17   8____    FS___     16 :    __/__/__  _____   _____
   2 :    81/02/18   8____    FS___     17 :    __/__/__  _____   _____
   3 :    81/02/19   8____    FS___     18 :    __/__/__  _____   _____
   4 :    __/__/__   _____    _____     19 :    __/__/__  _____   _____
   5 :    __/__/__   _____    _____     20 :    __/__/__  _____   _____
   6 :    __/__/__   _____    _____
   7 :    __/__/__   _____    _____     Sick Time Calc Date: 77/02/01
   8 :    __/__/__   _____    _____     Sick Time Schedule:  A
   9 :    __/__/__   _____    _____
  10 :    __/__/__   _____    _____     Sick Time Allowed:   _32__
  11 :    __/__/__   _____    _____     Sick Time Taken:     24
  12 :    __/__/__   _____    _____     Sick Time Available: 8
  13 :    __/__/__   _____    _____
  14 :    __/__/__   _____    _____
  15 :    __/__/__   _____    _____


                                              F10-CANCEL AND EXIT
```

Figure 14.14 History file—employee sick time

```
XYZ COMPANY
POSITION/GRADE ANALYSIS BY DEPARTMENT AS OF: 10-16-1985
*************************************************************************

DEPARTMENT: ADM

       NAME                POSITION CODE    GRADE    HIREDATE     SALARY       SUPV POS

MORGAN ELLYN              CLERK             01      69/10/05    $21000.00     MCORD
HALPRIN JOHN             ACLER             01      82/06/01    $8800.00      MROFF
CLOCK KAREN              OFMGR             09      79/09/06    $22576.00     MROFF
LOYAL CAROLYN            MCORD             10      75/06/12    $33200.00     MRMKT
JONES RANDY              MROFF             11      77/06/15    $41600.00     VPADM


TOTAL NUMBER OF EMPLOYEES =  5
TOTAL SALARIES = $ 127176
------------------------------------------------------------------------------

DEPARTMENT: DP

       NAME                POSITION CODE    GRADE    HIREDATE     SALARY       SUPV POS

JONES MARY               SCOMP             06      78/08/16    $30600.00     SCOOP
STEELE JONATHAN          CCORD             10      80/08/01    $44655.00     VPDP


TOTAL NUMBER OF EMPLOYEES =  2
TOTAL SALARIES = $ 75255
------------------------------------------------------------------------------

DEPARTMENT: FIN

       NAME                POSITION CODE    GRADE    HIREDATE     SALARY       SUPV POS

DOE JOHN                 ACCT              06      77/02/01    $16000.00     CONTR
SMITH LAWRENCE           ACCT              07      76/06/15    $26400.00     VPFIN


TOTAL NUMBER OF EMPLOYEES =  2
TOTAL SALARIES = $ 42400
------------------------------------------------------------------------------

DEPARTMENT: MKT

       NAME                POSITION CODE    GRADE    HIREDATE     SALARY       SUPV POS

ROSEN ROGER              MASST             08      78/03/18    $28600.00     MCORD


TOTAL NUMBER OF EMPLOYEES =  1
TOTAL SALARIES = $ 28600
------------------------------------------------------------------------------
```

Figure 14.15 Position/grade analysis by department

```
XYZ COMPANY
POSITION/GRADE ANALYSIS BY SALARY AS OF: 10-16-1985
***************************************************************************
SALARY            NAME                      GRADE     DEPT      POSITION CODE

$ 8800            HALPRIN JOHN               01       ADM          ACLER
$ 16000           DOE JOHN                   06       FIN          ACCT
$ 21000           MORGAN ELLYN               01       ADM          CLERK
$ 22576           CLOCK KAREN                09       ADM          OFMGR
$ 26400           SMITH LAWRENCE             07       FIN          ACCT
$ 28600           ROSEN ROGER                08       MKT          MASST
$ 30600           JONES MARY                 06       DP           SCOMP
$ 33200           LOYAL CAROLYN              10       ADM          MCORD
$ 41600           JONES RANDY                11       ADM          MROFF
$ 44655           STEELE JONATHAN            10       DP           CCORD

---------------------------------------------------------------------------

TOTAL SALARIES              = $ 273431
TOTAL NUMBER OF EMPLOYEES   =   10

***************************************************************************
```

Figure 14.16 Position/grade analysis by salary

```
XYZ COMPANY
GRADE SUMMARY AS OF: 10-16-1985
*****************************************************************************
GRADE: 01

        NAME              SALARY        DEPT      POS CODE      SUPV POSITION
HALPRIN JOHN            $8800.00        ADM        ACLER          MROFF
MORGAN ELLYN            $21000.00       ADM        CLERK          MCORD

TOTAL NUMBER OF EMPLOYEES =   2
AVERAGE SALARY = $ 14900
------------------------------------------------------------------------------
GRADE: 06

        NAME              SALARY        DEPT      POS CODE      SUPV POSITION
DOE JOHN                $16000.00       FIN        ACCT           CONTR
JONES MARY              $30600.00       DP         SCOMP          SCOOP

TOTAL NUMBER OF EMPLOYEES =   2
AVERAGE SALARY = $ 23300
------------------------------------------------------------------------------
GRADE: 07

        NAME              SALARY        DEPT      POS CODE      SUPV POSITION
SMITH LAWRENCE          $26400.00       FIN        ACCT           VPFIN

TOTAL NUMBER OF EMPLOYEES =   1
AVERAGE SALARY = $ 26400
------------------------------------------------------------------------------
GRADE: 08

        NAME              SALARY        DEPT      POS CODE      SUPV POSITION
ROSEN ROGER             $28600.00       MKT        MASST          MCORD

TOTAL NUMBER OF EMPLOYEES =   1
AVERAGE SALARY = $ 28600
------------------------------------------------------------------------------
GRADE: 09

        NAME              SALARY        DEPT      POS CODE      SUPV POSITION
CLOCK KAREN             $22576.00       ADM        OFMGR          MROFF

TOTAL NUMBER OF EMPLOYEES =   1
AVERAGE SALARY = $ 22576
------------------------------------------------------------------------------
GRADE: 10

        NAME              SALARY        DEPT      POS CODE      SUPV POSITION
LOYAL CAROLYN           $33200.00       ADM        MCORD          MRMKT
STEELE JONATHAN         $44655.00       DP         CCORD          VPDP

TOTAL NUMBER OF EMPLOYEES =   2
AVERAGE SALARY = $ 38927.5
------------------------------------------------------------------------------
GRADE: 11

        NAME              SALARY        DEPT      POS CODE      SUPV POSITION
JONES RANDY             $41600.00       ADM        MROFF          VPADM

TOTAL NUMBER OF EMPLOYEES =   1
AVERAGE SALARY = $ 41600
```

Figure 14.17 Grade summary

```
XYZ COMPANY
SENIORITY SUMMARY AS OF: 10-16-1985
**************************************************************************
HIREDATE            NAME             BIRTHDATE     DEPT     GRADE      SALARY

69/10/05      MORGAN ELLYN           33/06/13      ADM       01      $21000.00
75/06/12      LOYAL CAROLYN          45/06/18      ADM       10      $33200.00
76/06/15      SMITH LAWRENCE         38/06/12      FIN       07      $26400.00
77/02/01      DOE JOHN               53/01/01      FIN       06      $16000.00
77/06/15      JONES RANDY            48/12/06      ADM       11      $41600.00
78/03/18      ROSEN ROGER            52/11/01      MKT       08      $28600.00
78/08/16      JONES MARY             58/12/03      DP        06      $30600.00
79/09/06      CLOCK KAREN            58/12/14      ADM       09      $22576.00
80/08/01      STEELE JONATHAN        37/07/14      DP        10      $44655.00
82/06/01      HALPRIN JOHN           63/11/12      ADM       01       $8800.00


**************************************************************************
```

Figure 14.18 Seniority summary

```
XYZ COMPANY
 2 EMPLOYEE(S) HIRED DURING 1978 AS OF: 10-16-1985
**************************************************************************
HIREDATE            NAME        EEO CODE  BIRTHDATE    DEPT   GRADE    SALARY

78/08/16   JONES MARY              2H      58/12/03     DP     06    $30600.00
78/03/18   ROSEN ROGER             5C      52/11/01     MKT    08    $28600.00
**************************************************************************
```

Figure 14.19 Specific hire date analysis

```
XYZ COMPANY
BIRTHDATE SUMMARY AS OF: 10-16-1985
**************************************************************************
BIRTHDATE           NAME          EEO CODE      POS CODE     HIREDATE

33/06/13      MORGAN ELLYN           5G           CLERK      69/10/05
37/07/14      STEELE JONATHAN        1B           CCORD      80/08/01
38/06/12      SMITH LAWRENCE         1D           ACCT       76/06/15
45/06/18      LOYAL CAROLYN          1I           MCORD      75/06/12
48/12/06      JONES RANDY            1C           MROFF      77/06/15
52/11/01      ROSEN ROGER            5C           MASST      78/03/18
53/01/01      DOE JOHN               2B           ACCT       77/02/01
58/12/03      JONES MARY             2H           SCOMP      78/08/16
58/12/14      CLOCK KAREN            5G           OFMGR      79/09/06
63/11/12      HALPRIN JOHN           5B           ACLER      82/06/01

**************************************************************************
```

Figure 14.20 Birthdate summary

```
XYZ COMPANY
 2 EMPLOYEE(S) BORN DURING 1958 WERE FOUND AS OF: 10-16-1985
*********************************************************************************

        BIRTHDATE              NAME                HIREDATE

        58/12/14        CLOCK  KAREN               79/09/06
        58/12/03        JONES MARY                 78/08/16


*********************************************************************************
```

Figure 14.21 Specific birthdate analysis

```
XYZ COMPANY
 6 EMPLOYEE(S) WITH STATUS CODE A     WERE FOUND AS OF: 10-16-1985
*******************************************************************************
         NAME                CHANGE OF STATUS DATE       DEPT      SUPV POS

CLOCK  KAREN                     79/09/06                ADM        MROFF
DOE JOHN                         78/09/01                FIN        CONTR
MORGAN ELLYN                     80/01/01                ADM        MCORD
ROSEN ROGER                      78/03/18                MKT        MCORD
SMITH LAWRENCE                   76/06/15                FIN        VPFIN
STEELE JONATHAN                  83/01/01                DP         VPDP


*******************************************************************************
```

Figure 14.22 Specific employee status analysis

```
XYZ COMPANY
10   EMPLOYEE(S) WITH MEDICAL       DEDUCTION WERE FOUND AS OF: 10-16-1985
********************************************************************************
            NAME             EE AMOUNT        ER AMOUNT        DATE       DEPT

CLOCK KAREN                   $135.00          $50.00        79/09/06      ADM
DOE JOHN                      $100.00          $70.00        77/02/01      FIN
HALPRIN JOHN                   $70.00          $35.00        82/06/01      ADM
JONES MARY                     $70.00          $78.00        78/08/16      DP
JONES RANDY                   $150.00          $45.00        77/06/15      ADM
LOYAL CAROLYN                  $90.00          $35.00        75/06/12      ADM
MORGAN ELLYN                   $70.00          $35.00        69/10/05      ADM
ROSEN ROGER                    $35.00          $12.00        78/03/18      MKT
SMITH LAWRENCE                 $35.00          $35.00        76/06/15      FIN
STEELE JONATHAN                $70.00          $17.00        80/08/01      DP
--------------------------------------------------------------------------------
TOTALS                        $ 825           $ 412


********************************************************************************



XYZ COMPANY
SUMMARY OF INDIVIDUAL EMPLOYEE PAYROLL INFORMATION AS OF: 10-16-1985
********************************************************************************
         NAME            EXEMPTIONS    FED WTHL      STATE WTHL        FICA
CLOCK KAREN                  1          $100.00        $2.00         $10.00

SALARY           $22576.00          TOTAL EE BENEFIT AMOUNT   $ 235
GROSS/PAY PERIOD $359.00            TOTAL ER BENEFIT AMOUNT   $ 245
--------------------------------------------------------------------------------

DOE JOHN                     2          $147.69        $61.50        $73.80

SALARY           $16000.00          TOTAL EE BENEFIT AMOUNT   $ 145
GROSS/PAY PERIOD $615.38            TOTAL ER BENEFIT AMOUNT   $ 190
--------------------------------------------------------------------------------

HALPRIN JOHN                            $78.00         $2.00         $8.00

SALARY           $8800.00           TOTAL EE BENEFIT AMOUNT   $ 70
GROSS/PAY PERIOD $252.00            TOTAL ER BENEFIT AMOUNT   $ 35
--------------------------------------------------------------------------------
```

Figure 14.23 Specific deduction analysis

```
XYZ COMPANY
SUMMARY OF EMPLOYEE VACATION/PERSONAL LEAVE/SICK TIME BY DEPARTMENT
********************************************************************
DEPARTMENT: ADM                              AS OF: 10-16-1985

                    VACATION         PERSONAL LEAVE        SICK TIME
                  ----------------  ----------------  ----------------
        NAME      ALLOW TAKEN LEFT  ALLOW TAKEN LEFT  ALLOW TAKEN LEFT

CLOCK KAREN       10.00   9     1   24.00   0    24   48.00  40     8
HALPRIN JOHN      10.00   6     4   24.00  1.5  22.5  96.00  2.27  93.7
JONES RANDY       10.00  3.5   6.5  24.00  2.5  21.5  96.00   2    94
LOYAL CAROLYN     10.00   5     5   24.00   1    23            0     0
MORGAN ELLYN      10.00   7     3   24.00  16     8   48.00  16    32
------------------------------------------------------------------
DEPARTMENT: DP                               AS OF: 10-16-1985

                    VACATION         PERSONAL LEAVE        SICK TIME
                  ----------------  ----------------  ----------------
        NAME      ALLOW TAKEN LEFT  ALLOW TAKEN LEFT  ALLOW TAKEN LEFT

JONES MARY        10.00  4.5   5.5  24.00   8    16   48.00  16    32
STEELE JONATHAN   10.00   7     3   24.00  16     8   48.00   8    40
------------------------------------------------------------------
DEPARTMENT: FIN                              AS OF: 10-16-1985

                    VACATION         PERSONAL LEAVE        SICK TIME
                  ----------------  ----------------  ----------------
        NAME      ALLOW TAKEN LEFT  ALLOW TAKEN LEFT  ALLOW TAKEN LEFT

DOE JOHN          15.00  15     0   24.00 14.5  9.5   48.00  24    24
SMITH LAWRENCE    15.00  6.5   8.5  24.00   8    16   48.00   0    48
------------------------------------------------------------------
DEPARTMENT: MKT                              AS OF: 10-16-1985

                    VACATION         PERSONAL LEAVE        SICK TIME
                  ----------------  ----------------  ----------------
        NAME      ALLOW TAKEN LEFT  ALLOW TAKEN LEFT  ALLOW TAKEN LEFT

ROSEN ROGER       10.00   2     8   24.00  16     8   48.00   0    48
------------------------------------------------------------------
********************************************************************
```

Figure 14.24 Summary of employee vacation/personal leave/sick time by department

```
XYZ COMPANY
SUMMARY OF BASIC EEO DATA AS OF: 10-16-1985
********************************************************************

                          EEO-1 JOB CATEGORY
                  ----------------------------------
     RACE/SEX     1   2   3   4   5   6   7   8   9      TOTALS
------------------------------------------------------------------
B = M WHITE       1   1   0   0   1   0   0   0   0        3
C = M BLACK       1   0   0   0   1   0   0   0   0        2
D = M HISPANIC    1   0   0   0   0   0   0   0   0        1
G = F WHITE       0   0   0   0   2   0   0   0   0        2
H = F BLACK       0   1   0   0   0   0   0   0   0        1
I = F HISPANIC    1   0   0   0   0   0   0   0   0        1
------------------------------------------------------------------
        TOTALS    4   2   0   0   4   0   0   0   0

********************************************************************
```

Figure 14.25 Summary of basic EEO data

```
XYZ COMPANY
SUMMARY OF JOB GROUP AND WORK FORCE ANALYSIS DATA AS OF: 10-16-1985
********************************************************************
DEPARTMENT: ADM

POSITION CODE       GRADE        EEO=1 CATEGORY       RACE/SEX        SALARY

      ACLER          01               5                  B          $8800.00
      CLERK          01               5                  G         $21000.00
      MCORD          10               1                  I         $33200.00
      MROFF          11               1                  C         $41600.00
      OFMGR          09               5                  G         $22576.00
      ------------------------------------------------------------------------

DEPARTMENT: DP

POSITION CODE       GRADE        EEO=1 CATEGORY       RACE/SEX        SALARY

      CCORD          10               1                  B         $44655.00
      SCOMP          06               2                  H         $30600.00
      ------------------------------------------------------------------------

DEPARTMENT: FIN

POSITION CODE       GRADE        EEO=1 CATEGORY       RACE/SEX        SALARY

      ACCT           06               2                  B         $16000.00
      ACCT           07               1                  D         $26400.00
      ------------------------------------------------------------------------

DEPARTMENT: MKT

POSITION CODE       GRADE        EEO=1 CATEGORY       RACE/SEX        SALARY

      MASST          08               5                  C         $28600.00
      ------------------------------------------------------------------------

********************************************************************
```

Figure 14.26 Summary of job group and workforce data

```
XYZ COMPANY
 2  EMPLOYEE(S) WITH EEO CODE OF 5G WERE FOUND AS OF: 10-16-1985
********************************************************************
      NAME              POSITION CODE     GRADE     DEPT       SALARY
CLOCK KAREN                 OFMGR           09       ADM      $22576.00
MORGAN ELLYN                CLERK           01       ADM      $21000.00

********************************************************************
```

Figure 14.27 Specific EEO analysis

March 12, 1986

/NAME
/ADDRESS 1
/ADDRESS 2
/CITY/STATE/ZIP

Dear /NAME,

ABC Corporation prides itself in offering it's employees one of the most comprehensive and flexible benefits programs available in the working world.
Through your continued suggestions and comments, we have been able to offer
benefits that specifically meet your needs.

Below we have listed the benefits which you have to date chosen to include
within your benefits package. Please take a minute to review this information.

/BENEFITS

Employee Benefit Dollars Available: $250.00

BENEFITS
```
        Type        Effect Date  EE Amount   ER Amount   Covered Dependents
  1: MEDICAL FAM     82/07/01     $35.00      $135.00      1 2 3 4
  2: LIFE INS        82/07/01     $20.00      $20.00
  3: DENTAL          83/07/01     $20.00      $35.00       1 2 3
  4: PROFIT PLAN     83/07/01     $30.00      $60.00
  5: PEN PLAN        83/07/01     $0          $35.00
  6: UN WAY          83/12/06     $5.00       $10.00
  7: CHILD CARE      83/12/08     $50.00      $50.00        2
                     TOTALS       $160.00     $345.00
```
Dependents:
1. JANE DOE
2. SUSAN DOE
3. GEORGE DOE
4. EMMA SMITH

Life Insurance Beneficiary: JANE DOE
Relationship: Wife
SS Number: 222-22-2222

Please contact the human resources department if you would like to make changes
to your benefits package, or if you have any questions. We would be happy to
help in way we can!

Sincerely,

Jane Doe
Human Resources Manager

Figure 14.28 Summary of individual employee benefits

```
XYZ COMPANY
SUMMARY OF INDIVIDUAL EMPLOYEE BENEFITS BY DEPARTMENT AS OF: 10-16-1985
***************************************************************************

DEPARTMENT: ADM


      NAME            SALARY        TYPE          DATE      EE AMT     ER AMT

CLOCK KAREN          $22576.00   MEDICAL       79/09/06    $135.00    $70.00
                                 DENTAL        80/09/06     $50.00    $25.00
                                 PEN PLAN      80/09/06     $         $50.00
                                 PROFIT PLAN   81/10/12     $50.00   $100.00
                                                 /  /       $         $
                                                 /  /       $         $
                                                 /  /       $         $
                                                 /  /       $         $
                                              TOTALS =     $ 235     $ 245

---------------------------------------------------------------------------
HALPRIN JOHN         $8800.00    MEDICAL       82/06/01     $70.00    $35.00
                                                 /  /       $         $
                                                 /  /       $         $
                                                 /  /       $         $
                                                 /  /       $         $
                                                 /  /       $         $
                                                 /  /       $         $
                                                 /  /       $         $
                                              TOTALS =     $  70     $  35

---------------------------------------------------------------------------
JONES RANDY          $41600.00   MEDICAL       77/06/15    $150.00    $78.00
                                 DENTAL        78/06/15      $8.00     $4.00
                                                 /  /       $         $
                                                 /  /       $         $
                                                 /  /       $         $
                                                 /  /       $         $
                                                 /  /       $         $
                                              TOTALS =     $ 158     $  82

---------------------------------------------------------------------------
LOYAL CAROLYN        $33200.00   MEDICAL       75/06/12     $90.00    $45.00
                                 DENTAL        76/06/12     $10.00     $5.00
                                 UN WAY        75/06/15      $8.00     $4.00
                                 PEN PLAN      76/06/15     $         $50.00
                                                 /  /       $         $
                                                 /  /       $         $
                                                 /  /       $         $
                                              TOTALS =     $ 108     $ 104

---------------------------------------------------------------------------
MORGAN ELLYN         $21000.00   MEDICAL       69/10/05     $70.00    $35.00
                                 DENTAL        70/10/05     $35.00    $17.00
                                 PEN PLAN      70/10/05     $         $50.00
                                 UN WAY        73/12/04     $25.00    $50.00
                                                 /  /       $         $
                                                 /  /       $         $
                                                 /  /       $         $
                                                 /  /       $         $
                                              TOTALS =     $ 130     $ 152

---------------------------------------------------------------------------

TOTAL NUMBER OF EMPLOYEES =   5        TOTAL DEPT EE AMOUNT = $ 701
TOTAL SALARIES = $ 127176              TOTAL DEPT ER AMOUNT = $ 618
```

Figure 14.29 Benefit summary statement by department

continued

DEPARTMENT: DP

NAME	SALARY	TYPE	DATE	EE AMT	ER AMT
JONES MARY	$30600.00	MEDICAL	78/08/16	$70.00	$35.00
		DENTAL	79/08/16	$30.00	$15.00
		PEN PLAN	79/08/16	$	$50.00
			/ /	$	$
			/ /	$	$
			/ /	$	$
			/ /	$	$
			/ /	$	$
			TOTALS =	$ 100	$ 100
STEELE JONATHAN	$44655.00	MEDICAL	80/08/01	$70.00	$35.00
		DENTAL	81/08/01	$30.00	$15.00
		PEN PLAN	81/08/01	$	$50.00
		UN WAY	82/06/12	$15.00	$30.00
			/ /	$	$
			/ /	$	$
			/ /	$	$
			/ /	$	$
			TOTALS =	$ 115	$ 130

TOTAL NUMBER OF EMPLOYEES = 2   TOTAL DEPT EE AMOUNT = $ 215
TOTAL SALARIES = $ 75255   TOTAL DEPT ER AMOUNT = $ 230
****

DEPARTMENT: FIN

NAME	SALARY	TYPE	DATE	EE AMT	ER AMT
DOE JOHN	$16000.00	MEDICAL	77/02/01	$100.00	$50.00
		DENTAL	78/02/01	$15.00	$30.00
		PEN PLAN	78/02/01	$	$50.00
		PROFIT PLAN	78/02/01	$25.00	$50.00
		UN WAY	78/06/01	$5.00	$10.00
			/ /	$	$
			/ /	$	$
			/ /	$	$
			TOTALS =	$ 145	$ 190
SMITH LAWRENCE	$26400.00	MEDICAL	76/06/15	$35.00	$17.00
		MEDICAL S	76/06/15	$35.00	$17.00
		MEDICAL 1	76/06/15	$35.00	$17.00
		DENTAL	77/06/15	$50.00	$25.00
		UN WAY	77/06/23	$5.00	$10.00
		PEN PLAN	77/06/15	$	$50.00
		ADD LIFE	80/03/12	$15.00	$30.00
		PROFIT PLAN	82/06/24	$10.00	$20.00
			TOTALS =	$ 185	$ 186

TOTAL NUMBER OF EMPLOYEES = 2   TOTAL DEPT EE AMOUNT = $ 330
TOTAL SALARIES = $ 42400   TOTAL DEPT ER AMOUNT = $ 376
****

Figure 14.29 *(cont.)*

```
XYZ COMPANY
 10 EMPLOYEE(S) HAVING REVIEW DATE IN 01 WERE FOUND AS OF: 10-16-1985
*********************************************************************************
            NAME              REVIEW DATE        SUPV NAME      DEPT

       CLOCK KAREN             83/01/01            MROFF         ADM
       DOE JOHN                81/01/01            CONTR         FIN
       HALPRIN JOHN            84/01/01            MROFF         ADM
       JONES MARY              82/01/01            SCOOP         DP
       JONES RANDY             83/01/01            VPADM         ADM
       LOYAL CAROLYN           79/01/01            MRMKT         ADM
       MORGAN ELLYN            81/01/01            MCORD         ADM
       ROSEN ROGER             82/01/01            MCORD         MKT
       SMITH LAWRENCE          81/01/01            VPFIN         FIN
       STEELE JONATHAN         83/01/01            VPDP          DP


*********************************************************************************
```

Figure 14.30 Review date summary

```
XYZ COMPANY
 2 EMPLOYEE(S) IN POSITION ACCT   WERE FOUND AS OF: 10-16-1985
*********************************************************************************
        NAME              DATE          SCHOOL        EEO CODE     DEPT

DOE JOHN                80/03/04       NORTH CEN         2B        FIN
SMITH LAWRENCE          76/06/15       UNIV CHIC         1D        FIN


*********************************************************************************
```

Figure 14.31 Specific position code analysis

```
XYZ COMPANY
 4 EMPLOYEE(S) WITH PR REASON FOR CHANGE IN POSITION WERE FOUND AS OF:
 10-16-1985
*********************************************************************************
                        POSITION
        NAME             CODE      DATE        SALARY      SALARY RANGE   GRADE    DEPT

CLOCK KAREN             OFMGR    83/12/01    $22576.00      3RD    QTR      09      ADM
LOYAL CAROLYN           MCORD    81/01/14    $33200.00     +MAX    QTR      10      ADM
ROSEN ROGER             MASST    83/12/28    $28600.00     +MAX    QTR      08      MKT
STEELE JONATHAN         CCORD    82/04/01    $44655.00     +MAX    QTR      10      DP


*********************************************************************************
```

Figure 14.32 Specific reason for change in position analysis

```
XYZ COMPANY
SALARY RANGE ANALYSIS BY GRADE AS OF: 10-16-1985
*********************************************************************i
GRADE: 01


                                         SALARY RANGE
                                  -----------------------------
          NAME          DEPT      SALARY    MIN 1ST 2ND 3RD 4TH   MAX      C-RATIO
     HALPRIN JOHN       ADM      $8800.00        1ST                        .88
     MORGAN ELLYN       ADM     $21000.00                           +MAX    2.1

     TOTAL NUMBER OF EMPLOYEES =  2        TOTAL SALARIES = $ 29800
     TOTAL EMPLOYEES BELOW MIN =  0        AVERAGE SALARY = $ 14900
     TOTAL EMPLOYEES ABOVE MAX =  1        AVERAGE C-RATIO =  1.49

----------------------------------------------------------------------------
GRADE: 06


                                         SALARY RANGE
                                  -----------------------------
          NAME          DEPT      SALARY    MIN 1ST 2ND 3RD 4TH   MAX      C-RATIO
     DOE JOHN           FIN     $16000.00            2ND                    .993
     JONES MARY         DP      $30600.00                           +MAX    1.90

     TOTAL NUMBER OF EMPLOYEES =  2        TOTAL SALARIES = $ 46600
     TOTAL EMPLOYEES BELOW MIN =  0        AVERAGE SALARY = $ 23300
     TOTAL EMPLOYEES ABOVE MAX =  1        AVERAGE C-RATIO =  1.4465

----------------------------------------------------------------------------
GRADE: 07


                                         SALARY RANGE
                                  -----------------------------
          NAME          DEPT      SALARY    MIN 1ST 2ND 3RD 4TH   MAX      C-RATIO
     SMITH LAWRENCE     FIN     $26400.00                           +MAX    1.47

     TOTAL NUMBER OF EMPLOYEES =  1        TOTAL SALARIES = $ 26400
     TOTAL EMPLOYEES BELOW MIN =  0        AVERAGE SALARY = $ 26400
     TOTAL EMPLOYEES ABOVE MAX =  1        AVERAGE C-RATIO =  1.47

----------------------------------------------------------------------------
GRADE: 08


                                         SALARY RANGE
                                  -----------------------------
          NAME          DEPT      SALARY    MIN 1ST 2ND 3RD 4TH   MAX      C-RATIO
     ROSEN ROGER        MKT     $28600.00                           +MAX    1.44

     TOTAL NUMBER OF EMPLOYEES =  1        TOTAL SALARIES = $ 28600
     TOTAL EMPLOYEES BELOW MIN =  0        AVERAGE SALARY = $ 28600
     TOTAL EMPLOYEES ABOVE MAX =  1        AVERAGE C-RATIO =  1.44

----------------------------------------------------------------------------
GRADE: 09


                                         SALARY RANGE
                                  -----------------------------
          NAME          DEPT      SALARY    MIN 1ST 2ND 3RD 4TH   MAX      C-RATIO
     CLOCK KAREN        ADM     $22576.00                3RD                 1.02

     TOTAL NUMBER OF EMPLOYEES =  1        TOTAL SALARIES = $ 22576
     TOTAL EMPLOYEES BELOW MIN =  0        AVERAGE SALARY = $ 22576
     TOTAL EMPLOYEES ABOVE MAX =  0        AVERAGE C-RATIO =  1.02

----------------------------------------------------------------------------
```

Figure 14.33 Salary range analysis by grade

```
XYZ COMPANY
SALARY RANGE ANALYSIS BY DEPARTMENT AS OF: 10-16-1985
*********************************************************************************
DEPARTMENT: ADM

                                           SALARY RANGE
                                   ------------------------------
         NAME             GRADE      SALARY   MIN 1ST 2ND 3RD 4TH   MAX    C-RATIO
CLOCK KAREN               09       $22576.00                3RD           1.02
HALPRIN JOHN             01       $8800.00        1ST                    .88
JONES RANDY              11       $41600.00                      +MAX    1.50
LOYAL CAROLYN           10       $33200.00                      +MAX    1.34
MORGAN ELLYN            01       $21000.00                      +MAX    2.1

TOTAL NUMBER OF EMPLOYEES =   5        TOTAL SALARIES = $ 127176
TOTAL EMPLOYEES BELOW MIN =   0        AVERAGE SALARY = $ 25435.2
TOTAL EMPLOYEES ABOVE MAX =   3        AVERAGE C-RATIO =   1.368
-----------------------------------------------------------------------------------
DEPARTMENT: DP

                                           SALARY RANGE
                                   ------------------------------
         NAME             GRADE      SALARY   MIN 1ST 2ND 3RD 4TH   MAX    C-RATIO
JONES MARY               06       $30600.00                      +MAX    1.90
STEELE JONATHAN        10       $44655.00                      +MAX    1.81

TOTAL NUMBER OF EMPLOYEES =   2        TOTAL SALARIES = $ 75255
TOTAL EMPLOYEES BELOW MIN =   0        AVERAGE SALARY = $ 37627.5
TOTAL EMPLOYEES ABOVE MAX =   2        AVERAGE C-RATIO =   1.855
-----------------------------------------------------------------------------------
DEPARTMENT: FIN

                                           SALARY RANGE
                                   ------------------------------
         NAME             GRADE      SALARY   MIN 1ST 2ND 3RD 4TH   MAX    C-RATIO
DOE JOHN                 06       $16000.00            2ND               .993
SMITH LAWRENCE         07       $26400.00                      +MAX    1.47

TOTAL NUMBER OF EMPLOYEES =   2        TOTAL SALARIES = $ 42400
TOTAL EMPLOYEES BELOW MIN =   0        AVERAGE SALARY = $ 21200
TOTAL EMPLOYEES ABOVE MAX =   1        AVERAGE C-RATIO =   1.2315
-----------------------------------------------------------------------------------
DEPARTMENT: MKT

                                           SALARY RANGE
                                   ------------------------------
         NAME             GRADE      SALARY   MIN 1ST 2ND 3RD 4TH   MAX    C-RATIO
ROSEN ROGER             08       $28600.00                      +MAX    1.44

TOTAL NUMBER OF EMPLOYEES =   1        TOTAL SALARIES = $ 28600
TOTAL EMPLOYEES BELOW MIN =   0        AVERAGE SALARY = $ 28600
TOTAL EMPLOYEES ABOVE MAX =   1        AVERAGE C-RATIO =   1.44
-----------------------------------------------------------------------------------
*********************************************************************************
```

Figure 14.34 Salary range analysis by department

```
XYZ COMPANY
MERIT RATING AND PLACE IN RANGE MATRIX (ORGANIZATION-WIDE) AS OF: 10-16-1985
****************************************************************************

RATING                        PLACE IN RANGE
        -----------------------------------------------------------------------
          - MIN     1ST     2ND     3RD     4TH     + MAX     TOTALS
        -----------------------------------------------------------------------
E           0        1       1       1       0        5         8
S           0        0       0       0       0        2         2
        -----------------------------------------------------------------------
TOTALS      0        1       1       1       0        7        10


****************************************************************************
```

Figure 14.35 Merit rating and place in range matrix

```
XYZ COMPANY
SALARY INCREASE ANALYSIS BY DEPARTMENT AS OF: 10-16-1985
***************************************************************************************
DEPARTMENT: ADM

SALARY              NAME              PERF RATING    PERF DATE   % CHANGE  $ CHANGE

$22576.00   CLOCK KAREN                  E           83/01/01     15.00    $2200.00
$8800.00    HALPRIN JOHN                 E           84/01/01     10.00    $800.00
$41600.00   JONES RANDY                  E           83/01/01     10.00    $3800.00
$33200.00   LOYAL CAROLYN                S           79/01/01     10.00    $3020.00
$21000.00   MORGAN ELLYN                 E           81/01/01     10.00    $2000.00

TOTAL SALARIES     = $ 127176      AVERAGE MERIT $ =   $ 2364
TOTAL MERIT $      = $ 11820       AVERAGE MERIT % =     11 %

------------------------------------------------------------------------------------

DEPARTMENT: DP

SALARY              NAME              PERF RATING    PERF DATE   % CHANGE  $ CHANGE

$30600.00   JONES MARY                   E           82/01/01     10.00    $2800.00
$44655.00   STEELE JONATHAN              E           83/01/01     12.00    $4241.00

TOTAL SALARIES     = $ 75255       AVERAGE MERIT $ =   $ 3520.5
TOTAL MERIT $      = $ 7041        AVERAGE MERIT % =     11 %

------------------------------------------------------------------------------------

DEPARTMENT: FIN

SALARY              NAME              PERF RATING    PERF DATE   % CHANGE  $ CHANGE

$16000.00   DOE JOHN                     E           81/01/01     10.00    $1000.00
$26400.00   SMITH LAWRENCE               E           81/01/01     10.00    $2400.00

TOTAL SALARIES     = $ 42400       AVERAGE MERIT $ =   $ 1700
TOTAL MERIT $      = $ 3400        AVERAGE MERIT % =     10 %

------------------------------------------------------------------------------------

DEPARTMENT: MKT

SALARY              NAME              PERF RATING    PERF DATE   % CHANGE  $ CHANGE

$28600.00   ROSEN ROGER                  S           82/01/01     10.00    $2600.00

TOTAL SALARIES     = $ 28600       AVERAGE MERIT $ =   $ 2600
TOTAL MERIT $      = $ 2600        AVERAGE MERIT % =     10 %

------------------------------------------------------------------------------------


***************************************************************************************
```

Figure 14.36 Salary and dollar increase by department

```
XYZ COMPANY
SALARY INCREASE ANALYSIS BY EEO CODE AS OF: 10-16-1985
**************************************************************************
EEO CODE: 1B

   SALARY      NAME                        GRADE   RATING   MERIT %   MERIT $    C-RATIO
 $44655.00   STEELE JONATHAN                10       E      12.00   $4241.00      1.81

 TOTAL SALARIES       = $ 44655          AVERAGE MERIT $ =    $ 4241
 TOTAL MERIT $        = $ 4241           AVERAGE MERIT % =     12 %
------------------------------------------------------------------------

EEO CODE: 1C

   SALARY      NAME                        GRADE   RATING   MERIT %   MERIT $    C-RATIO
 $41600.00   JONES RANDY                    11       E      10.00   $3800.00      1.50

 TOTAL SALARIES       = $ 41600          AVERAGE MERIT $ =    $ 3800
 TOTAL MERIT $        = $ 3800           AVERAGE MERIT % =     10 %
------------------------------------------------------------------------

EEO CODE: 1D

   SALARY      NAME                        GRADE   RATING   MERIT %   MERIT $    C-RATIO
 $26400.00   SMITH LAWRENCE                 07       E      10.00   $2400.00      1.47

 TOTAL SALARIES       = $ 26400          AVERAGE MERIT $ =    $ 2400
 TOTAL MERIT $        = $ 2400           AVERAGE MERIT % =     10 %
------------------------------------------------------------------------

EEO CODE: 1I

   SALARY      NAME                        GRADE   RATING   MERIT %   MERIT $    C-RATIO
 $33200.00   LOYAL CAROLYN                  10       S      10.00   $3020.00      1.34

 TOTAL SALARIES       = $ 33200          AVERAGE MERIT $ =    $ 3020
 TOTAL MERIT $        = $ 3020           AVERAGE MERIT % =     10 %
------------------------------------------------------------------------

EEO CODE: 2B

   SALARY      NAME                        GRADE   RATING   MERIT %   MERIT $    C-RATIO
 $16000.00   DOE JOHN                       06       E      10.00   $1000.00      .993

 TOTAL SALARIES       = $ 16000          AVERAGE MERIT $ =    $ 1000
 TOTAL MERIT $        = $ 1000           AVERAGE MERIT % =     10 %
------------------------------------------------------------------------

EEO CODE: 2H

   SALARY      NAME                        GRADE   RATING   MERIT %   MERIT $    C-RATIO
 $30600.00   JONES MARY                     06       E      10.00   $2800.00      1.90

 TOTAL SALARIES       = $ 30600          AVERAGE MERIT $ =    $ 2800
 TOTAL MERIT $        = $ 2800           AVERAGE MERIT % =     10 %
------------------------------------------------------------------------

EEO CODE: 5B

   SALARY      NAME                        GRADE   RATING   MERIT %   MERIT $    C-RATIO
 $8800.00    HALPRIN JOHN                   01       E      10.00   $800.00       .88
```

Figure 14.37 Salary and dollar increase by EEO code

OTHER SAMPLE HRM REPORTS AND FORMATS

Computerization of HRM Processes

Type of Sample Format or Report

Scheduled Interview Report* (Figure 14.38)

Software Product Name and Overall Functions

The APPLICANT MANAGEMENT SYSTEM™ is designed to streamline the hiring process through maintaining a thorough and up-to-date record on each applicant. The system automatically tabulates data entered to generate a number of reports.

Specific Functions Performed by Format or Report

The Scheduled Interview Report provides a summary of interviews, plant visits, or any other activity that may be scheduled along with the date and time. This report is run on a scheduled basis to ensure that timely interview arrangements are accomplished.

Explanation of Terms, Column Headings, and Codes

All reports in the Applicant Management System are straightforward in their operation and terms; all headers are in English and no codes are used. The reports can be configured by date, position titles, and applicant status.

```
                         VSI INC.  /  ATLANTA, GA.
                         SCHEDULED INTERVIEW REPORT


POSITION APPLIED FOR
APPLICANT NAME                  INTERVIEWER/EVENT             DATE       TIME

ATM SYSTEMS ANALYST
BROWN, SCOTT                    BILL ROGERS                  05-25-84   09:30

ATM SYSTEMS ANALYST
DANIELS, WILLIAM                BILL ROGERS                  05-24-84   11:00

PROGRAMMER/ANALYST
JOHNSON, FRED                   CALVIN CLINE                 06-15-84   11:00

PROGRAMMER/ANALYST
JOHNSON, FRED                   HARRY SMITH                  07-10-84   08:30

PROGRAMMER/ANALYST
LOGGINS, KEN                    JOHN JONES                   06-01-84   12:00

ATM SYSTEMS ANALYST
POLO, JOHN                      HARRY SMITH                  10-12-84   10:00
```

Figure 14.38 Scheduled interview report

* Courtesy of VSI INC., 6425 Powers Ferry Road, Suite 365, Atlanta, GA 30339.

Computerization of HRM Processes

Type of Sample Format or Report

Applicant EEO/Flow Report* (Figure 14.39)

Software Product Name and Overall Functions

The APPLICANT MANAGEMENT SYSTEM™ is designed to streamline the hiring process through maintaining a thorough and up-to-date record on each applicant. The system automatically tabulates data entered to generate a number of reports.

Specific Functions Performed by Format or Report

The Applicant EEO/Flow Report provides a summary of the applicant flow through the organization. A breakdown of data into 5 categories is provided: sex, race, disability status, veteran status, and age group. For each category, data are shown as progressing from entered, interviewed, offers, and hires.

Explanation of Terms, Column Headings, and Codes

All reports in the Applicant Management System are straightforward in their operation and terms; all headers are in English and no codes are used. The reports can be configured by date, position titles, and applicant status.

(See following page)

* Courtesy of VSI INC., 6425 Powers Ferry Road, Suite 365, Atlanta, GA 30339.

```
                    VSI INC.  /  ATLANTA, GA.
                    APPLICANT EEO REPORT

                ENTERED   INTERVIEWED OFFERS      HIRES

ALL POSITION APPLIED FOR
ALL STATUS

SEX
------------------------------------
      MALE                5         3          2          2
      FEMALE              2         0          0          0


RACE
------------------------------------
      CAUCASIAN           4         3          1          1
      BLACK               1         1          1          1
      AMERICAN INDIAN     2         1          0          0


DISABILITY STATUS
------------------------------------
      NO DISABILITY       5         3          1          1
      PHYSICAL/PARTIAL    2         2          1          1


VETERAN STATUS
------------------------------------
      NON VETERAN         3         2          1          1
      VETERAN             1         1          1          1
      VIETNAM VETERAN     1         1          0          0
      DISABLED VETERAN    1         1          0          0
      WORLD WAR II VET.   1         0          0          0


AGE GROUP
------------------------------------
      UNDER 40            4         4          1          1
      40-55               1         1          1          1
      UNKNOWN             1         0          0          0
      OVER 55             1         0          0          0


UNCLASSIFIED
------------------------------------
      UNCLASSIFIED       26         1          1          1
```

Figure 14.39 Applicant EEO/flow report

Computerization of HRM Processes

Type of Sample Format or Report

Applicant EEO-1 Report* (Figure 14.40)

Software Product Name and Overall Functions

The APPLICANT MANAGEMENT SYSTEM™ is designed to streamline the hiring process through maintaining a thorough and up-to-date record on each applicant. The system automatically tabulates data entered to generate a number of reports.

Specific Functions Performed by Format or Report

The Applicant EEO-1 Report provides a breakdown by EEO-1 category, race, and sex. It is similar to the EEO-1 report prepared on employees, but it provides this information on applicants.

Explanation of Terms, Column Headings, and Codes

All reports in the Applicant Management System are straightforward in their operation and terms; all headers are in English and no codes are used. The reports can be configured by date, position titles, and applicant status.

```
ALL JOB CATEGORY
ALL STATUS


                          CAUCASIAN
                          ---------------------------
EEOC CODE                 MALE        FEMALE
---------                 ---------------------------
MANAGEMENT                3            1
PROFESSIONAL
TECHNICAL



                          BLACK
                          ---------------------------
EEOC CODE                 MALE        FEMALE
---------                 ---------------------------
MANAGEMENT
PROFESSIONAL              1
TECHNICAL



                          AMERICAN INDIAN
                          ---------------------------
EEOC CODE                 MALE        FEMALE
---------                 ---------------------------
MANAGEMENT
PROFESSIONAL                           1
TECHNICAL                 1
```

Figure 14.40 Applicant EEO-1 report

* Courtesy of VSI INC., 6425 Powers Ferry Road, Suite 365, Atlanta, GA 30339.

Computerization of HRM Processes

Type of Sample Format or Report

Applicant EEO/Status Report* (Figure 14.41)

Software Product Name and Overall Functions

The APPLICANT MANAGEMENT SYSTEM™ is designed to streamline the hiring process through maintaining a thorough and up-to-date record on each applicant. The system automatically tabulates data entered to generate a number of reports.

Specific Functions Performed by Format or Report

The Applicant EEO/Status Report provides complete EEO category information. In addition, the report provides information on each applicant concerning the position applied for, source, and current status. The report is useful in monitoring the effectiveness of Affirmative Action Plans, or in providing information for an EEO audit.

Explanation of Terms, Column Headings, and Codes

All reports in the Applicant Management System are straightforward in their operation and terms; all headers are in English and no codes are used. The reports can be configured by date, position titles, and applicant status.

(See following page)

* Courtesy of VSI INC., 6425 Powers Ferry Road, Suite 365, Atlanta, GA 30339.

```
                        VSI INC. / ATLANTA, GA.
                     APPLICANT EEO/STATUS REPORT


ALL POSITION APPLIED FOR                    ALL JOB CATEGORY
ALL STATUS
   INDEX #                    SEX                    POSITION APPLIED FOR
   NAME                       RACE                   EEO JOB CATEGORY
   DATE ENTERED               HANDICAP               SOURCE
                              VETERAN                STATUS
                              AGE

-------------                 --------               ---------------------
   4                          MALE                   ATM SYSTEMS ANALYST
   BROWN, SCOTT               CAUCASIAN              MANAGEMENT
   08-06-84                   PHYSICAL/PARTIAL       REFERRAL
                              DISABLED VETERAN       REJECT/EXPERIENCE
                              UNDER 40


   2                          MALE                   ATM SYSTEMS ANALYST
   DANIELS, WILLIAM           BLACK                  PROFESSIONAL
   08-06-84                   PHYSICAL/PARTIAL       AD CHICAGO TRIB 4/09
                              VETERAN                REJECT/EXPERIENCE
                              40-55


   25                         FEMALE                 ACCOUNTING MGR.
   DAVIS, SHIRLEY             CAUCASIAN              MANAGEMENT
   08-06-84                   NO DISABILITY          WALK IN
                              WORLD WAR II VET.      REJECT/EXPERIENCE
                              OVER 55


   3                          MALE                   PROGRAMMER/ANALYST
   JOHNSON, FRED              AMERICAN INDIAN        TECHNICAL
   08-06-84                   NO DISABILITY          ATL CONST AD 12-20
                              VIETNAM VETERAN        REJECTED OFFER
                              UNDER 40


   5                          MALE                   PROGRAMMER/ANALYST
   LOGGINS, KEN               CAUCASIAN              MANAGEMENT
   09-18-84                   NO DISABILITY          EMPLOYEE REFERRAL
                              NON VETERAN
                              UNDER 40


   17                         FEMALE                 UNKNOWN
   PEEK, CHAR                 AMERICAN INDIAN        PROFESSIONAL
   08-06-84                   NO DISABILITY          UNKNOWN
                              NON VETERAN            REJECTED OFFER
                              UNKNOWN


   1                          MALE                   ATM SYSTEMS ANALYST
   POLO, JOHN                 CAUCASIAN              MANAGEMENT
   08-06-84                   NO DISABILITY          RECRUITMENT
                              NON VETERAN            INTEREST
                              UNDER 40
```

Figure 14.41 Applicant EEO/status report

Computerization of HRM Processes

Type of Sample Format or Report

Applicant Expense Report* (Figure 14.42)

Software Product Name and Overall Functions

The APPLICANT MANAGEMENT SYSTEM™ is designed to streamline the hiring process through maintaining a thorough and up-to-date record on each applicant. The system automatically tabulates data entered to generate a number of reports.

Specific Functions Performed by Format or Report

The Applicant Expense Report provides information on any and all expenses related to applicants. Individual applicant expenses are summarized in the applicant's file, and a similar report summarizes expenses relating to a specific position: advertisements, agency fees, and so on.

Explanation of Terms, Column Headings, and Codes

All reports in the Applicant Management System are straightforward in their operation and terms; all headers are in English and no codes are used. The reports can be configured by date, position titles, and applicant status.

(See following page)

* Courtesy of VSI INC., 6425 Powers Ferry Road, Suite 365, Atlanta, GA 30339.

```
                    VSI INC.  / ATLANTA, GA.
                 EXPENSES BY POSITION APPLIED FOR


ALL POSITION APPLIED FOR
INDEX #
NAME                        POSITION                    EXPENSE DATE
                            EXPENSE                     AMOUNT
--------                    ----------                  --------------
4                           ATM SYSTEMS ANALYST         08-06-84
BROWN, SCOTT                RENTAL CAR                       35.00

4                           ATM SYSTEMS ANALYST         08-06-84
BROWN, SCOTT                AIRFARE                         325.00

4                           ATM SYSTEMS ANALYST         08-06-84
BROWN, SCOTT                HOTEL                            45.00

18                          UNKNOWN                     08-06-84
BROWN, MARY                 MEALS                            22.75

2                           ATM SYSTEMS ANALYST         08-06-84
DANIELS, WILLIAM            AIRFARE                         350.00

2                           ATM SYSTEMS ANALYST         08-06-84
DANIELS, WILLIAM            HOTEL                            75.00

3                           PROGRAMMER/ANALYST          08-06-84
JOHNSON, FRED               HOTEL                            55.00

3                           PROGRAMMER/ANALYST          08-06-84
JOHNSON, FRED               MEALS                            25.00

3                           PROGRAMMER/ANALYST          08-06-84
JOHNSON, FRED               RENTAL CAR                       78.00

5                           PROGRAMMER/ANALYST          08-06-84
LOGGINS, KEN                MEALS                            25.00

1                           ATM SYSTEMS ANALYST         08-06-84
POLO, JOHN                  AIRFARE                         275.00

1                           ATM SYSTEMS ANALYST         08-06-84
POLO, JOHN                  RENTAL CAR                       36.50


                            TOTAL:                       1,347.25
```

Figure 14.42 Applicant expense report

Computerization of HRM Processes

Type of Sample Format or Report

Applicant Hire Report* (Figure 14.43)

Software Product Name and Overall Functions

The APPLICANT MANAGEMENT SYSTEM™ is designed to streamline the hiring process through maintaining a thorough and up-to-date record on each applicant. The system automatically tabulates data entered to generate a number of reports.

Specific Functions Performed by Format or Report

The Applicant Hire Report provides information on applicants that have accepted offers of employment. This includes the position, supervisor, work location, applicant source, and start date.

Explanation of Terms, Column Headings, and Codes

All reports in the Applicant Management System are straightforward in their operation and terms; all headers are in English and no codes are used. The reports can be configured by date, position titles, and applicant status.

```
                    VSI INC.  /  ATLANTA, GA.
                    APPLICANT HIRE REPORT


ALL POSITION APPLIED FOR ALL DIVISION/BUREAU      ALL INTERVIEWER/SUPERVS

REQ. #                     HIRE(POSITION)
INDEX #                    SUPERVISOR             SOURCE
NAME                       LOCATION/DIVISON-BUREAU  START DATE
--------                   --------------------------  ----------
  0
  2                        ACCOUNTING MGR.        AD CHICAGO TRIB 4/09
DANIELS, WILLIAM           MAYORS OFFICE          12-12-89

 86125                     ATM SYSTEMS ANALYST
 1                         BILL ROGERS            RECRUITMENT
POLO, JOHN                 ACCOUNTING             01-05-87

  0                        ATM SYSTEMS ANALYST
 32                        SYSTEMS MANAGER        ADVERTISEMENT
STEVENS, JOE               ADMINISTRATION         09-01-86
```

Figure 14.43 Applicant hire report

* Courtesy of VSI INC., 6425 Powers Ferry Road, Suite 365, Atlanta, GA 30339.

Computerization of HRM Processes

Type of Sample Format or Report

Applicant Listing* (Figure 14.44)

Software Product Name and Overall Functions

RETRIEVE; RETRIEVE/TRACKING; RETRIEVE/COLLEGE™ These applicant retrieval and tracking systems allow an employment or recruiting manager to store and keep track of over 10,000 job applicants on a personal computer. These systems generate applicant form letters and keep track of dates sent, perform fast data base searches using flexible criteria, and produce a number of management reports. Representative reports include EEO statistics, recruiting source effectiveness, and interview/hire/start summaries by recruiter.

Specific Functions Performed by Format or Report

The Applicant Listing shows the position of each job applicant in the hiring cycle, and the dates associated with each step. The Applicant Listing may be produced for any subset of the data base after using any of a number of search criteria. Examples of search criteria are: specific jobs or skills, any date such as date résumé received, date interviewed or date hired, school, degree, former employer, source, status, recruiter, or hiring manager.

Explanation of Terms, Column Headings, and Codes

The Applicant Listing includes the I.D. number assigned to each applicant by the system, and the names of the hiring managers to whom each applicant was routed during the hiring cycle.

(See following page)

---

* Courtesy of Greentree Systems, Inc., 444 Castro Street, Mountain View, CA 94041.

RETRIEVE APPLICANT LISTING

ID	----- Candidate -----	--Offer--	------ Answer ------	---On---	--Start--	--Route--	--Date--	-Result--	--Date---
1	Hill, Anthony	10-Jan-86	Decline-Location	30-Jan-86		Myers	01-Dec-85	Invite	02-Dec-85
2	Cosbie, Douglas					Johnson	20-Nov-85	Invite	02-Dec-85
						Myers	20-Nov-85	Invite	16-Dec-85
3	Lockhart, Eugene					Johnson	19-Nov-86	Invite	05-Jan-87
4	Newsome, Timothy					Johnson	01-Nov-86	Reject	10-Nov-86
5	Cartwright, William					Myers	01-Dec-86	Invite	05-Dec-86
6	Short, Purvis	31-Jan-86	Accept	15-Feb-86	01-May-86	Johnson	01-Dec-85	Invite	03-Jan-86
7	Perry, William					Johnson	03-Nov-86	Invite	07-Nov-86
8	Watson, Kenneth					Bergman	05-Dec-86	Invite	10-Dec-86
9	Reynolds, Thomas					Myers	03-Mar-86	Invite	15-Mar-86
10	Burroughs, Edgar	15-Mar-86	Decline-Salary	20-Mar-86		Myers	07-Jan-86	Invite	
11	Cristopolous, Anthony					Johnson	20-Nov-86	Invite	01-Dec-86
12	Berenson, Marisa					Myers	20-Dec-86	Invite	05-Jan-87
13	Marino, Daniel	08-Jan-87	Accept	08-Jan-87	01-Mar-87	Johnson	02-Dec-86	Invite	10-Dec-86
14	Wagner, Alicia					Johnson	12-Nov-86	Invite	01-Dec-86
15	Jasper, Nancy	01-May-86	Decline-Salary	15-May-86		Johnson	12-Mar-86	Invite	01-Apr-86
16	Wilkerson, Thomas					Myers	06-Nov-86	Invite	30-Nov-86
17	Michaels, Marvin	10-Nov-86	Decline-Salary	10-Dec-86		Myers	15-Oct-86	Invite	20-Oct-86
						Johnson	15-Oct-86	Invite	22-Oct-86
18	Kim, Byung Hak	08-Jan-86	Accept	14-Jan-86	16-Feb-86	Myers	05-Dec-85	Invite	20-Dec-85
						Johnson	05-Dec-85	Invite	15-Dec-85
19	Ramirez, Gloria	02-Feb-86	Decline-Salary	28-Feb-86		Myers	08-Dec-85	Invite	03-Jan-86
20	Hernandez, Anna Maria					Myers	30-Oct-86	Invite	02-Nov-86
21	Smith, Mary Nelson					Myers	20-Oct-86	Invite	05-Nov-86
						Johnson	20-Oct-86	Reject	01-Nov-86
22	Nickson, Troy					Myers			
						Bergman			
23	Andrews, Leonard					Myers			
24	Misner, Tamara					Johnson			

Figure 14.44 Applicant listing

Computerization of HRM Processes

Type of Sample Format or Report

Applicant Profiles Report* (Figure 14.45)

Software Product Name and Overall Functions

RETRIEVE; RETRIEVE/TRACKING; RETRIEVE/COLLEGE™ These applicant retrieval and tracking systems allow an employment or recruiting manager to store and keep track of over 10,000 job applicants on a personal computer. These systems generate applicant form letters and keep track of dates sent, perform fast data base searches using flexible criteria, and produce a number of management reports. Representative reports include EEO statistics, recruiting source effectiveness, and interview/hire/start summaries by recruiter.

Specific Functions Performed by Format or Report

The Applicant Profiles Report displays "mini-résumés" for a group of job applicants extracted from an employment manager's RETRIEVE data base. Normally produced for review by hiring managers, the Profiles Report summarizes the background and qualifications of applicants in a particular job/skill group that have been recently reviewed by the employment department.

Explanation of Terms, Column Headings, and Codes

The Applicant Profiles Report shows the name of the recruiter to which each applicant is assigned so that a hiring manager can follow up with the recruiter if there is interest in a candidate.

(See following page)

---

* Courtesy of Greentree Systems, Inc., 444 Castro Street, Mountain View, CA 94041.

January 26, 1987

To: _____
From: Employment Manager
Subj: Engineer Candidates


```
JOB/SKILLS           APPLICANTS                                    RECRUITER
----------           ----------                                    ---------


Engineer         : Lockhart, Eugene                 3  15-Nov-84     Knox
Design           : 10010 Lovers Lane; Dallas, TX 75033
FORTRAN          : 214 543-9494(H)   214 222-5200x341(W)
                 : U of H      BSEE     MSEE     Yrs exper:  5
                 : TI       / 5 yrs, Design Engineer
                 :          /
                 :


Engineer         : Newsome, Timothy                 4  15-Nov-84     Knox
Design           : 8765 Greenville Ave.; Dallas, TX 75040
QC               : 214 235-4311(H)   214 330-3300x4555(W)
                 : Purdue       BSEE            Yrs exper:  6
                 : TI       / 4 yrs, Qual Cntrl Engineer
                 : Apple    / 2 yrs, Qual Cntrl Supvisor
                 : Assembly and packaging of microcomputers


Engineer         : Wagner, Alicia                  14  19-Nov-85     Mercer
Design           : 3923 112th Street; Miami, FL 33156
FORTRAN          : 305 385-2326(H)   305 564-3900x456(W)
                 : U Miami      None            Yrs exper:  5
                 : TI       / 5 yrs, Design Engineer
                 :          /
                 : Telecommunications System Design
```

Figure 14.45 Applicant profiles report

Computerization of HRM Processes

Type of Sample Format or Report

Applicant Source vs. Status Analysis* (Figure 14.46)

Software Product Name and Overall Functions

RETRIEVE; RETRIEVE/TRACKING; RETRIEVE/COLLEGE™ These applicant retrieval and tracking systems allow an employment or recruiting manager to store and keep track of over 10,000 job applicants on a personal computer. These systems generate applicant form letters and keep track of dates sent, perform fast data base searches using flexible criteria, and produce a number of management reports. Representative reports include EEO statistics, recruiting source effectiveness, and interview/hire/start summaries by recruiter.

Specific Functions Performed by Format or Report

The Source Applicant vs. Status Analysis allows a manager to compare and evaluate the effectiveness of the company's recruiting sources.

Explanation of Terms, Column Headings, and Codes

The Applicant Source vs. Status Analysis cross-tabulates recruiting sources (column headings) by applicant status (row labels). Each cell contains percentages calculated horizontally (H), vertically (V), and overall total (T).

(See following page)

* Courtesy of Greentree Systems, Inc., 444 Castro Street, Mountain View, CA 94041.

	Ad-Chronicle	Ad-Mercury	Ad-Tribune	Mail in	Total
Dclnd Offer	0	0	1	0	1
			V 25%		
			T 3%		T 3%
Future	2	0	0	2	4
	H 50%			H 50%	
	V 13%			V 22%	
	T 7%			T 7%	T 14%
Hired	5	0	0	1	6
	H 83%			H 17%	
	V 33%			V 11%	
	T 17%			T 3%	T 21%
Intvd-Rejected	3	0	0	1	4
	H 75%			H 25%	
	V 20%			V 11%	
	T 10%			T 3%	T 14%
Invite	0	1	1	0	2
		H 50%	H 50%		
			V 25%		
		T 3%	T 3%		T 7%
Rejected	3	0	1	1	5
	H 60%		H 20%	H 20%	
	V 20%		V 25%	V 11%	
	T 10%		T 3%	T 3%	T 17%
Route-Harrison	1	0	0	0	1
	V 7%				
	T 3%				T 3%
Route-Johnson	1	0	1	0	2
	H 50%		H 50%		
	V 7%		V 25%		
	T 3%		T 3%		T 7%
Route-Myers	0	0	0	4	4
				V 44%	
				T 14%	T 14%
Total	15	1	4	9	29
	T 52%	T 3%	T 14%	T 31%	

Figure 14.46 Applicant source vs. status analysis

585

Computerization of HRM Processes

Type of Sample Format or Report

New Hires Summary by Job/Skill* (Figure 14.47)

Software Product Name and Overall Functions

RETRIEVE; RETRIEVE/TRACKING; RETRIEVE/COLLEGE™ These applicant retrieval and tracking systems allow an employment or recruiting manager to store and keep track of over 10,00 job applicants on a personal computer. These systems generate applicant form letters and keep track of dates sent, perform fast data base searches using flexible criteria, and produce a number of management reports. Representative reports include EEO statistics, recruiting source effectiveness, and interview/hire/start summaries by recruiter.

Specific Functions Performed by Format or Report

The New Hires Summary by Job/Skill provides an analysis of the type of applicants who have been hired, or who still reside in the applicant data base. This report can be produced for any subset of applicants such as new hires or applicants with a particular degree, sex, race, or former employer.

Explanation of Terms, Column Headings, and Codes

The New Hires Summary by Job/Skill shows the number of applicants (count) and percentages of the total.

```
              RETRIEVE Analysis Function
                1987 New Hires Summary
                     By Job/Skill


                    Count  Percent

    App Programmer     2      3%
            COBOL     10     15%
           Design      4      6%
         Engineer      6      9%
      Fin Analyst      6      9%
          Fortran      7     10%
            Lotus      4      6%
              MVS      4      6%
  Product Engineer     2      3%
        Programmer    10     15%
               QC      3      4%
        Sales Rep      5      7%
    Sys Programmer     3      4%
       Other/None      1      1%

            Total     67
```

Figure 14.47 New hires summary by job/skill

* Courtesy of Greentree Systems, Inc., 444 Castro Street, Mountain View, CA 94041.

Computerization of HRM Processes

Type of Sample Format or Report

New Hires Summary by School* (Figure 14.48)

Software Product Name and Overall Functions

RETRIEVE; RETRIEVE/TRACKING; RETRIEVE/COLLEGE™ These applicant retrieval and tracking systems allow an employment or recruiting manager to store and keep track of over 10,000 job applicants on a personal computer. These systems generate applicant form letters and keep track of dates sent, perform fast data base searches using flexible criteria, and produce a number of management reports. Representative reports include EEO statistics, recruiting source effectiveness, and interview/hire/start summaries by recruiter.

Specific Functions Performed by Format or Report

The New Hires Summary by School allows a manager to evaluate the effectiveness of on campus recruiting efforts. This report can be produced for any subset of applicants in the data base, such as new hires (shown) total applicants, or by sex, race, job/skill, or degree.

Explanation of Terms, Column Headings, and Codes

The New Hires Summary by School shows the number of applicants (count) and percentages of the total.

```
             RETRIEVE Analysis Function
               1987 New Hires Summary
                     By School


                     Count Percent

        Berkeley       6      21%
         Clemson       1       3%
      Notre Dame       2       7%
          Purdue       2       7%
     Santa Clara       5      17%
        Stanford       6      21%
         U Miami       3      10%
          U of H       1       3%
      Other/None       3      10%


           Total      29
```

Figure 14.48 New hires summary by school

* Courtesy of Greentree Systems, Inc., 444 Castro Street, Mountain View, CA 94041.

Computerization of HRM Processes

Type of Sample Format or Report

Human Resources Chart* (Figure 14.49)

Software Product Name and Overall Functions

Continuity & Succession Planning (CSP) is a customized, fully integrated human resources information center. It is designed to accommodate existing systems and enhance user ability to analyze, report, and implement human resources action plans. CSP provides reports, statistics, organization charts, analytical tables, a downloading program to link it to other internal systems, and an interface to Lotus 1-2-3™ and word processing. CSP allows the user to integrate succession planning, labor-power planning, career planning and training and development administration at a pace that suits the organization's learning curve and priorities.

Specific Functions Performed by Format or Report

The Human Resources Chart provides an overview of the continuity dynamics within a given department or unit of the organization. The chart highlights situations where managers are "blocked" or "restrained" from moving due to readiness mismatches between hierarchical levels. It also highlights managers who are "at risk" of leaving the company unless certain continuity problems are remedied. The HR chart also shows where too many managers have chosen the same succession candidate, and many other continuity problems.

The HR chart allows the HR director to analyze, anticipate, and avert problems by setting up a simple feedback loop to line managers, who will have the vital information ahead of time. The HR chart also makes an ideal review tool. Using CSP, the manager can examine the chart, decide on a course of strategy, enter the new strategy into the computer, and then review the resultant situation on an updated HR chart.

Explanation of Terms, Column Headings, and Codes

(1) is "ready now" (for promotion, transfer, rotation, job enlargement, etc.) but is "restrained" from moving for lack of a successor who also is ready now. (2) is also ready now but is "blocked" by (3) who is not yet ready to be succeeded. (4) and (5) are "at risk" in that they are both ready to succeed the same individual but cannot do so simultaneously. The data in the boxes can be drawn from any information in the data base.

(See following page)

---

* Courtesy of Management Executive Center, 96 Beacon Street, Chestnut Hill, MA 02167.

HUMAN RESOURCE CHART

CONFIDENTIAL

Functional Organization: Finance
Affiliate/EEC-HQ: Switzerland

Vice President Finance
Alfred   J. Gelz
Rating: B   Ready: 2   Pot.: N
Reports to: NORTON

Completed by: Date:

DIRECT REPORTS FROM NODY

Manager Tax Coordination
Switzerland
Jane E. Chapman

Manager Accounting
Switzerland
Susan B. Heywood

Manager Budget and Reporting
Switzerland
Albert L. Hough

Manager Cost and Capital Expenditure
Switzerland
Janet R. Shalhoub

Treasurer
Switzerland
John T. Marlow

Manager Internal Controls
Switzerland
Donald L. Balcom

Financial Analyst Budget
Switzerland
Curtis M. Goodson

SUCCESSORS

Supervisor Tax Analysis
Switzerland
Karen C. Carter

Manager Cost Projects
Switzerland
Horace R. Ewo

Financial Analyst Cost
Switzerland
Clara P. Conrad

Financial Analyst Budget
Switzerland
Curtis M. Goodson

Manager Reporting
Switzerland
Edward W. Kidney

Manager Budget
Switzerland
Chee E. Chou

FROM OTHER UNITS/CANDIDATES

Financial Analyst Tax
Switzerland
David M. Moran

Supervisor Accounts Payable
Switzerland
Donald G. Darling

Supervisor Accounts Receivable
Switzerland
Susan C. Bump

Figure 14.49 Human resources chart

Computerization of HRM Processes

Type of Sample Format or Report

Succession Chart* (Figure 14.50)

Software Product Name and Overall Functions

Continuity & Succession Planning (CSP) is a customized, fully integrated human resources information center. It is designed to accommodate existing systems and enhance user ability to analyze, report, and implement human resources action plans. CSP provides reports, statistics, organization charts, analytical tables, a downloading program to link it to other internal systems, and an interface to Lotus 1-2-3™ and word processing. CSP allows the user to integrate successful planning, manpower planning, career planning and training and development administration at a pace that suits the organization's learning curve and priorities.

Specific Functions Performed by Format or Report

The Succession Chart lists the first and second choice successors to all the members of a given department or operating unit. It shows individuals chosen by more than one person as a successor, and individuals with fewer than two successors. If you track more than two successors, the Succession Chart will show the first two choices. Thus, upon preparing an initial continuity analysis, the manager may introduce changes into the continuity order and change charts automatically to reflect the new information. The additional data appearing in the boxes may be drawn from anywhere within the data base.

Explanation of Terms, Column Headings, and Codes

The Succession Chart may be printed singly or by group. Thus, the HR director may specify all the succession charts for a given department and have them printed out in succession for providing a report to a department head.

(See following page)

* Courtesy of Management Executive Center, 96 Beacon Street, Chestnut Hill, MA 02167.

CONFIDENTIAL

EEC HQ or name of affiliate: Switzerland

Functional Organization: Finance

Completed by: Date:
Reviewed by: Date:
Reviewed by: Date:
Reviewed by: Date:
Reviewed by: Date:
Reviewed by: B. Morton   Date:

Vice President Finance
Switzerland

Alfred J. Getz

Rating: B   Readiness: 2   Potential: N
Months in Job: 38   Age: 41.9   Grade: 50

Manager Budget and Reporting
Switzerland

Albert L. Hough

Rating: A   Readiness: 1   Potential: Y
Months in Job: 42   Age: 42.9   Grade: 40

Manager Accounting
Switzerland

Susan B. Henwood

Rating: C   Readiness: 1   Potential: Y
Months in Job: 38   Age: 45.9   Grade: 40

Manager Tax Coordination
Switzerland

Jane E. Chapman

Rating: A   Readiness: 3   Potential: N
Months in Job: 15   Age: 45.5   Grade: 40

Supervisor Tax Analysis
Switzerland

Karen C. Carter

Rating: C   Readiness: 2   Potential: N
Months in Job: 66   Age: 36.8   Grade: 30

Financial Analyst Tax
Switzerland

David M. Moran

Rating: C   Readiness: 3   Potential: N
Months in Job: 35   Age: 29.1   Grade: 30

Manager Accounting
Switzerland

Susan B. Henwood

Rating: C   Readiness: 1   Potential: Y
Months in Job: 38   Age: 45.9   Grade: 40

Supervisor Accounts Payable
Switzerland

Donald G. Darling

Rating: C   Readiness: 2   Potential: N
Months in Job: 22   Age: 46.6   Grade: 30

Manager Budget and Reporting
Switzerland

Albert L. Hough

Rating: A   Readiness: 1   Potential: Y
Months in Job: 42   Age: 42.9   Grade: 40

Manager Reporting
Switzerland

Edward W. Kidney

Rating: B   Readiness: 1   Potential: N
Months in Job: 65   Age: 34.4   Grade: 30

Financial Analyst Budget
Switzerland

Curtis M. Goodson

Rating: A   Readiness: 3   Potential: N
Months in Job: 54   Age: 44.8   Grade: 30

Manager Cost and Capital Expenditures
Switzerland

Janet R. Shalhoub

Rating: A   Readiness: 1   Potential: N
Months in Job: 42   Age: 46.8   Grade: 40

Manager Cost Projects
Switzerland

Horace R. Ewo

Rating: B   Readiness: 1   Potential: N
Months in Job: 41   Age: 44.7   Grade: 30

Financial Analyst Cost
Switzerland

Clara P. Conrad

Rating: A   Readiness: 4   Potential: N
Months in Job: 6   Age: 42.6   Grade: 30

Treasurer
Switzerland

John T. Harlow

Rating: B   Readiness: 3   Potential: N
Months in Job: 18   Age: 46.1   Grade: 40

Supervisor Accounts Receivable
Switzerland

Susan C. Bump

Rating: C   Readiness: 2   Potential: N
Months in Job: 30   Age: 46.8   Grade: 30

Manager Internal Controls
Switzerland

Donald L. Balcom

Rating: C   Readiness: 1   Potential: N
Months in Job: 86   Age: 45.6   Grade: 40

Financial Analyst Budget
Switzerland

Curtis M. Goodson

Rating: A   Readiness: 3   Potential: N
Months in Job: 54   Age: 44.8   Grade: 30

Manager Budget
Switzerland

Chee E. Chow

Rating: A   Readiness: 2   Potential: N
Months in Job: 52   Age: 31.6   Grade: 30

Figure 14.50 Succession chart

591

Computerization of HRM Processes

Type of Sample Format or Report

Organization Chart* (Figure 14.51)

Software Product Name and Overall Functions

Continuity & Succession Planning (CSP) is a customized, fully integrated human resources information center. It is designed to accommodate existing systems and enhance user ability to analyze, report, and implement human resources action plans. CSP provides reports, statistics, organization charts, analytical tables, a downloading program to link it to other internal systems, and an interface to Lotus 1-2-3™ and word processing. CSP allows the user to integrate succession planning, manpower planning, career planning and training and development administration at a pace that suits the organization's learning curve and priorities.

Specific Functions Performed by Format or Report

The Organization Chart requires no on-screen work by the manager and is always up to date. Whenever a manager makes a change to an individual's record such as to note a promotion or change of succession candidates, the Organization Chart automatically reflects that change.

This makes it very easy for a manager to prepare a series of charts for review purposes, and to examine "what-if" scenarios by compiling experimental organization charts that illustrate possible restructuring.

Explanation of Terms, Column Headings, and Codes

The chart can be printed for an individual or a group. For example, if all the charts for the finance department are required, all the manager needs to do is specify the department name and the entire series of charts will print out. No creating boxes, drawing lines, or adding and subtracting direct reports is required. The chart always is up to date, and draws directly from the CSP data base. It allows the manager to print data regarding individuals in their respective boxes of a chart.

(See following page)

* Courtesy of Management Executive Center, 96 Beacon Street, Chestnut Hill, MA 02167.

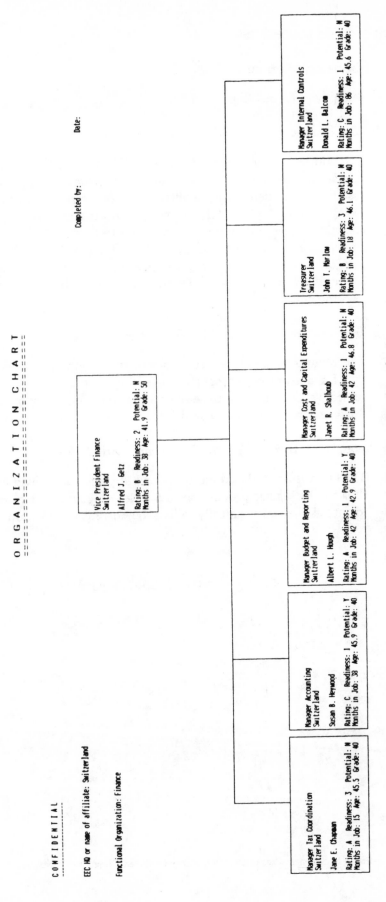

Figure 14.51 Organization chart

Computerization of HRM Processes

Type of Sample Format or Report

Manpower Audit* (Figure 14.52)

Software Product Name and Overall Functions

Continuity & Succession Planning (CSP) is a customized, fully integrated human resources information center. It is designed to accommodate existing systems and enhance user ability to analyze, report, and implement human resources action plans. CSP provides reports, statistics, organization charts, analytical tables, a downloading program to link it to other internal systems, and an interface to Lotus 1-2-3™ and word processing. CSP allows the user to integrate succession planning, manpower planning, career planning and training and development administration at a pace that suits the organization's learning curve and priorities.

Specific Functions Performed by Format or Report

The Manpower Audit is a summary of succession and development information for a given department or operating unit. It lists all the strategic (and subjective) data that comprise the Succession Plan, as opposed to the objective data (such as current salary grade) which is usually an auxiliary part of the plan.

Explanation of Terms, Column Headings, and Codes

The chart is printed at the touch of a button for an individual or for a group, thus facilitating the production of a series of charts. The charts always are up to date as they automatically reflect the current information in the data base.

(See following page)

(See following page)

---

* Courtesy of Management Executive Center, 96 Beacon Street, Chestnut Hill, MA 02167.

M A N P O W E R   A U D I T

Organisation/HQ: Switzerland

Function: Finance
Department: ################

Incumbent		Title	Months in job	Performance	Promotability	Potential	Potential Successors	Next Planned Position	Training Development Needs
SUPERVISOR: Getz	Alfred	Vice President Finance	3.3	B	2	N	Hough / Heywood (Albert / Susan)	VP Finance and Administration	Understudy Training; Language; Communication/Negotiation
FIRST SUCCESSOR: Hough	Albert	Manager Budget and Reporting	3.6	A	1	Y	Kidney / Goodson (Edward / Curtis)	Director Finance	Conceptual Ability; Language; Attendance Senior Level M
SECOND SUCCESSOR: Heywood	Susan	Manager Accounting	3.3	C	1	Y	Darling (Donald)	Director Finance	Leadership/Delegation; Attendance Senior Level Mtgs; Task Force Assignments
DIRECT REPORT: Chapman	Jane	Manager Tax Coordination	1.3	A	3	N	Carter / Moran (Karen / David)	Director Finance	Attendance Senior Level; Long Term External; Leadership/Delegation
FIRST SUCCESSOR: Carter	Karen	Supervisor Tax Analysis	5.6	C	2	N	Moran (David)	Manager Tax Coordination	Team Building; Language; Train the Trainer
SECOND SUCCESSOR: Moran	David	Financial Analyst Tax	3	C	3	N		Manager Tax Coordination	Communication/Negotiation; Job Rotation; Train the Trainer
DIRECT REPORT: Heywood	Susan	Manager Accounting	3.3	C	1	Y	Darling (Donald)	Director Finance	Leadership/Delegation; Attendance Senior Level Mtgs; Task Force Assignments
FIRST SUCCESSOR: Darling	Donald	Supervisor Accounts Payable	1.9	C	2	N	Bump (Susan)	Manager Accounting	Planning and Control; Decision Making
SECOND SUCCESSOR:									
DIRECT REPORT: Hough	Albert	Manager Budget and Reporting	3.6	A	1	Y	Kidney / Goodson (Edward / Curtis)	Director Finance	Conceptual Ability; Language; Attendance Senior Level M
FIRST SUCCESSOR: Kidney	Edward	Manager Reporting	5.5	B	2	N	Chow (Chee)	Manager Budget and Reporting	Conceptual Ability; Language; Job Enrichment
SECOND SUCCESSOR: Goodson	Curtis	Financial Analyst Budget	4.6	A	3	N		Manager Budget and Reporting	Attendance Senior Level Mtgs; Task Force Assignments; Replacement Assignments
DIRECT REPORT: Shabhaub	Janet	Manager Cost and Capital Expenditures	3.6	A	1	N	Ewo / Conrad (Horace / Clara)	Director Finance	Job Enrichment
FIRST SUCCESSOR: Ewo	Horace	Manager Cost Projects	3.5	B	1	N	Conrad (Clara)	Manager Cost and Capital Expenditures	Conference Leader/Instructor; Communication/Negotiation; Long Term External
SECOND SUCCESSOR: Conrad	Clara	Financial Analyst Cost	.6	A	4	N		Manager Cost and Capital Expenditure	Team Building
DIRECT REPORT: Marlow	John	Treasurer	1.6	B	3	N	Bump (Susan)	Director Finance	Long Term External; Task Force Assignments
FIRST SUCCESSOR: Bump	Susan	Supervisor Accounts Receivable	2.6	C	3	N		Treasurer	Language; Understudy Training; Team Building
SECOND SUCCESSOR:									
DIRECT REPORT: Balcom	Donald	Manager Internal Controls	7.3	C	1	N	Goodson / Chow (Curtis / Chee)	Director Finance	Conceptual Ability; Decision Making
FIRST SUCCESSOR: Goodson	Curtis	Financial Analyst Budget	4.6	A	3	N		Manager Budget and Reporting	Attendance Senior Level Mtgs; Task Force Assignments; Replacement Assignments
SECOND SUCCESSOR: Chow	Chee	Manager Budget	4.5	A	2	N		Manager Internal Controls	Decision Making; Language

Figure 14.52 Manpower audit

Computerization of HRM Processes

Type of Sample Format or Report

Training and Development Chart* (Figure 14.53)

Software Product Name and Overall Functions

Contnuity & Succession Planning (CSP) is a customized, fully integrated human resources information center. It is designed to accommodate existing systems and enhance user ability to analyze, report, and implement human resources action plans. CSP provides reports, statistics, organization charts, analytical tables, a downloading program to link it to other internal systems, and an interface to Lotus 1-2-3™ and word processing. CSP allows the user to integrate succession planning, manpower planning, career planning and training and development administration at a pace that suits the organization's learning curve and priorities.

Specific Functions Performed by Format or Report

The Training and Development Chart provides a summary of all the training needs and planned courses for each successor within a given department or operating unit.

Explanation of Terms, Column Headings, and Codes

The chart can be requested by individual or operating group, and reflects the most up to date changes in the data base.

(See following page)

---

* Courtesy of Management Executive Center, 96 Beacon Street, Chestnut Hill, MA 02167.

Function: Finance
Organization/HQ: Retailers Ltd.
Department: Headquarters

Manager: Vice President Finance
Alfred
J. Getz

Reports to: MORTON

BARRY

Completed by: Date:

B R E O C R T T

Manager Internal Controls
Donald L. Balcom
Ready: 1 Prom.: 2 Pot.: N Perf.: C
Yrs Co.: 12.9/ Yrs Job: 7.2 Age: 45.6

Treasurer
John T. Marlowe
Ready: 3 Prom.: 3 Pot.: N Perf.: B
Yrs Co.: 7.5/ Yrs Job: 1.5 Age: 46.1

Manager Cost and Capital Expenditure
Janet R. Shalhoub
Ready: 1 Prom.: 1 Pot.: N Perf.: A
Yrs Co.: 5.5/ Yrs Job: 3.5 Age: 46.8

Manager Tax Coordination
Jane E. Chapman
Ready: 3 Prom.: 1 Pot.: N Perf.: A
Yrs Co.: 14.5/ Yrs Job: 1.2 Age: 45.5

Manager Accounting
Susan B. Heywood
Ready: 1 Prom.: 1 Pot.: Y Perf.: A
Yrs Co.: 9.2/ Yrs Job: 3.1 Age: 45.9

Manager Budget and Reporting
Albert L. Hough
Ready: 1 Prom.: 2 Pot.: Y Perf.: A
Yrs Co.: 10.5/ Yrs Job: 3.5 Age: 42.9

S U C F C I E R S S T O R

Financial Analyst Controls
Chee K. Chou
Ready: 2 Prom.: 2 Pot.: N Perf.: A
Yrs Co.: 4.4/ Yrs Job: 4.4 Age: 31.6
1st Training Need:
Decision Making
Start Date:85/03 Complete Date:
2nd Training Need:
Language
Start Date:85/08 Complete Date:
3rd Training Need:
Replacement Assignments
Start Date:85/11 Complete Date:

Assistant Treasurer
Susan C. Bump
Ready: 2 Prom.: 4 Pot.: N Perf.: C
Yrs Co.: 11.5/ Yrs Job: 2.5 Age: 46.8
1st Training Need:
Language
Start Date:85/06 Complete Date:
2nd Training Need:
Understudy Training
Start Date:85/09 Complete Date:
3rd Training Need:
Team Building
Start Date:85/11 Complete Date:

Manager of Cost Projects
Horace R. Kwo
Ready: 1 Prom.: 1 Pot.: N Perf.: B
Yrs Co.: 9.5/ Yrs Job: 3.4 Age: 44.7
1st Training Need:
Conference Leader/Instructor
Start Date:85/04 Complete Date:85/06
2nd Training Need:
Communication/Negotiation
Start Date:85/08 Complete Date:
3rd Training Need:
Long Term External
Start Date:85/11 Complete Date:

Supervisor Tax Analysis
Karen C. Carter
Ready: 1 Prom.: 2 Pot.: N Perf.: C
Yrs Co.: 6.1/ Yrs Job: 5.5 Age: 36.8
1st Training Need:
Team Building
Start Date:85/02 Complete Date:85/06
2nd Training Need:
Language
Start Date:85/03 Complete Date:85/06
3rd Training Need:
=========================
Start Date: Complete Date:

Supervisor Accounting
Donald G. Darling
Ready: 2 Prom.: 3 Pot.: N Perf.: C
Yrs Co.: 15.9/ Yrs Job: 1.8 Age: 46.6
1st Training Need:
Team Building
Start Date:85/09 Complete Date:
2nd Training Need:
Decision Making
Start Date:85/11 Complete Date:
3rd Training Need:
=========================
Start Date: Complete Date:

Manager Reporting
Edward W. Kidney
Ready: 1 Prom.: 2 Pot.: N Perf.: B
Yrs Co.: 5.4/ Yrs Job: 5.4 Age: 34.4
1st Training Need:
Conceptual Ability
Start Date:85/01 Complete Date:85/06
2nd Training Need:
Language
Start Date:85/03 Complete Date:85/06
3rd Training Need:
Job Enrichment
Start Date:85/06 Complete Date:

S U S C U E B C O S M O D

Financial Analyst Budget
Curtis N. Goodson
Ready: 3 Prom.: 1 Pot.: N Perf.: A
Yrs Co.: 9.5/ Yrs Job: 4.5 Age: 44.8
1st Training Need:
Conceptual Ability
Start Date:85/01 Complete Date:85/06
2nd Training Need:
Task Force Assignments
Start Date:85/02 Complete Date:85/06
3rd Training Need:
Replacement Assignments
Start Date:85/04 Complete Date:

Financial Analyst Cost
Clara P. Conrad
Ready: 4 Prom.: 1 Pot.: N Perf.: A
Yrs Co.: 6.1/ Yrs Job: .5 Age: 42.6
1st Training Need:
Team Building
Start Date:85/01 Complete Date:85/03
2nd Training Need:
Long Term External
Start Date:85/02 Complete Date:85/05
3rd Training Need:
Attendance Senior Level Mtgs.
Start Date:85/08 Complete Date:

Financial Analyst Tax
David M. Moran
Ready: 3 Prom.: 3 Pot.: N Perf.: C
Yrs Co.: 2.9/ Yrs Job: 2.9 Age: 29.1
1st Training Need:
Attendance Senior Level Mtgs.
Start Date:85/01 Complete Date:85/04
2nd Training Need:
Job Rotation
Start Date:85/02 Complete Date:85/04
3rd Training Need:
Train the Trainer
Start Date:85/06 Complete Date:

1st Training Need:

2nd Training Need:

3rd Training Need:

Financial Analyst Budget
Curtis N. Goodson
Ready: 3 Prom.: 1 Pot.: N Perf.: A
Yrs Co.: 9.5/ Yrs Job: 4.5 Age: 44.8
1st Training Need:
Conceptual Ability
Start Date:85/01 Complete Date:85/06
2nd Training Need:
Task Force Assignments
Start Date:85/01 Complete Date:85/06
3rd Training Need:
Replacement Assignments
Start Date:85/02 Complete Date:85/06

Figure 14.53 Training and development chart

597

Computerization of HRM Processes

Type of Sample Format or Report

Ad-Hoc Report—Critical Development Candidates* (Figure 14.54)

Software Product Name and Overall Functions

Continuity & Succession Planning (CSP) is a customized, fully integrated human resources information center. It is designed to accommodate existing systems and enhance user ability to analyze, report, and implement human resources action plans. CSP provides reports, statistics, organization charts, analytical tables, a downloading program to link it to other internal systems, and an interface to Lotus 1-2-3™ and word processing. CSP allows the user to integrate succession planning, manpower planning, career planning and training and development administration at a pace that suits the organization's learning curve and priorities.

Specific Functions Performed by Format or Report

An Ad-Hoc Report may be prepared for a number of reasons: to highlight trouble spots, e.g. "managers restrained from moving for lack of a successor"; to examine trends, e.g., "high potential managers in the same position for more than three years"; or simply to report information, e.g., "candidates for the advanced management program." Ad-hoc reports can be generated by selecting any data base information. They are automatically archived for future use, and there is no limit to the number of reports in the library.

Explanation of Terms, Column Headings, and Codes

The information shown in an Ad-Hoc Report is chosen by the user. These reports are simple to create and print. Most reports can be prepared in a couple of minutes.

(See following page)

---

* Courtesy of Management Executive Center, 96 Beacon Street, Chestnut Hill, MA 02167.

Family Name	First Name	Title	Job Entry Date	Next Planned Position	1-Description
Balcom	Donald	Manager Internal Controls	78/05/01	Director Finance	Conceptual Ability
Boynton	Gale	Director, Wage & Salary Administration	79/02/28		
Bump	Susan	Supervisor Accounts Receivable	83/01/01	Treasurer	Language
Carey	Charlotte	Vice Director Process Development	79/02/09	Director Research and Development	Replacement Assignments
Chow	Chee	Manager Budget	81/03/01	Manager Internal Controls	Decision Making
Conway	Margaret	Director and Principal Scientist	85/01/01	Vice President Operations	Communication/Negotiation
Dare	Nancy	Director, Product Engineering	84/12/16		
Dodd	Herman	Manager EDP Support	79/09/22	Director Research and Development	Task Force Assignments
Duval	Ann	Manager, Project Analyst	75/09/19		
Eager	Susan	Manager, Basic Research	81/02/20		
Feldman	Eleanor	Project Leader	82/07/23	Vice Director Science and Technology	Leadership/Delegation
Ford	Wendell	Vice Director Engineering Services	85/06/05	Director Operations	Lateral Transfer
Gerardi	George	Junior Engineer	83/12/25	Industrial Engineer	Long Term External
Gilly	Lawrence	Manager, Organization Planning	85/01/26		
Hamilton	Mary	Manager Production Planning	80/12/14	Director Manufacturing Support	Communication/Negotiation
Hobbs	Cathy	Controller (Manager)	86/03/09		
Holmes	Lawrence	Industrial Engineer	86/03/15	Vice Director Engineering Services	Communication/Negotiation
Insling	Dianne	Manager, Credit & Collections	80/05/13		
Jumble	Alex	Mgr., Product Redevel. for Cost Reduct.	12/11/17		
Marlow	John	Treasurer	84/01/01	Director Finance	Long Term External
Moore	William	Director Operations Scotland	81/12/15	Director Manufacturing Support	Team Building
Moran	David	Financial Analyst Tax	82/08/15	Manager Tax Coordination	Communication/Negotiation
Newman	Claire	Manager, Sales Assistance	86/01/02		

23 records were input, 23 (100%) were selected.

Figure 14.54 Ad-hoc report—critical development candidates

Computerization of HRM Processes

Type of Sample Format or Report

Statistical Summary—Training Needs* (Figure 14.55)

Software Product Name and Overall Functions

Continuity & Succession Planning (CSP) is a customized, fully integrated human resources information center. It is designed to accommodate existing systems and enhance user ability to analyze, report, and implement human resources action plans. CSP provides reports, statistics, organization charts, analytical tables, a downloading program to link it to other internal systems, and an interface to Lotus 1-2-3™ and word processing. CSP allows the user to integrate succession planning, manpower planning, career planning and training and development administration at a pace that suits the organization's learning curve and priorities.

Specific Functions Performed by Format or Report

CSP provides elementary statistical reports such as the example shown.

Explanation of Terms, Column Headings, and Codes

This statistical report is instantly assembled by CSP and archived in a library. Using CSP's direct Lotus 1-2-3™ interface, this report can be converted into a bar chart, pie chart, or other graphic formats.

1-Description	Total Number	Percent Of Total
	69	57%
Attendance Senior Level Mtgs	6	5%
Communication/Negotiation	7	6%
Conceptual Ability	4	3%
Conference Leader/Instructor	1	1%
Decision Making	4	3%
Job Enrichment	6	5%
Language	4	3%
Lateral Transfer	2	2%
Leadership/Delegation	3	2%
Long Term External	2	2%
Planning and Control	1	1%
Replacement Assignments	1	1%
Task Force Assignments	3	2%
Team Building	5	4%
Understudy Training	3	2%
TOTALS:	121	100 %

Figure 14.55 Statistical summary—training needs

* Courtesy of Management Executive Center, 96 Beacon Street, Chestnut Hill, MA 02167.

Computerization of HRM Processes

Type of Sample Format or Report

Training Needs Pie Chart* (Figure 14.56)

Software Product Name and Overall Functions

Continuity & Succession Planning (CSP) is a customized, fully integrated human resources information center. It is designed to accommodate existing systems and enhance user ability to analyze, report, and implement human resources action plans. CSP provides reports, statistics, organization charts, analytical tables, a downloading program to link it to other internal systems, and an interface to Lotus 1-2-3™ and word processing. CSP allows the user to integrate succession planning, manpower planning, career planning and training and development administration at a pace that suits the organization's learning curve and priorities.

Specific Functions Performed by Format or Report

CSP has a direct Lotus 1-2-3™ interface which allows the user to produce a statistical report in CSP and view it as a pie chart in Lotus.

Explanation of Terms, Column Headings, and Codes

This chart is simple to produce. The user is transferred between programs automatically through user-friendly menus.

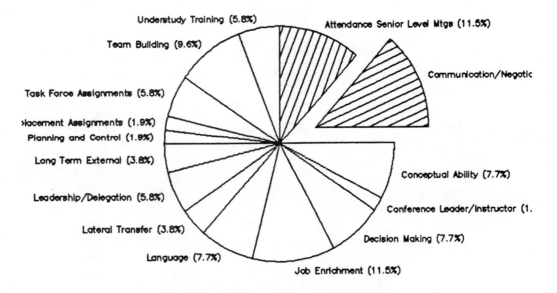

ABC WORLD, INC
TRAINING NEEDS

Figure 14.56 Training needs pie chart

* Courtesy of Management Executive Center, 96 Beacon Street, Chestnut Hill, MA 02167.

Computerization of HRM Processes

Type of Sample Format or Report

Statistical Summary—High Potential Managers* (Figure 14.57)

Software Product Name and Overall Functions

Continuity & Succession Planning (CSP) is a customized, fully integrated human resources information center. It is designed to accommodate existing systems and enhance user ability to analyze, report, and implement human resources action plans. CSP provides reports, statistics, organization charts, analytical tables, a downloading program to link it to other internal systems, and an interface to Lotus 1-2-3™ and word processing. CSP allows the user to integrate succession planning, manpower planning, career planning and training and development administration at a pace that suits the organization's learning curve and priorities.

Specific Functions Performed by Format or Report

CSP provides elementary statistical reports such as the example shown.

Explanation of Terms, Column Headings, and Codes

This statistical report is instantly assembled by CSP and archived in a library. Using CSP's direct Lotus 1-2-3™ interface, this report can be converted into a bar chart, pie chart, or other graphic formats.

```
                       STATISTICAL SUMMARY
                       ...................

                 BREAKDOWN OF HIGH POTENTIAL MANAGERS
             IN THE SAME POSITION FORE MORE THAN TWO YEARS
                           BY FUNCTION
                         Potential =  Y
                 Job Entry Date   .  <  84/12/09
                     Function    .  <>


                      Number      Total                   Percent
     Function         Matching    Number      Ratio       Of Total
     ....................................................................
     Finance          5           32          16 %        21%
     General Management  0         1           0 %         0%
     Human Resources  3           15          20 %        13%
     Marketing        7           31          23 %        29%
     Operations       6           23          26 %        25%
     R & D            3           19          16 %        13%
     ....................................................................
     TOTALS:          24          121         20%         100 %
```

Figure 14.57 Statistical summary—high potential managers

* Courtesy of Management Executive Center, 96 Beacon Street, Chestnut Hill, MA 02167.

Computerization of HRM Processes

Type of Sample Format or Report

High Potential Managers Bar Chart* (Figure 14.58)

Software Product Name and Overall Functions

Continuity & Succession Planning (CSP) is a customized, fully integrated human resources information center. It is designed to accommodate existing systems and enhance user ability to analyze, report, and implement human resources action plans. CSP provides reports, statistics, organization charts, analytical tables, a downloading program to link it to other internal systems, and an interface to Lotus 1-2-3™ and word processing. CSP allows the user to integrate succession planning, manpower planning, career planning and training and development administration at a pace that suits the organization's learning curve and priorities.

Specific Functions Performed by Format or Report

CSP has a direct Lotus 1-2-3™ interface which allows the user to produce a statistical report in CSP and view it as a bar chart in Lotus.

Explanation of Terms, Column Headings, and Codes

This chart is simple to produce. The user is transferred between programs automatically through user-friendly menus.

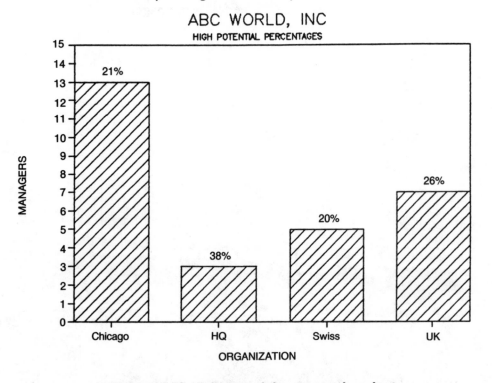

Figure 14.58 High potential managers bar chart

* Courtesy of Management Executive Center, 96 Beacon Street, Chestnut Hill, MA 02167.

Computerization of HRM Processes

Type of Sample Format or Report

Executive Record Report* (Figure 14.59)

Software Product Name and Overall Functions

Executive Track™ searches data base files and matches candidates to open positions. It creates reports on succession and development planning, organization and replacement charts, and basic manager profiles. By storing information on executive competencies (work history, demographics, educational background, career paths and performance levels); it finds appropriate candidates for open positions; creates organization and succession charts; produces standard and customized reports; and keeps detailed records on position requirements (general descriptions, function, required skills, replacement timing, candidates and their readiness and reporting relationships).

Specific Functions Performed by Format or Report

Three sample pages of this five-page format illustrate the extensive competencies and developmental requirements. Associated data provide the basis for generating a variety of effective reports which serve as the basis for succession and development planning.

(See following page)

---

* Courtesy of Corporate Education Resources, Inc., 116 West Burlington Street, Fairfield, IA 52556.

Executive Record Report: 1

```
ABC Corporation                                        Date: 09/28/85
Executive Record Report
```

Last Name, First, & Middle Initial		Soc. Sec. No.
HOBBS LISA		034-65-9821

Location	Citizenship	Status Code
PITTSFORD	US	1

Time in Position	Time in Service	Age
1 YR 11 MO	14 YR 6 MO	36 YR 9 MO

Salary Grade	Salary	Bonus	Bonus Date
0028	80	5000	12/82

Position Title		Code
SR VICE PRESIDENT/MARKETING CORP		C28

Function
MARKETING

Reports to		Code
PRESIDENT/CEO	CORP	C30

Dotted Line		Code
SR VICE PRESIDENT/FINANCE	CORP	C28

EDUCATIONAL HISTORY

	Degree	Code	Major	Institution	Code	Start	End
1.	MBA	MKT	MARKETING	HARVARD			
2.	BA	BUS	BUS ADM	UNIVERSITY OF IOWA			
3.							

WORK HISTORY

	Experience		Position Code	Code	Years
1.	VICE PRESIDENT/MARKETING	SDI	S26		81-83
2.	NATIONAL SALES MANAGER	SDI	S23		78-81
3.	REGIONAL SALES MANAGER	SDI	S19		75-78
4.	SALES REPRESENTATIVE	SDI	S15		72-75
5.					-
6.					-
7.					-
8.					-
9.					-
10.					-

DEVELOPMENT HISTORY

	Development Activity	Code	Start	End
1.	COMPUTER USE SEMINAR	CP		
2.	POLICY COMMITTEE	PC	01	01
3.	FOREIGN AFFAIRS COMMITTEE	FA	05	01
4.				

	Other History	Code	Start	End
1.	SCA: UNITED WAY			
2.				

Figure 14.59 Executive record report

continued

Executive Record Report: 2

```
ABC Corporation                                           Date: 09/28/85
Executive Record Report

Name: L. HOBBS              Position: SR VICE PRESIDENT/MARKETING    CORP
```

DEVELOPMENT PLAN				
Next Planned Positions	Code	Date		
1. INTERNATIONAL EXPERIENCE		15/05		
2. RETURN TO CORPORATE		01/01		
3.				
Development Activity	Code	Starts	Ends	
1. MARKETING TASK FORCE	M	01/01	01/06	
2.				
3.				
Education Activity	Code	Date	Code	Date
1. HARVARD ADV PROGRAM	4	15/11 3.		
2. FOREIGN LANGUAGE TRA	F	01/01 4.		

INDIVIDUAL PREFERENCE
1. FEELS NO PLACE TO GO
2. WANTS MORE RESPONSIBILITY

EXECUTIVE NARRATIVE
9/25/85 - LISA HAS DEMONSTRATED EXCEPTIONAL ABILITIES IN MARKETING AS HER WORK HISTORY RECORD SHOWS. HOWEVER, SHE NEEDS SOME ADDITIONAL EXPERIENCE AND DEVELOPMENT IN THE AREAS OF LEADERSHIP AND MANAGEMENT.

```
CONFIDENTIAL INFORMATION
Performance   Date of Rating                  Track Wildcards
8                25/05                         1 D    2      3

Readiness     Date of Rating  Readiness Date  Language Codes
85               25/05           01/10         1 S    2      3

Potential     Date of Rating                  Sex      Minority Code
0028             25/05                         F        1

Programmed Replacement Date  Retirement
01/01/87
```

Figure 14.59 *(cont.)*

Executive Record Report: 5

Name: L. HOBBS	Position: SR VICE PRESIDENT/MARKETING CORP

```
COMPANY                                     0
POSITION                                    0
PROFILES                                    0
                                            0
                                            0
                                            0
                                            0
                                            0
                                            0
                                            0
                                            0
                                            0
                                            0
                                            0
                                            0
                                            0
                                            0
                                            0
                                            0
                                            0
                                            0
                                            0
                                            0
                                            0
                                            0
                                            0
                                            0
```

```
POSITION      Marketing                9 ******************
PROFILES      Finance                  5 **********
              Operations               0
              Technical                0
              Strategy                 9 ******************
              Planning                 9 ******************
              Management Systems       5 **********
              Policy                   5 **********
              Human Resources          5 **********
              Governmental Relations   0
              Labor Relations          0
              U.S. Economy             5 **********
              International Business   7 **************
              Leadership Values        5 **********
              Business Ethics          9 ******************
              Leadership Styles        5 **********
              Communication            9 ******************
              Negotiation              0
              Political                5 **********
              Health Management        0
              Stress Management        0
              Analytic Approaches      6 ************
              Decision Methods-Quant.  6 ************
              Language Competence      5 **********
              Social Contribution      5 **********
              Entrepreneurship         9 ******************
              Creativity               9 ******************
              Cultural Awareness       9 ******************
```

Figure 14.59 *(cont.)*

Computerization of HRM Processes

Type of Sample Format or Report

Executive Record Report—Developmental Requirements* (Figure 14.60)

Software Product Name and Overall Functions

ExecuGROW™ is a system for use by human resource executives in the design and implementation of management development planning. It includes procedures to store multiple training needs for executives as well as recommend and/or assign various training and development activities to fulfill those needs. For example, comprehensive information about various development programs, including both in-house training courses and external academic programs. The administrator may specify objectives or developmental activities and track the effectiveness of the various courses. Numerous reports, including user-designed reports, facilitate the management development process.

Specific Functions Performed by Format or Report

This sample individual development plan incorporates performance-related problems and specifies training activities which are planned for developing skills needed to resolve these developmental deficiencies. Perspective is offered through information on the executive's "training and development history."

(See following page)

*Courtesy of Corporate Education Resources, Inc., 116 West Burlington Street, Fairfield, IA 52556.

```
Sample Company                                          Date: 11/03/86
GROW Executive Record Report
Name: M. J. BROWNING          Position: MANAGER, PRODUCT DESIGN

DEVELOPMENT PLAN APPROVAL
Discussion Date    Date Last Changed    Approval Date
  08/01/86             06/30/86            06/30/86

Plan Supervisor
  WALLOW HERB S.

Present Supervisor
  WALLOW HERB S.


Comments




EXECUTIVE SUMMARY NARRATIVE
MARY IS NOT MEETING DEADLINES AND MUST IMPROVE IN THIS AREA.  SHE HAS NOT LIVED
UP TO HER ASSUMED POTENTIAL.


EXECUTIVE NEEDS

Need:  1    MARY HAS PROBLEMS MEETING DEADLINES, NEEDS WORK IN THE AREA
            OF TIME MANAGEMENT

Source:     BOB FIELDING
Date:       10/31/86
Code:       SDC

Need:  2    MARY NEEDS TO WORK ON HER MANAGEMENT SKILLS


Source:     ED YOULIAN
Date:       11/01/86
Code:       GRET

TRAINING AND DEVELOPMENT ACTIVITIES
Pri  Activity                              Code   Sch Start    Complete
     TIME MANAGEMENT                       TMFUNC    06/01/86
        Activity Assigned to Need:  1

     MANAGEMENT II                         MMMGT     04/01/87
        Activity Assigned to Need:  2

     CAREER DEVELOPMENT WORKSHOP           CDFUNC    08/20/87
        Activity Assigned to Need:  2

TRAINING AND DEVELOPMENT HISTORY
Activity                             Code   Effect   Start   Complete
DUKE PMD                                                     07/15/82
MANAGEMENT II                                               08/10/81
MANAGEMENT I                                                02/14/81
TIME  MANAGEMENT                                            11/28/77
```

Figure 14.60 Executive record report—developmental requirements

Computerization of HRM Processes

Type of Sample Format or Report

Training Budget* (Figure 14.61)

Software Product Name and Overall Functions

ExecuGROW™ is a system for use by human resource executives in the design and implementation of management development planning. It includes procedures to store multiple training needs for executives as well as recommend and/or assign various training and development activities to fulfill those needs. For example, comprehensive information about various development programs, including both in-house training courses and external academic programs. The administrator may specify objectives or developmental activities and track the effectiveness of the various courses. Numerous reports, including user-designed reports, facilitate the management development process.

Specific Functions Performed by Format or Report

This budget format for training activities outlines planned courses, locations, dates, and expenditures. Scheduled course costs versus actual costs also are shown.

```
Database:  SAMPLE                        Sample Company
                                              Budget                           Page      1

                        Time Period From: 01/01/85   To: 01/01/87


Activity                              Location                 Date     Code    Plan  Sched  Actual

TIME MANAGEMENT                                                06/01/86  TMFUNC   590     0      0
MANAGEMENT I                          TRAINING CENTER          02/10/87  LMMGT      0     0      0
ASPEN ES                              ASPEN, COLORADO          03/16/87  HUFUNC  4000  4000   4000
MANAGEMENT II                         TRAINING CENTER          04/01/87  MMMGT      0     0      0
CAREER DEVELOPMENT WORKSHOP           TRAINING CENTER          06/01/87  CDFUNC     0     0      0
MIT EPCS                              DEDHAM, MASSACHUSETTS    07/06/87  STFUNC  2750     0      0
CAREER DEVELOPMENT WORKSHOP           TRAINING CENTER          07/15/87  CDFUNC     0     0      0
CAREER DEVELOPMENT WORKSHOP           TRAINING CENTER          08/20/87  CDFUNC     0     0      0
DUKE PMD                              DURHAM, NORTH CAROLINA   09/07/87  MMMGT   3600     0      0
COLUMBIA MMP                          HARRIMAN, NEW YORK       11/07/87  MKFUNC     0     0      0
THE BROOKINGS INSTITUTION UFGO        WASHINGTON, D.C.         04/06/88  PAFUNC  2040  2040   2000
MANAGEMENT III                        TRAINING CENTER          09/14/88  UMMGT      0     0      0


                                                         Totals:      12980  6040   6000
```

Figure 14.61 Training budget

* Courtesy of Corporate Education Resources, Inc., 116 West Burlington Street, Fairfield, IA 52556.

Computerization of HRM Processes

Type of Sample Format or Report

Salary Survey Market Comparison—Using Weighted Average* (Figure 14.62)

Software Product Name and Overall Functions

This human resource product is designed specifically to perform salary survey analysis with output to the surveying organization and to participants. Comparisons using simple and weighted averages, weighted means, and percentiles are available. Reports to participating organizations are coded for security and one job is equal to one report. The program has easy input screens and builds tables or participants, jobs to be surveyed, and salary data. It allows for any participant to be the "pivot" organization, and customized analysis is available by organization or type or organization. Options allow projecting salaries to a future date by using a multiplier factor assigned to each participant.

Specific Functions Performed by Format or Report

Compares the "pivot" organization against the weighted averages in the market. Uses the population in the "pivot" organization to answer these questions: "What do I pay my own workers in the benchmark populace?" and "What would the market pay my benchmark populace?" The result is a figure representing how far above or behind the market the pivot organization is.

Explanation of Terms, Column Headings, and Codes

Job = benchmark job title; Base Employees = number of employees in the base or "pivot" organization; Participant Av Salary = average salary in the "pivot" organization; Mrkt Emps = the number of incumbents in that job in the surveyed market. The rest of the measurements are standard statistical measurements and self-explanatory.

```
                           Salary Survey Expert
                     Market Comparison for Newsales Inc.
```

Job	Base Employees	Particpnt Av Salary	Low	High	Average	Difference	Pcnt	Stnd Dev	Mrkt Emps
			===== Weighted Market =====						
1 Clerk Typist	2	9,840.00	9,840.00	12,563.00	12,105.16	-2,265.16	-23.0	878.72	63
3 Telephone Operator	1	9,900.00	9,900.00	13,790.00	12,512.92	-2,612.92	-26.4	1,144.05	13
5 Receptionist	1	9,900.00	9,900.00	10,747.00	10,533.15	-633.15	-6.4	221.28	20
6 Secretary I	3	10,471.00	10,471.00	12,563.00	11,859.55	-1,388.55	-13.3	892.13	11
7 Secretary II	5	11,719.00	11,719.00	14,102.00	13,006.45	-1,287.45	-11.0	881.16	20
	=====	==============				=============			=====
Working Totals:	12	129,488.00*				-18,379.28*			127
Position Against Market:						Weighted:	-14.2%		

```
    * Working totals weighted by base employee counts.
```

Figure 14.62 Salary survey market comparison—using weighted average

*Courtesy of Human Resource Management—Personnel Systems, 883 East 2850 North, North Ogden, Utah 84404.

Computerization of HRM Processes

Type of Sample Format or Report

Salary Survey Market Comparison—Using Percentiles* (Figure 14.63)

Software Product Name and Overall Functions

This human resource product is designed specifically to perform salary survey analysis with output to the surveying organization and to participants. Comparisons using simple and weighted averages, weighted means, and percentiles are available. Reports to participating organizations are coded for security and one job is equal to one report. The program has easy input screens and builds tables or participants, jobs to be surveyed, and salary data. It allows for any participant to be the "pivot" organization, and customized analysis is available by organization or type or organization. Options allow projecting salaries to a future date by using a multiplier factor assigned to each participant.

Specific Functions Performed by Format or Report

Shows any five percentiles specified by the operator. Gives a visual picture of the "pivot" organization's average salary in each case compared with the various percentiles in the market.

Page 1

Salary Survey Expert
Market Comparison for Newsales Inc.

| Job | Base Organization | | | ===================== Percentile ========================= | | | | | # |
	Employees	Av Salary	Pcntile	10	25	50	90	95	Srvyd
1 Clerk Typist	2	9,840.00	25	9,840.00	9,840.00	10,404.00	12,472.60	12,517.80	4
3 Telephone Operator	1	9,900.00	33	9,900.00	9,900.00	10,937.00	13,245.20	13,517.60	3
5 Receptionist	1	9,900.00	33	9,900.00	9,900.00	10,152.00	10,644.10	10,695.55	3
6 Secretary I	3	10,471.00	33	10,471.00	10,471.00	11,151.50	12,343.70	12,453.35	3
7 Secretary II	5	11,719.00	25	11,719.00	11,719.00	12,933.00	13,973.20	14,037.60	4

Figure 14.63 Salary survey market comparison—using percentiles

* Courtesy of Human Resource Management—Personnel Systems, 883 East 2850 North, North Ogden, Utah 84404.

Computerization of HRM Processes

Type of Sample Format or Report

Salary Survey Output to Participants* (Figure 14.64)

Software Product Name and Overall Functions

This human resource product is designed specifically to perform salary survey analysis with output to the surveying organization and to participants. Comparisons using simple and weighted averages, weighted means, and percentiles are available. Reports to participating organizations are coded for security and one job is equal to one report. The program has easy input screens and builds tables or participants, jobs to be surveyed, and salary data. It allows for any participant to be the "pivot" organization, and customized analysis is available by organization or type or organization. Options allow projecting salaries to a future date by using a multiplier factor assigned to each participant.

Specific Functions Performed by Format or Report

This report is the "reward" for participating in the salary survey. It is the organization-by-organization listing of reported averages. One page is equal to one job, so the participants receive as many pages as there are benchmark jobs. Participants are coded to provide security of data.

```
                          Market Salary Report                    Page    1
                    SAMPLE SURVEY OUTPUT TO PARTICIPANTS
Job:    1 - Clerk Typist
                                  Range                 Actual
                     Emplyees    Low        High         Low        High       Average
Participant  202        2      8,448.00   13,272.00    9,600.00   10,080.00    9,840.00
Participant  203        8     12,168.00   15,808.00   12,168.00   13,520.00   12,337.00
Participant  206       10      9,853.00   14,606.00                           10,404.00
Participant  212       43     11,419.00   14,851.00   11,419.00   14,851.00   12,563.00
                             =========   =========   =========   =========   =========
     Weighted Averages:      11,171.22   14,883.51   11,463.42   14,470.06   12,105.16
     Simple Averages:        10,472.00   14,634.25   11,062.33   12,817.00   11,286.00
```

Figure 14.64 Salary survey output to participants

---

* Courtesy of Human Resource Management—Personnel Systems, 883 East 2850 North, North Ogden, Utah 84404.

Computerization of HRM Processes

Type of Sample Format or Report

Employee Attitude Survey* (Figure 14.65)

Software Product Name and Overall Functions

Q-FAST™ is a general testing system that allows you to computerize questionnaires, surveys, interviews, etc. After entering your questionnaire (guided with step-by-step instructions) your computer will do the testing for you. Questionnaires may be administered by computer, scored by computer, and the results may be stored in a format accessible by other software (e.g., statistical packages, data bases, word processors, etc.) including microcomputer-to-mainframe communication packages. If you do not want to administer your questionnaires via computer, Q-FAST™ also can be used as a powerful scoring program.

Specific Functions Performed by Format or Report

Up to 600 questions may be included in a single questionnaire. Questions may be open-ended (allowing entry of the respondent's name, address, etc.), or multiple choice (up to 10 response choices). You can score the questionnaire on up to 25 user-defined scoring scales. Q-FAST™ produces detailed and summary reports of individual results, and accumulates and stores data for analysis and reporting by word processing and statistical software.

(See following page)

* Courtesy of Stat Soft, Inc., 2832 E. 10th, Suite #4, Tulsa, OK 74104.

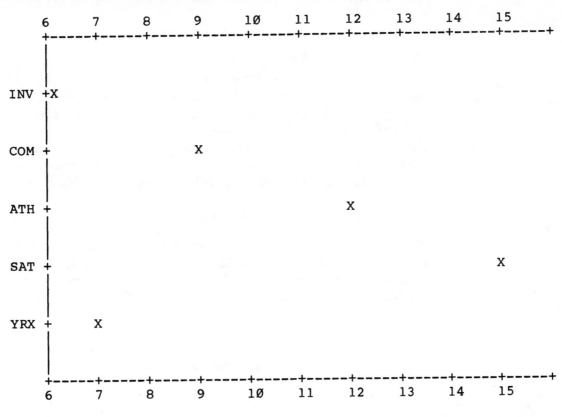

Q-FAST

Employee Attitude Survey I.   Ø1-28-1987   Ø8:46:Ø6

Respondent: SSN# 5Ø5-ØØ-1234
Questionnaire taken: Ø1-28-1987   Ø8:33:31

Job Involvement   6
Organizational Commitment   9
Attitude Toward Authority   12
Job Satisfaction   15
Years Experience   7

Figure 14.65 Employee attitude survey

Computerization of HRM Processes

Type of Sample Format or Report

Organization Chart—Feather and Tree Structures* (Figure 14.66)

Software Product Name and Overall Functions

Corporate CHARTER™ produces organization and reporting relationship charts from the human resources data base. It generates charts in either wall map or book formats with multiple chart structures. User-designed box styles can display any field of information, and comments may be placed inside or adjacent to the boxes. A compression feature efficiently organizes branches on the page. Charts may be customized readily to display "what-if" scenarios. This software utilizes data downloaded from mainframe or other micro data bases, and automatically updates charts to reflect changes in the data base.

Specific Functions Performed by Format or Report

This sample includes feather structures, e.g., "Corporate Officers", and tree structures, e.g., "SR VICE PRESIDENT 2". The chart is "levelized"—that is, all equivalent positions such as VPs are shown on the same horizontal level. Assistants also are shown, e.g., ADM ASST and SPECIAL ASST.

(See following page)

* Courtesy of Corporate Education Resources, Inc., 116 West Burlington Street, Fairfield, IA 52556.

Sample chart 1
Compressed print
20 cpi, 9.6 lpi

Corporate CHARTER
Feather & Tree structures
Levelized

PRESIDENT
BRIAN BROOKS

ADMIN ASST
LISA BROWN

VP INTERNATIONAL
JOHN MCDONALD

Corporate Officers

SR VICE PRESIDENT 1
DOUGLAS GRIMES

SPECIAL ASST
NORMAN COOPER

VP CONTROLLER
RUTHERFORD NELSON

TREASURER
CLAUDE VOLCKER

ASST CONTROLLER
SHARON SMITH

ASST TREASURER
LEONARD BLACK

MGR INFO SYSTEMS
REGINALD DIAZ

DIR INSURANCE
ROGER SMITH

GEN MGR DISTRIBUTION
DEAN JEFFREYS

DIR SECURITY
ROBERTA PETERS

DIR TRAFFIC
MARILYN JOHNSON

GENERAL COUNSEL
RONALD WHITE

DIR TAX
WALTER JOHNSON

VP PERSONNEL
JOHN THOMAS

DIR PERSONNEL SERVICES
ADAM JONES

VP PUBLIC RELATIONS
TED LANGLEY

DIR PUBLIC RELATIONS
VIVIAN JOHNSON

VP INTL DEVELOPMENT
DAIN WEMBLEY

EXECUTIVE VICE PRESIDENT
STANLEY BENSON

SPECIAL PROJECTS
CHARLES SANDS

ADMIN ASST
CHERYL BROWN

VP MARKET SERVICES
KEN RICHARDS

VP OPERATIONS
THOMAS MCARTHUR

DIR CORP SALES
ROBERT WHITE

MGR OFFICE OPERATIONS
REGINALD HUNT

VP ADVERTISING
NORMAN JAMES

VP PURCHASING
PETER OLIVER

VP CONSUMER PRODUCTS
PATRICK CAMPBELL

VP TECHNOLOGY
RANDOLPH WHITE

DIR TRADE RELATIONS
JOHN WILLIAMS

VP ENGINEERING
HAROLD ROBINSON

DIR MARKET RESEARCH
PAUL WHITE

VP CORP RESEARCH
GERARD VAUGHAN

SR VICE PRESIDENT 2
VERNON KATZ

ADMIN ASST
RUTH BROWN

VP GEN MGR DIV A
ARETHA STIMSON

VP GEN MGR DIV B
GEORGE BLACK

VP GEN MGR DIV C
HUGH FLINT

VP GEN MGR DIV D
RALPH TROMBLEY

VP GEN MGR DIV E
JAMES WASHINGTON

VP GEN MGR DIV F
DONNA WOODS

VP GEN MGR DIV G
ADRIEN HENDRICKS

VP GEN MGR DIV H
JIM SATURLEY

VP GEN MGR DIV I
VINCE CHARLES

VP GEN MGR DIV J
FRANK KENDROS

VP GEN MGR DIV K
HELEN MARION

VP GEN MGR DIV L
ED MONK

VP GEN MGR DIV M
DANIEL CROW

VP GEN MGR DIV N
RITA NELSON

VP GEN MGR DIV O
WILLIAM THORP

VP GEN MGR DIV P
ANTHONY MUSANTI

VP GEN MGR DIV Q
GREGORY JAMESON

VP GEN MGR DIV R
J. T. WYMAN

SR VICE PRESIDENT 3
GERALD CARSON

VP CORP DEVELOPMENT
ROBERTA CHARLES

MGR CORP DEVELOPMENT
JAMES HAYES

Figure 14.66 Organization chart—feather and tree structures

617

Computerization of HRM Processes

Type of Sample Format or Report

Organization Chart—Succession Planning* (Figure 14.67)

Software Product Name and Overall Functions

Corprate CHARTER™ produces organization and reporting relationship charts from the human resources data base. It generates charts in either wall map or book formats with multiple chart structures. User-designed box styles can display any field of information, and comments may be placed inside or adjacent to the boxes. A compression feature efficiently organizes branches on the page. Charts may be customized readily to display "what-if" scenarios. This software utilizes data downloaded from mainframe or other micro data bases, and automatically updates charts to reflect changes in the data base.

Specific Functions Performed by Format or Report

This sample demonstrates the versatility of Corporate CHARTER™ by displaying structures needed for planning strategic organizational changes. The wide variety of box drawing capabilities, based on a library, which stores up to 200 user-defined box types, is employed for presenting data on key management personnel and their potential successors.

(See following page)

* Courtesy of Corporate Education Resources, Inc., 116 West Burlington Street, Fairfield, IA 52556.

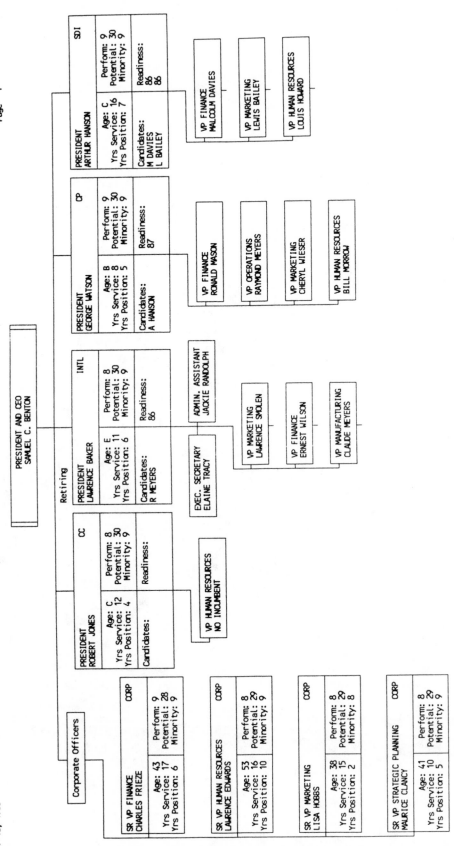

Figure 14.67 Organization chart—succession planning

Index